EX·LIBRIS·SUNE·GREGERSEN

PAPERS FROM THE 5TH ICEHL

AMSTERDAM STUDIES IN THE THEORY AND HISTORY OF LINGUISTIC SCIENCE

General Editor
E.F. KONRAD KOERNER
(University of Ottawa)

Series IV – CURRENT ISSUES IN LINGUISTIC THEORY

Advisory Editorial Board

Henning Andersen (Los Angeles); Raimo Anttila (Los Angeles)
Thomas V. Gamkrelidze (Tbilisi); Hans-Heinrich Lieb (Berlin)
J. Peter Maher (Chicago); Ernst Pulgram (Ann Arbor, Mich.)
E. Wyn Roberts (Vancouver, B.C.); Danny Steinberg (Tokyo)

Volume 65

Sylvia Adamson, Vivien Law, Nigel Vincent and Susan Wright (eds)

*Papers from the 5th International Conference
on English Historical Linguistics*

PAPERS FROM THE 5TH INTERNATIONAL CONFERENCE ON ENGLISH HISTORICAL LINGUISTICS
Cambridge, 6-9 April 1987

Edited by

SYLVIA ADAMSON, VIVIEN LAW,
NIGEL VINCENT and SUSAN WRIGHT

JOHN BENJAMINS PUBLISHING COMPANY
AMSTERDAM/PHILADELPHIA

1990

Library of Congress Cataloging-in-Publication Data

International Conference on English Historical Linguistics (5th: 1987: St. John's College, Cambridge, England)
  Papers from the 5th International Conferrence on English Historical Linguistics: dedicated to the memory of James Peter Thorne (1933-1988) / edited by Sylvia Adamson ... [et al.].
        p.   cm. -- (Amsterdam studies in the theory and history of linguistic science. Series IV, Current issues in linguistic theory, ISSN 0304-0763; v. 65)
  Half t.p. title: Papers from the 5th ICEHL
  Includes bibliographical references and index.
  1. English language--History--Congresses. 2. English language-Middle English, 1100-1500--Congresses. 3. English language--Old English, ca. 450-1100--Congresses. I. Thorne, James Peter, 1933-1988. II. Adamson, Sylvia. III. Title. IV. Title: Papers from the 5th ICEHL. V. Series.
  PE1075.I57   1987
  420.9--dc 20   90-681
  ISBN 90 272 3562 7 (alk. paper)   CIP

© Copyright 1990 - John Benjamins B.V.
No part of this book may be reproduced in any form, by print, photoprint, microfilm, or any other means, without written permission from the publisher.

Dedicated to the memory of
JAMES PETER THORNE
(1933-1988)

CONTENTS

In Memoriam James Peter Thorne, 1933-1988 by John Lyons   xi

PREFACE   xxi

LIST OF PARTICIPANTS   xxv

Alex Agutter
   Restandardisation in Middle Scots   1
John Algeo
   British and American English: *odi et amo*   13
Laurel Brinton
   The stylistic function of ME *gan* reconsidered   31
Cecily Clark
   Historical Linguistics - Linguistic Archaeology   55
Robert Coleman
   The assessment of lexical mortality and replacement between Old and Modern English   69
Xavier Dekeyser
   Preposition stranding and relative complementiser deletion: implicational tendencies in English and the other Germanic languages   87
David Denison
   The Old English Impersonals Revived   111
B. Elan Dresher
   On the unity of the Mercian Second Fronting   141
Thomas Frank
   Hugh Blair's theory of the origin and the basic functions of language   165
Ossi Ihalainen
   Methodological preliminaries to the study of linguistic change in dialectal English: evaluating the grammars of Barnes and Elworthy as sources of linguistic evidence   189

Dieter Kastovsky
   The typological status of Old English word-formation   205
Willem Koopman
   The double object construction in Old English   225
Roger Lass
   Where do Extraterritorial Englishes come from? Dialect input and recodification in transported Englishes   245
David Lightfoot
   Obsolescence and Universal Grammar   281
Peter Lucas
   On the role of some adverbs in Old English verse grammar   293
Donka Minkova
   Adjectival inflexion relics and speech rhythm in late Middle English and Early Modern English   313
Terttu Nevalainen
   Modelling functional differentiation and function loss: the case of *but*   337
Ray Page
   Dating Old English inscriptions: the limits of inference   357
Frans Plank
   Paradigm arrangement and inflectional homonymy: Old English case   379
Pat Poussa
   A contact-universals origin for periphrastic *do* with special consideration of Old English-Celtic contact   407
Geoffrey Russom
   A new kind metrical evidence in Old English poetry   435
Małgorzata Tecław
   The development of ME ǭ from open syllable lengthening in the West Midlands   458
James P. Thorne
   Some Modern Standard English filters   471
Ingrid Tieken-Boon van Ostade
   Exemplification in eighteenth century grammars   481
Elizabeth Closs Traugott
   From less to more situated in language: the unidirectionality of semantic change   497
Wim van der Wurff
   The *easy-to-please* construction in Old and Middle English   519

Anthony Warner
   Reworking the history of English auxiliaries 537
Brita Wårvik
   On grounding in English narratives: a diachronic perspective 559

AUTHOR INDEX 577

J.P.THORNE 1933-1988

They told me, Heraclitus, they told me you were dead,
They brought me bitter news to hear and bitter tears to shed.
I wept as I remember'd how often you and I
Had tired the sun with talking and sent him down the sky.

And now that thou art lying, my dear old Carian guest,
A handful of grey ashes, long, long ago at rest,
Still are thy pleasant voices, thy nightingales, awake;
For Death, he taketh all away, but them he cannot take.

IN MEMORIAM JAMES PETER THORNE
1933-1988

JOHN LYONS

Trinity Hall
Cambridge

The paper that Professor Thorne gave to the Fifth International Conference on English Historical Linguistics, in Cambridge, on 9 April 1987, 'Some Modern English filters', was, to the best of my knowledge, the last one that he ever delivered, and the last that he himself prepared for publication. Indeed, it was during the Conference that he was first alerted to the possible seriousness of the symptoms of which he had been complaining for some time, and it was only a few days later, on his return to Edinburgh, that their actual seriousness was confirmed and the cancer diagnosed which was to lead, indirectly, to his death eleven months later. It is therefore appropriate - poignantly appropriate for those who were with him at the Conference - that the volume which contains this particular paper should be dedicated to him. And on behalf of his many friends and colleagues, and also of his family, I must begin by thanking the editors for having decided to dedicate the volume to him, and for having given me the opportunity of writing this brief tribute.[1]

James Peter Thorne was born on 29 January 1933 in Penarth, in South Wales. He was educated at Penarth Grammar School and at Jesus College, Oxford, where he graduated in English Language and Literature and subsequently obtained his B.Litt., the subject of his thesis being *Renaissance theories of logic and poetry*. After a brief period as a Research Fellow at Bedford College in London (1958-1959), he was appointed to an Assistant Lectureship in English Language in Edinburgh, where he spent the rest of his academic career (with, however, several periods abroad on secondment or as a visiting professor). In 1962 he was promoted to a full Lectureship, in 1970 to a Readership and in 1979, on the retirement of Professor Angus McIntosh, to the Forbes Chair of English Language. Among the more significant of his other academic appointments, may be listed the following: Assistant Directorship of the USAF Mechanical Analysis of Language Project, Indiana University (under the Directorship of Professor Fred W. Householder, 1961-1962); Visiting Associate Professorship, University of California at Berkeley (1967); Visiting Associate Professorship, University of California at San Diego (1969); LSA Visiting Professorship, University of Massachusetts, Amherst (Summer Institute of Linguistics, 1976); Visiting Professorship, University of Paris 3 (Nouvelle Sorbonne)

(1978-1979); Visiting Professorship, the National University of Singapore (1982 and 1985).

Such was his curriculum vitae, set out baldly in conventional obituary style. It remains to add, in the same vein, that his publications (some thirty articles and perhaps as many reviews) ranged over the fields of literary criticism, English philology, linguistics and the computational analysis of texts; that as the first Secretary of the School of Epistemics, in Edinburgh, in the early 1970s, he played an important part in the foundation and development of what has now become the University's world-famous centre for Cognitive Science; that at the time of his death, as well as being head of the English Language Department, he was also the Director of the Edinburgh University Gayre Institute in Medieval Dialectology and Convener of the Joint Universities Council for the Dictionary of the Older Scottish Tongue; and, finally, that, like any other established professor, he was, or had been, a member of several important committees and other bodies inside and outside the University, including the Council of the Philological Society and the Council for National Academic Awards (CNAA).

So much then, for a straightforward conventional account of his life and work. Presented in these terms, it might seem to be indistinguishable, to those who did not know him, from the life and work of any one of a host of successful university professors of his (and my) generation. But anyone who did know Jimmy Thorne (and 'Jimmy' he was to all who could claim any degree of acquaintance with him) would also know that he was far from being a typical professor. More to the point, in the present context, anyone who did not know him - anyone who had not been taught by him, had not heard him lecture or had never met him socially - would find it impossible, on the basis of a straightforward recital of his official appointments and a list of his publications, to account for the reputation and influence that he undoubtedly enjoyed, not to mention the affection and esteem in which he was universally held. Any appreciation of Jimmy's life and work must try to answer, on behalf of those that did know him, the perhaps unspoken question that arises in the mind of those who did not: What was there about him that was so special?

Some idea of the nature of Jimmy's work and of the basis of his academic reputation can of course be got from reading his publications, several of which are widely quoted and, reprinted in students' readers and anthologies, have now been made accessible to a larger audience. It is easy enough to see, sometimes even from the titles, that his intellectual interests were diverse and wide-ranging. A reading of the papers themselves will also show that his work was, not merely interdisciplinary, but also integrative and catalytic. The paper that appears in the present volume is typical in this respect: bringing to bear upon an issue of general import in theoretical linguistics a philologist's evidence from Middle English, it demonstrates a mastery of both disciplines and of two characteristically different modes of thought and argument. Many of his published articles are of this kind: one thinks particularly of 'Stylistics and generative grammars' (1965), of 'The grammar of jealousy: a note on the character of Leontes' (1977) or of 'A computer model for the perception of syntactic structure' (1968). To say that such works are interdisciplinary would be almost to misrepresent them, for it would imply that there are, at least temporarily, real boundaries between currently established disciplines, between linguistics and literary criticism, or between philology and computer science; and in his own thinking Jimmy did not recognize the existence of such interdisciplinary boundaries. As a graduate student at Oxford, many years ago, he had reconciled for himself the conflicting attitudes that divided the two factions in the Renaissance battle of the books. One of his abiding and passionate interests was poetry, which he not only read, but wrote (never, as far as I know, for publication). But sensitive though he was as a reader of poetry and skilled practitioner though he was of literary criticism, he never felt any conflict between what is referred to, in the jargon of school and university curricula, as language and literature. Not for him the philosophy-will-clip-an-angel's-wings philosophy! This much is clear, as I have said, even from the titles of some of his better-known articles.

But his publications give only a very partial view of the range and quality of his interests. Regrettably, there is nothing apart from his very early paper, 'A Ramistical commentary on Sidney's *Apology for Poetry*' (1957), to testify to the deep knowledge of

scholastic and Renaissance theories of language and
logic that he acquired when he was working on his
B.Litt. dissertation. (This work ought to have earned
him a Ph.D. and no doubt would have done, if it had been
more respectful of the conventional disciplinary
boundaries.) By the early 1970s there was a greater
interest in the history of linguistics than there had
been a generation previously; there was also by then a
greater awareness on the part of linguists and
philosophers of the importance and renewed topicality of
scholastic logic and grammatical theory; and at that
time Jimmy did consider revising and updating his
dissertation for publication. But writing did not come
easy to him at the best of times (he was a perfectionist
and agonized over every phrase), and he abandoned the
project. It so happens that, by the accident of my own
upbringing and school-education (rather than from having
studied classics and comparative philology at
university), I too had some knowledge of scholastic
philosophy (though superficial by comparison with his)
when I first met Jimmy (in 1961). One of our earliest
topics of conversation, and one to which we frequently
returned in the years that followed, had to do with the
links between the aims of Chomskyan generativism and
those of the speculative grammarians of the later Middle
Ages.(Chomsky himself was, of course, completely unaware
of these links - as he was also unaware, at that time,
of the work of his Cartesian and Humboldtian
predecessors.) For me, therefore, it is the absence
from Jimmy's 'Nachlass' of any major work on the history
and philosophy of linguistics, written from this
viewpoint, that is the most to be regretted.(I should

perhaps add, for the record, that, although Jimmy was one of the earliest fully-committed adherents of generativism in this country, and one of its most influential advocates in the early 1960s, it was Michael Halliday's lectures in Edinburgh in 1959-1961 that first excited his interest in modern linguistics. Jimmy himself readily acknowledged his indebtedness to Halliday, as he also acknowledged his indebtedness to his other Edinburgh mentor, Angus McIntosh, whose chair he was in later years proud to occupy.) But there are many other topics upon which he conversed and lectured with authority that are not represented in his published writings. And it is as a lecturer and as a conversationalist that he will be remembered. *Scripta absunt; verba manent!*

I have said that writing did not come easily to him. It may surprise many of those who heard him lecture that he did not find lecturing all that easy either. He was of course an outstandingly successful lecturer, with a style that was unique to him; histrionic and inspirational (in the best sense of both of these words), rather than soundly and conventionally discursive; allusive, rather than transparently erudite. But the platform fluency for which he was justly renowned was far from being as spontaneous as, in performance, it appeared. It was the product of long and careful preparation ('rehearsal' is perhaps a better word - the "actor-like qualities" of his lectures, it has been said, "raised memories of Richard Burton".[2] Nor was it only the prestigious set lecture or conference paper that he prepared with such care. The same thought and time went into the preparation of his day-to-day teaching, both in his own Department in Edinburgh and also in the several universities in which he held visiting appointments. Many of his students, in this country and abroad, are by now well established in fields of research and scholarship to which Jimmy first introduced them, but which they have since made thoroughly their own and to which, in many cases, they have made strikingly original contributions. He was proud of them; and they, I am sure, will remember him with gratitude and affection.

So too will all those - and, happily, they were many - who were privileged to know him and enjoy his conversation. For conversation was Jimmy's forte: conversation of all kinds, from casual everyday gossip with close friends to high-level intellectual discussion with specialists in an astonishingly wide range of disciplines. Much of his very considerable knowledge of up-to-date research in fields other than English studies and linguistics derived from conversation with experts, many of them friends of long standing; and much of the knowledge of linguistics that he propagated among representatives of other disciplines was similarly transmitted in conversation. It was not for nothing that (working closely with Christopher Longuet-Higgins, its Chairman) he was such a successful Secretary of the School of Epistemics in its early days.

On a more personal and social level, Jimmy was not merely an amusing companion and an accomplished raconteur of well-chosen anecdotes, but also and always a sympathetic and interested listener. His outward cheerfulness concealed, however, an inner melancholy, which not surprisingly in the circumstances of his illness, took a firm grip on him in the last months of his life and made them painfully unendurable. He died on 11 March 1988.

They told me, Heraclitus, they told me you were dead,...

I do not know what Jimmy thought of Callimachus's elegy, which, in Cory's translation (or paraphrase), he must have learned at school, as we all did in those days. But, as I have now frequently remarked to mutual friends, every line of this elegy seems relevant. Have we not all, in company with him, so often *tired the sun with talking and sent him down the sky*? And can we not all take comfort from the knowledge that his *nightingales still live?* (Here, to evoke a purely private memory that he shared and treasured, I translate literally from the penultimate line of the original Greek: 'nightingales' in its intended metaphorical sense of "utterances" or, as Cory puts it, "voices" will, of course, command more public assent, and I continue it, and conclude, with the more familiar final line from the Cory version.)

For Death, he taketh all away, but them he cannot take.

NOTES

1. In preparing this tribute, I have had before me, and have drawn freely upon, the Memorial Address delivered by Professor K.A. Fowler at the Funeral on 18 March 1988, the obituaries by Alan Davies (*The Times*, 29 March 1988) and Norman Macleod (*Edinburgh University Bulletin*, May 1988; *The Scotsman*, 6 April 1988; *The Independent*, 24 March 1988); and recent *curriculum vitae* and list of publications kindly supplied to me by Norman Macleod and Virginia Barnes, the late Professor Thorne's secretary. But most of what I have written is based solely on personal knowledge, and the judgements that I make are my own.

2. Alan Davies, *The Times*, 29 March 1988.

PREFACE

The Fifth International Conference on English
Historical Linguistics (ICEHL5) was held in St John's
College, Cambridge from 6th to 9th April 1987. In the
number of its participants, it was comparable with the
Amsterdam meeting of 1985 (ICEHL4), but--as witness the
size of the present volume--there was again a sharp rise
in the number of papers that survived the successive
selection procedures for presentation and publication.
Clearly the ICEHL series has established itself as a major
forum for debate in the field; indeed, a number of the
papers in this volume explicitly continue (or controvert)
lines of enquiry initiated in ICEHL4.

The conference was organised as a series of thematic
sections, and we took advantage of our position as
organisers to promote the discussion of topics in which
Cambridge has established a particular interest: so there
were sections on the auxiliary system, on historical
stylistics and on the history of the study of the English
language, as well as a valuable workshop discussion (which
unfortunately cannot be represented here) on methods and
problems in teaching. For the rest, the balance of both
conference and volume reflects pretty accurately the state
of English Historical Linguistics at the end of the 1980s:
the continued expansion of syntax at the expense of

phonology; the revitalisation of dialectology, begun under the influence of sociolinguistics and now given new impetus and directions by the growth of interest in creoles and the dynamics of languages in contact; and the emergence of grammaticalisation as a major field of study which challenges many of the traditional lines of demarcation, whether between syntax and semantics or synchrony and diachrony. We believe that many of the papers in this volume, some of them specially commissioned by the conference, will become important reference points for English Historical Linguistics in the 1990s.

The volume is dedicated to the memory of one of its contributors, Professor James Thorne. As Sir John Lyons explains in his memorial, the paper that Jimmy gave at the conference was his last, and it was memorable--and entirely characteristic--in the way it combined the interests of the philologist and the theoretical linguist. It is therefore appropriate that his name should stand at the head of a collection of papers whose subjects range from Old English to Modern American, from justifying the form of grammars to evaluating the physical remains on which linguistic histories are built. One of the delights of attending the ICEHL series of conferences and one of the most valuable features of the volumes that result from them is that they promote the kind of interdisciplinary understanding that was the hallmark of Jimmy's own work.

The process of translating the conference into volume form ran into difficulties through the early loss of two of the three original conference organisers: Nigel Vincent moved from Cambridge to become Montfollick Professor and Head of the Linguistics Department in Manchester; less happily, Vivien Law suffered a prolonged and incapacitating illness. The situation was saved only by the arrival of Susan Wright, who took on the task of working with contributors and producing camera-ready copy for those who, for one reason or another, were unable to do so themselves. It is perhaps unusual for one editor to thank another, but in this case it is true to say that without Susan the volume would have been further delayed or else seriously depleted in contents.

The conference and volume owe many other debts of gratitude. Among individuals, we would like to record our thanks to: Professor Peter Matthews for advice and support throughout the period of planning and staging the conference; Sir John Lyons for inviting the conference to stage one of its sessions in Trinity Hall; Dr Richard Beadle and the library staff of St John's College for arranging a special exhibition of medieval manuscripts in the Upper Library of St John's; Professor Ray Page and Mrs Alison Wilson of Corpus Christi College for opening the Parker collection to conference participants; the graduate students of the Department of Linguistics for acting as conference stewards; the secretarial staff of the English Faculty for helping in the preparation of materials for the conference; the editorial staff of Benjamins for their patience and co-operation during the preparation of the volume; Jonathan Hope for compiling the index of names; and--last but not least--all the anonymous readers who gave so generously of their time and advice to ensure the high quality of the papers included in this collection.

We also wish to acknowledge the support of a number of institutions: The British Academy and the Cambridge English Faculty paid the travel expenses of some of our commissioned speakers; the Cambridge Local Examinations

Syndicate marked the inauguration of the new Centre for English as an International Language by sponsoring an academic and social evening in which Professor Braj Kachru's paper 'On the Linguistic Hegemony of English across Cultures' opened up issues new to many European participants; other evening receptions were hosted by the General Board of the University of Cambridge and by Cambridge University Press in association with Heffer's bookshop. But our greatest obligation is to the Master and Fellows of St John's. The College provided all the domestic and academic facilities for the conference as well as the adminstrative and catering staff who ran it so smoothly; it provided a memorable conference dinner; but above all it was the College's financial generosity which enabled us to commission papers by some of the most distinguished scholars in the field and, no less valuably, to offer bursaries that brought talented young graduate students to their first international conference.

Sylvia Adamson
Cambridge, 1989

LIST OF PARTICIPANTS

V. Adams, University College London, U.K.
S.M. Adamson, University of Cambridge, U.K.
H. Aertsen, Free University of Amsterdam, The Netherlands.
A. Agutter, University of Edinburgh, U.K.
K. Aijmer, University of Lund, Sweden.
J. Algeo, University of Georgia, U.S.A.
M. Annams, University of Naples, Italy.
F.O. Austin, University of Liverpool, U.K.
A.C. Benzi, University of Naples, Italy.
P. Bibire, University of Cambridge, U.K.
C.P. Biggam, University of Strathclyde, U.K.
L. Brinton University of British Columbia, Canada.
J.D. Burnley, University of Sheffield, U.K.
J. De Caluwé-Dor, University of Liège, Belgium
P. Carter, Cambridge University Press, U.K.
J. Cheshire, Birkbeck College, London.
P. Christophersen, Cambridge, U.K.
C. Clark, Cambridge, U.K.
R. Coleman University of Cambridge, U.K.
E. Daams, University of Amsterdam, The Netherlands.
M. Davenport, University of Odense, Denmark.
X. Dekeyser, University of Antwerp, Belgium.
D. Denison, University of Manchester, U.K.
G. Di Martino, University of Naples, Italy.
B. Elan Dresher, University of Toronto, Canada.
J. Elsness, University of Oslo, Norway.
M.J. Evans, University of Heidelberg, West Germany.
C.J. Ewen, University of Leiden, The Netherlands.
J. Fisiak, A. Mickiewicz University, Poland.
A. Finell, Åbo Academy, Finland.
A. Fischer, University of Zürich, Switzerland.
T. Frank, University of Naples, Italy.
C. Franzen, Somerville College, Oxford, U.K.
H.J. Giegerich, University of Edinburgh, U.K.
J.S. Gomez Solino, University of Laguna, Spain.
M. Görlach, University of Cologne, West Germany.

LIST OF PARTICIPANTS

J. Holm, Hunter College, U.S.A.
J. Honey, University of Bophutatswana, South Africa.
L. Houwen, University of Sheffield, U.K.
O. Ihalainen, University of Helsinki, Finland.
M. Ingels, University of Leuven, Belgium.
B. Jansan, John Benjamins, Amsterdam, The Netherlands.
S.W. Jolly, University of Sussex, U.K.
A.H. Jucker, University of Zürich, Switzerland.
B. Kachru, University of Illinois, U.S.A.
T. Kaminska, University of Edinburgh, U.K.
D. Kastovsky, University of Vienna, Austria.
C.J. Kay, University of Glasgow, U.K.
A. King, University of Glasgow, U.K.
C.D. King, Univ of St Andrews, U.K.
E. Klimczak, Worcester College, Oxford, U.K.
W. Koopman, University of Amsterdam, The Netherlands.
L. Lagerquist, Oxford, U.K.
S. La Rana, University of Naples, Italy.
R. Lass, University of Cape Town, South Africa.
V. Law, University of Cambridge, U.K.
D. Lightfoot, University of Maryland, U.S.A.
P.J. Lucas, University College Dublin, Ireland.
A. Lutz, University of Munich, West Germany.
A.A. MacDonald, University of Groningen, The Netherlands.
L.H. Malmberg, University of Durham, U.K.
H. Mausch, A. Mickiewicz University, Poland.
G. Mazzon, University of Naples, Italy.
F. McDonald, Oxford University Press, Oxford, U.K.
A.M. McMahon, University of Cambridge, U.K.
M. Messina, University of Naples, Italy.
V. Micillo, University of Potenza, Italy.
A. Meurman-Solin, University of Helsinki, Finland.
D. Minkova, University of California, Los Angeles, U.S.A.
A. Muskita, University of Amsterdam, The Netherlands.
T. Nevalainen, University of Helsinki, Finland.
S. Nevanlinna, University of Helsinki, Finland.
H.F. Nielsen, University of Odense, Denmark.
M.H. Noteboom, University of Leiden, The Netherlands.

LIST OF PARTICIPANTS

W. O'Neil, Massachusetts Institute of Technology, U.S.A.
L.L. Opas, Linacre College, Oxford, U.K.
R.I. Page, University of Cambridge, U.K.
N. Pantaleo, University of Bari, Italy.
A. Pisa, University of Naples, Italy.
F. Plank, University of Konstanz, West Germany.
P. Poussa, University of Helsinki, Finland.
H. Raumolin-Brunberg, University of Helsinki, Finland.
M. Rissanen, University of Helsinki, Finland.
D. Rodier, McGill University, Canada.
G. Russom, Brown University, U.S.A.
R.W. Rutherford, University of Bielefeld, West Germany.
A.E. Rutten, University of Brabant, Tilburg, The Netherlands.
R. Ruyten, University of Nijmegen, The Netherlands.
M. Ryden, University of Umeå, Sweden.
K.I. Sandred, University of Uppsala, Sweden.
W. Schipper, International Christian University, Tokyo, Japan
A. Seppanen, University of Gothenburg, Sweden.
T. Shannon, University of California, Berkeley, U.S.A.
R.D. Smith, University of Leiden, The Netherlands.
J. Söderlind, University of Uppsala, Sweden.
M-J Sole, University of Barcelona, Spain.
K. Sorensen, University of Aarhus, Denmark.
R. Sornicola, University of Naples, Italy.
D. Stark, University of Hannover, West Germany.
J. Staun, University of Copenhagen, Denmark.
R.P. Stockwell, University of California, Los Angeles, U.S.A.
M. Suphi, University College London, U.K.
L. Sylvester, King's College London, U.K.
I. Taavitsainen, University of Helsinki, Finland,
B. Tebrunsvelt, University of Amsterdam, The Netherlands.
M. Tecław, University of Gdańsk, Poland.
L. Thornburg, California State University, U.S.A.
J. Thorne, University of Edinburgh, U.K.
I. Tieken-Boon van Ostade, University of Leiden, The Netherlands.

LIST OF PARTICIPANTS

E.C. Traugott, Stanford University, U.S.A.

N. van den Eynden, University of Louvain, Belgium.

W. van der Wurff, University of Amsterdam, The Netherlands.

B.E. van Kinsbergen, University of Amsterdam, The Netherlands.

J. van Marle, P.J. Meertens Institute, The Netherlands.

J. Verdonck, University of Ghent, The Netherlands.

N.B. Vincent, University of Manchester, U.K.

A.R. Warner, University of York, U.K.

B. Wårvik, Åbo Academy, Finland.

X. Wełna, University of Warsaw, Poland.

S.M. Wright, University of Cambridge, U.K.

P. Young-Bae, School of Oriental and African Studies, U.K.

RESTANDARDISATION IN MIDDLE SCOTS

ALEX AGUTTER
University of Edinburgh

1.0 Introduction.

Although a great deal of variation was permissible within the variety of English known as Middle Scots, especially in the orthography, there is a body of Middle Scots texts which share a number of linguistic characteristics and which contain few, if any, clues to their geographical sources within Scotland. In Agutter (forthcoming (a)) I argue that Middle Scots developed an autonomous standard dialect during the fifteenth and sixteenth centuries. This is the only dialect that compares in development and uses to the standard dialect which was developing in England at the same time. Unlike the southern standard dialect, however, the Scots standard did not continue its independent progress, but underwent rapid change in the late sixteenth and early seventeenth centuries. This process could be interpreted as a process of 'Anglicisation'. (Devitt, forthcoming) or of restandardisation: the replacement of one national written standard by another. If this interpretation is correct, then this is the earliest known case in English of restandardisation without a temporal break.

2.0 The Linguistic Data.

In the late sixteenth century and especially in the seventeenth century, the language of Scots texts changed rapidly. In many cases it is clear that the changes were made deliberately: for example, James VI and his printer modified the text of <u>Basilicon Doron</u> from the original holograph MS to the 1599 printed edition and again for the 1603 printed edition. All these changes were in the direction of the written southern standard, though many involved the choice of linguistic forms shared between Scots and English in place of characteristically Scots forms. There is little argument over what changes occurred in Scots at this period, but changes which appear in retrospect to have been part of a unified process may have been separately motivated.

2.1. <u>Orthography and Phonology</u>. Of the changes which appear to be purely othographic with no phonological implications, two can be attributed to the practice of printers. The letters <ȝ> and <þ> were not included in the printers' founts and were regularly replaced by <z> and <th> respectively. The second of these changes brought Scots practice in line with southern standard practice, but the first did not. Words with /j/ appeared in printed texts with <z>, a representation so unfamiliar in standard English that it resulted in spelling pronunciations such as /mɛnziz/ in place of the native Scots development /mɪŋəs/ for <u>Menzies</u>. Other changes in orthographic practice cannot be accounted for by the technology of printing and may have been deliberate introductions of southern forms e.g. the replacement of Middle Scots <sch> with southern <sh> for /ʃ/ (see below). This also seems to be the explanation for some of the cases in which the Middle Scots convention of using <Vi, Vy> to represent long monophthongs was replaced. For instance in <u>The Basilicon Doron</u> <braithing> in the original was replaced by <breathing> in the 1599 edition (presumably the vowel represented was /e:/ in both dialects at that time). However, in many cases <Vi, Vy> was replaced by a form which was as acceptable in Middle Scots as these digraphs but which, unlike <Vi, Vy> for /V:/, also occurred regularly in southern standard English e.g. <heire> by <here>.

There are several instances of changes in orthographic practice which suggest the representation of a southern phonology for individual lexical items. The most widespread change was the replacement of Middle Scots <a> forms by <o> forms e.g. <lang> by <long>; <na> by <no>; <knaw> (<u>know</u>) by <no>. Palatalisation is also sometimes represented in the orthography e.g. <such> for earlier <sik>.

In many cases it is hard to tell whether an orthographic change represented any phonological change. When <wh> replaced <quh> did it represent a more labial, less velar pronunciation? Evidence from the early seventeenth century suggests that some pronunciation such as /xw/ was still current in Scotland in contrast to /ʍ/ in the south (Alexander Hume cited in Barber (1976: 33)). Did the use of <gh> in place of Middle Scots <ch> suggest to the contemporary reader the loss of /x/, or was it a purely orthographic change in the direction of southern standard? Several spelling forms in Middle Scots show loss of /x/ word finally in words of English origin, so the loss of /x/ was presumably in progress in Scots. On the other hand, those words which still retain /x/ for most Scots (including Scottish Standard English speakers - see Abercrombie (1979: 71)) were never assimilated to the southern <gh> convention e.g. <loch>, <clarsach>, <McKechnie> (NB all such words are of Gaelic origin). In both of these cases, even if a change in phonology is assumed, the motivation for the change is still open to question. The changes concerned could have been deliberate assimilations of southern accent characteristics, or they could have been 'natural' changes i.e. changes which took place in all the dialects of English and which, purely by coincidence, occurred in Scots at the same period as the other linguistic changes being discussed. Similarly, when <oo> was used in place of Middle Scots <ui, uy> was it still read with a Scots phonology i.e. as /o:/, or with a southern-like phonology as post-Great Vowel Shift /u:/; and if the latter, was this merely an instance of a recurrent trend in English to dispense with front rounded vowels?

Problems of interpretation occur not only in relation to widespread changes but also to modification in the spelling of individual lexemes e.g. the original <u>Basilicon Doron</u> text has <lees> (<u>lies</u>, N), the 1599 edition had <lyes>: in Middle Scots the expected phonology would be post-Great Vowel Shift /i:/ as opposed to southern /ai/, but the spelling in the 1599 edition could represent either pronunciation.

2.2. <u>Morphology</u>. Although there are changes in the morphology of Middle Scots in the late sixteenth and seventeenth centuries, only one regular, systematic change could be explained in terms of southern influence: the loss of the distinction between the present participle inflection - {and} [1] and the verbal noun (gerund) inflection {ɪŋ}, such that {ɪŋ} came to be used syncretically for both morphological categories. Although southern influence is a possible motivation for the change, it is not the only possible explanation. All the dialects of English had separate morphemes for these categories but now have a single syncretic form which is conventionally written as <-ing>. Even in Scots texts of the early and mid fifteenth centuries, occasional <-ing> forms are found for the present participle where {and} <-and> would be expected. This predates by more than a century the changes usually explained in terms of 'Anglicisation' (Bald, 1927; Devitt, forthcoming). In an extract from the Lanark Burgh Records of 1610, in a supposedly verbatim account, <-and> forms were used for present participles in simple sentence structures, but <-ing> and <-in> were used for present participles in complex structures (and, of course, verbal nouns). This evidence; occasional <-in> and <-an> inflections; knowledge of the common reduction of the consonant cluster /nd#/ to /n#/ in Middle Scots; and the modern dialect pronunciations of {ɪŋ} as /ən/, all lead me to suppose that this syncretism was phonologically motivated in Middle Scots, with both {and} and {ɪŋ} being pronounced as /ən/. This, and the fact that similar syncretism happens in all the dialects of English, seems sufficient to account for this morphological change without recourse to explanations of deliberate borrowing of southern forms.

The occurrence in late Middle Scots of increasing numbers of <-es, -s> and <-ed, -d> forms for {S} and {T} respectively has also been attributed to southern influence; but here the case is even weaker than the <-and>/<-ing> case. Of these spellings, only those with <e> were previously unfamiliar in Middle Scots, but even then, sequences of <es> and <ed> did occur when the stem ended in <-e> e.g. in a <VCe> convention. The apparent borrowing of <-es> and <-ed> was not as frequent as the occurrence of these sequences might suggest, therefore, nor would these forms have seemed particularly 'un-Scots' at the time. The use of these spelling conventions could imply a change in the allomorphies of {S} and {T} (Agutter, forthcoming (b)), or they could simply be orthographic changes.

The most distinctive aspect of Middle Scots morphology, the treatment of present tense verbs, was quite resistant to change towards the southern standard. Although {Est} and {Eθ} inflections for second and third person singular were still commonly used in southern standard texts, these forms appeared only comparatively rarely in Scots texts, and even then only with common verbs - particularly the auxiliaries have and do. Although the second person singular pronoun thou was maintained in Scots, it regularly appears with the Middle Scots morpheme {S} not southern {Est}. Of course, southern standard was in the process of adopting a northern morphology for present tense verbs (without the northern personal pronoun rule) (Agutter, forthcoming (b)) but there were innumerable southern texts (including versions of the Bible) which had the more conservative morphological system and which could have provided a model for writers and printers in Scotland at the time. Moreover, the use of {S} in many Scots texts continued to be subject to the northern personal pronoun rule for some time after the adoption of the modern use of {S} in southern standard English.

On balance, changes in the morphology appear to be at least as readily explained in terms of a continuing process of standardisation in Middle Scots as by deliberate assimilation of a southern system. In cases where the southern standard dialect was also in a state of change, there were few instances of adoption of the conservative more complex morphological system. Instead, changes in the morphologies of the Middle Scots and southern standard dialects were in the direction of syncretism: Middle Scots morphology modified towards southern standard morphology only when this condition was met. In other cases, southern morphology modified towards the Middle Scots standard - NB this is never described as the Scotticisation of standard English.

Exceptions to this criterion are confined to the morphology of individual lexical items e.g. the occurrence of hath and doth showing {EƟ}. Sporadically, lexical items could change declensional or conjugational class e.g. give could be conjugated as strong as in southern English, rather than as weak as in standard Middle Scots; but such changes occurred only slowly and were dependent on the frequency of occurrence of the lexical item concerned.

2.3. Lexis. The lexis of Middle Scots was also affected by the rapid changes of the late sixteenth and early seventeenth centuries. Southern influence seems the only reasonable explanation for the replacement of common word forms such as gif by if, quhilk by which (orthography and phonology are also involved in this case), and thir by these (often <theis>). Sometimes a characteristically Scots lexeme was avoided in favour of a shared or southern lexical item e.g. gar replaced by make, kirk by church. Throughout the period, and even in present-day Scottish Standard English, Scots items may be retained alongside their equivalent southern forms e.g. kirk is now confined in use to specifically Scottish churches: it cannot be used of, say, the Roman Catholic Church even in Scotland. Many survivals of characteristically Scots lexical items can be explained by differences in culture: Scots still do not translate <u>provost</u> into <u>mayor</u> or <u>minister</u> into <u>vicar</u> to conform with southern practice. Other Scots lexical items may have survived because Scots speakers were unaware that they were not southern standard items e.g. <u>pinkie</u> (A, 'little'; now especially N, little finger), <u>chap</u> (V, 'knock').

3.0 <u>Motivation</u> <u>for</u> <u>change</u>? Whatever the motivation for the changes which took place in Middle Scots in the late sixteenth and the seventeenth century, the effect of these changes was to refocus the direction of standardisation of Scots to such an extent that it has become difficult for us to tell a standard Scottish text from a standard English one. Since the term <u>Anglicisation</u> is so often taken to imply a simplistic and essentially non-liguistic motivation for these changes, I have preferred the term <u>restandardisation</u> for this process. We are culturally programmed to perceive all shared forms as English, so that when the proportion of characteristically Scots forms drops to a very low level, we may consider a text to be non-Scots: perception may have been different in sixteenth and seventeenth century Scotland - shared forms may have been regarded as Scots and a text might have required a high proportion of characteristically southern forms before it was perceived as non-Scots.

There is little doubt that the changes which occurred in standard Middle Scots in the late sixteenth and early seventeenth centuries were in the direction of southern standard English usage. The argument that increasing English cultural dominance was a major factor at this period is supported by a number of historical events. For instance, the fact that England already had a reformed Protestant church by the time of the Reformation in Scotland in 1560/1 clearly made it possible for a number of English Protestant texts to be imported for use in Scotland. Undoubtedly, the most important of these texts was the Bible. There was no printed Scots translation of the Bible until centuries later; Nisbet's translation of The New Testament (c1520) was not printed at the time. After the Scottish Reformation there was also a single, enlarged market for Protestant literature; force of numbers as well as precedence guaranteed that southern standard English would be chosen for such works (see e.g. the contrast in language use between John Knox's religious and non-religious works (Jack, 1981). For these reasons, few religious texts of any importance were written in Middle Scots, although many sermons were. However, the fact that Middle Scots was hardly used for written religious texts cannot be taken as evidence that it was not considered to be a standard dialect: the initial use of English in Reformation literature was as much a historical accident as the pre-Reformation use of Latin. On the other hand, the widespread use of southern standard English forms in such an important area set a precedent for their spread in Scotland.

In the late sixteenth century it became more and more likely that James VI would inherit the English throne from Elizabeth. James, who had had a less than happy life in Scotland, was eager to move south. He had been a major patron of Scottish literature, and it is clear that the permanent removal of the Court from Scotland after 1603 had an adverse effect on the status of Middle Scots both in terms of the social range of its speakers, and the sylistic range of its uses. The Union of Parliaments in 1707 did not so much cause any further advance of English as ensure that there was no return to the official use of a Scots standard.

Comparatively few people were directly affected by the political changes, though all literate people would have come into contact with written southern English in the Bible. Nonetheless, there was no sign of widespread deliberate adoption of southern English e.g. through elocution lessons (Templeton, 1973: 8; Aitken, 1979: 96) until the mid eighteenth century. Such a change in the eighteenth century was partly motivated by Augustan concepts of correctness which were of course not confined to Scotland, but was probably further encouraged in Scotland by a desire to be distanced from the defeated Jacobites.

Up until this point, there is little evidence to suggest that linguistic changes were brought about by any sudden perception of southern cultural superiority. The changes were first and foremost consistent with general trends in the development of English. Where southern standard English had linguistic forms which ran counter to those trends, or which were more conservative than those already in existence in Middle Scots, then a change was less likely to occur.

Even some apparently purely orthographic changes could be regarded in this way. For instance, present-day English has few trigraphs: despite having been very stable throughout the Middle Scots period, the trigraphs <sch> and <quh> were replaced by digraphs. (I would not wish to extend this into a generalisation about economy in the orthographic system, which would be a patently indefensible position with regard to the spelling system of any English dialect.)

It could be argued that right from its inception, the whole process of standardisation in Scots as in other dialects of English was focussed on the developing written standard of southern England. This view is apparently supported by the following evidence. Some of the linguistic forms which came to be typical of the late sixteenth and the seventeenth centuries were found sporadically in formal Middle Scots texts, especially courtly verse, as early as the fifteenth century. This has been taken to indicate that such changes were motivated by a desire to adopt southern forms because southern forms were considered more respectable, or more appropriate in formal contexts: in other words, southern English was considered to be a standard dialect but Middle Scots was not. However, the occurrence of these English forms was extremely sporadic even in the most heavily influenced texts e.g. those which used Chaucer, Lydgate etc as literary models. The commonest of these forms are: the occurrence of {ɪŋ} for the present participle which I have argued could have developed in Middle Scots without overt borrowing from southern dialects; and the apparent attempt to represent in spelling the southern phonology of rounding of OE /ɑː/. The representation of a rounded reflex of OE /ɑː/ is particularly interesting since it frequently involved the use of characteristically Scottish spelling conventions for this non-Scots phonology e.g. <quhois> rather than typical Middle Scots <quhais> for southern <whose>. Dunbar used several such forms, many in The Thrissil and the Rois, a poem to celebrate the marriage of the reluctant James IV to Margaret Tudor in 1503; given the circumstances and the distribution of these linguistic forms, it is possible that they were an anti-English joke. Whatever their explanation, they never amount to more than occasional English forms in texts which are clearly written in Middle Scots. Middle Scots was therefore a perfectly acceptable medium for even the most formal texts; it was southern standard English forms which had a restricted stylistic range in medieval Scotland.

4.0. Conclusion. Middle Scots seems to provide a very close parallel to the development of standard English in England in the late Middle English and Early Modern English periods. Even if it is argued that the standardisation of Middle Scots was never completed, the fact that it was undoubtedly begun means that Scots still provides the only other comparable example of this process in English.[2] If, as I contend, the written standard dialect of Middle Scots was replaced in a process of restandardisation, then Scots provides the earliest known example of this process, predating the replacement of British standard English by American standard English in America by a couple of centuries.

Even the most conservative interpretation of the data suggests that Middle Scots has a lot to offer to sociohistorical linguists and to English historical linguistics as a whole.

NOTES

1. { } is used for morphemes. Lower case letters in such brackets represent phonemic transcription; upper case letters indicate that the segments show allomorphy.
2. I discount West Saxon (a) because it is chronologically so distant from these dialects and there was no continuous use of standard dialects of English to link them; and (b) because of the relative scarcity of sizable OE texts in other dialects.

REFERENCES

Abercrombie, David. 1979. 'The accents of Standard English in Scotland'. In A.J. Aitken and Tom McArthureds. *Languages of Scotland*, 68-84. Edinburgh: Chambers.

Agutter, Alex. 1987. 'A taxonomy of Older Scots orthography'. In Caroline Macafee and Iseabail MacLeod eds. The Nuttis Schell, 75-82. Aberdeen: Aberdeen University Press.

Agutter, Alex. Forthcoming a. 'Standardisation in Middle Scots' *Scottish Language*.

Agutter, Alex. Forthcoming b. Morphological change in Early Modern English: Present tense verbs.

Aitken, A.J. 1979. Scottish speech: a historical view with special reference to the Standard English of Scotland. In A.J. Aitken & Tom McArthur (eds.) *Languages of Scotland*, 85-118. Edinburgh: Chambers.

Bald, Marjory, A. 1927. 'The pioneers of anglicised speech in Scotland'. *SHR* 24. 179-193.

Barber, Charles. 1976. *Early Modern English* (The Language Library Series). London: Andre Deutsche.

Craigie, J. 1950. ed. *The Basilicon Doron of King James VI*. Vol 2. (STS 3rd series, Vol 18) Edinburgh: Scottish Text Society.

Devitt, Amy. Forthcoming. *Standardizing written English*. Cambridge: Cambridge University Press.

Hume, Alexander. c1617. *Orthographie and Congruitie of the Britan Tongue*, (cited in Barber, 1976, *op. cit.*)

Jack, R. D. S. 1976. 'The prose of John Knox: a re-assessment'. *Prose Studies* 4.239-251.

Kinsley, James. 1979. ed., *The Poems of William Dunbar*. Oxford: Clarendon Press.

Law, T. Graves. 1901-5. ed. *The New Testament in Scots. Being Purvey's revision of Wycliffe's version turned into Scots by Murdoch Nisbet c1520*. (STS 1st series, Vols 46, 49, 52) Edinburgh: Scottish Text Society.

Templeton, Janet M. 1973. 'Scots: an outline history'. In A. J. Aitken ed. *Lowland Scots* (ASLS Occasional Papers no. 2) 4-19.

BRITISH AND AMERICAN ENGLISH: ODI ET AMO

JOHN ALGEO
University of Georgia and University College London

Linguistic relations between the United Kingdom and the United States--and the attitudes of speakers of each national variety toward the other--are a matter of some interest, since British and American are the two main national varieties of the English language today, and their historical separation marks the beginning of separate standards for English.[1]

American Speech, the journal of the American Dialect Society, is concerned primarily with the English language in the US. However, it pays attention also to English in the UK and especially to the relationship between British and American English. An examination of its first 62 volumes of publication, beginning in 1925, uncovers a goodly number of treatments of British English from various approaches. The account in this essay is based on those treatments.

Almost from the beginning of the English settlement of America, Englishmen had been aware of American departures from the speechways of the motherland. English visitors to the American colonies commented on the diverging use of English in the New World, and such comment has continued to the present day. In the beginning, the reaction of Englishmen to the usage of Americans was relatively unemotional, and travelers often commented favorably on the speechways of the colonies. They noted the lack of provincial dialects throughout the length of the land (there being not much breadth to the country in those early days, the settlement being a thin strip along the coast). After the War for Independence, however, a different tone--on both sides of the Atlantic--gradually came into comments about variations in the common tongue. Thereafter, linguistic differences were magnified, both in fact and in perception. And the differences were assigned moral values.

Americans found themselves in a Catch-22 long before one of them invented the term. As a result of the bad feelings engendered by the War of Independence, a dislike of all things English became the fashion in the new nation. Yet the dislike had to be expressed in the English language. Various ways of resolving the problem were proposed. Perhaps apocryphal is the proposal reported by a French traveler that the United States should adopt Hebrew instead of English as its national language. And American children never really took to the republican version of Mother Goose, illustrated by this stanza from the rime about the four and twenty blackbirds:

> And when the pie was opened
> The birds they were songless--
> Wasn't that a dainty dish
> To set before the Congress?

However, linguistic patriots like Noah Webster did band together in 1788 to form a Philological Society, a kind of New World Academy, "for the purpose of ascertaining and improving the *American Tongue*" and of promoting "the principles of a *Federal* language" (9: 131-36, esp. 131, 133).[2]

Not all American opinion, however, favored a division between British and American language use. Some Americans were alarmed at the prospect of linguistic, in addition to political, separation from the homeland. Indeed, they supported a general adherence to British standards, except for such new words as the circumstances of the new nation required. Such a position was advanced in the *Monthly Magazine and American Review* in 1800 (1: 454-55). However, Webster's concept of an American Federal language distinct from the English of Britain was far more patriotically appealing.

To such American linguistic chauvinism, Britons responded in kind. John Davis from Salisbury, Wiltshire, traveled in the United States between 1798 and 1802 and, upon his return to England, published an account of those travels in which he illustrated the linguistic gaucheries of the new nation. For example, he observed:

> *Lengthy* is the *American* for *long*. It is frequently used by the *classical* writers of the New World.

He went on to cite the opinion of an Irishman named Mr. George about the word:

> The English language is not written with purity in America (says George). The structure of Mr. Jefferson's sentences is, I think, French; and he uses words unintelligible to an Englishman. Where the devil did he get the word *lengthy*? (4: 473-76)

The language of American literature, as well as of its politics, became the focus of unsympathetic comment. When Joel Barlow's bit of patriotism in epic verse entitled *The Columbiad* was published in England in 1809, it was assessed by the Edinburgh *Review:*

> ... this American bard frequently writes in a language utterly unknown to the prose or verse of this country. We have often heard it reported, that our transatlantic brethren were beginning to take it amiss that their language should still be called English; and truly we must say, that Mr Barlow has gone far to take away that ground of reproach. (2: 497-99)

American scholarship was thought to be, if not quite a contradiction in terms, at least in the category of Dr. Johnson's preaching women and walking dogs. When Noah Webster's *American Dictionary* was brought out in England in 1830, the *Gentleman's Magazine* had this to say:

> A Dictionary of the English language, by an American, is an annunciation prone to excite alarm or ridicule; but nevertheless the fact is such, and we rejoice, because it may tend to prevent American-English from lapsing into that slang to which the late Mr. Mactaggart and others have pronounced it to be in speedy progress of approximation. (2: 156-57)

A British conviction that American English is on the verge of decay, if not quite toppled over, was still held nearly a hundred years later, when in 1929 the *Spectator* responded to an *American Speech* article on "Popular Variants of *Yes*":

> These variations of a single English word are inevitable in a country with a polyglot population, and it is clear that the English language in America is in grave danger of

disruption. It is "Americanisms" of this sort which we have cause to dread and deplore, for they are the result of illiteracy or awkwardness. When an American immigrant says "Yah" or "Yep" he is probably trying to say "yes," just as a baby when it mispronounces a word is trying to pronounce it correctly. (2: 413-14)

Throughout the 19th century, *Punch* magazine used as a stock comic figure a stereotyped American, recognizable by his use of pronunciations like *warn't* for 'were not', of fustian like *splendiferous*, of neologisms like *shyster*, and of general informality, for example, "Look here, you know, this game's about played out" as the American translation of British "We may be excused for feeling that the trend of events makes a change in our present policy an imperative necessity." Which of those two versions is preferable stylistically is at least moot. They are, however, obviously on quite different levels of formality. The trick of comparing highly informal, intimate or familiar, American English with highly formal, literary or bureaucratic, British English is a common ploy, one that H. L. Mencken used frequently.

Between 1841 and 1900, the role of the stock American in *Punch* fluctuated with the diplomatic relations between the UK and the US. When relations were good, *Punch*'s American spoke standard English, using only an occasional, amiably eccentric expression like *dubitate*. When they were bad, he lapsed into egregious vulgarisms and outlandish modes of expression. However, supposed Americanisms in *Punch* were often nothing of the kind, being rather drawn from the language of the stage Yankee, a figure created by British comedians. Indeed, when an actor from the United States, James H. Hackett, played an American role on the London stage, he was criticized as sounding too little like a "real" American—that is, like a British comedian in an American role.

When British authors of the 19th and 20th centuries have wanted to depict an American character, and to establish that character's Americanness by linguistic features, they have also sometimes blundered in using supposed Americanisms incorrectly (7: 255-56). A frequently misused form is the past participle *gotten*. Having become aware that Americans use that old form, the British author may suppose that they use it always in place of *got*, whereas in fact American English uses *gotten* for processes but not for states (6: 314-16). John Galsworthy, a British novelist and playwright of considerable popularity in the United States during the early years of this century, often included American characters in his works, and just as often got their language wrong (7: 297-301). Misuse of a language variety not one's own is, or course, no British monopoly. Americans doubtless do it at least as often when they try to reproduce British speech (1: 511).

Punch also objected to "Americanisms" like *enjoyable* and *reliable*, which are in fact common English, not American in provenience (28: 171-80). There is still today a tendency for Britons to assume that any term with which they are unfamiliar must be an importation from across the Atlantic. In fact, the UK is fully as capable of neology as the US, and is daily making innovations, many of a type that seem just as odd to a contemporary American ear as *Punch*'s Americanisms were to Victorian Britons.

Other powerful sources in forming British stereotypes of Americans were Charles Dickens's novels, his *American Notes*, and his periodical *Household Words*. All of these freely satirized American manners, morals, and morphemes (22: 124-30; 37: 83-94). The actress Fanny Kemble spent some time in America during the 1830s and commented on the Northern "snuffle," the Southern "thick and inelegant pronunciation," which she attributed to Negro influence, and a general "national nasal twang" (13: 8-12). This British attribution of nasality to American is noteworthy, for it is precisely that same nasal quality that has seemed to Americans to typify stereotypically British upper-class speech. Perhaps we simply notice those linguistic features that we dislike and identify them as characteristic of the other nationality.

Histories of American English generally describe the reactions of Britons to the new national variety on the west side of the Atlantic. Less attention has been paid, however, to the reactions of Americans to the English spoken by Britons, as the two national varieties continued to diverge. As Americans came to regard their own speechways as the norm for English, they naturally developed a new set of responses to the differences in pronunciation, vocabulary, and grammar in the quondam motherland. The appendix at the end of this essay focuses on a small part of the story: the view of British English (and also of British reactions to American English) presented on the pages of the journal *American Speech* from its inception in 1925 to the present.

American reactions to British English have always been characterized by ambivalence. On the one hand, British English is regarded as "correct," elegant, exact, decorous, proficient, and prestigious. Early volumes of *American Speech* sometimes included remarks that now seem quaintly prissy in tone, such as the cautionary tale of a lad from Belfast who got a good job in New York because he had learnt diction and realized that "Americans don't speak good English" and thus found it easy to impress them, whereas a slangy go-getter from America lost out in Britain because the English who listened to him refused to believe he could possibly be a college graduate (1: 132).

On the other hand, upper class forms of British English are regarded as snobbish, effete, effeminate, and inarticulate, and its lower-class forms as vulgar, inaccessible, comic, and inarticulate. Americans have two negative linguistic stereotypes of the Briton. Either he speaks in pansy-like fluting tones just below the pitch level audible only to hounds, or his speech is a succession of glottal stops, diversified by an occasional vowel of a quality not otherwise attested in human language.

The aspects of British English thus ambivalently treated in *American Speech* are some measure of American concern with and response to the English of the other major national variety. They demonstrate the fluctuating responses of Americans to British English, but especially they show the interest Americans have in the language of their cousins across the Pond. The journal has treated a variety of subjects: general comparisons of British and American English, historical attitudes, and reviews of contrastive dictionaries; linguistic terms for the two varieties and their treatment as distinct languages; the relative prestige of the two varieties and the study of American English in Europe; mutual influence between British and American and predictions about the future of the varieties, including divergence and convergence; British pronunciation, BBC guides to it, and the prestige value of a British accent; British vocabulary, parallel lists of British-American correspondences, British and American versions of the same literary work, shared lexical items used in slightly, or sometimes drastically, different ways, British neology, and collocational differences; and a variety of other topics in British grammar, lexicography, dialectology, and onomastics.

Many of the articles in *American Speech* treating British English have been straightforward accounts of linguistic facts, but some also have dealt with the emotional values attached to those facts. The affective side of British-American relations in language, as in other cultural affairs, has been a mixture--on both sides of the Atlantic--of scorn and admiration, of rejection and imitation, of hate and love. And perhaps, in the long run, that is not a bad thing. It shows that the relationship between British and American English is a vital one.

NOTES

1. For support during the preparation of this essay, the author is grateful to the John Simon Guggenheim Memorial Foundation and to the Fulbright Commission.
2. Citations are to the journal of the American Dialect Society, *American Speech*, by volume and page number, with complete bibliographical information in the following appendix.

APPENDIX

TREATMENTS OF BRITISH ENGLISH IN *AMERICAN SPEECH*

1 (1925-26): 1-17. George H. McKnight. 'Conservatism in American Speech' (the greater influence of traditional usage rules in American than in British).

1 (1925-26): 26-31. Kemp Malone. 'A Linguistic Patriot' (Noah Webster's promotion of an independent American standard).

1 (1925-26): 121-25. Arthur G. Kennedy. rev. inter alia of *The Pocket Oxford Dictionary of Current English*, by F. G. Fowler and H. W. Fowler (containing Briticisms and lacking American coverage; cf. 2: 508-10).

1 (1925-26): 132. (untitled note on the effect of speech on business success, contrasting a well-spoken youth from Belfast who succeeds in New York with a slangy New Yorker who is thought uneducated in England).

1 (1925-26): 159-60. Helen McM. Buckhurst. 'Some Recent Americanisms in Standard English' (American influence on British).

1 (1925-26): 246. George F. Babbitt. 'Ice-Cream Cones' (*cornet* as the British equivalent).

1 (1925-26): 269-70. William Feather. 'Anglicizing Americanisms' (rewording of an American text for British readers; cf. 1: 565-66, 2: 215-16).

1 (1925-26): 288-90. Arthur G. Kennedy. rev. of "Ueber den Amerikanischen Sprachgebrauch" in *Englisches Englisch*, by Paul Heyne (an increased though factually flawed recognition of American as a standard distinct from British).

1 (1925-26): 350-51. H. L. Mencken. 'Notes' (one on supposedly American *gap* as a generic in a British place name).

1 (1925-26): 363-67. Elizabeth Avery. 'Standards of Speech' (Daniel Jones's phonetics, with general comparisons of British and American).

1 (1925-26): 446. R. Howard Claudius. 'Different--To, From, or Than?' (explanation of British *to* and American *than* as confusions).

1 (1925-26): 454-55. 'Notes and Quotes' (quotations from an 1800 protest in the *Monthly Magazine and American Review* against the name, concept, and substance of a separate language in the United States).

1 (1925-26): 462. (untitled note on American slang defined for British theater-goers).

1 (1925-26): 490-94. Claude de Crespigny. 'American and English' (differences in words, idioms, and turns of phrase).

1 (1925-26): 511. (untitled note on American turns of phrase in a novel about Britons).

1 (1925-26): 565-66. Claude de Crespigny. 'Peculiar Anglicizing' (a criticism of the Briticizing of American English in 1:269-70; cf. 2: 215-16).

1 (1925-26): 570. 'American or British?' (the effect of radio on the national variety of English used internationally).
1 (1925-26): 685. 'Meaning What?' (British use of *less* for *fewer*).
1 (1925-26): 686. 'Automobile Nomenclature' (a list of equivalent British and American terms).
2 (1926-27): 19. R. Howard Claudius. '"Up" and "Down"' (differences of use in the UK and the US).
2 (1926-27): 34-38. Steven T. Byington. 'The Attributive Noun Becomes Cancerous' (headline use of attributive nouns likely to spread to England).
2 (1926-27): 71-74. Claude de Crespigny. 'English English' (social and regional variation within British English).
2 (1926-27): 107-8. 'Notes and Quotes' (common British surnames, for comparison with a similar American list in 1: 470-77; cf. 2: 332-33).
2 (1926-27): 112. (untitled note on Dickens's *whistling shop* as an equivalent of *speakeasy*).
2 (1926-27): 115-32. J. M. Steadman, Jr. 'The Language Consciousness of College Students: A Study of Conscious Changes in Pronunciation' (British influence as one factor).
2 (1926-27): 156-57. 'Notes and Quotes' (British reaction to Webster's *American Dictionary* (1830)).
2 (1926-27): 164. (untitled note citing George Jean Nathan on Americanisms in England).
2 (1926-27): 165-81. Marguerite E. DeWitt. 'Stage Versus Screen' (stage diction and British influence).
2 (1926-27): 203. William Feather. 'Anglicizings' (rewording of an American text for British readers).
2 (1926-27): 214. Edwin Deller. 'Americanisms' (noted by the Registrar of the University of London).
2 (1926-27): 215-16. Alfred Pemberton. 'Anglicizing Americanisms' (current British usage and American equivalents, comment on 1: 269-70, 565-66).
2 (1926-27): 332-33. Howard F. Barker. 'Surnames' (comment on 2: 107-8).
2 (1926-27): 335-36. 'Pronunciations for Broadcasters' (recommended by a BBC advisory committee).
2 (1926-27): 413-14. (untitled comment on 2: 132 recording a British complaint against American variants for *yes*).
2 (1926-27): 444-45. Arthur G. Kennedy. rev. of *A Dictionary of English Pronunciation with American Variants (in Phonetic Transcription)*, by H. E. Palmer, J. Victor Martin, and F. G. Blandford.
2 (1926-27): 495-96. George O. Curme. 'Gotten' (American preservation of an older use).
2 (1926-27): 497-99. Leon Howard. 'A Historical Note on American English' (Edinburgh *Review*'s criticism of Americanisms in Joel Barlow's *Columbiad* (1809)).
2 (1926-27): 508-10. A. G., and L. E. B. Kennedy. rev. of *The Pocket Oxford Dictionary of Current English*, by F. G. Fowler and

H. W. Fowler, American ed. rev. George Van Santvoord (an improved record of American use, comment on 1: 121-25).

3 (1927-28): 68-69. H. L. Mencken. 'English Terms for American Readers.'

3 (1927-28): 75-77. Katherine Buxbaum. rev. of *History in English Words*, by Owen Barfield.

3 (1927-28): 146-51. Arthur G. Kennedy. rev. of *A Comprehensive Guide to Good English* and of *The Knowledge of English*, by George Philip Krapp (compared with Fowler).

3 (1927-28): 157-59. 'Notes and Quotes' (one on an Anglo-American International Council for English).

3 (1927-28): 167. R. Schaupp. 'American Slang in London'.

3 (1927-28): 261-75. Kemp Malone. 'The International Council for English'.

3 (1927-28): 347. Anne Currie. 'British and American Pronunciation'.

3 (1927-28): 377-83. H. P. Johnson. 'Who Lost the Southern R?' (source of Southernisms in British or Black usage).

3 (1927-28): 492. G. L. Masters. 'More Vocabulary Divergence'.

4 (1928-29): 43-47. E. C. Hills. 'The English of America and the French of France' (divergence and convergence of British and American).

4 (1928-29): 48-53. Howard F. Barker. 'How We Got Our Surnames'.

4 (1928-29): 150-53. J. S. Kenyon. 'Correct Pronunciation'.

4 (1928-29): 473-76. Kemp Malone. 'John Davis on American English'.

5 (1929-30): 86-87. Willa Roberts. '"Flatlet"' (on that term and *bare minute*).

5 (1929-30): 168-69. A. G. Kennedy. rev. of *The Phonetics of English*, by Ida C. Ward, and of *The Mollusc*, phonetic ed. by Dorothee Palmer.

5 (1929-30): 169-70. A. G. Kennedy. rev. of *The B.B.C.'s Recommendations for Pronouncing Doubtful Words*, ed. Robert Bridges.

5 (1929-30): 175. Atcheson L. Hench. 'Anglo-Saxon Readers'.

5 (1929-30): 175. Kemp Malone. 'Output and Throughput'.

5 (1929-30): 253-55. J. S. Kenyon. 'On "Who" and "Whom"'.

5 (1929-30): 280-81. Robert Withington. '"Guy"--A Case of Rehabilitation'.

5 (1929-30): 297-300. Kemp Malone. 'On Linguistic Unity'.

5 (1929-30): 323-26. J. S. Kenyon. 'Flat A and Broad A'.

5 (1929-30): 414-16. Kemp Malone. 'Anglo-Saxon Parlance'.

6 (1930-31): 1-9. B. W. A. Massey. 'The Divergence of American from English'.

6 (1930-31): 29-35. Robert Withington. 'A Note on "Bloody"'.

6 (1930-31): 314-16. Stuart Robertson. 'A British Misconception'.

6 (1930-31): 391-93. John W. Birss, Jr. 'English Underworld Slang'.

7 (1931-32): 143-45. J. S. Kenyon. (untitled column in the Usage Department devoted to "some details in the pronunciation of the great public men and women of England and America," noting their departures from supposedly correct norms).

7 (1931-32): 219-22. Charles Wendell Townsend. 'Concerning Briticisms'.

7 (1931-32): 255-56. Mildred Wasson. 'Cockney American'.
7 (1931-32): 297-301. Stuart Robertson. 'American Speech according to Galsworthy'.
7 (1931-32): 302-5. Howard Frederick Barker. rev. of *A History of Surnames of the British Isles*, by C. L'Estrange Ewen.
7 (1931-32): 412-19. Marvin Theodore Herrick. 'Current English Usage and the Dramas of Galsworthy'.
8 (1933): 1.72-73. H. L. Mencken. 'Notes and Queries' (4 on British expressions and 1 on a British misconception about American).
8 (1933): 2.3-14. A. Lloyd James. 'Standards in Speech' (a paper read before the Philological Society at University College London).
8 (1933): 2.48-50. Lee S. Hultzen. rev. of *An Outline of English Phonetics*, 3d ed., by Daniel Jones.
8 (1933): 2.75. R. H. '"His Grace" and "To Tin"' (corrections to 8: 1.72-73).
8 (1933): 4.3-12. Arthur G. Kennedy. 'The Future of the English Language'.
8 (1933): 4.69-71. George Philip Krapp. rev. of *The Universal Dictionary of the English Language*, ed. Henry Cecil Wyld.
9 (1934): 3-10. R. W. Zandvoort. 'Standards of English in Europe'.
9 (1934): 131-36. Allen Walker Read. 'The Philological Society of New York, 1788'.
10 (1935): 180-83. Edmund E. Miller. 'American and English Translations of "The Oppermanns"'.
10 (1935): 218-19. C. Greet. rev. of *The Broadcast Word*, by A. Lloyd James.
11 (1936): 50-63. Elbridge Colby. 'Soldier Speech'.
11 (1936): 167-68. (phonetic transcription of a radio broadcast by King Edward VIII).
12 (1937): 63-64. 'English Place Names', rev. of *The Concise Oxford Dictionary of English Place-Names*, by Eibert Ekwall.
12 (1937): 82-83. Chad Walsh. 'Refined Speech'.
12 (1937): 164. D. L. Canfield. 'Intervocalic *r*: American, British, Spanish'.
12 (1937): 202. Steven T. Byington. 'Bean in America'.
12 (1937): 207-8. Daniel Jones. 'On "Received Pronunciation"'.
12 (1937): 296-97. C. K. Thomas. 'An English Pronouncing Dictionary', rev. of 4th ed., by Daniel Jones.
13 (1938): 8-12. Robert J. Menner. 'Two Early Comments on American Dialects'.
13 (1938): 294-96. The Editors. 'The Sociological Background', rev. of *The Tongues of Men*, by J. R. Firth.
14 (1939): 127-29. Harry Morgan Ayres. 'Cockney Past and Present', rev. of that book by William Matthews.
14 (1939): 243-54. Stuart Robertson. 'British-American Differentiations in Syntax and Idiom'.
15 (1940): 38. Chad Walsh. 'Broad "A" in Virginia'.
15 (1940): 305-6. Allen Walker Read. 'These Parallel Lists', rev. of *An Anglo-American Interpreter*, by H. W. Horwill.

15 (1940): 328-29. C. A. Lloyd. 'Comments' (on 14: 243-54).
15 (1940): 444-45. William Feather. 'Anglo-American Equations'.
16 (1941): 85-87, 136. William Bell Wait. 'Richardson's "O.K." of 1815'.
16 (1941): 153. William Feather. 'British and American' (comment on 15: 444-45).
16 (1941): 186. 'Army Slang'.
17 (1942): 3-9. A. F. Hubbell. 'A List of Briticisms'.
17 (1942): 70. F. W. B. '"Thriller" and "Shocker"'.
18 (1943): 273-78. Henry W. Wells. 'Kipling's Barrack-Room Language'.
19 (1944): 3-15. H. L. Mencken. 'War Words in England'.
19 (1944): 81-90. Elliott V. K. Dobbie. 'The Word "Commando"'.
19 (1944): 276-80. Henry Alexander. 'Words and the War'.
19 (1944): 292-95. Bob Trout. 'Some Notes on H. L. Mencken's "War Words in England"' (comment on 19: 3-15).
19 (1944): 311. E. V. K. Dobbie. '"Paratroop"' (comment on 19: 3-15).
21 (1946): 45-47. Sir St Vincent Troubridge. 'Some Notes on Rhyming Argot'.
21 (1946): 51-60 (esp. 54-56). Eva Mackintosh. 'A Letter from East Africa to Mr. Mencken'.
21 (1946): 151. Robert J. Menner. 'Affirmative "Any More" in England'.
21 (1946): 307. Paul R. Beath. 'Exit "Queue"'.
22 (1947): 124-30. Louise Pound. 'The American Dialect of Charles Dickens'.
24 (1949): 148-49. Jess Stein. '"Lieutenant" in the British Navy'.
25 (1950): 280-89. Allen Walker Read. 'The Adjective "American" in England'.
27 (1952): 39-42. Herbert Penzl. 'A German Anglist's Description of American English', rev. of *Die Sprache des Amerikaners*, vol. 1, by Hans Galinsky.
27 (1952): 191-96 (esp. 192-93). E. Bagby Atwood. 'A Survey of English since 1900', rev. of *British and American English since 1900*, by Eric Partridge and John W. Clark.
28 (1953): 67-79. Thomas Pyles. 'British Titles of Nobility and Honor in American English'.
28 (1953): 171-80. Jane W. Stedman. 'American English in Punch, 1841-1900'.
28 (1953): 199-200. Sir St Vincent Troubridge. 'British Titles' (comment on 28: 69-79).
29 (1954): 56-59. Herbert Penzl. 'A German Anglist's Description of American English', rev. of *Die Sprache des Amerikaners*, vol. 2, by Hans Galinsky.
30 (1955): 172-75. John Lyman. '*Chantey* and *Limey*'.
31 (1956): 202-8. Mitford M. Mathews. 'Of Matters Lexicographical' (putative Americanisms in the *DA* for which evidence exists in the *EDD* or elsewhere).
31 (1956): 278-83. Mitford M. Mathews. 'Of Matters Lexicographical' (continuation of 31: 202-8).

32 (1957): 130-35. Mitford M. Mathews. 'Of Matters Lexicographical' (prior British use of putative Americanisms in the *DA* uncovered by St. Vincent Troubridge).
33 (1958): 47-49. Herbert Penzl. 'Two German Descriptions of American English', rev. of *Amerikanisches und Britisches Englisch*, by Hans Galinsky, and of *Phonetik des amerikanischen Englisch*, by Kurt Wittig.
34 (1959): 197-201. Dwight L. Bolinger. 'The Intonation of "Received Pronunciation"', rev. of *English Intonation*, by Maria Schubiger.
34 (1959): 243-50. W. Nelson Francis. 'Some Dialect Isoglosses in England'.
34 (1959): 280-86. Thomas L. Crowell. '*Have Got*, A Pattern Preserver'.
35 (1960): 24-28. Anne Lohrli. '"Knocked Up" in England and the United States'.
37 (1962): 83-94. Anne Lohrli. 'Dickens's *Household Words* on American English'.
37 (1962): 142. E. V. K. Dobbie. rev. of *Die Amerikanismen im 'Manchester Guardian Weekly' (1948-54)*, by Gunter Panten.
37 (1962): 275. S. V. Baum. (bibliographical note on 'British Aide Talks on Global English in English English' and other popular pieces on British-American divergence).
38 (1963): 55-58. Seymour Chatman. 'Cockney Phonology', rev. of that book by Eva Sivertsen.
38 (1963): 124-29. Hans Kurath. 'The "Survey of English Dialects"', rev. of *Introduction*, by Harold Orton, and *Basic Material*, vol. 1, by Harold Orton and Wilfred J. Halliday.
38 (1963): 141. E. V. K. Dobbie. rev. of *The Uses of English*, by Randolph Quirk.
39 (1964): 213-16. George W. Hibbitt. 'Pshaw for Shaw's British Alphabet', rev. of *On Language*, by George Bernard Shaw, ed. Abraham Tauber.
42 (1967): 38-44. William Edwin Bettridge. 'American Borrowings of British Motoring Terms'.
43 (1968): 238. Ben Harris McClary. '"Brummagem"--Then and Now' (British pronunciation of *Birmingham*).
44 (1969): 33-54. Albert F. Moe. 'On Haber's "Canine Terms Applied to Human Beings and Human Events"' (comment on 40: 83-101, 243-71, distinguishing British and American uses of the terms).
44 (1969): 200-209. John F. Runcie. 'Truck Drivers' Jargon' (ref. on p. 201 to British Studies of lorry-drivers' jargon and British-American differences).
44 (1969): 234. Raven I. McDavid, Jr. 'The English Can't Make Up Their Mind' (on number agreement of the verb with *management*).
45 (1970): 60-68. Hans Kurath. 'English Sources of Some American Regional Words and Verb Forms'.
45 (1970): 159. 'Query' (on British-American use of *US, USA, US of A,* etc.).

45 (1970): 304-5. Sarah Lawson. '*Immigrant* in British and American Usage'.
47 (1972): 155-57. Donald Kay. '*Tea-Hounds* in Carolina: British Fops and American Hair'.
47 (1972): 159-60. Ashby Bland Crowder. 'Browning's Use of *Kennel*'.
47 (1972): 256-60. Neil G. Grill. 'The *New Monthly Magazine* and American English, 1814-1824'.
47 (1972): 301-3. Esther K. Sheldon. '*Project* and *Scheme*: Switchmates'.
47 (1972): 306-7. Sarah Lawson. '*Mugging* in Britain'.
48 (1973): 108-17. Thomas Pyles. 'British and American English', rev. of *A Concise Pronouncing Dictionary of British and American English*, by J. Windsor Lewis; *A Dictionary of Modern American and British English on a Contrastive Basis*, by Givi Zviadadze; and *British Self-Taught*, by Norman W. Schur.
48 (1973): 276-78. Henry R. Stern. 'British and American', rev. of *What's the Difference? A British/American Dictionary*, by Norman Moss.
49 (1974): 67-78. Patricia A. Moody. '*Shall* and *Will*: The Grammatical Tradition and Dialectology'.
49 (1974): 79-89. Sidney Greenbaum. 'Some Verb-Intensifier Collocations in American and British English'.
49 (1974): 278-81 (esp. 279). Gordon R. Wood. 'Five Analyses of Twentieth-Century English', rev. inter alia of *Varieties of English*, by G. L. Brook.
50 (1975): 313-15. Dwight Bolinger. 'Are You a Sincere *H*-Dropper?' (on *an* before words beginning with *h*).
50 (1975): 317-19. Sarah Lawson. 'Traduit de l'americain'.
51 (1976): 44. '*To Part Brass Rags*'.
51 (1976): 219-22. Raven I. McDavid, Jr. 'Harold Orton, 23 October 1898 - 7 March 1975'.
51 (1976): 223-34. J. Derrick McClure. 'The Linguistic Atlas of Scotland', rev. of vol. 1, by J. Y. Mather and H. H. Speitel.
51 (1976): 234-38. Frederic G. Cassidy. 'The Scottish National Dictionary', rev. of that work, ed. William Grant and David D. Murison.
51 (1976): 285-92. Lea Bussey Lane. 'Automotive Terms in British and American English'.
53 (1978): 221-31. W. Nelson Francis. 'Word Geography of England', rev. of that book by Harold Orton and Nathalia Wright.
55 (1980): 79-80. Sarah Lawson. '*Macho* and *Machismo*'.
56 (1981): 97. 'From Womanly *Ms* to Gentlewomanly *Loz*'.
56 (1981): 139-41. Morton Dilkes. 'U and Non-U', rev. of *U and Non-U Revisited*, ed. Richard Buckle.
56 (1981): 143-44. Sarah Lawson. 'Confusables/Confusibles', rev. of *Room's Dictionary of Confusibles*, by Adrian Room.
56 (1981): 219-34. Raven I. McDavid, Jr. 'Linguistic Atlas of England', rev. of that book, ed. Harold Orton, Stewart Sanderson, and John Widdowson.

56 (1981): 234-36. Ronald R. Butters. 'British Dialects', rev. of *English Accents and Dialects*, by Arthur Hughes and Peter Trudgill.
57 (1982): 43. Ronald R. Butters. 'Media Watch' (on a literary dialect spelling for /h/-less *who*).
57 (1982): 197. 'Words Words Words' (including a note on *Britglish* 'British English').
58 (1983): 84-85. Sarah Lawson. '*Girl* in British Newspapers'.
58 (1983): 368-71. Sarah Lawson. 'A Curate's Egg', rev. of *Longman Dictionary of English Idioms*.
59 (1984): 99-122. Thomas E. Murray. '*Poppy Show*'.
59 (1984): 165-72. Richard W. Bailey. 'Brits Broadcasting', rev. of *The Spoken Word: A BBC Guide*, by Robert Burchfield.
59 (1984): 246-49. Thomas E. Murray. 'Of Dictionaries and Dictionary Makers', rev. of *Harmless Drudges* by Israel Shenker.
59 (1984): 310-31. Alan Crozier. 'The Scotch-Irish Influence on American English'.
60 (1985): 88. Ronald R. Butters. 'The Editor Recommends', rev. of *A Bibliography of Writings on Varieties of English, 1965-1983*, ed. Wolfgang Viereck, Edgar W. Schneider, and Manfred Gorlach.
61 (1986): 60. Ronald R. Butters. 'Query: *Sorry* "Excuse Me"'.
62 (1987): 84-89. Yakov Malkiel. '(American) English *Perspire, Transpire*'.
62 (1987): 99-119. Douglas Biber. 'A Textual Comparison of British and American Writing'.
62 (1987): 242-48. John Algeo and Mary Gray Porter. 'Among the New Words' (British neologisms).
62 (1987): 346-53. John Algeo. 'Among the New Words' (British neologisms).
62 (1987): 369-75. Keith Walters. 'Advances in Cartographic Dialectology', rev. of *Studies in Linguistic Geography: The Dialects of English in Britain and Ireland*, ed. John M. Kirk, Stewart Sanderson, and J. D. A. Widdowson.

THE STYLISTIC FUNCTION OF ME *GAN* RECONSIDERED*

LAUREL J. BRINTON
University of British Columbia

0. *Introduction*. A characteristic feature of Middle English verse style is the occurrence of *gan* 'began' with an accompanying infinitive; this collocation appears in the earliest Middle English and is common throughout the period.[1] Despite the morphological relation of ME *ginnen* to NE *begin*, an ingressive interpretation of *gan* is frequently not possible. Earlier suggestions that *gan* served an 'intensive-descriptive' function in Middle English in emphasizing the action expressed by the infinitive and in isolating it from the surrounding actions of the narrative are now dismissed as subjective and indemonstrable. *Gan* is generally considered to be a meaningless filler, serving as a metrical expedient (see, e.g., Visser 1969:1572),[2] a dummy tense carrier (see, e.g., Traugott 1972: 138, 141), and otherwise as a precursor of *do*. However, this view of *gan* leaves unanswered diachronically interesting questions concerning the choice of this particular verb and semantic changes undergone by it in its evolution as a metrical filler. Significantly, such questions are central to discussions of the origin and development of the comparable *do*

form (see, e.g., Ellegård 1953:20-21, 28-33; Visser 1969:1492; Denison 1985).

Since both the arguments given in favor of the stylistic function of *gan* and the linguistic evidence adduced against it seem misguided, I propose, in light of current work in discourse analysis, to approach the problem of ME *gan* quite differently. It is widely acknowledged that there is a varied set of linguistic forms whose meaning, syntactic distribution, or function defies analysis on the clausal level, but which can be satisfactorily explained with reference to the larger organization of discourse (Stubbs 1983:67, 82; see Longacre 1979a for a list of such forms). The central role of tense and aspect forms in discourse is also recognized (Hopper 1983a). Given the nature of discourse markers and the kinds of linguistic evidence significant in establishing discourse functions, therefore, I will argue that ME *gan* serves as a discourse structure marker rather than as a stylistic indicator of emphasis or importance. Additionally, given semantic and pragmatic principles of grammaticalization (Traugott 1982), I will present a plausible semantic development for *gan* from aspectual to discourse meaning.

1. *The stylistic function of gan.* Though claims about the stylistic function of *gan* are now rejected, I believe that they warrant re-examination to determine ways in which they were both misguided yet insightful.

The stylistic function was first described by Otto Funke:

> Tatsache ist, dass es [*gan*] in vielen Fällen nicht perfektiv fungiert, sondern den Ansatzpunkt einer neuen Handlung und

damit diese selbst als Glied einer Reihe heller beleuchtet und
hervorhebt. Hierbei handelt es sich nicht um eine perfektiv-
aktionelle Betonung der im Infinitiv gelegenen Aktion an und
für sich, sondern um die Art der An- und Einreihung dieser
Aktion in den Gesamtverlauf der Vorstellungen. Dass mit dieser
Verschärfung eines Handlungsansatzes in lebhafter Schilderung
dieses Handlungsglied selbst gehoben wird oder gehoben werden
kann, dürfte wohl nicht bezweifelt werden. Hier gehen also
Wege zu einem Intensivum weiter. Im allgemeinen aber ist heir
ein Mittel gegeben zur Erhöhung der Situation, zu kräftigem
Handlungseinsatz und zur Belebung des Aktionsverlaufes
(1922:8).

Funke proposes the term 'descriptive' to account for this function of *gan*. Mustanoja (1960:610-15) substitutes the term 'intensive-descriptive' and suggests that as a 'mere intensifier of the main verb [*gan* may] enable the speaker or writer to describe the dynamic qualities of an action in a more vivid and forceful way than would be possible by using a simple verb form'. The only detailed study which sets out to demonstrate this function is Homann (1954); she claims that Chaucer uses *gan* to make distinctions of tempo, intensity, and manner, and to indicate dramatic moments, nuances of character, or vivid and exciting contexts. However, her study has been seen as a case of 'hinein-interpretieren', or reading into a text grammatical or semantic distinctions which are not present or were not intended.[3]

    I believe that Funke's proposal is misguided in three ways. First, in suggesting that the function of *gan* is to 'intensify', 'emphasize', 'heighten', or 'strengthen' the situation expressed by the infinitive, Funke attributes to the form a marked or intensive quality (Funke 1922:2, 8,

13) and thus departs quite far from Alfred Wuth's original claim (which he is trying to clarify) that *gan* has the neutral meaning 'da geschah dass ... da setzte das nun ein' (1915:56). It has been easy for critics of Funke's theory to show that *gan* is frequently not used in semantically important contexts (see, e.g., Koziol 1932:131-32), and to argue that intensive or emphatic meanings, where they exist, derive from the context, not from the semantics of *gan* (see, e.g., Smyser 1967:72). Proponents of the theory would have done well to heed the warning of Funke's student, Hans Häusermann, that the 'Hervorheben' (highlighting or foregrounding) of the action by *gan* does not in fact constitute an 'intensive Aktionsart':

> Die deskriptive Ausdrucksform lässt das Wesen der Handlung selbst unverändert, sie appelliert nur an die Aufmerksamkeit des Lesers oder Hörers durch die Ankündigung von etwas Neuem, Unerwartetem (1930:19).

Second, Funke establishes three separate functions of *gan*: perfective, descriptive, and pleonastic (1922:2, 15; Häusermann 1930:18-22). However, his attempts to determine which of these functions *gan* has in any particular instance are often arguable. Scholars have found these functions difficult to distinguish (see, e.g. Koziol 1932:131-32; Kerkhof 1966:30-32), and Visser (1969:1379) concludes that classification is 'largely arbitrary'. Rather than discrete functions, *gan* seems to serve multiple functions: 'We have good reason to believe', Mustanoja observes (1960:612), 'that in addition to metre and rhyme other stylistic considerations play a certain role in a good poet's choice between the simple preterite and *gan*-periphrasis'. Third, Funke gives no explicit criteria, either for the impossibility of aspectual meaning[4] or for the presence of descriptive meaning in *gan*. Lack of linguistic evidence, other than individual assessments of where emphasis falls in a text, causes arguments for the stylistic function of *gan* to appear 'kaum beweisbar' (Koziol 1932:131-32).

2. *Evidence against the stylistic function of* gan. Linguistic evidence adduced against the stylistic function of *gan* consists of two types, the apparent synonymy of the *gan* construction and other forms, and the restriction of the *gan* periphrasis to certain types of metrical texts.

2.1. The *gan* periphrasis appears to have two rival constructions in Middle English. The first is periphrastic *do*, which may alternate with *gan* in different manuscripts of the same text; the second is the historical present, which sometimes co-occurs with *gan* in the same contexts.[5] From the interchangeability and assumed equivalency of these constructions, it is concluded that *gan* is meaningless. However, while Visser has argued that the historical present serves as a meaningless metrical filler in Middle English (1966:711, 718; cf. Ness and Duncan-Rose 1982:301-06) and several scholars have suggested that *do* serves a similar function (see Ellegård 1953:208; Smyser 1967:81-82; Visser 1969:1498), there is still considerable uncertainty concerning the meaning and function of both forms during this period. It could equally well be argued (see below) that all three serve a stylistic function. Furthermore, the overlapping of these constructions is far from complete; their distribution is more or less complementary over time, genre (or author), and perhaps dialect.[6] *Gan* is common during the entire ME period and antedates both the historical present and *do*. The rise in frequency of *do* in

the 15th century coincides with the decline of *gan*.
Whereas Chaucer uses *gan* and the historical present
equally, alliterative versifiers use the historical present
but seldom *gan*; neither uses *do* frequently (see Funke
1922:17ff., 22ff., 26; Mustanoja 1960:603, 614; Smyser
1967:1967:69, 79; Tajima 1975:435). Given the lack of
parallel distribution and uncertainty about the meaning of
all three constructions, therefore, I believe that evidence
for their similar function and lack of meaning is
inconclusive.

2.2. The second kind of evidence produced against the
stylistic function of *gan* is the restricted distribution of
the periphrasis: *gan* is very rare in prose and not at all
frequent in unrhymed alliterative verse (see Funke
1922:22ff.; Koziol 1932:131-34). For example, while
Chaucer uses *gan* over seven hundred times in his rhymed
verse (Smyser 1967:69), he uses it only three times in the
'Melibeus' and not at all in his other prose works (Kerkhof
1966:31). *Con* (the Northern form of *gan*) is common in the
rhymed alliterative poem 'Purity', less common in the partially rhymed 'Gawain and the Green Knight', and rare in
the unrhymed 'Patience' and 'Purity'; in fact, it occurs
only eleven times in unrhymed portions of the 'Gawain'
poet's verse (Tajima 1975:432, 434). From such negative
evidence, it is concluded that *gan* must serve as a meaningless expedient in metrical verse: that it provides an extra
syllable in a line or allows the infinitive to be placed in
line-final, rhyme position. Positive evidence is the
appearance of the infinitive in rhyme position in a majority of cases where *gan* is used (95% of time for the
'Gawain' poet, see Tajima 1975:433; 73% of the time for
Chaucer, see Smyser 1967:74). Although the statistical

evidence for the metrical function of *gan* appears quite
convincing, prose narratives in this period are very
scarce, so the rarity of this characteristically 'narrative
idiom' (Taylor 1917:575) in ME prose is not surprising.[7]
More importantly, the metrical usefulness of *gan* is important only to the spread of the construction and possibly to
its ultimate loss; it says nothing about the origin,
semantic development, and primary function of *gan*.[8] I
think that it must have been the case that a pre-existing
(and meaningful) *gan*-construction provided the poet with a
ready expedient in composing his verse and that the metrical utility of the periphrasis contributed to its popularity and wide-spread use, not that the periphrasis developed
originally to serve this function.

3. *The discourse function of gan*. While the spread of
gan can be explained by its metrical usefulness, its meaning and function must be a consequence of its original
meaning. OE *onginnan*, from which ME *gan* derives aphetically, functions unambiguously as a marker of ingressive
aspect with the meaning of 'to begin'. I will argue in the
remainder of the paper that *gan* develops the secondary
functions generally observed in aspectual forms and undergoes a similar semantic development.

3.1. Because a central task in discourse, especially
narrative discourse, is the placement and sequencing of
events in time, tense and aspect forms perform a crucial
function (Longacre 1979a:258). That aspect serves primarily a global discourse function rather than a local semantic function is the premise of a recent collection of
articles (Hopper 1982a) and of a series of articles by Paul
Hopper (1979a; 1979b; 1982b), who defines aspect as fol-

lows: 'Aspect considered from a discourse perspective is a device or set of devices that exists in order to guide the language user through a text' (1979b:219).[9] The focus of attention in discourse studies of aspect has been on functional differences between the perfective and imperfective: perfective aspect, it is generally agreed, indicates the strict chronological sequence of events viewed as wholes, while imperfective aspect indicates simultaneous or overlapping events viewed as happening (see Hopper 1979a:61). Furthermore, according to Hopper (1979a:61; 1979b:213, 216), the perfective marks 'foregrounded' 'event[s] indispensable to the narrative' and the imperfective marks 'backgrounded' 'state[s] or situation[s] necessary for understanding motives, attitudes, etc.', and according to Longacre (1983:14-17), aspect functions along with other formal markers in distinguishing 'mainline' or 'backbone' events from supportive material.

When attention is focused on ingressive aspect markers, however, an important difference is apparent: while perfective and imperfective forms are distributed evenly throughout the discourse, ingressive forms occur only at certain points. In discourse studies, it is widely recognized that there exists a set of formal markers, termed 'overt sequence signals' of 'closure' (Longacre 1979b:117) or 'discourse structure signalling devices' (Polanyi and Scha 1983:263), which occur at the beginning and/or end of coherent units of discourse; on the surface, these units correspond more or less to 'paragraphs', while on a semantic level, they are characterized as 'episodes' (van Dijk 1982). It is also generally agreed that a significant change in temporal or spatial setting, participants, action, or theme brings about a break between episodes (Chafe 1979:179, 177-78; also van Dijk 1982:177; Brown and Yule 1983:96). A variety of formal devices may mark these structural breaks: major hesitations in oral discourse or paragraph indentations in written discourse, sentence adverbs or conjunctions, deictic pronouns, back reference, frame-shifting adverbs of time or place, indications of change of cast, or change of perspective markers, including markers of aspect, tense, and mood (see Longacre 1979b: 117-18; van Dijk 1982:181; Polanyi and Scha 1983:266). The particular signals used appear to be genre-specific (Brown and Yule 1983:95). I would like to suggest, then, that ME *gan* serves just such a 'delimiting' function. It occurs at stages in the narrative sequence, at points of transition between episodes. Specifically, it indicates the beginning of a new or significant event in the discourse. A suitable paraphrase for the *gan* construction in its discourse function might be 'it then happened that ...' or 'it chanced that ...'.

3.2. Furthermore, the progression from aspectual to discourse meaning is semantically transparent and compatible with changes observed in the process of grammaticalization. In essence, there is no change in meaning, only an extension of the scope of 'beginning' from an action considered in isolation to an action or actions considered in relation to the other actions in the discourse. The course followed by *gan* conforms to the principles of semantic and pragmatic change noted by Traugott (1982:256) for lexical items undergoing grammaticalization: namely, from propositional to textual to expressive meaning. Whereas aspectual meaning belongs within the 'propositional' domain, episode boundary meaning belongs within the 'textual' domain. Furthermore, since situations marked by *gan* represent new or important stages in the plot development and sometimes happen suddenly, unexpectedly, or fortuitously, *gan* may acquire the 'expressive' (emphatic, intensive) meanings mentioned by Funke and followers.

4. *Evidence for the discourse function of gan*.
Evidence for the discourse function of *gan* is of two types: textual and comparative. When considering the evidence, one must keep in mind two general qualities of discourse markers which cause their distribution to appear unsystematic. First, since discourse markers are non-obligatory (see Brown and Yule 1983:107), they do not always appear where expected; Stein (1985:299) argues that the best one can say is that given certain factors, the appearance of a discourse marker is 'likely' but not 'categorical'. Second, since such markers may have multiple functions, operating on the morphophonemic, syntactic, semantic, or pragmatic level as well as the discourse level (van Dijk 1982:179; Stubbs 1983:83; Stein 1985:283, 299, 300), they will often not be serving exclusively, or even primarily, as discourse markers in any particular context; it may prove difficult in individual cases to differentiate a discourse-motivated from a non-discourse-motivated occurrence of the form.

4.1. The textual evidence significant for establishing the discourse function of *gan* is quite different from the evidence cited either to support or to refute its stylistic function. Rather than noting its distribution among different types of texts, one must carefully observe its distribution within an individual text. One would not expect it to be evenly spaced in the text, as one would if it were merely a metrical filler (see Ness and Duncan-Rose

1982:312), since in its discourse function, its occurrence is determined by the larger content structure, not the structure of the individual verse line. One would also not expect it to co-occur regularly with particular syntactic, semantic, or even 'stylistic' features, but rather with other discourse boundary markers, such as frame-shifting temporal and spatial adverbs and conjunctions.

I have looked at the occurrence of *gan* in *Troilus and Criseyde*, in which Chaucer uses the form more frequently than in any other text (Beschorner 1920:10; Smyser 1967:82-83). By my count there are 302 examples of *gan* or *gonnen* in 8239 lines of text.[10] Though the use of *gan* here is sometimes attributed to Italian influence, the preponderance of this form in *Troilus and Criseyde*, considered by many to represent the height of Chaucer's poetic achievement, has not been explained other than as a metrical filler.

The occurrences of *gan* in *Troilus and Criseyde* can in fact be convincingly explained by its discourse function.[11] *Gan* is very unevenly distributed both in respect to the five books constituting *Troilus and Criseyde* and within individual books. Per hundred lines, *gan* occurs 3.11 times in Book I, 5.24 times in Book II, 3.85 times in Book III, 2.47 times in Book IV, and 3.42 times in Book V. This distribution corresponds closely to the amount of narrated action as opposed to reported speech or thought in each book. For example, whereas Book II includes all the actions which bring Troilus and Criseyde together and hence has the highest proportion of *gan*'s, Book IV consists almost entirely of discussion of the imminent separation of Troilus and Criseyde and hence has the lowest proportion.

Gan appears only four times in direct discourse; in three of the four cases, there is an embedded narration (II 194, II 509ff., V 1467ff.)[12] Otherwise, *gan* always marks 'complicating actions' as opposed to 'evaluation' or 'orientation' (to use Labov's distinction 1972:363ff.); in the case of *Troilus and Criseyde*, complicating actions are as often mental as physical. *Gan*'s generally occur in multiples rather than singly, and these clusters seem to signal the essential plot actions. In fact, a list of the actions expressed with *gan* (see Appendix A) could well serve as a plot synopsis of *Troilus and Criseyde*. More specifically, *gan* occurs in a number of identifiable contexts, all representing junctures in the narrative sequence:

(a) changes in the time of day (II 65-71, II 906, III 1418, IV 1690; V 276, V 515, V 1108);

(b) changes in scene or cast (e.g. II 80, II 614, II 943, II 1096, II 1318, II 1460, II 1668, II 1702, III 57-72, III 206, III 424, III 554-56, III 1528-35, III 1556, III 1594, IV 355, IV 813, IV 1128, IV 1693, V 82, V 294);

(c) introduction to or conclusion of speeches (e.g. I 204, I 329, I 506, I 596, I 1044, II 253-54, II 428, II 505, II 825, II 884, IV 519, IV 521, V 637, V 870, V 925, V 1006, V 1456-57, V 1538);

(d) character internal changes--resolutions, responses, etc. (e.g. I 866, I 1085, II 455, II 674, II 806, II 1159-67, II 1337, III 155, IV 631, IV 1427, V 433, V 1667);

(e) turns in the general course of events (e.g. I 139, III 1696-99, IV 8, V 1, V 1546, V 1745);

(f) fortuitous occurrences (e.g. I 275, II 1250, III 626, III 743, IV 131, IV 1213, V 1656-59).

The co-occurrence of adverbs with *gan* (see Appendix B) also provides very convincing evidence for the discourse function of *gan*. The most common adverbs are temporal sequencers, followed by resultative and causal adverbs which express a temporal as well as a logical relation. *Gan* occurs most frequently in clauses following a *whan* clause. All of the adverbs thus function as temporal frame-shifters and reinforce the boundary marking features of *gan*. Furthermore, though manner adverbs are fairly common with *gan*, they are restricted to two forms, one of which (*thus*) can also express a resultative connection.

The uneven distribution of *gan* throughout *Troilus and Criseyde*, therefore, and the frequent co-occurrence of sequencing adverbs both point to the delimiting function of *gan* in discourse: *gan* serves to mark structurally significant transitions and the beginning of new episodes in the advancement of the plot.

4.2. Comparative evidence for the discourse function of *gan*, though weaker, is of two kinds: first, the existence of parallel functions in *do* and the historical present, and second, the development of parallel functions in other ingressive markers.

4.2.1. It is occasionally observed that *do* has a 'stylistic' function similar to that of *gan*. For example, Mustanoja (1960:602) notes that *do* may 'intensify the force of the verb', while Funke (1922:15-16) suggests tentatively that *do* may be an 'intensive'. Stein (1985:294ff.) argues that in Early Modern English, at least, *do* occurs at the juncture of structural parts of a texts and marks the beginning of a complicating action. A number of stylistic functions are also attributed to the historical present in Middle English: it may denote transitions, new phases of the action, or changes in person (Mustanoja 1960:487); when accompanied by connective adverbs and with verbs of motion, it can mark important turning points (Trnka 1930:17); it provides the syntactic correlate to style switching (Ness and Duncan-Rose 1982:306ff.); and it takes over the 'descriptive' function of *gan*, though incorporating a somewhat different world-view (Funke 1922:16, 23). Accounts of the function of the historical present in Modern English[13] argue that rather than increasing the vividness, liveliness, and drama of a text, as traditional accounts assert, the switch from past to present tense (and back) serves to organize a discourse into segments, signal breaks, and give focus to textual divisions (Wolfson 1979), a function identical to that of ME *gan*.

4.2.2. The use of a number of other ingressive aspect markers in a 'delimiting' function in discourse attests to the naturalness of the development for which I am arguing. First, though the verb *comsen*, ultimately deriving from Lt. *com-* + *initiare* meaning 'to begin', had a limited distribution (occurring primarily in two texts) and lifespan (from c. 1250 - 1400), the *MED* (s.v. *comsen*, def. 2; also Visser 1969:1375-76) sees *gan* as a model for *comsen*, suggests that it is 'usually, if not always simply stressing the fact that something actually is done or occurs', and compares it with *do*. Funke (1922:23-24) likewise attributes both 'perfective' and 'descriptive' functions to *comsen*. Second, two hendiadic structures involving ingressive as-pectualizers, *take and* V and *go and* V, are attested in late Old English or Middle English to the present (see Rynell

1960:128-31; Visser 1969:1397-98) which, because of the presence of aspectually incompatible elements, more plausible express discourse rather than ingressive meaning. Both periphrases are still current, with acquired expressive meanings (see *OED* s.v. *go*, def. 32c and *OED* Supplement, s.v. *take*, def. IV, 25d). Third, the ingressive aspectualizers, *break* and *burst (out)*, common in Middle English but quite restricted in Modern English, appear to have had a discourse function when occurring in hendiadic structures. Finally, Visser (1969:1377) suggests that the ingressive aspectualizer *fall* sometimes means 'something like *happen*', citing examples from Middle English to the present.

5. *Conclusion*. In conclusion, Otto Funke's original description of the stylistic function of *gan* now appears more credible. In suggesting that the function of *gan* was to indicate 'the kind of sequencing and placement of [the] action in the entire succession of events', Funke seems to have come close to articulating the textual function of *gan* as a marker of discourse structure. However, his insistence on the discreteness of the propositional, textual, and expressive functions and on the primacy of the emphatic and intensive meanings, combined with his failure to provide linguistic evidence, weakens his arguments. Here I have tried to provide evidence based on the placement of *gan* within the narrative structure of an extended text and on the co-occurrence of sequencing adverbs, as well as comparative evidence of parallel functions in other stylistic markers and ingressive aspectualizers, of the role of *gan* in Middle English in marking significant transitions or junctures in the narrative plot. In addition to clarifying the function of this 'mystery particle' in

Middle English, this study has perhaps also contributed to our general understanding of discourse markers: of their sources, of their semantic developments, of their spread, and of their transience (Stein 1985:300). *Gan* seems a particularly clear case of the ephemerality of discourse markers, since its use did not last beyond the Middle English period.

NOTES

* Research for this paper was supported in part by a Leave Fellowship (1986-87) from the Social Sciences and Humanities Research Council of Canada, which also supplied travel funds for my attendance at ICEHL5. I am grateful for this support.
1. For brief accounts of the history of *gan*, see Funke (1922:26), Mustanoja (1960:610), and Visser (1969:1571-75).
2. In a recent article (1983), Tauno Mustanoja questions his earlier (1960) arguments for the 'intensive-descriptive' function of *gan* and ultimately finds himself in agreement with the majority of scholars that *gan* serves an exclusively metrical function (see Taylor 1917:574, 590; Beschorner 1920:15-16, 17-19; Koziol 1932:132, 133; Smyser 1967: 69, 74, 81; Visser 1969: 1372; Tajima 1975: 434, 437-38; Ness and Duncan-Rose 1982:303).
3. Homann's study is deemed unconvincing by a number of scholars (Kerkhof 1966:31; Smyser 1967:72-74; Visser 1969:1572; cf. Mustanoja 1983). Despite the rather impressionistic nature of her study, I believe that at times she comes close to seeing the real function of *gan*, e.g.: 'the primary behest in narrative communication is to emphasize the important points along the span of movement, to make clear the relationship between these points, and to suggest the tempos and duration of movement ... [the *gan*] form helped the narrator to choose out and stress the beginning or the end of the action or the continuance of time in which the action existed' (1954:398; cf.390, 392).
4. In Brinton (1983), I present criteria based on a theory of aspect: the occurrence either of verbs with punctual aktionsart or of durative/iterative adverbs prevents an ingressive reading of *gan* (cf. Smyser 1967:69).
5. On the equivalency of *gan* and *do*, see Taylor (1917:573), Funke (1922:15-16, 18), Trnka (1930:34, 52), Mustanoja (1960:602, 611, 614), Visser (1969:1492, 1571, 1572, 1577, 1579), Traugott (1972:138, 141), Tajima (1975:435), *MED* (svv. *ginnen*, def. 3b, *beginnen*, def. 6, and *can* v2). Wuth (1915:55) is alone in rejecting the equation of *gan* and *do*; he observes that although

both seem superfluous according to our 'Sprachgefühl', they have very different 'Grundbedeutungen'.

On the equivalency of *gan* and the historical present, see Beschorner (1920:13), Funke (1922:15, 16, 19-20), and Mustanoja (1960:486, 614).

6. According to Traugott (1972:141), the *gan* periphrasis developed in the northeast in the 13th century and spread to the south in the 14th century. However, its rarity in the Ormulum and frequency in La amon casts doubt on this course of development. Apparently, *gan* was common in the north, east, and south and uncommon in the northwest and west. The distribution of *gan* is a complex question deserving much fuller examination.

7. Significantly, the three instances of *gan* in Chaucer's 'Melibeus' occur in the few truly narrative passages of this prose tract, and they mark important stages in the narrative: Melibeus's reaction to the attack by his enemies (ll. 972, 974) and his decision to accept Prudence's advice (l. 1870).

8. In general, metrical exigency is a convenient, but not very convincing explanation of the function of linguistic forms. The requirements of verse alone cannot motivate the use of basic grammatical forms such as those of tense and aspect (see Ness and Duncan-Rose 1982:305). As Denison observes (1985:45) of similar arguments about *do*, 'The implication is that but for the advent of rhyming verse there would have been no motivation' for the periphrases.

It is telling that though Chaucer parodies all of the contemporary metrical expedients in 'Sir Thopas', neither *gan* nor the historical present is included (Funke 1922:26; Smyser 1967:312; Ness and Duncan-Rose 1982:312).

9. Hopper (1982b:10, 13, 15-16) contends that discourse/pragmatic functions are primary, and that the standardly recognized aspectual meanings are synchronically 'additive', 'sedimented', or grammaticalized, merely the 'sentence-level correlates of discourse structure'. However, as Friedrich observes (1985:186), proponents of this view 'assume the "primacy" of discourse ... but leave unsolved the question of its priority--perhaps because this is unknowable, or because the question is trivial'. I think it more likely, given diachronic evidence, that discourse meanings derive from original aspectual meanings. Stein (1985:299) argues that textual or discourse meanings are always peripheral: 'these meanings seem to have to depend for their surface realisations on what happens to be left over by the structural make-up of a language at a given evolutionary stage'.

10. In contrast, the present tense of *gan* occurs only three times (IV 12, V 657, V 1286), and forms of *beginnen* only fourteen times (II 408, II 511, II 518, II 1276, III 961, IV 240, IV 1218, V 13, V 214, V 247, V 519, V 1026, V 1091, V 1800).

11. Surprisingly, it is a scholar who argues most forcefully for the metrical function of *gan* who supplies some evidence for its discourse function. Beschorner (1920:9-11) first notes that *gan*

does not appear at regular intervals in Chaucer's verse. He then observes that infinitives following *gan* fall into a number of lexical classes: verbs of motion, vision, sound, desire or its expression, and emotion and its expression. Furthermore, *gan* occurs when the action expressed happens suddenly or in haste, as denoted by the following: the verb *hye*; adverbs such as *anoon*, *right anoon*, *anoon-right*, *sodenly*, *swythe*; and conjoined sentences, either with explicit conjunctions (e.g. *and also sone*) or not. Finally, *gan* often denotes changes in the time of day, especially the transition from day to night or vice versa (see also Homann 1954:391). The verbs occurring typically with *gan* thus denote aspectually definite changes or events which happen unexpectedly or by chance; both kinds of events would naturally initiate a new episode. In *Troilus and Criseyde*, however, *gan* appears with a wide variety of verbs, frequently in conjoined clauses. It occurs only rarely with adverbs expressing suddenness (T 278, III 691, III 000, IV 1001, V 1505).

12. The use of *gan* in the passage (II 509ff.) is quite marked; *gan* appears four times in the first eighteen lines of the narrative along with two occurrences of *beginnen*. The exaggerated use of *gan* here may either point to the colloquial nature of the form or underscore the fictivity of Pandarus's story.

13. Visser (1966:725) argues that the use of the historical present in Middle English and in Modern English is not connected, primarily because whereas the form is now sustained throughout an entire text, earlier it occurred only sporadically in a text. However, Wolfson (1979) and others have shown that in Modern English the historical present is sustained through very short texts such as jokes, but that under normal circumstances it occurs only occasionally. It is the switch from one tense to another which is signifilcant (Wolfson 1979:173-74).

14. All line numbers refer to Robinson's (1957) edition of Chaucer's work; T = Troilus, C = Criseyde, P = Pandarus. Space limitations prevent a complete listing of the occurrences of *gan* in all of the books of *Troilus and Criseyde*, but this may be obtained from the author.

APPENDIX A: OCCURRENCES OF *GAN* IN *TROILUS AND CRISEYDE*[14]

Line	Verb of Infinitive	Action
Book I		
139	whielen 'turn'	Trojan war begins to take its course
189	preise 'praise'	T speaks disparagingly of love
190	wayten 'observe'	
192	syke 'sigh'	
204	caste 'cast'	T's words provoke the God of Love

206	loken 'look'	
275	biholde 'behold'	T sees C for the first time
278	sprede & rise 'spread & rise'	
289	like 'like'	T is pleased with C's appearance
293	lighte 'soften'	C changes her look
295	quyken 'quicken'	T responds to the look
297	stiken 'stick'	T receives lasting impression of C
322	dissimulen & hide 'dissemble & hide'	T regrets his words, hides his love
329	smyle 'smile'	
360	sike & grone 'sigh & groan'	Alone, T begins to show his love
364	avise 'consider'	T remembers C's look
365	make 'make'	T visualizes C
390	wynne 'overcome'	T conquers sorrow by giving into love
391	assente 'consent'	
443	quiken & encresse 'grow & increase'	T's love increases, he seeks release
446	presse 'hasten'	
486	multiplie 'multiply'	T's sickness begins to show
488	borwe 'borrow'	
506	pleyne 'complain'	T rebukes himself for his foolishness
546	multiplie 'multiply'	Nonetheless, his woe continues
596	syke 'sigh'	T tells P of his love
749	caste 'consider'	T will not reveal lover's identity
751	syken 'sigh'	T awakes from his stupor
827	syke 'sigh'	T begins to accept P's reasoning
866	blede 'bleed'	T capitulates to P and names C
869	shake 'shake'	
871	quake 'quake'	
1044	falle 'falle'	P will act for T
1085	chaunge 'change'	T is a changed man on account of love

Book IV

8	writhe 'turn'	T's fortunes change
131	biseke 'beseech'	Chalcus asks Greeks for his daughter
150	chaungen 'change'	T learns of the exchange
154	drye 'dry'	
168	deliberen 'deliberate'	T tries to decide on course of action
178	withstonde 'oppose'	Hector opposes plan
242	sterte 'leap'	Alone in his chamber, T reacts to news
348	breyde 'start'	P reacts to news
355	gon 'go'	P goes to T
361	byholden 'behold'	
367	melte 'melt'	T's responds to P's visit
373	bresten 'burst'	
519	distille 'distill'	T ends his speech rejecting P's solace
521	holde 'hold'	P holds his tongue but then continues
631	quyken 'recover'	T decides to take action, speak to C

702	spende 'tell'	Trojan women visit C
709	welle 'well'	
722	comforten 'comfort'	
733	falle 'fall'	C begins her lament
813	trete 'treat'	P goes to C, finds her desolate
819	desire 'desire'	
820	hide 'hide'	
826	pleyne 'complain'	
912	wepen 'weep'	C wants T to come to her
1128	mete 'meet'	C and T meet
1129	twiste 'twist'	
1144	wayken 'awaken'	T and C's feelings
1145	ebben 'ebb'	
1156	biholde 'behold'	T looks at apparently lifeless C
1173	wypen 'wipe'	
1174	preye 'pray'	
1182	dresse 'dress'	
1213	sike 'sigh'	C revives
1224	espie 'see'	C sees T's sword
1225	crye 'cry'	
1229	biholde 'behold'	C embraces T
1230	folde 'fold'	
1249	byholde 'behold'	T and C look at each other sadly
1427	wreste 'constrain'	T decides to trust C's plan
1690	rise 'rise'	Daylight comes
1691	byholde 'behold'	T looks at C in bed
1693	recomaunde 'recommend'	T takes leave of C

APPENDIX B: CO-OCCURRENCE OF *GAN* AND ADVERBS

Adverbs of temporal sequence:
1. preceding *whan*-clause: I 329, I 360-64, I 506, I 546, I 751, II 5, II 80, II 768, II 1172-73, II 1492-96, III 424, III 54-56, II 1232, III 1416-18, IV 820, IV 1129, IV 1182, IV 1249 V 107, V 182, V 515, V 532, V 535-38, V 637, V 1546, V 656
2. within *whan*-clause: III 89, III 1123, III 1416-18, IV 1128, IV 1144-45, V 37, V 181, V533
3. a. (*right*) *tho*: I 866, I 871, I 1044, II 141, II 505, II 519, II 1128, II 1639, III 72, III 348, III 1170, III 1203, III 1396, III 1646, IV 826, IV 1173-74;
   b. *fro this forth tho*: I 486-88
   c. *than(ne)*: I 596, III 561
   d. *forth*: V 1745
4. a. *after that*: I 293, II 806, II 1082, IV 1690
   b. (*soone/so*) *after this*: II 150, II 1076, III 568, III 1672
   c. *after noon*: II 1186
   d. *after soper*: III 610   e. *afterward*: I322

      f. *after compleynte*: II 1583
      g. *hereafter soone*: III 674
      h. *as soone as*: V 520
      i. *ful sone*: V 294
5. a. *therwith*: I 278, II 884, II 1199, III 1115, III 1359, V 504, V 1214
    b. *therwithal*: II 1573, III 1448, V 1006
6. a. *first*: II 1065, V 1457
    b. *at the laste*: II 825, III 1119
    c. *til at the last*: II 825, V 433
    d. *tyl*: II 153
    e. *fynaly*: IV 1427

Other temporal adverbs:
7. a. *day by day*: I 443; V 1538
    b. *day and nyght*: II 1339
    c. *fro day to night*: V 1436
    d. *this other day*: II 509
    e. *withinne the nyght*: V 1182
    f. *ofte*: II 1321
    g. *whil*: II 1322
    h. *right as*: II 1250
    i. *in his walk*: I 190

Adverbs of resultative sequence:
8 a. *with that*: II 253-54, II 428, II 541, II 542, II 614, II 1257, III 155, III 1569
   b. *with that word*: I 204, I 869, II 264, III 741, III 812 V 925 (cf. *with hire goodly wordes* III 1133; *with tho wordes* V 632; *these wordes said* IV 912)
   c. *with that thought*: I 827, II 657, III 1541
   d. *with the noyse*: II 70
   e. *at which*: I 206, III 561
   f. *so (...) that*: I 297; II 768-70, III 57
   g. *that*: III 626

Adverbs of causal sequence:
9. a. *therfor*: I 448
    b. *forthi*: I 446
    c. *for which*: IV 168
    d. *and of hire look*: I 295
    e. *and for the harme*: II 455

Adverbs of manner:
10. a. *(right) so*: II 694, II 971, II 1345, IV 242, IV 1129, V36, V 82
    b. *(right) thus*: I 139, I 365, I 506, II 522, III 1251, V 1456

REFERENCES

Beschorner, Franz. 1920. *Verbale Reime bei Chaucer*. Studien zur englischen Philologie 60. Halle: Max Niemeyer.

Brinton, Laurel J. 1983. 'Criteria for Distinguishing the Non-aspectual Functions of ME *ginnen*'. *GL* 23.235-45.

Brown, Gillian and George Yule. 1983. *Discourse Analysis*. Cambridge Textbooks in Linguistics 14. Cambridge: Cambridge University Press.

Chafe, Wallace. 1979. 'The Flow of Thought and the Flow of Language'. In Givón, ed. 1979: 159-81.

Denison, David. 1985. 'The Origins of Periphrastic *do*: Ellegård and Visser Reconsidered'. In Eaton et al., eds. 1985: 45-60.

van Dijk, Teun A. 1982. 'Episodes as Units of Discourse Analysis'. In Tannen, ed. 1982: 177-95.
Eaton, Roger et al., eds. 1985. *Papers from the 4th International Conference of English Historical Linguistics*. CILT 41. Amsterdam & Philadelphia: John Benjamins.
Ellegård, Alvar. 1953. *The Auxiliary do: the Establishment and Regulation of its Use in English*. Gothenburg Studies in English 2. Stockholm: Almqvist & Wiksell.
Friedrich, Paul. 1985. Review of Hopper (1982a). *Lg* 61.182-87.
Funke, Otto. 1922. 'Die Fügung *ginnen* mit dem Infinitiv im Mittelenglischen.' *Englische Studien* 56.1-27.
Givón, Talmy, ed. 1979. *Discourse and Syntax*. SynS 12. New York: Academic Press.
Häusermann, Hans Walter. 1930. *Studien zu den Aktionsarten im Frühmittelenglischen*. Wiener Beiträge zur englischen Philologie, 54. Wien & Leipzig: Wilhelm Braumüller.
Homann, Elizabeth R. 1954. 'Chaucer's Use of "gan"'. *JEGP* 53.389-98.
Hopper, Paul J. 1979a. 'Some observations on the Typology of Focus and Aspect in Narrative Language'. *SLang* 3.37-64.
———— 1979b. 'Aspect and Foregrounding in Discourse'. In Givón, ed. 1979: 213-41.
———— ed. 1982a. *Tense-Aspect: Between Semantics & Pragmatics*. Typological Studies in Language 1. Amsterdam & Philadelphia: John Benjamins.
———— 1982b. 'Aspect between Discourse and Grammar: an Introductory Essay for the Volume'. In Hopper, ed. 1982a: 3-18.
Kerkhof, Jelle. 1966. *Studies in the Language of Geoffrey Chaucer*. Diss. Rijksuniversiteit te Leiden. Leiden: Universitaire Pers Leiden.
Koziol, Herbert. 1932. *Grundzüge der Syntax der mittelenglischen Stabreimdichtungen*. Wiener Beiträge zur englischen Philologie 58. Wien & Leipzig: Wilhelm Braumüller.
Labov, William. 1972. *Language in the Inner City: Studies in the Black English Vernacular*. Philadelphia: University of Pennsylvania Press.
Longacre, Robert E. 1979a. 'Why We Need a Vertical Revolution in Linguistics'. In Wolfgang Wölck and Paul L. Garvin, eds. *The Fifth LACUS Forum 1978*, 247-70. Columbia, SC: Hornbeam Press.
———— 1979b. 'The Paragraph as a Grammatical Tool'. In Givón, ed. 1979: 115-34.
———— 1983. *The Grammar of Discourse*. New York & London: Plenum Press.
Middle English Dictionary. 1952-present. Hans Kurath, Sherman M. Kuhn, et al., eds. Ann Arbor: University of Michigan Press. [=*MED*. in text].
Mustanoja, Tauno F. 1960. *A Middle English Syntax*. I Parts of Speech. Helsinki: Société Néophilologique.
———— 1983. 'Chaucer's Use of *gan*: Some Recent Studies'. In Douglas Gray and E.G. Stanley, eds. *Middle English Studies*

Presented to Norman Davies in Honour of his Seventieth Birthday, 59-64. Oxford: Clarendon Press.
Ness, Lynn and Caroline Duncan-Rose. 1982. 'A Syntactic Correlate of Style Switching in the Canterbury Tales'. In J. Peter Maher et al., eds. *Papers from the 3rd International Conference on Historical Linguistics*, 293-322. CILT 13. Amsterdam: John Benjamins.
Oxford English Dictionary and *Supplement to the Oxford English Dictionary*. Oxford: Clarendon Press. [=*OED* in text].
Polanyi, Livia and R.J.H. Scha. 1983. 'The Syntax of Discourse'. *Text* 3.261-70.
Robinson, F.N. 1957. *The Works of Geoffrey Chaucer*. 2nd ed. London: Oxford University Press.
Rynell, Alarik. 1960. 'On Middle English *take(n)* as an Inchoative Verb'. *Studier i modern Språkventenskap*, New series 1.115-31.
Smyser, H.M. 1967. 'Chaucer's Use of *gin* and *do*'. *Speculum* 42.68-83.
Stein, Dieter. 1985. 'Discourse Markers in Early Modern English'. In Eaton et al., eds. 1985: 283-302.
Stubbs, Michael. 1983. *Discourse Analysis: the Sociolinguistic Analysis of Natural Language*. Language in Society Series 4. Oxford: Basil Blackwell.
Tajima, Matsuji. 1975. 'The *Gawain*-poet's Use of *con* as a Periphrastic Auxiliary'. *NphM* 76.429-38.
Tannen, Deborah, ed. 1982. *Analyzing Discourse: Text and Talk*. GURT 1981. Washington, D.C.: Georgetown University Press.
Taylor, Rupert. 1917. 'Some Notes on the Use of *can* and *couth* as Preteritive Auxiliaries in Early and Middle Scottish Poetry'. *JEGP* 16.573-91.
Traugott, Elizabeth Closs. 1972. *A (The) History of English Syntax*. Transatlantic Series in Linguistics. New York: Holt, Rinehart & Winston.
_____ 1982. 'From Propositional to Textual and Expressive Meanings: Some Semantic-pragmatic Aspects of Grammaticalization'. In Winfred P. Lehmann and Yakov Malkiel, eds. *Perspectives on Historical Linguistics*, 245-71. CILT 4. Amsterdam & Philadelphia: John Benjamins.
Trnka, B. 1930. *On the Syntax of the English Verb from Caxton to Dryden*. Travaux du Cercle Linguistique de Prague 3.
Visser, F. Th. 1966, 1969. *An Historical Syntax of the English Language*. Part two: Syntactical Units with One Verb. Part three, Second half: Syntactical Units with Two Verbs. Leiden: E.J. Brill.
Wolfson, Nessa. 1979. 'The Conversational Historical Present Alternation'. *Lg* 55. 168-82.
Wuth, Alfred. 1915. *Aktionsarten der Verba bei Cynewulf*. Diss. Universität Leipzig. Weid i. Thüringen: Thomas & Hubert.

HISTORICAL LINGUISTICS -- LINGUISTIC ARCHAEOLOGY

CECILY CLARK

The history of language is part of 'history' in the wider sense, and can therefore be tapped for evidence of past socio-cultural patterns. The resultant discipline - already well-established - might be called 'Applied Historical Socio-Linguistics' or, as the title more succinctly puts it, 'Linguistic Archaeology', this latter formulation having the merit of indicating that linguistic phenomena can be to socio-cultural historians much as artefacts are to archaeologists. Linguistic 'finds' vary in context much as do those of artefacts: some items are scattered on the present-day surface, whereas others lie buried at varying depths; and, in both categories, some occur in quasi-isolation, but most of them amid complexes of interrelated material.

Relevant finds upon the present-day surface of the language are infinitely numerous, because any linguistic feature, from the orthographical to the syntactic, may have socio-onomastic bearings that prove explicable only in historical terms. For vocabulary, and especially for the loanwords that have over the centuries been adopted into any language, this is a cliché. Thus, a well-ordered thesaurus reveals the world-view adopted by the users of the language in question. The common Indo-European roots deducible by means of comparative philology can be scanned for clues as to likely habitat and cultural patterns of the original Indo-European tribes.

Especially rich testimony to the socio-cultural history of any people is offered by its heritage of name-material.

Taking name-material as historical evidence is nothing new. The English Place-Name Society, for instance, was founded - now well over sixty years ago - partly by historians and principally for historical ends; and, although it has over the years perforce numbered many philologists among its county editors, philosophically it continues to the present day serving those same historical ends. Its work illustrates admirably what 'linguistic archaeology' involves. Place-names form part of the present-day surface of the language and are constantly before our eyes and in our mouths; yet few, other than professional toponymists, give them much thought. As soon as one does reflect upon current place-names, one finds oneself ranging them into two categories: on the one hand, there are occasional forms which, like Ashford, Blackheath and Eastfield are seemingly transparent in present-day terms; on the other, there looms a host of ones that are to greater or lesser degrees opaque, including many which, like London and like York, are wholly unintelligible. Being unintelligible does not, of course, disable a name: freedom from 'sense' has indeed been deemed essential to perfect fulfilment of the onomastic function. But no name ever began as a simple pointer: no-one ever gazed upon, for instance, a nascent settlement at the confluence of the Ouse and the Foss and then, fired with mystic inspiration, cried out, 'York!' Names of all kinds are created out of elements taken from ordinary language: a place-name, that is to say, normally begins as a description of the place originally concerned. The capacity of names to long outlive their intelligibility is indeed what enables them to rank as archaeological finds, and in some cases as prehistoric fossils. So, whether or not a present-day name-form may look intelligible, the linguistic archaeologist's duty is always to excavate deeper and deeper around it until a definitive interpretation be unearthed. 'Excavation' means burrowing back as far as may be possible through the successive strata of archive material (the palaeographical and diplomatic dating of which is the linguist's equivalent of dendrochronology and radio-carbon analysis), and then interpreting the findings in terms of the languages current at the places and times to which the records relate. This is what the county surveys published by the English Place-Name Society illustrate so well. Under each present-day place-name there is ranged, in chronological order, a selection of corresponding forms from ancient records, sometimes going back as far as Romano-British times. Then, on the basis of these early forms and in the light of all available topographical and tenurial information, an interpretation is suggested or, if none be possible, the obscurities are indicated. Some obscurity has in the end to be accepted: no-one has yet, I think, established any certain interpretation of the name London and that of York is also, as we shall see, in part somewhat speculative.

Establishing an etymology is, in any case, only the first stage in a linguistic archaeologist's work. With any sequence of early place-name forms, the aim is to use it - irregularities, obscurities, and all - much as one might a sequence of artefacts excavated from a site: that is, for throwing light upon the successive inhabitants of the locality and upon their linguistic and cultural affiliations. The Romans it was who transmitted to us the earliest known forms corresponding to the place-name York: Eburācum or Eborācum (transmitted by them also to the geographer Ptolemy). That name is not, however, of true Roman or Latin origin, but represents either a Celtic possessive formed upon a personal name Eburos or else a Celtic adjective derived from a plant-name whose meanings apparently varied from dialect to dialect, ranging from 'yew-tree' to 'hogweed'. The exact etymology may, luckily, be beside the point: what counts is that an undoubtedly Celtic name had been adopted by the occupying Romans from the usage of the local inhabitants. After the Romans had left, the English settlers made this district their own; and they did something at once strange and yet commonplace in the transmission of names. Their name for this place was Eoforwīc. Had no earlier form survived, that would have passed as an ordinary enough Old English place-name; for its second element represents the frequent Old English generic -wīc, adapted from the Latin vicus and carrying various meanings, such as 'settlement associated with a Roman camp' and 'landing-place, port', potentially applicable to Dark-Age York, and its first - the specific or qualifier - looks like Old English eofor 'boar', a term found several times elsewhere in a similar role (the boar, being a symbolic beast, might have been found apt either as eponymous patron for a settlement or else as source of a personal nickname for its founder or overlord). But, when compared with the Romano-British name, Eoforwīc looks less like an Old English creation than like a rendering into Old English terms of what the Germanic-speaking newcomers thought they heard the Celtic-speaking natives say. Such remodellings - usually called 'folk-etymology' - are not uncommon in place-name history, and imply that our remote ancestors, whose own place-naming was still at an early and therefore literally descriptive stage, were less at ease than we are with unintelligible onomastic pointers. Such a process implies communication of some kind between the two groups of people, yet at the same time little appreciation by the newcomers of the existing inhabitants' language. The next strangers to make York their own were the Vikings, and they too adapted its name to suit them. For the Old English first element Eofor- they substituted their own similar-sounding and cognate, term jofurr, which had through metaphor acquired the connotation 'princely warrior'; and, as often, they also imposed upon the form as a whole their own articulatory habits, to wit, their tendencies to prefer rising diphthongs to falling ones, to elide medial [v] in certain contexts and not to assibilate palatal consonants. Old English Eoforwīc therefore gave place to Anglo-Scandinavian *Jǫfurvík > Jórvík > York. The place's whole history is thus summarily exhibited in this sequence of the forms successively given to its name. For the political shifts behind this thousand-year series of linguistic dislocations we do, of course, possess other sources of information; but, none the less for that, the linguistic evidence is invaluable for fleshing out the social and cultural concomitants of war and politics, for suggesting what sorts of everyday compromise may have been entailed by the invasions and the shifts of hegemony.

Linguistic finds usually form part of interrelated complexes of material. The name York, as well as carrying individual significance, also belongs to two of the major strata formed by 'English' place-names; the Romano-British one, and the Anglo-Scandinavian. Over the last quarter-century, the evidential value of such complexes has come to be more and more appreciated and exploited. Often, study of place-name strata has been combined with that of artefact archaeology, as in the many, still-continuing endeavours to identify more accurately the earliest types of truly English place-names and to plot their distributions as an aid towards tracing the course of the earliest settlements. Scandinavian-influenced place-names too have been, and are still being, intensively surveyed on archaeological lines. All over the former Danelaw - everywhere, that is, north and east of Watling Street - the Viking settlers imposed their stamp, in varying styles and to varying degrees, upon the nomenclature of the districts where they settled. The place-names that they created, or adapted, are classified by scholars according to modes of formation (Jórvík, for instance, represents Scandinavianization of a pre-existing form), and then analyzed geographically and chronologically, again with the aim of throwing light on patterns of settlement. Such modes of research are now the principal tools of place-name study, in which linguistic analysis constitutes a preliminary stage, not an end in itself.

There are other ways too in which place-names throw light upon the settlements and migrations that have shaped English history. For seven or more centuries such names have been serving not only to denote localities but also as bases for personal by-names (or surnames) helping to identify individual people and individual

families. Among present-day family-names, there abound forms that
coincide with those of current place-names, typical examples being
Appleby, Barton, Bolton, Burton, Crossland, Lancaster, London,
Satterthwaite, Spofforth, Stow(e), Warwick, York(e), and so on by the
thousand. Toponymic family-names like these mainly reflect the
internal migrations underlying our present population-structure; and
study of them on these lines has indeed become the most popular branch
of personal-name research. One of its attractions to would-be
practitioners may sometimes be suspected to be a seemingly minimal
need for philological competence; but matters are far from being as
simple as they may appear to the uninitiated. A basic problem is
exemplified by several forms in the token list just given: Barton,
Burton, and Stow(e), for instance. Early English place-naming was a
pragmatic business, where wit and originality were at a discount, and
many names simply specified in standard terms the type of settlement
concerned. Certain such standard forms, of which Barton is typical,
therefore recur over and over again throughout the country, so that a
family-name representing one of these can give little clue to the
original family home. In the end, only a minority of place-names
forms prove to be of unique occurrence, and this restricts the
usefulness of toponymic family-names as raw material for studies in
migration. Furthermore, a family-name may - because of a
predominantly oral transmission - represent a line of development
different from that behind the current form of the place-name from
which it is derived: thus, the family-name Coxall represents the
directly developed form of the Essex place-name spelt ⟨Coggeshall⟩ and
now commonly given the spelling-pronunciation [kɒgrʃɔ:l]. Yet a
further dimension of difficulty arises from the fact that there never
had been a time when the English population was stable and that the
'surname-creating period' - running approximately from the twelfth to
the fifteenth centuries - was also one of especially rapid urban
development, with all the shifts of population that this involved.

Using family-names as a basis for studies in migration is thus no business for the amateur (however enthusiastic) but demands a trained name-archaeologist, accomplished in socio-economic history as well as in philology and in archive-work. The possibilities that such studies can, when rightly exploited, bring to realization are well illustrated in the county surveys that have since the early 1970s been appearing in the English Surnames Series.

Analysis of toponymic family-names is, however, only one branch of personal-name archaeology. The general socio-onomastic bearings of personal-naming are, of course, familiar even to laypeople: if someone is called, say, 'Moira McLaren', one straightaway assumes that either she possesses family connections with the Scottish Highlands or else she, or her parents, have for some reason chosen to give that impression. That particular deduction involves, admittedly, not 'Anthroponymical Archaeology', merely the synchronic level of 'Applied Socio-Anthroponymics'; but, the historical dimension apart, the two disciplines differ little. In an historical context, too, personal identity may be encapsulated in a name; and assessing how far the etymology or the associations of a particular form may throw light upon its bearer's background and status can often assist the genealogist and the prosopographer. Archaeologically and methodologically, on the other hand, such individual exercises are of less moment than studies of whole communities. Every name-corpus encapsulates - if at times hermetically - the cultural influences that have over the centuries converged upon the community to which it belongs; and this should enable a name-archaeologist to deduce from any such corpus the cultural allegiances of the local or social group in question.

The archaeological potentialities of personal names are virtually the converse of those associated with place-names. People are - self-evidently - vastly more numerous than named places, so that, even if we reckon up under 'place-names' all the so-called 'minor' forms (such as names of landmarks, fields and streets), personal names will still be for any given time vastly more numerous than place-names. Moreover, whereas a place-name corpus, once established, is significantly increased or modified only in exceptional circumstances (such as those of the Viking settlement in the Danelaw), every personal-name one is inherently unstable, changing day by day as individuals die and others are born and baptized, and thus being entirely renewed in under a century. People, besides, move freely about the world, taking their own names on their backs and their former community's traditional name-stock in their heads. For all these reasons, personal names constitute a far fuller and more sensitive guide to socio-cultural history than place-names could ever be.

These great potentialities entail, unfortunately, problems no less great. For a voluminous personal-name corpus (amounting perhaps to tens of thousands of items), statistical analysis may offer the only means of imposing order upon the material and drawing conclusions from it; such analysis is in any event likely to be more and more often undertaken as computers become more and more widely used. Need for statistics faces us not simply with controversy but with fundamental difficulties. The trouble is not that 'statistics' as understood by mathematicians is a domain inaccessible to most scholars in the humanities: that could in the long run be remedied by different policies for recruiting and training onomasticians and, in particular, by assembling - as has already upon occasion been done, most notably at Münster and at Freiburg - teams in which philologists, historians and statisticians would work side by side. The true problems reside in the material itself. Even a comprehensive census of the modern kind involves some arbitrariness, in that even one day later the population, and with it the name-corpus, would have been modified by deaths and by births. Medieval records were, in any case, never meant to be comprehensive, but only to specify which individuals were responsible for certain duties, rents or taxes, or which of them had fallen foul of the law, and so on. These varying types of selectivity, as well as increasing the essential arbitrariness of the sample, also put at some risk any comparison between records of different types: setting, for instance, a gaol-delivery roll alongside a guild-roll of identical provenance and date might prove profitable, so too might comparing two guild-rolls either from the same town but of different dates or else of the same date but from different towns; but what significance to read into contrasts or agreements between unlike records from different places and/or dates must always remain problematic. Nor is that all: anyone who has ever tried to classify medieval names knows that always there remain a good few ambivalent forms, such as might with equal plausibility be assigned to any of several origins. Given these multiple uncertainties, it is not surprising that some anthroponymists should have counselled against any reliance at all upon statistics. Others, however, no less scrupulous and no less learned, have displayed personal-name distributions in percentages refined to two decimal places. What is then best to do? Common sense suggests a compromise: whether or not the difference between 52.37% and 54.13% ought, in the sort of contexts with which we are concerned, to be allowed any great statistical weight, that between 10% and 90% is likely to mean something; and so it may be safe even for non-mathematicians to allow themselves some 'coarse statistics', such as lend weight only to discrepancies of at least 5% and preferably 10% between samples and then only when the types of material seem adequately comparable. A fail-safe methodology has, in its unheroic way, something to commend it.

There remain questions of how to base any calculation. Personal names can be reckoned up in at least two ways: in terms either of the number of individuals named or of the number of distinct forms current in the stock represented. The latter method is by far the easier, because determining how many separate individuals are mentioned in a set of medieval records can in itself constitute a substantial

research project. Choice is not, however, a matter just of diligence
versus sloth, for the two techniques are not interchangeable: a point
well illustrated by baptismal names current in twelfth-century
England. Many records show a mixture of several types of name: some
of native Old English origin, others introduced by the Viking
settlers, and others again by the more recent post-Conquest ones. The
two foreign influences are not on the same footing, and do not
therefore lend themselves to identical modes of analysis. The
so-called 'Norman' one was fresh and still increasing in popularity,
and may thus be most effectively assessed in terms of the number of
individuals named, in so far as ten different peasants all called
William have more significance than a solitary one. By contrast, the
Viking influence was at this time spent and indeed recessive, and so
can best be assessed by the number of forms it had contributed to the
name-stock rather than by the number of individuals currently bearing
such names. Both techniques can, of course, be applied to each
category in turn, because each has its own contribution to make to the
whole analysis; but to attempt direct comparison between two such
disparate influences would be pointless.

Etymologizing and counting the specimens is again only a
preliminary procedure, because the personal-name archaeologist's aim
is to assess the socio-cultural implications of the corpus as a whole.
Now, trying to work out _in vacuo_ the implications of a name-corpus is
- to employ a simile that I have used before - rather like trying to
deduce the familial, social and commercial relationships of any
household solely from the stamps on its incoming letters: one observes
a frequent connection with, say, Germany and sporadic ones with France
and with Denmark, but whether such connections are recent or ancestral
ones, whether they are based upon ties of kindred or affection or upon
business relationships, one cannot tell. Similarly, the motivations
and the implications behind the adoption and the perpetuation of
particular personal names can be determined only by taking into
account the whole context, in so far as it may be knowable; that is,

by discovering as much as possible about the conquests, settlements, trade-patterns, religious movements and literary fashions that may have impinged upon the community concerned. Linguistic archaeology is indeed a branch of history rather than of linguistics.

Such a classification, indeed, such an affinity is already partly acknowledged in some quarters: for instance, by those bibliographers and librarians who place Onomastics under 'History: Auxiliary Sciences'. There was, however, a deliberate intent behind my choice of 'Linguistic', rather than 'Onomastic', 'Archaeology' as the title of this paper, because I regard the approach outlined as potentially extensible to all aspects of language. The historical bearings of vocabulary have already been mentioned in the passing. For orthography, I have myself elsewhere endeavoured to exhibit some socio-linguistic bearings, with special reference to the half-century following the Norman Conquest; and I have lately attempted to extend this study to include scribal choices between alternative letter-forms. As for pronunciation and for morpho-syntax, present-day experience constantly reveals both as sensitive indicators of social disarray. If one sees life as a continuum, synchronically as well as diachronically, as a seamless fabric in which language is woven together with politics, religion, economic developments and socio-cultural relationships, then all linguistic manifestations are - if rightly understood - capable of illuminating these other spheres, in the same measure as language is enriched, impoverished, reshaped by the contexts in which it is used. In order to reveal these cross-illuminations, all that is needed is appropriate technique.

WORKS CONSULTED

Benveniste, Emile. 1969. *Le Vocabulaire des institutions indo-européennes*. 2 vols. Paris: Les Editions de Minuit.

Brattö, O. 1956. *Notes d'anthroponymie messine*. (=Göteborgs Universitets Årsskrift, 62, part 4.)

Cameron, Kenneth. 1976. 'The Significance of English Place-Names'. *Proceedings of the British Academy* 62. 135-55.

Cameron, Kenneth, ed. 1977. *Place-names Evidence for the Anglo-Saxon Invasion and Scandinavian Settlements: Eight studies collected by K.C.* Nottingham: English Place-Name Society.

Clark, Cecily. 1978. 'Women's Names in post-Conquest England: Observations and speculations'. *Speculum* 53. 223-51.

Clark, Cecily. 1979. 'Clark's First Three Laws of Applied Anthroponymics'. *Nomina* 3. 13-19.

Clark, Cecily. 1980. 'Battle c. 1110: An anthroponymist looks at an Anglo-Norman New Town'. *Proceedings of the Battle Conference on Anglo-Norman Studies*. Ed. R. Allen Brown, 21-41; 168-72. Woodbridge: Bodell and Brewer.

Clark, Cecily. 1982-3. 'The Early personal Names of King's Lynn: An essay in socio-cultural history'. *Nomina* 6.51-71; 7.65-89.

Clark, Cecily. 1983. 'On Dating *The Battle of Maldon*: Certain evidence reviewed'. *Nottingham Medieval Studies* 27. 1-22.

Clark, Cecily. 1984. 'L'Angleterre anglo-normande et ses ambivalences socio-culturelles'. *Les Mutations socio-culturelles au tournant des XIe-XIIe siècles: Actes du Colloque international du CNRS -Études anselmiennes (IVe session)* ed. Raymonde Foreville, 99-110. (= Spicilegium Beccense, 2.) Paris: Editions du CNRS.

Clark, Cecily. 1985. 'Certains éléments français de l'anthroponymie anglaise du Moyen Age: Essai méthodologique'. *L'Onomastique, témoin de l'activité humaine*. Ed. G. Taverdet, 259-67. Fontaine lès Dijon: Association Bourguigonne de Dialectologique et d'Onomastique.

Clark, Cecily. 1986. Review of *Surnames and Genetic Structure*. By G.W. Lasker et al. (Cambridge: CUP, 1985). *Nomina* 10. 180-3.

Clark, Cecily. 1987a. 'English Personal Names ca. 650-1300: Some prosopographical bearings'. *Medieval Prosopography* 8, part 1: 31-60.

Clark, Cecily. 1987b. 'Spelling and Grammaticality in the *Vespasian Homilies:* A reassessment'. *Manuscripta* 31, part 1: 7-10.

Clark, Cecily. 1987c. 'A Witness to post-Conquest English Cultural Patterns: The *Liber Vitae* of Thorney Abbey'. *Studies in Honour of Rene Derolez*. Ed. A.M. Simon-Vandenbergen, 73-85. Ghent: Seminarie voor Engelse en Oud-Germaanse Taalkunde. Rijksuniversiteit Gent.

Clark, Cecily. In press. '*Willelmus rex? vel alius Willelmus?* *Nomina* 11.

Ekwall, Eilert. 1956. *Studies on the Population of Medieval London.* (= Kungl. Vitterhets Historie och Antikvitets Akademiens Handlingar: Filologisk-Filosofiska Serien, 2.) Stockholm: Almqvist & Wiksell.
Ekwall, Eilert. 1964. *Old English wīc in Place-Names.* (= Nomina Germanica, 13.) Uppsala: A.-B. Lundequistska Bodhandeln.
Ellegård, Alvar. 1958. 'Notes on the use of Statistical Methods in the Study of Name Vocabularies'. *Studia Neophilologica* 30. 214-31.
Fellows-Jensen, Gillian. 1975. 'The Vikings in England: A review'. *Anglo-Saxon England* 4. 181-206.
Fellows-Jensen, Gillian. 1976. 'Place-Names and Settlement History: A review'. *Northern History* 13. 1-26.
Fellows-Jensen, Gillian. 1987. 'York'. *Leeds Studies in English*, new Ser. 18. 141-55.
Gardiner, Alan H. 1940. *The Theory of Proper Names: A controversial essay.* London: Oxford University Press.
Gelling, Margaret. 1973-1976. *The Place-Names of Berkshire.* 3 vols. (= English Place-Name Society, 49-51.) Cambridge: CUP.
Gelling, Margaret. 1977. 'Latin Loan-Words in Old English Place-Names'. *Anglo-Saxon England* 6. 1-13.
Gelling, Margaret. 1978. *Signposts to the Past.* London: J.M. Dent & Sons Ltd.
Jackson, Kenneth. 1953. *Language and History in Early Britain.* Edinburgh: Edinburgh University Press.
McClure, Peter. 1979. 'Patterns of Migration in the Late Middle Ages: The evidence of English place-name surnames'. *Economic History Review*, 2nd Ser. 32.167-82.
McKinley, Richard. 1975. *Norfolk and Suffolk Surnames in the Middle Ages.* (= English Surnames Series, 2.) London and Chichester: Phillimore & Co. Ltd.
McKinley, Richard. 1977. *The Surnames of Oxfordshire.* (= English Surnames Series, 3.) London: Leopard's Head Press Ltd.
McKinley, Richard. 1981. *The Surnames of Lancashire.* (= English Surnames Series, 4.) London: Leopard's Head Press Ltd.
Martinet, André. 1986. *Des Steppes aux océans: l'indo-européen et les "Indo-Européens".* Paris: Payot.
Mawer, Allen, & Stenton, Frank Merry, eds. 1924. *Introduction to the Survey of English Place-Names.* (= English Place-Name Society, 1, part 1.) Cambridge: Cambridge University Press.
Michaëlsson, Karl. 1947. 'Questions de méthode anthroponymique'. *Onomastica* 1. 190-204.
Michaëlsson, Karl. 1954. 'L'Anthroponymie et la statistique'. *IVe Congrès international de Sciences onomastiques.* ed. Jöran Sallgren et al., 380-94. Uppsala: A.-B. Lundequistska Bokhandeln.
Nicolaisen, W.F.H., ed. 1970. *The Names of Towns and Cities in Britain*, compiled by Margaret Gelling, W.F.H.N. and Melville Richards. London: B.T. Batsford Ltd.
Reaney, P.H. 1935. *The Place-Names of Essex.* (= English Place-Name Society, 12.) Cambridge: Cambridge University Press.

Reaney, P.H. 1967. *The Origin of English Surnames.* London: Routledge and Kegan Paul.

Reaney, P.H. 1976. *A Dictionary of British Surnames.* 2nd edn. Revised by R.M. Wilson. London: Routledge and Kegan Paul.

Redmonds, George. 1973. *Yorkshire: West Riding.* (= English Surnames Series, 1.) London & Chichester: Phillimore & Co. Ltd.

Rivet, A.L.F., and Smith, Colin. 1979. *The Place-Names of Roman Britain.* London: B.T. Batsford Ltd.

Smith, Albert Hugh. 1937. *The Place-Names of the East Riding of Yorkshire and York.* (= English Place-Name Society, 14.) Cambridge: Cambridge University Press.

Smith, Albert Hugh. 1956. *English Place-Name Elements.* 2 vols. (= English Place-Name Society, 25 & 26.) Cambridge: CUP.

THE ASSESSMENT OF LEXICAL MORTALITY AND REPLACEMENT
BETWEEN OLD AND MODERN ENGLISH

ROBERT COLEMAN
Emmanuel College
University of Cambridge

1.1   This paper is an attempt to rehabilitate the quantitative study of lexical change after the débacle into which glottochronology precipitated it more than two decades ago.

1.2   The lexical corpus used for the purpose is the basic vocabulary of 224 items employed in Bergsland-Vogt 117ff. It is of course possible to argue about the composition of this or any other such list. Some of the items are clearly too culture-specific to be of legitimate use globally; for instance *clothes, dance, road* and *spear*. For the present study this is perhaps not a serious objection, since we are in a position to monitor changes in the English extra-linguistic culture over the millennium that separates OE from MoE. But there are other more serious difficulties. For instance, why include *father, full, give, hand, neck* but not *son, empty, take, arm, face*? How many pronouns or numerals should be included? To acknowledge these difficulties and then proceed as if they did not exist might seem to be nothing more than docile acquiescence in what Bergsland and Vogt (1962) and their predecessors arbitrarily laid down. In defence it can be argued that a high proportion of the items chosen would surely appear in any basic list of 224, and that, so long as the items are publicly known, it is possible for anyone who has misgivings about any of them to make the appropriate changes.

1.3 Similar considerations apply in the choice of exponents of the 224 lexical meanings. Do we select MoE *wide* or *broad? small* or *little? big* or *large?* The decision matters if we are making diachronic comparisons. Thus OE *wid* and *brad* seem also to be near-synonyms but *smæl* 'fine, slender' is at best a hyponym of *lytel*, while *large*, a French loan-word, and *big*, probably Scandinavian in origin, did not enter the language until late ME and remained minor exponents of the meaning 'big' until well after 1400. In fact relative frequency and range of usage justify the choice of MoE *wide*, *small* and *big*. If the choice between two words really turns out to be impossible, then we must either devise some way of counting both of them or, if this is methodologically impracticable, omit the item altogether from our calculations.

1.4 The selection of OE exponents is of course much more difficult. There is, to begin with, the general problem of comparability between data drawn from different stages of the same language. In a living language like MoE it is possible to distinguish standard phenomena from those that are restricted in dialect or register. (For this research all lexemes that are not classed as obsolete, technical, or dialectal in OED are treated as standard; cf. §2.2.1.) We can even infer what contributions the more restricted groups have made and are making to the standard language. However, for earlier periods the volume and range of material is relatively small. As a result besides the indeterminacies noted in §1.3 there are large holes all over the lexicon and rare or unique items are hard to assess. Thus OE *left* occurs only in a Kentish gloss on Lat. *inanis* (§2.3.3), and we cannot tell how widespread the lexeme was (for instance, is the absence of *lyft from W. Saxon merely accidental?)

and what semantic relation it already had with *winestra*. We do not know in what dialects *docga*, attested only in a late gloss on Lat. *canis* (§6.4.2), occurred and how serious a rival it was in them to *hund*.

1.5 The overwhelming volume of OE material is from one dialect, West Saxon, which has no direct linear relationship with any MoE dialect, let alone standard MoE. However, like most of the earliest records of living IE languages, the West Saxon material belongs to the literary and administrative registers and its lexicon is therefore dialectally impure. In fact its basic vocabulary can be treated as if it were standard OE. The phonological variations noted in §2.2.1 are in this context insignificant, and substantial additions to the volume and range of the known OE lexicon, in so far as they might fill some of the gaps specified in §6.4.1 and could resolve some of the uncertainties noted in §1.6 and elsewhere, would only increase, though not be very much, the proportion of material common to the OE and MoE basic vocabularies.

1.6 In choosing the OE exponents, Skeat (1879) and Buck (1949) have been relied on extensively and, where they disagree, the decision has been reached on the basis of a word's frequency, as established from the Microform Concordance, and -- more importantly -- on its semantic range, as exhibited in Bosworth and Toller etc. Thus for 'die' *steorfan* is preferred to *sweltan*, for 'say' *cweþan* to *secgan*, for 'smoke' *rēc* to *þrosm* (and *smoca*) and for 'cut' *snīþan* to *sceran* and the more frequent *ceorfan* and *hēawan*. Where mistakes have been made, the offending items can once again be replaced without invalidating the method.

2.1 The conventional procedure for lexical comparison is based upon the mere recording of pairs of words, selected either on morphological grounds, e.g. *wamb* and its MoE reflex *womb*, or more often on semantic grounds, e.g. *wamb* and its MoE synonym *belly*. ('Synonym' is used, as in Buck, to refer to semantic equivalents whether they co-exist in the same language or belong to different periods of the same language or to different languages.) This is satisfactory where the two words correspond both in form and in meaning, e.g. *cuman* and *come*, or where the two words are synonyms but neither has a formal correspondent synchronic with the other, e.g. *rīman* and *count*, *sealtian* and *dance*. But there are many instances where a simple binary citation cannot recapture the complexity of the relationship. Thus not only is OE *wamb* reflected in *womb* but its synonym *belly* in turn reflects OE *belg* 'bag, pouch'. Again *wēpan* is reflected in *weep* but its synonym *cry* (< ME *crien* a French loanword) has no OE cognate. Conversely *orþian* has no MoE cognates but its synonym *breathe* is a denominative from OE *brǣþ*. Words do not come and go abruptly. Their rise or fall may be a long gradual process, in which changes in status, form and meaning may all contribute. Hence, whenever an OE word X has been replaced by a MoE word Y, we need to know what the nearest cognates are for X in MoE and for Y in OE, and to classify the latter pair by status, form and meaning.

    2.2.1 The STATUS of a word may be **(a)** standard, by which is meant that it appears to be either in general use or at least recognised and even used now and then in dialects or registers where a synonym is preferred. Thus OE *swīþra* 'right (side)' and *bearn* 'child' are standard and can be classed as **(a)**, while their nearest MoE cognates are both dialectal and hence, being non-standard, are classed as **(b)**: *swith* 'quickly, at once' (cf. OE *swīþ* 'strong') and *bairn*. In general, a standard word is given precedence over a non-standard one, even if the latter corresponds more closely in meaning; e.g. OE *gangan* is paired with standard MoE *gangway* rather than dialectal *gang* 'go'; *mycel* with *much*, even though dialectal *mickle* corresponds better semantically.

This preserves comparability, since dialectal variants at the lexical level are much more difficult to establish in a dead language. Purely phonological variations in OE dialect usage are sometimes more easily recovered; but these are not taken account of here either, even when they show a closer relationship to the relevant words in MoE; e.g. Anglian *cald*, *hēran*, *hlæhhan*, *tēn* and Kentish *left*, as against the W.Saxon forms cited below for *cold*, *hear*, *laugh*, *ten* and *left*.

2.2.2 Words belonging to special literary or technical registers have after some hesitation been classed under **(a)**; e.g. *welkin* and *slay*. There may be a case for putting them in **(b)** or even in some third status-category, but in the end they have been differentiated instead under the semantic heading (§2.4.2) and classed as minor synonyms etc.

2.3.1 In MORPHOLOGY the MoE word may be **(a)** a straightforward reflex of the OE one, as *much* is of *mycel*, *belly* of *belg*. *Much* and *belg* are therefore both classed as **(a)**. MoE *he* appears twice -- with OE *he* and *hīe*. In both instances it is classed morphologically as **(a)**; for although it directly reflects *he* not *hīe*, the two OE words are different paradigmatic forms of the same lexical root in contrast to *they* and *hie*, which belong to different lexical roots (§6.4.2).

2.3.2 Again one word may be **(b)** a complex form containing the exact correspondent of the other in its root but with different derivational morphology. Thus *winestra* 'left' is derived by suffixation from the root attested in *wine* 'friendly', which appears with a different suffix in *wynsum*, reflected in the MoE complex *winsome*; *dirty* reflects the adjectival formant *-ig* suffixed to the root of *gedrītan* 'to shit'; *swīþra* has the comparative formant suffixed to the root reflected in *swith*. Although OE *hundred* reflects a

PGmc compound *xund-raþ* 'hundred-number', the second constituent does not survive into OE as an independent lexeme; so *hundred* is classed as a complex also. Thus *winsome*, *gedrītan*, *swith* and *hundred* are all classed as **(b)**. Derivations entailing a change in the part of speech, e.g. *cook* (v.) < *cōc* (n.), might be included here but have been classed instead under **(a)** and differentiated under the semantic heading (§2.4.2).

2.3.3 A word may be **(c)** a compound, one of whose constituents is the exact correspondent of the other word. Thus *werewolf* and *wer* 'men', *lyftādl* 'palsy' and *left* (< Kentish *left* 'weak'), with the two compounds classed as **(c)**. Again the two may be merely **(d)** cognates; e.g. *scrapian* 'scratch' and MoE *sharp*; *wallow*, which < OE *walwian* 'roll' (intr.), and OE *wealt*, the participle of *wielwan* (tr.), which appears in the compound *seonuwealt* 'round' (lit. 'always rolled'). It would be possible to place *he*, paired with *hie* (§2.3.1) in this category.

2.3.4 Words whose cognation is established by reference not to any common form in English but to PIE or even PGmc are treated separately as 'external' cognates and classed simply as **(x)**. Thus (i) *blōstm* and *flower* (< ME *flour*, which displaced ME *blosme*) are derived via PGmc and PItalic from PIE < *bhleə3-s-*. (ii) MoE *give* < ME *given* a Scandinavian loanword (cf. OSw *giva*) beside *yeven*, which < OE *giefan*. It might be argued that *give* does reflect *giefan* and the abnormal phonology is evidence for its origin in a dialect (perhaps Early Northumbrian?) where palatalization was not complete. But it is better to treat *give* as an external cognate of *giefan*. (iii) *dēad* (> *dead*) reflects PGmc *dauðaz* beside **dau̯i̯an*, reflected in ON *deyja*, which was borrowed as ME *deyen*, whence MoE *die*. (The existence of an OE **diegan* is unlikely in view of the large number of 'die' synonyms that are actually attested in OE). (iv) *dig* < ME *diggen*, which like Fr. *diguer* is probably borrowed from the Low Countries and so an external cognate of OE *dīc* 'dyke' (> MoE *ditch*). If, however, *dig* < **dīcigian* a compound of *dic*, it would of course be transferred to class *(a)*.

2.4.1 SEMANTICALLY the two words may be *(a)* major synonyms, each being the major exponent of the meaning in question. Thus *mycel* and *big*, *fugol* and *bird*, where both members of each pair are classed as *(a)*. Alternatively one may be *(b)* a minor synonym of the other, being less often used as an exponent of the meaning in question; e.g. *cild* beside *child* and *delve* beside *delfan*. *Cild* and *delve* are both classed as *(b)*. In this way account can be taken of both *broad* and *wide* etc. (§1.3).

2.4.2 One word may be *(c)* a hyponym (or conversely hyperonym) of the other. Thus *brid* beside *bird*, *fowl* beside *fugol*. *Brid* and *fowl* are both classed as *(c)*. Here also are included minor synonyms that are restricted to certain formulaic phrases, like *to wit*, *quoth*, *weeds*. Again one may be *(d)* a plesionym of the other, having a meaning that is adjacent to it or even partly overlapping; e.g. *hefig* and *heavy*, *starve* and *steorfan* 'die'. *Hefig* and *starve* are therefore classed as *(d)*. Here, as elsewhere, we are very much at the mercy of our data. The semantic shift from *wealcan* 'roll' to *walken* 'walk' is not clearly attested till well into the ME period, but the isolated testimony of an early eleventh century gloss (Meritt 855) of Lat. *emensus* by ȝewealcon 'having traversed' justifies classing *wealcan* as *(d)*. Complete heteronyms are classed as *(e)*; e.g. *belg* beside *belly*, *team* beside *tēon* 'pull'. There may be grounds for reallocating some items semantically -- from *(e)* to *(d)*, from *(d)* to *(c)* or *(e)* and so forth -- but such reallocations are unlikely to extend beyond one category.

3.1 The advantages that a more elaborate system of classification has over the conventional division into occurrence/non-occurrence (§2.1) can be demonstrated by reference to the six pairs of (major) synonyms cited by Swadesh (1952:455): *eall -- all, æsce -- ash, dēor -- animal, hrycg -- back, yfel -- bad, rind -- bark*. On the binary scheme the first two pairs score a plus, the remaining four a minus. On the present classification the two pairs *eall -- all* and *æsce -- ash* can be classed as **(aaa)**, viz. **(a)** in status and morphology and semantics. In the remaining pairs all four OE words are directly reflected in MoE: *deor* and *yfel* in *deer* and *evil*, which as *hyponyms* of *animal* and *bad* are **(aac)**, *rind* in *rind*, which as a plesionym of *bark* is **(aad)** and *hrycg* in *ridge*, a heteronym of *back* and therefore **(aae)**.

3.2 Conversely two of the MoE words reflect OE forms: *back* < *bæc*, a minor synomym of *hrycg* and therefore **(aab)**; *bad* < ME *badde* < *bæddel* 'hermaphrodite', a plesionym of *yfel*, and therefore **(aad)**. The other two, *animal* and *bark*, are ME loan- words from French or Latin and Scandinavian respectively, the latter being perhaps an external cognate to *birch* (< OE *birce*). Both therefore come out as **(x)**. The *all* and *ash* pairs clearly stand out, as they did in the binary scheme, but the more elaborate classification enables the variety of relationships within the other four pairs to be captured more accurately. To score all four simply as **minus** would be to suppress important information about the diachrony of this part of the lexicon.

4.1 In the following lists the 224 MoE words appear alphabetically in the left-hand column. Each is paired with its closest OE cognate. Where the latter is not also its major synonym in OE the word that is appears immediately underneath with its own nearest MoE cognate in the left-hand column opposite. Thus *belly* appears beside *belg*, *wamb* beneath *belg* and *womb* beneath *belly*. The three-letter code indicates the relationship with the paired major exponent as explained in §2.1.1 - 2.4.2.

MoE		OE		MoE		OE	
all	aaa	eall	aaa	cook		cōc (n.)	aad
and	aaa	and	aaa	--	x	gecōcsian	
animal		(animal)	x	count		(counten)	x
deer	aac	dēor		(rimen)	x	rīman	
ashes	aaa	æsce	aaa	cry		(crīen)	x
at	aaa	æt	aaa	weep	aab	wēpan	
back		bæc	aab	cut		(cutten)	x
ridge	aae	hrycg		snithe	bbb	snīþan	
bad		bæddel	aad	dance		(dauncen)	x
evil	aac	yfel		--	x	sealtian	
bark		(barke)	x	day	aaa	dæg	aaa
rind	aad	rind		die		(deyen)	x
because		(bī cause)	x	starve	aad	steorfan	
for that	baa	for þam þe		dig		(diggen)	x
belly		belg	aae	delve	aab	delfan	
womb	aac	wamb		dirty		gedrītan	abd
berry	aaa	berie	aaa	foul	aac	ful	
big		(big)	x	dog		docga	aab
much	aad	mycel		hound	aac	hund	
bird		brid	aac	drink	aaa	drincan	aaa
fowl	aac	fugol		dry	aaa	drȳge	aaa
bite	aaa	bītan	aaa	dust	aaa	dūst	aaa
black	aaa	blæc	aaa	ear	aaa	ēare	aaa
blood	aaa	blōd	aaa	earth	aaa	eorþe	aaa
blow	aaa	blāwan	aaa	eat	aaa	etan	aaa
blunt		(blont)	x	egg	aaa	æg	aaa
stunted	ace	astynt		eight	aaa	ehta	aaa
bone	aaa	bān	aaa	eye	aaa	ēage	aaa
breast	aaa	brēost	aaa	fall	aaa	feallan	aaa
breathe		bræþ(n.)	aad	far	aaa	feor	aaa
(orpiæn)	x	orpian		fat(n.)		fætt	aad
brother	aaa	brōþor	aaa	fatness	aad	fætnes	
burn	aaa	beornan	aaa	father	aaa	fæder	aaa
child		cild	aab	fear		fǣr	aad
bairn	baa	bearn		(eʒe)	x	ege	
claw	aaa	clawu	aaa	feather	aaa	feþer	aaa
clothes		clāþas	aab	few	aaa	fēawe	aaa
weeds	aac	gewæde		fight	aaa	feohtan	aaa
cloud		clūd	aae	fire	aaa	fȳr	aaa
welkin	aad	weolcen		fish	aaa	fisc	aaa
cold	aaa	ceald	aaa	five	aaa	fīf	aaa
come	aaa	cuman	aaa				
float		flotian	aab	kill		(killen)	x
fleeting	abd	flēotan		quell	aad	cwellan	
flow	aaa	flōwan	aaa	knee	aaa	cnēow	aaa

flower		(flour) **x**	know		cnāwan **aab**
blossom**aac**		blōstm	to wit**aac**		witan
fly	**aaa**	flēogan **aaa**	lake		lacu **aac**
fog		(fogge) **x**	mere	**bab**	mere
mist	**aac**	mist	laugh	**aaa**	hliehhan**aaa**
foot	**aaa**	fōt **aaa**	leaf	**aaa**	lēaf **aaa**
four	**aaa**	fēower **aaa**	left		lyftādl**ace**
freeze	**aaa**	frēosan **aaa**	winsome**abe**		winestra
full	**aaa**	full **aaa**	leg		(leg) **x**
give		(given) **x**	shank**aab**		sceanca
(yeven)	**x**	giefan	lie	**aaa**	licgan **aaa**
good	**aaa**	gōd **aaa**	live	**aaa**	libban **aaa**
grass	**aaa**	græs **aaa**	liver	**aaa**	lifer **aaa**
green	**aaa**	grēne **aaa**	long	**aaa**	lang **aaa**
guts	**aaa**	guttas **aaa**	louse	**aaa**	lūs **aaa**
hair	**aaa**	hǣr **aaa**	man		mann **aac**
hand	**aaa**	hand **aaa**	werewolf**acc**		wer
he	**aaa**	hē **aaa**	many	**aaa**	manig **aaa**
head	**aaa**	hēafod **aaa**	meat		mete **aac**
hear	**aaa**	hīeran **aaa**	flesh	**aad**	flǣsc
heart	**aaa**	heorte **aaa**	moon	**aaa**	mōna **aaa**
heavy		hefig **aad**	mother	**aaa**	mōdor **aaa**
sweer	**bbd**	swǣr	mountain		(mountaine)**x**
here	**aaa**	hēr **aaa**	barrow**aae**		beorg
hit		hittan **aad**	mouth	**aaa**	mūþ **aaa**
slay	**aad**	slēan	name	**aaa**	nama **aaa**
hold	**aaa**	healdan **aaa**	narrow	**aaa**	nearu **aaa**
horn	**aaa**	horn **aaa**	near		nēar **abd**
how	**aaa**	hū **aaa**	nigh	**aab**	nēah
hundred		hundred**aab**	neck		hnecca **aab**
hundred	**aba**	hund	hause	**baa**	heals
hunt	**aaa**	huntian **aaa**	new	**aaa**	nīwe **aaa**
husband		hūsbonda**aad**	night	**aaa**	niht **aaa**
werewolf**acc**		wer	nine	**aaa**	nigun **aaa**
I	**aaa**	ic **aaa**	nose	**aaa**	nosu **aaa**
ice	**aaa**	īs **aaa**	not		nāwiht**acd**
if	**aaa**	gif **aaa**	no	**aac**	nā
in	**aaa**	in **aaa**	old	**aaa**	eald **aaa**
			one	**aaa**	ān **aaa**
other	**aaa**	ōþer **aaa**	sit	**aaa**	sittan **aaa**
person		(persoune) **x**	six	**aaa**	siex **aaa**
man	**aac**	mann	skin		scinn **aab**
play	**aaa**	plegian **aaa**	hide	**aac**	hȳd
pull		pullian **aac**	sky		(skye) **x**
team	**aae**	tēon	--	**x**	swegel
push		(pushen)**x**	sleep	**aaa**	slǣpan **aaa**
shove	**aab**	scūfan	small		smæl **aab**
rain	**aaa**	regnian **aaa**	little	**aab**	lytel
red	**aaa**	rēad **aaa**	smell		(smellen)**x**
right	**aaa**	riht **aaa**	stink	**aad**	gestincan
right		riht **aae**	smoke		smoca **aab**

swith	*bbe*	swiþra		reek	*aad*	rēc	
river		(river) *x*		smooth	*aaa*	smēþe	*aaa*
ea	*bbc*	ēa		snake	*aaa*	snaca	*aaa*
road		rād	*aad*	snow	*aaa*	snāw	*aaa*
way	*aac*	weg		some	*aaa*	sum	*aaa*
root		(rote) *x*		speak		specan	*aab*
wort	*acd*	wyrttruma		(spreken) *x*		sprecan	
round		(rond) *x*		spear	*aaa*	spere	*aaa*
wallow	*ade*	seonuwealt		spit	*aaa*	spittan	*aaa*
rope	*aaa*	rāp	*aaa*	split		(split) *x*	
rotten		(roten) *x*		cleave	*aab*	clēofan	
rotted	*abb*	gerotod		squeeze		cwysan	*abb*
rub		(rubben) *x*		thrutch	*bbc*	geþryccan	
(gniden) *x*		gnīdan		stab		(stabben) *x*	
salt	*aaa*	sealt	*aaa*	thud	*aae*	þyddan	
sand	*aaa*	sand	*aaa*	stand	*aaa*	standan	*aaa*
say		ocogan	*aab*	star	*aaa*	steorra	*aaa*
quoth	*aac*	cweþan		stick	*aaa*	sticca	*aaa*
scratch		(scrattin) *x*		stone	*aaa*	stān	*aaa*
sharp	*add*	scrapian		straight		strehte	*aad*
sea	*aaa*	sǣ	*aaa*	right	*aac*	riht	
see	*aaa*	sēon	*aaa*	suck		sūcan	*aaa*
seed	*aaa*	sǣd	*aaa*	sun	*aaa*	sunne	*aaa*
seven	*aaa*	seofon	*aaa*	swell	*aaa*	swellan	*aaa*
sew	*aaa*	siwan	*aaa*	swim	*aaa*	swimman	*aaa*
sharp	*aaa*	scearp	*aaa*	tail	*aaa*	tægl	*aaa*
shoot	*aaa*	scēotan	*aaa*	ten	*aaa*	tīen	*aaa*
short	*aaa*	sceort	*aaa*	that	*aaa*	þæt	*aaa*
sing	*aaa*	singan	*aaa*	there	*aaa*	þær	*aaa*
sister		(süster) *x*					
(suster)		sweoster					
*		*	*	*		*	
they		(þei)	*x*	water	*aaa*	wæter	*aaa*
he	*aad*	hīe		we	*aaa*	we	*aaa*
thick	*aaa*	þicce	*aaa*	wet	*aaa*	wǣt	*aaa*
thin	*aaa*	þynne	*aaa*	what?	*aaa*	hwæt	*aaa*
think	*aaa*	þencan	*aaa*	when?	*aaa*	hwænne	*aaa*
this	*aaa*	þes	*aaa*	where?	*aaa*	hwǣr	*aaa*
you		īow	*aac*	white	*aaa*	hwīt	*aaa*
thou	*aab*	þū		who?	*aaa*	hwa	*aaa*
three	*aaa*	þrī	*aaa*	wide	*aaa*	wīd	*aaa*
throw		þrāwan	*aae*	wife		wīf	*aab*
warp	*aae*	weorpan		bedded	*aae*	gebedda	
tie	*aaa*	tīgan	*aaa*	wind	*aaa*	wind	*aaa*
tongue	*aaa*	tunge	*aaa*	wing		(wengen) *x*	
tooth	*aaa*	tōþ	*aaa*	feather	*aae*	feþra	
tree	*aaa*	trēow	*aaa*	wipe	*aaa*	wīpian	*aaa*
turn		turnian	*aac*	with		wiþ	*aac*
wend	*aad*	wendan		midwife	*aca*	mid	
twenty	*aaa*	twentig	*aaa*	woman		wifmann	*aab*
two		twā	*aac*	wife	*aac*	wīf	

twain	aac	twegen		woods	aaa	wudu	aaa
vomit		(vomyt)	x	work	aaa	wyrcan	aaa
spew	aab	spīwan		worm	aaa	wyrm	aaa
walk		wealcan	aad	year	aaa	gēar	aaa
gangway	aca	gangan		yellow	aaa	geolu	aaa
warm	aaa	wearm	aaa	you		īow	aac
wash	aaa	wæscan	aaa	ye	aab	gē	

*   *   *   *   *   *

5.1   Of the OE major exponents 146 (65.2%) are directly reflected in their respective MoE major synonyms: *eall* and *æt* and all the others that are marked **(aaa)**. Another 28 (12.5%) are directly reflected in minor synonyms or hyponyms in MoE: *wēpan, delfan, ceosan, seūfan, lytel, clēofan, spīwan, nēah, þū, gē* (all **aab**) and *dēor, yfel, wamb, gewǣde, fugol, fūl, hund, blōstm, mist, witan, nā, mann, weg, cwepan, hȳd, riht, twegen, wīf* (all **aac**). Thirteen (5.8%) are directly reflected in MoE plesionyms: *rind, mycel, weolcen, steorfan, fætnes, fǣr, slēan, cwellan, flǣsc, gestincan, rēc, hīe, wendan* (all **aad**). Seven (3.1%) are directly reflected in MoE heteronyms: *hrycg, beorg, tēon, þyddan, weorpan, gebedde, feþra*. Thus no less than 86.6% of the OE basic vocabulary has direct reflexes in the MoE lexicon, 77.7% being broadly synonymic (**aaa -- aac**).

5.2   Eight of the OE major exponents (3.6%) are reflected only in MoE dialect usage (**baa** etc.): *bearn, snīþan, swǣr, mēr, heals, swīþra, ēa, geþryccan*. Perhaps only *bairn* could be counted as a major synonym in the dialects where it occurs, *swith* is a heteronym and the rest come semantically in between.

5.3   Thirteen OE major exponents (5.8%) have MoE correspondents in **(aba -- ade)**. These include the simple forms *flēotan* and *hund*, the participle *gerotod* and the complexes *gecōcsian* and *winestra*, all with correspondents in MoE complexes, **(aba** etc*)*. *gecōcsian* and *hund*, already coexisting in OE with the noun *cōc* (< Lat. *coquus*) and the complex *hundred*, are, together with *gerotod*, semantically close to the respective MoE words. *wer* (listed twice under 'husband' and 'man'), *gangan* and *mid* have reflexes in MoE compounds: *werewolf* (**acc**) *gangway* and *midwife* (**aca**). *scrapian* has its closest cognate in MoE *sharp* (**add**). The constituents of three OE compounds in simple MoE forms: *astynt* 'blunt' and *seonuwealt* 'round' beside their MoE heteronyms *stunted* and *wallow*, *wyrttruma* 'root' beside its MoE plesionym *wort*.

5.4 Only nine (4.0%) of the major exponents in OE have no cognates in MoE. Two were replaced by other native words: *orþian* by a ME denominative from *breeth* 'breath' (< OE *bræþ* 'odour'); *sprecan* by *specan*, not attested before late OE, though there are parallel pairs in continental Gmc, e.g. OHG *sprehhan, spehhan*. Four were replaced by Scandinavian loan- words in ME: *gnīdan* by *rubben* (cf. Icel. *rubben*); *swegel* by *skye* (cf. ON *sky* 'cloud'), an external cognate to OE *sceo* 'cloud'; and the other two by their own external cognates -- *giefan* by *give* (§2.3.4), *sweoster* (> ME *suster*) by *süster* (cf. ON *systir*). Three were replaced by words of French origin: *rīman* by *counten;* *sealtian*, itself a Latin loanword, by *dauncen;* for *þām þe* etc. by *bī cause* (cf. *par cause*). The survival of *for that* at least into rare nineteenth century usage reminds us that 'obsolete' is always a treacherous label.

6.1 As we have seen, 146 (65.2%) major exponents in MoE are direct reflexes of their major synonyms in OE. Fifteen more (6.7%) reflect minor synonyms: *back, child, clothes, dog, float, hundred, know, neck, say, skin, small, smoke, speak, wife, woman* (all **aab**). Eleven (5%) reflect hyponyms: *bird, husband, lake, man, meat, pull, thou, turn, two, with, you* (all **aac**).

6.2 Ten (4.5%) reflect OE plesionyms (**aad**): *bad, breathe, cook, fat, fear, heavy, hit, road, straight, walk*.

Four (1.8%) reflect OE heteronyms (**aae**): *belly, cloud, right (side), throw*. Thus 83.1% of the MoE basic vocabulary directly reflects attested items in the OE lexicon, 76.9% being still broadly synonymic (**aaa** -- **aac**).

6.3 Five (2.2%) have more indirect morphological relations with their OE cognates: *dirty, near, squeeze* (< ME *queisen* < *cwysan*) and the compounds *not* (*nā-wiht*) and *left*; cf. ME *lüft* reflecting the first constituent of *lyft-ādl* (§2.2.1).

6.4.1 Thirty-three major exponents in MoE (14.7%) do not reflect any material recorded from the OE lexicon. For four of these, *count, dance, give* and *sky*, the OE major exponents have no MoE cognates either. Only one of the thirty-three emerges after the ME period: *split* is a seventeenth century loanword from Dutch *splitten*, an external cognate of ME *splatten* 'to lay open'. Four could on phonological grounds be given an OE origin, though the relevant forms have not survived: (i) *blunt* < *blont*, a participial cognate of *blinnen* (< OE *blinnan*) 'to cease', which appears in the thirteenth century, meaning 'dull-witted'; (ii) *cutten*, an ME minor synonym of *scheren, cerven*, though of Scandinavian origin (cf. Norw. *kutte*) may have come in as OE **cyttan*; (iii) *kill* < *killen*, which though also perhaps of Scandinavian origin (cf. OFris. *kullen* 'to strike') may have come in as OE **cyllan*, a minor synonym to *cwellan*, an external cognate, since both reflect different grades of the same PGmc root **kulįan, *kualįan*; (iv) *smell* < ME *smellen*, which could reflect OE **smiellan*, sometimes connected with Dutch *smuelen* 'to emit fumes or smoke'; it replaced **ystincen* (< *gestincan*) when aphaeresis produced homophony with *stincen* 'to stink'.

6.4.2 Sixteen are ME loanwords from other Germanic languages. All but one -- *dig*, which is probably from Dutch (§2.3.4) -- are from Scandinavian. *leg* and *wing* are straightforward; *bark, die, give, rub, sister* and *sky* have already been noted (§2.3.4, 3.2, 5.4). The following also deserve comment. (i) *big* first appears as 'stout, strong' in north-eastern dialects (cf. Norw. *bugge* 'strong man'). (ii) *fog* < ME *fogge* 'rank grass' (cf. Norw. *fogg*) with *foggy* 'murky, thick' already recorded in mid-sixteenth century. (iii) *root* < *rōte*, from ON *rót*, which < PGmc *wrōt*; a different gradation *wurt > OE *wyrt* 'plant', with which *root* is thus an external cognate. (iv) *rotten* < ON *rotinn*, an external cognate of OE *gerotod*. (v) *scratch* < *scratten*; cf. OSw *kratte* and for *s-* squeeze and squash. (vi) *stab* a denominative from *stabbe* 'stab-wound'; cf. Icel. *stabbi* 'stump'. (vii) *they* < *þei* (from ON *ðeir*, an external cognate to OE *þes, þæt*, MoE *this, that*), which spread from northern dialects to replace *þa*, the deictic that had itself replaced OE *hīe*. *dog* (< ME *dogge*) would naturally have been assigned to this group, had it not been for the late OE gloss *docgena* for Lat. *canum* (Meritt 1959: 724), which reveals an OE *docga*. Nine of the sixteen loanwords are in fact external cognates: *give, root, rotten, bark, die, dig, sister, sky* and *they*. Of these the first three are related to items in the OE basic vocabulary.

6.4.3 Twelve are of Latinate origin. From Latin itself probably come ME *animal* and *vomyt* (though the noun *vomyte* may be from Fr. *vomite*). Of the French loanwords *because, count, dance, flower, person, push, river* and *round* are straight- forward. A few deserve comment: (i) *cry* < ME *crien* originally 'shout' and not even a minor synonym to *wepen* before the fifteenth century; (ii) *mountaine* < OFr *montaigne* < Lat. *montanam*, an adjectival derivative of *mont(em)*, which was borrowed as OE *munt* (minor synonym to *beorg*), whence ME *mont* (beside minor synonym *mountaine*) > MoE *mount*, to which *mountain* is thus an external cognate.

6.4.4 It is well known that a large number of words from Scandinavian, Low German and Latin-French sources first appear in the Middle English period. What is perhaps surprising is that as much as 14.7% of the MoE basic vocabulary came from these sources (or 12.1% if *blunt, cut, die, dig, kill* and *smell* go back to OE: §§2.3.4, 6.4.1), and that only one of these entered the language after 1350. It is beyond the scope of this paper and indeed the competence of the author to chronicle the stages by which each of these words gradually penetrated the basic vocabulary, displacing as they advanced the existing exponents, but the work would obviously be worth doing.

7.1 The figures in §6 are brought together in Tables 1 and 2. These figures will no doubt need modification in the light of further research -- in particular as a result of changes in the view of what constitutes a basic vocabulary, further refinements in the system of classification employed here and more efficient trawling of the relevant dictionaries, historical grammars and above all the written sources themselves. Even as they stand, it is interesting to compare them with those reported by earlier scholars, which are summarised in Bergsland and Vogt (1962:116).

Table 1 *OE survivals into MoE basic vocabulary*

	aaa	aab-c	aad-e	ab-ad	b-	x
Total	146	28	20	13	8	9
%		65.2	12.5	8.9	5.8	3.6	4.0
cum. %		65.2	77.7	86.6	92.4	96.0	100

Table 2 *MoE retentions from OE basic vocabulary*

	aaa	aab-c	aad-e	ab-ad	b-	x
Total	146	26	14	5	--	33
%		65.2	11.7	6.2	2.2	--	14.7
cum. %	65.2	76.9	83.1	85.3	--	100

Arndt's (1959) figure for lexical retention in English was
67.8%, which is a little above the 65.2% for our category
(aaa) (= exact morphological correspondents that are major
synonyms in the standard language). Lees's (1953) figure of
76.6% is a little below the combined totals for our
categories *(aaa aab aac)* (= exact morphological
correspondents that are broadly synonymic in the standard
language): 76.9% for MoE retentions and 77.7% for OE
survivals. Swadesh's (1952) figure of 85% is not far from
the totals for all our *(aa)* categories (= exact
morphological correspondents in the standard language
without regard to meaning): 83.1% for MoE retentions and
86.6% for OE survivals. It is clear that the Swadesh '15%
mortality rate per millennium' that became canonical for the
glottochronologists is far too high, unless we are to attach
greater weight to morphological than to semantic criteria.
Since the morphology of words is usually more durable than
their meanings, this overweighting in favour of morphology
must be very misleading.

    7.2   A few further general observations can be made.
Firstly, while 14.7% of the MoE basic vocabulary embodies
material that is not directly attested in OE, only 4.0% of
the OE basic vocabulary has actually disappeared from the
language. Many items that have been displaced from the basic
vocabulary have still survived with changes in their status,
morphology or meaning. Indeed no word can ever be declared
to be completely dead, even though it may show a steady
decline over the centuries. By contrast it is possible, as
we have seen (§6.4), to identify lexical innovations, even
when the date of their first appearance in the language
cannot be made more precise than the *terminus ante quem*
provided by their earliest written attestation. How swiftly
and by what steps these and the upwardly mobile native words
established themselves in the basic vocabulary will have of

course to be investigated word by word. Such an investigation would also establish whether replacements occurred at a more or less constant rate over the millennium or, as seems at present more likely, they were much more rapid in the period 1200- 1450 than they were before or after. There is still plenty of work to be done.

REFERENCES

Arndt, W.W. 1959. 'The performance of glottochronology in Germanic.' *Language* 35. 180-92.
Bergsland, K. & Vogt, H. 1962. 'On the validity of glottochronology.' *Current Anthropology* 3. 115-53.
Bosworth, J. & Toller, T.N. 1898. *An Anglo-Saxon Dictionary.* Oxford. [Supplement. ed. Toller, 1921. Oxford; Enlarged Addenda and Corrigenda, ed. A. Campbell, 1972. Oxford.]
Buck, C.D. 1949. *A Dictionary of Selected Synonyms in the Principal Indo-European Languages.* Chicago.
Kurath, H. & Kuhn, S. 1954. *Middle-English Dictionary.* Ann Arbor.
Lees, R.B. 1953. 'The basis of glottochronology'. *Language* 29.113-27.
The Microform Concordance of Old English. 1980. Delaware.
Meritt, H.D. ed. 1959. *The Old English Prudentius Glosses of Boulogne-sur-Mer.* Stanford.
Murray, J.A.H., Bradley, H., Craigie, W.A. & Onions, C.T. 1933. *The Oxford English Dictionary.* Oxford.
Onions, C.T., Friedrichsen, G.W.S. & Burchfield, R.W. 1966. *The Oxford Dictionary of English Etymology.* Oxford.
Skeat, W.W. 1879. *An English-Anglo-Saxon Vocabulary.* Cambridge.
Stratman, F.H. & Bradley, H. 1891. *A Middle-English Dictionary.* Oxford.
Swadesh, M. 1952. 'Lexicostatistic dating of prehistoric ethnic contacts'. *Proceedings of the American Philosophical Society* 96. 452-63.

PREPOSITION STRANDING AND RELATIVE COMPLEMENTIZER DELETION:
IMPLICATIONAL TENDENCIES IN ENGLISH AND THE OTHER
GERMANIC LANGUAGES

XAVIER DEKEYSER
Universiteit van Antwerpen/ UFSIA
Katholieke Universiteit Leuven

0. *Introduction*. 0.1. In this paper I shall argue that both preposition stranding and deletion of a relative complementizer can best be viewed as implicational tendencies, accommodated by the 'movement or deletion' hypothesis proposed by Grimshaw(1975) for Middle English, and Bresnan(1976) for Old English. The bulk of the data will be drawn from the history of English, while Dutch, German and Scandinavian will be used as collateral evidence.[1]

0.2. The grammar of Old and Middle English has the following types of Relative Clause, with THAT representing a complementizer and WH- standing for a relative pronoun:

Type I: NP THAT(S.........)   Type III: NP WH- THAT(S.........)

Type II: NP WH-(S.........)   Type IV: NP {THAT / WH-} (S....PRO......)

Type I: Old English

(1) AE CHom i.18.33...*mid þam deofle þe hine forlærde*.

(Mitchell II: 109)[2]

Middle English

(2) Best.24 *þat defte meiden, Marie bi name, þe him bar to manne frame*.   (Mustanoja: 188)

(3) Best.112 *(þe neddre) sekeþ a ston þat a þirl is on*.

(Mustanoja: 189)

Type II: Old English

(4) A.S.Chron. 1022 *Leofwine abb se wæs unrihtlice of Elig adræfed wæs his gerefa*.

(Plummer: 157)

Middle English

(5) Lamb.Hom.11 *twa stanene tables breode on hwulche Almihti heofde iwriten þa ten lawe*.

(Mustanoja: 195)

Type III: Old English

(6) Bede 222.23...*þæt heo ne woldon heora Gode hyran, þone þe heo gelyfden*.

(Mitchell II: 125)

Middle English

(7) Chaucer CT A Kn.931 *I, wrecche, which that wepe and wayle*.   (Mustanoja: 197)

Type IV: Old English

(8) Or.102.24 7 *ic gehwam wille þærto tæcan þe hiene his lyst ma to witanne*.   (Mitchell II: 132)

In Middle English there are numerous attestations of THAT...PRO as well as WH-...PRO (Geoghegan, 1975: 47 or Traugott,1972: 157-158). One example with THAT from the *Paston Letters* may suffice here:

(9) *with other dyveres* that I know not ther names.

(Traugott: 157)

0.3. Following Grimshaw(1975), I assume that relative clauses are formed either by deletion *in situ* of the relative NP or by WH-movement. In Type I relative clauses are introduced by a (non-pronominal) Complementizer: the only transformation that applies here is deletion of the relative NP in its original position. In both II and III the relativized NP is moved into Complementizer position adjacent to the antecedent NP by a transformation of WH-fronting; in II fronted WH- replaces the subordination marker in surface structure, while in III this marker is preserved. Type IV is a variant of either I or II, with the relative NP given surface realization as a resumptive personal pronoun. As this paper crucially revolves around the 'movement or deletion' dichotomy, we needn't concern ourselves here with III and IV, which are of no importance for the present purposes; they have been included here only for the sake of completeness.

The 'movement or deletion' model allows us to make strong generalizations about Relative Clause Formation (hence RCF), both diachronically and cross-linguistically; more particularly it adequately accommodates preposition stranding and non-introduced relative clauses of the type: $NP_{\emptyset}(S\ldots\ldots\ldots)$ with which we are concerned in the present paper.

Let us now probe the data as regards stranding and

pied-piping, first in English and then in Dutch, German and Scandinavian.

1. *Stranding in English and the other Germanic languages*
1.1. *Stranding in Old English*. Relativization involving PP can be captured as follows:
a) Type I was always characterized by stranded prepositions: the relative NP was deleted while the preposition was obligatorily kept in its original position as a surface trace of the deleted NP, which normally occurred before V (SOV) in an Old English dependent modifier clause; see also Allen (1980: 267-268):

(1) AE CHom I.14.10...*þu geearnast*... *þone stede þe se deofol of afeoll*. (Mitchell II: 151)
(2) A.S.Chron.1087 *Se cyng Willelm þe we embe specaþ was swiþe wis man.* (Plummer: 219)

b) Pied-piping was an obligatory feature of both Types II(3) and III(4):

(3) AE CHom II.292.9 *þæt fyr getacnode þone Halgan Gast, þurh þone we beoþ gehalgode*.
(Mitchell II: 151)
(4) AE CHom II.346.11 *Hwæt sind þas buton þrymsetl heora Scyppendes, on þam þe he wunigende mannum demþ?* (Ibidem)

Clearly, the particle status of *þe* accounts for there being no attestations of pied-piping with Type I, and *vice versa* (see Mitchell's data, vol.II: 156-157). But what about *þæt*, which is strictly speaking the neuter nominative/accusative (singular) of the relative pronoun paradigm? As we may expect pied-piping occurred here (e.g. *þurh* or *umbe þæt*), but Mitchell's data prove stranding to be the prevailing structure, sometimes coupled with a violation of case constraints (Vol.II: 153-154), which undoubtedly

foreshadowed Middle English *that*.
(5) CP 331.18...*he forgiet þæt grin <u>þæt he mid awierged wirþ</u>*.
(Mitchell II: 154)

1.2. *Stranding in Middle English.* 1.2.1. Basically the grammar of Old English stranded and pied-piped prepositions was continued in Early Middle English; for the data, see Visser (I: 399-400).
With COMP:
(6) Layamon 13966 *Woden, ure lauerd, <u>þe we on bi-liued</u>*.
(Visser I: 400)
(7) Havelok 2105 *Crist, <u>þat alle folk on leues</u>*. (Ibidem)
With WH-:
(8) Orm 69995 *Jesu Crist ... <u>of whamm profetess Haffdenn forrlannge cwiddedd</u>*. (Visser I: 401)
With WH- and Comp:
(9) Chaucer HF 1243 *Ther herde I trumpen Messenus, <u>Of whom that speketh Virgilius</u>*.
(Kivimaa, 1966: 17)
The only difference there was involved the place of the stranded preposition: this shifted from pre-verbal, as shown in (6-7), to post-verbal, which of course was tied up with the change-over from SOV to SVO in Middle English embedded clauses. The earliest attestations of post-verbal stranding seem to date from ca.1200:
(10) ca.1200 Orm 304 *Elysabeþ, <u>þatt we nu mælenn ummbe</u>*.
(Visser I: 400)
(11) ca.1200 Trin.Coll.Hom. 86 *þe drige stedes <u>þat þe fule gost wandreþ abuten</u>*. (Ibidem)
The crucial change in the grammar of stranded and pied-piped prepositions took place in the course of the Late

Middle English period, when stranding was extended to WH-(THAT), which means that pied-piping was no longer obligatory with types II and III:

With WH-:

(12) Layamon 27487 *þeo at þan laste nuste nan kempe <u>Whæm he sculde slæn on</u>*. (Visser I: 401)

(13) 1422 Secr.Secret. (EETS) 9,18 *y shalle teche the science of phisik abreggid, <u>the which y had not purposid to haue spokene of</u>*.
(Ibidem)

With WH- + THAT:

(14) Chaucer, The Canon's Yeoman's Tale, 879
  ...*for nadde they but a sheete, <u>Which that they myghte wrappe hem inne a-nyght</u>*.   (Grimshaw, 1975: 41)

The scarcity of examples in Visser: 401-402 before 1500 seems to suggest that stranding with WH-relatives was still rare in Late Middle English. To some extent this also holds for Early Modern English; it appears from Ingels' 16th century data that stranding accounted for roughly 10% of PPs with WH- (10 out of 87 examples), as compared with 17% in Quirk (1968: 104). A comparison of the Early Modern English and the 20th century corpora also reveals another interesting feature concerning the diffusion of stranding: Ingels recorded only 8 PPs with THAT and 7 with Ø, which yields a total of 25 instances of stranded prepositions out of 112 PPs, i.e. 22% or 1/5; in Quirk's material, on the other hand, there are 34 examples of THAT and 42 of Ø, which together with stranding in WH-relatives yields 94 cases out of a total of 180, or 52%. Though we should be wary of interpreting data from such diverse corpora as these, the expansion of stranding in Modern English seems to be an unassailable fact.

1.2.2. Stranding was not only expanding in RCF, it also spread to other structures in the course of Late Middle and Early Modern English, viz. WH-questions and passives. With stranding extended to WH-relatives, it became possible also to form questions with a non-pied-piped preposition. In her Chaucerian material Grimshaw did not record stranded prepositions except in one casual example of an indirect question from *Troilus and Criseyde* , Bk.1.819: ... *And thoughte anon what folie he was inne.* (Grimshaw, 1975: 41). The fact that Visser's earliest quotations (on page 406) date from the late 16th century allows us to hypothesize that the overall introduction of stranding in questions was posterior to stranding with WH-relatives. As far as passives are concerned, it is commonly known that subjectivalization of indirect objects and PPs started in Late Middle English (Mustanoja, 1960: 440-441); the latter very nicely fitted in with the stranding potential in relative clauses. Here, apart from a few dubious sporadic occurrences, the earliest attestations seem to date from the 14th century; see also Denison (1985: 196).

(15) ca. 1370-80 Wyclif, Eng.Wks.366 *Criste and his colage myght not be dispensid with.* (Visser III: 2123)

(16) Ibidem 369 *þes oþir wordis of þis bischop oughte to be taken hede to.* (Mustanoja, 1960: 441)

1.2.3. The Old and Middle English data presented here prove that preposition stranding originated as an obligatory feature of relative clauses introduced by a non-pronominal Complementizer (*þe* or *þat*), while pied-piping was obligatory with WH-relativization. During the Middle English period stranding spread to WH-relatives and much later to WH-questions as well, where it applied optionally. The scope of stranding was also extended by the new potentials of of passivization on PPs.

1.3. *Stranding in Scandinavian, Dutch and German.*
As is generally known (see also 2.4.1), the Scandinavian languages have always used a non-pronominal Complementizer and, accordingly, preposition-stranding has invariably been a feature of RCF just like in English. "None of these (my note: particles) can be governed by preceding prepositions; the preposition is always final", Haugen (1982: 172) writes; see also Maling (1978: 81-82). In present-day Scandinavian stranding roughly has the same range of potential as in English, including relativization, WH-movement in questions and prepositional passives (but no stranding with passives in Danish); see Herslund (1984: 48-51). It would be worthwhile to examine whether stranded prepositions were introduced in the same diachronic order as the one described above for Middle English.

Typically, Dutch and German, which can only form relative clauses by WH-movement, and so have no particle Complementizer in their surface structures, have never known stranded prepositions. One point needs clarifying here: while Old and Middle High German used relative particles next to WH-movement, there seem to be no attestations of stranding; in none of the historical grammars that I have consulted, such as Behaghel (1923-1933), Paul (1969) or Dal (1966), have I come across any reference to the possibility of placing or keeping prepositions at the end of the relative clause. The reason, I think, is to be found in the grammatical function assigned to these particles. Behaghel (III: 712) states that the particles *the*, *so* and *wo* filled the subject or object function. If this is correct, they never occurred in PP, so the issue of stranding or pied-piping is not relevant here.

The evidence from English and Scandinavian, both diachronic and synchronic, suggests that stranding is a concomitant feature or relativization by *in situ* deletion of the relative NP. In the following sections I shall argue that this also holds for the occurrence of contact clauses.

2. *Contact clauses in English and the other Germanic languages.*

2.1. *The Germanic background.* In present-day English, and also in the Scandinavian languages, contact clauses are all of the restrictive type: they are closely linked to their antecedents, semantically and prosodically. It is often pointed out that the origin of this construction is "Germanic or rather Indo-Germanic", as Curme (1912: 12) puts it. While this may be true, the question arises why precisely it has survived in English and Scandinavian, but not in Modern Dutch and German. Before attempting to answer this question, I shall first turn to the primitive Germanic data.

The existing literature in this field is impressive; see Helgander (1971: 36ff.). Most scholars are agreed that contact clauses, which seem to have occurred in most of the Germanic dialects, originated in asyndetic parataxis, often of the *apo koinou* type with an 'omitted' subject or object, and that such structures antedated the 'true' relative clause. Meritt (1938: 95) points out that the early attestations of non-introduced clauses may be regarded as reflexes of "an early asyndetic means of joining before the use of relatives", or, alternatively, may be due "to the omission of the relative"; he decides in favour of the latter interpretation, so hypotaxis, because asyndeta always occur "along with similar expressions where a kind of relative is used".

2.2. *The Old English data.* Whatever their origin may have been, occurrence and frequency of contact clauses were determined by the colloquiality of the language. Helgander (1971: 39-40) points out that in the Eastern dialects of Old Norse non-introduced clauses were considerably more frequent than in the West, where "the literary tradition was much better established and the texts were compiled by learned scholars". The same holds for Old English: in spite of a number of occurrences in a variety of texts the construction did not fully develop in the language of the learned Anglo-Saxon writers, while in Old High German, e.g. in Otfrid, it was much more common; see Curme (1912: 23), Helgander (1971: 39); for German also Dal (1966:198). Actually, the potential of the contact clause in Old English was severely constrained: nearly all of the examples cited by Bourcier (1977: 55-56, 138-139 and 464), Mitchell II (1985: 184ff.) and Bastiaensens (1983: 130ff.) are stereotyped naming constructions with a fronted proper name as the pivotal noun: *X wæs haten/wæron hatene*, or *X hatte/hatton* (Bourcier: 55). Other attestations of contact clauses are scarce in Old English and mostly involve a copula, as in:

(1) A.S.Chron.901 *on þys ilcan gere forþferde Aeþered, <u>wæs on Defenum ealdormon</u>*. (Plummer: 92)

In such sentences a NP in subject position is deleted; examples of deletions in other functions are extremely rare (Mitchell II (1985: 187-188). It should also be stressed that, unlike Modern English, most Old English contact clauses fitted a non-restrictive context; Bourcier (1977: 56) speaks of "une faible solidarité syntaxique qu'on doit poser entre les deux segments".

2.3. *Contact clauses in Middle English.*

2.3.1. As we shall see later, non-introduced clauses, whether paratactic or hypotactic, gradually fell into disuse, in Middle High German (Curme, 1912: 23, Dal, 1966: 198, or Paul, 1969: 423) as a result of the growing ascendancy of the literary tradition in the language; this also holds for Middle Dutch. In Middle English, however, and as we shall see in section 2.4.1. also in Scandinavian, the primitive Germanic construction was not only preserved, but developed new potentials, in sharp contradistinction to the Old English stereotypes.

2.3.2. The distribution of Middle English contact clauses is stylistically determined: some texts, such as the Middle English *Homilies* (Van den Eynden (1984)) or Trevisa's *Polychronicon* (Grommersch (1986) and Martens (1986)) contain hardly any examples, while in other works like the *Continuations of the Peterborough Chronicle* (Chevillet (1981) and Dekeyser (1986b)) *Havelok* (Chevillet) and *Piers Plowman* (Chevillet),they are comparatively common. It is an acknowledged commonplace that Middle English was generally characterized by the growing ascendancy of the colloquial language (Phillipps, 1965: 323-324). This was the channel through which the old tradition of asyndeta could be passed on, but it does not account for what Kurzova (1981: 93) calls "die Grammatikalisierung des Relativsatzes ohne Einleitungselement", which she ascribes to three parameters: most importantly, the existence of a relative particle; next, fixed (SVO) word order in the embedded clause as a marker of clause boundaries; finally, "Kontakt-stellung" between the antecedent and its relative clause; see also Dekeyser (1986a: 112-113).

As far as the Germanic dialects are concerned, the first condition is met: they all had particles as relative Complementizers: e.g. *þe* in Old English and also in Old High German (Dal, 1966: 205), *sum*, *är*, *þär* in the Scandinavian languages (see Wessén (1965)); but they usually had SOV word order, which was not a preferred environment for the non-introduced clause to develop. It is difficult to assess the impact of contact position as this is a clause variable. I can only refer to the Old English data in Bastiaensens (1983: 22-23): she has calculated that in nearly one fifth of the clauses in her *Anglo-Saxon Chronicle* sample the clause did not immediately follow its antecedent, in which cases deletion of the relative marker could give rise to opaque structures.

German and Dutch are prototypes of languages in which contact clauses cannot develop: they lost their particle strategy several centuries ago, and, in addition, have preserved SOV in embedded clauses. I have argued elsewhere (see Dekeyser 1986a)) that Middle English provided the ideal environment for the development and spread of contact clauses: not only was there a relative Complementizer *that*, also the rapid generalization of SVO must have contributed to the grammaticalization of the contact clause.

I suggest that we now look at the Middle English evidence in some detail. I shall confine myself to those structures which have broadly the same characteristics as the Modern English contact clause, thus leaving aside Middle English examples of naming constructions and the like with a deleted subject (Visser I: 12), which dropped out of use.

2.3.3. As pointed out before, contact clauses were virtually blocked from formal (Latinate) registers; so one of the factors that contributed to the continuation and expansion of asyndetic relative clauses was the colloquial nature of particular works, such as *Havelok*, *Genesis and Exodus*, *Ancrene Wisse*, *Piers Plowman*, etc., for which Chevillet (1981: passim) lists a fair number of examples. The data in Visser (I: 537ff. and 541ff.) and in Chevillet (passim) also suggest that the majority of contact clauses with a deleted object or PP were short clauses consisting of a sequence: (ANTECEDENT) (Ø + NP + VP); in addition, the NP was often a pronoun in the nominative case; typically this also holds for present-day spoken usage (Quirk, 1968: 107).

(2) Havelok 907 *Wel is set þe mete þu etes*.
        (Chevillet II: Illustrations, p.21)
(3) Robert of Brunne, Chron.3838 *The tresor they hadden, he it hem reft.* (Visser I: 538)
(4) Destr. Troy 4865 *We mut bye it full bitterly, þe baret we make.* (Ibidem)
(5) Paston Letters I, 390 *he hath thynges to showe ye saw nevyr yit.* (Ibidem)
(6) Towneley Pl. 280,33 *Thus He gettis many fees cf thym he begyles.* (Ibidem)

Clearly, it was such perceptually simple and unambiguous configurations that promoted the use of contact clauses. But also in sentences with a subject noun perceptual misunderstanding was ruled out after the generalization of SVO:

(7) Gen.& Ex. 3672 *And ches þo men god made wis*.
        (Chevillet II: Illustrations, p.21)
(8) Lamb. Hom. A X/107/17 *nu ye habbeþ iherd hu þes haie mihten ouercumaþ þa sunnan þe deouel bisaweþ on us*.(Chevillet II: Illustr.,p.75)

In a sentence like (7) *god* could only be interpreted as the subject, not as the object.

It is obvious that fixed SVO could also promote clauses with a deleted subject. However, this type of contact clause fell into disuse for a number of reasons, syntactic and socio-linguistic, into which we cannot go here; see Romaine (1980) and (1981), or Bever and Langendoen (1971); also Dekeyser (1986a).

2.3.1. I shall now adduce evidence that proves Middle English contact clauses to be structurally related to clauses introduced by a particle Complementizer, not to WH-. I have pointed out in 1.2. that in Early Middle English, and to some extent also in Late Middle English, preposition stranding was bound to the particle, while WH- obligatorily involved pied-piping. It follows from this that contact clauses with a relativized PP, like (9-11), are only derivable from an underlying structure with relative *that*, or earlier also *þe*:

(9) Poema Mor. T 157 *Ich wulle nu cumen eft to þe dome ic eow ar of sæde*. (Chevillet II: Illustr., p.21)

(10) Brunne, Chron. A 1402 *And that ilde thou hast of herd With se on alle halve ys spred*. (Visser I: 541-542)(Visser adds that MS.T has *that)*

(11) Chaucer, Troil. I, 577 *There is another thing I take of hede*. (Visser I: 542)

Such data allow us to assume that contact clauses could only derive from clauses with a particle, not from clauses with a pronominal Complementizer. In addition, pronominal Complementizers were very rare in the early stages of Middle English when contact clauses began to diffuse; see Van den Eynden (1984: 167 and 169) and Martens (1986: 16).

This relationship is also borne out by numerous instances of alternation between *that* and zero as recorded in more or less identical sentences in different manuscripts. Examples are rife in Chevillet's Middle English material, so a few quotations may suffice here; see also (10) above and Dekeyser (1986a: 114). Chevillet quotes 2 examples from *Horn*, Laud and Cambr., where the younger manuscript typically shows Complementizer deletion:

(12) Cambr. *þe ring þat þu þrewe, þu seie whar þu hit nome.*
     (Chevillet II: 671)

To be compared with:

(13) Laud: *þe ring þou here þrewe*...(Ibid.: 215)

Similarly in *Piers Plowman*:

(14) A-version (ca.1360-70) *I performede the penaunce. that the prest me en-ioynede.*

(15) B-version (ca.1377-79) *I parfourned the penaunce. the preest me enioyned.*

(16) C-version (ca.1390-93) *And parfourne the penaunce. that the preest me highte.*
     (Chevillet II: 754, note 188)

I have also recorded a few instances where clauses with and without Complementizer deletion occur side by side, as in:

(17) Trin. Hom. xxxii/203 *he seide þos word to alle þo þe þo weren. and siþen hauen ben. and þo þe nu ben. and þo her after comen.* (Chevillet II: Illustr., p.21)

There is also persuasive diachronic evidence on the performance level which substantiates the claim about contact clauses and the particle Complementizer being structurally related. While *that* could introduce restrictive as well as non-restrictive clauses in Middle English (Mustanoja, 1960: 190), its distribution in (Early) Modern English got increasingly confined to a restrictive context; interestingly, the history of contact clauses was characterized by a similar distributional development; see Dekeyser (1984a: 66) (Tables IIIa and b) and Saito (1961: 78).

Another feature that shows *that* and contact clauses to correlate is their stylistic distribution in Early Modern English: in my data these two strategies are significantly more frequent in simple registers (Drama) than in the more complex ones (Informative Prose), as shown in the Table below; see Dekeyser and Ingels (forthcoming) and Dekeyser (1984b); also Romaine (1980) and (1981) as far as Scots English is concerned.

THAT and Ø correlated with register

	WH	TH	Ø	Totals
ca.1550-1600 DRAMA	286(44.2%)	313(48.4%)	48(7.4%)	647
ca.1550-1600 INF.PR.	562(66.6%)	252(29.9%)	30(3.5%)	844
Totals	848(56.9%)	565(37.9%)	78(5.2%)	1,491

$x^2 = 76$ (highly significant)

	WH	TH	Ø	Totals
ca.1600-49 DRAMA	397(37.9%)	526(50.1%)	126(12%)	1,049
ca.1600-49 INF.PR.	803(75.7%)	226(21.3%)	32(3%)	1,061
Totals	1,200(56.9%)	752(35.6%)	158(7.5%)	2,110

$x^2 =$ ca.311 (highly significant)

2.4. *The Scandinavian, Dutch and German evidence*

2.4.1. The correlation between contact clauses, relative particles and SVO is also substantiated by the evidence from Scandinavian, Dutch and German. Let us first turn to the Scandinavian languages, whose relative clause system broadly shows the same potential as in English.

The three Scandinavian languages have an indeclinable particle *som*, Danish also has *der* in subject function; Danish and Swedish occasionally use interrogative pronouns as relative markers (Walshe, 1965: 134-135; 153). As Haugen (1982: 172) observes,

> Scandinavian has no vernacular forms for a relative pronoun proper... but has always managed with relative particles: *es/er* in CSc., replaced in OSc. by *sum/sem* 'as', from which the modern *som* of the mainland languages... in Da varying with *der*.

In addition, Scandinavian, just like English, has a long-standing tradition of SVO in embedded clauses (Haugen: 177). As both the particle and word order conditions are met, contact clauses have always constituted an inherent feature of RCF in these languages. For detailed diachronic data see Wessén (1965: 246ff.). In Modern Scandinavian the relative Complementizer is deletable under much the same conditions as in English (Jespersen, 1965: 135) and, as we have seen above, requires preposition stranding:

(18) Swedish: *huset, (som) jag bor i*. (the house (that) I live in) (Walshe, 1965: 135)

(19) Danish: *Du er ikke den første jeg har sagt nej til*.
(You are not the first I've said no to)
(Jespersen, 1969: 67)

2.4.2. Modern Dutch and German are at the other side of the scale: they have preserved SOV in embedded clauses and only know case-coding relative Complementizers in their present-day standard varieties: German exclusively uses deictic relatives, while Dutch has deictic and interrogative relatives, which occur in fixed paradigmatic distribution (Dekeyser, forthcoming). As is commonly known, neither of them can form contact clauses.

Historically the situation was as follows: in Old and Middle High German relative clauses were introduced either by relative pronouns or particles; the primitive Germanic asyndetic construction, or its reflex, is also attested (Lenerz, 1984: 58ff., Dal, 1966: 198ff.). As pointed out above, Standard German has only preserved its pronominal strategy. Middle Dutch, with data from ca.1200, knew (deictic and interrogative) relative pronouns, sometimes followed by the particle *dat* 'that' (Stoett, 1923: 32ff.), but unlike Old German no independent particle Complementizer. Again asyndeta of the type :
(20) *Ic wille u tellen van twee vrienden, <u>waren ghesellen</u>.*
    'I will you tell of two friends, were mates.
                                            (Stoett: 42)
fell into disuse by the end of the Middle Dutch period.

3. *Conclusions.* Typologically speaking, two strategies of RCF characterize the Germanic languages: relativization by deletion of the relative NP in place and relativization by movement of the WH-phrase to the Complementizer position; in the surface structure the former has a particle Complementizer, the latter a case-coding pronoun. Modern German and Dutch, with only case-coding Complementizers, are at one side of the RCF scale, while Scandinavian, with its almost exclusive use of an invariable Complementizer, is at the opposite end. Typically, English occupies an intermediate position: it knows both strategies in an intricate distributional system determined by syntactic, semantic (restrictive vs. non-restrictive) and stylistic (often also dialectal)

parameters.

The first divide that runs through these languages arises from preposition stranding: WH-movement obligatorily implies pied-piping, as in Dutch and German, while relativization through deletion is always coupled with stranded prepositions, no movement having occurred, as in the Scandinavian languages. English has both pied-piping and stranding, which follows from it having two relativization strategies. However, the Old and Early Middle English evidence unmistakably demonstrates that stranding was linked up with deletion, pied-piping with movement. Only later was it systematically extended to WH-relatives, then WH-interrogatives, and, with the development of passivization on PPs, to this syntactic structure as well. Typically, Modern Scandinavian has the same range of stranding potential (Herslund, 1984: 48-51).

The second divide, which coalesces with the first, bears on the occurrence and cross-linguistic distribution of non-introduced relative clauses. Grimshaw's 'movement or deletion' hypothesis implies that only particle Complementizers are deletable, while moved WH-pronouns are not (Grimshaw, 1975: 39). This assumption is persuasively borne out by the Germanic evidence, both diachronic and synchronic. Again, Scandinavian and the Dutch/German group are each other's opposites. As far as English is concerned, we have clearly demonstrated that the Middle English contact clause derived from deletion of a particle Complementizer, so from clauses with relativization by an *in situ* deletion of the relative NP, not from clauses with WH-movement. Actually, for no stage in the history of English is it necessary to posit a rule of WH-deletion.

Preposition stranding and contact clauses have to be regarded as implicational tendencies in Scandinavian and English: if a language has property Y, it is likely to have property X as well (Downing, 1978: 381). However, the evidence suggests that, unlike stranded prepositions, the mere presence of a particle Complementizer in the surface structure does not automatically lead to its grammaticalized deletion under certain conditions; see Old English or Old High German for that matter. Kurzova's claim about SVO (in embedded clauses) promoting particle deletion (Kurzova, 1981: 93) is fully substantiated by the English and Scandinavian evidence. The Middle English and Early Modern English data also suggest that particle deletion was stylistically determined on two counts: to a greater or lesser extent contact clauses were a feature of colloquial English; in addition, they tended to occur in simple syntactic configurations, often a two-constituent string in contact position, where no perceptual problems were likely to arise. Finally, the importance of the Old Germanic paratactic asyndeta should not be underrated, as it was probably these structures that provided the substratum on which grammaticalization of contact clauses was to develop in English and Scandinavian.

To conclude, this data-based analysis has proved the 'movement or deletion' hypothesis to be very adequate, because it allows us to make the correct diachronic and cross-linguistic generalizations covering the entire history of RCF in the Germanic languages dealt with in this paper.

NOTES

1. I am very grateful to Dr. Ria Vranckx of Leuven University, who gave generously of her time to help me through the Scandinavian data; all errors and lacunae are of course my own responsibility.
2. For typological reasons the dental fricative is uniformly represented as <þ>.

REFERENCES

Allen, Cynthia. 1980.'Movement and deletion in Old English'. *LIn* 13.261-323.

Bastiaensens, Anna. 1983. *Aspects of relativization in the Anglo-Saxon Chronicle: a dynamic synchronic approach*. Unpublished dissertation, K.U.Leuven.

Behaghel, Otto. 1923-1932. *Deutsche Syntax. Eine geschichtliche Darstellung*. Vol.3. Heidelberg: Winter.

Bever, T. and Langendoen, D.T. 1971. 'A dynamic model of the evolution of language.' *LIn* 2.433-463.

Bourcier, G. 1977. *Les propositions relatives en vieil-anglais*. Publications de l'Université de Paris X Nanterre. Paris: Honoré Champion.

Bresnan, Joan. 1976. 'Evidence for a theory of unbounded transformations.' *Linguistic Analysis* 2.353-393.

Chevillet, François. 1981. *Les relatifs au début du moyen-anglais*. Thèse présentée devant l'Université de Paris X. 2 vols. Paris: Honoré Champion.

Curme, G.O. 1912. 'A history of the English relative constructions.' *JEGP* 11.10-29, 180-204, 355-380.

Dal, Ingerid. 1966. *Kurze deutsche Syntax auf historischer Grundlage*. 3. verbesserte Auflage. Tübingen: Max Niemeyer Verlag.

Dekeyser, Xavier. 1984a. 'Relativizers in Early Modern English: a dynamic quantitative study.' In J. Fisiak, ed. *Historical syntax*, 61-87. The Hague: Mouton.

_____ 1984b. *Socio-historical linguistics and relativization in 17th century English: ca.1600-1649*. Unpublished paper, K.U.Leuven.

_____ 1986a. 'English contact clauses revisited: a diachronic approach.' *FLH* 7.107-120.

_____ 1986b. 'Relative markers in the *Peterborough Chronicle*: 1070-1154 or linguistic change exemplified.' *FLH* 7.93-105.

_____ (forthcoming). 'Relativization in English and Dutch: a comparative historical survey.'

_____ and Ingels, Mia.(forthcoming). 'Socio-historical aspects of relativization in late 16th century English: ca.1550-1600.' *Studia Anglica Posnaniensia*.

Denison, D. 1985. 'Why Old English had no prepositional passive.' *ES* 66.189-204.

Downing, Bruce T. 1978. 'Some universals of relative clause structure.' In Joseph H. Greenberg, ed. *Universals of human language*,375-418. Stanford University Press.

Emonds, J.E. 1976. *A transformational approach to English syntax.* New York: Academic Press.

Geoghegan, Sheila Graves. 1975. 'Relative clauses in Old, Middle and New English.' *OSU WPL* 18.30-71.

Grimshaw, Jane B. 1975. 'Evidence for relativization by deletion in Chaucerian Middle English.' In Jane B. Grimshaw, ed. *Papers in the history and structure of English*, 35-43. University of Massachusetts Occasional Papers in Linguistics, 1.

Grommersch, Claudine. 1986. *The Middle English relative pronouns in Higdin's 'Polychronicon', as translated by Trevisa and an anonymous 15th century writer.* Unpublished dissertation, Université Catholique de Louvain-la-Neuve.

Haugen, Einar. 1982. *Scandinavian language structures: a comparative historical survey.* Tübingen: Max Niemeyer Verlag.

Helgander, John. 1971. *The relative clause in English and other Germanic languages.* Department of English, Göteborg University.

Herslund, Michael. 1984. 'Particles, prefixes and preposition stranding.' In *Topics in Danish syntx*, 34-71. Nydanske Studier & Almen Kommunikationsteori 14. Akademisk Forlag.

Ingels, Mia. 1975. *Socio-historical aspects of relativization in 16th century English (ca.1550-1600).* Unpublished dissertation, K.U.Leuven.

Jespersen, Otto. 1965. *A Modern English grammar on historical principles.* Vol.3. London: George Allen and Unwin Ltd.

——————. 1969. *Analytic syntax.* Transatlantic Series in Linguistics. New York: Holt, Rinehart and Winston, Inc.

Kivimaa, Kirsti. 1966. *The pleonastic That in relative and interrogative constructions in Chaucer's verse.* Commentationes Humanarum Litterarum, vol.39/3. Helsinki: Societas Scientiarium Fennica.

Kurzova, Helena. 1981. *Der Relativsatz in den indoeuropäischen Sprachen.* Hamburg: Buske.

Lenerz, J. 1984. *Syntaktischer Wandel und Grammatiktheorie. Eine Untersuchung an Beispielen aus der Sprachgeschichte des Deutschen.* Linguistische Arbeiten, 4. Tübingen: Max Niemeyer Verlag.

Maling, Joan M. 1978. 'An asymmetry with respect to WH-Islands.' *LIn* 9. 75-89.

Martens, Livine. 1986. *The process of relativization and personal pronouns in Middle English: a diachronic approach based on the analysis of two translations of Higdin's 'Polychronicon' (ca.1380-1440).* Unpublished dissertation, K.U.Leuven.

Mitchell, Bruce. 1985. *Old English syntax.* Vol.1 and 2. Oxford: Clarendon Press.

Meritt, Herbert Dean. 1938. *The construction apo koinou in the Germanic languages.* Stanford University Series, Language and Literature,VI/2. Stanford.

Mustanoja, Tauno F. 1960. *A Middle English syntax. Part I: Parts of Speech.* Mémoires de la Société Néophilologique de Helsinki, XXIII. Helsinki: Société Néophilologique.

Paul, H. 1969. *Mittelhochdeutsche Grammatik*.20.Auflage von Hugo Moser und Ingeborg Schröbler. Tübingen: Max Niemeyer Verlag.
Phillipps, K.C. 1965. 'Asyndetic relative clauses in Late Middle English.' *ES* 46.323-329.
Plummer, C. 1892. *Two of the Saxon Chronicles Parallel*...ed. by Charles Plummer. Oxford: Clarendon Press.
Quirk, Randolph. 1968. 'Relative clauses in educated spoken English.' In *Essays on the English language, Medieval and Modern*,94-108. London: Longmans, Green and Co Ltd.
Romaine, Suzanne. 1980. 'The relative clause marker in Scots English: diffusion, complexity and style as dimensions of syntactic change.' *LiS* 9.221-247.
_____ 1981. 'Syntactic complexity, relativization and stylistic levels in Middle Scots.' *FLH*.2.71-97.
Saito, Toshio. 1961. 'The development of relative pronouns in modern colloquial English. A statistical survey of the development of their usage seen in British prose plays from the 16th century to the present time.' *The Scientific Reports of Mukogawa Women's University*, 8.67-89.
Stoett, F.A. 1923. *Middelnederlandsche spraakkunst*. 's Gravenhage: Martinus Nijhoff.
Traugott, Elizabeth Closs. 1972. *A history of English syntax: a transformational approach to the history of English sentence structure*. Transatlantic Series in Linguistics. New York: Holt, Rinehart and Winston, Inc.
Van den Eynden, Nadine M. 1984. *The process of relativization in Middle English: a diachronic approach based on the analysis of 12th-late 14th century theological prose*. Unpublished dissertation.
Visser, F.Th. 1963-1973. *An historical syntax of the English language*. Parts I and III, second half. Leiden: E.J.Brill.
Walshe, M.O'C. 1965. *Introduction to the Scandinavian languages*. London: André Deutsch.
Warner, Anthony. 1982. *Complementation in Middle English and the methodology of historical syntax: a study of the Wyclifite sermons*. London: Croom Helm.
Wessén, E. 1965. *Svensk språkhistoria III. Grundlinjer till en historisk syntax*. Stockholm: Almqvist & Wiksell.

THE OLD ENGLISH IMPERSONALS REVIVED

DAVID DENISON
University of Manchester

0. *Introduction.* This paper arose from queries about examples cited in Olga Fischer and Frederike van der Leek's paper, 'The Demise of the Old English Impersonal Construction' (1983), which had seemed to be the definitive account. I will refer to it and them as 'FL'. My material has now grown quite extensive, and though I have a very high regard for FL (the friends who wrote it as well as the paper itself!), I no longer think it the last word — hence my title. Nor do others. At least five publications on English impersonals by different authors have appeared since I started work, several explicitly in response to FL, plus one from Fischer and van der Leek themselves (1987). The latter avoids some of the problems discussed here, but its focus is more on case theory and semantic explanation and hence further from my present concerns.

Here I shall be considering serial relationships among OE impersonal (and other) verbs.[1] First I will summarise FL's analysis (§1). Then I shall re-interpret some of FL's data and introduce a selection of other data, hoping to show that you can't adequately capture with a single analysis all the impersonal verbs that FL discuss (§2). I shall then discuss the alternative strategy of grouping the impersonals into different classes. Again, I shall claim that no one grouping works very well, as demarcations between classes, whether syntactic or semantic, are often unconvincing (§3). Furthermore, the boundary between impersonals and not-impersonals is very fuzzy indeed (§4). So I shall explore instead the merits of a verb-by-verb analysis, capturing some of the evident similarities by means of Quirk's (1965) notion of serial relationship (§5). Then I shall sketch some particular advantages of this approach in both synchronic (§6) and diachronic (§7) analysis. Finally I will comment on the relationship between a surface-y and apparently taxonomic approach like this and generative approaches (§8).

1. *FL's account.* FL remains one of the most coherent accounts available, and it is convenient to start from it and to keep to its terminology. (I don't want to tangle here with the question of terminology.) Thus an *impersonal construction* is a subjectless construction in which the verb has 3 sg. form and there is no nominative NP controlling verb concord; an *impersonal verb* is a verb which can, but need not always, occur in an impersonal construction (1983: 346-7). FL also define the subject-matter semantically as follows:

> The term 'impersonal' verbs refers to a class of verbs which have a common semantic core: they all express a physical or mental/cognitive experience which involves a 'goal', in this case an animate 'experiencer', and a 'source', i.e. something from which the experience emanates or by which the experience is effected (in this article we shall mostly refer to the 'source' as 'cause' ...).

1.1. FL's account of OE impersonal verbs can be summarised in three examples from Ælfric (handily gathered by John Anderson, 1986: 170-1), and a lexical entry. Examples (1) to (3) illustrate FL's types (i) to (iii), respectively:[2]

(1) *him ofhreow þæs mannes*
     to-him(DAT) there-was-pity because-of-the man(GEN)
     'He pitied man' (*ÆCHom* I (Thorpe) 192.16)
(2) *Þa ofhreow ðam munece þæs hreoflian mægenleast*
     then brought-pity to-the monk(DAT) the leper's feebleness(NOM)
     'Then the monk pitied the leper's feebleness' (*ÆCHom* I (Thorpe) 336.10)
(3) *se mæssepreost þæs mannes ofhreow*
     the priest(NOM) because-of-the man(GEN) felt-pity
     'The priest pitied the man' (*ÆLS* 26 (Oswald) 262)

Example (1), the type otherwise called 'neutral', or 'true impersonal', has no subject. The cause is in the genitive, the experiencer is in the dative. (2) has the cause as nominative subject[3] and the experiencer in the dative. (3) has the experiencer as subject and the cause in the genitive. FL's lexical entry for an OE impersonal is my (4), their (20):

(4) $\begin{bmatrix} \text{NP NP} - (\bar{\text{S}}) \\ \text{NP: DATIVE; } \theta\text{-role: experiencer} \\ \begin{Bmatrix} \text{NP: GENITIVE} \\ \bar{\text{S}} \end{Bmatrix} \theta\text{-role: cause} \end{bmatrix}$

The entry encapsulates a number of claims. It suggests that OE impersonals are characteristically two-place verbs, with an experiencer and a cause argument. The experiencer is a (typically animate) NP, the cause is either an NP or a clause but not both (unless the NP is a provisional non-argument, that is, an NP with no referential function). Typical surface cases are dative for the experiencer and genitive for a nominal cause, though one also finds accusative for either and PP for cause. This is FL's type (i) pattern. By means of syntactic processes in Government Binding theory that I won't discuss here, either argument of the verb may, if it is an NP, wind up as subject of the verb in the nominative, giving type (ii) or (iii). The range of examples (1-3) for *OFHREOWAN 'rue' is claimed to be typical of *all* OE impersonal verbs (four exceptions are noted at 1983: 344 n.7). This is the essence of the account of OE impersonals given by FL.

1.2. FL's account goes on to claim that type (i) died out in ME, and that eventually only one of types (ii) and (iii) survived for a given verb. This is to be contrasted with the traditional account put forward by van der Gaaf (1904) and Jespersen (1927, 1949) and adopted by Lightfoot (1979, 1981) and others, which assumes that type (i) or (ii) was basic in OE and was reanalysed as type (iii) in the course of the ME period. In the accounts of Jespersen and his followers, LIKE rather than RUE is usually taken as the prototypical impersonal.

2. *A single class of impersonals?* First I discuss some patterns and individual examples from FL which permit or even require a different analysis from the one they give.

2.1. *LICIAN in types (i) and (iii)?* The most-discussed verb in the literature, thanks partly to Jespersen, has been OE (GE)LICIAN, ModE LIKE. For FL, (GE)LICIAN is a member of their 'fully productive' system of impersonals, which implies that type (i) (true impersonal) should be basic and that types (ii) and (iii) should both occur too. Yet type (ii) seems to be in the overwhelming majority, to the extent that it is doubtful whether the others are grammatical at all given the commonness of the verb (over 400 citations in the *Concordance to OE*, Healey & Venezky 1980). Are there *any* examples of types (i) or (iii) with (GE)-LICIAN?

First, type (i). FL cite (5) (our glossing differs here and elsewhere):

(5) & *him gelicade hire þeawas & þancode Gode*
and him(DAT) liked/pleased(3 SG) her behaviour(ACC/NOM PL) and (he) thanked God
'And he liked her behaviour and thanked God' *(ChronD* 201.32 (1067))

The *Concordance* leads to perhaps four other examples of type (i) (GE)LICIAN, all of which have the cause argument apparently in the accusative — certainly (in at least four out of five instances) not in the genitive.[4] Others have a sentential cause, or a nominal cause indeterminately nominative or accusative, and are thus ambiguous between types (i) and (ii) — what I shall call type (i/ii) — since the cause is indeterminately object or subject, for example:

(6) *þa gelicode us, þæt man sceolde hi gehalgian ...*
then pleased(3 SG) us(DAT) that one should it [*sc.* a church] hallow ...
'then it pleased us that it should be consecrated ...' *(GD* 235.19)

So even if type (i) (GE)LICIAN exists in OE, it is rare and shows a case combination (DAT for experiencer, ACC for cause) which differs from FL's prototypical DAT-GEN frame.

As for type (iii), FL quote (7):

(7) *þu eart sunu min leof, on þe ic wel licade*
you are son my beloved, in you I(NOM) well liked(1/3 SG)
L. ... in te complacui *(MkGl(Ru)* 1.11)

However, it comes from an interlinear gloss of poor evidential value for OE syntax. We can corroborate the lack of independence with further biblical examples of (GE)LICIAN, this time from a translation, all of which mirror the Latin syntax very closely:

(8) *on þe me gelicode*
 in you me(DAT/ACC) liked(3/1 SG)
 L. *in te complacuit me* (*Lk(WSCp)* 3.22)
(9) *hit beforan þe swa gelicode*
 it(NOM/ACC) before you thus liked(3 SG)
 L. *sic placuit ante te* (*Lk(WSCp)* 10.21)

Not only is the OE almost a word-for-word gloss of the Latin, but examples (7-8) express the apparent cause argument in a prepositional phrase.[5] How are we to analyse the PP? Useful clues come from similar PPs in other examples:

(10) *ac me swa þeah no ne licede on him, þæt he þa weorþuncge Eastrena on riht ne heold ne nyste*
 but me(DAT) however not-at-all not liked/pleased in him, that he the celebration of Easter aright not kept nor not knew
 L. *nequaquam in eo laudans uel eligens hoc, quod de obseruatione paschae minus perfecte sapiebat*
 'however I did not like in him his not keeping Easter rightly' (*Bede* 206.2)

Example (10) suggests that the PP with *on* is peripheral and is not an argument of the verb LICIAN, since there is a regular experiencer (*me*) and cause (the *þæt*-clause). The possibility of an extra *on-* (later *in-*) phrase in collocation with LIKE has remained in the language, as the English translation of (10) shows: '... I did not like *in him* his ...'. A similar PP is found nearby in the same text in collocation with the personal verb LUFIAN:

(11) *Ðas þing ic on þam foresprecenan bisceope swiþe lufie*
 these things I in the aforementioned bishop very-much love
 'these things I love very much in the aforementioned bishop' (*Bede* 206.18)

Analogous PPs turn up in the complementation of other impersonal verbs too. There are many examples with ÞYNCAN containing a *be*-phrase in addition to FL's predicted types of complement:

(12) *Ac hu þincð þe ðonne be ðæm þe nanwuht goodes næfð, gif he hæfð sumne eacan yfeles?*
 but how seems/thinks(3 SG) to-you(DAT/ACC) then concerning the-one who nothing of-good not-has, if he has an increase of evil
 'But what, then, do you think about someone who has no goodness, if he has evil in addition?' (*Bo* 119.6)

Example (12) can be interpreted as having pronominal experiencer, *þe*, and adverbial cause, *hu*, with an additional PP of (roughly) location and an *if*-clause both associated with the cause. Another apposite example, this time from ME, involves a HAPPEN verb:

(13) *Of swuch witunge is muchel vuel ilumpen ofte siðen.*
from such guarding is much evil happened often
'from such looking-after (of possessions) much evil has often come about' (*Ancr.*(Corp-C) 113a.18)

Here we have a cause-subject construction with an extra source PP (and with no experiencer expressed).[6]

Returning to (7), then, the obvious explanations are that it is a Latinism — Elmer (1981) and Allen (1986) have made similar observations — and/or that it shows personal, one-place use of LICIAN without cause argument (§2.4 below). Given that type (i) (at least with nominal cause) is rare or absent and type (iii) is only used in glossing, we can say that (GE)LICIAN does not share in the pattern of impersonals described by FL. However, it is not enough to dismiss (7-9) and similar biblical and homiletic examples as Latinisms: one should try to explain *why* OE writers felt able to mirror a Latin construction, i.e. in what way the construction was sufficiently close to OE idiom to seem acceptable. This I hope to do later (§6.2).

2.2. ÞYNCAN in passive? Several impersonal verbs occur in what look like passive constructions, e.g.

(14) *ac forþon hit mæg beon tweod fram tyddrum & unstrangum modum, hwæþer ...*
'but because[?] it may be doubted by weak and feeble minds whether ...' (*GD* 177.7)

Example (14) *is* passive, but not all colligations of BEON/WESAN 'be' + past participle are. (Example (13) and similar OE examples are clear instances of non-passives.) FL needed to cite 'passives' of ÞYNCAN to prove the existence of a receptive sense for this verb in OE, as they found no active type (iii) examples. One of their examples is:

(15) *& se leoma þe him ofstod. wæs swiðe lang geþuht suðeast scinende*
and the light(NOM) which (from) it shone was very long(NOM) seemed/thought(PAST PTCP) south-east shining(NOM)
'And the light which shone from it (had) seemed very long, shining towards the south east.' (*ChronE* 233.28 (1097))

Their translation is: 'the light which shone (from it) towards the south east was considered to be very long'. But since ÞYNCAN is never attested in active use with an accusative object, the most natural interpretation here is not passive but 'perfect' (conjugated, as might be expected, with BEON/WESAN). In that case we would have the typical type (ii) use of this verb. 'Perfect' here is shorthand for a colligation of BEON/WESAN + intransitive past participle where the participle may be adjectival but is not passive; I don't commit myself to the view that it is a true verbal perfect.

Something very similar happens with LICIAN:

(16) *Ic nat ... for hwi eow Romanum sindon þa ærran gewin swa wel gelicad & swa lustsumlice ... to gehieranne*
I not-know ... why you Romans(DAT) are(PL) those earlier conflicts(NOM PL) so well pleased(PAST PTCP) and so enjoyable ... to hear
'I don't know why those earlier conflicts are so pleasing and so enjoyable for you Romans ... to hear' (*Or* 65.25)

The translation I have given ('are pleasing' is a tentative suggestion of Bruce Mitchell's) reflects my belief that this is again a 'perfect' conjugated with BEON/WESAN, and hence a normal type (ii) pattern. Ogura notes that glosses of *beneplacitum est* in the *Psalter* include *(wel)gelicad is, gecwemed is* (i.e. past ptcp + BEON/WESAN), *gecwem(lic) is, (wel)licwyrðe is* (i.e. adj + BEON/WESAN), and *gelicode* (past tense), all apparently equivalent (1986b: 36-9, a reworking of 1986a: 168-9). This point supports the analysis of the past participles as adjectival, and it also reminds us that many of the impersonals in OE are phrasal.

Returning now to the ÞYNCAN example (15), in favour of a 'perfect' analysis are the facts that ÞYNCAN is essentially intransitive in OE; that (15) then shows a typical subcategorization for that verb; that there are no examples of a HABBAN-perfect with ÞYNCAN; and that in example (17) there is a dative experiencer rather than the agent-phrase one would expect with a passive:

(17) *þa wæs he geðuht ðam folce þæt he witega wære, and Iohannes Crist*
then had/was(3 SG) he(NOM) seemed(PAST PTCP) to-the people(DAT) that he prophet was, and John Christ
'Then it (had) seemed to the people that he was a prophet, and that John was Christ' (*ÆCHom* I (Thorpe) 356.31)

(This is an interesting example in its own right which I shall mention again in §5.2.)

Now some examples do look just like passives of ModE THINK, a verb which — unlike OE ÞYNCAN or its ModE equivalent SEEM — *can* be transitive. Which is the most appropriate gloss for (18)?

(18) *and we earfoðlice him filiað tomerigen. se ðe nu todæg is ure folgere geðuht*
and we with-difficulty him follow tomorrow who now today is our follower thought [passive] / is our apparent follower [adjectival] / has our follower seemed [true perfect]
'And tomorrow we trail behind the one who today apparently follows us' (*ÆCHom* II 5 48.199)

In my opinion neither the superficial resemblance to ModE passives, the present time reference of the adverbials, nor even the use in some examples of auxiliary WEORÐAN, is decisive for a passive interpretation. My preferred interpretation is one of the other two, adjectival or perfect.[7]

In any event ÞYNCAN is another, very common impersonal verb which, as noted by FL (1983: 366 n.18), displays a different range of constructions from that predicted by the general analysis, and once again the uniform treatment falls down.

2.3. *Different surface forms.* Also serious is the fact that there are rather more surface possibilities in OE than the lexical entry (4) allows for. Prepositional phrases are envisaged by FL as an alternative to genitive, but the use of the accusative case, either for experiencer or for cause, is mentioned and then simply ignored. It seems to be reasonably common in OE and indeed to be the normal surface case for the experiencer argument of e.g. TWEOGAN 'doubt' and for both arguments of MÆTAN 'dream', and of course since many NPs, including pronouns, show no acc/dat distinction even in OE, the potential total is even higher. (The revised analysis of Fischer & van der Leek (1987) makes the contrast between nominative/accusative and dative/genitive central.)

2.4. *One-place use.* All the verbs are discussed by FL as if they were two-place verbs, but some can occur in one-place use too, with omission either of the cause argument or of the experiencer argument. It can be maintained on semantic grounds that verbs like HREOWAN and LICIAN are essentially two-place predicates and that one-place use is elliptical, but it is not so obvious that two-place use is fundamental either with what I shall provisionally call the HAPPEN class or with the HUNGER class, the former having only the cause (or theme — Anderson 1986: 174-5) as semantically obligatory argument, the latter only the experiencer:

(19) *Hit gelamp gio ðætte an hearpere wæs on ðære ðiode ðe Ðracia hatte*
 it happened formerly that a harper was in the nation that Thracia is/was-called
 'Once there was a harpist in the country called Thracia.' (*Bo* 101.22)
(20) *& ne þyrst þone næfre ðe on me gelyfð*
 and not thirsts the-one(ACC) never who in me believes
 'and he who believes in me will never thirst' (*Jn(WSCp)* 6.35)

There is no plausible 'experiencer' of the happening mentioned in (19), and no specific 'cause' of the thirst in (20). Indeed one-place use of HREOWAN could be explained as having the cause incorporated in the verb, as with ÞYRSTAN.

2.5. *Summary.* Let me draw together what has been established so far. We have evidence that the PLEASE verbs and the main SEEM verb (to adapt Elmer's labels) — which provide between them a substantial proportion of the evidence for OE impersonal usage — do not conform to FL's analysis. In fact the productive use of all three types in OE seems to be a property not of all impersonals but of only a small subset, namely the RUE verbs and some of the DESIRE and BEHOVE verbs. The template is also too rigid in its surface case assignments and in the number of arguments subcategorized for. On these points see also Anderson (1986). Finally, type (i/ii), the neutralization of types (i) and (ii), is so frequent that it should be given due recognition in its own right. Outside the domain of impersonals it is worth noting some fuzzy distinctions which we have come across in the OE data: idiomatic OE vs. 'translation OE', argument of a verb vs. non-argument, perfect vs. passive.

3. *Several classes of OE impersonal?* An obvious response to certain of the problems I have mentioned is to admit the existence of more than one class of impersonal in OE. Everyone, for example, FL included, treats the WEATHER verbs, which are zero-place verbs, as a class on their own. Among the remaining impersonals John Anderson (1986) recognises two main classes: those with potential theme and experiencer arguments and those with potential cause and experiencer arguments; subclasses take account of arguments which are optional. Elmer (1981) recognises five main classes, and Ogura (1986a) divides her material up somewhat similarly. In certain respects subclassification is an obvious improvement, but every actual subclassification I have looked at raises intractable problems of demarcation. I shall discuss a selection now.

3.1. I have argued that (GE)LICIAN is only marginally impersonal, that ÞYNCAN is an exceptional verb which does not fit FL's template, yet each has a very common subcategorization frame, type (i/ii) — that is, without nominal subject. Not only are they similar enough to permit coordination with each other, as in:

(21) *Ac me nu þynceð & bet licað, þætte ...*
but me(DAT) now seems and better pleases that
'But it now seems to me, and I prefer, that ...' (*Bede* 66.19)

but the syntax is apparently identical to one pattern found with true impersonal verbs.

3.2. (GE)LUSTFULLIAN 'desire', unlike (GE)LICIAN, is an impersonal that occurs often in type (iii), so presumably they belong to different subclasses, yet they can share a dative object by VP-reduction:

(22) *ðeah ðæt ðonne ðæm mode licige & lustfullige*
though that then the mind(DAT) please and desire
'although it pleases and delights the mind' (*CP* 71.23)

Precisely what this proves is questionable, but *prima facie* it suggests that both verbs have a similar relation to the dative NP.

3.3. OE ÞYNCAN is in a class of its own, the SEEM class, requiring the cause to be a clause or alternatively allowing it to be a nominative NP but with a subject complement (= predicative adjunct). (FL analyse the latter as raising examples.) If the HAPPEN verbs form another class — and their subcategorization possibilities are not the same — where should the various DREAM verbs go? HAPPEN and SEEM share the possibility of a raising analysis, in ME if not earlier. HAPPEN and DREAM share the possibility of a nominative cause without subject complement. SEEM and DREAM are semantically closer in being verbs of genuine mental experience. All three classes allow type (i/ii).

3.4. Ogura treats ÞYRSTAN 'thirst' as a verb of physical affection. A cause argument — i.e. not the one incorporated in the verb itself — is optional for this verb. When expressed, however, the cause is often in the genitive or is a clause, and then the verb behaves much like LYSTAN 'desire':

(23) *Mine sawle þyrst and lyst, þæt heo mæge cuman to Gode*
my soul(ACC) thirsts and desires that it may come to God (*Ps* 41.2)
(24) *þonne seo sawl þyrsteð & lysteð Godes rices*
when the soul(NOM) thirsts-for and desires God's kingdom(GEN)
'when the soul thirsts for and desires the kingdom of God' (*GD* 244.27)

The examples illustrate types (i/ii) and (iii), respectively.

3.5. TWEO(GA)N 'doubt' and SCEAMIAN 'feel shame', each showing most of the properties of FL's basic impersonal type, belong in the RUE class. Here are two phrasal impersonals, *on tweon* CUMAN and *sceame* ÞYNCAN (or ÞYNCAN + predicative adjunct), which are semantically similar but which seem to straddle the RUE, SEEM and HAPPEN classes:

(25) *þy læs unc cuman on tweon þa word þara unlifigendra*
lest us-two(DAT/ACC DUAL) should-come(PRES SUBJ PL?) in doubt the words(NOM/ACC PL) of-the unliving
'lest we should have doubts about the words of the dead' (*GD* 346.9)
(26) *hit is sceame to tellanne. ac hit ne þuhte him nan sceame to donne.*
it is shame to tell but it not seemed to-him(DAT) no shame to do
'It is a shameful thing to report, but it did not seem to him a shameful thing to do.' (*ChronE* 216.27 (1085))

3.6. Elmer (1981) and following him Anderson (1986) identify two separate verbs BEHOFIAN, with meanings 'need' and 'befit', respectively. Fischer & van der Leek point out (1987: 91-2) that a generalization is lost by so doing, and with it the possibility of relating two kinds of syntax, type (iii) for 'need' and (ii) or (i/ii) for 'befit', as well as the common element of meaning. On the latter see also Ogura (1985, 1986a). Similarly, several scholars have noted the overlap in membership of the HAPPEN and BEHOVE classes.

3.7. In a way, of course, the various bridges between classes argue for a uniform account of the kind attempted by FL. In semantics, too, there are many overlapping lexical fields. One possible chain through some impersonal verb meanings is as follows:

(27) feel obligation ~ feel emotion (bad sense: rue, shame, etc) ~ hate ~ like ~ hunger/thirst for ~ hunger/thirst ~ be weary ~ feel emotion (bad) ~ happen (bad) ~ happen (appropriate) ~ befit ~ happen ~ dream ~ seem ~ seem good ~ like

In short, subclassification of impersonals is a Procrustean venture.

4. *What is an impersonal?* We talk about 'impersonal verbs' as a coherent domain of OE lexis and syntax. The previous section dealt with the internal boundaries, if any, of that domain. Now I want to look at the outer perimeter. Is it a well-defined area? Once again we find gradience: while differences between impersonals and non-impersonals do exist, the boundary is very hard to draw.

4.1. FL excluded the weather verbs as being obviously different from the kinds of impersonal they wanted to explain (1983: 346-7 n.8). WEATHER verbs usually take no arguments. But RIGNAN 'rain', say, at least shares with *OFHREOWAN 'rue' the noteworthy property of often occurring in a subjectless construction or with a *hit* subject. It can certainly have a cognate object (or maybe subject), and in glosses the verb may be used with a lexical subject and even a dative recipient:

(28) & he rinde heom þane heofonlican mete to etanne
and he rained them(DAT) the heavenly food to eat
L. et pluit illis manna ad manducandum (*PsGl(I)* (Lindelöf) 77.24)

4.2. The verb SWEORCAN 'grow dark' is semantically like a weather verb except that it frequently has a lexical subject:

(29) *Wedercandel swearc*
      weather-candle darkened
      'the sun grew dark' (*And* 372)

But it can also occur with a dative:

(30) *ne him inwitsorh | on sefan sweorceð*
      nor him(DAT) malice-sorrow in heart darkens
      'nor does malice [*or* problem caused by malice] darken his heart' (*Beo* 1736)

Him in (30) is a dative of possession or interest (disadvantage), but it is not unlike the dative experiencers subcategorized for by certain impersonal verbs (cf. *Wand* 41 *Þinceð him on mode þæt* ...). In (31) SWEORCAN occurs between a personal verb and an impersonal and it is unclear whether its construction is more like type (iii) or type (i):

(31) *Siteð sorgcearig, ... | on sefan sweorceð, sylfum þinceð | þæt sy endeleas earfoða dæl*
      sits sorrow-careworn, ... in mind (it/he) darkens(3 SG), self(DAT) seems that is endless of-troubles share
      'the sorrowful one sits, ... his mind darkens, it seems to him that the portion/number of troubles is endless' (*Deor* 28)

The boundaries between dative of disadvantage, possessive dative and experiencer are very fuzzy, as exemplified by (32-4):

(32) *Him on mod bearn | þæt healreced hatan wolde, | ... men gewyrcean*[8]
      him(DAT) in mind ran(PAST SG) that hall-building command wished ... men to-build
      'It came into his mind that he would command men to build a hall.' (*Beo* 67)
(33) *þæt him ne getweode treow in breostum*
      that him(DAT) not doubted faith(NOM) in breast
      'that faith did not waver in his heart' (*GuthA,B* 543)
(34) *Denum eallum wearð | æfter þam wælræse willa gelumpen*
      Danes all(DAT PL) became(PAST SG) after the murderous-attack desire/ delight(NOM) happened(PAST PTCP)
      'the desire of all the Danes came to pass after that murderous attack' (*Beo* 823)

Such examples hover on the margins of the OE impersonal.

4.3. Verbs of saying like CWEÐAN, SECGAN are not usually thought of as impersonal verbs, but in certain contexts they occur in subjectless clauses with a clause complement, and sometimes also a dative:

(35) swa hit her beforan sægð
 as it here before says
 'as mentioned above' (*Or* 70.20)
(36) *Her sægþ, men þa leofestan, be þisse halgan tide arwyrþnesse, hu ...*
 here says men the dearest concerning this holy time's honour how ...
 'It says here about the honouring of this holy time, dearest men, how ...' (*BlHom* 65.27)
(37) *Þæt us tacnaþ þæt he ...*
 that to-us(DAT/ACC) signifies that he ...
 'That signifies to us that He ...' (*BlHom* 19.27)

These syntactic patterns[9] are of course characteristic of impersonals.

4.4. The verb EGL(I)AN 'ail' is an impersonal, the verb DERIAN 'harm' is not, yet DERIAN + dative is sufficiently like the type (ii) use of EGL(I)AN in syntax and semantics for the two verbs to share a dative object by VP-reduction:

(38) *& ðeah sua sua hit him no ne derige, ne ne egle*
 and yet such that it them(DAT) not-at-all not injure nor not ail
 'and yet so that it does not injure or annoy them at all' (*CP* 199.12)

Similarly, SCEAMIAN 'shame' is an impersonal while FÆGNIAN 'rejoice in' and WEOPAN 'bewail' are not, yet type (iii) use of SCEAMIAN is exactly like the ordinary use of the other verbs with an object, respectively genitive or accusative:

(39) *oððe forhwy hi ne mægen hiora ma scamian þonne fægnian*
 or why they not may of-them(GEN) more feel-shame than rejoice
 'or why they may not be more ashamed of those things/themselves than glad' (*Bo* 68.15)
(40) *... ongan his scylde weopan & scamian*
 ... began his offence(ACC/GEN) to-bewail and to-be-ashamed-of
 '... began to bewail and be ashamed of his offence' (*GD(C)* 130.4)

The verb LYSTAN 'desire' is impersonal, GITSIAN 'covet' and FRICLAN 'desire' are not, yet all take a genitive of the object desired. In LYSTAN's rare type (iii) occurrences its subcategorization is just like the other two.

4.5. LICIAN 'please' is usually classed as an impersonal, CWEMAN 'please' is not. In fact their normal subcategorizations are identical, and they can share a dative object by VP-reduction:

(41) *And ic ... him tilode to licianne, & to cwemanne*
 and I(NOM) ... them(DAT) strove to please and to please (*Ps* 34.14)

The verb HELPAN 'help' is normally regarded as a dative-governing personal verb, yet HELPAN can be subjectless (or at least type (i/ii)), and HELPAN and FREMIAN 'profit' are MS. variants in constructions that look subjectless and indeed impersonal:

(42) Wiþ fefre eft hylpð syndrigo marubie to drincanne
against fever again helps(3 SG) alone/especially marrubium to drink
'For fever again it helps to drink marrubium alone.' (*Lch* ii 134.27)

(43) Ic wat, þæt þe na ne helpeð [MS. H: fremað] þæt þu ga fram me þus unrotum
I know that you(DAT/ACC) not-at-all not helps(3 SG) that you go from me thus dejected (*GD(C)* 81.12)

4.6. *Phrasal impersonals.* There are many phrases, most commonly a noun or adjective with the verb BEON/WESAN, which in semantics and syntax seem to be closely related to the impersonals. Some, like *lað/leof* BEON/WESAN 'be hateful/dear', are actually more common than their simple cognates. (44-6) are examples, and cf. also (25-6) and (49):

(44) þa him wæs manna þearf
when him(DAT) was men(GEN PL) need/lack
'when he had need of men' (*Beo* 201)

(45) mid þy sumum monnum cwom in tweon hwæðer ...
with this some men(DAT PL) came(SG) in doubt whether ...
'seeing that some men doubted whether...' (*Bede* 316.18)

(46) ðonne we for synderlecum synnum synderleca hreowsunga doð
when we for separate sins separate repentances do
'when we separately repent of separate sins' (*CP* 413.28)

If phrasal impersonals are properly taken account of, as for example by Elmer (1981), they contribute a useful range of data and insights, though they perhaps weaken the notion of a clear prototypical impersonal verb in the competence of speakers of OE. I argue that there is no single impersonal prototype.

4.7. *Impersonal passives.* This is a traditional term for passives of non--accusative-governing verbs, as in (47):

(47) ac him næs þære bene getiðod
but to-him(DAT) not-was(3 SG) that prayer(GEN/DAT) granted
'but he was not granted this request' (*ÆCHom* II 35 302.115)

Here we have a (passive) verb with BEON/WESAN in the 3 sg, lacking a nominative subject, and governing a dative NP that can be regarded as an experiencer (better a recipient) and a genitive NP (other examples have a clause) that is something like a cause. Example (47) is apparently very much like FL's type (i) construction in both semantics and syntax. Impersonal passives could be incorporated with advantage into the analysis, but such passive verbs could hardly be allowed *optional* case assignment. Fischer & van der Leek have now sketched how impersonal passives might fit in (1987: 113).

The impersonal passive, phrasal impersonal and true impersonal can resemble one another very closely, as illustrated in examples (48-50):

(48) *þæt heom næs alyfed, þæt hi ...*
that(OJ) thom(DAT PL) not-was(3 3G) allowed, that they ...
'that they were not allowed to ...' (*GD(C)* 104.16)

(49) *Him þæt gifeðe ne wæs | þæt ...*
to-him(DAT) that granted-by-fate not was that ...
'It was not granted to him by fate that ...' (*Beo* 2682)

(50) *Þa gelamp him þæt ...*
then happened to-him(DAT) that ...
'Then it befell him that ...' (*BlHom* 113.7)

Intuitively we would want an account of OE impersonals to keep such patterns together.

4.8. *Semantics.* To repeat a quotation in part, impersonal verbs are said to be 'a class of verbs which have a common semantic core: they all express a physical or mental/cognitive experience which involves a "goal", in this case an animate "experiencer", and a "source", i.e. something from which the experience emanates or by which the experience is effected' (FL p.346). Elmer, too, talks of *his* 'verb classes typically occurring ... with two semantic arguments, usually a "person" and a "thing", the latter in the form of a nominal or sentential complement' (1981: 5). Actually the criteria are perhaps not necessary (HAPPEN verbs don't always have an experiencer), and certainly not sufficient, since verbs of apparently similar meaning can be normal personal verbs (e.g. BLISSIAN 'rejoice', HATIAN 'hate', HEDAN 'heed', IRSAN 'be angry', LUFIAN 'love', MURNAN 'mourn'). There is an obvious risk of circularity in identifying some semantic property which appears to delimit the required set of verbs.[10] Nevertheless, in general terms FL's characterization seems apt, and there is apparently cross-linguistic support (see FL's n.7). I accept FL's implicit assumption that semantic similarity is likely to have some correlation with syntactic similarity.

5. *Gradience and serial relationship.* An alternative way of describing the patterning of OE impersonals is along the lines suggested by Randolph Quirk (1965) for various syntactic phenomena of ModE. A matrix, possibly polydimensional, is arranged to show the partial and overlapping relationships among the syntactic patterns entered in by different items, and thereby helps predict the behaviour of items on the borderline between two subtypes.

5.1. Quirk illustrates this with a handful of examples. In the most elaborate (1965: 210-13 = 1968: 174-7), thirteen ModE verbs are tested for occurrence ("+") or non-occurrence ("−") in eight syntactic patterns. The results are reproduced in table 1. Diagonals dividing off areas of pluses from minuses indicate gradience, and near such diagonals one actually expects to find free variation and doubtful usage (both represented by "?"). Quirk argues that the passive of SAY in *He is said to be Adj.*, which has no corresponding active, is accounted for by the fact that FEEL and KNOW have such a passive and that SAY is related to both by other similarities of distribution. The matrix may also help to account for the growth of forms like *He is regarded insane*, without *as*.

Quirk's suggestion, then, is that such a presentation is not merely a descriptive tool, it also represents an explanatory model for speakers' behaviour. He does not set out to replace the generative accounts which were becoming fashionable in the mid-sixties, rather to supplement them in an area where they were, and still are, weak. I haven't seen this particular formalism followed up, though the ideas behind it are easy to detect in the various Quirk grammars of modern English.

1. They V so.
2. They V that he is Adj.
3. It is Ved that he is Adj.
4. They V him to be Adj.
5. He is Ved to be Adj.
6. They V him Adj.
7. He is Ved Adj.
8. They V him$_i$ N$_i$.

	1	2	3	4	5	6	7	8
pretend	+	+	+	?	−	−	−	−
feel	?	+	+	+	+	?	−	−
say	+	+	+	−	+	−	−	−
know	−	+	+	+	+	−	−	−
find	−	+	−	?	+	+	?	+
think	+	+	+	+	+	+	+	+
declare	−	+	+	+	+	+	+	+
regard	−	−	?	?	?	+	?	?
like	−	−	+	+	−	?	−	−
persuade	−	−	−	+	+	−	−	−
make	−	−	−	−	+	+	+	+
call	−	−	−	−	−	+	+	+
elect	−	−	−	−	−	−	−	+

Table 1

5.2. *Blends.* Quirk's paper has to do with resemblances of surface pattern rather than abstract underlying structures. That stretches of surface pattern can influence language production is confirmed by the appearance of blends, also discussed by Quirk. A number of examples of impersonals in OE and ME are best regarded as blends. Ideally we should be able to explain these examples, whether or not they are regarded as grammatical:

(51) *þæt þu la, Petrus, ne tweost na þone ungesewenlican God, þæt he is scyppende ...*
that you(NOM) indeed Peter not doubt(2 SG) not-at-all the invisible God(ACC) that he is creating ...
'that indeed you, Peter, have no doubt of the invisible God, that He creates ...' (*GD* 268.21)

(52) (= (12)) *Ac hu þincð þe ðonne be ðæm þe nanwuht goodes næfð, gif he hæfð sumne eacan yfeles?*
but how seems/thinks(3 SG) to-you(DAT/ACC) then concerning the-one who nothing of-good not-has, if he has an increase of evil
'But what, then, do you think about someone who has no goodness, if he has evil in addition?' (*Bo* 119.6)

In (51) two different type (iii) constructions are combined: NP cause and clausal cause, the subject of the clause being coreferential with the NP in question. In (52) a clause in some sense 'picks up' a previous argument (the *be*-PP), its subject again a pronoun coreferential with the NP in that argument; arguably (10) belongs here too. Anthony Warner has noted a number of such appositions between NP and clause in his rather later corpus of Wyclifite English (1982: 91-9), calling them 'CLAN'-sentences (= 'clause and nominal'). In Warner's CLAN-sentences 'nominal and clause both separately fulfil the subcategorization and selection restrictions imposed by the verb' (1982: 95). They are blends, therefore, but not necessarily anacolutha given their frequency in his corpus; for OE cf. also Mitchell (1985: §§1968, 2067).

Omission from a CLAN-sentence either of the NP or of the clause would leave a grammatical residue. In other examples this is not true:

(53) (= (17)) *þa wæs he geðuht ðam folce þæt he witega wære, and Iohannes Crist*
then had/was(3 SG) he(NOM) seemed(PAST PTCP) to-the people(DAT) that he prophet was(SUBJ), and John Christ
'Then it (had) seemed to the people as if He were a prophet, and John were Christ' (*ÆCHom* I (Thorpe) 356.31)

(54) *& euch her þunched þet stont in his heaued up*
and each hair seems that stands in his head up
'it seems that (= as if) each hair on his head stands on end'/ 'and each hair on his head seems to stand on end' (*SWard*(Bod) 64)

Sentence (53) as far as *folce* looks like a common construction of ÞYNCAN, namely type (ii) with NP theme and subject complement (= predicative adjunct). However, it continues in a different but equally normal way with the clausal theme of a type (i/ii) instead of the subject complement, and is completed with a gapped clause which would match either construction. A few similar examples elsewhere (e.g. *GD* 159.1, *ÆLS*(Basil) 470) suggest that the pattern of (53), even if a blend in origin, may be acceptable OE idiom. The early ME (54) is stranger — I am tempted to label it as raising out of a finite clause — but nevertheless is comprehensible as a blend.

Confusion between related lexemes probably underlies these two early ME examples:

(55)   & swetest him þuncheð ham
       and sweetest him(OBL) seem(s)/thinks(3 SG or PL) them(OBL)
       'and sweetest they seem to him' (*Ancr.*(Corp-C) 52a.15)
(56)   *As ofte as ich am ischriuen: eauer me þuncheð me unschriuen*
       as often as I am confessed ever me(OBL) seems(3 SG) me(OBL) unconfessed
       'However often I confess myself, still I seem to myself to be unconfessed' (*ibid.* 90a.15)

The partly-phonetically-motivated falling together of the two verbs PUNCHEN 'seem' and PENCHEN 'think' in many dialects of ME is well known. Examples (55-6) seem to show a blending of the type (ii) use of PUNCHEN with subject complement and the transitive use of PENCHEN with object complement. Alternatively, PUNCHEN may have developed a type (i) use with what now must be an object complement, rather as new type (i) uses of other impersonal verbs develop in ME. Here the explanation would be serial relationship involving PUNCHEN and such verbs as REOWEN 'rue'.[11]

Most of the examples in this section are nonce-occurrences and even perhaps mistakes, but they testify both to the influence of one surface form on another and to the existence of conflicting choices among variants.

6. *Synchronic analysis.*

6.1. *Variation.* Most generative analyses are uncomfortable with the existence of variation. Some kinds of variation *within* a particular variety may be describable — for example, the types (i) - (iii) in FL's analysis — but usually without convenient means of indicating relative frequencies. Degrees of acceptability are rarely indicated. Variation across dialects or speakers is either ignored altogether or treated as a peripheral and secondary phenomenon. Yet synchronic variation is widely acknowledged to be the prerequisite for diachronic change, so a description which ignores it or relegates it to a minor place is unlikely to give an optimal account of change. Mappings of gradience and serial relationship, even in the simple form advocated by Quirk, actually *focus* on areas of marginal or variable acceptability. It should be possible to change from a crude plus-query-minus trichotomy to a more sophisticated taxonomy that indicates degrees of acceptability or frequency.

6.2. *Latinisms.* Some allegedly Latinate uses of (GE)LICIAN discussed earlier on (examples (7-8)) make more sense if fitted into a context such as that of table 2. I use 'experiencer/patient' as a crude device to represent an obligatorily animate, non-agentive argument.

1 = NOM experiencer, PP/GEN cause — type (iii)
2 = DAT experiencer, PP/GEN cause — type (i)
3 = DAT experiencer, ACC cause — ?type (i)
4 = DAT experiencer, clausal cause — type (i/ii)
5 = DAT experiencer/patient, NOM cause/agent — type (ii)

	1	2	3	4	5
BEFEOLAN 'apply (o/s) to'	−	−	−	−	+
CWEMAN 'please'	−	−	−	−	+
HELPAN 'help'	−	−	−	+	+
LAÞIAN 'loathe'	−	−	−	+	+
MÆTAN 'dream'	−	−	?	+	+
(GE)LICIAN 'like, please'	?	?	?	+	+
HREOWAN 'rue'	+	+	+	+	+

Table 2

Continuation of the table as far as BEFEOLAN, which can occur with both animate and inanimate dative NPs, hints at an extension towards *non*-animate object arguments. The matrix makes clear that (GE)LICIAN is much like HELPAN in syntax but overlaps sufficiently with HREOWAN to allow the sporadic analogical use of impersonal-like syntax. (Allen makes interesting observations on a statistical difference between LICIAN and CWEMAN as far as potential volitionality on the part of the cause argument is concerned (1986: 404); this is consistent with the different placings of the verbs in table 2.)[12]

A converse process may underlie sporadic *non*-impersonal use of HYNGRIAN 'hunger', which Mitchell (1985: §1038) regards as a possible Latinism. The transitive, agentive use of *rinde* 'rained' in (28), probably a calque of a similar use of late L. *pluit*, can also be viewed in the same light.

6.3. *Passive ~ perfect.* Auxiliary BEON/WESAN/WEORÐAN + past participle is a taxonomic problem. With a transitive verb it can safely be labelled 'passive', and with a mutative intransitive, 'perfect', but what of verbs such as PYNCAN which do not fall neatly into either division? Bruce Mitchell and Michiko Ogura have both worried in print over individual decisions (and cf. §2.2 above). Describing examples syntactically purely as surface strings (though perhaps taking account of semantic notions like perfectivity) allows one to avoid false demarcations and to bring out the differing degrees of resemblance to one or other clear pattern.

6.4. *Indeterminacy between types (i) and (ii).* A common use of *hit* 'it' allows either a dummy pronoun (non-argument) reading or an anaphoric, referential reading:

(57) *Hi synd ungeryme swa swa hit gerisð gode*
 they [*sc.* holy servants] are countless just as it befits God
 'They are countless, as befits God' (*ÆLS* Pr 69)

In (57) *hit* might either be a dummy subject or anaphoric for the preceding clause: the difference between types (i) and (ii) is obscured. Similar indeterminacy often accompanies the use of subject *hit* with *OFHREOWAN (and is perhaps found also in the second clause of (26)), and with RIGNAN 'rain' there are several examples indeterminate between 'weather-*hit*' and *hit* anaphoric for *wolcn* 'cloud'. In ModE there seems to be gradience from dummy to anaphoric *it*, whether or not you follow Bolinger (1977: 66-90) in attributing referential function to most uses of *it*. One merit of a surface structure account is that the many examples like (57) need not be treated as embarrassingly indeterminate but can simply take their place in the spectrum of possibilities for a given verb.

6.5. *Subclasses of impersonal.* In §3 I gave examples of differences and similarities among (subclasses of) impersonal verbs. A taxonomy of impersonals should allow for these multiple and overlapping relationships. The kind of matrix used by Quirk does just that.

6.6. *Cline from impersonals to non-impersonals.* In §4 I discussed gradience from impersonal to non-impersonal verbs. Table 3 illustrates one such gradience.

1 = NOM cause, ACC experiencer/patient (type (ii))
2 = Ø cause, ACC experiencer/patient
3 = GEN/clausal cause, ACC experiencer/patient (type (i))

	1	2	3
SLEAN 'strike'	+	−	−
GEYFLIAN 'injure, suffer'	+	+	−
CALAN 'grow cold'	−	+	−
*ÞREOTAN 'grow weary'	−	+	−
HYNGRIAN 'hunger'	−	+	?
AÞREOTAN 'grow weary'	−	+	+
ÞYRSTAN 'thirst'	−	+	+
TWEOGAN 'doubt'	−	+	+
ONHAGIAN 'be convenient'	−	+	+

Table 3

Poles apart are a personal verb like SLEAN 'strike' and an impersonal like *ÞREOTAN 'grow weary' or ONHAGIAN 'be convenient'. Consider now the verb GEYFLIAN 'suffer', which can be an impersonal verb with just an experiencer argument, like *ÞREOTAN. The cause argument of GEYFLIAN, however, appears in the nominative if expressed, giving FL's type (ii) pattern, and the verb can then equally be viewed as an ordinary, personal, transitive verb − 'injure' − like SLEAN. The table gives a simple illustration of serial relationship from personal to impersonal verbs.

Another example can be plotted in a preliminary fashion as in table 4. This matrix does not reveal gradience or serial relationship, merely a complex overlapping similarity. A gradient from impersonal to non-impersonal might be demonstrable by extension and rearrangement of the matrix, perhaps in more than two dimensions.

1 = NOM agent, ACC/clausal theme, (DAT experiencer)
2 = ACC theme, DAT experiencer — ?type (i)
3 = clausal theme, (DAT experiencer) — type (i/ii)
4 = NOM theme, DAT experiencer — type (ii)
5 = NOM theme, NOM subject complement, DAT experiencer
6 = NOM theme

	1	2	3	4	5	6
OÐIEWAN/ÆTIEWAN 'show, appear'	+	−	+	+	+	+
MÆTAN 'dream'	−	+	+	+	−	−
ÞYNCAN 'seem'	−	−	+	−	+	−

Table 4

7. *Diachronic change.*

7.1. *Lexical diffusion.* A mapping of serial relationship is in effect a snapshot of potential lexical diffusion in progress. For anyone who believes that much syntactic change proceeds by lexical diffusion, serial relationship could play a useful part both in description and explanation. A couple of suggestions follow, though I have not had time to explore them in depth.

7.2. *Loss of the impersonal construction.* Many of the ME and post-ME changes explained by FL can be described in terms of analogy: analogy with more common syntactic patterns and/or with more common types of verb. Such ideas could be given more substance by plotting matrices over time, showing for instance how (if true) the sentence patterns of LIKE and HELP both converged on the patterns of ordinary transitives like LOVE. Matrices of gradience could easily allow for the possibility of dative-marked subjects, as envisaged in Allen (1986) and elsewhere, if such an analysis were thought justifiable. To what extent such matrices would *explain* the changes — even for those scholars who would be prepared in principle to use the term 'explanation' — cannot be anticipated.

7.3. *New ME impersonal usages.* A converse influence — away from the norm — is shown by the appearance in ME of a sporadic impersonal use of phrasal and modal verbs like HAVE *liefer* 'prefer', MUST, OUGHT, ÞURFE 'need' (see Visser 1963: §33, Plank 1984: 32-3):

(58) *Us moste putte oure good in aventure*
us(OBL) must(SG) put our goods in jeopardy
'We have to put our goods at risk.' (Chaucer, *CYT* VIII.946)

(59) *and if he have taken grace, to use it noght als hym aght*
and if he has not received grace, to use it not as him(OBL) ought
'... as he ought' (Rolle, *FLiving* 99.83)

Type (i/ii) seems to become available to a small group of verbs which had not normally been impersonals in OE. Here we must reckon on mutual syntactic influence of verbs from the same lexical field, e.g. impersonal and non-impersonal verbs of obligation like BEHOVEN and MOTEN, simplex and compound verbs like ÞURFE and BEÞURFE 'need'. Similarly we get type (i) uses of the verbs PUNCHEN and LIKEN, which had not appeared in type (i) in OE (see e.g. Allen 1986: 397-400). When influence can work in either direction, a principled account of relative frequency and salience would be necessary to save this approach from excessive *post-hoc-ery*.

7.4. *Subject raising*. From OE to early ModE the HAPPEN verbs have a type (i/ii) construction with a dative (or oblique) experiencer argument in the higher clause and a clausal theme which can be non-finite and therefore subjectless only if the unexpressed subject is coreferential with ('controlled by') the experiencer NP. Here is a late example:

(60) *And at the laste by fortune hym happynd ... to com to a fayre courtelage*
and at the last by chance him(OBL) happened ... to come to a fair courtyard
'And eventually by chance he happened ... to come to a fair courtyard' (Malory *Wks.* [1-vol. edn.] 162.26)

In a newer construction there is no experiencer argument but instead a subject NP — not necessarily animate and not an argument of the higher verb — often said to be raised out of the lower clause, as in:

(61) *The door happened to be open.*

The two patterns coexisted for quite some time before the older one disappeared. An account which enforces a rigid distinction between the two constructions cannot do justice to the surface structure relationships of (62):

(62) *Therfore yf eny suche parsone happen to se this boke ...*
'therefore if any such person happens to see this book' (*Mirror Our Lady* 8.9)

Examples like (62) with an animate but non-case-marked NP represent a striking surface overlap between two different constructions. I don't want to enter the questions of (a) if and when subject raising entered the syntax of English, and (b) whether or not subject raising examples derive historically by re-analysis of oblique experiencer examples. Whatever the answers, however, the surface overlap exemplified in (62) must play an important part.[10]

8. Conclusion and theoretical observations.

8.1. *Future work.* The matrices given here are provisional and unsatisfactory. It is clear that polydimensional plotting is needed, with computer techniques necessary both for the manipulation of entries and for the presentation of two-dimensional slices (or perhaps pseudo-3D diagrams) for visual inspection. One obvious suggestion is that variation in the distribution of (what we may continue to call) the cause argument should be plotted on a different axis from variation in the experiencer argument. It may be necessary to introduce numerical scaling for entries rather than mere $+/?/-$, in which case statistical treatment of frequency and covariance can be tackled. The status of a minus entry is anyway dubious where a dead language is concerned.

It is also unclear whether we can maintain Quirk's plotting of the verbs themselves along one linear dimension. Perhaps we should just plot patterns along the axes and insert verbs into particular cells. But both the collection of data and the mechanics (or rather statistics) of organising them are far bigger tasks than I had envisaged when I started, and much further work is necessary.

8.2. *Adequacy of generative grammar.* If the present observations have any merit, they suggest that generative models of language like GB theory which place high priority on economy of statement are not likely to be good models of actual human linguistic behaviour. What they may be instead is useful heuristics for homing in on a restricted area of syntax and systematically increasing the data coverage. (One reason for focusing on FL is indeed that a generative account is explicit and testable.) By schematizing the data they then facilitate the search for deeper, non-syntactic explanations of certain regularities (as in Fischer & van der Leek 1987) — that is, of patterns taken to be prototypical.

8.3. *Serial relationship and generative grammar.* I regard the form of an individual sentence as controlled simultaneously and independently both by its semantico-syntax (and indeed pragmatics, discourse function, etc) and by the complex analogies of related surface structures. Fischer & van der Leek (1987) deals with (some of) the former, I have been looking at (some of) the latter.

If this sketch is ever worked into a full analysis, what are the likely benefits? An optimistic forecast is that much that is so grandly explained in generative theories, with their elaborate superstructure of axioms, modules, levels of structure, and so on, would fall out more simply under fewer and less counter-intuitive assumptions. The approach envisaged here is compatible with numerous recent proposals that particular aspects of language use are determined probabilistically by the interplay of various factors, often arranged in hierarchies. Like them it is neither generative nor falsifiable (except where an implicational series could be set up).

Plotting surface structure relationships can show how one part of a synchronic system influences another. What it cannot in itself explain is why the system has the shape it has, so there is no question of making other approaches wholly redundant. A safer bet, then, is to claim that mapping of surface relationships will fill in some of the gaps left by synchronic generative theory and contribute significantly to the explanation of change from one synchronic state to another.

8.4. *Idealization*. Returning to the immediate topic in hand, the question is whether the impersonal verbs of OE can be neatly captured by one (or even two) type(s) of lexical entry, thus whether there is an underlying system where any gaps are caused by semantic conditioning or by chance, or whether the very range of variation is more fundamental. The account which covers the greatest range of data in the neatest way will score highest as far as parsimony and elegance are concerned, and is therefore most likely, other things being equal, to be considered descriptively and explanatorily adequate. (I don't suggest that these are the only criteria for judging work in linguistics.) It is always difficult to focus an investigation in such a way that 'all and only' the appropriate data fall under the scope of the analysis offered. FL shifted the focus of previous study of impersonals and managed to capture a lot of data very elegantly. Some idealization was necessary, however, to fit everything into a unitary analysis.

The present sketch adjusts the focus yet again but is undoubtedly messier, despite its potentially greater data coverage. Does that mean that too much has been included (or that the analysis is faulty)? Not necessarily: language *is* messy. My analysis deals with surface patterns and highlights some of the diverse interconnections between what is called 'the impersonal verb' and the rest of OE and ME grammar, connections which help to make up the 'seamless web' of language. But impersonals do constitute a viable subject of study, whose coherence, in my opinion, should be captured not — or not just — by the prototypical analysis of FL's account but rather by a cluster of family resemblances.

NOTES

1. An aspect of impersonal usage more amenable to generative analysis is discussed in Denison (forthcoming). Concerning the present paper I am grateful for helpful discussions with, or extensive written comments from, Olga Fischer, Frederike van der Leek, Anthony Warner, students at the University of Amsterdam, and an audience at the University of Nijmegen, where a very early version was read.

2. Unfortunately the labelling in Elmer (1981) is confusingly similar. The main correspondences are as follows:

FL	Elmer
type (i), neutral	type N (cause is NP) / type S (cause is clausal)
type (ii), cause-subject	variant type I (cause is NP)
type (iii), experiencer-subject	variant type II (cause is NP) / variant with nominative subject (cause is clausal)

3. N.b. another MS. has *non*-nominative *mægenleaste*, so (2) may not be an ideal example.
4. An alternative analysis of (5) treats the cause argument as *nominative* and *gelicade* as showing a failure of verbal concord (Allen 1986: 388). Anthony Warner, drawing my attention to Mitchell (1985: §§19-20), points out that *gelicade* could actually be plural. Either way (5) would be type (ii). Other examples, all with pres. *licað*, are *PPs* 146.12, *Instr* 185, *ÆCHom* II 12.1 120.367, *Alc* 26 (Foerst) 13.
5. Type (iii) examples like (7), also translating Latin COMPLACEO, are found in Psalter glosses; see Healey & Venezky (1980) s.v. *gelicode* etc.
6. In the revised theory of FL, such PPs are more readily accommodated: 'We will assume that PPs whose NP object bears a θ-role other than the one(s) explicated in the entry ... are generated freely in the VP provided they are compatible with the semantic and thematic information in the entry of the verb' (1987: 106). But then (7) can be taken as a one-place use of LICIAN.
7. The *is geþuht* construction is common in *GD* and the works of Ælfric (see Ogura 1986a: 285-6). Since L. *videtur* is a passive of 'see' used in the sense 'seems', it may have been the morphology of the Latin that was uppermost in Ælfric's mind, especially in a teaching context; *ÆColl* 211, 213, 217 has the gloss *uidetur ~ (ys) geþuht*. So the pattern may have started out as a teacher's or glossator's device. Mitchell has a long and non-committal discussion of apparent passives of ÞYNCAN (1985: §§1049-51; cf. also §§734-5, 739, 777-81, 1965). Anthony Warner reminds me of the calque *is geworden* 'became' = *factum est* (Visser 1973: §1900) and says that if passive, it shows non-passive semantics and the same relationship to nominative subject as the intransitive verb, and if perfect, renders a L. deponent by a non-passive participle. Either way it supports the analysis of (15) as type (ii).
8. Example (32) is discussed as an impersonal by Ogura (1986a: 131-2).
9. I was alerted to their existence by yet-to-be-published work of Elizabeth Traugott.
10. Compare the claim by Malcolm Godden, adducing personal verbs like GLADIAN 'be glad' and expressions like *gif ... ure mood nimð gelustfullunge* 'if our mind takes delight', that as far as the Anglo-Saxons were concerned, passions or feelings towards someone or something typically involved an act of will — the exact opposite of the involuntariness detected by writers on the impersonal (1985: 286, in an article on metaphysics rather than language).
11. Or there is Allen's analysis of *him* in (55) as a dative subject (1986: 397-8).
12. Xavier Dekeyser reminds me of the discussion in Coates (1983) of semantic gradience and fuzzy set membership (in the context of ModE modals). The gradient phenomena I discuss in this paper are probably as much matters of semantics as of syntax, though I concentrate on the latter.
13. Palmer (1972) discusses some rather similar problematic distinctions in ModE, arguing that they are artefacts of the transformational generative model.

REFERENCES

Allen, Cynthia L. 1986. 'Reconsidering the History of *like*'. *JL* 22.375-409.
Anderson, John. 1986. 'A Note on Old English Impersonals'. *JL* 22.167-77.
Bolinger, Dwight. 1977. *Meaning and Form*. London & New York: Longman.
Coates, Jennifer. 1983. *The Semantics of the Modal Auxiliaries*. London & Canberra: Croom Helm.
Denison, David. forthcoming. 'Auxiliary + Impersonal in Old English'.
Elmer, Willy. 1981. *Diachronic Grammar: The History of Old and Middle English Subjectless Constructions*. Linguistische Arbeiten 97. Tübingen: Niemeyer.
FL = Fischer, Olga C. M. & Frederike C. van der Leek. 1983. 'The Demise of the Old English Impersonal Construction'. *JL* 19.337-68.
Fischer, Olga & Frederike van der Leek. 1987. 'A "Case" for the Old English Impersonal'. In Willem Koopman *et al.*, ed. *Explanation and Linguistic Change*, 79-120. Current Issues in Linguistic Theory 45. Amsterdam & Philadelphia: John Benjamins.
Gaaf, W. van der. 1904. *The Transition from the Impersonal to the Personal Construction: In Middle English*. Anglistische Forschungen 14. Heidelberg: Carl Winter's Universitätsbuchhandlung.
Godden, M. R. 1985. 'Anglo-Saxons on the Mind'. In Michael Lapidge & Helmut Gneuss, eds. *Language and Literature in Anglo-Saxon England: Studies Presented to Peter Clemoes on the Occasion of his Sixty-fifth Birthday*, 271-98. Cambridge, etc: Cambridge University Press.
Healey, Antonette DiPaolo & Richard L. Venezky. 1980. *A Microfiche Concordance to Old English*. Toronto.
Jespersen, Otto. 1927, 1949. *A Modern English Grammar on Historical Principles*, III, VII. Heidelberg: Carl Winters Universitätsbuchhandlung, Copenhagen: Ejnar Munksgaard.
Lightfoot, David W. 1979. *Principles of Diachronic Syntax*. Cambridge Studies in Linguistics 23. Cambridge: Cambridge University Press.
Lightfoot, David. 1981. 'The History of Noun Phrase Movement'. In C. L. Baker & John J. McCarthy, eds. *The Logical Problem of Language Acquisition*, 86-119. Cambridge, Mass. & London: MIT Press.
Mitchell, Bruce. 1985. *Old English Syntax*, I, II. Oxford: Clarendon Press.
Ogura, Michiko. 1985. 'Old English "Impersonal" Verbs denoting "to happen", "to befit", or "to belong to"'. *Senshu Jimbun Ronshu* 34.1-45.
Ogura, Michiko. 1986a. *Old English 'Impersonal' Verbs and Expressions*. Anglistica 24. Copenhagen: Rosenkilde & Bagger.
Ogura, Michiko. 1986b. 'Old English "Impersonal Periphrasis", or the Construction "Copula + Past Participle" of "Impersonal" Verbs'. *Poet* 23.16-52.
Palmer, F. R. 1972. 'Noun-phrase and Sentence: A Problem in Semantics/Syntax'. *TPS* 20-43.
Plank, Frans. 1984. 'The Modals Story Retold'. *SLang* 8.305-64.
Quirk, Randolph. 1965. 'Descriptive Statement and Serial Relationship'. *Lg* 41.205-17. (Repr. in *Essays on the English Language, Medieval and Modern* by R. Quirk, 167-83. London: Longmans, 1968.)
Traugott, Elizabeth Closs. forthcoming. 'Old English Syntax'. In Richard M. Hogg, ed. *The Cambridge History of the English Language*, I. Cambridge: Cambridge University Press.
Visser, F. Th. 1963, 1973. *An Historical Syntax of the English Language*, I, III-ii. Leiden: E. J. Brill.
Warner, Anthony. 1982. *Complementation in Middle English and the Methodology of Historical Syntax: A Study of the Wycliffite Sermons*. London & Canberra: Croom Helm.

ON THE UNITY OF THE MERCIAN SECOND FRONTING

B. ELAN DRESHER
University of Toronto

0. *Introduction.* In Dresher (1980), it is proposed that the controversial Mercian Old English sound change known as the 'Second Fronting' actually consisted of two separate changes: the addition of a raising rule, and the loss of a backing rule. Various implications concerning phonological organization were shown to follow from this analysis. This account has been criticised by Colman and Anderson (1983), who offer new arguments on behalf of the unity of the Second Fronting. A consideration of their position, however, reveals a number of difficulties which can be better explained by an analysis in which the Second Fronting is not treated as a single phenomenon. Moreover, it can be shown that the analysis proposed here accords more with the observed distribution of Mercian dialects, as recorded in the surviving texts. In this connection, I will consider the evidence of the *Omont Leaf*, a document brought to light by Schauman and Cameron (1977).

Section 1 reviews the facts which originally motivated the analysis of Second Fronting as two separate processes. Section 2 takes up the criticisms and proposals of Colman and Anderson (1983). In Section 3, I consider the evidence

of the *Omont Leaf*. Colman and Anderson's attempt to unify
Second Fronting with *i*-Umlaut, and an alternative approach
to accounting for generalizations in Old English phonology,
is discussed in Section 4.[1]

1. *The Mercian Second Fronting*. In the Mercian
dialect of Old English, changes occurred whereby, in
certain environments, stressed *ae* became *e* and stressed *a*
became *ae*. These changes can be seen in progress in the
early *Epinal* and *Corpus* glossaries, and are completed in
the later *Vespasian Psalter*. Their effects on sample forms
are illustrated in (1):

(1) Mercian Second Fronting
    a. *ae > e*   (but not before a back consonant)
    b. *a > ae (ea)* (except before a back sonorant)
    Before Second Fronting:

a.	*daeġ*	*faet*	*aeldra-*	*naeht*
	'day'	'vessel'	'older'	'night'
b.	*dagas*	*fatu*	*ald*	*hwalas*
	'days'	'vessels'	'old'	'whales'

    After Second Fronting:

a.	*deġ*	*fet*	*aeldra-*	*naeht*
b.	*daegas*	*faetu~featu*	*ald*	*hwalas*

In traditional accounts, such as that of Campbell (1959,
§§164-169), these changes are considered part of a single
process known as Second Fronting. However, Second Fronting
has several problematic characteristics which are clearly
revealed when we consider it in the light of the grammars
of successive stages of Mercian.

At an early stage of Mercian Old English--call it
Stage I--it is possible to motivate a grammar in which all
stressed *a*'s are derived from underlying /ae/ by the
application of two different rules: a rule of Retraction,

given in (2), which operates in the environment of a back sonorant, and a rule of a-Restoration, as in (3), which applies when a back vowel follows in the next syllable:

(2) Retraction

$$\begin{bmatrix} +\text{syll} \\ +\text{low} \end{bmatrix} \longrightarrow [+\text{back}] \ / \ \underline{}_{[+\text{stress}]} \begin{bmatrix} -\text{syll} \\ +\text{son} \\ +\text{back} \end{bmatrix}$$

(3) a-Restoration

$$\begin{bmatrix} +\text{syll} \\ +\text{low} \end{bmatrix} \longrightarrow [+\text{back}] \ / \ \underline{}_{[+\text{stress}]} \ [-\text{syll}] \begin{bmatrix} +\text{syll} \\ +\text{back} \end{bmatrix}$$

The back sonorants referred to by Retraction (2) include *w* and back *l*, i.e. *l* followed by a consonant or back vowel.[2] Despite the similarity of these two rules, it is quite difficult to combine them. Moreover, the rule of Breaking (see 2.1 below) is ordered between them.[3]

At Stage I, then, we have the grammar shown in (4), which derives the sample forms *ald*, *faet*, *fatu*, *hwael*, and *hwalas* from forms which all have underlying /ae/. It should be noted that though on the surface the *ae~a* alternation in *faet~fatu* looks just like the one in *hwael~hwalas*, the *a* in *hwalas* is derived by Retraction, since it precedes a back *l*, while the *a* in *fatu* is derived by a-Restoration:

(4) Early Mercian: Stage I
```
Underlng  /aeld/  /faet/  /faet+u/  /hwael/  /hwael+as/
Ret (2)   ald     -       -         -        hwal+as
Breaking  -       -       -         -        -
a-Rest (3) -      -       fatu      -        -
Surface   [ald]   [faet]  [fatu]    [hwael]  [hwalas]
```

Subsequently, Second Fronting occurred:

(5) After Second Fronting
        ald   *fet*   *faetu~featu*   (*hwel*)   *hwalas*

ald and *hwalas* remained, *fatu* became *faetu* (or, if Back Mutation intervened, *featu*), and *faet* became *fet*. Similarly, we expect that *hwael* became **hwel*, but the form is unattested. We do, however, find *hel* 'concealed', from **hael*, supporting the positing of **hwel*; cf. Hogg (1977, 76), Dresher (1980, 59).

How can we account for these changes? Consider the two analyses sketched in (6):

(6) Two Analyses of the Second Fronting
    a. *ae > e*: In both analyses, the result of the addition of a rule of *ae*-Raising.
    b. *a > ae*

        Rule Addition Analysis (e.g. Campbell 1959): Related to (a); the result of the addition of a rule fronting *a* to *ae*.

        Rule Loss Analysis (Dresher 1980): Unrelated to (a); the result of the loss of the rule of *a*-Restoration.

In both analyses, the raising part of Second Fronting—the change of *ae* to *e*—is quite straightforward: it is the result of the addition of a rule of *ae*-Raising, or, in traditional terminology, a sound change. It only has to be noted that the change does not occur before a back consonant—hence, forms like *aeldra* and *naeht* even after the Second Fronting.[4]

The change of *a* to *ae*, however, is more problematic, for it has the peculiar property of exactly undoing the effects of *a*-Restoration. Thus, it applies to *a* when it occurs in the *a*-Restoration environment, but not when the intervening consonant is *l*. This failure of the Second Fronting before *l* is suspiciously reminiscent of Retraction. However, in an analysis such as Campbell's, given in (6b), the change of *a* to *ae* is a sound change connected to the change of ae to e, and there is no satisfactory way to explain its resemblance to both Retraction and a-Restoration. If we suppose, however, that the change of a to ae results from the loss of the rule of a-Restoration, these consequences follow immediately. Thus, if a-Restoration is removed from the grammar in (4), only *fatu* will be affected, but not the forms derived by Retraction.[5]

A second problem with the traditional account of Second Fronting concerns its interaction with the rule of Back Mutation, given in (7):

(7) Back Mutation

$$\emptyset \longrightarrow \schwa\ /\ \begin{bmatrix} +syll \\ -back \\ -long \\ +stress \end{bmatrix} \underline{} \begin{bmatrix} -syll \\ -back \end{bmatrix} \begin{bmatrix} +syll \\ +back \end{bmatrix}$$

As a result of Back Mutation, [ae] becomes [aeə] (written *ea*), [e] becomes [eə] (written *eo*), and [i] becomes [iə] (written *io*) before a back vowel when a single non-back consonant intervenes. Back Mutation applies to short front vowels which are followed by a back vowel. Thus, it can apply to forms which had previously undergone a-Restoration, as is illustrated in the evolution of the *Epinal Glossary* dialect, outlined in (8):

(8) *Epinal Glossary* Dialect: Historical Evolution
    a. Stage I: As in (4)

```
        Underlying      /faet+u/    /wer+as/
        a-Restoration   fat+u         -
        Surface         [fatu]      [weras]
        Orthography     fatu        weras
```
    b. Stage II: a-Restoration is lost
```
        Underlying      /faet+u/    /wer+as/
        Surface         [faetu]     [weras]
        Orthography     faetu       weras
```

c. Stage III: Back Mutation is added

Underlying	/faet+u/	/wer+as/
Back Mutation	faeət+u	weər+as
Surface	[faeətu]	[weəras]
Orthography	*featu*	*weoras*

Beginning with the sample forms *fatu* 'vessels' and *weras* 'men' in Stage I, the loss of *a*-Restoration, shown in (8b), subsequently produces *faetu*. Then, Back Mutation is added, producing *featu* and *weoras*. This is the expected sequence, and forms from every stage are recorded.[6]

The history of the *Corpus Glossary* dialect was slightly different. Kuhn (1939, 13-14) has shown that the Back Mutation of *e* and *i* occurred before the Back Mutation of the low vowel in this dialect. He proposes that Back Mutation began at a time when the low vowel was still *a*, i.e. before the change of *a* to *ae*. As can be seen in (9b), *a*-Restoration would initially bleed Back Mutation, producing back-mutated non-low vowels, as in *weoras*, but with *a* remaining in *fatu*:

(9) *Corpus Glossary* Dialect: Historical Evolution

a. Stage I: As in (4)

Underlying	/faet+u/	/wer+as/
a-Restoration	fat+u	-
Surface	[fatu]	[weras]
Orthography	*fatu*	*weras*

b. Stage II: Back Mutation is added

Underlying	/faet+u/	/wer+as/
a-Restoration	fat+u	-
Back Mutation	-	weər+as
Surface	[fatu]	[weəras]
Orthography	*fatu*	*weoras*

c. Stage III: *a*-Restoration is lost

Underlying	/faet+u/	/wer+as/
Back Mutation	faeət+u	weər+as
Surface	[faeətu]	[weəras]
Orthography	*featu*	*weoras*

On the traditional account of Second Fronting, this *a* would first have to be fronted to *ae* before it could be back-mutated to *ea*. However, unlike the *Epinal Glossary*, the *Corpus Glossary* records no intermediate forms with front vowel *ae*, like *faetu*, although forms like *fatu*, with *a*, and *featu*, with *ea*, are both recorded. The lack of intermediate forms in *ae* is a problem for the traditional analysis, but it is predicted by the rule loss analysis, as can be seen in (9c). As soon as *a*-Restoration is lost, Back Mutation can apply to the underlying /ae/ in /faetu/, creating, on the surface, a phonetic leap from *a* to *ea*, which is what we find in the written record.

2. *On the Unity of Second Fronting.* The rule loss analysis accounts for two separate problems: it explains why the change of *a* to *ae* (or *ea*) simply reverses the effects of *a*-Restoration, except for *a*'s derived by Retraction, which remain untouched; and it explains why Back Mutation appears to apply directly to *a* in the *Corpus Glossary*. However, we must give up the traditional view that the change of *a* to *ae* was related to the raising of *ae* to *e*. At first, this appears to be an undesirable consequence. Thus, it could be argued that the two changes occur in similar environments and are both forms of 'brightening' ('Aufhellung'). Moreover, they occur at about the same time, and the change of *a* to *ae* appears to occur only in dialects which had the change of *ae* to *e*. As the unity of the Second Fronting has been defended by Colman and Anderson (1983), it is worth considering these issues in some detail.

2.1. *The Environment of the Second Fronting.* One of the arguments against the unity of the two parts of the Second Fronting is that, despite initial appearances, they do not really operate in the same environments: *ae*-Raising is blocked before any back consonant, while *a*-Fronting (actually the loss of *a*-Restoration) is blocked before a back sonorant, i.e. in the environment of Retraction. Colman and Anderson dispute this argument on several grounds, suggesting instead that both rules are blocked before *l*.

First, though, they maintain that even in the case of indisputably unitary phonological phenomena, different parts of a rule may be subject to different conditions-- e.g. in some dialects the breaking of /e/ fails in some contexts in which the breaking of /ae/ is found. There are indeed many such examples, and they pose no problems in cases where there is little doubt that the various parts of a rule have similar origins and conditioning environments. In the case of the Second Fronting, though, the unity of the phenomenon is what is at issue, and the claim that there is a common environment takes on more importance than in other less controversial cases. The argument for a unified rule is weakened if it can be shown that the environments are different.

I have claimed above that *ae*-Raising is blocked before any back consonant, and not just before back *l*. Forms such as those in (10) can be adduced as evidence for this general restriction on the rule:

(10) Mercian Unraised *ae*
    a. *naeht*   'night'   *slaeh*   'killed'
    b. *cwaecian*   'quake'   *plaegian*   'applaud'

Colman and Anderson do not find these forms relevant, since they argue that an unraised *ae* would be expected here even in the absence of any special restriction on *ae*-Raising.

Consider first forms of type (10a): these forms underwent a series of historical changes whereby an original ae was subject first to Breaking, producing *neaht, and then to Smoothing, which undid the diphthong and restored naeht. According to Colman and Anderson, Smoothing was later than Second Fronting, so we would not expect forms like naeht to be susceptible to ae-Raising, since such forms would still have had a diphthong which did not undergo ae-Raising:

(11) Chronology According to Colman and Anderson

West Germanic	naht
Anglo-Frisian Brightening	naeht
Breaking	neaht
ae-Raising	-
Smoothing	naeht

They assert (168) that 'there is no reason to question the ordering of [Anglian Smoothing] after i-umlaut and second fronting.' But this ordering is only uncontroversial given their view that Second Fronting was a prehistoric rule--the documents suggest that Smoothing was earlier than both parts of Second Fronting. However, even if for the sake of discussion we accept their historical ordering, we must still take into account the synchronic consequences of the successive addition of the rules of Breaking, ae-Raising, and Smoothing to the grammar.

Breaking originally diphthongized a front vowel which stood before h and rC, where C represents any consonant (we consider here only the breaking of short ae; the breaking of other vowels involved various complications that are not relevant to this discussion):

(12) Early Breaking of ae

$$ae \longrightarrow ae\partial \ / \ \underline{[+stress]} \ \left\{ \begin{array}{c} h \\ rC \end{array} \right\}$$

The sample forms in (13) all had /ae/ prior to Breaking:

(13) Early Breaking: Sample Forms
a. *neaht* 'night'   *sleah* 'killed'
b. *beard* 'beard'   *earm* 'arm'
c. *bearht* 'bright'   *heargas* 'idols'

Smoothing subsequently monophthongized vowels standing before a back consonant, whether or not a liquid intervened:

(14) Smoothing

$$\text{ə} \longrightarrow \emptyset \;/\; \begin{bmatrix} +syll \\ +stress \end{bmatrix} \underline{\hspace{1cm}} \begin{bmatrix} +cons \\ +son \\ -nasal \end{bmatrix} \begin{bmatrix} +cons \\ +back \end{bmatrix}$$

Once Smoothing has been added to the grammar, there is no longer any motivation for a language learner to acquire Breaking in its original form, for Smoothing reverses the effects of Breaking in forms of type (13a) and (13c).

We would expect, then, a reanalysis of the grammar to occur. A simpler, more transparent grammar can be obtained by restricting Breaking before back consonants, as in (15):[7]

(15) Later Breaking

$$ae \longrightarrow ae\text{ə} \;/\; \underline{\hspace{1cm}}_{[+stress]} \; r \begin{bmatrix} -syll \\ -back \end{bmatrix}$$

After the reanalysis of Breaking, forms like *naeht* become susceptible to *ae*-Raising (even if Smoothing had been the historically later rule). Unless it is prevented from raising vowels followed by a back consonant, *ae*-Raising would apply to *naeht*.

There is in fact evidence that smoothed forms not

immediately followed by a back consonant were affected by
ae-Raising. Forms like those in (13c) appear in the *Vespasian Psalter* with e, not ae. This result is unexpected if
ae-Raising could not affect smoothed forms, but it is consistent with the analysis proposed here, as shown in (16):

(16) Raising of Smoothed Forms

	/naeht/	/haerg+as/	/baerd/
Underlying			
Breaking	-	-	beard
ae-Raising	-	hergas	-

The restriction that ae-Raising does not operate before a
back consonant is thus shown to be independently necessary,
whether or not ae-Raising historically preceded Smoothing.[8]

Consider now forms of type (10b), *cwaecian* 'quake' and
plaegian 'applaud'. Colman and Anderson correctly point out
that these forms are Class II weak verbs, whose original
stem vowel ae had been subject to a-Restoration before a no
longer visible back vowel suffix. This a was subsequently
restored to ae by Second Fronting. In all crucial respects,
then, these forms act like the sample form *daegas*. Since,
in the analysis being proposed here, the change of a to ae
is the result of the loss of the rule of a-Restoration, in
a synchronic grammar such forms would become susceptible to
ae-Raising, were it not for a restriction preventing raising before back consonants. In this way, forms of type
(10b) fall together with forms of type (10a) synchronically, despite their different histories.[9]

As a further objection, Colman and Anderson cite the
form *kaelid* 'cools' from the *Corpus Glossary*, presumably to
demonstrate that ae-Raising was blocked before any l, and
not before back consonants. The force of this example is
unclear, as the *Corpus Glossary* often has unraised ae where
in the *Vespasian Psalter* we find e. Moreover, they later

assert (179) that, while the fronting of *a* to *ae* was blocked before any *l* (and not just *l* followed by a consonant or back vowel), the raising of *ae* to *e* was not so affected. So, even on their own account, the conditioning environments of the two parts of Second Fronting were different.

2.2. *The Use of Manuscript Evidence*. Colman and Anderson raise a number of objections to the way manuscripts were used to support particular sound changes, as well as synchronic and diachronic ordering of rules.

First, they find an equivocation in the use of the term 'dialect' in Dresher (1980)--sometimes, the various manuscripts are treated as having their own dialects (e.g. the *Corpus Glosssary* dialect vs. the *Epinal Glossary* dialect), while at other times they are treated as representing the development of a single 'Mercian dialect'. While it is true that the term 'dialect' is used in these two ways, there is nothing unnatural or ambiguous about this usage. We can talk of a 'Mercian dialect' which is represented by a number of manuscripts sharing enough features that we can group them together in opposition to manuscripts representing the 'West Saxon' or 'Kentish' dialect. To the extent that the manuscripts differ from each other, it is useful to talk also of the dialect of a particular manuscript, as representing a subdialect of Mercian. This usage is quite conventional: the relationship between the (sub-)dialects represented by the various manuscripts which emerges from the work summarized above is consistent with that proposed by Kuhn (1970).[10]

There is nothing 'internally inconsistent' about an analysis which assigns different rule orders to different manuscripts, 'while yet insisting that the three manuscripts all represent diachronic developments of the same dialect', as Colman and Anderson (172) put it. Colman and Anderson themselves, like most students of Old English, recognize the existence of a Mercian dialect, represented by manuscripts which nevertheless differ in certain ways among themselves.[11] However, they appear to regard these differences as being limited to orthographic practice, at least in the crucial cases.

Colman and Anderson maintain that the analysis proposed in Dresher (1980) and summarized above rests on an 'over-literal interpretation of spelling forms.' They suggest that the variation between the graphs <ae>, <a>, and <ea> in the *Corpus Glossary* should not be taken as indicating variation in pronunciation. They propose instead (172) that '<ae>, <a>, and <ea> before a back consonant + back vowel all represent [ae], while <a> and <ea> before a non-back consonant + back vowel represent [ae̜]...the sounds represented by <a ae ea> are in complementary distribution, and the spelling system need not systematically record allophonic variations.' Colman and Anderson require some such interpretation of the documentary record in order to maintain their view that the Second Fronting was an early, pretextual change.

This interpretation of the variation in the glossaries is not an appealing one on several grounds. First, it does not take account of the arguments of Kuhn (1939), and the subsequent work of Toon (1983), which argues rather for the more literal interpretation of these spellings. Second, the varied distributions of the various graphs in the different manuscripts is left unaccounted for, and the lack of <ae> before non-back consonants + back vowel in the *Corpus Glossary* is left unexplained, as they themselves concede.

Third, the sounds represented by <a ae ea> were not in complementary distribution at the surface in the *Corpus Glossary* dialect. In the analysis of Dresher (1980) (and in more detail Dresher 1978/1985), it is argued that [a], [ae], and [aeə] (*ea*) were in fact allophones of a single phoneme, but only if one allows a certain amount of abstractness in phonological derivations. For example, in the dialect of the *Corpus Glossary* we could have found minimal pairs such as *alde*, the acc. pl. masc. of the adjective *ald*, and *aelde*, the pret. ind. 3 sg. of the verb *aeldan* 'delay'. In fact, Hockett (1959), who held to the view that allophones must be in complementary distribution on the surface, argued at some length that the sounds represented by <ae>, <a>, and <ea> had to belong to separate phonemes in the *Vespasian Psalter* dialect; his arguments would go through equally for the glossaries.

I assume, given the rest of their discussion, that Colman and Anderson would not want to argue that Old English orthography was sensitive to the somewhat abstract level of the derivation at which the low vowel allophones are in complementary distribution. Moreover, for the sake of consistency they would have to adopt a similarly 'non-literal' approach to the graphic alternations occasioned by other changes, such as Breaking and Smoothing, which are allophonic in the same sense that Second Fronting is allophonic. Again, they do not appear willing to take such a step. Given these various considerations, it appears that the more literal interpretation of the variation found in the manuscripts yields the most consistent and believable account. This interpretation supports the view that the Second Fronting was relatively late, and can be observed in progress in the documents.[12]

2.3. *Second Fronting in Mercian Dialects*. Let us turn now to a remaining apparent bad consequence of the Rule Loss analysis. If the two parts of the Second Fronting are in fact separate processes, we cannot explain, as Colman and Anderson point out, why they occur in the same texts. The distribution of the two parts of the Second Fronting in the existing texts is, according to Campbell (1959, §168), as depicted in (17):

(17) Mercian Dialects
   a. Lacking both ae > e and a > ae (or ea):
      Rushworth Gospels
   b. Having both ae > e and a > ae (ea): *Epinal Glossary*, *Corpus Glossary*, *Vespasian Psalter*
   c. Having ae > e but not a > ae (ea): *Royal Glosses*, *Life of St. Chad*
   d. Having a > ae (ea) but not ae > e: ?

There were dialects which did not undergo either change, such as the dialect of the Mercian portion of the *Rushworth Gospels*, in (17a);[13] there were dialects such as in (17c), which underwent the raising of *ae* but not the fronting of *a*; and there were dialects which had both rules, such as the ones in (17b). One might think, then, that the fronting of *a* is a further development of the raising of *ae*, and we would seem to have a kind of pull chain, with some dialects having the first part, and others adding the second.

This account would be undermined if we could find a dialect with the characteristics of (17d) -- one having the fronting of *a*, but not the raising of *ae*. The existence of such a dialect would be inconsistent with the view that the fronting and raising are parts of the same process, with one part being a further development of the other. The *Omont Leaf*, described by Schauman and Cameron (1977), appears to be such a dialect.

3. *The Omont Leaf*. Schauman and Cameron (1977) report on a hitherto unnoticed leaf of Old English in the collection of the Bibliothèque Centrale de l'Université Catholique de Louvain. Cameron (1977, 309f.) points out that this fragment, which came to Louvain from the library of Henri Omont, is written in an Anglian dialect, similar to the dialect of the *Corpus Glossary*. It has such characteristic Mercian features as long $\bar{e}$ for Primitive Germanic long $\bar{ae}$, Retraction of *a* before a consonant cluster beginning with *l*, lack of Breaking in the word *afirrad*, unrounding of *o* to *a* in the word *maren*, and so on. Also, the Back Mutation of *e* and *i* is common.

With respect to the Second Fronting, Cameron does not treat the raising and fronting rules separately, and the result is a seemingly paradoxical situation. Thus, he observes (310) that the *Omont Leaf* dialect 'is not close to the language of the *Vespasian Psalter* gloss as there are no sure signs of "second fronting"...' Certainly, there are no sure signs of the raising of *ae* to *e*. Hence, we find the forms listed in (18c), which all have an unraised *ae*:

(18) *Omont Leaf* Dialect (Schauman and Cameron 1977)
   a. Retraction: *alne* 'all', *calde* 'cold', *all* 'all', *salfe* 'salve', *-alo* 'ale'
   b. *a*-Restoration does not apply
   c. *ae*-Raising does not apply: *baed* 'bath', *aesc* 'ash', *waetre* 'water', *hraefnes* 'ravens'
   d. Back Mutation of *ae*: *eapul* 'apple'
   e. Back Mutation of *e*, *i*: *beolonan* 'henbane', *peopor* 'pepper'...

While *ae*-Raising does not exist in this dialect, *a*-Restoration has nevertheless been lost. According to Cameron (306), '"Second fronting", the characteristic of the *Vespasian Psalter* gloss, does not seem to appear here, although the form of *eapul* shows back mutation of an *ae* which might presuppose it.'[14] In terms of our analysis, the Back Mutation in *eapul* presupposes the loss of *a*-Restoration, as can be seen in its derivation in (19); for otherwise, *a*-Restoration would not allow Back Mutation to apply to /ae/:

(19) *Omont Leaf* Dialect: Sample Derivations

UR	/baed/	/caeld+e/	/-ael+o/	/aepul/	/belon+an/
Ret	-	cald+e	-al+o	-	-
a-Rest	L		O	S	T
BckMut	-	-	-	aeəpul	beəlon+an
ae-Rais	A	B	S	E	N	T
PR	[baed]	[calde]	-[alo]	[aeəpul]	[beəlonan]
OR	*baed*	*calde*	*-alo*	*eapul*	*beolonan*

One further apparent paradox in Cameron's account can also be resolved in terms of this analysis; according to Cameron (306), '*a* is restored before a back vowel in *-alo*', '*ale*', listed in (18a). If *a*-Restoration was lost, as it had to be to allow Back Mutation in *eapul*, why is it still applying in *-alo*? We have already seen the answer, with respect to the word *hwalas*: the *a* in *-alo* precedes a back *l*, and so is derived, not by *a*-Restoration, but by Retraction, like the other words in (18a).

In short, the *Omont Leaf* represents the missing dialect (17d): it is a dialect in which *a*-Restoration has been lost, although it has not added *ae*-Raising. The discovery of the *Omont Leaf* thus removes the last remaining argument for the unity of the changes traditionally grouped under the name of the Second Fronting. It thereby further supports the rule loss analysis, in which these changes are the results of two separate processes.

4. *Generalizations in Old English Phonology*. Colman and Anderson's arguments in favour of the unity of the Second Fronting are a prelude to a further generalization: they propose that the Second Fronting should be collapsed with *i*-Umlaut as 'alternative manifestations of a single impulse' (186). They observe that binary features of the familiar type cannot adequately express this impulse, for it appears to involve movement along two dimensions: from back to front (*a* to *ae*), and from low to mid (*ae* to *e*). They suggest that the impulse can be uniformly characterized as a movement toward *i*, and propose how this can be expressed in terms of a theory of dependency components.

Given the arguments against the unity of the Second Fronting, the larger unification with *i*-Umlaut also cannot be maintained. However, there is something appealing in Colman and Anderson's attempt to account for similarities in rules that have usually been treated as being completely unrelated, and I would like to consider here an alternative approach to this question.

Let us consider first the raising of *ae* to *e*. Colman and Anderson's claim that *ae*-Raising and *i*-Umlaut originated historically in the same period is not supported by the documents, which show rather that *i*-Umlaut was considerably earlier than *ae*-Raising--see Toon (1983, Chapter 4) for detailed discussion. Moreover, *i*-Umlaut was triggered by a following unstressed *i*, while *ae*-Raising applied whenever it was not impeded by a back consonant. Toon argues that early Old English *a was at first umlauted to *ae*; then *ae*'s from a variety of sources were raised in umlaut environments. According to Toon (141), 'the raising of the *aes* produced from several umlaut processes formed an early Mercian phonological conspiracy, the effect of which was an extended general tendency to raise [ae] to [ɛ].' Since the unstressed *i* which originally conditioned the change had in most cases become irretrievably lost at the surface, the stage was set for a generalization of the conditioned raising of *ae* to an unconditioned raising. On this account, the raising component of the Second Fronting is not a part of the raising caused by *i*-Umlaut, but rather a later generalization of it. In a synchronic grammar of the *Vespasian Psalter* dialect there is no motivation for a raising rule corresponding to the historical raising associated with *i*-Umlaut, for it has become subsumed under the more general rule of *ae*-Raising.

The situation is quite different with regard to the fronting aspects of *i*-Umlaut and Second Fronting. There is evidence in the synchronic grammar of the *Vespasian Psalter* for a rule of *i*-Umlaut which fronts *a* to *ae* when an unstressed *i* follows (this *i* is seldom observed directly at the surface--see Dresher 1978/1985); however, there is no motivation for a rule of Second Fronting, as we might expect, since the latter was due to the loss of the rule of *a*-Restoration. Nor is one of these processes in any sense a more general version of the other, since the contexts in which they occur are complementary: *i*-Umlaut occurs before *i*, while *a*-Restoration--and hence, Second Fronting--occurs before a back vowel. Relating this part of the Second Fronting to *ae*-Raising obscures its much closer connection to *a*-Restoration. I think there is a connection here with *i*-Umlaut, but not the one proposed by Colman and Anderson.

I propose that *i*-Umlaut be viewed not as part of a shared movement toward *i*, but rather as part of a general process whereby an unstressed vowel spreads its specification for [back] to the stressed vowel to its left. In this respect, *i*-Umlaut is quite similar to *a*-Restoration as well as to Back Mutation. The similarity between the latter two rules is obscured by their formulations in (3) and (7); both, however, involve the spreading of [+back] to a stressed short vowel that is [-back]. The difference is that, in *a*-Restoration, the spreading [+back] replaces the [-back] specification of the stressed vowel, while in Back Mutation, the stressed [-back] is preserved, resulting in a 'contour segment', expressed as a diphthong. A schematic view of these processes, abstracting away from a number of details, is given in (20):

(20) Spreading [back]: *a*-Restoration and Back Mutation
    a. *a*-Restoration

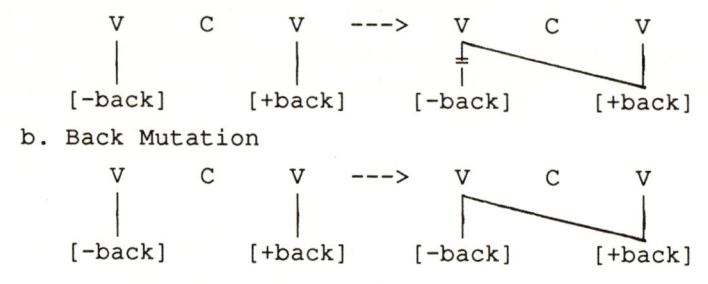

```
    V       C       V     --->    V       C       V
    |               |                     
 [-back]         [+back]        [-back]         [+back]
```

    b. Back Mutation

```
    V       C       V     --->    V       C       V
    |               |                     
 [-back]         [+back]        [-back]         [+back]
```

On this view, the second element of the diphthong is created mainly to support the [+back] feature.

    In these general terms, *i*-Umlaut involves a similar spread of the feature [-back]. The susceptibility of the stressed vowel to backness assimilation extends also to following consonants: the rules of Retraction, Breaking, and perhaps even Smoothing, may all be viewed in this way. This does not mean that these rules can all be conflated into a single process--an analysis along these lines would have to take into account the many details omitted from (20), as well as considerations of ordering. Such an account is beyond the scope of this paper. It is nevertheless clear that even if there is no unified rule of Second Fronting, there are a number of overarching formal generalizations in the phonology of Old English which remain to be adequately characterized.

NOTES

1. Section 3 of this paper was presented at the annual meeting of the LSA in New York City, December 1981. I would like to thank Ashley Amos and Richard Hogg for their helpful comments on an earlier draft. I have also benefitted from discussions with Patricia Keating and Aditi Lahiri. I would like also to recall the late Angus Cameron, who first called my attention to the *Omont Leaf*.
2. Cf. d'Ardenne (1961, 185), Hogg (1977, 76). Rules are given in a traditional format, though I now think that they can be better characterized in terms of nonlinear phonology; cf. Section 4.
3. See Campbell (1959, §157), Dresher (1979, 436), for the ordering of Breaking before a-Restoration; the rule of Breaking can be simplified if it follows Retraction--see Dresher (1978/1985, 58-62) for discussion. The decision to treat Retraction and a-Restoration as separate rules is further supported by subsequent diachronic developments, whereby a-Restoration was lost, while Retraction remained. The synchronic status of the rules at any point does not necessarily mirror diachronic changes. Hogg (OEGN XII, §§5.10-5.15) has revived the idea that the a in Retraction environments was not derived from *ae, but represents the retention of West Germanic *a; i.e. the First Fronting of WG *a to OE ae (Anglo-Frisian Brightening) failed in the Retraction environment. Language learners are usually ignorant of the history of their language, however, and it can be shown that the optimal synchronic grammar resulting from these changes would still derive forms with a in Retraction environments from underlying /ae/; cf. Dresher (1980, 68-72). Be that as it may, the argument advanced below will hold even if such forms are derived from /a/.
4. This restriction on ae-Raising has been contested by Colman and Anderson (1983); see 2.1 below for discussion.
5. The recognition that the restriction on the Second Fronting of a is connected to the prehistoric Retraction rule is one of the motivations for continuing attempts to date the Second Fronting to the prehistoric period, against the evidence of the documents. In the analysis proposed here, this connection can be established without dating the onset of the two rules to the same period. It is only important that Retraction remain in the grammar as a synchronic rule until the loss of a-Restoration. Colman and Anderson (1983, 174) ask why 'the positing of a rule of Retraction before ⟨1⟩̃ [is] more explanatory than the inclusion of a restriction on

the fronting of [ɑ] before ⟨l⟩?' It is more explanatory because Retraction exists independently of Second Fronting. It would be required in Old English even if there were no Second Fronting. Since such a rule is independently motivated, an analysis which relates it to the restriction on the fronting of a is more explanatory than an analysis in which two different rules coincidentally incorporate the same generalization.

6. Ball and Stiles (1983), contrary to many earlier commentators, maintain that there are no clear cases of Back Mutation in the *Epinal Glossary*, which, in their view, was compiled prior to its inception. If their conclusions are correct, then Stage III in (8c) would have to be omitted. This emendation, however, would not affect the argument being presented here in any crucial respect.

7. An even more general formulation of Breaking can be attained by allowing the rule to apply before r followed by any consonant, with Smoothing applying to undo Breaking before r followed by a back consonant. In that case, Smoothing would have to precede ae-Raising in the synchronic grammar of the *Vespasian Psalter* (no matter what the diachronic order), to adequately account for forms like *hergas* in (16) below. Whatever the optimal formulation of Breaking in these cases, there appears to be no justification for Breaking before h following the introduction of Smoothing.

8. R.M. Hogg has called my attention to the fact that e is the product of the Smoothing of ae before r-clusters also in Anglian dialects which do not have a general rule of ae-Raising. It might be supposed, then, that the raising of forms like *hergas* is due, even in the dialects discussed here, not to ae-Raising, but to some other rule. Resolution of this issue must await an account of what this other process is; in the meantime, we cannot exclude the possibility that these raisings, though achieving the same result, are due to different rules in different dialects. The fact remains that in the dialect of the *Vespasian Psalter*, the raising of smoothed ae before r-clusters but not before h participates in a wider generalization about the raising of ae.

9. In dialects with Back Mutation, it is possible that the correct (synchronic) grammar is one in which forms of type (10b) are subject to both Back Mutation and Smoothing. If Back Mutation is ordered before ae-Raising, then such forms would not bear on the question of whether that rule should be made sensitive to back consonants. As in the case of Breaking (see n. 7), the correct formulation of Back Mutation and its ordering with respect to ae-Raising depend on a number of points of detail, including, again, the determination of the correct synchronic formulation of Smoothing in the various dialects.

10. See further Dresher (1980,67n.) and the references cited there.

11. Contrary to the assumption of Colman and Anderson (169), no rule ordering considerations were responsible for the exclusion of the *Royal Glosses* and the *Life of St. Chad* from Dresher (1980). These manuscripts are not particularly relevant to the discussion there.

But as they note, both of these texts show *ae*-Raising but not *a*-Fronting, a fact which further weakens the case for the unity of Second Fronting. Colman and Anderson do not comment on this feature of these manuscripts; for more discussion, see 2.3 below.
12. The *Rushworth Gospels* has very occasional examples of *ae>e*.
13. Cameron's caution as to whether Back Mutation in fact presupposes Second Fronting may be due to the possibility of suffix variation in the form *eapul*, which appears elsewhere as *aep(p)el*. Thus, it is possible that an original *aepel* would have bypassed *a*-Restoration; a late suffix shift, to *aepul*, would then have been subject to Back Mutation. However, if *a*-Restoration was still in the grammar, it must be explained why it would not have applied, preventing Back Mutation, and yielding **apul*. I am grateful to Ashley Amos and R.M. Hogg for help with this point.

REFERENCES

d'Ardenne, S.R.T.O. 1961. *þe liflade ant te passiun of seinte Iuliene*. Early English Text Society, 248. London: Oxford University Press.

Ball, C.J.E. and P. Stiles 1983. 'The Derivation of Old English *geolu* "yellow", and the Relative Chronology of Smoothing and Back Mutation.' *Anglia* 101:5-28.

Campbell, A. 1959. *Old English Grammar*. Oxford: Clarendon Press.

Colman, F. and J. Anderson. 1983. 'Front Umlaut: A Celebration of 2nd Fronting, i-Umlaut, Life, Food and Sex'. In M. Davenport, E. Hansen and H.F. Nielsen, eds, *Current Topics in English Historical Linguistics*. Odense: Odense University Press.

Dresher, B.E. 1978/85. *Old English and the Theory of Phonology*. New York: Garland. [University of Massachusetts Doctoral dissertation. Also reproduced by the GLSA. University of Massachusetts, Amherst.]

Dresher, B.E. 1979. 'Review of R. Lass and J.M. Anderson, *Old English Phonology*'. *Language* 54:432-445.

Dresher, B.E. 1980. 'The Mercian Second Fronting: A Case of Rule Loss in Old English'. *Linguistic Inquiry* 11:47-73.

Hockett, C.F. 1959. 'The Stressed Syllabics of Old English'. *Language* 35:575-597.

Hogg, R.M. 1977. 'The Chronology and Status of Second Fronting'. *Archivum Linguisticum* (n.s.) 8:70-81.

Hogg, R.M. 1977-. *Old English Grammar Notes*. Unpublished ms. Department of English Language and Literature, University of Manchester, Manchester.

Kuhn, S.M. 1939. 'The Dialect of the Corpus Glossary'. *PMLA* 54:1-19.

Kuhn, S.M. 1970. 'On the Consonantal Phonemes of Old English'. In J.L. Rosier, ed, *Philological Essays: Studies in Old and Middle English Language and Literature in Honour of Herbert Dean Meritt*. The Hague: Mouton.

Schauman, B. and A. Cameron. 1977. 'A Newly-found Leaf of the Old

English from Louvain'. *Anglia* 95:289-312.
Toon, T.E. 1983. *The Politics of Early Old English Sound Change*. New York: Academic Press.

HUGH BLAIR'S THEORY OF THE ORIGIN
AND THE BASIC FUNCTIONS OF LANGUAGE

THOMAS FRANK

University of Naples

In the history of English studies, the figure of Hugh Blair, the Scottish divine and prominent member of the Edinburgh literati of the second half of the 18th century is of particular interest. When he was appointed Regius Professor of Rhetoric and Belles Lettres in the University of Edinburgh in 1762, the institutional study of what later became the English Language and Literature course can, in a very real sense, be said to have been initiated. It should perhaps be pointed out that, provided this interpretation of Blair's role is accepted, England was well over a century behind Scotland in setting up comparable chairs either in the ancient universities or in the more recently founded 19th century institutions. My claim is this: in courses like that taught by Blair at Edinburgh, or by Adam Smith in Glasgow[1], by Robert

Watson[2] at St.Andrews or James Beattie[3] in Aberdeen, we have the nucleus of what in time became what I would like to call the 'Oxford model' of the English Language and Literature course. I am not concerned here with the 'belles lettres' or strictly rhetorical aspect of these courses, though the subject is by no means devoid of interest. In saying that this tradition goes back to Blair, I am not claiming that he was the first to lecture on the subject in a Scottish university: even before Smith became Professor of Logic at Glasgow, he had lectured in an informal capacity on rhetoric in Edinburgh[4], and according to John Millar (quoted by Dugald Stewart, Stewart, 1795: 274) he completely transformed the barren course of logic offered by his predecessors at Glasgow "illustrating the various powers of the human mind...from the several ways of communicating our thoughts by speech." It is a curious sidelight on the culture of 18th century Scotland, that the author of <u>The Wealth of Nations</u> in some of his earliest published work concerned himself with the problems of language, and in fact his <u>Considerations Concerning the First Formation of Languages and the Different Genius of Original and Compounded Languages</u> (a greatly expanded version of the language part of the Rhetoric lectures) first appeared in 1761. It is noteworthy that Blair acknowledged his debt both to Smith's published treatise on language and to his unpublished lectures on rhetoric[5]. As is well known[6], a MS of these lectures was discovered as recently as 1961 and first published in 1963. But Smith's was by no means the only treatment of language with the Scottish rhetoric courses. Watson's lectures at St. Andrews consisted basically of a digest of Harris's <u>Hermes</u> and there is evidence that this work was studied at Edinburgh too[7], and even Leechman's lectures on pulpit oratory[8] at Glasgow contained observations on linguistic matters.

Blair tells us in the Preface to his Lectures (Blair I 1785: iv) that the text now published represented the lectures he had been delivering at Edinburgh over the previous twenty-four years, and it is clear that during this period of time his ideas on language, as on other subjects, must have matured considerably. A synopsis of the Lectures (Blair 1777) had already appeared six years before their publication in book form and there are numerous MS student notes preserved in the Edinburgh University Library. He considered his <u>Lectures</u>

> neither as a work wholly original, nor as a Compilation from the writings of others. On every subject contained in them, he thought for himself. He consulted his own ideas and reflections; and a great part of what will be found in these Lectures is entirely his own. (Blair 1785 I: iv)

Perhaps it is precisely this capacity as an expounder of of received ideas, his exposition of a 'consensus' view of the subjects he treats - we may remember that Blair was one of the leading moderates within the Church of Scotland at the time - that accounts for his extraordinary popularity not only in the English-speaking world, but also throughout Europe. Within a few years of the first publication of the Lectures, there appeared translations into French, German, Italian, Dutch and Spanish. To mention only those I am most familiar with: I have counted no fewer than twenty different editions or adaptations of the Italian translation[9], published between 1801 and 1859 in five different Italian cities, but the list is almost certainly incomplete. Let us put it this way: Blair's Lectures became an internationally acknowledged textbook and we may therefore assume that generations of students were brought up not only on his digest of classical rhetorical theory and on his comments on the great authors of the past, but also on his ideas on the nature, history and structure of language.

Let us now look at these ideas a little more closely. I have mentioned what I called the 'Oxford model' of the English syllabus and its development from the end of the 19th century onwards. The language part of this was - and, to some extent still is - largely concerned with the historical study of the English language, with some Gothic and Old Norse thrown in for good measure. We all know this, since I suppose most of us were brought up on it. Blair's language sections (Lectures 6-9, but there are passages of considerable interest for linguists also in Lectures 10-16, i.e. those dealing with rhetorical theory) partly also deal with historical matters, though much of this is what in the 18th century was known as 'conjectural history', a term I shall return to shortly. His brief account of the origin and history of the English language, whose "irregular grammar" is said to be due to the fact that English is of hybrid origin, is disappointing and shows little direct knowledge of the earlier phases of the history of our tongue. Blair is far more interested in language as a general phenomenon of human societies than in any particular language. In choosing this approach, he is squarely within the tradition of 18th century rational grammar, a philosophical rather than a philological discipline, although he complains that "few authors have written with philosophical accuracy on the principles of General Grammar, and what is more to be regretted, fewer still have thought of applying those principles to the English Language" (Blair I 1785: 172-73), unlike the French who have "considered its construction and determined its propriety with great accuracy" (Blair I 1785: 174). Some attempts have been made, but much remains to be done. I am not concerned here with refuting Blair's claim that little had been written on general grammar in English, though this would not be difficult, bearing in mind influential authors like Harris, Smith or Priestley, but I do want to go back for a moment to the concept of 'conjectural history', because I believe this is central to our understanding of how Blair, like most of his contemporaries, approached the study of language. The term, which came to be widely used of all forms of history, was coined by Dugald Stewart in talking about Smith's Considerations

> In this want of direct evidence we are under a necessity of supplying the place of fact by conjecture; and when we are unable to ascertain how men have actually conducted

themselves upon particular occasions, of considering in
what manner they are likely to have proceeded, from the
principles of their nature, and the circumstances of their
external situation. In such enquiries, the detached facts
which travels and voyages afford us, may frequently serve
as land-marks to our speculations, and sometimes our conclusions <u>a priori</u> may tend to confirm the credibility of facts,
which on a superficial view, appeared to be doubtful or
incredible.
(Stewart 1975: xli-xlii)

If this was true in general of human history, it was true in particular of the history of language; an account of the history of human speech is above all an account of its nature, and vice versa, the nature of language can be understood by reconstructing not its more or less docu- mented stages, but by an <u>a priori</u> reasoning, on 'how it must have happened', where 'must' is to be interpreted in terms of an objective rather than subjective epistemic modality, since the facts described arise out of consid- erations based on the general principles of communication, which give the term 'conjectural' objective validity.
To a considerable extent, this explains the recurrent con- cern of 18th century writers on language, both in France and in Britain as well as in Germany (we remember Herder's prize-winning essay for the Berlin Academy in 1771) with the question of origins. It was a subject that loomed as large in most 18th century accounts of language as it is conspicuous by its absence in practically all contemporary writing on the subject. I am not sure that I would go all the way with Aarsleff's interpretation of the origins question, when he affirms that what these authors were

interested in was a model, rather than a historical state of things

> the philosophical question of the origin of language first formulated by Condillac sought to establish man's linguistic state of nature in order to gain insight into the nature of man... the search for origins concerned the present state of man, not the establishment of some 'historical' fact or 'explanation' of how things actually were at some point in the past.
> (Aarsleff 1974: 107-8)

Blair of course cites Condillac among his sources, together other French authors like the Port-Royal grammarians, Du Marsais, Beauzée, Batteaux, de Brosses, Girard, Rousseau as well as English works like those of Adam Smith and Harris, and in a long note in Lecture 7 he discusses Monboddo's account of "some of the first articulate sounds" of certain primitive tongues, in which he accepts Monboddo's contention, in its turn based on a hypothesis enunciated by Smith and ultimately traceable to Condillac, that they

> denoted a whole sentence rather than the name of a particular object; conveying some information, or expressing some desires or fears, suited to the circumstances in which that tribe was placed, or relating to the business they had most frequent occasion to carry on; as the lion is coming, the river is swelling & c.
> (Blair I 1785: 176)

It is certainly true that much of the discussion of the origins of speech is conducted in philosophical terms. For Condillac, as for Rousseau and Monboddo, arises in response to human need, primitive men

n'ont pas dit, <u>faisons une langue</u>: ils ont senti besoin
d'un mot, et ils ont prononcé le plus propre à représenter
la chose qu'ils vouloient faire connaître
(Porset 1970: 162-63)

Beauzée too talks of <u>sociabilité</u> as the source of the universal phenomenon of human language, emphasizing that the elements that all human languages have in common are far more numerous and basic than the superficial elements of time, place and custom that determine the difference between individual tongues, an idea that we also find in other 18th century philosophers: Blair, for example, would have found it in the writings of the most prominent Scottish philosopher of his time, David Hume, and another Scot, Thomas Reid, distinguishes between 'natural' and 'artificial' signs (Reid 1764: 103), a distinction much insisted upon also by Monboddo when he talks of the 'language of nature' vs. the 'language of art': it is only the latter which has the full status of language, since the former, especially in Reid's formulation, is nothing but the direct expression of the passions not mediated by the double articulation characteristic of human speech.[10]

But let me return to my previous point: Aarsleff's 'metaphorical' reading of 18th century concerns with origins. Since the subject is not dealt with in detail by Blair, I will limit myself here to saying that the interest shown in Britain by such writers as Monboddo or in France in the numerous accounts of the customs and speech of primitive tribes (echoed, for example, in de Brosses) is surely proof that these 18th century scholars were concerned not merely with the general principles of human speech, which is undeniable, or with primitive languages as somehow representing the basic functions of language, which too I believe to be beyond doubt, but that they sought to provide a concrete and empirically verifiable account of what the speech of primitive man was actually like. I do not believe one necessarily excludes the other, though in the case of Blair the philosophical as opposed to the empirical interest appears to be predominant.

There are several aspects of the origin question that were widely debated and that Blair too is concerned with. I shall not deal with the vexed question of whether language was of human or divine origin (Blair is inclined to accept the latter view), since this is not my central concern here. Blair, like Rousseau, whose <u>Discours sur l'origine de l'inégalité parmi les hommes</u> he quotes, is caught up in what we might rougly call the chicken or the egg dilemma, i.e. of whether we can conceive of a society prior to the 'invention' of language, or whether language is a condition necessary to the existence of society:

> So that, either how Society could form itself, previously to Language, or how words could rise into a Language previously to Society formed, seem to be points attended with equal difficulty.
> (Blair I 1785: 126)

Since there is no obvious answer to this question, Blair skates over the problem in order to consider just what this language must have been like. Like most of his contemporaries, he identifies the 'language of nature' with the grammatical category of interjections, which must therefore have been the first words, though the term 'word' may be inappropriate for such direct expressions of the passions. "Those exclamations, therefore," he affirms, "which by Grammarians are called Interjections, uttered in a strong and passionate manner, were beyond doubt, the elements of beginnings of Speech" (Blair I 1785: 128-29). Like de Brosses, Blair rejects a purely arbitrary origin for the first linguistic signs, for

> To suppose words invented, without any ground or reason, is to suppose an effect without a cause. There must have always been some motive which led to the assignation of one name rather than another
> (Blair I 1785: 128-29)

although he concedes in a different passage that sound symbolism can have affected only a very limited sphere of the vocabulary.[11]

The problem is twofold: what words were first 'invented' and how did they develop in the course of human history to form the languages of the polite nations of Europe, which are now greatly refined and not only have words for all the objects of the world, but also a series of ornaments, a state of affairs which has been in existence "among many nations for some thousand years" (Blair I 1785: 124). In the second place he sought to ascertain how these words were arranged in structures to convey propositional, not merely atomistic meanings. It is to these two subjects that I now wish to turn my attention.

Early man had few words at his disposal, since his experience of the world was limited and he therefore had to help himself out by an abundant use of metaphor, since Blair, like practically all his contemporaries, holds that abstract terms all have their origin in concrete nouns denoting the objects of the world:

> The names of sensible objects were, in all languages, the words most early introduced, and were by degrees, extended to those mental objects, of which men had more obscure conceptions, and to which they found it more difficult to assign a distinct name
> (Blair I 1785: 353)

so that primitive speech was

> strong and expressive...(and) could be no other than full of figures and metaphors, not correct indeed, but forcible and picturesque... Mankind never employed so many figures of speech, as when they had hardly any words for expressing their meaning
> (Blair I 1785: 141)

That the men of letters of the Enlightenment were fascinated by 'primitive' (or what they believed to be primitive) poetry is a commonplace: as is well known, Blair was one of the chief defenders of the authenticity of Macpherson's *Ossian*, which he considered to be the perfect example of primitive, but powerful poetry. Like other writers on rhetoric, Blair is distinctly wary of the use of figures of speech, which must be strictly subordinate to the supreme requirement of clarity, or as the oft quoted

Quintilian had put it, "nobis prima sit virtus perspicuitas" (<u>Inst. Or.</u> VIII, ii,2).

Figurative language is associated with primitive societies, whereas "Language is become, in modern times, more correct indeed, and accurate, but however less striking and animated" (Blair I 1785: 157). Ours is, in other words, an age of reason and philosophy, not of poetry and oratory. I do not know if Matthew Arnold knew this passage of Blair's; it would certainly have been grist to his mill in his contention that the 18th century was essentially an age of prose.

The earliest vocal sounds were interjections, but the first real words were

> substantive nouns, which are the foundation of all Grammar, and may be considered as the most antient part of Speech; For, assuredly, as soon as men got beyond simle interjections, or exclamations, of passions, and began to communicate themselves (<u>sic</u>), they would be under a necessity of assigning names to the objects they saw around them; which, in Grammatical Language is called the invention of substantive nouns.[12]
>
> (Blair I 1785: 176)

The idea that the naming process is the basis of all language goes back at least as far as the mediaeval so-called 'modistae' school of grammarians, who insisted on the primacy of the 'modus entis' over the 'modus esse'. In English linguistic theory this is particularly evident in Wilkins's <u>Essay</u>, where everything, except the purely grammatical operators called 'particles', is reduced to the basic category of the noun. In Blair this must be seen in his almost Bloomfieldian account of the first linguistic utterances, which are treated in terms of stimulus and response[13]. However, unlike his 17th century predecessors, who in one way or another tend to subsume the verb in the naming process, for Blair

> Verbs must have been coëval with men's first attempts towards the formation of Language
> (Blair I 1785: 203)

and, following Smith's suggestion (Smith 1983: 215-16), as we have already had occasion to mention, he opines that impersonal verbs must have been the first to appear, so that the origin of speech must be seen not in the mere naming process, envisaged as a mythical savage pointing to a tree laden with apples and uttering the word 'apple', but in 'event verbs' in elementary one argument propositions like 'it is raining'.

Blair follows Harris's scheme of dividing lexical words into substantives and attributes, and he is of the opinion that since adjectives, the simplest form of attributes, are found in all languages, they must have been among the first words to be invented, whereas adverbs, which can generally be reduced to nouns plus prepositions

> may be conceived as of less necessity, and of later introduction in the System of Speech, than any other classes of words
> (Blair I 1785: 210)

In other words, for Blair, most ancient means most essen-
or necessary. The whole concept of the 'necessary' elements of a language is fully developed in Beauzée, who mentions "éléments necessaires" on the very title-page of his Grammar. Shortage of space does not permit me to go into Blair's many points of contact with this influential French work, published some 16 years prior to the <u>Lectures</u>. Necessary is seen in terms of basic, so we come back once again to the idea that, at least to some extent, and in the case of Blair rather more so than in an author like Monboddo, the origins question is intimately connected with what are seen to be the basic structures of language: richness of vocabulary, elegance, harmony, ornament are the additions of a politer age, which make language suitable for scientific and philosophical discourse, but do not constitute the essential categories that serve to convey meaning as invented by the first men. To what extent we are justified in equating these basic categories with our contemporary concept of deep structure is a question I would like to leave open for the time being, but I suspect it may well be possible to draw some sort of parallel between the two.

Finally, I would like to turn to the question of how words are arranged in sentences so as to convey propositional rather than purely lexical meaning. The problem of word order, i.e. the order of words considered to be most natural, was much debated during the 18th century. That word order constitutes one of the principal criteria of modern typological studies hardly needs emphasizing.[14] The problem was seen terms of rigid as opposed to (comparatively) free word order, with particular attention to the position of the subject. Girard, whose <u>Les vrais principes</u> is cited by Blair among his list of sources, had divided languages into 'analogous' and 'transpositive' types, roughly what later linguists called 'analytic' and 'synthetic' languages, and this division is followed, among others, by Beauzée in France and in Britain by the anonymous author of the article on 'Language' in the first edition of the <u>Encyclopaedia Britannica</u> (1771). In both cases, analogous languages are said to respect the order of nature. Beauzée calls this the "analytical order" or "analytical succession of ideas", since according to him

> La succession analytique des idées est le fondement unique
> & invariable des loix de la Syntaxe dans toutes les langues
> imaginables
>
> (Beauzée 1947: 467-68)

and Du Marsais, another much quoted author in English treatments of the subject, in his article for the <u>Encyclopaedie</u> (Porset 1970: 232) is of much the same opinion. A full examination of word order as treated by 18th century grammarians and philosophers (but there is often little difference between the two) would be out of place here. I have referred to it since Blair approaches the question from a rather different point of view. Word order, like the question of word categories, is seen in terms of origins:

> Let us go back...to the most early period of Language. Let
> us figure to ourselves a Savage, who beholds some object,

> such as fruit, which raises his desire, who requests another
> to give it to him... He would not express himself, according
> to an English order of construction, 'Give me fruit',
> 'Fructum da mihi': For this plain reason, that his attention
> was wholly directed towards fruit, the desired object
> (Blair I 1785: 148-49)[15]

In other words, Blair is concerned with a psychological as opposed to a logical succession of ideas, an order which he calls "though not the most logical...the most natural order (Blair I 1785: 149), and in view of the importance focusing has acquired in recent linguistic theory, this dichotomy of natural (i.e. psychological) vs. logical order is of considerable interest. This question had been the cause of controversy between Beauzée and Batteaux, another French source quoted by Blair, and nearer home, Campbell in his highly influential <u>The Philosophy of Rhetoric</u> (1776), a work Blair greatly esteemed, had talked of a grammatical vs. a rhetorical order, ascribing universal status to the latter, but only local and particular validity to the former

> I imagine that the only principle in which this subject
> can safely rest, as being founded in nature, is that what-
> ever most strongly fixes the attention, or operates on
> the passion of the speaker, will first seek utterance by
> the speaker... In these transpositions, therefore, I main-
> tain that the order will be found, on examination, to be
> more strictly natural than when the more general practice
> in the tongue is followed.
> (Campbell 1850: 357-58)

Within the context of 18th century Enlightenment culture the question could not but be seen in terms of the superiority of the classical languages as compared with their modern successors, or vice versa. Unlike some of his contemporaries, who came down very decidedly on the side of the moderns[16], Blair tries to reconcile the two positions in some way: Latin order is said to be "more animated", English "more clear and distinct", the Latin order reflecting the succession in which ideas rise in the speaker's mind, ours "the order in which the understanding directs those ideas to be exhibited (Blair I 1785: 153)[17].

The above remarks by no means aim to give an exhaustive account of Blair's ideas on the nature, structure and development of language: there are a great many points, both in the chapters strictly concerned with language and in his treatment of the laws of rhetoric, that would repay much more detailed study, especially within the wider framework of the contribution of the thinkers of the Scottish Enlightenment to linguistic theory, than is possible in a short paper. In conclusion, I would not claim any great originality for Blair's ideas, but I do think that it was precisely because he was <u>not</u> original that he became so popular and that both as the first Professor of Rhetoric and Belles Lettres and as the author of an internationally acclaimed text-book he deserves more than an honourable mention in the history of English Studies.

NOTES

1. Smith was appointed Professor of Logic and Rhetoric at Glasgow in 1751 and following year he succeeded Thomas Craigie as Professor of Moral Philosophy. The rhetoric lectures, as they have come down

to us in the Glasgow University Library MS, go back to the session 1762-63, but according to Bryce (in Smith 1983: 9) he began lecturing on rhetoric as soon as he took up his appointment in Glasgow.

2. Robert Watson was appointed to the Chair of Logic at St. Salvator's College, St. Andrews in 1756 and Principal of the same in 1778. There are five sets of student notes of his lectures on universal grammar delivered at St. Andrews preserved in the University Library dating from between 1758 and 1778. With the exception of MS PN 173, they are substantially identical and consist of an abstract of Books I and II of Harris's Hermes. Watson never published anything on the subject.

3. James Beattie was appointed Professor of Moral Philosophy and Logic at Marischal College, Aberdeen in 1760. The following year he was elected member of the Aberdeen Philosophical Society, of which George Campbell, Principal of Marischal College, was a founder member. Though Rule 17 of the statutes of the Society states that "all Grammatical Historical and Philological Discussion being conceived to be foreign to the Design of this Society", Campbell certainly read a number of papers on rhetoric to the Society. These papers were later transformed into The Philosophy of Rhetoric, and there are other contributions on such matters as the word order of the ancient compared with those of the modern languages (George Skene), the characteristics of a polished language (James Dunbar) or writing systems (Thomas Gordon). See Aberdeen University Library MS 539, reprinted in Humphries 1931. Beattie's The Theory of Language too is based on lectures delivered at Aberdeen. Copies of the Session Journals of Marischal College preserved in the Aberdeen University Library give a very clear idea of how his Rhetoric course was structured.

4. In 1748 at the suggestion of Lord Kames. At the time Smith was 25 years old. Cf. Bryce in Smith 1983: 8.

5. Smith's Considerations are mentioned among his sources in Lecture V, whereas in Lecture XVIII we read: "On this head...several ideas have been taken from a manuscript treatise on rhetoric, part of which was shewn to me many years ago, by the learned and ingenious Author, Dr. Adam Smith; and which, it is hoped, will be given by him to the Public" (Blair II 1785: 24).

6. Cf. Introduction to Smith 1983: 1.

7. For example there is a notebook (MS 3125) in the National Library of Scotland entitled 'Universal Grammar written by James Trail" which is very similar to the Watson notes in the St. Andrews

University Library. James Trail was educated at Edinburgh, but the notes were apparently originally taken down by his brother David, who was a student at St. Andrews. It would therefore appear that Watson's Universal Grammar course, based on Harris, was also in use at Edinburgh. There are frequent echoes of Harris in Blair's treatment, for example his division of words into substantives and attributives in Lecture VIII or his definition of adjectives in the same Lecture.

8. 'Lectures on Composition by the Reverend Mr. Leechman'. The parts that have some linguistic interest are Lectures 11-18. Leechman (1706-1785) was appointed Professor of Divinity in the University of Glasgow in 1743 and Principal in 1761. He gave lectures on composition and the Evidences of Christianity in alternate years (Wodrow I 1779: 49).

9. <u>Lezioni di Retorica e Belle Lettere di Ugone Blair...Tradotte dall'Inglese e commentate da Francesco Soave C.R.S.</u>, Parma: dalla Real Tipografia MDCCCI-MDCCCII.

10. In case it may be thought that I am arbitrarily using contemporary concepts and terminology (e.g. double articolation) in referring to different ways of conceptualizing these matters, I would refer the reader to Monboddo's extended treatment of the enormous conceptual jump represented not only by the use of sounds to symbolize ideas, as compared with the direct expression of the passions which are said to their origin in animal cries, but by what he calls the <u>matter</u> of language, i.e. the sound system and the development of articulate, that is to say significant sounds, which in Monboddo's view provide the real dividing line between true language and the <u>language of nature</u>.

11. "natural connexion (i.e. sound symbolism) can affect only a small part of the fabric of language; the connexion between words and ideas may, in general, be considered as arbitrary, and conventional, owing to the agreement of men among themselves" (Blair I 1785: 123). Even the most outstanding exponent of the view that there exists a natural correspondence between certain sounds and some of the basic human needs or sentiments like de Brosses (e.g. "Dans tous les siècles et dans toutes les contrées on emploie la lettre de lèvre ou à son default la lettre de dent, ou tous les deux ensemble, pour exprimer les premieres mots enfantins papa et maman" de Brosses 1798 I: 222) has to accept that conventional words are far more numerous than 'natural' words.

12. Cf. Smith's much fuller account of the origin of common nouns: "Those objects only which were most familiar to them, (i.e. to the

first men) and which they had most frequent occasion to mention, would have particular names assigned to them. The particular cave whose covering sheltered them from the weather, the particular tree whose fruit relieved their hunger, the particular fountain whose water allayed their thirst, would first be denominated by the words <u>cave</u>, <u>tree</u>, <u>fountain</u>...Afterwards when the more enlarged experience of these savages had led them to observe, and their necessary occasions obliged them to make mention of other caves, and other trees, and other fountains, they would naturally bestow, upon each of those new objects, the same name, by which they had been accustomed to express the similar objects they were first acquainted with. The new objects had none of them any name of its own, but each of them exactly resembled another object, which had such an appellation... And thus, those words, which were originally the proper names of individuals, would each of them insensibly become the common name of a multitude" Smith 1983: 203-204).

13. Like Bloomfield in his account of Jack and Jill and the apple tree (Bloomfield 1935: 22), he talks of a savage who desires a fruit.
14. Among recent treatments, see for example the special issue on typology of <u>Folia Linguistica</u>, Plank 1986.
15. Condillac in the chapter entitled "Des Mots" discusses the question of 'natural' word order at some length: "l'ordre le plus naturel des idées vouloit qu'on mit le régime avant le verbe: on disoit, par example, <u>fruit vouloir</u>...les mots se construissoient dans la même ordre dans lequel ils se régissoient; unique moyen d'en faciliter l'intelligence. On disoit <u>fruit vouloir Pierre</u> pour <u>Pierre veut du fruit</u>; & la premiere construction n'étoit pas moins naturelle que l'autre l'est actuellement" (Condillac 1792: 263-64). The example, it will be noted, is almost identical to Blair's, but Condillac's reason for preferring OV order is grammatical-conceptual, whereas Blair's is psychological.
16. For example Beauzée and even more strongly the anonymous author of the above-mentioned article on "Language" in the first edition of the <u>Encyclopaedia Britannica</u>.
17. Cf. "Le français suit l'ordre de l'intelligence, mais le latin suit l'ordre du sentiment et des mouvements du coeur" (de Brosses I 1798: 71). Beauzée dedicates a great deal of space to refuting Batteaux's thesis that languages like Latin represent the order in which ideas arise in the mind, since his interest is not so much in the input as in the output of language. As to ornament or elegance "l'ordre analytique peut donc être contraire àl'élo-

quence sans être contraire à la nature du Langage, pour lequel l'éloquence n'est qu'un accessoire artificiel" (Beauzée II 1974: 530).

REFERENCES

Aarsleff, H. 1974. 'The Tradition of Condillac. The Problem of the Origin of Language in the Eighteenth Century and the Debate in the Berlin Academy before Herder'. In D. Hymes, ed. Studies in the History of Linguistics, 93-156. Bloomington: Indiana University Press.
Batteaux, Charles. 1764 (1746). Traité de la Construction Oratoire. Vol.5 of Principes de la Litterature. Nouvelle Edition. Paris: Desaint & Saillant.
Beattie, James. 1788. The Theory of Language. London: A. Strahan. Microfiche reproduction in English Linguistics 1500-1800. Menston: Scolar Press, 1968.
Beauzée, Nicolas. 1974 (1767). Grammaire générale ou exposition raisonnée des éléments nécessaires du langage. Nouvelle impression en facsimile de l'édition du 1767 avec une introduction par Barrie E. Bartlett. 2 vols. Stuttgart-Bad Caunstatt: Fromman.
Blair, Hugh. 1777. Heads of the Lectures on Rhetoric and Belles Lettres in the University of Edinburgh. Edinburgh: W. Creech.
------------ 1785 (1783). Lectures on Rhetoric and Belles Lettres. 3 vols. Second edition corrected. London: W. Strahan and T. Cadell; Edinburgh: W. Creech.
Bloomfield, L. 1935 (1933). Language. Revised British edition. London: Allen & Unwin.
de Brosses, Charles. 1798 (1765). Traité de la formation méchanique des langues. Paris: chez Terrelonge.
Burnett, James (Lord Monboddo). 1773-1792. On the Origin and Progress of Language. 6 vols. Edinburgh: Kincaid & Creech; London: T.Cadell. Microfiche reproduction in English Linguistics 1500-1800. Menston: Scolar Press, 1968.
----------------------------- 1779-1799. Antient Metaphysics.6 vols. Edinburgh: J. Balfour; London: T. Cadell. Both works were published anonymously.
Campbell, George. 1850 (1776). The Philosophy of Rhetoric. London: W. Tegg.

Condillac, Etienne Bonnot de. 1792 (1746). Essai sur l'origine des connoissances humaines. Troisième Edition revue & augmentée. Paris: chez le Libraires Associés.
---------------------------- 1775. Cours d'étude pour l'instruction du Prince de Parme. In Porset 1970: 149-211.
Du Marsais, César Chesneau. In Porset 1970: 210-301.
Encyclopaedia Britannica. 1771. "by a Society of Gentlemen in Scotland". 3 vols. Edinburgh: Bell & Macfarquhar.
Frank, T. 1979. Segno e significato. La lingua filosofica di John Wilkins. Napoli: Guida.
Girard, Gabriel. 1747. Les vrais principes de la langue françoise. 2 vols. Paris: Le Breton.
Harris, James. 1751. Hermes; or a Philosophical Inquiry concerning Language and Universal Grammar. London: H. Woodfall. Microfiche reproduction in English Linguistics 1500-1800. Menston: Scolar Press, 1968.
Herder, Johann Gottfried. 1772. Abhandlung über den Ursprung der Sprache. English translation by A. Gode, Essay on the Origin of Language. Chicago: Chicago University Press, 1986.
Humphries, W.R. 1931. 'The First Aberdeen Philosophical Society'. Transactions of the Aberdeen Philosophical Society, 5.203-38.
Lancelot, Claude and Antoine Arnauld. 1660. Grammaire Générale et Raisonnée. Paris: Presse Le Petit. Repr. Menston: Scolar Press, 1968.
Leechman, William. 1779. Sermons. London: A. Strahan & T. Cadell; Edinburgh: E. Balfour & W. Creech.
--------------------- c. 1770. Glasgow University Library MS Gen 51. The last six leaves of this contain an abstract of Harris's Hermes.
---------------------- 1770 (but delivered 1754-55). 'Lectures on Composition'. Edinburgh University Library MS Dc.7.86. Student notes.
Plank, F. (ed.) 1986. Folia Linguistica. Special Issue.20/1-2.
--------------- 'The Smith-Schlegel Connection in linguistic typology: forgotten fact or fiction?'. To appear in Zeitschrift für Fonetik, Sprachwissenschaft und Kommunikationsforschung.
Porset, C. 1970. Varia Linguistica. Bordeaux: Ducros.
Quintilian (M. Fabius Quintilianus). Istituto Oratoria, ed. H.E. Butler. London: Heinemann, 1921.
Reid, Thomas. 1764. An Inquiry into the Human Mind on the Principles of Common Sense. London: A. Millar; Edinburgh: Kincaid & Bell.
Rousseau, Jean-Jacques. 1755. Discours sur l'origine et les fondements de l'inégalité parmi les hommes. English transaltion by M. Cranston, A Discourse on Inequality. Harmondsworth: Penguin Books. 1984.

Smith, Adam. 1983. (1762-63?). Lectures on Rhetoric and Belles Lettres, ed. J. Bryce. Oxford: Clarendon Press.
---------- 1761. Considerations Concerning the First Formation and the Different Genius of Original and Compounded Languages in Smith 1983.
Soublin, F. 1976. 'Rationalisme et grammaire chez Dumarsais' in H. Parret ed. History of Linguistic Thought and Contemporary Linguistics, 383-409. Berlin-New York: de Gruyter.
Stewart, Dugald. 1795. An Account of the Life and Writings of Adam Smith LL.D., published as an introduction to Smith's Essays on Philosophical Subjects. London: T. Cadell Jun. & W. Davies; Edinburgh: W.Creech.
Watson, Robert. Student notes on Watson's lectures on universal grammar delivered at St. Andrews University and preserved in the St. Andrews University Library:
1. MS PN 173 (1762).
2. MS 36978 (1776).
3. MS BC 6 W1 (1776).
4. MS BC W2 (1778).
5. MS PN 173 (1758) contains an earlier version.
Wilkins, John. 1668. An Essay towards a Real Character and Philosophical Language. London: Gellibrand. Microfiche reproduction in English Linguistics 1500-1800. Menston: Scolar Press, 1968.
Wodrow, James. 1779. Life of William Leechman in Leechman 1779 I: 1-102.

METHODOLOGICAL PRELIMINARIES TO THE STUDY OF LINGUISTIC CHANGE IN
DIALECTAL ENGLISH: EVALUATING THE GRAMMARS OF BARNES AND ELWORTHY
AS SOURCES OF LINGUISTIC EVIDENCE

OSSI IHALAINEN
University of Helsinki

One important source of data for the study of change in modern regional dialects is dialect grammars and word books written in the late nineteenth and early twentieth century. In this paper I shall concentrate on South-Western British English, which seems to be particularly well covered by these early grammars. The following works specifically treat some variety of South-Western English: Jennings (1825), Barnes (1863, 1886), Bonaparte (1875-6), Elworthy (1875, 1877, 1886), Hewett (1892), Kruisinga (1905) Wilson (1913). Kruisinga is a grammarian, but his knowledge of the Somerset dialect appears to be highly academic and he draws heavily on the work of others. The others were not trained philologists, but seem to have known several foreign languages and enough formal grammar to be able to write quite intelligibly about the structure of the dialect of their home county.

Besides the fact that the early authorities list the characteristic forms of the dialect and explain how these are used, i.e. formulate "rules," they also discuss things like the frequency of various forms, their regional distributions, and occasionally even comment on ongoing changes. For example, Barnes (1863: 26) points out that periphrastic *do*, which he calls "a great mark of south-western English", is not found in Devon. The SED material shows that this is in fact the case. Elworthy (1877: 41) points out that the word *as* is not used as a relative pronoun in West Somerset. He also says that in West Somerset the periphrastic form is being replaced by the *s* form (1886: xx-xxi). There is recent evidence that both generalizations are accurate (Ihalainen: 1980, to appear a, b).

On the other hand, some of the claims, although they may seem quite specific and convincing at first, look suspicious in the light of the evidence available. Thus, Elworthy (1877: 35) claims that in West-Somerset the nominative form *I* is exceptional as a direct object and non existent as a prepositional object ("We should never say *Give it to I*, but always *to me*"). Yet tape-recordings from West-Somerset show that *I* as a prepositional object occurs in the vernacular. Also dialect stories from the 1920's suggest that *I* as a prepositional object is in no way exceptional. Elworthy's claim is therefore difficult to accept unless we assume that the loss of the constraint was rather abrupt -- my oldest West-Somerset informant who uses *I* as a prepositional object was born in 1892. However, since we know very little about the rate of grammatical change in dialect, one cannot, of course, rule out the possibility of hyperdialectism in the speech of the generation following Elworthy. Close analysis of the relevant SED data might throw further light on this problem.

In addition to the fact that these early writers had no systematic corpus to rely on, their descriptions may at times be biased because of their desire to show that dialects are respectable. The respectability argument takes two forms. The writer may want to show that in comparison to Standard English a specific dialect is pure. By this he means that the dialect is closer to Anglo-Saxon than Standard English is. I shall call this kind of argument the pedigree argument. The second type of argument consists of showing that dialects are not simply distorted Standard English but have grammars of their own which may differ from the grammar of Standard English quite considerably. While the former line of argument looks somewhat pathetic now, the second type of argument looks quite modern and makes highly interesting reading for anyone concerned with linguistics.

In the following I shall briefly look at the work of William Barnes and Thomas Elworthy and try to give a general picture of what they were doing. Although I shall be critical of some aspects of their work, I cannot help feeling that these grammars are extremely valuable and can be read with profit by modern readers. I add my critical comments mainly because I feel that they might help the modern reader to avoid certain errors of interpretation. I shall also comment on what kind of material could be used to supplement the data in these early grammars.
aa
It will be seen that in many places these two writers offer almost identical descriptions. To what extent the writers were aware of each other's work is an interesting question, but cannot be pursued here.

THE PEDIGREE ARGUMENT

I shall first look at the pedigree argument, i.e. the argument that a particular dialect is closer in structure to Anglo-Saxon than Standard English is. The thinking underlying it is conveniently and quite explicitly stated by Hewett:

> The speech of the peasantry of Devon and the adjacent counties is undoubtedly the purest remains of the Anglo-Saxon tongue extant in England at the present time. Many words are almost as pure as when spoken by our Saxon ancestors. (1892: v)

The same line of thinking permeates the work of Barnes[1] and can be found in Elworthy. Just to give a characteristic example, for

Barnes the fact that Dorset has retained the the participial prefix is a mark of the purity of his dialect as against the corruption of Standard Engish:

> The true Dorset retains, what one could wish
> the English had not lost, an affix or syllabic
> augment to the perfect participle, answering to
> one in the Saxon-English and German.
> (Barnes 1863: 30)

This kind of comparison as a descriptive method may look rather harmless at first, but there is a danger that the desire to see Anglo Saxon forms in the dialect makes the analyst blind to features that, although they are part of the strucure of the dialect, are not "pure". Bearing this in mind, it is instructive to look at the passage where Barnes shows that the forms of the verb *to be* are alike in Dorset and Anglo-Saxon. The paradigms are given below.

The verb TO BE in Dorset and Anglo-Saxon:

I be	ic beo
thou bist	thu byst
He is	he is
we be	we beoth
you be	ge beoth
they be	hi beoth

Compare Barnes's paradigm with the following Dorset responses elicited by SED:

"You are." (SED IX.7.7.)
1. thee art
2. thee art
3. thee art
4. thee art
5. thee art
(The numbers refer to SED Dorset localities)

The second person singuar pronoun is given as *thou*. As can be seen from the SED responses above, the pronoun is *thee* invariably rather than *thou* in present-day Dorset. This makes the form *thou* look suspicious because it is unlikely that it would have disappeared without a trace if it was firmly established in Barnes's day. However, if it was only a variant, possibly a recessive variant, it could have in fact have been replaced by *thee* by the 1950's when the SED material was collected. But if this is true, the only explanation for Barnes's not mentioning it would have been that it was not the original Anglo-Saxon subject form, whereas *thou* was. Given a choice, then, anyone committed to showing the purity of the dialect, would have chosen *thou* rather than *thee*.

Also the non-appearance of *art* is problematical. The SED responses above show a unified *art* in the declarative sentence. However, there is some evidence for *bis* in questions:

"Are you married?" (SED IX.7.2.)
1. Bis thee...
2. Bis thee...
3. Art thee...
4. Be you...
5. At thee...

Yet it is difficult to believe that *art* could have replaced *bist* since Barnes's day to the extent that it seems to have done if we take Barnes's paradigm literally. It is more likely that *art* existed as a variant. But if *art* was a Dorset form, why didn't

Barnes mention it? Again one possible explanation is that he quotes only those forms that he believes to be closest to Anglo-Saxon.

Another point to note about Barnes's paradigm is that, while it is still true that in the south-west the usual third person singular form is *he is*, one will occasionally hear forms like "He be tired". The form "he be" is also given by Jennings (1825: 7) as an occasional albeit rare variant of "he is", and it must have existed in Dorset in Barnes's day as well. But again the variant *he be* would have been less pure than the "he is" that occurs in Barnes's paradigm.

Another interesting omission is *they'm*. According to Jennings (1825: 8), this form occurred in south-western English in the early nineteenth century and it certainly occurs there today. But, of course, this form is not a "pure" Anglo-Saxon form.

It would seem, then, that when the local dialect is compared to what the writer believes to be Anglo-Saxon, there may be a definite tendency to idealize one's paradigms for the sake of a more dramatic presentation. That the picture of the dialect is somewhat simplified will probably not matter a great deal if one is interested only in synchronic description. But what this kind of suppression of data that does not fit might do, is to lead a later scholar to postulate a change that never occurred. Thus if we take Barnes's description literally, we have to conclude that the form *thee art* is replacing the form *thou bist* in Dorset. Since there is a great deal of evidence that the second person singular forms are disappearing rather than spreading, this is not a likely development. Therefore, one might assume that both forms were found there to start with, but for some reason Barnes recorded only one of them.

THE "DIFFERENT FROM STANDARD ENGLISH" ARGUMENT: TWO CLASSES OF THINGS AND THE CHOICE OF PRONOUNS

Besides the desire to show that dialects are closer to Anglo-Saxon than Standard English is, there is another strong tendency: early writers want to show that dialects are independent languages and that they show grammatical distinctions that do not exist in the Queen's English. This aspect of their research is highly original and makes delightful reading. Their treatment of pronouns illustrates the point well. Barnes (1863: 20-23) and Elworthy (1877: 29-33) point out that "things" are divided into those that have a shape (countables) and those that do not (uncountables). The former take an indefinite article and can be referred to by the personal pronoun *he*. These two different noun classes also take different demonstratives. "Indefinite" (i.e. uncountable) nouns take *this/that*, while "definite" nouns take *thik/thease*. Thus, when one refers to a knife one might say "I don't like thease knife. He's too sharp", but when one refers to tea, one would say "I don't like this tea. It's too sweet."

As far as the personal pronoun is concerned, there is much evidence that its use is correctly described,[2] but I have not seen the demonstrative system tested against modern data. At the University of Helsinki we have a number of dialect stories from the nineteen-twenties in machine-readable form. The concordances that are available at the moment are too small to test the whole demonstrative system, but they do suggest that *thik* is used only with countables. Since this is the kind of thing that a dialect writer could not possibly dream up on his own, it seems plausible to assume that the pronouns *thik* and *that* had different distributions.

PARS PRO TOTO GENERALIZATIONS (ONE ENVIRONMENT REPRESENTING THE WHOLE DISTRIBUTION): NOMINATIVE OBJECTS

Since the early grammarians had no corpus to rely on, there was always the danger that the description was based on partial data. I would like to call an argument that is based on restricted data a pars pro toto argument. By this I mean that one characteristic environment comes to represent the whole distribution. It seems to me that this is precisely what happened with the so-called nominative objects. Nominative objects, that is objects like *he* in the sentence *You know he then?*, are commonly found in South-Western English.

According to Barnes (1863: 23), Elworthy (1877:36), and quite recently Wakelin (1977: 113), nominative objects only occur if the pronoun is emphatic, emphasis here meaning contrastive stress. Thus, Barnes describes the situation as follows: "When a pronoun in an objective case is emphatical, it is given in its nominative case: Gi'e the money to I, not HE."

However, the SED material and tape-recordings made in the seventies and early eighties suggest that nominative objects do not have to be stressed. In fact sentences like, *I had a firkin and I had he filled up twice a day* (J.Ch. T7)[3] are in no way exceptional. Therefore, if the early grammars are right there has been a change in the distribution of nominative objects. The stress constraint has been removed. Removal of a constraint is not of course an impossible development as such: Peter Trudgill (1986: 70-71) has recently suggested that this is precisely what has happened with periphrastic *do* in the south-west.

However, as far as nominative objects are concerned, dialect stories published in the Somerset Yearbook in the twenties show no signs of the stress constraint: nominative objects seem to occur in unstressed positions as well as in stressed positions.

In the light of the above it seems that Barnes and Elworthy simply got the distribution wrong. They noted one environment and overgeneralized on the basis of that. It is easy to see how this kind of misinterpretation could come about. Naturally, it is the exceptional, the highly marked forms that attract our attention if we have no systematic body of data to study. What it seems has happened here, then, is simply an error due to inattention.

CONFLICTING DESCRIPTIONS

Above we had examples where grammarians agreed about a description. In the case of the pronouns the treatments were almost identical. However, in some places descriptions of a specific point may differ considerably. Under these circumstances, we have two alternatives. We might conclude that the descriptions are good, but the dialects are different, or we might conclude that there is something wrong with the description or descriptions and no conclusions can be drawn about the structure of the dialects under discussion.

This kind of situation is illustrated by the various descriptions of the so-called free infinitive ending, as in *Ain't many can sheary now*. The different descriptions of this feature will be discussed in the following section.

CONFLICTING DESCRIPTIONS: THE INFINITIVE MARKER *EE* (ALSO SPELT *Y*)

Jennings seems to have been the first to point out that infinitives in the south-west end in *ee*, or the letter *y*, as he puts it:

> "Another peculiarity is that of attaching to many
> of the common verbs in the infinitive mode, as
> well as to some other parts of different conjugations
> the letter *y*. Thus it is very common to say *I
> can't sewy*; but never, I think without an auxiliary
> verb, or the infinitive *to*.
> (Jennings 1825: 6-7)

Barnes refines this, adding that only intransitive verbs take the *ee* ending:

> The truth is that in Dorset the verb takes *y* only
> when it is free, and never with an accusative case
> (i.e. one says *Can ye zewy?*, but not *Wull
> ye zewy up thease zeam?*). (Barnes 1863:25)

Elworthy's description differs from the above in that the
intransitive ending is not restricted to infinitives:

> "Our intransitive verbs have an inflection which
> is only just referred to in p. 51 of W. S. Gram.
> It is *us*, and it is quite peculiar to W. Som.,
> or if not, I have not seen it alluded to by other
> observers. (*They says how they workus to factory,
> Our Handy always barkus so long's any strangers
> be about.*) In all these cases the inflection
> distinctly conveys a continuance of action;
> and in certain districts it is a commoner form
> than the well-known periphrastic one, so fully
> illustrated in W. S. Grammar, pp. 50-79"
> (Elworthy 1886: xx-xxi).

That is, in addition to forms like *They do workee*, the affix,
written *u*, occurs in finite forms as well, as in *They workus*. For
Elworthy, then, the affix, which he calls an "inflection," marks
intransitive verbs in general rather than intransitive infinitives.

SED has some instances of the type *there ain't many can
sheary*; that is, the ending is attached to an infinitive.
However, there are no signs of the type *They workus* as described
by Elworthy. The dialect stories that I have looked at show no
sign of this kind of construction either. It would seem to me
that we should look at Elworthy's description with some
suspicion. On the other hand, one can deduce from Elworthy that
the verb system was rather unstable at the time, the *s* ending
being in the process of replacing the periphrastic form, which in

turn had replaced the *th* ending. But the truth is that there is
no independent evidence to support Elworthy's analysis and it is
possible that the *us* form, which Elworthy analyses as consisting
of the intransitive marker and the present tense marker, is
simply a variant of the present tense marker *s*. It may or may not
be possible to work this out on the basis of the dialect material
in Elworthy's works. The main probem is finding all the
evidence, as it is scattered in various places in his writings. I
shall come back to this problem later.

ALTERNATION EXPLAINED IN TERMS OF STYLE

So far we have been looking at alternation that can be explained
in terms of linguistic structure. Sometimes, early grammarians
explain alternation in terms of style. This is, for example, the
case with the alternation between the inflectional and the periphrastic genitive, as in the following sentences:

> Look at the veet o'n.
> Look at his veet.

Both Barnes and Elworthy explain this variation stylistically.
Barnes (1886: 19) claims that the periphrastic form is used in
derision. Elworthy takes the same line. The dialectal form is
less polite (1877: 13). When the problem of politeness does not
arise, Elworthy feels dialect speakers would prefer the
periphrastic genitive. They would say, *the belly of en* rather
than *his belly*.

    That there is stylistic variation in dialect seems quite
clear. My informants for example regard the dialectal form *ain't*
as more polite than the form *bent*. However, one feels that in the
case of the genitive some questions concerning the data have
remained unasked. The grammarians have admitted defeat too early,
so to speak. Consider the following Swedish sentences:

Han lagade sin bil. 'He fixed his (own) car.'
Han lagade hans bil. 'He fixed his (someone else's) car.'

In certain languages there are reflexive genitives and one feels that the various genitive forms found in south-western English should be looked at from this viewpoint. I have not been able to study this in detail, but it is beginning to seem that the periphrastic genitive is not used reflexively whereas the inflectional genitive is. This observation is based on tape-recorded material from the seventies and dialect stories from the twenties. Although the results so far are tentative one can at least say that the evidence does not contradict the assumption that the periphrastic genitive is not used reflexively. That is, sentences like *I can't remember the name of her* are possible but sentences like *Harry burnt the finger o'n* 'Harry burnt his finger' are not.

Elworthy's examples do not throw much light on this problem: there is only one instance of the periphrastic genitive in a larger context (*Thee'st swuat the finger oa'n* 'You have squeezed his finger'). It is true that this does not contradict the rule given above, but it is not really much to go by. Clearly, what is needed is independent supplementary evidence.

TESTING THE RELIABILITY OF THE EARLY EVIDENCE

The early dialect grammars themselves contain a great deal of information but their reliability should be tested somehow. One important test is internal consistency. Obviously, when a writer argues for a particular rule he illustrates his point by giving examples that support his claim. Thus if he feels that the third person pronoun *un* is realized as *um* after *f*, he is not likely to give examples that contradict this claim. However, since third person object pronouns also occur in a great many sentences that are used to illustrate some other points of grammar, these sentences could be used to check the reliability of the pronoun rule. The difficulty here is that it is almost impossible to

predict where information about a particular form might occur.
Thus, since every sentence has a verb, there is a lot of
information about verbs scattered all over these grammars. In
order to be able to do one's testing in a reasonable time,
therefore, the texts under investigation should be in machine
readable form. If they are in machine readable form, searching
for a specific pattern is a trivial task. One can easily generate
a concordance of the contexts where the feature being analysed
occurs, and determine from that whether or not there are reasons
for accepting a specific generalization.

In addition to the grammars themselves, there is a considerable amount of literary dialect available. For example, the
Somerset Yearbook abounds with dialect material written in the
early twentieth century. The only problem is the evaluation of
this material. However, it seems to me that fairly reliable
samples can be found by simply making sure that the writers are
accurate about those features that we are sure of. For example,
we know that the early authorities got the distribution of non-
personal *he* and periphrastic *do* right because their descriptions
are confirmed by present-day evidence. Frequent violations of the
syntax of the periphrastic form in some document should therefore
be indication enough that the writer is not entirely familiar
with the dialect he is trying to imitate. I have recently
analysed the use of *do* in a text from *The Somerset Yearbook* and
found the grammar of *do* that emerges from this text quite
accurate (W.M. Jones's story "Jarge Balsh goes to Lunnon" in *The
Somerset Yearbook* 1928). A combination of tests like this would
give one a reasonably good picture of the quality of the text in
general. However, this kind of checking is practicable only if it
can be done automatically. That is, if the texts are in machine
readable form.

CONCLUSION

In his *Word Book* Elworthy discusses a number of ongoing changes in the Somerset dialect. He concludes his discussion of these changes with the wish that his readers would carry on this line of research. The early works on south-western English are rich in suggestions as to what to study. My paper has only scratched the surface, but I hope it has given some kind of picture of the love, care and insight with which these writers treated their local dialect.

NOTES

1. For an interesting discussion of this aspect of Barnes's work, see Gachelin (1987).

2. For a discussion, see Ihalainen (1985).

3. The references are to my tape-recordings of Somerset speech from the 1970's and 1980's. The transcripts are being stored in computer memory and will be part of the University of Helsinki Corpus of Dialectal British English.

REFERENCES

Jennings, James. 1825. *Observations on Some of the Dialects in the West of England, Particulary Somersetshire.*
Barnes, William. 1863. *A Grammar and Glossary of the Dorset Dialect with the History, Outspreading and Bearings of South-Western English.* Berlin: Asher and Co.
---- 1886. *A Glossary of the Dorset Dialect, with a Grammar.* Dorchester: M. & E. Case, County Printers. (much as 1863)
Bonaparte, L.-L. 1975-6. "On The Dialects of Monmouthshire,

Herefordshire, Worcestershire, Gloucestershire, Berkshire, Oxfordshire, South Warwickshire, South Northamptonshire, Buckinghamshire, Hertfordshire, Middlesex, and Surrey, with a New Classification of the English Dialects." London and Strassburg: Trubner.

Elworthy, Thomas. 1875. *The Dialect of West Somerset*. (From the Transactions of the Philological Society for 1875-6, pp. 197-271, London: Trubner & Co.). Vaduz: Kraus Reprint Limited, 1965.

---- 1877. *An Outline of the Grammar of the Dialect of the West Somerset*. (From the Transactions of the Philological Society for 1877-9, pp. 143-257, London: Trubner & Co.). Vaduz: Kraus Reprint Limited, 1965.

---- 1886. *The West Somerset Word-Book: A Glossary of Dialectal and Archaic Words and Phrases Used in the West of Somerset and East Devon*. (London: Trubner & Co.). Vaduz: Kraus reprint Ltd., 1965.

Gachelin, Jean-Marc. 1987. "The Ultimate Purist." *English Today*, No 10, 34-36.

Hewett, Mary. 1892. *The Peasant Speech of Devon*.

The Somerset Year Book. 1927-28. London: Folk Press Limited.

Ihalainen, Ossi. 1980. "Relative Clauses in the Dialect of Somerset. *Neuphilologische Mitteilungen*, 81, 187-196.

---- 1985. "*He took the bottle and put 'n in his pocket*: the Object Pronoun *it* in Present-Day Somerset." Varieties of English Around the World, General Series, Volume 4, *Focus on England and Wales* ed. by Wolfgang Viereck, 153-161. Amsterdam: John Benjamins Publishing Company.

---- to appear a. "Towards a Grammar of the Somerset Dialect." To appear in *Neuphilologishe Mitteilungen*, 1987.

---- to appear b. *A Study of Folk Speech in Somerset*.

Jones, W.M. 1928. "Jarge Balsh Goes to Lunnon." *The Somerset Year Book*, 68-70. London: Folk Press Limited.

Orton, Harold and Martyn Wakelin. 1967-1968. *Survey of English Dialects* (B): *The Basic Material*. Leeds: E. J. Arnold.

Wakelin, Martyn. 1977. *English Dialects: An Introduction*. 2nd ed. London: Athlone Press.

THE TYPOLOGICAL STATUS OF
OLD ENGLISH WORD-FORMATION[1]

DIETER KASTOVSKY
University of Vienna

0. The historical development of English has usually been characterized as a typological change from a synthetic to an analytic language, which is a rather gross generalization[2]. More refined evaluations are rare, especially since typological investigations have not really been of general interest in the past twenty or thirty years, the work of Greenberg being the exception rather than the rule. It is only recently that interest in language typology has been renewed, and the following considerations, which will be limited to the area of morphology, are just a small contribution to this resurrected branch of linguistics. But even these first limited investigations already indicate that typological considerations of the kind outlined here might help explain quite a number of otherwise rather mysterious phenomena such as the all-but-complete loss of ablaut nouns in English in contrast to German, cf. Kastovsky (1987a).

1.1. Morphology is usually subdivided into word-formation or derivational morphology and inflectional morphology. The primary function of word-formation is the enrichment of the vocabulary by creating new lexical items on the basis of morphological material already present in the language.

Inflectional morphology, on the other hand, does not create new lexical items, at least not normally; if this does happen, it is usually due to the lexicalization/petrification of some individual inflectional form. Inflectional morphology derives the word-forms that represent lexical items in syntactic constructions, i.e. it converts abstract lexemes into words as syntactic units. Because of their different functions, word-formation and inflectional morphology are usually differentiated - correctly so, I think - although there is undeniably close interdependence between these two levels. And the degree of interdependence is a matter of language typology, in particular, morphological typology, in so far as the typological status of word-formation (viz. whether it is root-based, stem-based, or word-based), is largely dependent on the kind of inflectional system characterizing the language in question. Changes in the latter will invariably lead to changes in the former. The most important factors in this regard are the relationship between the categories lexeme, word-form, word, stem, root, base form, and citation form, and the question of which of them are required for a description of the overall morphological system.

1.2. This relationship suggests a brief terminological clarification, although I will mainly use the terms in question as they are defined in Lyons (1977: 18ff.) and Matthews (1974: 20ff.), cf. also Kastovsky (1982: 70-76). The term "lexeme" refers to a lexical item in the sense of "dictionary entry", the dictionary being understood here as a component of a grammatical model. Lexemes are thus abstract lexical units, actualized in concrete syntactic contexts by "word-forms" (= inflectional forms). A lexeme may only have one word-form, e.g. Modern English $butter_N$, or it may involve a whole paradigm of word-forms, e.g. Old English *bindan*.

A "word" is an independent, meaningful syntactic element, susceptible of transposition in sentences (cf. Marchand 1969: 1); it may be simple or complex, and is thus the concrete realization of a word-form in an utterance. From this point of view, the term "word-formation" is a misnomer and strictly ought to be replaced by the term "lexeme-formation". In languages like Modern English, lexemes tend to be coextensive with words, because the citation forms and base forms are forms without inflectional endings and can occur as words in utterances. It is only in such languages that word-formation is basically equivalent to lexeme formation[3]. However, I will retain the term "word-formation", because it is the established term, even if it is sometimes not totally appropriate.

A "base form" is that form representing a lexeme from which all other word-forms can be derived by appropriate morphophonemic and/or morphological rules. Sometimes only one base form is necessary, e.g. for Modern English regular nouns and verbs; sometimes one has to specify several "principal parts", as in Old English *bringan - brōhte*, or Latin *ferro - tuli - latus*, i.e. in cases of partial or total suppletion.

The "citation form" is that form in which the lexeme is referred to in the dictionary and in metalinguistic usage. This form may coincide with the base-form, and thus may not be characterized by any inflectional ending, as in Modern English; in this case, the lexeme as such has word status. In other languages, such as Old English, the citation form is itself an inflected word-form, e.g. the infinitive.

A "stem" is a word-class-specific lexeme representation stripped of inflectional endings, but it may contain stem-formatives or genuine derivational affixes.

A "root", finally, is the element that is left over when all derivational, stem-forming and inflectional elements are stripped away. Such roots can either be affiliated to a particular word-class, or they may be word-class neutral, the word-class affiliation being added by a word-formative process.

1.3. Table (1) contains examples of these categories from both Modern English and Old English. The interpretation of any form clearly presupposes a corresponding overall morphological analysis, and interpretations may vary considerably in accordance with the degree of abstractness that is allowed or required for underlying morphophonemic representations.

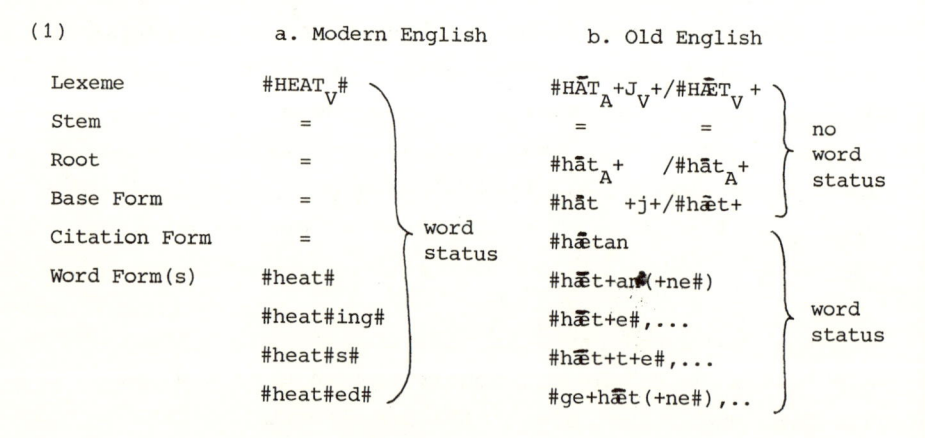

(1)

	a. Modern English	b. Old English	
Lexeme	#HEAT$_V$#	#HĀT$_A$+J$_V$+/#HǢT$_V$+	no word status
Stem	=	= =	
Root	=	#hāt$_A$+ /#hāt$_A$+	
Base Form	=	#hāt +j+/#hæt+	
Citation Form	=	#hǣtan	word status
Word Form(s)	#heat#	#hǣt+an(+ne#)	
	#heat#ing#	#hǣt+e#,...	word status
	#heat#s#	#hǣt+t+e#,...	
	#heat#ed#	#ge+hǣt(+ne#),..	

{a. Modern English bracket: word status}

In Modern English, all the categories involved have word-status. In Old English, only the actual word-forms have word-status, while lexeme, stem and base form do not, at least not with verbs (see 2.3.1. below). The analysis of the Old English forms depends, as has already been pointed out, on the degree of abstractness allowed. If *i*-mutation is still regarded as a living morphophonemic process, then we might just as well postulate an underlying stem formative *-j-* also acting as a derivational morpheme, which produces *i*-mutation (as well as consonant lengthening under the appropriate conditions). If not, the alternation *hāt* ~ *hǣtan* will have to be considered to be purely morphologically conditioned, as in Modern High German *rot* ~ *röten*. The decision will, however, have to be based on an overall analysis of the Old English morphological/morphophonemic system including derivational morphology, and the latter has usually not been sufficiently taken into consideration so far.

1.4. The typological status of word-formation now depends on the kind of input to (and output of) the word-formation rules, i.e. whether the input is a word, a stem, or a root. As mentioned above, in Modern English the input is typically a word-like unit, i.e. word-formation is word-based, except for the formations involving combining forms. Cases such as *de-sist*, *con-sist*, *re-sist*, *de-ceive*, *con-ceive*, *re-ceive*, have nothing to do with word-formation as it is defined here; the pseudo-constituents do not have word-status, nor do they have any identifiable meaning, as would be the case in real word-formation syntagmas. For Old English, on the other hand, no such generalization is possible; word-formation here is typologically heterogeneous. More precisely, Old English is obviously a linguistic system in transition.

2.1.1. Before I turn to the analysis of the Old English system, it must be stressed once again that any overall morphological characterization is basically model-dependent.

A simple example will illustrate this. The noun *cyme* 'coming' derived from the root or stem of the verb *cuman*[4], is, historically speaking, an *i*-stem with the following paradigm:

```
(2)              Sg              Pl

    NA           cyme            cyme/cymas
    G            cymes           cyma/cymigea
    D            cyme            cymum
```

This allows three possible analyses, viz.

```
(3) a.  kum+i+-ǰ     =   root + stem formative + case/number
    b.  kym+e        =   stem + case/number
    c.  kyme+        =   stem + case/number
```

In (3a), *i*-mutation is treated as a living morphophonemic process triggered by an appropriate underlying segment (in this case +*i*+), which eventually surfaces as -*e*/ə/. This segment may be regarded as a stem-formative, but it might at the same time be invested with derivative force, i.e. it might be interpreted as a derivative morpheme. The NA Sg. in this case, as with the original *a*-stems, has no case/number-exponent and may or may not be regarded as an unmarked (uninflected) base/citation form. Such an analysis is probably justified for the Early Old English period.

In (3b), *i*-mutation is considered as a purely morphologically conditioned alternation, i.e. umlaut vowels are treated as underlying segments, and the final -*e* in the NA Sg. is interpreted as the case/number exponent (Nominative Singular). Under this analysis, the Old English *i*-stems differ from the *a*-stems in that the former would have an overt NA Sg. exponent, which is absent with the latter, cf. (4):

(4)   Sg   Pl
NA   #cyning#   #cyning+as#
G   #cyning+es#   #cyning+a#
D   #cyning+e#   #cyning+um#

This analysis probably represents a transitional stage before analysis (3c) is fully generalized.

In (3c), finally, umlaut is also no longer triggered by an underlying segment, and final -e in the NA Sg. is treated as stem-final. Here the original reflex of the stem formative is interpreted as having merged with the stem, and is deleted before an inflectional ending beginning with a vowel. This analysis, which is probably justified for Late Old English, is certainly due to analogy with a pattern such as (4), where the NA Sg. is unmarked, a situation which generally became characteristic for masculine and neuter nouns. In actual fact, analyses (3b) and (3c) were probably not really successive stages, but rivalling segmentations after an analysis along the lines of (3a) was no longer possible, with (3c) eventually winning out[6].

2.1.2. Each of these analyses has certain consequences for the overall structure of derivational and inflectional morphology. An analysis along the lines of (3a) provides us with a derivational suffix, which is absent in (3b,c). In the latter analyses, the derivatives will have to be regarded as instances of conversion or zero-derivation, depending on one's stand in this somewhat controversial matter. Notice, incidentally, that similar considerations also play a role in the analysis of denominal verbs, cf.

(5) a. $hāt_A + j_V + an$: $+j+$ = derivational affix
    b. $\begin{Bmatrix} h\bar{æ}t + \emptyset_V + an \\ h\tilde{ā}t_A \end{Bmatrix}$: no derivational affix, or $\emptyset_V$ as derivational affix

Furthermore, analysis (3b) treats the noun as a case of stem-inflection, since the stem *cym+* is a bound form, i.e. does not have word status. But analyses (3a,c), where *-e* is stem-final, and the NA Sg. has no exponent, allow an interpretation as word-inflection, just as in Modern English. The stem *cyme* has word-status, and acts as both base form and citation form.

The fact that several such analyses are plausible indicates that the Old English morphological system is unstable and already in a state of restructuring.

2.1.3. In the following, no definite stand will be taken in this matter, since this would presuppose a general reappraisal of the available analyses in the light of the typological consequences discussed above. Moreover, for the abstractness problem and the status of *i*-mutation and other morphophonemic alternations such as consonant lengthening (gemination) etc., no general solution covering the whole Old English period is possible. Rather, we will have to assume a good deal of restructuring throughout the whole period, with many morphophonemic alternations becoming progressively opaque. Thus, the individual analyses presented below might be subject to some reinterpretation, but this will not change the overall picture that will emerge.

2.2.1. The first observation that can be made now with regard to derivation is that the three major word classes, i.e. nouns, adjectives, and verbs, do not show the same typological behaviour. Rather, nouns and adjectives are more progressive than verbs, and within the nouns, the various declension classes provide an additional differentiation.

THE TYPOLOGICAL STATUS OF OLD ENGLISH WORD FORMATION   213

As (4) has already demonstrated, the original masculine and neuter a-stems, and, depending on the analysis, also the i-stems, have developed an unmarked base form, viz. the NA Sg., which does not contain any overt case/number ending[7]. Derivatives such as

(6) hōc   'hook'   : hōc+ede   'hooked'
    trēow   'tree'   : trēow+en   'wooden'
    þorn   'thorn'   : þorn+ig   'thorny'
    bēam   'ray'   : bēam+ian   'to shine'
    cist   'coffin' : cist+ian   'to put in a coffin'
    fers   'verse'   : fers+ian   'to make verse'

are thus word-based: *hōc, trēow, þorn, bēam, cist, fers* are unmarked base forms, i.e. lexemes having word-status without the addition of an inflectional morpheme, to which the derivational suffix is added.

A similar analysis holds true for all deadjectival derivatives, since the masc. NA Sg. of the definite declension does not have an inflectional ending and can therefore also be regarded as an unmarked base form; the same form also acts as citation form, cf.

(7) ādlig   'sick'   : ādlig+ian   'to be sick'
    behȳdig   'careful' : behȳdig+ness 'care', etc.

2.2.2. Other noun classes, e.g. feminines like *talu* and the whole category of weak or consonantal nouns, however, manifest stem-inflection, i.e. the inflectional endings are added to a stem that does not have word-status without them, cf.

(8)a. tal+u, +e, +a, +um
   b. ġum+a, +an, +ena, +um

Consequently, derivatives from such lexical items are stem-based, cf.

(9) luf (+u)   'love'   : luf+sum 'lovable', luf+ian 'to love'
     angrisl (+a)   'terror' : angrisl+īc 'terrible'[8]
     eorþ (+e)   'earth'   : eorþ+en/eorþ+līc 'earthen'
     lag (+u/+a)   'law'   : lag+ian 'to make a law'

According to Quirk/Wrenn (1957: 20), masculine and neuter *a*-stem nouns are, quantitatively, the dominant inflectional pattern. If we add adjectives, we can safely conclude that denominal (including deadjectival) derivation in Old English is already predominantly word-based, and only in a minority of cases stem-based. The same is true, of course, for inflectional morphology.

2.3.1. Deverbal derivation, however, differs in many respects from denominal derivation. First of all, verbs exhibit a full set of inflectional endings, and there is no unmarked base or citation form. Consequently, verbs are characterized by stem inflection, and deverbal derivation would seem to be stem-based, too, cf.

(10) feorm (+ian) 'to entertain' : feorm+end,
      feorm+ere 'entertainer', feorm+ung 'entertainment'

For weak verbs, such an analysis is generally quite straightforward. But complications arise with derivatives from strong verbs. Strong verbs are characterized by ablaut alternations with a variety of origins. At least some of them were originally partly phonologically conditioned, e.g. by stress and pitch variation, although these in turn might have been tied up with some morphological factors. These ablaut alternations were to some extent reinterpreted as tense markers in the Germanic languages, although this morphologization has only partly become really functional. Thus we have overdifferentiation in some classes, i.e. different root vowels in the 1., 3.sg.pret. and 2.sg. and pl.pret. forms (cf. class V æt — ǣton), a distinction which is plainly nonfunctional.

And we have underdifferentiation, i.e. identical root vowels for different categories, e.g. preterite and 2nd participle in *writon - gewriten*, or present and 2nd participle in *bacan - gebacen*.

2.3.2. There have been several attempts to describe Old English ablaut alternations on the basis of phonological rules, albeit with partial morphological conditioning, and not just as a case of morphologically conditioned stem-allomorphy. The extent to which such an approach is really feasible is a difficult matter and will again depend on the degree of abstractness that one allows. Moreover, all the attempts that I am aware of have basically restricted themselves to verbal inflection and have not included deverbal derivation, where, as we shall see, ablaut also figures prominently. Before I turn to these latter instances, at least one such abstract analysis should be mentioned, viz. Lass/Anderson (1975), and this for a special reason. Lass/Anderson (1975: 25ff.) assume that the root of ablaut verbs contains an unspecified vowel, and that all stems, the infinitive/present stem included, are derived from this root by phonological rules. More precisely, the infinitive/present-stem does not hold a privileged place as it does with the weak verbs, where it acts as a quasi-base for the remaining paradigm. This analysis is quite interesting for its consequences for morphology, both from a synchronic and a diachronic point of view, although no morphological interpretation is offered by the authors themselves. If ablaut is treated as a morphological exponent of tense, and if roots are, as suggested above, lexical elements that remain when all derivational, stem-forming and inflectional elements are stripped away, then strong verbs are a clear case of root inflection. And Lass/Anderson's analysis involving an unspecified root vowel, although arrived at on purely phonological considerations, would seem to corroborate this assumption.

There is further corroboration from another point of view. The Germanic tense system, where the infinitive/present stem acts as a kind of unmarked base form (= non-past) and thus has a privileged position, evolved from a verb system that was aspect-, and not tense-oriented. We might now assume that each aspect had equal status, at least originally, so that it would not really make sense to derive one form from another. Rather, derivation from a common, minimally specified root would seem to be a much more plausible interpretation. These considerations together with the fact that at least some of the ablaut grades were originally partly phonologically conditioned make Lass/Anderson's unspecified vowel analysis a likely candidate for the (Early) Germanic situation. But this situation was not stable for two reasons: emergence of weak verbs and reorientation towards a tense system, where a marked form (past) contrasts with an unmarked form (non-past) which clearly holds a privileged position as base form. The emergence of weak verbs introduces stem inflection into the verbal system, since they are all characterized by stem formatives in contradistinction to most strong verbs (exceptions are -*j*-presents such as *licgan*, *hebban*, *sittan*, etc.). And eventually the existence of a verb class with stem inflection and a contrast between marked and unmarked base form must have also led to a reinterpretation of the strong verbs, where the infinitive/present stem attained a privileged position as a morphological base form, too. This reinterpretation at the same time obscures the status of root inflection and leads to a reinterpretation as stem-inflection.

Derivation from strong verbs seem to corroborate this hypothetical typological development and at the same time introduces a third type of derivation, viz. root-based derivation.

2.3.3. A cursory glance at the Old English vocabulary shows that strong verbs - or rather their roots - had been the starting point for numerous derivational patterns resulting in nouns, adjectives and verbs. Derivation is made from practically all stem forms or ablaut grades without any systematic correlation between ablaut grade, inflectional class and semantic category (action noun, agent noun, object noun) in Old English. There are certain preferences - agent noun and reduced grade, masc. action noun and full grade, etc., but they are not absolute, cf. the following examples:

(11) a. Inf.: *drepe, drinc, steorfa, sceaþa, faru, giefu, feohte, geberst, feoht, rīp*
 b. Pret.sg.: *drenc, sang, stalu, bād, grāp*
 c. Pret.pl.(lengthened grade): *ǣt, sǣta, sprǣc, gewǣge*
 d. Past part.(reduced grade): *frore, bite, cyrf, fuora, sopa, bedu, geswicu, bed, broc, flit, glida*

This holds also true for suffixal derivatives and deverbal adjectives:

(12) *fricgan* 'to ask', *frig(e)ness* 'interrogation', 'question', *gefricgan* 'to learn, find out by inquiry', *unfricgende* 'unquestioning'
 gefrǣge 'hearsay, knowledge', *gefrǣge* adj. 'well-known, celebrated, notorious',
 ungefrǣge(lic) 'unheard of, unusual, inconceivable',
 frægning 'questioning', *fregen* 'question'
 fregensyllic 'very strange'
 fregnung 'questioning', *(ge-)frignan* 'ask, inquire, learn by inquiry',
 frignung 'question', *friht* 'divination', *frihtere* 'diviner, soothsayer',
 frihtrung 'soothsaying, divination'

Examples of this kind introduce a tremendous amount of morphophonemic variation into inflectional and derivational patterns, which was increased by the effects of *i*-mutation, West Germanic consonant lengthening and the later lengthening and shortening processes. Thus, Old English is characterized in large parts of its vocabulary by a rather striking morphophonemic variability of its roots - basically inherited from Indo-European, and subsequently augmented by further phonological changes. But most of this morphophonemic variation was non-functional. The only attempt to functionalize it had been made in connection with the tense-characterization of strong verbs, where it had only been partially successful, because of the under- and overdifferentiation mentioned above.

2.3.4. While ablaut was functionalized up to a point in the inflectional system of the verb, no such functionalization can be postulated for derivation, i.e. ablaut certainly did not function as a derivative element comparable to the vowels in Semitic languages. Ablaut merely provides several root variants as the starting point for further derivation. Being non-functional, it was of course in a position of jeopardy, but nevertheless this non-functional variation at some period must have been so prominent that it was even extended to weak verbs, viz. in connection with the suffix *-ness*, which forms deverbal abstract nouns. This suffix derives from the infinitive stem as well as from the past participle and the present participle stem - sometimes even with one and the same verb. But no semantic difference seems to accompany this variation; and whether it reflects a dialectal difference is not quite clear, although one is commonly assumed[9]. All the following examples denote simple action nouns.

(13) a. Inf.: *brecness* 'breach', *ymbceorfness* 'circumcision' *blinness* 'cessation', *ambehtness* 'service', *andetness* 'confession'

b. 2nd part.: *gecoreness* 'election', *wiþcwedenness* 'contradiction', *ūpārisenness* 'resurrection', *ācwelledness/ācwealdness* 'killing', *gedreccedness/gedrehtness* 'affliction', *cirredness* 'turning'

c. pres.part.: *āblinnendness* 'cessation', *āstandendness* 'continuance'

d. doublets: *tōcnāwness/tōcnāwenness* 'knowledge, understanding' *onginness/onginnenness* 'undertaking' *dǣlnimeness/dǣlnimendness* 'participation' *gecīgness/gecīgedness* 'call, summons' *gedrēfness/gedrēfedness* 'disturbance' *lēorness/lēorendness/lēoredness* 'departure, passing away', *ālīsness/ālīsendness/ālīsedness* 'redemption'

As the examples demonstrate, participles of weak verbs are used as derivative bases, but without any trace of participial meaning, in the same way as ablaut grades do not influence the meaning of their derivatives. But *-ness* is a fairly recent acquisition among the nominal suffixes, and therefore at the time of its establishment this kind of stem variability must have still been a living principle in the language.

2.3.5. How do we best interpret this kind of variability? I have suggested interpreting the original situation as a case of root-inflection, which would match Lass/Anderson's phonological analysis involving an unspecified root vowel. The same would seem to hold for derivation: with derivatives from strong verbs, we originally had a case of root derivation, still recognizable as such in Old English. Whether the type of ablaut vowel had originally characterized a particular derivational pattern (as was probably the case to some extent) is no longer relevant; this correlation if it did exist, must have broken down in the Pre-Germanic

period. For the Germanic period, and also for the individual
Germanic languages, the most likely interpretation is that
there was a root with a variable vowel, where the variability was strongly constrained by the existence of certain
morphophonemic patterns. Derivation was made from this root
by supplying one of the morphophonemically possible vowels
and adding a stem-formative, which can also be regarded as
a derivative morpheme, thus converting the root into a stem,
to which the inflectional endings were added. Such an analysis actually follows automatically from the definition of
"root" in 1.2. If the vowel is treated as a tense/aspect
exponent, it has to be "stripped away", and we are left with
an "unspecified vowel", i.e. a root, not a stem. Whether
these roots were word-class specific items or not, is difficult to decide; in the Germanic period they probably were,
but this does not really matter for our purposes here.

2.3.6. So we have three types of derivational pattern
in Old English: root-based, stem-based and word-based. The
root-based pattern, restricted to derivatives from strong
verbs, is the oldest, and is probably no longer productive.
The loss of productivity is perhaps due to the emergence of
stem-based derivation as a consequence of the appearance of
the weak verbs, possibly in conjunction with the functionalization of the ablaut as a tense marker. The introduction
of the weak verbs and the new past - non-past tense system
provided a privileged base form, the infinitive/present stem.
This must have eventually led to a reanalysis of the strong
verbs as well, where the infinitive/present stem is reinterpreted as the basis of the paradigm. Whether this reinterpretation was extended to the derivatives or not, is beside
the point, since the patterns were no longer productive.
Productive derivation was made from the infinitive - except

in the case of -*ness*, where participles also acted as bases. And in this case, derivation was stem-based, and stem-based derivation was probably the "system-defining structural property" in the sense of Wurzel (1984). But alongside stem-based derivation, we already find a good deal of word-based derivation as well. And it is this type that will eventually win out in Middle English, as a consequence of the progressive loss of inflectional endings and the establishment of an unmarked base form in all three major word-classes. But it is obvious that the typological reorientation of morphology generally postulated for Middle English is already well under way in Old English, i.e. these restructurings begin much earlier than is generally assumed.

NOTES

1. I should like to thank the participants, in particular Angelika Lutz (Munich), Donka Minkova (Los Angeles) and Roger Lass (Cape Town) for their helpful comments. I am also grateful to Ardith J. Meier (Vienna) for her help with the manuscript.
2. From a purely morphological point of view, and if we restrict ourselves to noun inflection, the change might actually be interpreted as going from a synthetic to an agglutinative type, cf. *child-ren*, (Pl)-*s*(Gen), *ox-en*(Pl)-*s*(Gen), etc., and Kastovsky (1985).
3. Cf. also Aronoff's statement: "All regular word-formation processes are word-based. A new word is formed by applying a regular rule to a single already existing word" (Aronoff 1976: 21). This is basically correct, if one disregards so-called combining forms such as those present in *astrology*, *astronomy*, *astro-botany*, *cosmology*, *cosmography*, *cosmonaut*, *cosmo-dog*, etc., which require special treatment. They in fact represent loan patterns preserving the typological characteristics of their source languages, where "word-formation" was stem/root-based.
4. For this indeterminacy, see 2.3.5.f. below.
5. I have not added slashes or double slashes here as marking the level of representation, because that would add another variable. For our purpose, only the morphological segmentation is relevant.
6. The same kind of reinterpretation is also suggested in Keyser - O'Neill (1985a: Ch.3; 1985b: 94ff., 101f.), which I had not seen at the time when I wrote this paper. I am grateful to an anonymous reviewer for bringing this parallel analysis to my attention, and also for a number of other helpful suggestions.

7. Such an analysis of course presupposes that each paradigm is treated separately, so that the analysis of *tal + u (+ u* = N Sg.), *gum + a (+ a* = N Sg.) does not force us to analyse *cyning* as *cyning + ∅* with a zero allomorph of N Sg. If we do not make this proviso, we will have to litter our inflectional paradigms with zeros that do not really have any explanatory function.
8. From *angrisl + līc* with automatic degemination, a feature *-ly* has partly preserved even in Modern English, cf. *singly, fully, cruelly* vs. *solely, coolly*, etc. (Kastovsky 1987b).
9. This was also pointed out by Angelika Lutz in the discussion, but seems to require a new analysis, with the help of the Old English Concordance, before we can definitely attribute this variation to dialectal differences. But even if we have a case of dialect variation, there still remains the problem that the difference of deriving base (infinitive stem, past participle, present participle) does not seem to be accompanied by a corresponding semantic difference, e.g. 'action' vs. 'result or state' across the dialects.

REFERENCES

Aronoff, M. 1979. *Word-formation in Generative Grammar*. Linguistic Inquiry Monographs 1. Cambridge, Mass., London: MIT Press.

Kastovsky, D. 1982. *Wortbildung und Semantik*. Studienreihe Englisch 14. Tübingen: Francke.

───── 1985. 'Typological Changes in the Nominal Inflectional System of English and German' *Studia Gramatyczne* 7, 97-117.

───── 1987a. "What Happened to the Old English Ablaut Nouns and Why Didn't it Happen to the German Ones?" Paper read at the Eighth International Conference on Historical Linguistics, Lille, 1987.

───── 1987b. 'Boundaries in English and German Morphology'. In W. Lörscher and R. Schulze, eds. *Perspectives on Language Performance. Studies in Linguistics, Literary Criticism and Foreign Language Teaching Methodology. In Honour of Werner Hüllen on the Occasion of His Sixtieth Birthday*, 159-170. Tübingen: Narr.

Keyser, S.J. and W. O'Neil. 1985a. *Rule Generalization and Optionality in Language Change*. Dordrecht, Holland: Foris Publications.

───── 1985b. 'The Simplification of the Old English Strong Nominal Paradigms'. In R. Eaton et al., eds. *Papers from the 4th International Conference on English Historical Linguistics*. Current Issues in Linguistic Theory 41, 85-107. Amsterdam: John Benjamins.

Lass, R. and J. Anderson. 1975. *Old English Phonology*. Cambridge Studies in Linguistics 14. Cambridge.

Lyons, J. 1977. *Semantics*. 2 vols. Cambridge: Cambridge University Press.

Marchand, H. 1969. *The Categories and Types of Present-Day English Word-Formation*. 2nd rev.ed. Munich: Beck.

Matthews, P.H. 1974. *Morphology. An introduction to the Theory of Word-Structure*. Cambridge: Cambridge University Press.

Quirk, R. and C.L. Wrenn. 1957. *An Old English Grammar*. 2nd ed. London: Methuen.

Wurzel, W. 1984. *Flexionsmorphologie und Natürlichkeit. Ein Beitrag zur morphologischen Theoriebildung.* Studia grammatica 21. Berlin: Akademie-Verlag.

THE DOUBLE OBJECT CONSTRUCTION IN OLD ENGLISH

WILLEM F. KOOPMAN
University of Amsterdam

0. *Introduction.** Old English has many verbs that take two objects. I will restrict myself to three-place verbs taking an accusative and a dative object (traditionally the direct and indirect object). The order in which these objects appear shows great variety. I will argue that it is not easy to account for the variation if we assume that Old English had one underlying order from which the surface word order patterns were derived in various ways (Extraposition, NP Movement, V-Second rule, etc.). Assuming that there was no fixed order in Old English makes it possible to account for the various patterns quite naturally. I will use Government-Binding theory as a theoretical framework.[1]

1. *One base order.* Let us first of all investigate how the word order patterns can be accounted for if there is one underlying order (taking Old English as a configurational language). With others (Canale 1978, van Kemenade 1984a, Fischer/ van der Leek 1983) I will assume that the base order is SOV. This is exemplified in (1):

(1) GD 1(C)9.62.7 ær ðon þe he Gode (DAT) þone lofsang (ACC)
         before   he God   the psalm   said
     asægde[2] 'before he said the psalm to God'

In main clauses there is a V-Second rule (I will not go
into the details here) which accounts for the position of
the verb in (2):

(2) ÆCHom i.30.452.17 ða bead se biscop þam ceastergewarum (DAT)
              then offered the bishop the citizens
              heora sceattas (ACC)
              their treasures
    'then the biscop offered the citizens their treasures'

There is also Extraposition in Old English, for instance of
clauses, NP's and PP's. In (3) the accusative object has
been extraposed, and in (4) the dative object:

(3) HomS21(BlHom 6)139 þæt we urum Drihtne (DAT) bringaþ godra
                      that we our Lord   bring   of good
         weorca swetne stenc (ACC)
         works the sweet smell
        'that we bring our Lord of good works the sweet smell'
(4) HomU26(Nap 29)49 þæt we ure gyltas (ACC) andetton anum
                    that we our sins   confess   one
         men (DAT) her on life
         man here on earth'
        'that we confess our sins to one man here on earth'

If we assume that the V-Second rule only applies in main
clauses and that in subordinate clauses movement of V to
COMP is impossible because the COMP is lexicalized, thus
leaving the V in its base position (see den Besten (1983)),
then we have to assume extraposition of accusative and
dative object in (5) and (6):

(5) HomS35(Trist 4)150 þæt he andette his scrifte (DAT) ealle
                       that he confesses his confessor all
    his synna (ACC)
    his sins
    'that he confesses all his sins to his confessor'
(6) HomS11.1(Belf 5)84 forþan ðe Drihten behæt þone heofenlice
                      'because God promised the heavenly
    beah (ACC) þam wacigendum (DAT)
    crown   to those who keep watch'

The order of the objects in (5) and (6) is different. We
could explain this by assuming that in (5) the dative

object has been extraposed first and in (6) the accusative object. The V-Second rule in main clauses ought to ensure that (nominal) objects always follow the verb. On the whole this is true, but there are sporadic exceptions, such as in (7) and (8):

(7) ÆCHom i.31.460.8   se apostol þa þam cinge (DAT) bodade
                       the apotle than the king preached
    ealne Cristendom and middaneardes alysednysse (ACC)
    all Christianity and world's redemption
    'then the apostle preached the redemption of all Christianity and the world to the king'

(8) LawPromRegis 1   Ic þreo þing (ACC) behate Cristenum folce
                     I three things promise Christian people
    7 me underðeoddum (DAT)
    and my subjects
    'I promise three things to Christian people and my subjects'

We cannot claim a V-Second rule for (7) and (8) despite the fact that they are main clauses, because the verb is preceded by one of the objects and is not in COMP. The best way is to treat them as main clauses where V-Second fails, which happens occasionally in Old English (see also Mitchell (1985: § 3914)):

(9) Or 1.10.44.22   Hi þa þæt lond forleton
                    they then that country left
    'they then left that country'

Failure of V-Second will have to be explained separately. In (7), then, the accusative object has been extraposed, and in (8) the dative object, while the verb remains in its base position.

1.1. So far I have mainly given examples with the order dative object - accusative object. And if we always found this order, then the construction would be substantially the same as for instance in Modern Dutch, and we could try one of the analyses proposed to account for the word order distribution and case assignment (see Kerstens

(1985) and Berendsen (1983)). However, a glance at the Old English material reveals sentences such as (10):

(10) HomS16(Ass 12)8 þæt he his synna (ACC) Gode (DAT) andette
that he his sins God confesses
'that he confesses his sins to God'

The same order is found in main clauses (with V-Second):

(11) Or 3.9.126.7 þa bead Darius healf his rice (ACC)
then offered Darius half his kingdom
Alexandre (DAT)
Alexander
'then Darius offered half his kingdom to Alexander'

Is there a way to determine which order (DAT ACC or ACC-DAT) is the base order? It appears far from simple to find an answer. There are hardly any reliable statistics to go on. Either no detailed information is given about the construction (Barrett 1953, Gardner 1971, Kohonen 1978) or no distinction is made between nominal and pronominal objects (Carlton 1970), a distinction which is in fact relevant for Old English (see van Kemenade (1984a), Mitchell (1985: § 3907)). Even when nominal and pronominal objects are distinguished, the statistics also include clauses where one of the objects is extraposed (Brown 1970), which tells us nothing about the underlying order. Alternatively, the actual numbers are too small to base any conclusions on (Shannon 1964, Shores 1971).

1.2. So I have tried to supply the relevant statistics myself. I have looked at a sample of the verbs with two objects.[3] Unequivocal information about the base order is provided by main clauses with V-Second (only the verb is moved from its base position) and by subordinate clauses with both objects preceding the verb in its base position (final) (no possibility of extraposition of one of the objects). It is also important to exclude all cases with pronominal objects because the different syntactic behaviour of pronominal objects obscures the base order. My findings are given in (12):

(12) both objects nominal

	V-DAT-ACC	V-ACC-DAT
main clause	43	48
	DAT-ACC-V	ACC-DAT-V
subordinate clause	20	21

It must be noted that the numbers involved are rather small and that there is no significant preference for either of the orders on the basis of my material.[4] I can only conclude that there does not seem to be a good basis for choosing one of the orders as the base order.[5]

1.3. Because a configurational approach requires a base order I will choose the DAT-ACC order (perhaps influenced by the later order in English). The choice, though, is arbitrary and the following discussion would not be substantially changed (apart from the examples) if the order ACC-DAT had been chosen as base order.

If the base order is DAT-ACC-V, how can we derive the other order (ACC-DAT-V) from it? We could say that Scrambling accounts for it. I take Scrambling to be a local rule. After its application the two objects should be next to each other. Quite clearly this is not the case, see (13), (14), and (15):

(13) ÆLet 6(Wulfgeat) 304 Boda þu godes word (ACC) bealdlice
              preach you God's words boldly
      mannum (DAT)
      men
      'preach God's words boldly to men'

(14) ÆCHom ii.39.1.288.22 He æteowode ða soðan life(ACC)
　　　　　　　　　　　　　　he showed the true life
　　symle his geferum (DAT)
　　always his companions
　　'he showed his companions always the true life'
(15) ÆChom ii.8.68.51 forðan ðe he ða liflican bodunge (ACC)
　　　　　　　　　　　　because he the living message
　　on his andwerdnysse hæðenum leodum (DAT) bedigelode
　　'because while present he concealed the living message
　　from heathen nations'

Scrambling does not provide the right answer, unless we assume that it is not a local rule and that it can affect non-adjacent nodes. But then it loses much of its explanatory power.

What other possibilities are there? Is there VP internal topicalization as has been suggested for German? (see Thiersch (1982)). The only possible position for such a Topic is at the beginning of VP. If the Topic were immediately to the left of V, NP movement would lead to a trace governing the NP, and thus to an ungrammatical sentence. In (16) I have given a possible structure for the VP internal Topic position:

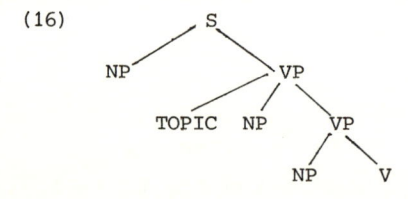

(16)
```
          S
       /    \
      NP     VP
           /  |  \
        TOPIC NP  VP
                 /  \
                NP   V
```

In Old English there is a Topic position in main clauses and there is some reason to assume that subordinate clauses also have a Topic position (Allen 1980), see (17) and (18):

(17) ÆCHom ii.25.206.25 forðan ðe on ðam dæge astah se hælend
because on that day ascended the Saviour
æfter his æriste up to his heofonlican fæder
after his resurrection to his heavenly father
'because on that day the Saviour ascended to his father after his resurrection'

(18) HomS10(BlHom 3)196 Hwæt we gehyrdon þæt Gode bið þæt
Lo, we heard that to God   is
fæsten swyþe gecweme
fasting very pleasing
'Lo, we heard that fasting is very pleasing to God'

Thus, with a VP Topic, there would be a Topic position on three different levels, and it would be preferable if we could derive them from one principle, though it is not clear to me how this could be done.

The VP Topic position looks odd, though. There are examples where the topicalized NP is clearly not the first item in the VP:

(19) Conf 3.1.1.(Raith Y)2.5 þæt man for swylcum men mæssan
that people for such a man mass
singe oððe mid ænigum sealmsange þæt lic (ACC) eorðan (DAT)
sing or with any psalmsinging the body   earth
befæste
entrust
'that people sing mass for such a man or entrust the body to the earth with any psalmsinging'

Should we say that the PP and the accusative object are both in Topic position? That would involve claiming that all VP initial elements occupy Topic position and (for the accusative object to be included) it sometimes has two elements in it. As far as I am aware there is no independent motivation for this Topic position, and it only seems to be needed for double object constructions. So, I am not convinced that a VP Topic position can be motivated. Within a configurational approach there does not seem to be a reasonable explanation for the various word order patterns of dative and accusative objects.

2.*Free order*. Let us now assume that Old English was a non-configurational language and that case assignment does not depend on the VP structure, but takes place through subcategorization. Let us further specify that the VP is head final, i.e. the V is in final position. Because we do not specify the order of the elements within the VP, we do not impose a structure upon it. We would then expect there to be a great variety in surface word order patterns. More specifically we expect that in double object constructions the objects can occur in both orders, and that they can be separated by PP's and adverbials. As the examples given earlier ((2), (10), (13), (14), and (15)) show, this is indeed the case. A non-configurational approach seems to make the right predictions.

2.1. The variety in word order exhibited by other constructions also follows naturally from a non-configurational structure. Elsewhere I have tried to show that the distribution of verb and particle (in verb-particle combinations) can be explained in this way, making it unnecessary to invoke a particle movement rule (Koopman 1985). A similar explanation is available for verbs which can take an object and a PP (precursors of the *I gave the book to John* construction), by the side of a double object. There are not many of these verbs in Old English (see Mitchell 1985: 1210), but my hypothesis would predict that object and PP can occur in both orders. This appears to be the case. It is illustrated in (20) and (21) for the verb *bringan*:

(20) LS18.1(NatMaryAss 10N) 74 þe to Gode (PP) heoræ lac
                                  who to God   their gift
    onsægednes (OBJ) brohten
    of sacrifice brought
    'who brought to God their gift of sacrifice'

(21)　LS17.1(MartinMor)224 þonne man hwylcne dæl his
　　　　　　　　　　　　that they a part　　of his
　　　hrægles (OBJ) to untruman men (PP) brohte
　　　garment to a sick man brought
　　　'that they brought part of his garment to a sick man'

2.2. So far I have only given examples with nominal objects. Let us now see what happens when both objects are pronominal. In Dutch they tend to cluster in the order direct object - indirect object:

(22)　omdat Jan 't 'm gegeven had
　　　because John it him given had
　　　'because John had given it to him'

Both objects in (22) are clitics as their phonological form indicates. Van Kemenade (1984a, 1984b,1987) argues that in Old English pronominal objects can be clitics. I will return to this later. The same pronominal order as in Dutch is found in Old English:

(23)　GDPref and 4(C)54.341.10　Ac he ondred, þæt he hit (ACC)
　　　　　　　　　　　　　　　　but he (reflexive) feared　that　he it
　　　him (DAT) asæde
　　　him　　　said
　　　'but he feared that he would say it to him'
(24)　Ch1489(Whitelock 26)4　swa he hit (ACC) me(DAT) to handa let
　　　　　　　　　　　　　　　　as he it　　　　me　in hands　let
　　　'as he gave it in my possession'

If pronominal objects always occurred in the order ACC - DAT, this would be evidence against a free order analysis, because we would not expect a fixed order when the order in the VP is not determined by its structure. A reason for the clustering seems difficult to give in a non-configurational approach, but with a fixed underlying order there are possible explanations (see e.g. Kerstens (1985) and Berendsen (1983) for Dutch). The Old English material, however, shows that the order of (23) and (24) is certainly not the only one (though it is much more frequent than the other order). So far I have found five examples with the pronominal objects in the order DAT-ACC and further research may unearth more. I give them in (25) to (29):

(25) Ch 322 (Birch507) 2.2 7 me (DAT) hit (ACC) for gode leanie
                             and me   it   for God repays
eow to elmessum
you as alms
'and for God repays it to me as alms for you'

(26) ChronE 251.19(1123) 7 he hem (DAT) hit (ACC) wolde tyþian[7]
                          and he them   it   wanted to grant
'and he wanted to grant it to them'

(27) LS1.1 (AndrewBright) 146 and hraþe he me (DAT) hine (ACC) æteowde
                           and quickly he me   him
showed
'and he showed himself quickly to me'

(28) LS1.1(AndrewBright)110 nu þonne, Drihten, ic þe bidde þæt
                          now then, Lord, I you pray that
þu me (DAT) þe (ACC) æteowe on þisse stowe
you me   you   show   in this place
'now then, Lord, I pray you to show yourself to me in this place'

(29) LS8 (Eust)46 þæt ic þurh þis nyten þe (DAT) me (ACC) ætywde[8]
                that I through this beast you me
showed
'that I showed myself to you through this beast'

My provisional conclusion is that with two pronominal objects too the free order hypothesis is a distinct possibility

2.3. In the examples given so far the pronominal objects cluster. We would also expect examples with the objects separated. (30) and (31) seem possible examples:

(30) Solil 1.12.4 ne agyf me (ACC) næfre eft hym (DAT)
                not give me   never again   him
'do not give me ever again to him'

(31) Or 6.30.280.5 oð hiene (ACC) þa burgleode him (DAT) ageafon
               until him   the citizens him   gave
'until the citizens gave him to him'

Different explanations are, however, possible. For (30) we can assume that the pronominal *hym* is not a clitic. Van Kemenade (1987) regards pronominal objects as clitics, occurring immediately left of their governor (V, VP) or in pre-S position.[9] She does not give phonological evidence for clitichood. Such evidence exists for the pronoun *þu* when it follows the verb immediately. Occasionally it clearly shows clitic properties:

(32) ÆCHom i.18.256.5 hu mihtu (= miht þu) for sceame æniges
                       how could you   for shame anything
      þinges æt Gode biddan?
      of God ask
      'how could you for shame ask anything from God'

This proves only that *þu* sometimes cliticizes. For other pronominal forms clitic behaviour must be proven syntactically. To van Kemenade's arguments (clitic-climbing in V-raising complements, and the form resumptive pronouns take) I can add that it is striking with double object constructions that they can precede nominal subjects, but follow pronominal subjects. See (33) and (23) (here repeated):

(33) Or 4.11.202.34   oð Philippus hira cyning friðes bæd, 7
                       until Philippus their king peace asked, and
      hit him Romane (SUBJ) aliefdon
      it him Romans   gave
      'until their king Philippus asked for peace and the Romans gave it to him'
(23) GDPref and 4(C)54.341.10 Ac he him ondred,þæt he (SUBJ) hit
                               but he (reflexive) feared that he   it
      him asæde
      him said
      'but he feared that he would say it to him'

It would be interesting to see whether this is a systematic difference.

2.4. Some pronominal objects quite clearly are not

clitics. They can occur in Topic position:

(34) HomS 10(BlHom 3)19   hine þa forlet se costigend
                          him then left   the tempter
'the tempter then left him'

They can also be used with contrastive stress. Clear examples are hard to find, but *hine* in (35) allows of no other interpretation:

(35) ÆCHom i.9.136.35 He bær þæt cild and þæt cild bær hine
'he carried the child and the child carried him'

If pronominal objects are clitics only if they occur immediately left of their governors (V, VP) or in pre-S position,[10] then we must assume that *hine* in (36) and *him* in (37) are not clitics, and in fact behave as nominal NP's:

(36) GD 2(C)24.154.21 þæt hi woldon þære byrgene (DAT) hine (ACC)
                      that they wanted the grave   him
eft befæstan
again entrust
'that they wanted to entrust him again to the grave'
(37) ÆLS (Maur) 262 sume eac befæstan heora suna (ACC) him (DAT)
                    'some also committed their sons   to him
to Godes þeowdome
for God's service'

Similarly, *hym* in (30) cannot be a clitic, and (30) is in fact a clause with one pronominal clitic object and one pronominal non-clitic object.

Back then to (31). We could say that (31) is support for the free order hypothesis, for the pronominal object occurs in pre-S position. But there is some doubt about this example. We could also say that *hiene* occurs in Topic position. As indicated above there is some reason for assuming a Topic position for subordinate clauses. Can we still maintain that *hiene* is a clitic? In (30) and (31) we can claim there is only one clitic object. This raises the question why pronominal objects should cluster. If no clear examples can be found with clitic objects separated, this needs to be explained. I will not attempt it here.

2.5. Finally, let us look at the largest group of examples, those with one nominal and one pronominal object. Here we run into the problem that we can only find support for our hypothesis if the pronominal object is not a 'van Kemenade' clitic, as clitichood disturbs the word order patterns. Obviously it is not easy to find many examples of the required type, but I have found a few and they show the characteristic variety in word order to be expected if Old English is non-configurational: with a non-clitic pronominal object we can expect it to precede or follow the nominal object as examplified in (37) (here repeated) and (38):

(37) ÆLS (Maur) 262 sume eac befæstan heora suna (ACC) him (DAT)
                'some also committed their sons   to him
to Godes þeowdome
for God's service'

(38) ÆLS (Basil) 364 gif he mid his syncræfte him (DAT) þæt
               if he with his magic   him   the
mæden (ACC) mihte gemacian to wife
maiden   could make   to wife
'if by his magic he could make the maiden become his wife'

In (37) and (38) *him* is not in one of the clitic positions, and therefore cannot be regarded as a clitic.

With one nominal and one pronominal object, too, the the free order hypothesis seems to make the right predictions.

3. *Case assignment*. So far I have assumed that case assignment takes place through subcategorization. That is a

position that must be modified. Passive constructions in Old English show that only accusative objects can become nominative in the passive (the personal passive). When the object is in the genitive or dative, it retains the case form in the passive (impersonal passive). If case assignment takes place through subcategorization (in D-structure) we cannot explain this systematic difference. Genitive and Dative are oblique cases. Nominative and Accusative are structural cases (assigned on S-structure level). A verb can only assign one structural case, but we can sometimes expect an oblique Accusative (also after certain prepositions), for instance with the small group of verbs that have two accusative objects. One of the objects must be oblique and cannot passivize. This may well be hard to prove conclusively, but the verb *læran* seems to offer reasonable supporting evidence. It has one accusative object denoting the person learning something, and the other accusative object denotes what is being taught. The available Old English evidence shows that there are only passives with the 'learner' as subject and the other accusative object still present. I have found no examples of the 'thing taught' as subject accompanied by a 'learner' accusative. There are passives with the 'thing taught' as subject, but it is striking that they are never accompanied by an accusative 'learner'. I would regard these simply as the passives of an active construction with one (structural) object.

4. *Structure of Old English*. I have argued that Old English was non-configurational, crucially that the position of dative and accusative objects is not determined by the VP structure. Diverse word orders in various constructions (NP - PP constructions with *bringan*, verb-particle

combinations, and double object constructions) can be explained quite naturally without resorting to a battery of movement rules, which are difficult to motivate. But how do we envisage the structure of Old English?

4.1. Haider (1981, 1985a, 1985b) has claimed that German has a 'flat' S without a VP.[11] The V-max projection, he claims, coincides with S. The subject NP, as well as the object NP's come under one S-node. In German passives there is then no NP movement. Because there is no VP to act as a barrier, INFL can assign Nominative case. In English, the object NP, which does not get case from the past participle, must move out of the VP to a position where it can get case from INFL. Haider explains the range of word orders in German through this 'flat' S structure. He argues that German does not show the asymmetry of subject and object that English does. The constructions he uses to argue his point are for instance:

(39) i. Extraction from a subject clause.
     ii. Relative pronoun extraction from a subject clause.
    iii. fronting (and extraction) from an object clause.

For Old English we cannot prove asymmetry of subject and object because it depends on grammaticality judgements which are not available. We can only prove symmetry through Haider's tests. Considering the nature of the constructions this must be difficult to do. There cannot be many examples of these constructions, if they can be found in the surviving material at all.

4.2. There is, however, some supporting evidence for the existence of a VP node in Old English. It comes from verb-particle combinations, to be compared with the separable verbs of Dutch and German. If Old English is non-configurational but has a VP, the distribution of verb and particle is fairly straightforward to explain. The particle can have any position within the VP. It only occurs outside the VP if it is moved along with the V (cases of reanalysis see Koopman (1985)). Significantly, there are, as far as I know, no cases where the particle precedes the subject. If Old English had no VP we would expect the particle to occur anywhere in S, thus also in pre-subject position.

4.3. If Old English indeed had a VP, it should also show NP movement in the passive. (40) seems a counterexample:

(40) GD 1(C)2.15.35 þa þam Godes mæn (DAT) his agen hors (NOM)
                     when God's   man   his own horse
gegifen wæs
given was
'when his own horse was given to God's man'

This is the word order that Haider claims German shows when the accusative NP gets Nominative case without movement. For Old English the order of (40) can also be explained by assuming that the dative NP has been topicalized.

5. *Conclusion*. The various word order patterns of dative and accusative objects are difficult to explain satisfactorily within a configurational approach. It is not at all clear what is the basic order. Movement rules are needed, while there is little to no independent motivation for the landing sites. Making the assumption that Old English is non-configurational allows us to explain the word order variety quite naturally. I have also argued that unlike German, Old English most probably had a VP, but one without internal structure (a 'flat' VP). Old

English would be partly configurational in having a VP, and partly non-configurational in having no structure within the VP.

NOTES

* I am grateful to David Denison, Olga Fischer, Frederike van der Leek, and Wim van der Wurff for comments on earlier drafts of this paper.
1. I leave out of account here the cases where one of the objects is a clause. They always have end position in the clause. Similarly, I will not take into account the relative weight of an object, because it seems only an explanation in some cases, certainly not in all. It could very well have been a contributing factor.
2. The examples are taken from the Old English Concordance (Healey and Venezky 1980). I have often cited only part of the concordance quotation while keeping the concordance line reference. Where possible the quotations have been checked against the texts.
3. I have looked at about one-fifth of the verbs listed by Visser (1963: 682).
4. No attempt has been made to establish which examples could be regarded as exhibiting marked order, because it is extremely hard, perhaps impossible, to reach any firm conclusions.
5. This is, I think, an important argument against analysing Old English as a configurational language.
6. The VS order is a problem I do not want to go into here.
7. It should be noted that (25) and (26) are very late Old English.
8. The context makes the interpretation of (28) and (29) clear.
9. Van Kemenade's theory seems to me essentially sound. She regards pronominal subjects as clitics too. Her theory is here supported by the word order in sentences with topicalized nominal direct objects. When the subject is pronominal the word order is always OSV, but when the subject is nominal the word order can be OSV or OVS. A clear difference therefore in the syntactic behaviour of nominal and pronominal subjects.
10. The large number of V-second main clauses with SpronOV order, and the few examples of main clauses with SVpronO order strongly suggest that object clitics can only occur left of V if V is a full verb, and cannot occur on the trace of V when V has been moved away.
11. For a different interpretation see den Besten (1985).

REFERENCES

Allen, Cynthia. 1980. 'Movement and Deletion in Old English.' *LI* 11, 261-323.
Barrett, Charles R. 1953. *Studies in the Word-Order of Ælfric's Catholic Homilies and Lives of the Saints*. Cambridge: The Department of Anglo-Saxon.
Berendsen, Egon. 1983. "Objectsclitica in het Nederlands.' *NTg* 76, 209-24.
Besten, Hans den. 1983. 'On the interaction of Root Transformations and Lexical Deletive Rules.' In Werner Abraham, ed. *On the Formal Syntax of the Westgermania*, 47-131. Amsterdam & Philadelphia: John Benjamins.
Besten, Hans den. 1985. 'The Ergative Hypothesis and Free Word Order in Dutch and German.' In J.Toman, ed. *Studies in German Syntax*, 23-62. Dordrecht: Foris.
Brown, William H., Jr. 1970. *A Syntax of King Alfred's Pastoral Care*. The Hague & Paris: Mouton.
Canale, William. 1978. *Word Order Change in Old English: Base Reanalysis in Generative Grammar*. Unpublished PhD Dissertation, McGill University.
Fischer, Olga C.M. and Frederike C. van der Leek. 1983. 'The Demise of the Old English Impersonal Construction.' *JL* 19, 337-68.
Gardner, Faith F. 1971. *An Analysis of Syntactic Patterns of Old English*. The Hague & Paris: Mouton.
Haider, Hubert. 1981. 'Empty Categories: on Some Differences between English and German.' *Wiener linguistische Gazette* 25, 13-36.
Haider, Hubert. 1985a. 'The Case of German.' In J.Toman. ed. *Studies in German Grammar*, 65-101. Dordrecht: Foris.
Haider, Hubert. 1985b. 'A Unified Account of Case and θ-Marking.' *Papiere zur Linguistik* 32, 3-36.
Healey, Antonette DiPaolo and Richard L.Venezky. 1980. *A Microfiche Concordance to Old English*. Toronto: Pontifical Institute of Medieval Studies.
Kemenade, Ans van. 1984a. 'Verb Second and Clitics in Old English.' In Hans Bennis and W.U.S. van Lessen Kloeke, eds. *Linguistics in the Netherlands 1984*, 101-109. Dordrecht: Foris
Kemenade, Ans van. 1984b. 'Clitic Movement and Preposition Stranding in Old English.' Unpublished Paper, University of Utrecht.
Kemenade, Ans van. 1987. *Syntactic Case and Morphological Case in the History of English*. PhD Dissertation, University of Utrecht.
Kerstens, Johan. 1985. 'Zijn indirecte objecten zinnen?' *Ntg* 78, 525-36.
Kohonen, Viljo. 1978. *On the Development of English Word Order in Religious Prose around 1000 to 1200 A.D.* Åbo: Åbo Akedemi.
Koopman, Willem. 1985. 'The Syntax of Verb and Particle Combinations in Old English.' In Hans Bennis and Frits Beukema, eds. *Linguistics in the Netherlands 1985*. 91-99. Dordrecht: Foris

Mitchell, Bruce. 1985. *Old English Syntax*. Oxford: Clarendon Press.
Shannon, Ann. 1964. *A Descriptive Syntax of the Parker Manuscript of the Anglo-Saxon Chronicle from 734 to 891*. London, The Hague & Paris: Mouton.
Shores, David L. 1971. *A Descriptive Syntax of the Peterborough Chronicle from 1122 to 1154*. The Hague & Paris: Mouton.
Thiersch, Craig. 1982.'A Note on 'Scrambling' and the existence of VP.' *Wiener Linguistische Gazette* 27-28, 83-95.
Visser, F.Th. 1963. *An Historical Syntax of the English Language*. Part I. Leiden: Brill.

WHERE DO EXTRATERRITORIAL ENGLISHES COME FROM?
DIALECT INPUT AND RECODIFICATION IN TRANSPORTED ENGLISHES*

ROGER LASS
University of Cape Town

1. ETEs and 'History of English'.

Extraterritorial Englishes (ETEs) haven't traditionally been the sexiest of specializations in historical Anglistics. Partly, I suppose, because they only really begin in the 17th century, and the big guns have typically been trained on earlier periods; and because the ETEs (American to some extent, South African and Australasian much more) lack the cachet of the 'mainstream' -- which appears to be the line leading to the southern British standard. This reflects an old ethnocentrism: straight-line evolution to the southern Received Standard (which is 'English'), and side-paths of antiquarian or specialist interest leading to 'the dialects'.

Whatever the cause, one result has been a relative lack of sophistication in diachronic ETE studies, and a failure to integrate them into the larger discipline, and to use well-tested materials and techniques for investigating their history. Much of what has been done is vitiated by various kinds of sociolinguistic and historical ineptitudes (see Lass & Wright 1986 for a case-study, and some of the discussion below). This had led Wolfgang Viereck, in a recent paper (1985: 566) to refer to 'the largely deplorable state of the art, so-called, in the field of the origins of the American Englishes and their development'; the picture isn't a lot rosier for the other ETEs.[1]

An 'English' bounded by the Tweed, the Irish Sea, the North Sea and the Channel is now rather out of date; but I'm not convinced that our progress has been in keeping with our enlightened attitudes. My rather modest aim in this paper is to sketch out a diachronic gradus ad Parnassum for ETE studies; to explore the value of some hitherto under-utilized materials for ETE history, and to try and integrate these rather neglected stepchildren into the main body of English historical studies. In a way, the real aim is to establish ETE study specifically in regional sense--as a quite traditional branch of English historical dialectology. This is particularly worth doing now, I think, because of the very strong (and largely uninformed) condemnation of precisely this approach recently mounted by J.L. Dillard (1985). In arguing for an almost exclusively 'contact' or 'mixing and levelling' origin for American English, Dillard says (1985: 21):

> Much of what can be said about the early spread of pidgins is ... frankly speculation. It could hardly be said to be more speculative, however, than statements about the importation of British regional dialects, which are never attested in the Americas.

He claims later (51) that there has been a 'failure to find any clear-cut correlations between ... features of American English and British dialects', and that this 'means that the region-to-region framework of the history of American English can hardly be supported by phonological considerations'. We must in fact 'give up the notion that British regional dialects hold the key to the history of American English'.

Unless Dillard is simply arguing against manifest absurdities like the idea that a New England village settled mainly from Norfolk in the 17th century should still show features that are clearly Norfolk (not Suffolk or

Northamptonshire), then what he says is demonstrably wrong. And dangerously so, since his earlier dismissal of the 'reconstructive tradition' and his highly fashionable 'social' approach are clearly retrograde steps in developing rigorous ETE histories.

I would claim rather that all the ETEs show certain broad regional provenances in a very clear way, and that most present-day ETE features can be shown to be coherent developments of specifiable Mainland regional types -- subject of course to later endogenous evolution, and some contact-effects. In principle the sorting out of ETE origins -- even in 'melting-pots' like the U.S. -- is no different from sorting out the developments of the Germanic or Romance dialects. A bit more micro- than macro-, yes, and often tricky: but even the trickinesses are of the same old traditional kind. Writing the history of U.S. English, for instance, is not very different from writing that of one of the hairier continental West Germanic dialects -- say Dutch.

Perhaps a definition of the ETE domain would be useful before going any further. The most fundamental division is between what I call 'Mother Tongue' and 'Contact' ETEs. The first are reasonably straightforward developments of particular social/regional varieties or variety-clusters of Mainland English (if often posing special problems because of their complex and heterogeneous inputs); they have evolved with no major structural influence from languages other than English.[2] The second group consists of L_2 Englishes on one hand (Indian, West African, Singaporean, etc.) and English-based pidgins and creoles on the other.[3] I will restrict myself here to the Mother-Tongue ETEs, since these are in my view simply part of the inventory of what can uncontroversially be called 'regional dialects of English', and pose none of the specialist problems of pidgin and creole study.

There were two major waves of ETE formation, separated by about three-quarters of a century, and geographically distinct; this has implications for their etymological typology (the nature of their reflex sets for early phonological categories), and the geographical clustering of certain features. The first wave was from the late 16th to the early 18th century, exclusively in the northern hemisphere: the results are Hiberno-English[4] and American English (U.S. and Canadian). The second wave, from the 1780s-1840s, covered the southern hemisphere, and produced Australasian and Southern African English. The ETE Stammbaum is shown in (1) below.[5]

(1) NORTHERN HEMISHPERE ETEs

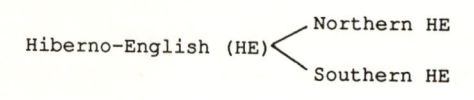

Hiberno-English (HE) ⟨ Northern HE
                      Southern HE

American English (AmE) ⟨ Canadian English (CE)
                         U.S. English

SOUTHERN HEMISHERE ETEs

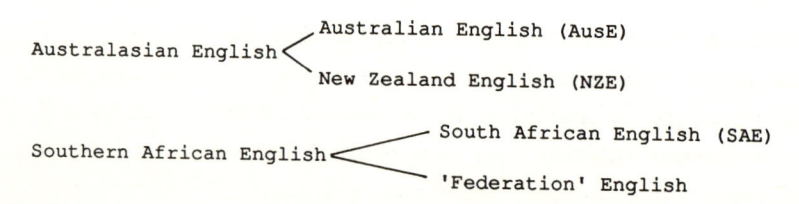

Australasian English ⟨ Australian English (AusE)
                       New Zealand English (NZE)

Southern African English ⟨ South African English (SAE)
                           'Federation' English

One of the striking features of this N/S dichotomy is that aside from HE (which is contiguous to Mainland English), the characteristic lay differentia of 'British' and 'American' English have an ETE projection: the 'British' features typify the southern hemisphere ETEs. (E.g. South African cars run on petrol not gas, people sit on bums not asses, etc.) The 'Britishness' of these varieties is further reinforced by their being generally non-rhotic, and having not only a length distinction between the vowels of cat and fast (which is universal in ETEs), but a sharp quality distinction as well (I will return to this important feature in § 3).

In terms of overall regional type, I will start with a simple characterization which is true without exception: there is no ETE that is not a dialect of Southern English.[6] This is an evolutionary and sociolinguistic, not necessarily a demographic fact. It is worth spending some time on the definition of 'southern'; it is complex and interesting, and the features clustering below the major N/S isoglosses in England play a major role in unpacking ETE histories and characterizing the various ETEs.

2. Southern English: Excluding the Far North.

This and the next section will define ETE regional typology, as well as its historical correlates; the idea is to be able to identify, with respect to certain salient features, the place of any ETE on the (admittedly squishy) 'archaic'/'innovative' scale, and to identify its main regional as well as temporal sources. The term 'southern' will therefore be given a rather elaborate ostensive definition. I am not using it in what to historians may be its more familiar Middle English sense; my 'south' includes not only 'true South' (Zummerzet, Kent, Sussex), but a good chunk of the Midlands as well. In this extended post-ME definition, everything south of a line running roughly from SW Gloucestershire northwest to the Norfolk/Lincolnshire border counts as 'the South'; parts of both the EML and WML are therefore at least marginally southern. Areas like N Gloucester and Oxfordshire are 'northern' in that they do not distinguish the vowels of cut and put, and 'southern' in having a long vowel in bath, etc.[7]

The first step is to isolate Scots from the rest of the North; the second to distinguish a dialectologists' 'True North' from the larger non-South.

I. The Scots Exclusion Features

(a) Vowel Length. All non-Scots dialects retain at least relics of the old Germanic (and OE/ME/EModE) vowel-length contrast. Not necessarily in the form of strict duration-pairs (though many N and NML dialects have [a]/[a:] in Sam/psalm, and AusE and SAE have [e]/[e:] in shed/shared). For a dialect to 'have length' it's sufficient that some subset of its vowels be ceteris paribus longer than some other, and that the short subset be excluded from terminating the strong syllable of a foot. By this criterion RP [ɪ]/[i:], [ɒ]/[ɔ:] instantiate a 'length contrast'.

In Scots on the other hand all vowels are underlyingly short, with (generally) all except the reflexes of ME /i u/ having long allophones before voiced fricatives, /r/, and boundaries (the latter giving the uniquely Scots possibility of phonetic minimal pairs like [brʉd] brood vs. [brʉ:d] brewed). This pattern is now generally called Aitken's Law (Vaiana Taylor 1972, Lass 1974, Aitken 1981).

(b) The pull/pool Merger. Non-Scots dialects have a qualitative and durational contrast between ME /u/ unlowered (see § 3) and the isolative vowel-shift reflex of ME /o:/, usually of the type [ʊ~ʉ̈] vs. [u:]. Scots has one vowel in both sets, typically around [u].

(c) The cot/caught Merger. Most varieties of Scots (if not excessively Anglicized) do not distinguish ME /o/ isolative from ME /au/, but have a single quality [ɔ] in both sets (vs. southern [ɒ]/[ɔ:] etc.).

(d) Non-Merger of ME /-ir(C), -er(C), -ur(C)/. In the 17th century all non-Scots dialects merged these categories; Scots still keeps all three distinct (e.g. /ɪ ɛ ʌ/ in fir, fern, fur respectively, or fir/fur merged in /ʌ/ vs. fern with /ɛ/ (cf. Lass 1987: § 5.7.1). With the exception of (variable) distinct ME /e/ in Ireland (e.g. /ɝ/ in urn vs. /ɛ/ in earn), which is an archaism rather than a Scotticism, no dialect outside Scotland lacks the full merger, which affects both rhotic and non-rhotic dialects.

II. The Far North Exclusion Features

The canonical North can be delimited as in (2) below.

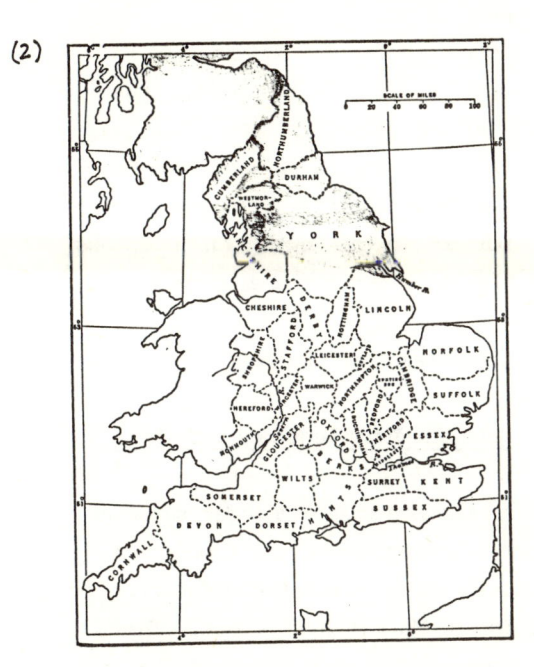

(2)

The Far North

(a) Unshifted ME /u:/ (house, out). The layman's North ('the land of flat caps and flat vowels'-- Beale 1985) is not coterminous with the dialectologists'; they distinguish a True or Far North from the North Midlands and other ML areas (cf. Wakelin 1972: ch.5, Lass 1987: § 5). One major isogloss defining the Far North and making Newcastle N and Liverpool NML, for instance, is the division between unshifted and shifted ME /u:/ (Ellis' 1889 house/hoose line). Briefly, the Far North, including vernacular Scotland, has no vowel-shift of /u:/; the modern reflexes are typically long back to centralized front monophthongs in the [u: - Y:] range in England, and short [u - ʉ - ÿ] in Scotland.[8]

(b) Front ME /o:/ (boot, school). In Northern ME, /o:/

fronted to /ø:/ in the 14th century, and later unrounded, giving reflexes in the North of England like [ɪə], [i:], and a wide range including [i - e - ø] in Scotland. Front ME /o:/ in other areas with normal shift of /u:/ (e.g. West Country [Y:]) is a later and independent development.

(c) Front OE /a:/ (home, oak). While OE /a:/ rounded to [ɔ:] in non-northern ME, it fronted to [a:] in the North, thus falling together with early ME /a/ lengthened in open syllables, rather than as in the South with ME /o/ in the same environment. Thus home, same (OE hām, sāma) rhyme in the Far North (English [ɪə], Scots [e] are typical), but not in the South; while oak and smoke (OE āc, smŏca) rhyme in the South but not the North (for details Lass 1976: 129ff).

There are other features, but these are the most important.

3. The Great N/S Isophones: Main Southern Features and their ETE Projections.

We can now look at the South in its wider sense as 'non-North'; the most important features separating the larger Macro-North from the post-ME South and southern Midlands are:

(a) Lowering and unrounding of ME /u/ (but, come). This characterizes all southern dialects. The usual story is that /u/ split sometime in the 17th century, with the original higher rounded type [ʊ] (actually a lowering of ME [u]) retained in certain (mainly labial) contexts, and lowering and unrounding elsewhere. The innovating trajectory gives modern '/ʌ/' (but, come), and is joined by early shortenings of ME /o:/ (flood); the conservative trajectory gives modern '/ʊ/', joined by later ME /o:/ shortenings (good). The outline history is given in (3).

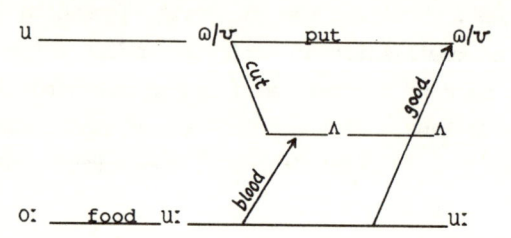

(3)

u ——————— ʊ/ʊ   put   ʊ/ʊ
              \\cut   \\good
                 ʌ ———— ʌ
              /blood
o: ——food— u: ——————————— u:

The conventional symbols /ʌ/, /ʋ/ are merely mnemonics for lexical classes, not 'transcriptions' or phonetic labels for reflex sets (hence the scare-quotes above). Something of the range of developments is illustrated below in (4).

(4)   '/ʌ/': Dublin [ɔ̈], Edinburgh [ʌ], RP [ɐ - Ä]
        Bristol [ə], London [ä], Cape Town [ɐ - ɜ - ɛ̈]
      '/ʊ/': RP [ɷ], New York [ÿ], Cape Town [ɷ̈], E. Texas [ɨ]

This is of course only an exemplary sample. (In most Irish varieties /u/-lowering is only partial, or at least variable -- probably another HE archaism. For details of incomplete diffusion here, see Wells 1982: §§ 5.3.2-4.)

Given a starting point of ME [u] (see Lass 1982 for justification of this value rather than traditional [ʋ]), it would seem that the fronter and lower the <u>but</u> nucleus is, the more historically advanced the dialect. Thus London [a], Cape Town [ɛ̈] are advanced, Dublin [ɔ̈], Edinburgh [ʌ] conservative. With <u>put</u>, the advanced forms are fronter and/or unrounded. The historical travels of ME /u/ can be visualized as in (5).

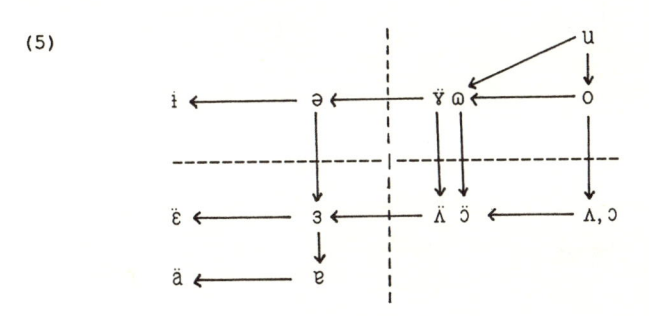

(5)
```
                          |         u
                          |         ↓
  ɨ ←——————  ə ←————+—— ÿ ɷ ←——————  o
                          |         ↓
  --------------------+-----+-------------
                          |         ↓
  ɛ̈ ←—————— ɜ ←————+—— Ä ɔ̈ ←—————— ʌ, ɔ
  ↓                       |
  ä ←—————— ɐ              |
```

Given this scenario, northern hemisphere ETE <u>cut</u> seems to be rather more archaic, as befits the earlier settlements; in general, all ETEs except HE show <u>cut</u> values fronter than centralized back and opener than half-close; though some rather old-fashioned U.S. varieties may have values around [Ä]. The extreme southern lowering and fronting of cut appears to be of 19th-century date. Ellis (1889: 238) describes this vowel in New Zealand as 'a much more open sound than I have been accustomed to, approaching the a in father'. Since Ellis' vowel here (1889: 3, if I'm right in my reading) is about [ä], this stage would have been reached in New Zealand but not London in the third quarter of the century. So in the 1880s New Zealand is ahead of London, the SE vernaculars, and the Received Standard; this development is thus not an importation but an endogenous change, probably convergent in Mainland (where it is now well established) and ETE.

The native /u/-lowering area, judging from SED data (see Wakelin 1972: 87) would seem to be delimited as in (6) below.

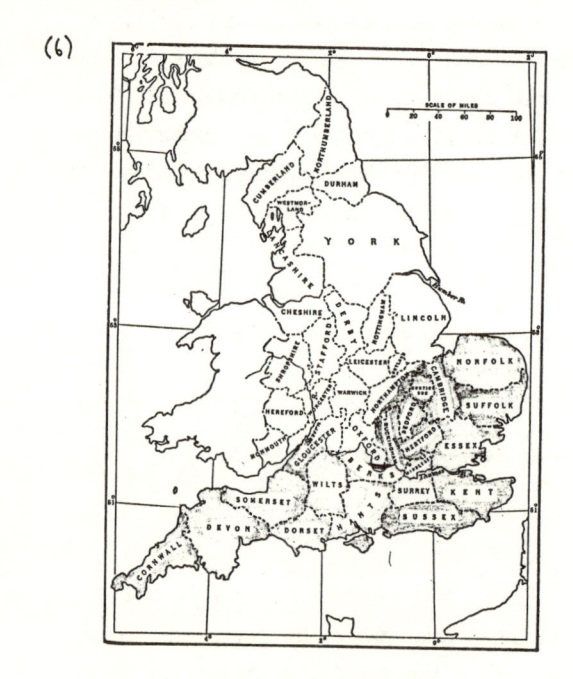

(6)

Lowering of ME /u/

(b) ME /a/ Isolative as [æ] or Higher. The development of [æ] < ME /a/ in about the 17th century is usually taken simply as a fact about 'the history of English'; the quality [æ] is so 'typically English' that it is not normally thought of as a regional marker. This is simply because essentially southern dialect-types have been institutionalized as standard since the 15th century or so, and this has had its effects on the ETEs as well. In actual fact the local dialect evidence from earlier times shows [æ] -- outside the Received Standard and the local vernaculars closest to it -- to be quite restricted.

The detailed survey in Ellis (1889) for instance shows [æ] in his southern and eastern divisions only; in the west in Wiltshire, Somerset, Dorset, parts of Gloucestershire, SE Devon, Berkshire and Hampshire (here ~ [a]); in the east in Kent, Sussex, Essex, Hertfordshire and East Anglia. At the turn of the century Wright (1905: § 23) has [a] or a backer value for the bulk of England north of Norfolk, and most of the Midlands; [æ] is reported as the norm only for Kent, Sussex, Hampshire and the Isle of Wight, and varies with [a] throughout the SWML, Buckinghamshire, Berkshire and Norfolk. Half a century later, with the benefit of a tighter grid and better-controlled transcription, the SED shows a more complex but not essentially different picture for the regional vernaculars. Aside from sporadic occurrences in Yorkshire (areas 21, 23) and the Isle of Man (which are suspicious, and may be accommodations to the fieldworker), [æ] is scattered in the WML (where the majority reflex is [a]); in the EML we find it in one area in Lincolnshire, in Norfolk ~ [a], and in Huntingdonshire, the rest of East Anglia, Essex and Middlesex/London. Further south, we get it in Surrey, Kent, Berkshire and Cornwall.

Combining the reports of Ellis, Wright and SED, the maximal 'native' (i.e. not standard-derived) domain of [æ] is as shown in (7).

(7)

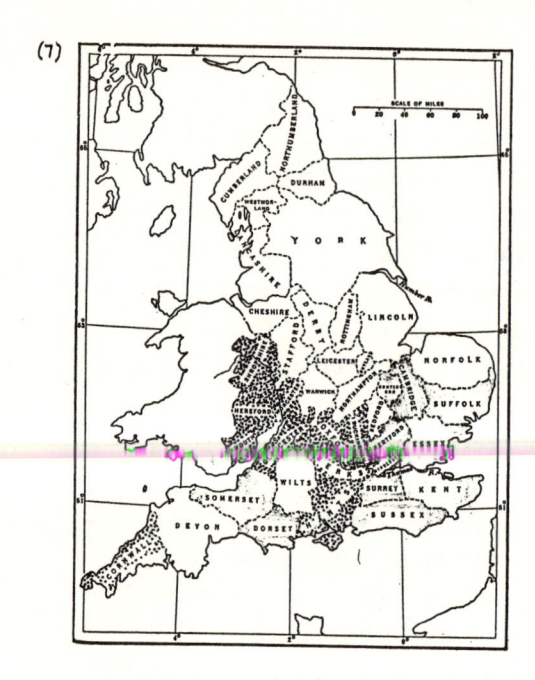

Distribution of [æ]
▨ [æ] only
▩ [æ] ~ [a]

Within the broader [æ]-Gebiet there is a localized further raising to [ɛ], either consistently or in a fair selection of lexical items in a given locale. This is essentially SE, but distinct from the familiar Old Kentish raising of OE /æ/ (10th century), since it affects OE /a/ words as well (cat, man, hand). By the 19th century this raising had begun to move from the Eastern Counties into London;[9] it is remarked on as early as the 1780s (see Jespersen 1909: § 8.6.2), and condemned by Batchelor (1809). It is not however well entrenched as prototypically London until quite late in the century; Ellis (1889) notes it, but says only that it 'may be growing'. It was thus not typically metropolitan as late as the 1880s; but it was widespread in the rural SE. Wright (§ 23) shows it as the norm for Middlesex, SE Bucks, S Herts, SW Essex and 'part of Kent'; SED shows scattered instances in the west as far north as Derbyshire and as far south as Devon, but the concentration is southeastern: mainly Essex, Surrey, Kent and Sussex, with a good

number of reports for Norfolk (though curiously, not for
Cambridgeshire or Suffolk). Taking these earlier reports
together, the core [ɛ]-areas seem to be those shown in (8) below.

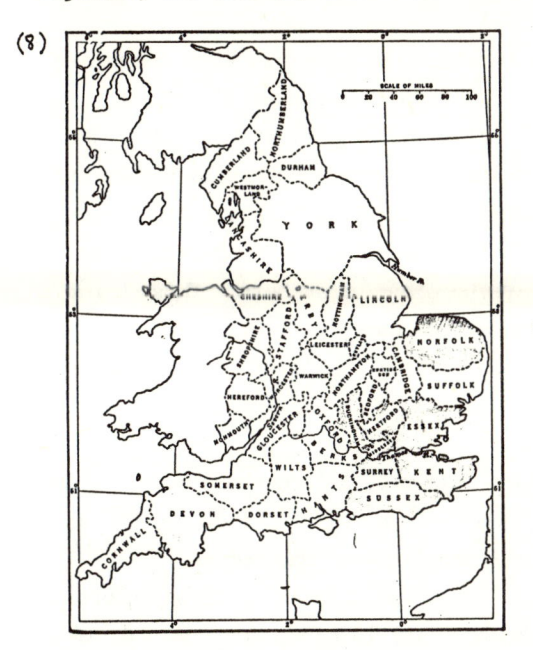

(8)

The core [ɛ] areas

So while [æ] is generally southern, [ɛ] is pretty strictly
SE; and its widespread occurrence in the southern ETEs (where it
is virtually a defining feature of local dialect-type) seems
likely to reflect primarily an input from the SE hinterland
rather than London itself. It could of course have been
reinforced by later immigration from London; but it is not
originally a London or 'Cockney' feature, since the base
dialect-types in the ETEs were established long before this
raising became characteristic of vernacular London. (Ellis is
percipient as usual in referring to 'Australian South Eastern'--
1889: 236ff.) The distribution of [ɛ] in the dialect records is
a useful example of the care required in attributing an ETE
feature to a specific Mainland locale; we have to know what that

locale was doing at the relevant time, rather than relying on what we may have later come to think of as 'typical' of it (for another cautionary example see Lass & Wright 1986: 204-7 on sources of rhoticity in ETEs).

(c) ME /a/ and /o/: Lengthening I (<u>bath</u>, <u>off</u>). Beginning in the 17th century, ME /a o/ began to lengthen in certain contexts: first before /r/ and voiceless fricatives, later (ME /a/ only) before nasal + obstruent. The lengthening before /r/ (<u>far</u>, <u>horn</u>) was nearly universal, and is not regionally diagnostic; it would appear in ETEs no matter where they came from. I will consider only the other cases here. This change does not have an institutionalized name, so I will call it Lengthening I, to distinguish it from the later lengthening in some dialects before voiced stops and nasals (<u>bag</u>, <u>man</u>); see below under Lengthening II.

(i) ME /a/ (<u>fast</u>, <u>bath</u>, <u>plant</u>). All southern d̲   ̲s show at least a length distinction between the nuclei of say <u>bat</u> and <u>bath</u>, with the former short; there may or may not be quality-difference as well. This lengthening is first reported in Cooper (1685, 1687), who has [æ:] in <u>pass</u>, etc.; we can take this as the initial lengthened value, and assume that lengthening and quality-shift are two distinct phases of the overall evolution. Later on lengthening, which started before voiceless fricatives and /r/, was extended variably and unevenly to nasal clusters, and in some parts of the country the long allophones lowered and retracted, giving an eventual range from archaic [æ:] to innovative [ɑ:] (there is some evidence that the quality shift began before /r/; Flint 1740 distinguishes [a:] before /r/ from [æ:] before /f θ s/). Some SW dialects went the other way, and raised the lengthened vowel to [e:] (see below). The history of the long reflexes in the standard is complex and not yet fully clear (see Holmberg 1964 for an admirable attempt at straightening it out); but it seems clear that the major qualitative change in non-/r/ environments was perceived in its early stages as vernacular, and lower and more retracted varieties of lengthened /æ/ were stigmatized when they first began to appear in quantity in the mid 18th century as provincial or vulgar. It took a long time before the new-fangled 'Italian a' was firmly established in more polite speech (Walker 1791 was very unhappy with it: see below under Lengthening II).

The distribution shown by Wright ($\overset{S}{\S}$ 23) is similar to what appears half a century later in the SED records. The northern limit of Lengthening I appears to be south Lincolnshire, and the isogloss runs roughly WSW through southern Leicestershire, dipping down into Worcestershire, and including most of Hereford and Gloucester. For Wright, whose information is a bit meagre, it seems that at least S Lincolnshire, Rutland, most of Leicestershire, N Shropshire, and the more southerly WML are within the lengthening zone, as are Berkshire, Buckinghamshire, East Anglia, Kent and the West Country. Wright doesn't mention Surrey or Cornwall, but this is clearly a data-fault.

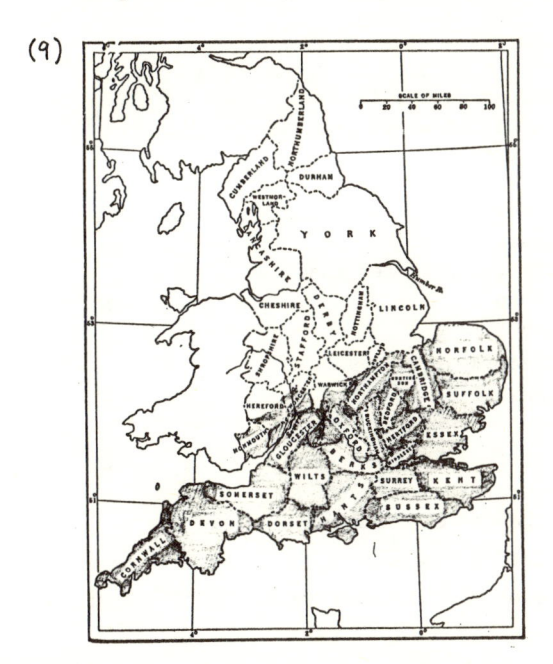

(9)

Lengthening I

Since there seems to have been little shifting of the isogloss since the 19th century, we can take the SED picture as representing the basic range of Lengthening I (all types), as shown in (9) above. Given an input [æ] and the furthest-distant value [ɑː], modern British dialects show virtually the whole range of possible outcomes of lengthening and non-lengthening, shift and non-shift of ME /a/. Only a small subset of these patterns shows up in the ETEs. I have discussed the Mainland patterning elsewhere (Lass 1976: 115ff), and I give only a summary here, based on selected examples from the SED Basic Materials for cat III.10.1 and last VII.£.£, following the taxonomy in my earlier treatment. The inventory is shown in (10) below.

(10)   Group A: No Lengthening
                A-1: Short Open V   cat   last
                     All Northumberland, Nottingham
                        Shropshire 2   a   a
                A-2: Raised Open V
                     Yorks 21, Hereford 5   æ   æ
        Group B: Lengthening only
                B-1: Both cat last Open
                     Lancashire 12, Warwickshire 2,
                     7, Somerset 9, 11   a   aː
                B-2: Both cat last raised
                     Hereford 6, Somerset 1-4, 13   æ   æː
        Group C: Lengthening & Quality Change
                C-1: cat closer than last, both front
                     (a) Shropshire 7, 10, Norfolk 2   æ   aː
                     (b) Sussex   ɛ   æː
                C-2: Front last, closer than cat
                     Shropshire 9   a   æː
                     Cornwall 5   a   eː
                C-3: Retracted or Back last
                     (a) Essex 2, 6, 10, 14   æ   äː
                     (b) Worcestershire 2, 7   a   ɑː
                     (c) Norfolk 4, 12   æ   ɑː
                     (d) Kent 1, 4, 5   ɛ   ɑː

If we assume no major changes of direction, we can sum up the relevant parts of the history represented in table (10) as in (11) below, with indications of which stages emerge in the major ETEs.

(11)

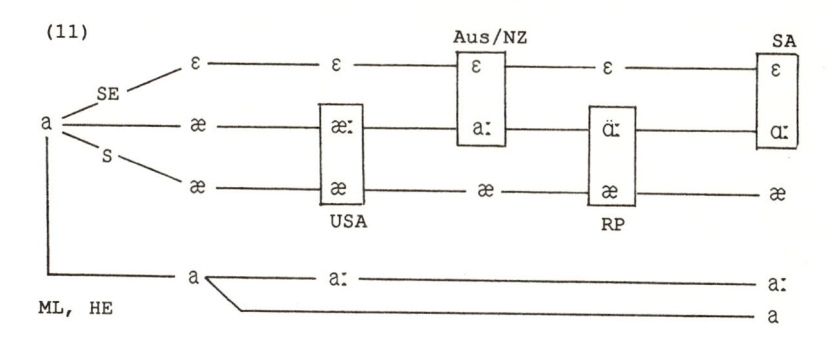

```
                              Aus/NZ                    SA
         ε ─────── ε ──────┌─ε─┐────── ε ──────┌─ε─┐
      SE                   └───┘                └───┘
   a ──── æ ─────┌─æː─┐────┌─aː┐──────┌─ɑ̈ː┐─────┌─ɑː┐
      S          └────┘    └───┘      └────┘     └───┘
         æ ─────┌─æ──┐────── æ ──────┌─æ─┐────── æ
                └────┘                └───┘
                 USA                   RP

   a ────── aː ──────────────────────────────── aː
ML, HE       └──────────────────────────────────── a
```

The most advanced types are those with [æ] or closer in <u>cat</u> and [aː] or backer in <u>last</u>. Since [æ] itself is a 17th-century innovation, the most archaic type is the N/NML with unaltered [a] in both classes, the next is [æ] in both, the next [æ]/[æː], etc. The ML and SW type with [a]/[aː] probably represents a separate line of development, with lengthening of unchanged [a]: since as we've seen [æ] was never a native quality in those parts. The same pattern also occurs in southern HE, which suggests either a large Midland input (not incompatible with the variable status of /u/-lowering); or it may simply be that Lengthening I in Ireland (more restricted lexically than on the Mainland) was superimposed on a southern dialect-type that had not yet developed [æ].

In an ETE perspective the most important patterns are B-1, typical of most of North America;[10] C-1(a) and C-3(a) which with <u>cat</u>-raising give something like the Aus/NZE pattern with front <u>last</u>; and C-3(c-d) which seems to have been codified in South Africa. C-1 [a]/[aː], which also occurs in certain parts of the eastern U.S. (where it can't represent a straightforward relic of the original settlement, which is too early) probably represents the mid-to-late 18th century state of play.

(ii) ME /o/ (<u>off</u>, <u>lost</u>, <u>moth</u>). At about the same time as Lengthening I of ME /a/, ME /o/ began to lengthen as well. (The

connection is probably that these two were the openest short
vowels in the system at this stage, and as such constituted a
kind of 'natural class'.) The first witness here also is Cooper
who in 1687 shows 'o guttural' (probably [ɔ]) long in lost, off,
and other items, and says that it is 'commonly long before rn,
rt, and st' (Part 2, ch. V). This change, like lengthening of
/æ/, is variable and lexically selective at this stage, and in
fact remains so throughout the 18th century; Nares (1784) for
instance has [ɔː] in cough, off, broth, cloth, dross, gloss, but
still a short vowel in moss, cost, frost. By the end of the
century at least some authorities are stigmatizing this
development; Walker (1791; cited by Jespersen §10.76) makes the
following interesting comment on both classes:

> ... and as it would be gross to a degree to sound the *a*
> in *castle*, *mask*, and *plant*, like the *a* in *palm*, *psalm*,
> etc., so it would be equally exceptionable to pronounce
> the *o* in *moss*, *dross*, and *frost*, as if it were written
> *mawse*, *drawse*, and *frawst*.

What Cooper simply notes as a fact a century earlier now has a
social meaning—for some writers a negative one. The merger of
lengthened MF /o/ and ME /au/ is now widespread enough to be a
vulgarism. I assume that the negative assessment of these
lengthenings, which later became fully standard (though
/o/-lengthening has now receded in Britain, and to some extent in
the posher ETE varieties) is due at least partially to quality
change. Mere length with no qualitative difference was probably
not salient enough for Cooper to be a social variable. But by
Walker's time lengthened /æ/ was certainly at least [aː], if not
[äː], and one would suspect that [ɔː] was salient either because
it had begun to raise toward current archaic/vernacular/southern
ETE [oː], or at least that ME /o/ isolative had lowered to [ɒ].

The 19th-century evidence shows lengthening of /o/ rather
more widespread than that of /a/; Wright (§82) reports it as far
north as mid Lancashire. But the main areas seem to be

Bedfordshire, Norfolk, Kent and the London area in the east, and Oxfordshire, Herefordshire and the West Country. The SED (s.v. cross VII.5.14) shows a similar picture: general lengthening in East Anglia (with some shorts in Norfolk), and in Kent, Sussex, Buckinghamshire, Bedfordshire, Essex, Middlesex, Herefordshire, Monmouthshire and the West Country. Both long and short reflexes occur in Lincolnshire, Hertfordshire, Cheshire, Derbyshire, Shropshire, Worcestershire and Warwickshire. The North and NML, as with /a/, show no lengthening, except for one area each in S Yorkshire (21) and E Central Lancashire (12). This change too then is basically of southern provenance, with only marginal occurrences north of Norfolk; though it is not particularly eastern. The SED distribution is shown in (12) below.

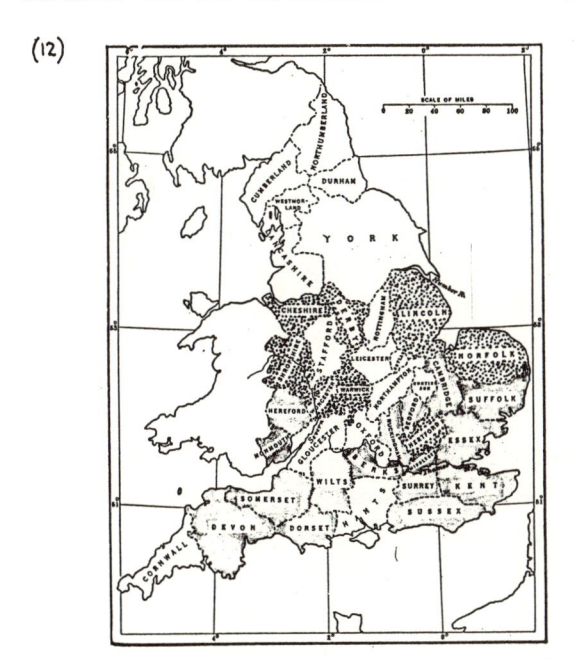

(12)

Lengthening I, ME /o/ (SED)
☐ only long reflexes
▨ both short & long reflexes

(d) ME /a/, Lengthening II (bag, hand). The ME /a/, EModE /æ/ story is even more complex in some southern areas. At some point after Lengthening I (for remarks on chronology see below), /æ/ lengthened before voiced stops and nasals (except /ŋ/). In all dialects showing quality change of the output of Lengthening I, the Lengthening II vowel is distinct both from that and from isolative /æ/: the most typical pattern is [æ] in cat, [aː] or the like in bath, and [æː] (often slightly raised and centralized, sometimes with a slight [ə]-offglide) in hand. In many U.S. dialects, where there was no shifting of the Lengthening I output, both categories have merged, i.e. [æ] in cat vs. [æː] in bath, hand. This change shows up in both northern and southern hemisphere ETEs, in much the same form, which raises some historical difficulties, as we will see below.

The reports in Wright and SED show a clear SE provenance, with minor northern and western enclaves. Wright reports [æː] before voiced stops and nasals only in Kent (§ § 23, 47); the SED shows a wider distribution, but still mainly eastern. The greatest concentrations are in Kent, Surrey, Berkshire and Middlesex, with scattered instances in Norfolk and Suffolk, one report each in Hereford and Dorset, and two marginal ones in Northumberland (S.v. bag V.8.5, hand VI.7.1). The picture for the traditional vernaculars is as in (13) below.

Absolute dating is difficult.[11] The evidence suggests that it's essentially vernacular in origin; it certainly is not noted as a possibility in the Received Standard in the 19th century. Ellis (1889: 3) gives a short vowel in man, sad and Sweet (1877: § 80) notes no difference between the nuclei of hat and man. I assume that if observers as sharp as Ellis and Sweet didn't hear it, it wasn't there. Since it wasn't stigmatized either, it seems that its entry into London vernacular as well as RP must be late, Ida Ward remarks in the 1940s that in RP this lengthening 'has long been noted' (1945: 202), which is not helpful.

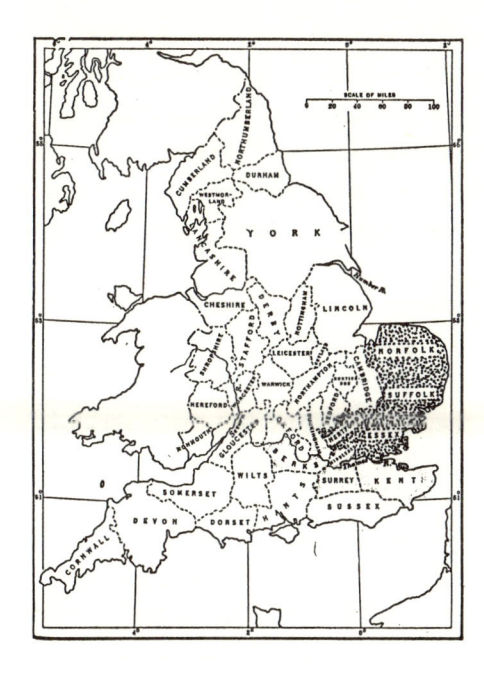

[Map of England with legend:]

Lengthening II, ME /a/
(bag, hand)

☐ only long reflexes
▨ scattered or marginal lengthening

Jones (1964: 874) gives a pattern suggesting rather recent lexical diffusion, i.e. he shows it only 'in certain words', usually long [æ:] in adjectives in -ad (bad, sad), short [æ] in nouns (lad, pad), common length before nasals, etc. This sort of pattern is not unusual for this change.

But this is clearly a case where any historiography based on RP developments is beside the point; Lengthening II is universal in the ETEs, and shows virtually identical exceptions and peculiarities in Mainland and ETE dialects. No single rule that entered RP in the late 19th century could have virtually identical idiosyncracies in Southampton, New York, and Cape Town -- which this one does. In other words, the paradox is that it must have originated in the vernaculars early enough to be exported and codified in the ETEs, but even the best observers didn't catch it at the right time.

Even though the rule seems 'phonetically natural' (what could be more expectable than lengthening of a vowel, especially an open one, before voiced stops and nasals?), it would be impossible to make out a case for convergence. First, Lengthening II occurs only in a very small part of the southern Mainland; second, it is so idiosyncratic in detail that convergence is unimaginable.

If we look only at presence vs. absence in some canonical lexical items, convergence would seem plausible; but certain segmental exclusions and morphosyntactic exceptions make anything except common origin hard to swallow. In the few cases where it has been exhaustively studied (Fudge 1977, Lass 1981), its results are odd, to say the least, and the correspondences between Mainland and ETE are striking. Taking Fudge's Southampton to represent a Mainland dialect in which (unlike conservative RP) Lengthening II is well advanced, my own New York City dialect as representing a typical northern ETE, and Cape Town standard for the southern ETEs, we find results like those in table (14).

(14)

	S	NY	CT		S	NY	CT
pal	−	−	−	hand	+	+	+
tank	−	−	−	and	−	−	−
grab	+	+	+	jazz	+	+	+
bad	+	+	+	has	−	−	−
badge	+	+	+	as	−	−	−
Madge	−	−	−				
				Pamela	−	−	−
man	+	+	+	Pam	+	+	+
can (aux)	−	−	−	Samuel	+	+	+
can (n, v)	+	+	+				
				bladder	+	−	−
				damn	+	+	+
				dam	−	+	+
				crag	−	+	+

Note the following: (i) although Lengthening II occurs before /-m(C), -n(C), it fails before /-ŋ (C); (ii) it fails before /l/; (iii) it fails in conjunctions, auxiliary verbs, and

have as both auxiliary and main verb (unlike can, where it fails
only in the auxiliary); (iv) certain full-name/hypocoristic
patterns show agreements too bizarre to be convergent. Further,
all dialects that show it also display the results of incomplete
lexical diffusion, aside from the morphosyntactic conditioning;
and this varies from dialect to dialect. Thus Fudge has long
[æ:] in candy, candle, but short [æ] in brandy, Randall; length
in bladder but not adder, in bag, brag but not crag, in damn but
not dam. My dialect has length in all except bladder and adder
of the examples above; but it has length in add, adds but not
adze, in mad, madder (comparative) but not the colour madder, in
badly but not Baddeley, Hadley.

Overall, Lenthening II always fails before /l ŋ/ and in
auxiliaries, and, as; and it is never apparently fully
implemented in major category words where it could be. This
suggests that the rule was exported at an early stage in its
evolution, where the segmental environments and morphosyntactic
constraints were firmly established, but where diffusion through
the lexicon was still relatively fluid and preliminary.

4. Swamping and Layering.

ETEs typically grow out of multiple migrations, and each
component wave tends to have a distinct regional character. But
it is not normally the case that all sub-migrations contribute
equally -- or at all -- to the character of the final product.
Nor does this product necessarily reflect in any very close way
the demography of the original wave, or any particular one, or
even all of them put together. There is a peculiar sort of
development in most cases, in which the overall profile of the
'finished' ETE tends to be of one regional type -- southern --
regardless of what other types are represented in the settlement
history.

Of course Mainland features, bolstered or not by population

movements, can enter an ETE at a relatively advanced stage of its evolution, and even override features already present. The New England and southeastern U.S. 'broad a' in bath, etc. is a case in point. The settlement areas that show [æ] in cat vs. [a: ~ ä:] in bath are all generally at least half a century too early for this to have been part of the input; the first Mainland testimony in the late 1670s suggests that lengthening (not to mention quality change) could not have occurred in the inputs to coastal settlements like Jamestown (1607), Plymouth (1620), etc. This must be an 18th-century feature superimposed on areas that had developed their own regional character much earlier (for the distribution today, see Kurath & McDavid 1961: Map 14).

Thus it is possible for ETEs (especially the older ones) to show both archaic and advanced features, often stemming from quite different layers of the Mainland evolutionary sequence; ETEs do not result from simple differential change in a monolithic input. (Though to say this is not to agree with Dillard; see below and § 5.) More rarely, ETEs may show distinctly 'odd' features, incongruous with both initial input and overall regional type; I will look at one such case below.

When a cluster of related but in detail dissimilar dialects moves into an ET situation, there are two main developmental options:
- (i) One particular input type will dominate, and this will determine the overall etymological type of the ET dialect.
- (ii) There will be (greater or lesser) 'mixture' or 'recodification', with etymological types from more than one input selected, and a 'compromise' output.

Despite the 'levelling and mixing' model of scholars like Dillard, and for complex and not entirely well understood reasons, option (i) is overwhelmingly the ETE choice: this is really what I mean by saying that all ETEs are southern. There is however a certain messiness in detail, with occasional (if rare) deviations in direction (ii); this creates a local 'palimpsest' effect, of a kind familiar from other ET languages. (Yiddish is a classic case: see Weinreich 1980 in its 'determinants'; it seems impossible to trace any dialect of Yiddish to any particular localized dialect of older German.)

Overall ETE histories appear similar enough from case to case to allow us to point out some general tendencies -- grandiosely 'laws'-- of ETE formation. What I say below is intended only to apply to English; whether anything similar is the case for other ET dialects depends on a number of factors, including the existence of a recognized and geographically coherent standard, and a host of 'quasi-standards' similar in local type. Thus the development of Yiddish, beginning in late OHG or early MHG times, would not be expected to follow the ETE pattern.

The most important of the ETE tendencies I will call the Law of Swamping:

(i) In cases of mixed input to an ETE, whatever the original demography, the output is (a) southern, and (b) more eastern than western.

(ii) Whatever the size of the non-southern input, it will normally leave only unsystematic relics (e.g. odd lexical items, idioms, or minor constructions); there will rarely be larger-scale structural effects (e.g. in the system of phonemic oppositions).

In short, outside of Ulster (see below), everything tends toward the southeast. I will look below at one of the few cases where this generalization fails -- the 'exception that proves the rule', as it were.

An example of swamping that shows the process fairly clearly is South African English; even though the 1820 Settler input was largely southeastern (see Lass & Wright 1985 and references), there were in later times considerable northern and Scottish inputs; yet the only clear feature of northern provenance, as far as I know, is the secondary-stressed unreduced vowel in the

The conservative Pattern 1 has in fact (as (16) suggests) re-surfaced in RP and many other southern varieties, with 'de-merger' of Lengthening I outputs and their return to the /ɒ/ class; this is now the case for most younger (quasi-) standard speakers in the south of England, though less so in some southern hemisphere ETEs, and not at all in the U.S. The important point to note here is that a northern dialect with /ɒ/ in cot/frost is 'archaic' or 'original'; a southern one with the same pattern is innovative (if 'pseudo-archaic'). An object-lesson in the importance of establishing historical chains that go beyond simple comparison, if there ever was one.

But there is yet another development, Pattern 3: merger of all three categories (ME /o/ isolative, Lengthening I, and /au/ under one value. This is typically Scots: central Scots with cot/frost/caught levelled under /ɔ/, and 'Core' Ulster Scots and some western Mainland Scots areas (e.g. Argyll) with levelling under /ɔ:/ (for details Harris 1985: 22ff). I will call these Patterns 3a and 3b respectively. Historically, they come about as shown in (17) below.

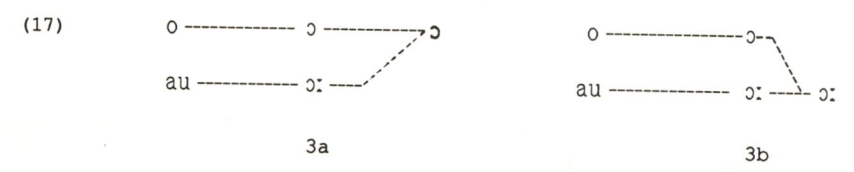

(17)
```
      o ----------- ɔ ----------→ ɔ           o --------------- ɔ-╮
                                  ↗                                ╲
      au ---------- ɔː ----⟋                  au ------------- ɔː --- ɔː
                 3a                                       3b
```

Pattern 3a is a natural outcome of Aitken's Law (§ 2), with /o/ remaining short and /ɔː/ shortening except in the long environments; 3b stems from an extension of the lengthening subpart of Aitken's Law, making the rule applicable to historical /a e o/ or some subset in all environments, thus producing new contrastive long vowels. Dialects of this type then may for instance show /aː/ in bath and /ɔː/ in frost not from Lengthening I but from Aitken-generalization; another nice example of the same outcome from quite different historical processes (cf. /ɒ/ in cot/frost/caught above).

WHERE DO EXTRATERRITORIAL ENGLISHES COME FROM?   271

prefix con-/com- (/kɒnfɜ́ː/ confer, /kɒmpjúːtə/ computer, etc.);
and the only Scots residues seem to be pinkie 'little finger' and
stay in the sense 'reside (habitually or permanently)'. All
non-SE features have been swamped by SE ones -- even though the
original and later inputs were fairly rich in settlers from other
areas.

    As I suggested above, however, not all developments are this
simple; there occasionally arise more complex situations, in
which the 'intrusion' of non-southern features into a southern
matrix can create partially hybrid systems, with a clearly
visible layering of etymological types -- what I referred to
above as a 'palimpsest'. A case in point is the well-known
cot/caught merger, which occurs not only in Scotland and Northern
Ireland (cf. § 2), but in the U.S. and Canada as well. The
overall history of the two categories involved is sketched out in
(15) below.

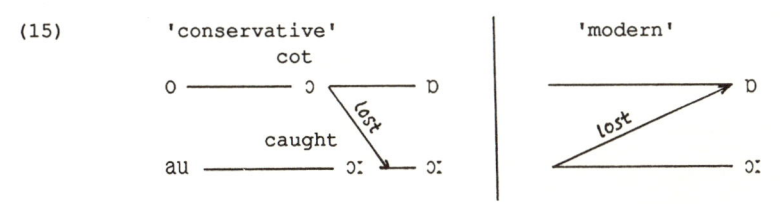

(15)   'conservative' | 'modern'
                cot
       o ——————— ɔ ⟍   ɒ | —————————————→ ɒ
                      lost | lost
            caught
      au ————————— ɔː ——— ɔː | ————————————— ɔː

That is, Lengthening II of ME /o/ (§ 3) produces a merger
with the monophthongal reflex of ME /au/. Thus for England (and
most ETEs) there are two major kinds of reflex-distribution,
which I will call Pattern 1 and Pattern 2, as in (16) below.

(16)	N, Adv RP	Cons RP, S	South HE	Mid Ulster	New York
cot		ɒ	ɑ	ɑ	ä
	ɒ				
lost		ɔː	ɑː	ɔː	ɔː – ɔə
caught	ɔː				

              PATTERN 1   PATTERN 2

The important typological point about Pattern 3 is that whether the merger-result is short or long, the development type is distinctly non-southern; in a framework where we can sensibly oppose 'Scots' and 'English' (cf. §2 and Lass 1976: ch. 1), it is non-English, but distinctly Scots. That is, not only do we have context-free merger of two vowel categories (common enough elsewhere: cf. ME/e:/ and /ɛ:/ in beet/beat); but complete merger of two quantitatively opposed categories under one quantitative type, i.e. a distinctly non-English kind of neutralization.

This merger has an important ETE projection. Most of Canada and a large (and apparently growing) part of the U.S. show a Pattern 3 merger (usually exemplified in writing on AmE by cot/caught or hock/hawk, and now by Wells 1982 as lot/thought). Phonetically the merger is quite variable; there are long and short, rounded and unrounded outcomes. In eastern New England the most typical value is [ɒ̈]; western Pennsylvania shows [ɑ~ɒ] (variably advanced or centralized), and Canada and most of the western U.S. [ɑ(:)~ɒ(:)], with long perhaps more common than short, and again variable peripherality. We thus have, over a range of dialects, the Pattern 3 types shown in (18) below.

(18)

	Central Scots	Ulster Scots	Canada	West Penn	E New England
cot lost caught	ɔ	ɔː	ɒ(ː)~ɑ(ː)	ɒ ~ ɑ	ɒ̈
	3a	3b			

The geographical spread is discontinuous; the merger covers Canada and two main U.S. areas: eastern New England, and a gradually widening belt beginning in western Pennsylvania around Pittsburgh, and moving west until it covers most of the western U.S. except for northern Washington state. According to data from the Linguistic Atlas of the Upper Midwest (Allen 1976: 24, cited in Wells 1982: §6.1.2) the merger has been moving north into Wisconsin, Michigan and Minnesota, largely in the past four decades or so. The current distribution, with arrows showing the direction of movement, is shown in (19) below (after Cassidy 1982).

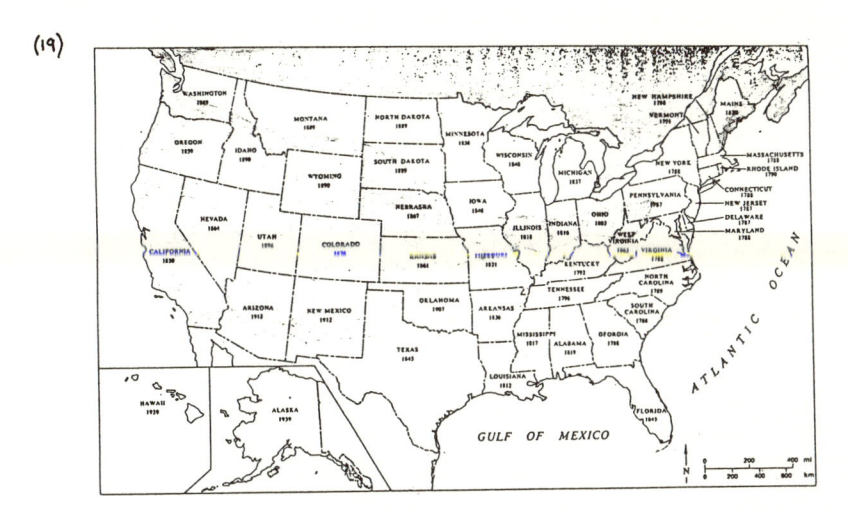

(19)

cot/caught Merger

Despite its recent spread into new areas, the merger itself is clearly an old one, and ties in well with settlement demography. The most likely source is Ulster Scots; and there was an extensive 'Scots-Irish' (the usual American term) influx into the U.S., beginning in the 1720s. These settlers first came to the inland south, and later to New England, and thence moved westward into the midwest and further. In most of the U.S., even in areas of majority Ulster Scots and other Scots settlement, the Scots element was totally swamped;[12] this one feature seems to be the only one that has established itself and overridden the native patterns (as in fact it appears to be doing again in the northern midwest).

From the point of view of origin type, then, American dialects with cot/caught merger are 'hybrid'. The southern features have swamped the pull/pool merger, the non-merger of the fir/fur/fern nuclei, and Aitken's Law; this one has swamped out the original length/quality contrast for these etymological sets. These dialects display a layered or composite structure, whose origins we can visualize as in (20) below.

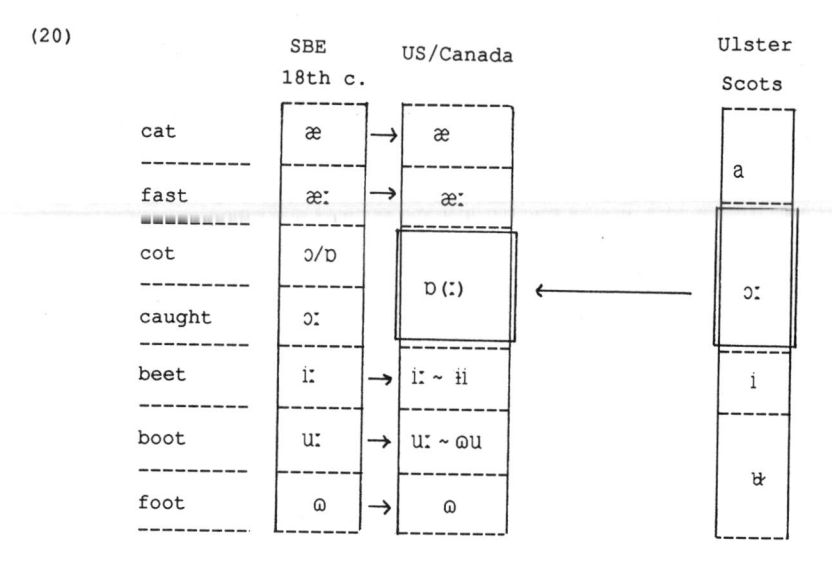

(20)

	SBE 18th c.	US/Canada		Ulster Scots
cat	æ	→	æ	a
fast	æː	→	æː	
cot	ɔ/ɒ		ɒ(ː)	ɔː
caught	ɔː			
beet	iː	→	iː ~ ɨi	i
boot	uː	→	uː ~ ɯu	ʉ
foot	ɷ	→	ɷ	

(arrow from Ulster Scots ɔː box pointing left to US/Canada ɒ(ː) box)

5. Regionality Revisited.

I think it's now clear that Dillard's contention (§ 1) that there are no 'clear-cut correlations between ... features of American English and British dialects' is untenable, and that there is no need to give up traditional assumptions about the origins of AmE (or any other ETEs). Certainly there is 'mixture', and certainly nobody is going to be silly enough to look for utterly unchanged 'living fossils'; even today's coelacanth is somewhat evolved and altered. But everything that has happened to the ETEs has happened within a clearly defined regional framework.

It might be interesting in this connection to sum all this up in a kind of 'southernness' league-table for some of the major

WHERE DO EXTRATERRITORIAL ENGLISHES COME FROM? 275

ETEs. The data is given in (21) below, and I think it makes my point as well as anything. In the table, circled values for particular features indicate 'aberration' or regional incongruity (deviation from 'south'); the fact that out of 84 possibles there are only five such divergences speaks for itself.

(21)   'Southernness' League Tables for ETEs

			eUS	wUS	sHE	SAE	AusE	NZE
N	Scots	1. Loss of V-Length	−	−	−	−	−	−
		2. *pull/pool* merged	−	−	−	−	−	−
		3. *cot/caught* merged	−	⊕	−	−	−	−
		4. ME /ir er ur/ distinct	−	−	⊕	−	−	−
		5. Unshifted ME /u:/	−	−	−	−	−	−
		6. Front ME /o:/	−	−	−	−	−	−
		7. Front OE /ɑ:/	−	−	−	−	−	−
S		8. *cut/put* split	+	+	⊕/−	+	+	+
		9. ME /a/ > [æ]	+	+	⊖	+	+	+
		10. ME /a/ Length I	+	+	+	+	+	+
		11. ME /o/ Length I	+	+	+	+	+	+
		12. ME /a/ Length II	+	+	⊖	+	+	+
	SE	13. Quality-shift in *last*	−	−	−	+	+	+
		14. ME /a/ > [ɛ]	−	−	−	+	+	+

NOTES

* Some of the material discussed here was presented in seminars at the University of Helsinki in 1986; I am grateful to the participants (especially Matti Rissanen, Fran Karttunen and Ossi Ihalainen) for valuable comments. The overall picture and point of view owes a lot to discussions with Susan Wright; see our work reported in Lass & Wright (1985, 1986). I also owe a great debt to Sylvia Adamson for believing that ETE study ought to be part of general Anglistics, and to Bob Stockwell for comments on the oral version of this paper, many of which I have foolishly disregarded in the interests of brevity. Much of the work on which this is based was supported by a grant from the Human Sciences Research Council.

Note: SED Survey of English Dialects. For all references in text, see Orton, et al. in bibliography.

1. A lot of 'history' of ETEs consists of programmatic accounts of Mainland sources of selected features (e.g. Kurath, 1928, 1964); there is little in the way of methodological discussion, or attempts at defining a broader framework. As far as I can tell, for instance, the historiography of U.S. English (in the detailed or 'philological' sense) hasn't proceeded much beyond the fine Problemstellung in Kurath (1964). There has however been some recent awareness of the sociohistorical complexities of ETE history, and some excellent preliminary work on Australian English (Horvath 1985: ch. 3). But detailed internal history of the traditional kind is sorely lacking; a notable exception is Harris (1985), a brilliantly worked and nearly unique example of the sort of thing I suggested over a decade ago ought to be done, and made a few preliminary attempts at myself (Lass 1976: ch. 5).
2. This is true even for SAE, which after its long coexistence with Afrikaans might be expected to show profound influences. But the loan-effects here are largely superficial, and where they do exist less direct than might be expected (Lass & Wright, 1985, 1986).
3. I am avoiding the vexed question of whether Mainland Englishes themselves might be part of a 'post-creole continuum', whether Anglo-French (Bailey & Maroldt 1977) or Anglo-Norse (Poussa 1982). I tend to side rather with the skepticism of Görlach (1986); but by the time English dialects are transported in bulk this is no longer an issue.
4. Southern HE is a bit of a hybrid, since it does show some contact-features; but fewer than are generally supposed (see Harris 1984).
5. This simplified taxonomy glosses over internal genetic complications in the interests of coverage. We might note (a) that the bulk of the early Canadian input was from the U.S. (migration of

6. Loyalists in the 1780s: Bailey 1982, Lass 1987: 5.8.2); (b) much of the early NZ settlement was Australian (Eagleson 1982); (c) the English of the 'Federation' (now white Zimbabwean, etc.) seems to have a large Transvaal component, and is in many respects probably a subtype of Transvaal SAE (a preliminary judgement, in the absence of detailed studies).

6. By the criteria to be given below, Southern HE is also southern English, if with a Midland admixture; but it has no northern features. Northern HE is a different story: Ulster Scots is ET Scots, not English, and Mid Ulster English is typologically a 'mixture' of HE and Scots (Harris 1985). The extremely complex profile of Mid Ulster (e.g. Belfast Vernacular), with its Scots vowel-length pattern and its non-Scots separation of ME /o/ and /au/ (cot/caught: see 4 below) is due to continuing contact with a Scots vernacular: a unique situation among the ETEs. I will look at a simpler 'mixture' in 4.

7. See the composite map in Wakelin (1972: 87), which shows the isogloss crossings. The Midlands have been noted as a special case ever since the 14th century; Anglicists are familiar with Ranulph Higden's comment in the 1320s about the 'mixed' nature of these dialects. In John of Trevisa's version, the Mercii, þat buþ men of myddle Engelond, as hyt were parteners of þe endes, undurstondeþ betre þe syde longages, Norþeron and Souþeron, þan Norþreon and Souþeron undurstondeþ eyþer oþer' (Mossé 1950: 289; cf. Lass 1976: 89). It should be noted that here and elsewhere my focus--for historical reasons--is on the rural 'traditional dialects' (Wells 1982), not modern urban ones, and on vernacular rather than standard features generally.

8. This criterion allows us to recognize late northern loans in the southern standard (e.g. *gruesome*: cf. G *grausam*<MHG *grusom*). The same is true for the fronted OE /a:/ criterion mentioned below: *hale* (cf. *whole*) < OE *hāl* is also a northernism.

9. Along perhaps with typical Essex features like (full or partial) merger of ME /i:/ and /oi/ (*bile/boil*). Ellis (1889: 227f) quotes an anonymous pamphlet of 1817 giving this as a typical 'London Errour'. Though it might also be a survival from an earlier standard type: Nares (1784: 25ff) gives 'long I' (= /ai/) in *joint, boil*, etc.

10. In many U.S. dialects it is now no longer appropriate to speak of a length distinction among allophones of /æ/; the effects of Lengthening I and II have been obscured by a context-free lengthening and diphthongization--often with raising--of *all* /æ/. Thus in much of the non-northeastern, non-southern U.S., both *cat* and *bad* are [æ·ə]. In those dialects affected by the 'Northern Cities Shift' (Labov et al. 1972), older /æ/ is long in all positions, and often as high as [e·ə] or [ɪ·ə].

11. The lengthening of /æ/ discussed here is to be distinguished from the minor lengthenings in similar environments reported from at least the 17th century (Luick 1965: § 576, Anm. 1-3). The

lengthening in question here has been more clearly
'phoneticized' (i.e. extended, made more salient), and there is
virtually always some qualitative difference from non-
lengthened /æ/. In addition, it is not an across-the-board
change; see below.

12. A possible exception to this may be inland U.S. rhoticity,
which is commonly believed to be an Ulster or general Scots
heritage. But -- given the times of settlement -- it could just
as easily be a provincial Mainland English feature from
anywhere except the EML; as late as the 1950s even rural Kent
and Surrey were still rhotic (cf. Lass & Wright 1986: 204ff).

REFERENCES

Aitken, A. J. (1981). The Scottish vowel length rule. In Benskin, M. &
  Samuels, M.L. (eds.), *So meny peple longages and tonges:
  Philological essays in Scots and mediaeval English presented to
  Angus McIntosh*. Edinburgh: Middle English Dialect Project,
  University of Edinburgh.
Allen, H.B. (1973-6). *The Linguistic Atlas of the Upper Midwest*. 3
  vols. Minneapolis: University of Minnesota Press.
Bailey, C-J. & Maroldt, K. (1977). The French lineage of English. In
  Meisel, J. (ed.), *Langues en contact -- pidgins -- creoles --
  languages in contact*, 21-51. Tübingen: Narr.
------ & Görlach, M., (eds.), (1982). *English as a World Language*.
  Ann Arbor: University of Michigan Press.
Batchelor, T. (1809). *An Orthoepical analysis of the English
  Language*. London: Didier & Tebbett.
Cassidy, F.G. (1982). Geographical variation of English in the United
  States. In Bailey & Görlach (1982).
Cooper, C. (1685). *Grammatica linguae Anglicanae*. Facsimile ed.,
  1968. Menston: Scolar Press.
------ (1687). *The English Teacher*. Ed. B. Sundby. Lund Studies in
  English XXII, 1953. Lund: Gleerup.
Dillard, J.L. (1985). *Toward a social history of American English*.
  Berlin: Mouton de Gruyter.
Eagleson, R.D. (1982). English in Australia and New Zealand. In
  Bailey & Görlach (1982).
Ellis, A.J. (1889). *On early English pronunciation, with especial
  reference to Shakespeare and Chaucer. Part V, Existing dialectal
  as compared with West Saxon pronunciation*. London: Trübner.
Flint, M. (1740). *Prononciation de la langue angloise*. In Kökeritz,
  H. (1944), Mather Flint on early eighteenth-century pronunciation.
  *Skrifter utgivna av Kungl. Humanistiska vetenskapssamfundet i
  Uppsala*, 37.
Fudge, E.C. (1977). Long and short [æ] in one Southern British
  speaker's English. *JIPA* 7. 55-65.
Görlach, M. (1986) Middle English -- a creole? In Kastovsky, D. &
  Szwedek, A., *Linguistics across historical and geographical
  boundaries in honour of Jacek Fisiak on the occasion of his*

fiftieth birthday. Vol 1, Linguistic theory and historical linguistics, 329-44. Berlin: Mouton de Gruyter.
Harris, J.M. (1984). Syntactic variation and dialect divergence. JL 20. 303-28.
------ (1985). Phonological variation and change: Studies in Hiberno-English. Cambridge: Cambridge University Press.
Holmberg, B. (1964). On the concept of standard English and the history of modern English pronunciation. Lund: Gleerup.
Horvath, B. (1985). Variation in Australian English: the sociolects of Sydney. Cambridge: Cambridge University Press.
Jespersen, O. (1909). A Modern English Grammar on Historical Principles. I, Sounds and Spellings. Copenhagen: Munksgaard.
Jones, D. (1964). An Outline of English Phonetics. 9th ed. Cambridge: Heffer.
Kurath, H. (1928). The origin of the dialectal differences in spoken American English. Modern Philology 25. 285-95.
------ (1964). British sources of selected features of American pronunciation. In Abercrombie, Fry, MacCarthy, Scott, Trimm (eds.), In Honour of Daniel Jones. Papers contributed on the occasion of his eightieth birthday, 12 September, 1961. London: Longman.
------ & McDavid, R.I. Jr. (1961). The pronunciation of English in the Atlantic States. Ann Arbor: University of Michigan Press.
Labov, W., Yeager, M., Steiner, R. (1972). A quantitative study of sound change in progress. Philadelphia: U.S. Regional Survey.
Lass, R. (1974). Linguistic orthogenesis? Scots vowel quantity and the English length conspiracy. In Anderson, J.M. & Jones, C. (eds.), Historical Linguistics: Proceedings of the First International Conference on Historical Linguistics, Edinburgh, 2-7 September 1973, II, 311-52. Amsterdam: North Holland.
------ (1976). English phonology and phonological theory: Synchronic and diachronic studies. Cambridge: Cambridge University Press.
------ (1981). Undigested history and synchronic 'structure'. In Goyvaerts, D. (ed.), Phonology in the 1980s, 525-44. Ghent: E. Story-Scientia.
------ (1982). John Hart vindicatus ? A study in the interpretation of early phoneticians. Folia Linguistica Historica 1. 75-96.
------ (1987) The shape of English: structure and history. London: J.M. Dent.
------ & Wright, S. (1985). The South African Chain Shift: order out of chaos? In Eaton, R. et. al. (eds.), Papers from the Fourth International Conference on English Historical Linguistics. 137-61.
---------------- (1986). Endogeny vs. contact: 'Afrikaans influence' on South African English. English Worldwide 7.201-23.
Luick, K. (1965). Historiche Grammatic der englischen Sprache. 2 vols. Reprint. Oxford: Blackwell.
Mosse, F. (1950). A Handbook of Middle English. Baltimore: Johns Hopkins Press.
Nares, R. (1784). Elements of orthoepy. Facsimile ed., 1968. Menston: Scolar Press.
Orton, H. & Barry, M.V. (1969). Survey of English dialects. B, Basic Material: the West Midland Counties. Leeds: Arnold.

-------- & Halliday, W. (1962). *Survey of English dialects. B, Basic Material: the Northern counties and the Isle of man.* Leeds: Arnold.
-------- & Tilling, P. (1969). *Survey of English dialects. B, Basic Material: the East Midland counties and East Anglia.* Leeds: Arnold.
-------- & Wakelin, M. (1967). *Survey of English dialects. B, Basic Material: the Southern counties.* Leeds: Arnold.
Poussa, P. (1982). The evolution of early standard English. *Studia Anglica Posnaniensia* 14. 69-85.
Sweet, B. (1877). *A Handbook of phonetics.* Oxford: Clarendon Press.
Vaiana Taylor, M. (1972). A study in the dialect of the southern counties of Scotland. Unpublished PhD thesis. Bloomington: Indiana University.
Viereck, W. (1985). On the origins and developments of American English. In Fisiak, J. (ed.), *Papers from the Sixth International Conference on Historical Linguistics,* 561-70. Amsterdam: John Benjamins.
Wakelin, M. (1972). *English dialects: An Introduction.* London: Athlone Press.
Ward, I.C. (1945). *The phonetics of English.* 4th ed. Cambridge: Heffer.
Weinreich, M. (1980). *History of the Yiddish Language.* Chicago: University of Chicago Press.
Wright, J. (1905). *The English dialect grammar.* Oxford: Frowde.

OBSOLESCENCE AND UNIVERSAL GRAMMAR

DAVID LIGHTFOOT
University of Maryland

1. *Triggers and obsolescence.* Work on language change can take on a new light when conducted in the context of a research program seeking the psychological basis for language. One such program focusses on the kinds of computations that are involved in natural language and seeks to find what a person's linguistic capacity consists of, how it functions, how it develops in us, etc. For language acquisition it adopts an explanatory model of (1). A child is genetically endowed with certain information and, when exposed to a typical linguistic environment, develops some particular mature capacity. (1.b) reflects the usual linguistic terminology.

(1) a. trigger (linguistic genotype --> phenotype)
    b. primary linguistic data (Universal Grammar --> grammar)

A person's mature linguistic capacity does not simply mirror the trigger experience that he or she had as a child, and is much richer than that. Because the stimulus is too poor to determine all aspects of the mature capacity, particular principles and parameters must be postulated at the level of Universal Grammar (UG) and language acquisition is then viewed as a process of setting the parameters defined at UG.

For example, many English-speakers contract *want to* in structures like (2.a) and pronounce one word *wanna*, but not in (2.b). Similarly, in (2.c) *is* is usually contracted and pronounced *z*, being attached, one can show, to the following word *in*; but not in (2.d).

(2) a. who$_i$ do you want [PRO to see e$_i$]
    b. who$_i$ do you want [e$_i$ to see New York]
    c. I wonder when$_i$ the game is in New York e$_i$
    d. I wonder where$_i$ the game is e$_i$ in two weeks

The correct generalization seems to be that phonological processes may be sensitive to empty positions which are the residues of syntactic movement rules ("e$_i$" above), but not to other empty elements. But how does the child "learn" this? Children are not informed that contracted forms do not occur in structures like (2.b) and (2.d), nor is there any evidence that they experiment with such forms and react to adverse or uncomprehending reactions from the people they are speaking to. Nor do children simply reproduce conservatively what they have heard. Children come to know where the contracted forms do not occur, but the relevant information is not part of the input to the acquisition process, not part of the stimulus or the trigger. Therefore, if certain aspects of what children come to know are not determined by their experience, they must come from somewhere else. Such arguments from the poverty of the stimulus have shaped proposals about what children must know independently of their linguistic experience, i.e. the principles and parameters of UG. I have alluded here to one of the simplest such arguments I know, but there are many arguments in the literature and there are several rich hypotheses about UG, whose consequences have been examined for several languages.

Any argument from the poverty of the stimulus is based on assumptions about the nature of the trigger experience, e.g. the availability of alternating forms like *want to* and *wanna*, *is* and *z*, but the unavailability of information about the non-occurrence of certain forms in certain environments. Much work on generative grammar is flawed through ignoring the trigger experience and postulating parameters of UG which could not be set by the kind of data that children have access to. However, if we ask what the trigger consists of, it is plausible to say that it is a haphazard set of simple utterances made in context and of a type that a child would hear frequently; for discussion and for a claim that the trigger consists only of unembedded material, see Lightfoot (1989). The trigger is clearly less than a child's total linguistic experience; for example, a child may be exposed to a foreign house-guest who speaks an unusual and defective form of English, but this typically has no noticeable effect on the child's mature speech and therefore is not part of the trigger.

Sometimes the trigger may be *systematically* less than what a child hears, which brings us to obsolescent forms and language change. As a form becomes obsolete, it is heard by children but does not become part of their productive system, i.e. it does not trigger something which would cause it to be generated by the child's emerging grammar. It is hard to see how this could be due to chance, and an explanation is required. The obsolescence of a form cannot be attributed directly to a foreign borrowing or to an innovation motivated by expressive factors, the two sources of externally induced change (see Lightfoot 1979: ch.7). Rather, it must have a grammatical explanation, being the by-product of a new parameter setting which is triggered by new primary data.

Therefore, obsolescent structures provide a novel window into UG and the limits of the trigger, for we must explain why children at certain stages "ignored" some of the available data, which, if part of the trigger, would have led to a different mature capacity, a different grammar (see Vincent 1989).

The significance of obsolescent structures will become clear as we examine three cases and ask how they might be explained.

2. *Null subject effects.* Much attention has been paid recently to the phenomenon of empty subjects, whereby forms like *saw New York* occur in certain languages, and are associated with a variety of other properties. The obsolescence of such forms in French casts interesting light on the treatment of this phenomenon.

Chomsky (1981) and Rizzi (1982) treated empty subjects of this type as instances of PRO, i.e. a NP which is unindexed at S-structure and which occurs only in ungoverned positions. It does not occur in English because the subject position is governed by INFL (3.a).[1] In Italian, however, INFL lowers on to the verb in the syntax, entailing that the NP is not governed by INFL or any lexical category at S-structure (3.b). The parametric difference between English and Italian lies in whether INFL lowers on to the verb in the syntax, and one might argue that the trigger for a positive setting of that parameter is the occurrence of sentences like *saw New York*.

(3) a. [NP INFL $_{VP}$[see New York]]
    b. [NP $_{VP}$[INFL+see New York]]

Another approach says certain kinds of PROs (i.e. those which are not of arbitrary reference) occur in *governed* positions (see Hornstein & Lightfoot 1987 and the references cited there). Thus *saw New York* in Italian etc has a subject NP which is governed. Italian has a subject postposing rule which adjoins the subject to the VP and yields structures like (4.a); that rule would also yield (4.b), where the postposed NP is empty and governed by the verb.

(4)   a.   Piero non crede [che e_i INFL $_{VP}$[$_{VP}$[mi possa spaventare] nessuno$_i$]]
          Piero not think that   can frighten me anybody
   b.   [e_i INFL $_{VP}$[$_{VP}$[see New York] PRO$_i$]]

Therefore, as the Italian child acquires the subject postposing rule, she automatically also acquires sentences with empty subjects. This approach becomes more plausible when one notes that languages may have other devices which render the empty subject governed. Adams (1987) argues that Old French showed verb-second properties and had a rule moving a verb to Comp in main clauses, just as in modern Dutch and German.[2] The resulting structure is (5), where the empty subject is governed by the preposed verb.

(5)   einsi corurent$_i$ $_S$[PRO e_i par mer tant que il vindrent a Cad]
      so   ran (they)   by   sea until they came to Cadmee

The fact that verbs do not move to Comp in embedded clauses explains the striking fact that in Old French empty subjects occur only in main clauses; so, *il* in (5) may not be omitted, which is the reverse of what a functional approach would lead one to expect. Under this analysis, the French child acquired empty subjects as a by-product of the verb movement process. Adams goes on to show that empty subjects became obsolete as the verb movement rule was lost; the verb movement rule was lost as structures like (6.a) were re-analysed as (6.b).

(6) a. Jean$_i$ aime$_j$ $_S$[e$_i$ e$_j$ Marie]
     b. $_S$[Jean aime Marie]

This is the right *kind* of explanation for the obsolescence of empty subjects in French: the loss is keyed to the re-analysis of simple NP V... sentences as subject-verb structures, which was in turn provoked by primary data. The account depends on a treatment of PRO whereby it may be governed.

3. *Inversion and negation*. It is well-known that earlier forms of English allowed inverted and negative sentences like (7), where a regular verb occurs initially and to the left of a negative, just like a modal auxiliary (8).

(7) a. saw Jay New York?
     b. Jay saw not New York
(8) a. can Jay see New York?
     b. Jay can not see New York

Forms like (7) dropped out of the language by the seventeenth century and this has been associated with the development of a new category of modal verbs (Lightfoot 1979, but see Lightfoot 1988 and forthcoming for some revisions to the earlier account in the light of observations by Warner 1983). But how exactly should that association be made? Lightfoot (1979) claimed that the inversion rule in Middle English was something along the lines of (9.a), where "V" covered both *saw* and *can*, which at that time were instances of V; but the later rule was (9.b), when INFL covered *can* but not *saw*, which now were members of different categories. (I shall focus here on the inverted forms, but exactly the same issues arise with the negatives).

(9) a. adjoin V to Comp
    b. adjoin INFL to Comp
    c. adjoin $\begin{Bmatrix} \text{INFL} \\ \text{V} \end{Bmatrix}$ to Comp

However, as the new modal category was introduced, children were hearing both (7.a) and (8.a). Such primary data should have triggered a rule like (9.c), allowing either a modal or a verb to prepose. However, we know that forms like (7.a) dropped out, even though children heard such forms and must have heard them frequently. An explanation might be that disjunctions like that in (9.c) are not permitted by UG, but it is hard to see how to state that limitation in a framework which allows only minimal rules of the form "Move alpha". That suggests the need for another approach.

One useful alternative postulates that in languages like Middle English, Dutch, French, German etc. verbs move to Comp in a two-step process via INFL. One might generalize along the lines of Chomsky (1986) and say that Move alpha moves heads only to other head positions. So in a structure like (10), a verb might move as indicated; it could not move directly to Comp without violating locality restrictions (whose form need not concern us here).[3]

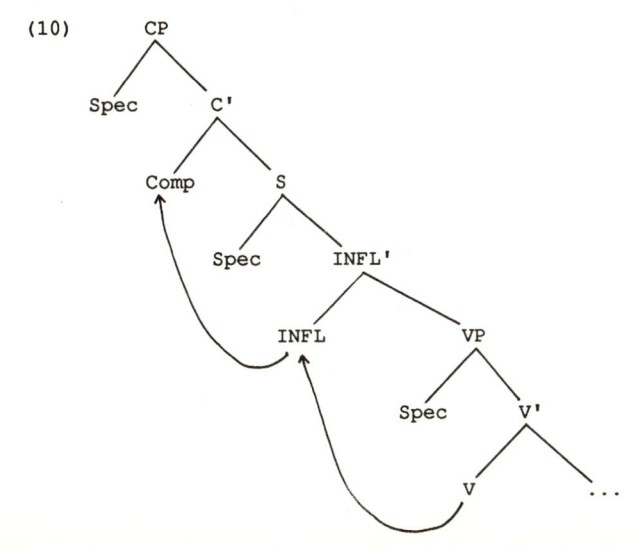

(10)
```
          CP
         /  \
       Spec  C'
            /  \
          Comp  S
                /  \
             Spec  INFL'
                   /    \
                INFL    VP
                        / \
                     Spec  V'
                          / \
                         V   ...
```

If something along these lines is correct, then one could attribute the obsolescence of (7.a) to the impossibility of moving V to INFL in modern English. This in turn is impossible because INFL is a lexical category, which may be occupied by the modal auxiliaries. Thus if INFL has an internal structure along the lines of (11) (where N features include person and number, i.e. "AGR", and V features include tense and, in modern English, modal auxiliaries), then UG would need to be structured in such a way that verbs may move into the righthand part of INFL only if that position is inherently non-lexical.

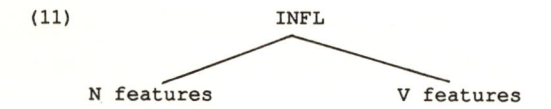

(11)
```
            INFL
           /    \
      N features  V features
```

I have identified two alternative possibilities but my general point is that something along these lines is needed to explain the obsolescence of highly productive forms like (7). As far as I know, nothing exists in the literature which is adequate, but the obsolescence of these forms suggests strongly that something more is needed. Studying the precise conditions under which these forms dropped out of the language will illuminate the exact UG condition.

4. *"Romance inversion" in Middle English.* Middle English had a process like that of modern Italian which allowed the subject to occur adjoined to the right of the VP. Thus while the language was still object-verb, one found sentences like *him like the priests*, where the initial NP was the object (as indicated here by the accusative case) and the final NP the subject (determining verb agreement) (12.a). The corresponding structure was either (12.b) or (12.c), depending on whether the pre-verbal *him* was in some pre-

sentential topic position (see below). This adjunction process occurred, as in modern Italian, with a class of "psychological" verbs, but dropped out of the language in late Middle English.

(12) a. him like the priests
         object-verb-subject
     b. $_S[e_i$ INFL $_{VP}[$ $_{VP}[$him like$]$ the priests$_i]]$
     c. him$_j$ $_S[e_i$ INFL $_{VP}[$ $_{VP}[e_j$ like$]$ the priests$_i]]$

These constructions have been discussed extensively from a variety of perspectives (see Allen 1986, Anderson 1986, Elmer 1981, Fischer & van der Leek 1983, Warner 1983, among others), but I raise them again here solely to consider how one might explain their obsolescence: if children heard such forms, why at a certain stage did they cease to use them?

One approach would link the demise of these forms to the new verb-object word order inside VP. As children fixed the V' parameter such that it contained verb-object instead of object-verb, so the relevant structure would become (13.a) (compare (12.b)).

(13) a. $_S[e_i$ INFL $_{VP}[$ $_{VP}[$like him$]$ the priests$_i]]$
     b. $_S[$him$_j$ INFL $_{VP}[$ $_{VP}[$like $e_j]$ the priests$_i]]$
     c. him$_j$ $_S[e_i$ INFL $_{VP}[$ $_{VP}[$like $e_j]$ the priests$_i]]$

To square this with what the child was hearing, *him like the priests*, it was necessary to move *him* forwards. There are three possible positions: a clitic position in front of the verb, the empty subject position, or a pre-sentential topic. First, there is no evidence that Middle English ever had French-style pre-verbal clitic positions but, even if it did, it would not suffice for non-pronominal objects. Second, moving *him* to the empty subject position would violate the theta-criterion; the resulting structure would be (13.b), where *him* is associated with two theta-positions and *the priests* with none. And that leaves only the third possibility, whereby *him* is a topic: it is unlikely that *him* would have the appropriate intonational contour to be treated as a topic, but, if so, it would conform to (12.c), where *him* was analyzed as a topic also in the earlier stage.

If we take these topic analyses seriously, then another explanation becomes possible for the obsolescence of the adjunction structures. There is some evidence that Old English was a null subject language (of section 0), and a structure like (12.c) would be one of the residual null subject effects, just as in Italian (cf (4.b) above). In that case, one could key the loss of the adjunction structures to the loss of whatever licensed empty subjects. So, (13.c) ceased to occur because empty subjects were no longer licensed.

There is obviously much more to be said about this case, but if we focus only on the loss of certain productive structures, there are plausible accounts available.

5. *Conclusion*. For each of the three cases we have looked at here I have considered at least two possible analyses, with different implications for UG. My goal has been to show the particular challenge raised by obsolescent structures for theories of UG, rather than to make any special claims about UG. Generative grammarians need to pay more attention to the nature of the child's trigger experience, because *all* of their analyses make claims about the trigger; those claims should be explicit and examined. In that context obsolescent structures are interesting because we know that they were heard but were not part of the trigger.

NOTES

1. Roughly, a lexical category *a* governs *b* if they share all maximal projections, i.e. if any maximal projection dominating *a* also dominates *b*, and vice versa.

2. This must be the Germanic-type verb movement rule, rather than the modern Romance subject postposing rule which moves subjects to the end of the VP (see section 2). One finds sentences like i. and ii., which need to be analyzed as indicated. If the subject were being postposed, one would expect *einsint aama Lancelot la damoisele* and *dont est venus ce?*.

   i. einsint aama$_i$ la damoisele $_{VP}$[e$_i$ Lancelot]
       thus   loved the girl   Lancelot
       thus the young lady loved Lancelot
   ii. dont est$_i$ ce $_{VP}$[e$_i$ venus]?
       whence is this come?

   If empty subjects are due to a Germanic-type verb movement rule in Old French, one must explain why Dutch and German lack them. Adams shows that an empty subject must be *canonically* governed. In French, a verb-object language, government was from left to right, but Dutch and German, being object-verb languages, have government from right to left. So the NP is canonically governed by *voit* in iii., but not by *ziet* in iv.

   iii. [(XP) voit$_i$ $_S$[NP INFL $_{VP}$[e$_i$ New York]]]
   iv. [(XP) ziet$_i$ $_S$[NP INFL $_{VP}$[New York e$_i$]]]

3. I adopt the structures used by Chomsky (1986), but I do not treat S as a phrasal category, IP. Although nicely symmetrical, if S is a phrasal category, it has many exceptional features: for example, given the discussion in section 2 above, one would have to allow a verb in Comp to govern a subject across an intervening maximal projection. See Lightfoot & Weinberg (1988) for discussion.

REFERENCES

Adams, Marianne. 1987. *Old French, Null Subjects, a Verb Second Phenomena*. Unpublished doctoral dissertation, UCLA.
Allen, Cynthia. 1986. 'Reconsidering the History of *like*'. *JL* 22.2.
Anderson, John. 1986. 'A Note on Old English Impersonals'. *JL* 22.1.
Chomsky, Noam. 1981. *Lectures on Government and Binding*. Dordrecht: Foris.
----. 1986. *Barriers*. Cambridge, MA: MIT Press.
Elmer, Willy. 1981. *Diachronic Grammar: The History of Old and Middle English Subjectless Constructions*. Tübingen: Niemeyer.
Fischer, Olga, and Fredericke van der Leek. 1983. 'The Demise of the Old English Impersonal Construction'. *JL* 19.2.
Hornstein, Norbert, and David Lightfoot. 1987. 'Predication and PRO'. *Language* 63.23-52.
Hyams, Nina. 1983. 'The Pro-drop Parameter in Child Grammars'. *Proceedings of the West Coast Conference on Formal Linguistics*. Stanford.
Lightfoot, David. 1979. *Principles of Diachronic Syntax*. Cambridge Studies in Linguistics 23. London: Cambridge University Press.
----. 1988. 'Syntactic Change'. In Fritz Newmeyer, ed. *Linguistics: the Cambridge Survey*. London: Cambridge University Press.
----. 1989. 'The Child's Trigger Experience: Degree-0 Learnability'. *Behavioral and Brain Sciences* 12.2.
----. Forthcoming. *New Parameter Settings*.
---- & Amy Weinberg. 1988. Review article on Chomsky (1986). *Language* 64.2.
Rizzi, Luigi. 1982. *Issues in Italian Syntax*. Dordrecht: Foris.
Vincent, Nigel. 1989. 'Observing Obsolescence'. *Behavioral and Brain Sciences* 12.2.
Warner, Anthony. 1983. Review article on Lightfoot (1979). *JL* 19.1.

ON THE ROLE OF SOME ADVERBS IN OLD ENGLISH VERSE GRAMMAR

PETER J. LUCAS

University College, Dublin

The foundations of Old English verse grammar were laid by Kuhn 1933, who divided the words that occur in Germanic verse into three categories corresponding to their function in the metre as determined by the extent to which metrical stress is accorded to them.

(1) Stress-words (<u>Satzteile</u>) 'are fully meaningful words which naturally carry a strong stress: nouns, verbal nouns (infinitives and participles), adjectives and many adverbs' (Bliss 1962: 7).

(2) Particles (<u>Satzpartikeln</u>) are words which do not naturally carry a strong stress but neither are they normally subordinated to any other word in particular: finite verbs, personal and demonstrative pronouns, conjunctions and some adverbs.

(3) Clitics (<u>Satzteilpartikeln</u>), if, as is usual, they are proclitics, are unstressed words dependent on a following stress-word: prepositions, demonstratives, possessives and possibly one or two adverbs; otherwise, if they are enclitics, they are unstressed words dependent on a preceding stress-word.

Two rules concerning the position of particles were observed and formulated by Kuhn.

Kuhn's First Law, his Law of Particles (<u>Satzpartikelgesetz</u>), states that all the particles in a verse clause must be grouped together in the first metrical dip, i.e. all before or (if the verse clause begins with a stressed element) all immediately after the first stress-word; if a particle does not occur in the first dip, it ceases to be a particle and becomes a stress-word (Kuhn 1933: 8-10). There are hardly any certain breaches of Kuhn's First Law in <u>Beowulf</u>, and none in <u>Exodus</u>.[1]

Kuhn's Second Law, his Law of Clause Openings (<u>Satzspitzengesetz</u>), states that if there is a metrical dip before the first lift in a verse clause then the dip must contain a particle; the dip may not be occupied solely by clitics (Kuhn 1933: 43-8). This law was less strictly adhered to than the First Law. But even in <u>Genesis B</u>, a poem which, in view of its Old Saxon pedigree, may be expected to show more frequent breaches of Kuhn's Second Law, there are only three breaches (Lucas 1988).

Kuhn's Laws are rules for the ordering and arrangement of words in the verse clause. As syntactical rules they contribute to the <u>structure</u> of OE verse. They are also part of a grammatical framework, which I call verse grammar. This verse grammar has categories of <u>class</u>: stress-word, particle, and clitic. These features of <u>structure</u> and <u>class</u>, in the linguistic sense employed, for example, by Halliday 1961 are more or less explicit in Kuhn's article. There are also categories of unit. The largest unit in OE verse grammar is the verse clause. A verse clause normally contains one finite verb, though occasionally the force of the finite verb, especially the verb 'to be', is taken over from the preceding clause. The other

category of <u>unit</u> implicit in Kuhn's analysis is the word, to
which he assigned his threefold mode of classification. In
between these two categories of <u>unit</u> comes the verse phrase,
which is a 'unit of sense' or 'breath-group', for example, a
stress-word 'with its attendant proclitics' (Bliss 1967: §42).
In OE verse grammar there is, then, a three-tiered ranked scale
of <u>units</u>: the verse clause, the verse phrase, and the word.

Despite the fact that we can observe in its rules of
<u>structure</u> and categories of <u>class</u> and <u>unit</u> OE verse grammar is
not complete in the sense that a grammar of a language is
complete. There seems to be nothing in OE verse grammar
corresponding to Halliday's <u>system</u>, and nothing to indicate the
<u>structure</u> of the sentence (how verse clauses are combined).
Although the categorization of <u>class</u> is complete in the sense
that all words are accounted for by it, evidently words also
belong to their appropriate <u>class</u> in the language, noun, verb,
etc.; the <u>systems</u> applicable to these classes of words operate in
OE poetry as they do in OE prose, but as part of the grammar of
the language, not as part of OE verse grammar. Evidently OE
verse grammar is, in the words of Lord (1960: 36), 'a grammar
superimposed, as it were, on the grammar of the language'. It is
an extra dimension of grammar to be mastered by the poet who
already had a command of the language, just as OE poetic diction
was an extra dimension of vocabulary.

The three classes of words in OE verse grammar, clitics,
particles, and stress-words, are mutually exclusive only to the
extent that a stress-word is always a stress-word: they
constitute a linguistic hierarchy (as defined by Halliday 1961:
§2.2, 3.2-3). By Kuhn's First Law, a particle becomes a
stress-word when it is not in the first metrical dip of the verse
clause. But a particle may become a clitic (i.e. proclitic) when
it is dependent on the following stress-word which it qualifies,

as with an indefinite adjective of quantity in eallra þrymma þrym
(Ele 483a),² or as with a personal pronoun in be him lifigendum
(Ex 324a, sim. Jln 133a, HbM 52a), or as with a conjunction (very
frequently) in, e.g., eafoð ond ellen (Bwf 902a). A particle
also becomes a clitic (i.e. enclitic) when it immediately follows
a stress-word in the same verse phrase (Lucas 1987). While the
top category, stress-words, remain at the top, the second of the
three categories, particles, can move up or down in the
hierarchy. For obvious reasons the bottom category, clitics,
can only move upwards in the hierarchy. It is of course implicit
in these statements that there is an interaction between verse
grammar and metre and that verse grammar has a bearing on
scansion and sometimes determines it.³

Adverbs are particularly interesting in that, according to
Kuhn, they occur in all three categories. Many adverbs are
stress-words. In Beowulf there are over 600 stressed adverbs,
approximately 5.5% of all words bearing a metrical stress, but
this figure includes some particles. According to Bliss (1962:
7) 'demonstrative adverbs' are particles. But on any
interpretation of 'demonstrative adverbs' Bliss's view will
require modification in respect of allowing a wider range of
adverbs into this category.⁴ Neither Slay 1952 nor Bliss 1962,
in their summaries and re-statements of Kuhn's Laws, include
adverbs among words classed as clitics, though Kuhn himself did.

It may be useful at this point to review briefly the ways in
which adverbs were formed in Old English:

(1) From adjectives by means of the ending -e, originally a
     locative inflexion.
(2) From adjectives by means of the ending -lice, originally the
     ending -e added to adjectives ending in -lic.

(3) By means of the adverbial ending, -a, which survives only in a relatively small number of words, notably sona 'soon', and adverbs ending in -inga/-unga.
(4) From adverbial uses of nouns and adjectives in various cases, accusative, genitive and dative.
(5) From combinations of preposition + noun etc.
(6) By historical development from earlier adverbs of place and time.

A particular problem for present purposes is that some adverbs are indistinguishable in form from conjunctions and prepositions. The following words, for example, function as both adverbs and conjunctions: hu, nu, siþþan, swa, þa, þeah, þenden, þonne. And the following words, for example, function as both adverbs and prepositions: æfter, beforan, eac, fore, fram, in, mid, of, on, to; they have been called 'prepositional adverbs' (Mitchell 1978). Sometimes glossary-makers display uncertainty in distinguishing the grammatical functions of a word: one editor, for example, categorizes both forþon and þenden as 'adv. and conj.' without distinguishing the two functions. Such grammatical distinctions may on occasion be difficult to make with certainty. In surveying their role in verse grammar it is necessary to bear in mind the function of these 'conjunctional adverbs' and 'prepositional adverbs' in the grammar of the language.

The majority of adverbs are stress-words in OE verse. I have found approximately 200, excluding those that occur with the prefix un- when the simplex has already been counted. Adverbs formed from adjectives by means of the ending -e, (1) above, are stress-words in all but exceptional instances: beorhte 'brightly', clæne 'entirely', deope 'deeply', etc. Even swiþe, which comes to be intensive of a following adjective or adverb, as in swiþe geneahhe 'very often' (Wan 56), is always stressed.

Adverbs in -lice, (2) above, are stressed without exception, and this group comprises over seventy of the 200 found. Adverbs in -inga/-unga, (3) above, are also stressed without exception: (un)dearninga 'secretly', eallunga 'entirely', eawunga 'openly', etc.

Whether any adverbs are clitics is problematical; hence, no doubt, the fact that Slay and Bliss omitted them. In theory the only possibilities are adverbs that are never stressed and never stand alone in the initial dip of a verse clause (where by Kuhn's Second Law a particle is required). In practice there is only one such adverb, ful, 'very', 'fully', which is always proclitic on a following word, usually an adjective or adverb, especially oft as in

  Ful oft ic for læssan lean teohhode   Bwf 951

Here ful occurs in the initial metrical dip of the verse clause so that even if it were a particle it would be metrically unstressed (by Kuhn's First Law). Elsewhere ful occurs outside the first metrical dip of the verse clause, and, since it cannot be stressed without obstructing the scansion, must be proclitic on the following word, be it adjective, past participle, or even finite verb:

  Þreaned þolian. Is þeos þrag ful strong   Jln 464
  wadan wræclastas. Wyrd bið ful aræd   Wan 5
  welegum biwedded; wyrd ne ful cuþe   Jln 33

In these instances ful could be a particle in proclitic position (see below), but in the absence of any positive evidence that it is a particle it seems reasonable to conclude that it is a clitic. Ful originated as an adverbial use of the adjective, (4) above. Since adjectives are always stress-words in OE poetry it is evident from its use as a clitic that the adverbial development has lost all trace of its formative origin. The only other possibility for an adverb-clitic is to when it is intensive, meaning 'too', before an adjective or adverb; see

Appendix, s.v. to 'too'.

Adverb-particles are particularly interesting because they can move both up and down in the hierarchy of word-classes, being either metrically stressed or unstressed. A good illustration of an adverb-particle that moves in both directions is swa 'so', 'accordingly'. Swa often occurs at the beginning of a sentence, as in

    Swa manlice   mære þeoden,   Bwf 1046

where, as the alliteration indicates, it is unstressed. If we apply Kuhn's Second Law, the Law of Clause Openings, to this example, then swa is the only word available to supply the clause opening with the necessary particle. That swa is a particle is confirmed by its occurrence in other positions typical of particles. When it is not in the first metrical dip of the verse clause it receives a metrical stress, as at Bwf 1709,

    hæleðum to helpe.   Ne wearð Heremod swa,

and this metrical stress may take the alliteration when appropriate:

    [hio stondað] simle singales   swa beclysed   Chrl 323

Equally, as a particle, swa may be promoted to take the alliteration even though theoretically (ignoring the requirements of alliteration) it could be unstressed in the first metrical dip of the verse clause, as in

    Searwum asettan,   gif hit swa meahte   Rag 6

Many particles are 'upwardly mobile' in this way. Apart from instances in the initial metrical dip of the verse clause swa is also 'downwardly mobile'. Before an adjective, adverb or certain nouns it may become proclitic, not receiving a metrical stress even when it occurs after the first metrical dip of a verse clause, as in

    þæs herewæðan   heafod swa blodig   Jud 126
    forð under fexe.   Næs he forht swa ðeh   Bwf 2967
    þæt næfre Grendel swa fela   gryra gefremede   Bwf 591

In these instances swa is proclitic on blodig, ðeh and fela respectively. Evidently swa, adv., is a particle, and it is notable that <u>swa</u>, conj., like all conjunctions, is also a particle.

In the Appendix over forty adverb-particles are listed with supporting evidence for their inclusion. Two other probable adverb-particles, <u>heonan</u> 'HENce', and <u>seþeah/swaþeah</u> 'however', have been omitted because the evidence seemed insufficient. It is notable that three particles, <u>þa</u>, <u>þeah</u> and <u>þonne</u>, never alliterate (unless accidentally) and some others are more commonly found either in unstressed position or in stressed position. It is possible that some poems differed from others in their treatment of some of these words. Many poems, for example, have no instance of stressed <u>a</u> (Ex, Dan, XSt, all the poems in the Vercelli Book, <u>Chr2</u>, <u>Chr3</u>, <u>GlcA</u>, etc.), yet <u>GenA</u> and <u>GlcB</u> have a lot. All the instances of <u>eft</u> (20) in <u>Bwf</u> are stressed and take the alliteration, yet <u>oft</u> occurs unstressed seven times. It seems more likely that these variations reflect differences of preferred usage rather than different conceptions of the categories to which words belonged in OE verse grammar. In any event for most words in most poems there is insufficient evidence to say definitively that, for example, a word that is normally a particle is a stress-word in one particular poem.

Apart form <u>swa</u>, instances of 'downwardly mobile' adverb-particles are quite common as the first word in pairs like <u>nu gen(a)</u>, <u>nu gyt</u>, <u>þa gen(a)</u>, <u>þa gyt(a)</u>, but otherwise not all that numerous outside the initial metrical dip of the verse clause. Two words that show this feature from time to time are <u>ne</u> 'not' and <u>nealles</u> 'not at all'. Neither ever receives a metrical stress but both are shown to be particles by the numerous instances in which each is the sole occupant of the initial metrical dip (Kuhn's Second Law): see Appendix, s.vv. 1.2. Outside the initial metrical dip <u>ne</u> is always proclitic on a following word or phrase, as in

Ac he hafað onfunden þæt he þa fæhðe ne þearf, Bwf 595

where a metrical stress on ne would obstruct scansion. Similarly nealles cannot be a stressed particle in Bwf 3019:

    [sceal]... oft nalles æne   elland tredan

In the following example nealles begins a phrase which complements a previous phrase, just as nalles ne complements oft in Bwf 3019.

    Wen ic þæt ge for wlenco,   nalles for wræcsiðum   Bwf 338

Other adverb-particles occur in proclitic position only sporadically. One instance occurs with eac 'also' at GenA 1215-17 (cp. 2042):

                fif ond syxtig

   wintra hæfde   þa he woruld ofgeaf

   ond eac þreohund.   Þ rage siððan

Evidently, eac, like the conjunction-particle ond, is proclitic on þreohund; so also R36 11, Jud 295. Another instance occurs with the adverb-particle a 'ever', 'at all':

   hales brucan: 'Ne scealt ðu in henðum a leng   And 1467

Here a must be proclitic on the comparative adverb leng, giving the sense 'not at all longer'. Similarly no, i.e. the adverb-particle formed from the ne...a of the previous example, must be proclitic in

   fyrst ferhðbana   no þy fægra wæs   Ex 399

Once again it is before a comparative. Another example occurs in

   lufade hine ond lærde   lenge hu geornor   GlcA 138

Here the adverb-particle hu must be proclitic on the comparative adverb geornor. Also before a phrase containing a comparative there is an instance with fre 'ever':

   [þæt ænig...] æfre marða þon ma   middangeardes
                gehede...   Bwf 504-5

All these instances of adverb-particles unstressed outside the initial metrical dip of the verse clause are proclitic on the following stress-word; for other instances see the Appendix, s.vv. eal(l), efne, eft (?), her (?), næfre, þus. In certain circumstances an adverb-particle may be enclitic on the stress-word immediately preceding it (Lucas 1987).

As must be evident by now adverb-particles are not confined to Bliss's 'demonstrative adverbs'. Bliss 1967 had difficulty with at least three adverb-particles, hraþe 'quickly', simle 'always', and sona 'at once', assigning them metrical stress or not inconsistently. For example, there are in Beowulf three instances of sona occurring in clause-initial position at the beginning of a line with s-alliteration, here given with Bliss's 1967 scansion:

1A*1b	Sona þæt gesawon	snottre ceorlas	Bwf 1591
1A*1b	Sona w s on sunde	se þe ær æt sæcce gebad	Bwf 1618
a2c	sona him seleþegn	siðes wergum	Bwf 1794

All these a-verses should be treated in the same way, preferably with sona unstressed, as it must be where it occurs clause-initially at the beginning of a line having alliteration on some sound other than s, e.g. Bwf 2928. As a particle occurring clause-initially sona should not be stressed, unless it is required to provide alliteration that would otherwise be lacking. This is one of the ways in which verse grammar may determine scansion.

In the discussion of swa above as an adverb-particle I noted that swa conj., is also a particle. Whatever its modern designation in the grammar of the language swa is a particle in OE verse grammar. The same identity of function in verse grammar applies to a number of 'conjunctional adverbs': forþon 'therefore', hu 'how', hwanon 'whence', nu 'now', siþþan 'afterwards', swa 'so', swilce 'likewise', þa 'then', þær 'there', þanon 'thence', þeah 'nevertheless', þenden 'meanwhile', þider 'thither', þonne 'then'. All these words are particles in OE verse grammar irrespective of whether they are adverbs or conjunctions in the grammar of the language. The close association between adverb-particles and conjunctions, which are always particles, in verse grammar is complemented by linguistic developments such as no hwæþere 'not at all however' > noþer 'and not'. In a line such as

    No hwæðre ælmihtig   ealra wolde   GenA 952

by Kuhn's Second Law either No or hwæðre, or both (in fact it is both), must be particles if the Law is not to be breached. Linguistically these two adverb-particles combined to form a new conjunction noþer, as in

    noðer hy hine ne moston,   syððan mergen cwom   Bwf 2124

The identity of function in OE verse-grammar at both the earlier and the later stage probably reflects an even earlier historical stage, proto- or pre-OE, when many conjunctions started out as adverbs (Mitchell 1984).

Prepositions are clitics, usually proclitic on the adjective or noun they govern. But when a preposition is displaced from this position, and occurs after the stress-word it governs, it receives a metrical stress. The actual process involved here is that a displaced clitic becomes a particle and is then accorded metrical stress when (as is virtually inevitable as far as prepositions are concerned) it does not occur in the first metrical dip of the verse clause (Lucas 1988). 'Prepositional adverbs' behave like displaced prepositions; in OE verse grammar they are particles and nearly always stressed. This identity of function in verse grammar applies to a number of 'prepositional adverbs', but because they are nearly always stressed only three can be positively identified as particles: eac 'also', mid 'alongside', and on 'on'. Probably also particles, but possibly stress-words, are: æfter 'afterwards', beforan 'in front', fore 'for it', fram 'away', in 'inside', innan 'inside', of 'off', to 'thereto', under 'underneath'.

This identity of function in OE verse grammar between words like swa which occur as 'conjunctional adverb-particles', whether they be adverbs or conjunctions in the grammar of the language,

and the similar identity of function between words like eac which
occur as 'prepositional adverb-particles', whether they be
adverbs or displaced prepositions in the grammar of the language,
together suggest the economy, explanatory power and inclusiveness
of the mode of analysis here employed. From the point of view of
verse composition Kendall 1983 has shown that verses may be
either (1) clause-initial, (2) clause-noninitial, or (3)
clause-unrestricted. Verses containing these words which occur
as 'conjunctional adverbs' and 'prepositional adverbs' will
therefore have the same status (assuming the word is in the same
position) irrespective of whether the particle is used as an
adverb or not; its designation in the grammar of the language
will be decided by the placement of an individual verse in its
linguistic context. This finding is relevant to what Bliss
(1981: 166) designated 'a central problem in the study of Old
English verse syntax; until it is solved the preference of an
Anglo-Saxon poet for parataxis or hypotaxis must remain a matter
for conjecture'. According to the present analysis the discovery
of such a preference is outside the scope of OE verse grammar.
It may well be that OE poets composed thinking more in terms of
clause-clusters than of parataxis and hypotaxis, which are terms
of modern grammatical analysis; cf. Mitchell 1980.

The mode of analysis employed here also has the capacity to
identify instances of faulty composition. Breaches of Kuhn's
Laws occur with adverb-particles as with other particles, e.g.,

 For þon we fæste sculon   wið þam færscyte
  symle wærlice   wearde healdan.   Chr2 766-7

As an adverb-particle symle should occur in the initial metrical
dip of the verse clause or receive a metrical stress, but it does
neither. Some other breaches of Kuhn's Laws involving adverb-
particles are noted in the Appendix, s.vv. eft (?), her (?),
hwæþ(e)re, na, næfre, þær. In identifying flaws in compositional

method, exceptional in the best poems but a little more frequent in some others, the study of verse grammar tends to confirm its own methodology by drawing attention to the high degree of regularity with which its Laws are kept.

In the discussion of clitics above I noted that the adverb ful had lost all trace of its adjectival origin. Similarly, though less dramatically, some adverb-particles have also thrown off their etymological traces. Perhaps the most obvious is hwilum 'at times', dat. pl. of the noun hwil 'time'. Another, disguised by linguistic shortening, is æfre 'ever', from a in feore 'at all in life', and its negative næfre 'never'. All three of these words, as particles, function differently in verse grammar from the nouns on which they were formed, nouns always being stress-words. (So also with efne 'exactly' and hraþe 'quickly', formed on adjectives, the adverbs functioning as particles, the adjectives a stress-words). Finally, in view of this observed development it is worth asking whether some other adverbs may have trodden the same path, from stress-word to particle. One such possibility is eaþe 'easily' in

Eaþe ic mæg freora   feorh genergan   R15 19

and also at WlE 18. Another possibility is micle 'much' in

    is hit mycle selre,   þæs þe ic soð talige   And 1563

and also at R40 42 and Bwf 2651 (cf. also Chr3 1317, where micle is an adj., also Mld 50, ECL 10). Both are adverbs formed from adjectives by means of the ending -e. But particles were useful, from the point of view of verse grammar the most flexible words in the word-hoard, and some poets, perhaps sensing the trend, may have thought it helpful to increase their number, even though, by the standards of their predecessors, they may have been 'stretching' the rules. In addition to its other advantages OE verse grammar has the capacity to reveal how OE poets may have refined the inherited norms by which they composed.

NOTES

1. References to OE texts are to Krapp & Dobbie 1931-53 except for *Beowulf* (Klaeber 1950) and *Exodus* (Lucas 1977). No instances are cited from Krapp & Dobbie 1931-53, vol. 5.
2. Apart from a few minor revisions I follow the contracted or abbreviated short titles for OE poems used by Bessinger 1978.
3. For a fuller discussion of the issues raised in the opening section of this paper see Lucas 1988.
4. But from Bliss 1981: 165-6 it would appear that he revised his earlier view.

REFERENCES

Bessinger, J.B. Jr 1978. *A Concordance to The Anglo-Saxon Poetic Records*. Ithaca: Cornell U.P.

Bliss, A.J. 1967. *The Metre of Beowulf*. Oxford: Blackwells (1st edn. 1958).

Bliss, Alan 1962. *An Introduction to Old English Metre*. Oxford: Blackwells.

Bliss, Alan 1981. "Auxillary and Verbal in *Beowulf*". ASE 9. 157-82.

Halliday, M.A.K. 1961. "Categories of the Theory of Grammar". *Word* 17.241-92.

Kendall, Calvin B. 1983. "The Metrical Grammar of *Beowulf*: Displacement". *Speculum* 58. 1-30.

Klaeber, Fr. 1950. *Beowulf and the Fight at Finnsburg*. Boston: Heath (1st end 1922).

Krapp, George Philip & Elliot van Kirk Dobbie 1931-53. *The Anglo-Saxon Poetic Records*. Vols 1-6. New York: Columbia U.P.

Kuhn, Hans 1933. "Wortstelling und -betonung im Altgermanischen". *PBB* 57.1-109. (Repr. Idem, *Kleine Schriften* I.18-103. Berlin: De Gruyter, where the original page numbers are also indicated.)

Lord, Albert B. 1960. *The Singer of Tales*. Cambridge, Mass.: Harvard U.P.

Lucas, Peter J. 1977. *Exodus*. London: Methuen.

Lucas, Peter J. 1988. "Some Aspects of *Genesis B* as Old English Verse". *Proc. Royal Irish Acad*. ser. C. 8 . forthcoming.

Lucas, Peter J. 1987. "Some Aspects of the Interaction between Verse Grammar and Metre in Old English Poetry". *SN* 59.145-75.

Mitchell, Bruce. 1978. "Prepositions, Adverbs, Prepositional Adverbs, Postpositions, Separable Prefixes, or Inseparable Prefixes, in Old English?". *NphM* 79.240-57, suppl. 81.313-7.

Mitchell, Bruce. 1980. "The Dangers of Disguise: Old English Texts in Modern Punctuation". *RES* 31:385-413.

Mitchell, Bruce. 1984. "The Origin of Old English Conjunctions: Some Problems". *Historical Syntax* (= *Trends in Linguistics: Studies and Monographs* 23) ed. by J. Fisiak, 271-99. Berlin: Mouton.

Slay, D. 1952. "Some Aspects of the Technique of Composition of Old English Verse". *TPhS*. 1-14.

APPENDIX

Table of Adverbs

The criteria for establishing that a word is a particle in OE verse grammar are 1. that it occurs metrically unstressed 1.1 in the initial metrical dip of a verse clause and/or 1.2 in proclitic position before another word or phrase, AND either 1.3 that it alone fulfils the requirements of Kuhn's Second Law, being the only possible particle in a clause opening comprising an initial metrical dip-- these instances are shown below by printing the appropriate line number in *italics* under 1.1/3-- or 2.1 that when it is not in the initial metrical dip of a verse clause it receives a metrical stress, or both 1.3 and 2.1 (or 2.2). 2.2 Sometimes such 2.1-particles take the alliteration. 3. On occasion a particle may also bear the metrical stress that takes the alliteration, even though theoretically (ignoring the requirements of alliteration) it could be part of the initial metrical dip of a verse clause. In the Table below instances are cited in columns under the numerical headings given for each relevant adverb; only unambiguous instances are cited, and are selective, followed by &c. where there are more than twenty instances available. Headwords are printed in the left-hand column in bold type, followed by the relevant OED headword in capitals where appropriate, followed if necessary by a gloss in inverted commas.

	Metrically Unstressed			Metrically Stressed		
	1.1/3	1.2	1.3	2.1	2.2	3
Æfre 'EVER' See also **nǣfre**	SB1 86 (= SB2 80), Chr1 73 Phx 128, R39 10, JgD1 31	Bwf 504	None	GenA 5 141 999 1480 Ele 403 507, GlcB 866, Phx 637, R40 9 R84 5, Jud 114	GenB 596, GenA 1954, Dan 753, XSt 50 633, And 553 1057, Ele 361 960, Chr1 75 311 Chr2 893, GlcB 1360, Phx 608, Jln 81, Prc 83, Whl 79, R40 65, Bwf 70 1314 &c.	GenB 398, GenA 1937 2567 2643, XSt 139 229 303 388 411, And 360 493 499, Ele 448 Chr2 479, GlcA 612, Deo 11, WfL 39
Ǣr ERE 'before'	GenB 338, GenA 1262 Ex 458, Dan 116 750, XSt 574, And 1449, SB 4, DrR 114, Ele 602, Chr1 45, Chr2 468, Chr3 984, Phx 252 Wan 113, Sfr 102, FtM 50, R1 12 Bwf 694 3038 &c **Ǣrest** WfL 6	None	None	GenA 78 2935, GenB 803, Ex 138, XSt 492 And 949, SB 7, DrR 154, Ele 101 1121, Chr1 115, Chr2 466, Chr3 916, GlcB 1014, Jln 304, Wan 43, R23 7, Bwf 778 3164, Jud 143 &c.	GenA 1508 2744, Ex 28, XSt 244, And 1274, SB 8, DrR 137, Ele 572, Chr1 39, Chr2 893, GlcA 27, GlcB 859, Aza 115, Jln 120, R11 10, R27 12, JgD1 42, Bwf 642 1787 2712 &c.	GenA 35 2266, GenB 539, Ex 285, XSt 74 688, And 188, Ele 74, Chr1 63, Chr2 615, Chr3 1056, GlcA 143, GlcB 844, Aza 128, Jln 75 634, R23 9, Bwf 83 3003 &c.
Ēac EKE 'also'	GenB 754, GenA 1372 Dan 518, And 584, Chr1 93, Chr2 662 790 Chr3 1152 1169 1383, GlcA 300, Aza 45, Jln 475, Sfr 119, DHl 98, Bwf 388, Jud 18 348, Fnb 45, Brb 37 &c.	GenA 1217, R36 11, Jud 295	None	GenB 386, GenA 1126 2042 2721, Dan 68 506, And 1592, FAp 50, DrR 92, Ele 3 741, Chr1 136 282, Chr3 943 1181, Phx 375, Jln 679, Bwf 1683, Brb 2 30 &c.	GenA 1440, Ele 1006, Chr3 1143 1276, Jln 307	Dan 271, Ele 1278, Chr3 1258 1457, GlcB 1182 1192, Jln 297

	1.1/3	1.2	1.3	2.1	2.2	3
eal(1) ALL 'entirely' See also n(e)alles	DrR 20, 48; **ealles** GlcA 469	Chr3 1220, Bwf 1708 3164	None	Chr3 969	And 1146 1483, Ele 1311, Chr1 97 305 366, Chr3 1283, GlcA 414, GlcB 1320, Phx 241, Vgl 26, R5 6, Mld 314. **ealles** GenA 1871, Dan 274, GlcA 601 662, R15 14 Bwf 1000, Jud 108	GenA 871, And 1097, 1627, Chr1 308, Chr2 666, Chr3 1005 1027, Phx 285, WfL 29, Bwf 680. **ealles** Dan 422
efne, emne EVEN 'just'	GenA 2300 2556, Dan 275, And 1234, Chr1 330, R3 13, Alm 5, Bwf 1571	GenA 1158 1943 2346, And 114 221 294 333, Bwf 943 1092 1223 1249 1283 3057	None	None	Ex 76, And 1104, SB 8, Chr1 300 436, GlcB 973	None
eft EFT 'back', 'later'	GenB 760, GenA 1446 2211, Ex 580, Dan 617, SB1 67 (=SB2 62), 101, DrR 101, Ele 1274, GfM 18, Mx1 104, R39 6, Mld 201, EgD 35 36	GenB 748 (or breach of Kuhn's First Law?)	None	GenA 1343 1413 1471 1603 1690 1101 1735, XSt 477, And 1356, Ele 382 500 923, GlcB 908 1243, Phx 277 433, Van 45, R2 14, R3 38 63 &c.	GenB 568, GenA 882, LA 452, DaN 87, XSt 211, And 466, Ele 255, Chr1 325, Chr2 614, GlcA 196, GlcB 920, Phx 224 648, Jln 231, GfM 17, FtM 60, R23 1, Bwf 22 2654, Jud 169 &c.	GenB 396, GenA 1117 2727, DaN 516, XSt 21, And 400, DrR 68, Ele 1154, Chr1 122, Chr2 455, Chr3 1156, GlcA 428, Phx 222, Jln 633, Sfr 61, R37 6, Bwf 853 1556 2790 Jud 146 &c.
forþam forþan forþon FOR-THON 'accordingly'	GenA 97 Ex 187, Dan 479, XSt 549 Hm1 40 GlcA 46, Aza 120, Van 37, Sfr 33	None	See 1.1/3	Ele 309, DH1 96	None	None
ful(1) FULL 'very'	GenB 444 XSt 151 321 Ele 167, Aza 135, Sfr 24, Wds 119, FtM 1 74, Mx1 147, R30 5, WfL 18 32 46, R83 6, R88 12, Bwf 480 951 1252, Mld 253 &c	GenB 634 688 705 728, XSt 683, And 496, SB1 35 (=SB2 32), Chr1 252 389 Jln 33 464, Van 5 R25 6, R40 104, WfL 1, JgD1 25 66	None	None	None	None
gēn, gīen 'yet'	GenA 2165 2197, And 601 727, Ele 924 1062 1217, Chr1 192, GlcA 521, Jln 191 290 293 345 417 589, Bwf 2149 2702	None	None	Ex 249, Ele 373 1077 1079 1091, Chr2 496 542, Chr3 1457, GlcA 515, Jln 317, R9 2, R49 8, Bwf 83 734 2081 2237 3006	Jln 110 169, Bwf 2070	GenB 413, GenA 2364 2742, Chr1 198, Chr2 734, GlcA 538, R20 25, Bwf 2859 3167
gēo, īu 'formerly'	XSt 81 150, DrR 87, Chr3 1488, Phx 41, Rui 32, Mnl 213	None	None	GenA 2310, XSt 44, And 438 661 1377 1386, Chr1 2 138, Jln 420, Vgl 57, OrW 11, R71 2, Mnl 158	And 489, DrR 28, GlcA 40, Van 22	SB1 60, Chr3 1476, Sfr 83, Bwf 1476 2459
gēt, gī(e)t, gȳt 'YET'	GenB 618, GenA 1245 1476 1510 Ex 520 XSt 159 224 And 632 1195 RsgB 117 Bwf 47 1050 1164 1866, Fnb 18 26 Mld 168 273	None	None	GenA 103 212 1038 2664, GenB 784, XSt 403, And 15 380 814 1039, SB1 135, Chr1 351, DH1 73, Bwf 536 583 1276 2141 2975,	Ex 235, Chr1 318	GenA 1793, And 1487, GlcB 1221, Bwf 944 956 1058 1134 1824 2512
hēr 'HERE'	GenA 112 XSt 92, And 724, FAp 96, DrR 137 Chr1 224, Chr2 521, Chr3 1322, GlcA 23, Phx 31, Van 108, Prc 74, R43 16, WfL 32 JgD1 40 Bwf 1228 Jud 177, Brb 1, EgC 1 &c	GenA 2882 (or breach of Kuhn's First Law?)	See 1.1/3	GenA 867 1139 2093 2170 2735, XSt 261, DrR 108, Chr1 116, Chr2 703, GlcA 14 792, GlcB 892 1248, Phx 536 638, Jln 116, Whl 43, R49 10, R88 20, Bwf 1061 &c.	GenB 474, GenA 2519 2741, SB1 42 (= SB2 39), 148, GlcB 1129, Bwf 397	GenA 103 935 2645, XSt 209, SB1 141, Chr3 1574, Aza 89, Phx 23, Jln 442, Sfr 102, Wds 134, RsgA 36, HbM 8, Bwf 1820, Fnb 26

SOME ADVERBS IN OLD ENGLISH 309

	1.1/3	1.2	1.3	2.1	2.2	3
(h)raþe hraþe RATHE 'quickly'	Bwf 1310 1437 1975, Mld 164	None	None	GenA 160 2727 Ex 502 XSt 227 And 947 1111 1272 1577, Ele 76 710, Chr3 1027, GlcA 422 687, Jln 254 370 Bwf 224 1541 2117 2968, Mld 30 &c.	And 1520	GenA 123 1584 2462, Dan 241 And 341 1106 Ele 372 406, Chr3 1525, Bwf 724 1390 1576 1937, Jud 37
hū 'HOW'	GenB 805, Ex 426 Dan 130, XSt 706, And 63 307 547 920, Ele 456 643, Chr1 183, Chr3 1059 1459, GlcA 366, GlcB 1011, Van 95, Bwf 1987, Sns 343, JgD2 92 123 &c.	GlcA 138	See 1.1/3	Bwf 2519 (conj.)	None	None
huru HURE 'indeed'	GenA 1503, XSt 170, And 549, FAp 48, SB 1, DrR 10, Ele 1046 1149, Chr1 82 337, GlcA 769, GlcB 1221, RsgB 102, DHl 15, Bwf 369 669 862 2836 3120, Jud 345 &c.	None	See 1.1/3	GenA 1581 2345	None	Chr2 789
hwǣr, hwār '(any)WHERE'	GenB 667, XSt 36, Van 92 93	None	None	FAp 111, Bwf 138 2029	None	None
hwæt WHAT 'why'	GenB 278 663, GenA 888 1010, And 629 1316 1413	None	See 1.1/3	None	None	None
hwæþere hwæþre WHETHER 'however'	GenA 214 1859, Dan 546, And 504 1487, DrR 18 Ele 719, Chr1 453, Chr2 709, Chr3 1377, GlcA 233, Phx 366 640 Jln 517, R31 9, R39 18, RsgB 70, Bwf 555 2298 2874 &c	None Breach of Kuhn's First Law: GenA 955	See 1.1/3	GenA 1863, R3 54, R22 17, R54 8, R58 5, RsgA 26	None	GlcA 520, GfM 32, Bwf 2442, Mnl 68
hwanan, hwanon, hwonan 'WHENCe'	And 256 258 683 GlcB 1223 Jln 259 Bwf 257 333 2403	None	See 1.1/3	None	None	None
hwider, hwyder WHITHER	GenA 2271, And 405, GlcA 26, Van 72, Bwf 163, Mz2 58	None	See 1.1/3	Jln 700, Bwf 1331	None	None
hwīlum WHILOM 'at times'	GenB 777 Ex 170, XSt 134, And 443, Hm1 22 DrR 23 Chr2 646 GlcA 86, GlcB 907 919 Sfr 19, R3 38 R12 7 R49 4 R73 25 R80 7 R93 9 Bwf 867 2016 2299 &c	None	See 1.1/3	R12 10, R20 5, R25 5 Hm2 5, R71 5, R73 7, R80 3, R95 12, Bwf 3044	XSt 131, R83 9, Bwf 1828	Jln 440, Van 43, R20 13, R62 6 and 7
mid MID 'there too'	XSt 564	None	None	GenA 1389, Dan 353, And 237 878 1638 DrR 106, Chr3 1521, Phx 532, Jln 676, OrW 54 R13 2, R22 18, R46 5 Bwf 1642 1649 SnS 174	None	Chr2 478

	1.1/3	1.2	1.3	2.1	2.2	3
nā nō NO 'not at all' See also **ā**	GenB 412, GenA 952, Dan 20 753, XSt 291, And 3 1265, SB1 97, Ele 779 Chr1 84 Chr3 1097, GlcA 407, Phx 80, Van 66, R39 9, JgD1 68 Bwf 841 1536 3307, Mld 258 &c.	Ex 399, WfL 4 Breach of Kuhn's First Law: Van 54	See 1.1/3	Dan 696, And 1704, Ele 1082, GlcA 492 506, Sfr 66, Bwf 567 1453, Jud 117, Mld 21 268, SnS 101	None	XSt 376 410 632, Ele 837, GlcB 833, Van 96, R6 4, Bwf 2585, SnS 203
nǣfre, nēfre 'NEVER' See also **ǣfre**	GenA 1953 2092 2188 2788, And 459, Ele 468, Chr1 54, GlcA 10, GlcB 1173, Aza 85, Phx 38, Jln 55, Van 69, GfH 16, R5 10, R72 17, Bwf 247 1041 1460, Fnb 37	Ele 388, GlcB 1170 Breach of Kuhn's First Law: GenA 1537	See 1.1/3	And 1382, Ele 659, Phx 567, Jud 91	And 1286, GlcA 648	GlcB 1013 1210, R39 7
ne 'not'	GenA 2200 2258 2531 2681, Ex 177, Dan 646, XSt 114, And 279 317, Ele 81, Chr1 78, Chr2 564, Chr3 1474 1555, GlcB 1064, Phx 134, Jln 210, R23 10 Bwf 336 1142 &c.	GenA 190 GenB 289 Ex 81 106 Dan 111 XSt 50 98 And 178 Ele 340, Chr1 198 Chr2 637, Chr3 1184 GlcA 282 R40 65, WfL 39, R70 1 Bwf 243 Mld 96 &c	See 1.1/3	None	None	None
n(e)alles nal(l)æs nal(l)as næs 'not at all' See also **eal(l)**	GenA 212 1198 2864, GenB 346, XSt 28 447 And 46 1042, Ele 359 1133 Chr3 1536, GlcA 461 583 616, Jln 118 Bwf 1076 1493 1537 1719 1919 &c.	GenB 582 Gen 2070 XSt 692, And 233 506 605, Ele 817 1252, Chr3 1170 1194, GlcA 261 672, Jln 356, Van 33, Prc 58 WlE 15 Bwf 338 1529 3019	See 1.1/3	None	None	None
nū 'NOW'	GenA 6, GenB 395, Ex 278, Dan 306, XSt 391, And 1364, Ele 313, Chr1 9, Chr3 1327, GlcA 6, GlcB 1263 1298 1366, Phx 470, Jln 341, Rim 43, HbM 43, R93 28, R95 7, Bwf 939, &c.	GenA 1038, And 422 475 814, Chr3 1457, R49 8, DH1 73	See 1.1/3	None	None	GlcA 42 49, Bwf 1174
oft 'OFTen'	GenA 2462, Dan 589, XSt 151, And 140 652 Ele 386, Chr1 870, GlcA 360 775, GlcB 894, Aza 80, Jln 22, R4 5, WfL 32, Rui 9, R61 1, R93 30, Bwf 4 2029, Mld 212 &c.	None	See 1.1/3	And 618 626, SB1 35 (=SB2 32), Ele 471, GlcA 108, Phx 108 261, Van 17, Sfr 29, R17 3, WfL 51, JgD1 25 70, R95 2, Mld 188, Brb 8	GenA 1539, XSt 270 640, Ele 301 1252, Chr3 1194, GlcA 315 718, GlcB 884, Phx 442, Van 40, Sfr 3, R31 11, R49 7, DH1 114, HbM 16, R84 40, Bwf 165 1885 3019 &c	GenB 766, GenA 1896 2588 2633, Ele 1140, Chr1 17, Jln 427, Sfr 6, R5 3, R67 13, Bwf 444, 907, 1252, 3116
on 'ON'	And 1334	GlcA 676	None	None	Ex 491	Chr3 1244, Bwf 1903
seoþþan sioþþan siþþan syþþan SITHEN 'afterwards'	GenA 1069 1150 1161 1392 1824 Ex 224 384 Dan 661 And 706 1223 FAp 54 Ele 913, Chr2 639, GlcB 852, R23 6 JgD1 118, Bwf 470 685 2072, Jud 189 &c	None	See 1.1/3	GenA 71 988 2698, GenB 343, XSt 376 632, Ele 483 1302, Chr1 39, Chr3 1409, GlcB 985, Aza 82, Phx 409, Jln 330, Sfr 78, R9 9, R26 2, Bwf 142 718 2920 &c.	GenB 345 482 566, GenA 1481, And 1514, Ele 507 639 1146, Chr1 346 438, Chr3 1494, GlcA 706 751, GlcB 866 1043 1196, R40 9, Bwf 2702 2806, Jud 114 &c.	GenA 1064 2014, XSt 396, And 1379, DrR 142, Ele 271 1315, Chr1 339, GlcA 665, GlcB 839 Phx 385 Jln 380 692, R15 22, R26 11, HbM 24, Bwf 567 1901 2071 2175 &c.

SOME ADVERBS IN OLD ENGLISH 311

	1.1/3	1.2	1.3	2.1	2.2	3
simle, symble symle 'always'	GenB 326, GenA 1325, And 157, Ele 914 1215, Chr1 432, GlcA 348 393 888, GlcB 913 1212 1238, Phx 146, Jln 238, Sfr 68, Wds 131, DH1 137 Bwf 2450 2497	None Breach of Kuhn's First Law: Chr2 767	See 1.1/3	And 1384, Chr1 477, Chr2 777, Phx 76 661 Jln 20, Prc 5 11 25 46 51, Vgl 79, RsgB 115	And 411 651, Chr1 53 88 103 108 128 323 376 393, Chr2 602, GlcB 966, Phx 601, Jln 269, Prc 80, Vgl 69, Mx1 88, R40 30 64	GenB 472, And 659 1153 1581, Ele 469, Chr3 1640, GlcA 785, Phx 108 369 375, Prc 29
sōna SOON 'at once'	GenB 429, XSt 628, R27 9, Bwf 750 1497 2011 2928, Fnb 46	None	See 1.1/3	GenA 2445 2492, And 1334 1567 1579, Ele 713, Jln 49 365 398, R25 9, R87 4, Bwf 1825, SnS 99 125	GenA 2566, Ele 47, GlcB 992, Ptg 8, R16 6, JgD2 36 108	GenA 862 1589 2860, Dan 161 XSt 534, And 72 849, SB1 67 (=SB2 62), Ele 85 222 887 1030 Chr1 10 460 Glc 1023, R27 7, Bwf 743 1280 2300 2713 &c.
swā 'SO'	GenA 1565 2106, Ex 549, Dan 333 XSt 279 And 461, Ele 1311, Chr1 85, Chr2 645, Chr3 972, GlcA 323 554 GlcB 1105 Aza 49 Phx 147 646, Bwf 144 2177 3178, Jud 28	GenB 425 655 GenA 989, Ex 338, XSt 83, And 1250 1562 Ele 653 1065 Chr3 1272 1399, GlcA 493, GlcB 940, Vgl 7, R58 11, Bwf 591 642 1929 2878, Jud 67 &c.	See 1.1/3	GenB 718, GenA 993 2833, XSt 22 700, And 1323 1393, Ele 1014, Chr1 148, GlcA 576, GlcB 854, Phx 405, Jln 504, Vgl 74, R27 16, R49 9, Bwf 538 1471 2091 2990 &c.	XSt 348 (2nd), Chr1 323	Chr1 86 233, Sfr 51, R9 12, R13 6, R29 6
swilce, swylce SUCH 'likewise'	GenA 1082 1615, Dan 506, XSt 665, And 1029 1687, FAp 16, Ele 1032 1112, Chr1 60 145, Chr2 688, Chr3 1437, Jln 307, Sfr 53, Bwf 830 1427 2258 3150, Brb 57 &c	None	See 1.1/3	GenA 2348	None	None
tō TOO 'also'	GlcB 844	None	None	GenA 1224	None	Sfr 119
tō TOO 'too'	Bwf 1748 Mld 150 164	GenA 1819 2582, And 98 612 1432 1609 Ele 63, Chr1 181 373 Chr3 1263 1567, GlcA 585, GlcB 1077 1343, Jln 99, R22 6, Van 66, WfL 51, Bwf 133 Mld 90 &c	Mld 55 66 (or breach of Kuhn's 2nd Law)	None	None	None
þā THO 'then'	GenA 126 144 1483, Ex 63 135, Dan 58 79 XSt 254, And 59 364, Ele 225 481, Chr1 195, Chr3 1281, GlcA 81, GlcB 1269, Aza 179, Jln 69, Bwf 86 1698 &c.	Gen 103 1189 1635 Ex 249, XSt 403, And 15 380, Chr1 351 GlcA 515 GlcB 1270, Bwf 83 734 1127 1276 2081 2141 2237 2975 3093, Jud 107, &c	See 1.1/3	GenA 1964 2083 2173 2338 2487 2498 2587 2691, Chr1 326, GlcB 932 997 1134 1152, Bwf 2192, Mnl 24 151	None	None
þǣr 'THERE'	GenA 28 1811, Ex 71, Dan 254, XSt 308, And 90 1542, DrR 101 Ele 231 284, Chr3 1515, GlcA 10, GlcB 1088, Phx 615, Jln 587, R46 4, Bwf 32 331 2214, Jud 307 &c	None Breach of Kuhn's First Law: Van 54 WlE 6	See 1.1/3	GenA 1893, XSt 509 645, And 48 445, Ele 864 1007 1281, Chr1 327, Chr2 540, Chr3 1237, GlcB 888, Phx 203 282, Jln 220, R15 9, Bwf 756 1299 2771 3039 &c.	XSt 325, Bwf 2235 3050	GenA 1811, XSt 234, Bwf 400 1837 3070
þanan þanon(ne) þonan (cont.)	GenA 1061, Ex 516, And 1065, Chr2 625 Chr3 999, GlcA 144, Phx 113, Wds 109,	None	See 1.1/3	GenA 2096 2928, XSt 326 633, Ele 143, Chr2 759, GlcA 325, GlcB 1353, Phx 415	None	XSt 719, Ele 348, Chr3 1595, Bwf 123 691, Jud 118

	1.1/3	1.2	1.3	2.1	2.2	3
þonon (cont.) THENNE 'from there'	Bwf 111 224 463 520 853 1265 1373 1960 2359, SnS 220			554, Jln 384, Van 23 R26 3, R29 10, R73 27, Bwf 763 1880 2140 2956 Jud 132 &c		
þē(a)h THOUGH 'nevertheless'	GenB 360 Dan 217 514 580, XSt 431 And 813 Ele 393 500, Chr3 1090 1308 1506, GlcA 240 374 380, Phx 563 638, Jln 397, R95 10 Jud 257, Mld 289 &c.	None	See 1.1/3	GenB 662, GenA 2391, Ex 339, Dan 126, And 1250, SB1 66, Hm1 5, Chr2 523, GlcA 493, GlcB 940, R6 8, R58 11, DH1 129, Bwf 972 1929 2442 2878 2967	None	None
þenden 'meanwhile'	Bwf 2418 2985	None	See 1.1/3	None	Bwf 1019	Rim 18
þider, þyder 'THITHER'	Dan 203 227 525, GlcA 22	None	See 1.1/3	XSt 216 529, And 282 Ele 548, GlcB 1044	Bwf 379 2970 3086 Jud 129	Ex 196, XSt 301 630, Sfr 118
þonne 'THEN'	GenA 228 1826, GenB 561, Dan 513 XSt 209 603, And 655 Ele 489 Chr1 13, Chr2 525, Chr3 867, GlcA 511, GlcB 1038, Phx 142, Jln 715 Van 45 R3 63 Bwf 377 525 1741 &c.	None	See 1.1/3	Chr2 827, Chr3 1115, FtM 11 Mx1 107 R3 2, RsgA 43 47 60, Bwf 3062	None	None
þus 'THUS'	XSt 729, And 62 354 539 818, FAp 85, Ele 189 400 528 1236, Chr1 196, Chr2 686, Phx 482 570 632, Jln 311 362, Prc 1, JgD1 116, Bwf 238 &c.	Chr1 156, GlcB 1015, Jln 432 451 JgD1 34, Bwf 337	See 1.1/3	XSt 655, And 1411, Ele 1119, GlcB 1011, Phx 621, Phr 4	None	XSt 532 568

ADJECTIVAL INFLEXION RELICS AND SPEECH RHYTHM IN LATE MIDDLE AND EARLY MODERN ENGLISH[1]

DONKA MINKOVA
University of California, Los Angeles

Schwa loss in English spans three centuries, c. 1150 - 1450. During the central years of the change (1200 - 1400) the data base produces a nebulous and confusing picture. At both chronological ends, however, the clouds disperse somewhat; textual evidence of early loss and late preservation of schwa becomes relatively more limited and tractable. In an earlier paper (Minkova, 1987) I proposed a prosodic account of the cases of schwa deletion predating the spread of the change across the board. Here I look at the other end of the continuum and deal with adjectival -e's which appear to have resisted deletion much longer than any other final -e's in the language.

The relative slowness of the disappearance of the final -e from the weak adjectival inflexion in Late Middle English has been noticed and commented on before. The explicit statement which has prompted the topic of this paper, is that 'for that stage of the language [Late Middle English]...-e should perform a range of varied functions, some old some new; *in the adjective, its older uses survive almost intact, but in nouns and verbs it has undergone a restructuring to carry other distinctions*'[2] (Samuels, 1972: 446).

A frequent assertion in more detailed descriptions of the adjectival morphological patterns in Middle English is that 'the *only* ones provided with flexions are *monosyllabic adjectives terminated by a consonant. These adjectives distinguish the weak and the strong flexion*' (Mossé, 1952/68: 64). Mossé's assumptions on this issue are representative of most standard textbook accounts of the adjectival patterns in Middle English, starting with Morsbach (1896: 112), and appearing again in e.g. Moore/Marckwardt (1951/68: 51-2, 148), Rastorguyeva (1983: 238-9), Schlauch (1959: 22), Fisiak (1970: 82-3), etc.

This presumed state of affairs has not remained unquestioned, especially in view of the general instability of final -e as an inflexional marker in the 14th c. Along with statements about the systematic preservation of the weak-strong adjectival pattern, one finds assertions that during the 14th c.'the last trace of inflexion died out' (Wardale, 1937: 80), or that 'the strong-weak contrast [for adjectives], being wholly contextually conditioned ... [was] particularly expendable' (Bourcier/Clark, 1978/81: 151). Three relatively recent studies have dealt in detail with the issue of whether or not adjectives continued to behave differently in weak and strong position in the late 14th c. Let me briefly summarize their arguments and conclusions.

Delores Topliff (1970: 78-90) was the first to attempt a numerical tabulation of singular weak adjectives in Chaucer following *that, the, this*. Her data is very lucidly presented; only 12% of the monosyllabic adjectives in the 'weak' frame remain uninflected, which supports Mossé's description cited above. However, if the entire set of adjectives (both monosyllabic and polysyllabic) are taken into account, only 55% are inflected. Topliff takes

this as a refutation of the statement that the weak
adjective inflection died out during the 14th century, but
obviously 55% is no overwhelming statistical evidence in
either direction. In fact, it is surprising that she
should accept this line of argument unquestioningly,
since, when broken up into groups depending on the number
of syllables, her figures show that 77% of the
polysyllabic adjectives remain uninflected. I will take
this ratio as a strong indication of the invariability of
these adjectives.[3]

The next important contribution to this particular
area of research is Samuels (1972: 445-8), who follows a
grammatical tradition earlier represented by Donaldson
(1948). The main claim in Samuels' paper is also that the
distribution of adjectival forms with and without final -e
in Chaucer is consistently grammatical. The same
grammatical distinction between weak and strong adjectives
is maintained consistently by the scribes trained in 'the
dialects of a large area of the southeast and the S. E.
Midlands, and date not only from Chaucer's time but also
from the early fifteenth century' (ibid: 445). This
statement is accompanied by an impressive list of
manuscripts, all of which are said to display the same
regularity with respect to adjectival inflexions.

The issue was followed up by Burnley (1982) who
concentrates on the inflexion of adjectives 'which may be
pronounced as monosyllables' in the Hengwrt MS.[4] Burnley's
study confirms the previous accounts: he comes up with an
extremely high figure, approximately 97%, for the
predictability of final -e in this MS. Unfortunately for
the idea I want to pursue here, Burnley does not make it

clear what portion of the -e's are weak singulars and how many of them mark plural concord.

In my discussion so far I presented the problem and its manifestations and proposed solutions in Chaucer. The question I want to address next is whether final -e was used consistently as an inflexional marker for singular weak monosyllabic adjectives ending in a consonant in non-Chaucerian material of the late 14th and early 15th c. Since Topliff's data is the only study compatible with my aims, I will take it as a point of comparison: she finds only 12% of the monosyllables of the type described above uniflected. Let us now look at some other sources:[5]

1. *Gower*. My sample is taken from the *Tale of Ulysses and Telegonus* and *The Tale of Nectanabus* (the entire Liber Sextus of *Confessio Amantis*, c.1390-1393, London). I counted 49 occurrences of singular monosyllabic adjectives. In this sample the pattern is very rigid; weak adjectival -e is preserved, and scanned. The only exceptions to the expected behaviour are syllabic final -e's within the frame Prep + Adj + Noun: *of pure dette* (1501), *for pure dredde* (4976), *under guile faith* (2049), *in strange place* (4791), where the meter requires them to be pronounced.[6] This high degree of regularity of the adjectival inflexions in Gower was first noticed by Macaulay (1900/69: CX-CXI):

> In the case of English monosyllables the exceptions are few. 'His *full* answere', i.1629, 'hire *good* astat', i.2764, '**here wrong condicion**', ii.295, '**his *slyh* compas**', ii.2341 (but 'his *slyhe* cast', ii.2374), 'the *ferst* of hem', iii.27, v.2863... 'my *riht* hond', iii.300, '<u>the *trew* man</u>', iii.2346 [but '*a trewe* assay ', vii.4785, DM], '**his *hih* lignage**', iv.2064 (due perhaps to the usual phrase 'of hih lignage'), '**the *hih* prouesse**', v.6428, 'hire *hih* astat', v.6597, 'the *gret* oultrage', vii.3413, 'hire *freissh* aray', vii.500, 'hire *hol* entente', vii,1222, cp. vii.1710, 2968.

Note that the exceptions listed by Macaulay are not all of the same type: most of them are potential cases of elision (left unmarked), and the boldfaced ones are adjectives + nouns whose first syllable is most probably unstressed, so there remains only one real exception, the underlined <u>trew man</u>.

Interestingly, Macaulay also remarks that 'other adjectives [i.e. polysyllabic ones], of which the termination is capable of accent may take the definite inflexion, *when the accent is thrown on the termination*, as 'this *lecherouse* pride', 'this *tyrannysshe* knyht'' (ibid.: CXI).

2. *The Bodley Version of Mandeville's Travels*, (Bodleian Library MS E Musaeo 116, ed. by M.C.Seymour). Absolute precision of the count is impossible for the reasons discussed by Burnley (1982: 172): uncertainty in the adjective - adverb distinction and possible elision before vowels or -h. There are, however, 188 occurrences of monosyllabic adjectives in the frame *the*, *that*, *this*, *his* + adj. + noun. Of these, 17 forms have no inflexion and 20 are questionable, because of ostensible elision. This leaves about 19% of the entire material "anomalous" in some way, and if we eliminate the elided forms, the statistics will resemble very closely Topliff's results, with only 10 to 11% of the forms in this frame violating the expected strong/weak pattern.

3. *Songs and carols from a Manuscript in the British Museum of the fifteenth century* (British Museum Sloane MS 2593 ed. by Thomas Wright). A count including just the singular adjectives shows a total of 80 occurrences of which 15 do not conform to the rules, i.e. about 18% of the cases go against the expected pattern. The violations

are most frequent in the direction of ungrammatical
addition of an -e, which must be syllabic, after the
indefinite article: *a newe 3er* (2), *a clene maydyn* (2), *a
powre man*, cf. *a riche feste* (Gower, CA,: vii.4702). If
such forms are excluded, the picture is more rigid;
exceptions amount to less than 7%. Like the previous
texts, this text is more regular than not, but it is no
model of perfection.

    More data can undoubtedly be presented along these
lines, but I cannot cover the non-Chaucerian material here
with the thoroughness, detail and dedication that
Chaucer's work has enjoyed. I am satisfied, however, that
the conclusions in studies based on Chaucerian material
are supported within an acceptable range of deviation by
non-Chaucerian data[7]. The rest of this paper concentrates
on an alternative interpretation of the reasons for the
regularity described and summarized above.

    The scholarship on adjectival final -e reveals two
contradictory beliefs about its function at the end of the
14th and the beginning of the 15th c:

    1. The sounding of final -e with adjectives, as well
as with all other word classes, was erratic in speech, and
in verse was *governed by the requirements of meter* [8]; like
all other final -e's in the language, it had lost its
power to signal systematically a specific grammatical
distinction (weak - strong).

    2. Final -e with adjectives has survived as a *marker
of a real grammatical distinction* in one part of the
country and within a particular stylistic register, even
after it has lost its grammatical distinctiveness in other
word classes. This, I believe, is the most widely accepted
view, though not always explicitly stated. There are

several aspects of this second hypothesis which I want to address:

(a) It allows continuing distinctiveness of final -e for *only one morphological class*, where it had clearly been functional across the board earlier. This is not an unprecedented situation[9], yet this line of reasoning still leaves open the question why adjectives, and not nouns, or verbs, were behaving in this aberrant manner.

(b) It allows continuing distinctiveness of final -e for *only one subclass of adjectives, defined in terms of their syllabic structure*, where it had clearly been functional with all adjectives. Again, this would not be an unusual morphological behaviour, yet the hypothesis in (2) still leaves open the question why monosyllabic adjectives were singled out in this way.

(c) In spite of the assertion that the forms present 'a distribution which is practically a mirror-image of the grammatical distinctions in Old English adjectives' (Samuels, 1972: 445), there is no clarity on the issue of *comparative and superlative adjectives*, which should display the same regularity of preserving the final -e. Topliff (1970: 83) has observed a somewhat higher rate of exceptions in their inflection: 18% of the comparatives and 21% of the superlatives remain uninflected. However, if we eliminate the *monosyllabic* and suppletive *more, most*, and *least* from her list, the figures look quite different: *only* 25% of the comparatives and 50% of the superlatives are, in fact, inflected.

(d) It relies on the dialectal provenance of the sources on which the evidence is drawn, the southeast and the S.E. Midlands, cf. quote above (Samuels, 1972: 445). It also refers to the rather elusive notion of register.

Analysing data from one regional variety of English, or any language, is no breach of scholarly decorum, of course. In this particular case, though, I believe that we can reasonably invoke a more general prosodic principle to account for the regularity in question. Dialectal and stylistic peculiarities should be kept in mind, yet by becoming pivotal such features may lose us the advantage of overall analytical coherence.[10]

An addition to and possible revision of this hypothesis is suggested by a comparison of the *metrical structures of the weak and the strong adjectival noun groups*. I want to go beyond the analysis of each adjective isolated from its head and from other units in the same noun group, such as determiners and look into the phrasal phonology of the unit as a whole. A familiar premise, which can serve as a starting point, is the long observed empirical fact that in human speech 'There is arguably a universal rhythmic ideal, one that favors a strict alternation of strong and weak beats' (Selkirk 1984: 37).[11] Typically, the two kinds of syntactic nodes in which the analysed adjectives appear, and which we want to compare, are the NP's and the VP's, thus:

(1) a. $_{NP}[_{Det}[þæt$ $_{AP}[blake$ $_N[smoke$
    b. $_S[_{NP}[_{Det}[his$ $_N[berd$ $_{VP}[_V[was$ $_{AP}[blak$

A familiar generalization about the metrical organization of such configurations is that in the default case they will be right branching[12], with tree structures of the following form:

ADJECTIVAL INFLEXION RELICS AND SPEECH RHYTHM   321

(2) a. þæt blake smoke   b. his berd was blak

```
      W   S   W   S            W   S   W   S
       \ / \ /                  \ / \ /
        W   S                    W   S
         \ /                      \ /
          S                        S
```

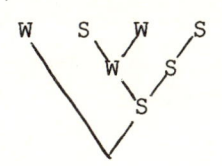

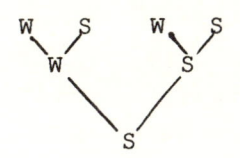

The representation in (2a) illustrates that an adjective in attributive position, always to the left of its head, will be metrically weak, and immediately adjacent to a strong node. In the configuration (2b), the same adjective occupies the metrically strongest position in the whole string. A metrically weak position is the domain of susceptibility to certain phonological rules, in particular to vowel reduction and deletion, which may be important for the future changes affecting adjectives filling that position. I'll come back to this point. Something else we can read off the first layer of metrical structure is that weak and strong positions are evenly spaced out, thus, both in grid and tree representation:[13]

(3)   x   x
                 x------x   x-------x
              x   x   x   x   x   x   x   x
    a. þæt blake smoke   b. his berd was blak

```
      W   S   W   S            W   S   W   S
       \ / \ /                  \ / \ /
        W   S                    W   S
         \ /                      \ /
          S                        S
```

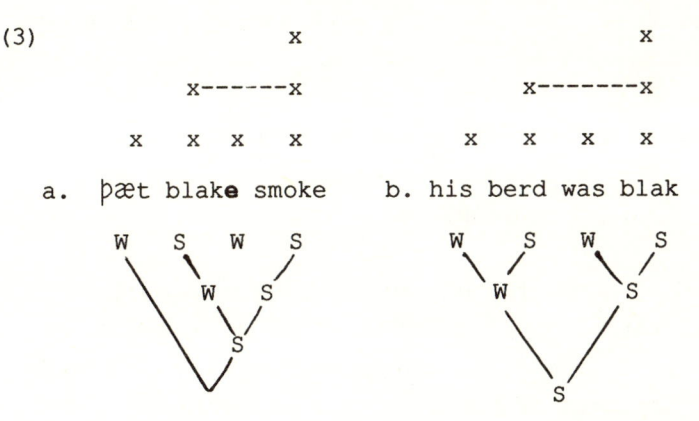

On the second horizontal level, the actual beats are also evenly spaced out, so the rhythmic organization of the phrases under consideration conforms with the *Principle of Rhythmic Alternation* which '...ensures that rhythmic clashes and lapses will be avoided, at all metrical levels, and that strong beats or demibeats will appear at regular intervals' (Selkirk, op.cit.: 19). In a further elaboration of this principle Hayes (1984) manifests that the notion of clash avoidance should cede to rules of eurhythmy, requiring a *'particular spacing of marks* to be found at some level of the grid'. The rules of eurhythmy are based on syllable count (ibid.: 70). In the examples analysed below the optimal interval is disyllabic. Thus if we can show that in (4):

```
(4)                    x                        x
            x------x       --->         x----x
        x   x   x   x              x    x    x
     a. þæt blake smoke       b. that black smoke
```

the elimination of the second syllable of the adjective *black* would produce dysrhythmy, we have a prosodically based rationale for expecting weak monosyllabic adjectives to be much more resistant to final schwa loss than other word classes in other positions.

The obvious objection raised by this analysis is that (4b) *is*, after all, what happened in the long run in English. Yes, it did, but the claim laid on rules of eurhythmy in English can be weakened and ultimately overruled by other factors such as the expansion of segmental phonological rules of final schwa deletion, a process which depends on and is augmented by the weak metrical position of the deletable syllable. The 15th century reversal of the strength of the eurhythmy rules relative to other rules is not surprising. Extremely powerful morphological analogy within the adjectives, analogy with the demorphologization of the -e in the other word classes, as well as sweeping changes in the syntactic structure of the language led to what may appear to be a tendency to 'dysrhythmy' in the prosodic organization of some adjectival phrases in Modern English. It has been claimed, I believe correctly, that 'phrasal stress in English can serve ends other than rhythmic ones,..thus the effects of eurhythmy rules become clear only when other factors are controlled for' (Hayes, 1984: 51). The entire history of schwa is, indeed, the result of a complex interaction of factors, and this is only an instance of the varying force of application of these factors.

An analysis referring to the realization of a preferred rhythmic configuration handles the data and answers some of the questions concerning the 'grammatical' status of final -e :

- Disyllabic adjectives are not "provided with flexions" (Mossé, op.cit: 64): in addition to the general weakness of final schwa in the entire system, there is no rhythmic pressure within the noun phrase for preserving the -e of such forms. The second unstressed syllable in disyllabic adjectives provides the convenient "spacing" between beats, as in (5):

```
(5) a.        x-------x
              x   x   x
       ...the comun clamour tolde/

     b.       x-------x
              x   x   x   x
       The ne we  shame of Sennes olde.
                           Gower, CA, (vii.5115-6)
```

The grid need not be extended beyond the first level of beats: what we see is enough to support the point: in

order to avoid contiguity of stressed syllables final -e
`is not needed in *comun* of (5a), while it is not so easily
expendable in *newe* of (5b).

The exceptions listed by Macaulay (1900/69: CX-CXI)
will also be covered by the same principle:

(6) a.　　　x--------x　　　　b.　　　　　x-------x
　　　x　x　x　x　　　　　　　　　x　x　x　x
　　　his slyh com pas　　　　　　his sly he cast

In both (6a). and b. eurhythmy is achieved: in the first
case the distancing factor between the beats is supplied
by the unstressed initial syllable of the noun, and in the
second by the inflexional -e on the adjective.

A similar case can be made for the exceptions in the
Sloane MS, (cf. footnote 6 and p. 5 above, as well as the
discussion of Smithers' *breaches of the rule* discussed in
footnote 10) In view of the ideal of spacing, (7a). below
will be preferable to (7b):

(7) a.　　　x-------x　　　　b.　　　　　x-----x
　　　x　x　x　x　　　　　　　　　x　x　x
　　　a riche feste　　　　　　　　a rich feste

Another group of exceptions to the postulated
grammatical requirements, easily accounted for by the
principle of rhythmic alternation, is represented by the
prepositional phrases mentioned in reference to Gower[14]:

(8)　　　　x---------x
　　　x　x　x　x
　　　of pu re dredde

Yet another case of the same type of rhythmic
preference can be seen in the nonconformity of ordinary

comparative and superlative adjectives with the
paradigmatic pattern of weak adjectives:

```
(9)             x---------x------x
        x    x  x       x   x  x    x
        the  fayrest    com pa ny   e
```

Since these forms are normally disyllabic, they pattern
with other disyllabic adjectives; in spite of the inherent
grammatical meaning of "definiteness" they appear without
the weak final -e. When monosyllabic, though, as in the
case of *more*, *most*, *least*, they are extremely obedient: in
Topliff's table *more* is always disyllabic, *most(e)* is
disyllabic in 17 out of 20 occurrences, and *least(e)* is
disyllabic in 14 out of 15 cases.

According to Peck (1967: XL) one of the 'predictable'
exceptions to the rules of the weak declension (though he
does not say why), is that if the adjective is of more
than one syllable, it does not inflect unless the accent
falls on the last syllable, in which case there might be a
final -e. cf. also Macaulay (op.cit: CXI)[15]. Thus:

```
(10)        x--------x--------x
        x   x   x   x   x   x
        this ty ran ny sshe knyht
```

Not surprisingly, then, the pattern in (10) does not
emerge when the first syllable of the following noun is
unstressed, as in:

```
(11)    x---------x--------x--------x
        x    x   x   x   x    x   x
        the  prou de  ty  ran nyssh Ro mein
```

as quoted in Macaulay (op.cit: CXI). The pattern in (10) will be predictably suppressed also when 'the final syllable of the adjective is incapable of accent...as in *croked*, *wicked*, *cruel*, *litel*, *middel*, *biter*, *dedly*, *lusti*, *sinful(l)*, *wilful*, *woful(l)*, *wrongful*, etc. (ibid.: CXI).[16]

Going outside the strictly adjectival morphology, yet staying within the same rhythmic pattern, we can find historical parallels supporting the buffer hypothesis.

- By Gower's day inflexional -e in the nominal paradigm appeared *only in the attributive genitive*, (traced back to OE gen.fem.sg.) or to weak declension endings), e.g. *myn herte rote*, or *the cherche keie*. (Peck, 1966: XXXVIII), i.e. if the nouns in the attributive phrase are monosyllabic, the -e would provide the rhythmic bridge between the two stresses, a role which the *of* of the prepositional genitive can fill.

- The eurhythmic principle will be in line with Samuels' assertion that in Late Middle English 'in nouns and verbs [the final -e] has undergone a restructuring to carry out other distinctions. Thus for the verbs *had* and *were* we find that a syllabic scansion more often calls for *monosyllables when they function as auxiliaries* [when they would naturally be in a weak metrical position, followed in most cases by a fully stressed lexical verb, and serving as a distancing device between stresses, for which one syllable is sufficient, DM], but for *disyllables when they function as lexical verbs*.' (op.cit.: 446)

Another diachronic pattern, which seems to make better sense if viewed from the eurhythmic perspective, is the Chaucerian distribution of the infinitival forms: 'The plain infinitive...is the commonest form following an auxiliary, but in other infinitive uses the prepositions *to* and *for to* may precede the verb' (Burnley 1983: 122). Without claiming that this was the crucial motivation behind the appearance of the new type of infinitive, it still seems worthwhile to point out that in terms of prosodic prominence this would imply that either the auxiliary, or the unstressed particle *to* can be called upon to keep the rhythmic beats apart, thus **I want go*, rhythmically imperfect, becomes *I want to go*, while *I should go*, with unstressed *should* preventing stress clash, remains unaltered.

The historical situation discussed in this paper is paralleled by phenomena in Modern English which have been extensively recorded and analysed. Bolinger (1965: 139)[17] refers to the operation of a rhythmic principle *'causing one of two alternative constructions to be preferred over the other, contributing to the preservation of a form that might otherwise have been lost...'* Here are some of the relevant cases he discusses:

- Adjectives originating from prepositional phrases: *asleep, afloat, aswim, aghast aglow, aslant,* etc. are restricted to predicative use (op.cit.: 145). A count reported by him (ibid.: 156-7) shows that in a sample of one thousand Modern English words, among the polysyllables 91% of the adjectives are non-oxytonic, while 63% of the verbs are oxytonic.

- Semantically identical "companion forms" are selected on the basis of this principle, thus: *The case is proved; a prov**en** case, The sailor is drunk; a drunk**en** sailor*, also *His knee is bent; on bend**ed** knee, The main had burst; a burst**ed** main* etc.(ibid.: 146-7).

- The existence of adjectives in *-id*: *solid, squalid, timid, vivid,* which did not undergo syncopation of the unstressed vowel because of the high frequency of prenominal use, has contributed to the survival of the phonetically identical [-id] in *dogged*, *crabbed*, *ragged*, *wicked*, *wretched*, *crooked*, *rugged*, *jagged*, *aged*, *learned*. (ibid.: 147-8).

-In verse, too, 'there is a connection between rhythmical and part-of-speech line composition. Lines with feminine word boundaries contain quite definite, usually attributive, syntactic patterns', i.e. a particular type of verse structure is contingent upon the syntactic and therefore the speech rhythmic properties of the words in a line (Tarlinskaya 1984: 16).

Before I conclude, let me also mention, comment on, and possibly preempt two possible objections to the proposed interpretation of the data:

1. Nobody has made an explicit commitment concerning the way in which attributive adjectives following the indefinite article should be classified in (Late) Middle English. The assumption is, I suppose, that such adjectives should follow the strong pattern, i.e., that they should have no final -e's.[18] My hypothesis links the *retention of* -e in attributive position to the mediation of eurhythmy, but there is no reason to expect the same principle *to insert an* -e in structures where it has never been an underlying grammatical marker; this would also run contrary to the loss of morphological distinctiveness of all other instances of final -e in the language. There are, however, as I have shown in (7) and fn. 6, some unsurprising, though not necessarily uniform and consistent, occurrences of -e in the frame Indef. Pron.+ Adj.+ Noun. A similar claim can be made in reference to

the exceptions discussed in (8), i.e. the frame Prep.+ Adj.+ Noun.

2. My analysis assumes that the status of the final -e as a grammatical marker is stable in the plural. Yet in maintaining the syntactically based strong - weak distinction in the singular, it is no longer independently viable. As a plural signal it is still salient, possibly because of the morphological stability of the category of number in all nouns, so that there is phrase-internal number concord within the adjectival NPs. Another argument supporting the survival of plural -e comes from the continuing number agreement between subject NPs and the predicate, in other words the singular-plural opposition continues to be realized across the system. On the other hand, to the extent that -e appears as a marker of the syntactic function of the adjective, attributive and predicative, weak and strong respectively, it surfaces only as a vehicle of rhythmic organization, an option increasing the eurhythmy of speech.

My argument appeals to a notion which has been around for a very long time: the sonorous saunter of syllables as a rhythmic target in English speech has lured scholars for over a hundred years. Within the narrower confine of adjectival morphological/syllabic patterns the earliest and most pertinent comments on this issue come from van Draat, followed by Bolinger and taken up in more recent synchronic studies in metrical phonology. Their analytical apparatus provides some genuinely new and promising insights into the processes of language change, too, and the present study aims in this direction. While my data would fit the notion of stress alternation no matter how this notion is formalized, I have chosen the grid representation and have referred to the rules of eurhythmy because of their simplicity, and, very importantly, their claim to universality.

In conclusion, the idiosyncratic behaviour of singular adjectival final -e in Late Middle English (for London and the South East, with earlier parallels for the North East Midlands) can be accounted for by mapping the prosodic structure onto the syntactic configurations in which it occurs. A singular weak adjective in attributive position triggers a rhythmic rule, whereby a syllable, consisting of the residual final -e, is preserved as a space marker, and sometimes, albeit rarely, even inserted as a buffer, between two beats, unetymologically, and 'ungrammatically'. I believe that final -e as a singular adjectival grammatical marker in Late Middle English appeared intact only as a result of the complex interaction between syntax, morphology, and the requirements of speech rhythm. Among the factors determining the surface realization of adjectival inflexion in the singular, analytical priority should be given to prosodic alignment within the relevant syntactic constituents.

NOTES

1 Between the time I wrote the conference version of this paper and now, two anonymous and one non-anonymous reviewers have commented on it extensively. For their helpful and insightful suggestions I am very grateful; infelicities and blunders in the paper remain my own.
2 Italics for emphasis are mine, unless otherwise indicated.
3 Topliff's data has been found inadequate because she used the *Concordance* and did not make sufficient distinction between types of adjectives (Burnley, 1983: 170), and failed to draw the

interesting conclusions, I might add. Nevertheless, I believe that the paper is important because it contains a complete list of all adjectives counted, and specifies the frequency of occurrence for each adjective.

4 Burnley narrows his investigation to adjectives ending in a consonant, e.g. *long, short, round, wyd, deep, hard* etc., and excludes from consideration cases in which elision could obscure the picture, as well as some other occurrences.

5 At the time of this version of the paper (January 1988) I have no access to machine readable texts of the relevant period. My figures are therefore more of an illustration and support of a theoretical hypothesis, rather than as a granitic body of data. Even if it turns out that preservation of final -e in weak monosyllabic adjectives in absolute numbers was not as regular as I am taking it to be, it is still worth considering the ways in which prosodic factors may have interacted with the morphological shape and the grammatical function of those items.

6 I have also noticed sporadic additions of final -e in the frame Indef. Article + Adjective + Noun e.g. *a riche* feste (4702), but predictably, not in *a wrongful thing, a good partie*. Also, in the MS E Musaeo 116 I found *a riche toun*, 81.1, *a riche lond*, 119.26 and 139.14, but not in *a strong contre*, 33.25, nor in *a wondyrful lyf*, 141.25 (with page and line number references from the Bodleian MS E Musaeo 116, Seymour: 1963). These instances, although not statistically striking, are worth mentioning because the apparent violation of 'gramaticalness' can only be attributed to the prosodic principle discussed here.

7 The data in (1-3) must be taken only as a spot-check on some of the 25 sources cited in Samuels; he mentions, but does not identify, at least ten more manuscripts in which the same situation obtains (1972: 446). One of the reviewers of this paper writes that there may be evidence in the *Equatorie of the Planets* to support my position. My attention has also been called to two recent publications, unavailable at the time I wrote the conference version of this paper: Cowen (1987) and Jefferson (1987). Cowen found no exceptions to the sounding of final -e with weak monosyllabic adjectives in *The Legend of Good Women* (op.cit.: 31-2). Jefferson encountered considerably less variation in the inflexion of adjectives than with other word classes (op.cit.: 106). Both studies confirm the preliminary statements about adjectival inflexions outlined at the beginning of this paper. Going through all possible manuscripts unassisted by a computer is a tall order, and I see little promise of novelty in such an undertaking.

8 For a summary of this view cf. Bihl (1916: 26): 'Maßgebend für die Verwendung des auslautenden e sind die Form des Adjektivs und die Betonungsverhaeltnisse des folgenden Wortes. Bei attributiven einsilbigen und auf der letzten Silbe betonten mehrsilbigen Adjektiven tritt die flektierte Form ausnahmlos

ein, wenn das folgende Substantiv auf der ersten Silbe betont ist: *ye fierse Mars, your excellente doghter.*' Note that Bihl treats all attributively used adjectives in the same way, which would include the groups *a, an, none, one* + Adj. + N. Bihl's view is, to my knowledge, the earliest attempt to relate specifically adjectival final -e's to the overall stress pattern of the noun phrase.

9   I have myself argued in print against the fallacy of treating all word classes as equal with respect to the process of schwa deletion, cf. Minkova: 1984b.

10 My attention has been called to observations on the possible rhythmic function of final -e made by Lehnert (1953), and Smithers (1983) on much earlier texts, and in a different part of the country. The thesis proposed in this paper relies on recent theoretical advances in metrical phonology which have lent, I believe, rigour and explicitness to the old intuitive notion of the inherently rhythmic nature of human speech. Lehnert (1953) speculated on the possibility of a rhythmic basis for the appearance of final -e in *both nouns and adjectives*. The evidence from the inexorably regular septenarius of the *Ormulum* certainly supports the view that in that text the appearance of final -e is no longer grammatically motivated, cf. also Minkova (1978). However, neither of these studies suggests an account of the data which would go beyond the vague statement that, roughly, what we find in verse should be attested in speech, nor has there been any attempt to recognize the syntactic function of adjectives as a factor related to prosodic behaviour.

In a recent study of *Havelok* Smithers (1983: 209-13) singles out the adjectives in that text as a group systematically resisting apocope. I am grateful to one of my reviewers for pointing out this important paper to me. Smithers relates the retention of -e 'with the desire for the regular alternation of an on-beat with an off-beat' (ibid.: 214), a phenomenon made possible by the analogical extension of elision to consonantal environemnts. I myself suggested the same strategy concerning Early Middle English in a paper read at the 1979 English Historical Linguistics Conference in Durham, available, after the usual publication odyssey, as Minkova (1984a: 61-3). The very important difference in the view expressed by Smithers and the view I want to defend here is that he considers 'the few *exceptions to the retention of final -e* in the weak inflexion of adjectives in the singular and in the plural both strong and weak...associated with the avoidance of two successive unaccented syllables between stresses' (ibid: 214),' whereas I regard the same prosodic principle responsible for the *bulk of the data*, i.e. all, or nearly all, monosyllabic singular weak adjectives. My suggestion covers both the cases which Smithers accounts for: *þe fairest þing* 2866, *þe faireste man* 1111, and cases which he considers "breaches of the rule": *þe beste* followed by þe fayrest 1082, þat fulę traytour 2534, þe godę charbocle-ston 2146, þe gretę laumprei 772, þe fayrest þing 2866 etc. In other words, in terms of chronological and dialectal distribution of final -e, we can treat the prosodic principle as providing an additional insight into the uneven rate of morphological changes in Middle English: at a time when the weak-strong distinction was breaking up as a purely grammatical opposition underlyingly, a speech rhythmic ideal, see below, kept the distinction alive on the level of performance.

11 The full quote is: 'There is arguably a universal rhythmic ideal, one that favors a strict alternation of strong and weak beats. Following Sweet 1875-76, we will call this ... the *Principle of Rhythmic Alternation* (PRA)'. And below: 'Our position is not that the PRA plays a direct role in linguistic description of a language's patterns of prominence, but rather that the rules of a grammar that define the possible metrical grid alignments of the sentences of that language *conspire in approximating this ideal*, on every level of organization' (ibid: 37).

12 'The phrasal stress rule for English is rather simple: of two metrical sister nodes, the right-hand one is strong'(Giegerich 1985: 16).

13 This is not the place for a discussion of the merits of the arboreal versus grid metrical representations. The argument has been developed in Giegerich 1985, Selkirk 1984, Hayes 1984. The material I am analysing is straightforward enough (no concatenations of prenominal adjectives, no adverb + adjective combinations etc.) to allow me to read off the predictions from either representation. However, I have chosen to refer to the grid because I am dealing with rhythm, rather than stress, and I accept Hayes' proposal that trees are better suited to the formulation of stress rules, while grids are more explanatory when talking about rhythm.

14 We might conceivably transfer the principle to the retention of -e in the *prepositional* Dative of substantives, as opposed to the *synthetic* Dative in earlier texts, as illustrated and discussed by Lehnert (1953: 135 ff.): 'So blieb das -e in zahlreichen formelhaften praepositionalen Wendungen aus rhythmischen Gründen erhalten (x ' x ' = Praep. + Subst. + -e + Starkdrucksilbe des folgenden Wortes'.

15 Adjectives of two or more syllables ending in a consonant are usually not inflected, either in the plural, or in circumstances which call for the use of the weak inflection; e.g.*mortal batailles*, A 61; *He which that hath the shortest shal biginne*, A 836 (Moore/Marckwardt 1951/68: 52) - such cases can be analysed as possible instances of avoidance of a concatenation of three unstressed syllables. The eurhythmic principle overrides the grammatical requirement for Adj. - head number agreement, cf.

[16] also Minkova (1987: fn.4) for the same type of rhythmic interpretation of e.g. OE *the semelieste man*.

[16] In poertry monosyllabic attributive adjectives regularly suppress the -e before nouns of French origin used with their Romance stress: *the chif cete*, 123.23, *that eche ymage*, 5.3, 5.10, *that iche ymage*, 5.11, (with elision), *that ich contre*, 89.9 (with page and line number references from the Bodleian MS E Musaeo 116, (Seymour: 1963). I agree with a reviewer's observation that a final -e followed by an unstressed initial syllable will make a very odd pentameter; in such configurations the requirements of poetic meter and the ideal of eurhythmy coincide conveniently.

[17] He attributes the first formulation of this principle to van Draat (1912), but goes on to criticize van Draat's extreme views and develops a convincing argument of his own supporting the operation of this principle. I am grateful to Bruce Hayes for drawing my attention to Bolinger's article.

[18] A reminder: the modern form of the indefinite article evolved in Middle English. The strong (indefinite) declension was used for attributive adjectives not preceded by a determiner. Indefinite attributive adjectives were mostly disyllabic: in 21 out of 24 possible paradigmatic variants monosyllabic adjectives acquired a syllabic case/number/gender morpheme. Disyllabic adjectives with a short stressed syllable were almost always uninflected; where the stressed syllable is long, syncope was usual (Quirk and Wrenn, 1957: 31-3).

References

Bihl, Josef. 1916. *Die Wirkungen des Rhythmus in der Sprache von Chaucer und Gower*. Anglistische Forschungen, Heft 50, Heidelberg, Carl Winters Verlag.

Bolinger, Dwight. 1965. 'Pitch Accent and Sentence Rhythm'. In: *Forms of English. Accent, Morpheme, Order*. Cambridge, Massachusetts: Harvard University Press.

Bourcier, Georges. 1978. *An Introduction to the History of the English Language*, English adaptation by Cecily Clark. 1981. Cheltenham.BORDAS, Paris and Stanley Thornes Publishers. Ltd.

Burnley, David. 1982. 'Inflexion in Chaucer's Adjectives'. *Neuphilologische Mitteilungen*, LXXXIII. 169-178.

Burnley, David. 1983. *A Guide to Chaucer's Language*. University of Oklahoma Press. Norman.

Cowen, Janet M. 1987. 'Metrical Problems in Editing *The Legend of Good Women*'. In: Derek Pearsall. ed. *Manuscripts and Texts. Editorial Problems in Later Middle English Literature. Essays from the 1985 Conference at the University of York*. Cambridge: D.S. Brewer.

Donaldson, E.T. 1948. 'Chaucer's Final -e'. *PMLA* LXIII, 1101-24.

Fisiak, Jacek. 1970. *A Short Grammar of Middle English*. Warszawa: Panstwowe Wydawnictwo Naukowe.

Giegerich, Heinz. 1985. *Metrical Phonology and Phonological Structure. German and English.* Cambridge: CUP.
Hayes, Bruce. 1984. 'The Phonology of Rhythm in English'. *Linguistic Inquiry,* 15.1, 33-75.
Jefferson, Judith A. 1987. 'The Hoccleve Holographs and Hoccleve's Metrical Practice'. In: Derek Pearsall. ed. *Manuscripts and Texts. Editorial Problems in Later Middle English Literature. Essays from the 1985 Conference at the University of York.* Cambridge: D.S. Brewer.
Lehnert, Martin. 1953. *Sprachform und Sprachfunktion im "Orrmulum" (um 1200).* Berlin: Deutscher Verlag der Wissenschaften.
Macaulay, G.C. 1900/69. ed, *The English Works of John Gower,* Vol. I, EETS, London, New York, Toronto: Oxford University Press.
Minkova D. 1978. 'Unstressed Final -e in the Ormulum'. *English Studies* 1. Sofia: Sofia University Press. 162-81.
_____ 1984a. 'Early Middle English Metric Elision and Schwa Deletion'. In N.F.Blake and Charles Jones, eds. *English Historical Linguistics: Studies in Development.* Sheffield: CECTAL Conference Papers Series, No. 3. 56-67.
_____ 1984b. 'On the hierarchy of factors causing schwa loss in Middle English'. *Neuphilologische Mitteilungen,* LXXX 4: 445-54.
_____ 1987. 'The Prosodic Character of Early Schwa Deletion in English'. In: *Papers from the 7th International Conference on Historical Linguistics,* ed, Anna Giacalone Ramat et al., Amsterdam/Philadelphia: John Benjamins. 445-59.
Moore, Samuel. 1951/68. *Historical Outlines of English Sounds and Inflections,* revised by Albert H. Marckwardt, Ann Arbor, Michigan: George Wahr Publishing Co.
Morsbach, Lorenz. 1896. *Mittelenglische Grammatik.* Halle.
Mossé, Fernand. 1952/68. *A Handbook of Middle English.* Translated by James A. Walker, Baltimore, London: The Johns Hopkins University Press.
Peck, Russel, ed. 1967. *Confessio Amantis* by John Gower. Toronto: 1980. Holt, Rinehart and Winston, Inc. Reprinted by University of Toronto Press,
Quirk, R. and C.L.Wrenn. 1957. *An Old English Grammar.* New York: Holt, Rinehart & Winston, Inc.
Rastorguyeva,T.A. 1983. *A History of English.* Moscow: Vyssaya skola.
Samuels, M.L. 1972. 'Chaucerian Final "-E"', *Notes and Queries,* CCXVII, 445-8.
Schlauch, Margaret. 1959. *The English Language in Modern Times. since 1400.* Warszawa: Panstwowe Wydawnictwo Naukowe.
Selkirk, Elisabeth. 1984. *Phonology and Syntax: The Relation Between Sound and Structure.* Cambridge, Massachusetts: The MIT Press.
Seymour, M.C. 1963. ed. *The Bodley Version of Mandeville's Travels.* EETS 253
Smithers, G.V. 1983. 'The Scansion of *Havelok* and the Use of ME *-en* and *-e* in *Havelok* and by Chaucer.' In Douglas Gray and E.G.Stanley, eds, *Middle English Studies Presented to Norman Davis in Honour of his Seventieth Birthday,* 195-235. Oxford: Clarendon Press.

Sweet, Henry. 1875-6. 'Words, Logic, Grammar.', *TPS*, 1875-6, 470-503.
Tarlinskaja, Marina. 1984. 'Rhythm-Morphology-Syntax-Rhythm.' *Style*, 18/1, 1-26.
Tatlock, John S. P., & Kennedy, Arthur G. 1927. *A Concordance to the Complete Works on Geoffrey Chaucer and to the Romant of the Rose.* Washington.
Topliff, Delores. 1970. 'Analysis of Singular Weak Adjective Inflection in Chaucer's Works.' *Journal of English Linguistics*, 4. 78-90.
van Draat, P. Fijn. 1912. 'Rhythm in English Prose. The Adjective.' *Anglia* XXXVI, Neue Folge XXIV. 1-59.
Wardale, E.E. 1937. *An Introduction to Middle English*, London.
Wright, Thomas. 1856. ed, *Songs and Carols from a Manuscript in the British Museum of the fifteenth century.* London: T. Richards.

MODELLING FUNCTIONAL DIFFERENTIATION AND FUNCTION LOSS:
the case of *but*

TERTTU NEVALAINEN
University of Helsinki

1. *Introduction.* Grammaticalization can be understood in syntactic terms as functional differentiation of a lexical item. Usually this process of category shift also involves semantic change. As the title implies, my paper is concerned with two aspects of grammaticalization: how a lexical item can acquire a grammatical function, and how it may lose one. I shall be looking at the semantic-pragmatic model proposed by Traugott (1982), which considers grammaticalization as a unilinear abstraction process within a basically Hallidayan framework. The model suggests that propositional items are first grammaticalized into textual functions, then shift into the expressive (interpersonal) component of language, and finally become dummy grammatical markers. All three shifts are not obligatory, but an item may also be directly syntactized or morphologized into a dummy, or it may stop at any of the earlier stages of the process (Traugott, 1982: 256).

In the first half of my paper, I shall discuss a paradigm case of a 'multi-shifter', the English morpheme *but(an)*. The second half focuses on one particular function of *but*, the focusing adverbial synonymous with *only*, and its rise and decline in English. Another implicational model of language change is briefly examined in the light of the data, namely Bailey's wave model (1973), which predicts that the decline of an element will reverse the process of its spread. In our case, the exclusive function of *but* is expected to prevail longest in environments where it was first grammaticalized. I hope to show in the course of my discussion that the two models, but especially Bailey's, may need further refinement in order to account for grammaticalization within the larger context of linguistic variation.

2. *Functional differentiation of* but. *The Oxford English Dictionary* recognizes over thirty different structures involving the morpheme *but* in English.[1] Only one third of that number will be discussed here. All the functions of *but* go back to the Old English place adverb *butan* (< *be utan* 'on the outside'), which was also used as a local preposition in the sense 'outside'. Both uses occur in example (1), taken from the *Anglo-Saxon Chronicle*.

 (1) Besæton þeah þæt geweorc utan sume twegen dagas, 7 genamon ceapes eall þæt þær *buton* wæs, 7 þa men ofslogon þe hie foran forridan mehton *butan* geweorce. (*Chronicle* 893)

  'they besieged the fortress for some two days, and seized all the cattle that was outside, and killed the men whom they could cut off outside the fortress.'

A shift in the prepositional meaning of *butan* from concrete to abstract can be seen in the OE use of the word in the senses 'without' and 'except', as in (2).

 (2) Sceotend swæfon/ þa þæt hornreced healdan scoldon/ ealle *buton* anum. (*Beowulf* 703-705)

  'The soldiers were sleeping, those who were guarding the gabled building, all except one.'

In Traugott's Hallidayan model both prepositions would still form part of the propositional component, which contains the linguistic resources for encoding human experience. So would the two uses of *butan* as a subordinating conjunction, which are based on the abstract preposition: 'except that' in real exceptions, as in example (3), and 'unless' in conditional exceptions, as in (4). The morphological distinction between the preposition and the conjunction is not, however, always clear even in OE (cf. Mitchell, 1985 II: 818-831).

(3) He sæde þeah þæt þæt land sie swiþe lang norþ þonan, ac hit is eal weste, *buton* on feawum stowum styccemælum wiciad Finnas, on huntode on wintra, & on sumera on fiscaþe be þære sæ. (*Ohthere*, p. 18)

'He said however that the country extends a very long way northwards from there, but it is all wasteland, except that in few places here and there some Lapps have their camps, hunting in winter, and in summer fishing in the sea.'

(4) For ðy ic wolde ðætte hie ealneg æt ðære stowe wæren, *buton* se biscep hie mid him habban wille, odde hio hwær to læne sie, odde hwa odre bi write. (*State of Learning*)

(lit.) 'Therefore I desire that they should always be at the same place, unless the bishop want to have it with him, or it be anywhere on loan, or anybody copying it.'

The functions of *but* as a coordinating conjunction also begin to develop in OE. Lacking an inherent propositional meaning in itself, the coordinating conjunction will link pieces of propositional information in different ways, and by doing so promote textual cohesion. The adversative conjunction *but* meaning 'on the contrary' (= German *sondern*) develops from the exceptive conjunction *but* after a negative principal clause. It is apparently quite rare in OE (cf. Mitchell, 1985 I: 728), but becomes more and more frequent in Middle English (see example (5)).

(5) Ne mihtestu þi lif helden none hwile, *bute* al þu it scoldest leten. (*The Proverbs of Alfred*, MED, s.v. *but*, conj. 6d)

This far the development of *but* is paralleled *eg* by its Swedish cognate *utan*, which also functions as a preposition meaning 'without', and as a conjunction meaning 'sondern'.

Unlike present-day Swedish *utan*, however, in ME *but* also replaces the conjunction *ac* in copulative juxtaposition meaning 'yet' and 'however' (= German *aber*), as in (6).

(6) He herde it wel, *but* he spak right not. (*Canterbury Tales*, MED, s.v. *but*, conj. 6d)

In (6) *but* connects the two clauses at the propositional level. We also get what might be called the expressive or interpersonal use of the conjunction in ME, illustrated by examples (7) and (8). Here *but* does not serve to make two clauses cohere syntactically as one sentence, but rather to promote discourse cohesion. Semantically it would represent Halliday's interpersonal language function indicating the speaker's attitude to the speech situation and what is being talked about (cf. Halliday & Hasan, 1976: 226-256). In (7), *but* introduces the speaker's comment; and the example in (8) can be identified as an instance of the speaker's countering move in the fictitious dialogue (cf. Donaldson, 1981, for Chaucer's uses of *but* in narration).

(7) Cutberd schal beo þat on .. þe þridde Alrid .. For hi beoþ of armes þe beste. *Bute* what schal vs to rede? Ihc wene we beþ alle dede. (*Horn*, MED, s.v. *but*, 7a)

(8) "Lat me go first!" "Nay, *but* let me!" (*House of Fame*, MED, s.v. *but*, 7b)

Studies exploring differences between speech and writing show that the conjunction *but* is twice as frequent in speech as in writing both in British and in American English today. Altenberg (1986), for instance, found that some 50% of the incidence of *but* in his spoken British English sample could be accounted for in terms of discourse functions. These uses include interactive countering, topic shifting, and resting point for planning, for example (cf. Altenberg, 1986: 26-35, Schiffrin, 1987: 152-177).

Two things emerge from this discussion of the diachronic

development of the conjunction *but*. The evidence suggests that what might be called the propositional-textual function of *but* meaning 'sondern' is clearly earlier than its textual function meaning 'aber'. However, it is not perfectly clear whether this 'aber' function was first used in propositional or interpersonal contexts. The textual evidence points to a near-simultaneous diffusion of these two, and the evidence is, of course, written-language biassed. We might argue in this case that there was perhaps no implicational relation between these two uses of the conjunction. Since the textual function reflects the mode of communication, it would not be surprising to find that the requirements of the spoken mode are reflected in the specialization of the textual function.

3. *The rise of the exclusive adverb* but. Going back to Old English, we have one more construction type involving *but*, *viz*. *ne ... butan* meaning 'only', 'no more than'. It is illustrated in (9).

> (9) þeah þe sume men sæden þæt þær nære *buton* twegen dælas: Asia, 7 þæt oþer Europe. (*Orosius* I.i.5-6)
>
> 'Some men said that there were no more than two parts /of the world/: Asia and, the other, Europe.'

Ne ... but is sometimes connected with the prepositional use of *but* meaning 'except', sometimes with the conjunction. The frequent lack of oblique inflections after *but* would support the latter interpretation; the connection of the construction with other negative phrases, the former. Another way to interpret *ne ... but* is to regard it as a complex exclusive structure parallel to French *ne ... que* meaning 'only'. This non-compositional interpretation would perhaps better fit in with the ME course of development as a result of which the negative particle *ne* is deleted, and *but* is grammaticalized into the adverbial function synonymous with 'only'. An early instance of the exclusive adverbial is quoted in (10).

(10) Fro londe woren he *bote* a mile. (*Havelok* 721)

In certain Northern varieties of English *but* is adverbialized through overt univerbation, with the resulting adverb *nobbut*. Omission of the negative particle in the other ME varieties can be considered an instance of Jespersen's cycle, a cyclical process from a single particle to a double, and back to a single again (cf. Dahl, 1979). The exclusive *but* is semantically conditioned by the negative particle, and hence not an independent development of the expective preposition or conjunction.

If we define the propositional component of language in terms of truth-conditional relations both the adverb *but* and the *ne* ... *but*-construction would presumably be placed in this component. In challenging examples (9) and (10), for instance, we are not denying the fact that the world has two parts in (9), or that the people were a mile away from land in (10). It is rather the semantic contribution of *but* that is denied, *i.e.* that there are more than two parts in (9), and that they were more than a mile away from land in (10).[2] The adverbialization of *but* would then seem to represent a simple reanalysis of the exclusive construction within the propositional component.

However, it can also be argued that focusing adverbials like *only*, *but*, and *just* also involve an act of evaluation on the part of the speaker. In the case of these exclusives, the evaluative aspect means placing the focus of the adverb on a scale the higher values of which are excluded from the discussion (cf. König, 1981; Taglicht, 1984: 90-93). Hence, example (10), above, could be paraphrased 'they were a mile away from land and no more than a mile away from land'. When *but* focuses on an item that represents the extreme value on a scale, the adverb is interpreted as an intensifier rather than as an ordinary exclusive.[3] In example (11), *but dead* can be paraphrased 'as good as dead', 'nearly dead', or 'about to die' (*MED*, s.v. *but*, conj. 2d).

(11) "þou es," coth golias, "*bot* ded." (*Cursor Mundi* 7576)

Similarly, *but right* would be synonymous with 'quite right', and so on.

In Traugott's model of grammaticalization, intensifier functions would be placed in the interpersonal component of language. According to dictionary evidence, the intensifying function of *but* is attested later than the purely exclusive one, although the *ne ... but* -construction had both. In the texts included in the Helsinki Corpus of English Texts the two functions of *but* occur in the second ME period, *i.e.* in texts dated between 1250 and 1350.[4] This would be natural if the adverbialization of *but* is not considered an independent development involving the morpheme *but*, but rather part of a more extensive process of negative simplification.

It has been suggested by Jack (1978) that the particle *ne* in such constructions as *ne ... not* and *ne ... but* was first dropped as redundant in the colloquial registers of language use. Purely phonetic reasons have also been given to explain similar processes in Dutch (Bossuyit, 1983) and French (Ashby, 1981). Ashby's variational study of Touraine French shows, among other things, a strong correlation between a number of phonetic environments and the loss or retention of *ne*.

In the computerized Helsinki Corpus, the frequencies shown in Table 1 can be found for the construction *ne ... but* and the adverb *but* per thousand words. The table indicates the gradual decline of *ne ... but* and steady rise of *but*.

Around the middle of the ME period *ne ... but* and *but* overlap, but towards the end of the period *ne ... but* recedes and almost disappears by 1500.[5] The hypothesis that the exclusive adverbial *but* emerges in the colloquial language is not contradicted by the data. In the second and third periods, *but* occurs more frequently in secular instruction and fictive narration than in religious instruction; for instance, it is more frequent in the verse of Chaucer's *Canterbury Tales* than in the prose of Wycliffite homilies or the documents of *The Book of London English*. Further study of its distribution will, however, be necessary because the present figures are too small to be statistically significant.

TABLE 1. Frequencies of *but* and *ne ... but* per thousand words in the ME texts of the Helsinki Corpus.

ME period	Frequency per 1000 words *NE ... BUT*	*BUT*	Sample size
1. 1150-1250	0.126	0.0	135,200 words
2. 1250-1350	0.099	0.054	130,800 words
3. 1350-1420	0.044	0.133	158,000 words
4. 1420-1500	0.010	0.436	202,600 words

4. *The decline of the exclusive* but. We know from present-day standard English that the exclusive *but* has suffered the same fate as the *ne ... but* -construction in LME. The 'life cycle' of the adverb can be seen in the Bible quotations in (12) ranging from OE to the present day.

(12a) þa 7swaredon hiġ. we *nabbað* her *buton* fif hlafas 7 twegen fixas. (*WS Gospels*, St Matthew XIV:17)

(12b) Thei answeriden, We han *not* heere, *but* fyue looues and twei fischis. (Wycliffe, *ibid.*)

(12c) Then sayde they vnto him: we have here *but* .v. loves and two fysshes. (Tyndale, *ibid.*)

(12d) And they say vnto him, We haue heere *but* fiue loaues, and two fisches. (*AV*, *ibid.*)

(12e) They said to him, "We have *only* five loaves here and two fish." (*RSV*, *ibid.*)

A systematic survey of the frequency of occurrence of *but* shows its gradual decline as an exclusive in Modern English. Early and Late Modern English data are compared in Table 2, where the figures are derived from similar, non-computerized corpora including private correspondence, plain and colloquial sermons, comic plays, and records of parliamentary debates (cf. Nevalainen, 1983, for the EModE data). As its incidence per thousand words indicates, *but* reaches its highest frequency in Elizabethan English, and then slowly declines towards the end of the LModE period.

TABLE 2. Frequency of the exclusive adverb *but* per thousand words in Early and Late Modern English.

Period	Frequency of *BUT* per 1000 words	Approximate sample size
EModE: 1500-1560	0.582	526,000 words
1570-1630	1.025	440,000 words
1640-1700	0.710	438,000 words
LModE: 1860-1900	0.196	520,000 words

The late Victorian data clearly show that the exclusive *but* is on its way out. According to Bailey's phonologically oriented wave model of language change, it ought to prevail longest in environments where it was first grammaticalized. In Bailey's words (1973: 82), what is quantitatively less is slower and later; what is more is earlier and faster. Two problems will arise in the case of a lexical item like *but*, however. One concerns the concept of relevant environment, and the other the difference between lexico-grammatical and phonetic changes in general. As far as *but* is concerned, the environments, phonetic and otherwise, that motivated the loss of *ne* are no longer relevant in LModE, because the negative particle was lost in all environments. It would be counter-intuitive to expect anything more than a chance cooccurrence of those initial conditioning contexts with the declining LModE adverb. In other words, certain conditioning factors may cease to be operative when a change within a system has reached its completion.

Another, more relevant approach to conditioning environments is the analysis of the syntactic-semantic contexts of the adverb. Both some general contextual features and some possible selection features of the adverb are included in my preliminary study of the ME and LModE data. The results are shown in Table 3.

TABLE 3. Contextual features of the exclusive adverb *but*.

Features	ME (N=28) 1250-1420	ME (N=88) 1420-1500	LModE (N=102) 1860-1900
CLAUSE TYPE:			
+ declarative - interrogative - imperative	28 (100.0%)	86 (97.7%)	98 (96.1%)
CLAUSE DEPENDENCE:			
+ main clause - subordinate cl.	18 (64.3%)	58 (65.9%)	69 (67.6%)
FOCUS FUNCTION:			
+ Cs/Co/Adv/V - S/O	20 (71.4%)	74 (84.1%)	79 (77.4%)
FOCUS SCALARITY:			
+ quantified/ measure phrase - non-quantified/ no measure phr.	14 (50.0%)	49 (55.7%)	56 (54.9%)

In spite of the smallness of the samples available, there seem to be remarkable similarities between the ME and LModE frequency patterns. The differences in distribution are not statistically significant. The exclusive *but* usually occurs in declarative main clauses. Although it may be argued that the figures only reflect the composition of the corpus, one would expect that a subordinate clause bias, for instance, would show up if there were any. More specific than the clause type and dependence features are focus function and inherent scalarity. The figures indicate that *but* clearly does not select a focus that is one of the two main referential items and discourse participants in the clause, the subject (S) or the direct object (O).[6] The focus of the exclusive usually constitutes, or forms part of, the subject complement (Cs) or an adverbial modifier (Adv). Occasionally it can also be the verb (V) or the object complement (Co). Semantically the focus of *but* is usually either a numerical quantifier, a measure phrase or a size modifier (cf. ex. (9) and (12)). The data indicate that *but* tends to select a naturally scalar focus.

The data in Table 3 would then seem to support the wave model of change. However, even these contextual features do not necessarily reflect anything other than the selectional properties of the exclusive adverb. If anything, they show that *but* has not changed much over the centuries. Rather than comparing its focus features with the new environments of an ongoing sound change, we should perhaps only compare them with the realization of phonotactic structures in the sound system. In this case, only some more data, especially from the intervening EModE period, could show whether *but* was at any time very differently distributed. My preliminary investigation does not provide much evidence to that effect (see also Walker, 1655: 25-26).

What we are left with then are the external selection criteria of the adverb. In this context, space only permits a discussion of the matter on the genre or text type level.

My EModE and LModE adverb data have been sampled from four comparable text types. To counterbalance the speech-related materials, educational writings have been included in the LModE corpus. Table 4 shows the distribution of *but* in the EModE subcorpus sampled around the turn of the 17th century, and in the late 19th century corpus.

TABLE 4. Frequency of the exclusive *but* per thousand words in different text types.

Text type	Frequency of BUT per 1000 words	Approximate sample size
EModE (1570-1640):		
Parliamentary diary	0.964	110,000 words
Private correspondence	0.891	110,000 words
Comic play	1.114	114,000 words
Popular sermon	1.132	106,000 words
LModE (1860-1900):		
Parliamentary Select Committee minutes	0.028	109,000 words
Private correspondence	0.047	106,000 words
Comic play	0.098	102,000 words
Popular sermon	0.350	103,000 words
Educational prose	0.480	100,000 words

The adverb is fairly evenly distributed in the Early Modern subcorpus, slightly dominating in the colloquial and plain sermons and comic plays. A comparison of these figures with the late Victorian data shows that, besides its frequency, its distribution pattern has changed. *But* is least frequent in the verbatim records of a parliamentary Select Committee, private correspondence and comedies, but it occurs at a considerable frequency in the sermons of Creighton, Parker and Spurgeon, and especially in the text books on education by Quick and Spencer sampled for the corpus.

In EModE *but* is a quantitatively prototypical exclusive, as it represents more than a half of all the occurrences of exclusive focusing adverbials in some of the more colloquial genres (cf. Nevalainen, 1985). In LModE its share has dropped to 7% in the present corpus. It represents less than 5% of all the exclusive adverbials in letters, plays and parliament records; some 15% in sermons, and nearly 20% in educational prose. In present-day standard English dictionaries *but* is commonly labelled as literary and archaic (see *e.g. Longman Dictionary of Contemporary English*, s.v. *but*, adv.). Two of its present-day contexts of use are illustrated by examples (13) and (14).

(13) As Theodore Silverstein pointed out in 1935, ... In 1938, *but* three years later, Carleton Brown, in an article entitled "*Beowulf* and the *Blickling Homilies* and Some Textual Notes", argued that the evidence which Silverstein had presented should be explained differently. (Collins, 1984: 63)

(14) Compared with the Declaration of Independence, a document vividly revered by millions of Americans, Magna Charta is *but* a dim, forgotten palimpsest. (*The Guardian Weekly*, Jan. 17, 1988, p. 6)

This survey of contextual cooccurrence features of *but* indicates that Bailey's phonologically-based wave model may not be ideally suited to account for lexical redistribution. Particular problems are presented by 'mixed' cases like *but* that continue to select fairly stable grammatical environments while reweighting their external situational and stylistic contexts of use.

5. *Discussion*. The slow decline of the exclusive *but* did not bring about a state of dysfunction in the English exclusive adverbial system. Since ME, the system has counted more than one member besides *but*, notably the derivatives of *one*, *only* and *alone* (cf. Rissanen, 1967). We may regard the decline of *but* as part of a process of lexical redistribution

within that system. To what extent the syntactic-semantic selection features of *only*, for instance, have been altered during the process still remains to be seen. It would seem that the notion of analogy would have an important role to play in this type of intrasystemic change (cf. Samuels, 1972: 55-61).

I would even go so far as to claim that analogy may reinforce shifts between grammatical functions. The cohesive conjunct function of *only* would be a good candidate for such a shift. In Present English we can say both *I would come, but I have no time*, and *I would come, only I have no time* (cf. Quirk *et al.*, 1985: 645-646). Textual evidence indicates that this function of *only* is more recent than that of *but*, while both words were used as exclusive adverbs before the syntactic extension of *only* took place in ME.

Another possible example of the influence of *but* is the marginal function of *only* as a preposition meaning 'except', well documented from the EModE period onwards (cf. ex. (15))

(15) Do not cross the line *only* by the bridge. (A notice at Bolton railway station; *OED*, s.v. *only*, B2)

The fact that the cohesive conjunct function of *only* seems to antedate its propositional function as a preposition may be another indicator of an anlogous rather than predictable course of development.

A further possible source of 'irregularity' in the grammaticalization of a lexical item is foreign contact influence. The negative relativizer function of *but*, for instance, that emerges in LME has often been attributed to Latin influence on English (cf. Sørensen, 1957: 135; Partridge, 1969: 53, 146, 162-163). The instance in (16) is quoted by Walker (1655: 23) as the recommended translation of Cicero's Latin *Nemo est, qui nesciat.*

(16) There is none *but* knowes.

While the relativizer *but* could still be understood as an extension of the exceptive preposition or conjunction, the more recent intensifier function of *but* is much less transparent. It is illustrated by example (17). Influence of the French conjunction *mais* is quoted as a possible source for this expressive function of the word in the *OED Supplement* (s.v. *but*, conj. 27c).

(17) She must never, *but* never, appear anything other than radiant, gracious and content. (*Observer Magazine*, June 28, 1981, p. 45)

6. *Conclusion*. The results of the present study on *but* can be summarized as follows. (1) The main claims of Traugott's implicational model of grammaticalization are supported by the data. The cohesive textual function of *but* derives from the propositional function of the word as a preposition and conjunction. Its expressive functions are not, however, very clearly differentiated. Within the textual 'aber' function, an ordering between the propositionally and interpersonally oriented meanings is not evident in the data, and the idea of a strong implicational hierarchy from propositional via textual to expressive meanings may have to be abandoned in this case.

Similarly, although in strict truth-conditional terms it takes place within the propositional component, the adverbialization of *but* also involves an evaluative, interpersonal meaning aspect. With certain inherently non-gradable items, an intensifier function is induced by the scalar reading of the focus. Hence, (2) it seems that expressive functions may also accompany propositional and textual grammaticalization processes rather than remain strictly compartamentalized.

The slow decline of the exclusive adverb *but* indicates that the contextual features of a lexical item do not always directly reflect the history of its diffusion. Some original conditioning contexts may have ceased to be operative, such as those environments that correlated with the loss of the negative particle *ne* in ME. Others, such as the scalarity of the adverbial focus, may be indicative of some fairly stable selection features of the lexical item. And yet others, *e.g.* stylistic environments, may be reweighted in the course of time. In these circumstances, (3) Bailey's wave model does not apply very well to recessive lexical variants like *but*. Further study of entire variant fields of lexical variables will be necessary to find out whether the model could account for other aspects of lexical redistribution.

NOTES

1. Apart from the historical dictionaries, *OED* and *MED*, the only extensive diachronic treatment of the functional differentiation of *but* is Varnhagen (1876). OE *butan* is discussed extensively in Mitchell (1985: 818-831, and *passim*). The exceptive and restrictive functions of *but* are outlined in Joly (1982), and the EModE exclusives, including *but*, in Nevalainen (1985).
2. This analysis of *but* is analogous to that of *only*, *even*, and *also* in Karttunen and Peters (1979), König (1981), and Taglicht (1984). It is based on semantic factoring of the contribution of the adverbial to the proposition. Exclusives seem to differ from other focusing adverbials in that they affect the truth conditions of the propositions in which they occur.
3. It would be possible to interpret all scalar exclusives like *but* as intensifiers (cf. downtoners in Quirk *et al.*, 1985: 597-602). In order to avoid multiple homonymy of the other exclusives, notably *only*, this has not been done in the present case.
4. The ME texts in the Helsinki Corpus of English Texts were selected and sampled by Professors Saara Nevanlinna and Matti Rissanen, Mrs. Irma Taavitsainen, Mr. Juha Hannula, Mrs. Leena Koskinen, Mrs. Tesma Outakoski and Dr. Kisti Peitsara. Their computerization was coordinated by Miss Merja Kytö. The Manual listing the texts in the corpus is forthcoming by the end of 1988.

5. These figures do not include constructions that involve other negative items, *e.g. nought* or *never*. The *not ... but* -construction still occurs dialectally, and also in certain collocations such as *cannot but* in the standard language (cf. Joly, 1982).
6. For the identification of the adverbial focus in written contexts, see Nevalainen (1982). The referential differentiation between subjects/objects and subject/object complements is based on a notion of prototypical nominal functions (Hopper & Thompson, 1984).

SOURCES

AV = *The Holy Bible. An Exact Reprint in Roman Type, Page for Page of the Authorised Version Published in the Year 1611*. Oxford: Oxford University Press. 1911.
Beowulf = *Beowulf and the Fight at Finnsburg*. Ed. Fr. Klaeber. London: D.C. Heath & Co. S.a.
Chronicle = *Two of the Saxon Chronicles Parallel*. Ed. C. Plummer & J. Earle. Oxford: Clarendon Press. 1892. Repr. 1965.
The Anglo-Saxon Chronicle. Transl. D. Whitelock *et al*. London: Eyre & Spottiswoode. 1961.
Collins, R.L. 1984. 'Blickling Homily XVI and the Dating of *Beowulf*'. In W.-D. Bald & H. Weinstock, ed. *Medieval Studies Conference, Aachen 1983*, 61-69. Frankfurt am Main: Peter Lang.
Cursor Mundi = *Cursor Mundi*. Part 2. EETS OS 59. Ed. R. Morris. London: Trübner & Co. 1875. Repr. 1966.
Havelok = *The Lay of Havelok the Dane*. Ed. W.W. Skeat. Second ed. Rev. K. Sisam. Oxford: Clarendon Press. 1915. Repr. 1939.
Ohthere = *Two Voyagers at the Court of King Alfred*. Ed. N. Lund. Transl. C.E. Fell. York: William Sessions Ltd. 1984.
Orosius = *King Alfred's Orosius*. Part 1. EETS OS 79. Ed. H. Sweet. London: Oxford University Press. 1883. Repr. 1959.
RSV = *The New Oxford Annotated Bible with the Apocrypha*. Revised Standard Version. Ed. H.G. May & B.M. Metzger. New York: Oxford University Press. 1946-1952. Repr. 1977.
State of Learning = *King Alfred's West-Saxon Version of Gregory's Pastoral Care*. Part 1. EETS OS 45. Ed. H. Sweet. London: N. Trübner. 1871. Repr. 1958.
Tyndale = *The New Testament*. Transl. W. Tyndale. 1534. Repr. Ed. N. Hardy Wallis. Cambridge: Cambridge University Press. 1938.
Walker, W. 1655. *A Treatise of English Particles*. A Scolar Press Facsimile. Menston: The Scolar Press Ltd. 1970.
WS Gospels = *The West-Saxon Gospels. A Study of the Gospel of St. Matthew with Text of the Four Gospels*. Ed. M. Grünberg. Amsterdam: Scheltema and Holkema. 1967.
Wycliffe = *The New Testament in English. According to the Version by John Wycliffe about A.D. 1380 and Revised by John Purvey about A.D. 1388*. Ed. J. Forshall & F. Madden. Oxford: Clarendon Press. 1879.

REFERENCES

Altenberg, B. 1986. 'Contrastive Linking in Spoken and Written English'. In G. Tottie & I. Bäcklund, ed. *English in Speech and Writing*. Studia Anglistica Upsaliensia 60, 13-40. Stockholm: Almqvist & Wiksell.

Ashby, W.J. 1981. 'The Loss of the Negative Particle *Ne* in French: A Syntactic Change in Progress'. *Language* 57.674-687.

Bailey, C.-J.N. 1973. *Variation and Linguistic Theory*. Arlington, Va.: Center for Applied Linguistics.

Bossuyt, A. 1983. 'Historical Functional Grammar: An Outline of an Integrated Theory of Language Change'. In S.C. Dik, ed. *Advances in Functional Grammar*, 301-325. Dordrecht: Foris.

Dahl, Ö. 1979. 'Typology of Sentence Negation'. *Linguistics* 17.79-106.

Donaldson, E.T. 1981. 'Adventures with the Adversative Conjunction in the General Prologue to the *Canterbury Tales*; or, What's before the *But*?' In M. Benskin & M.L. Samuels, ed. *So Meny People Longages and Tonges: Philological Essays in Scots and Mediaeval English Presented to Angus McIntosh*, 355-366. Edinburgh: The Editors.

Halliday, M.A.K. & R. Hasan. 1976. *Cohesion in English*. London: Longman.

Hopper, P.J. & S.A. Thompson. 1984. 'The Discourse Basis for Lexical Categories in Universal Grammar'. *Language* 60.703-752.

Jack, G.B. 1978. 'Negation in Later Middle English Prose'. *Archivum Linguisticum* 9.58-72.

Joly, A. 1982. '*But*, signe de l'exception et de la restriction dans l'histoire de l'anglais'. *Modèles linguistiques* 4.151-175.

Karttunen, L. & S. Peters. 1979. 'Conventional Implicature'. In C.-K. Oh & D.A. Dinneen, ed. *Syntax and Semantics 11: Presupposition*, 1-56. New York: Academic Press.

König, E. 1981. 'The Meaning of Scalar Particles in German'. In H.-J. Eykmeyer & H. Rieser, ed. *Words, Worlds, and Contexts*, 107-132. Berlin: W. de Gruyter.

Mitchell, B. 1985. *Old English Syntax*. 1-2. Oxford: Clarendon Press.

Nevalainen, T. 1982. 'Determining the Contextual Focus of Exclusive Focusing Adverbials'. *Papers on English Philology Read at the Symposium Arranged by the Modern Language Society at Tvärminne on 26-28 November, 1981. Neuphilologische Mitteilungen* 83, extra issue, 55-68.

Nevalainen, T. 1983. 'A Corpus of Colloquial Early Modern English for a Lexical-Syntactic Study: Evidence for Consistency and Variation'. In S. Jacobson, ed. *Papers from the Second Scandinavian Symposium on Syntactic Variation*. Stockholm Studies in English 57, 109-122. Stockholm: Almqvist & Wiksell International.

Nevalainen, T. 1985. 'Lexical Variation of EModE Exclusive Adverbs: Style Switching or a Change in Progress?' In R. Eaton, O. Fischer, W. Koopman & F. van der Leek, ed. *Papers from the 4th International Conference on English Historical Linguistics*. Current Issues in Linguistic Theory 41, 179-194. Amsterdam: John Benjamins.

Partridge, A.C. 1969. *Tudor to Augustan English: A Study in Syntax and Style from Caxton to Johnson*. London: André Deutsch.

Quirk, R., S. Greenbaum, G. Leech & J. Svartvik. 1985. *A Comprehensive Grammar of the English Language*. London: Longman.

Rissanen, M. 1967. *The Uses of* One *in Old and Early Middle English*. Mémoires de la Société Néophilologique de Helsinki 31. Helsinki.
Samuels, M.L. 1972. *Linguistic Evolution, with Special Reference to English*. Cambridge: Cambridge University Press.
Schiffrin, D. 1987. *Discourse Markers*. Cambridge: Cambridge University Press.
Sørensen, K. 1957. 'Latin Influence on English Syntax: A Survey with a Bibliography'. *Travaux du Cercle Linguistique de Copenhague* 11, 131-155. Copenhague: Nordisk Sprog- og Kulturforlag.
Taglicht, J. 1984. *Message and Emphasis: On Focus and Scope in English*. London: Longman.
Traugott, E.C. 1982. 'From Propositional to Textual and Expressive Meanings: Some Semantic-pragmatic Aspects of Grammaticalization'. In W.P. Lehmann & Y. Malkiel, ed. *Perspectives on Historical Linguistics*. Current Issues in Linguistic Theory 24, 245-271. Amsterdam: John Benjamins.
Varnhagen, H. 1876. *An Inquiry into the Origin and Different Meanings of the English Particle* "But". An Inaugural Dissertation. Göttingen: University Press.

DATING OLD ENGLISH INSCRIPTIONS: THE LIMITS OF INFERENCE

R.I. PAGE
University of Cambridge

For decades epigraphists have tried to establish principles for the linguistic dating of Old English texts, though without much success. The topic is raised again by the projected republication of the great runic crosses of Bewcastle (Cumbria) and Ruthwell (Dumfries and Galloway). Those concerned with the art historical aspects of the project are properly eager to find out what support they can get from linguistic techniques of dating, and indeed a comparison of the conclusions of the two disciplines may produce useful confirmation of the methodologies of each. On the whole I think it doubtful if any very firm conclusions will come from my reconsideration of the problem. I can point to difficulties, but I doubt if I can overcome them. At least, however, I may save other scholars from oversimplification.

There are few Anglo-Saxon inscriptions that can be dated precisely from their historical reference. The only runic example is, I think, St Cuthbert's coffin, presumably made by the monks of Lindisfarne for the translation of the saint's body in 698. But its texts are of very limited interest to the student of Old English, consisting only of the names of evangelists, archangels, apostles and of Christ and Mary (Dickins 1956: 305–7).

Non-runic inscriptions of historical significance are slightly more plentiful, though hardly abundant. Dr Okasha lists several Latin inscriptions (which may incorporate Old English personal name forms): there are individual examples from Deerhurst and Jarrow, there is St Cuthbert's portable altar, the Sherburn ring of Queen Eaðelswið and the Laverstock ring of King Ethelwulf and so on (Okasha 1971). But, if we except the Alfred jewel on the grounds that it is uncertainly attributed to the great king, the only inscription of any length in Old English firmly datable on historical grounds is the famous text of the Kirkdale (N. Yorkshire) sundial (inscriptions studied here are transliterated in the Appendix). This has referent points that put it between 1055 and 1065. Otherwise there are only coin legends, which have distinctive characteristics and problems, and in any case produce texts that consist largely of personal or place-names. Clearly there is nothing here on which a pattern of dating can be built up on historical evidence alone, to compare with the epigraphical evidence.

There are, of course, inscriptions whose dates can be inferred from the limiting dates of the institutions they derive from. Grave markers, if they can be ascribed to a particular ecclesiastical house, are not likely to pre-date its foundation or post-date its destruction. On such grounds we can give general dating limits to, for instance, the grave-markers at Lindisfarne, Monkwearmouth and probably Hartlepool, though even in these cases we should not be too confident that we have determined the absolute outer limits of Christian occupation of the sites. In any case, such dating can be only within a couple of centuries or so, and is a very blunt instrument indeed.

Art historians and archaeologists are often eager to help by adding their dating of monuments. Unfortunately there is equal imprecision in their methods. For sculptured stones, for instance, Professor Cramp has shown how much the scholar must rely for dating on the uncertain tools of typology and style (Cramp 1984: xlvii—xlviii). Here again there are too few examples clearly datable on external grounds to provide a matrix into which others can be fitted. The effects can be disconcerting. For instance, when I first wrote about the Great Urswick memorial cross I dated it on linguistic grounds to 750—850. To my surprise I found that art historians put it rather later, in the tenth century (Collingwood 1927: 53, 63). I was happy to find that the new Cumbria volume of the corpus of Anglo-Saxon sculptured stones brought it into the ninth century (Bailey and Cramp 1988: 150). Here, I thought, was a support to my own dating. It was something of a blow to learn that the art historians had moved the cross back into the ninth century in part because that is where the philologist had said it should be. What seemed to be an independent confirmation turned out to conceal a circular argument.

Datings by archaeologists may equally be tentative. The excavation report put into the fourth century the cremation urn that held the Caistor-by-Norwich runic bone (Myres and Green 1973: 46). Dr Catherine Hills, whose knowledge of East Anglian cremation pottery is unrivalled, tells me that there is no reason why this urn should not be fifth-century. The linguist can say only that the Caistor-by-Norwich inscription is very early, but has no means of deciding how early. Again, while an archaeologist or art historian may be able tentatively to date an object, he may not be able to date its inscription. Sonia Chadwick Hawkes pointed out, in a meticulous examination, that the inscription on the Chessell Down (Isle of Wight) scabbard mount was a late addition, probably shortly before burial, to a sword assembly which was already of some age (Hawkes and Page 1967: 17—18). The Chester-le-Street (Durham) stone has been assigned to the late ninth century (Cramp 1984: 54); the inscription does not look part of the original design, and may have been added to an existing stone at some later date.

Occasionally there is real coincidence of evidence. An example is the Franks casket. Art historians assure me that their dating for this piece is c. 700. The evidence of philology and runology suggests 700—750. Dr. T.A.M. Bishop, on consultation, observed that the few non-runic letters of the texts suggest a date c. 700. Here is an almost perfect case of three different types of evidence agreeing.

However, in general the philologist who enters upon epigraphy must beware. The physical context of an inscription must always be taken into account, for it may affect linguistic form. In a recent oral discussion of the early runic inscriptions of the Germanic world, a distinguished Danish scholar averred that what we needed was a full transliteration of all the available material from different parts of Europe, so that it could be examined dispassionately and as a purely linguistic exercise. To this I demurred for I was aware that a linguistic study alone could not allow for peculiarities that can only be understood if the texts are examined within their physical context. A simple example is the text cut in a censer-cover from Pershore: +GODRICMEWVORHT, 'Godric made me'. This is how it would appear in a transcript, divorced from its object. There appears to be loss of final -e in the verb, surely very early if this is, as the art historians assure us, a tenth-century piece (Wilson 1964: 158). But of course, this is not evidence of loss of the unstressed vowel. The explanation is that the carver did not lay out his inscription competently, and reached the end of his space before he completed his word (perhaps because he had added a superfluous V); so he had no option but to omit the final letter, whatever it was. So far so good. But the observation gives rise to further questions. Did the carver omit the vowel knowing that it was not required for the understanding of the text? Or was he only semi-literate (as Moltke has argued in parallel cases from Denmark: Moltke 1985: 95, 114)? If he had been literate, might he not have tried to ligature a final -E with his T — which would be both possible and easy to understand? Or was the unstressed -e at this date so imprecisely pronounced that a loss of the graph would be acceptable in a demotic written text? Our assessment of the inscription's language depends to some extent on the answer to questions like these.

In contrast there is the Great Edstone (N. Yorkshire) sundial's maker inscription: +LOÐAN|MEWRO|HTEA, 'Loðan made me' (Okasha 1971: 73). As it is thus given, the ending of the verb looks very odd indeed. When you see the text on the stone, however, you realise that though the carver provided a large panel for his wording, he cut on only a small part of it, and the text is almost certainly unfinished. Presumably it was to continue WROHTE A(ND) . . . . — there are no gaps between words — but was never completed.

In the case of the Kirkdale sundial we are fortunate in having a historical dating. It would be interesting to see what conclusions about date can be drawn from the language of the text alone. It is clear from a first glance that this inscription shows deviations from Standard Old English. There is decline in precision of inflexional endings in *svna, tofalan, tobrocan*: loss of the distinctive 2. weak infinitive ending in *macan*: an irregular ending to *newan* if *minster* is neuter, and to *ilcvm* if *tid* is feminine. On the other hand, the weakening of the dative (singular or plural) ending (often regarded as a later development) is not evidenced in *dagvm* (2x), *ilcvm*. Since there are some clearly latish features, what conclusion can properly be drawn from the uninflected genitives *Eadward dagvm cng* and *Tosti dagvm eorl*? The two panels holding the two sections of the main text are roughly the same size, yet they hold vastly different numbers of letters, 54 to the left (not counting punctuation symbols) and 90 to the right. Presumably what happened, and it is clearer from a photograph than a transcript, is that the carver found he had used up half his space when he had reached only a third of the way through the text. He may have spread out the beginning deliberately to give greater prominence to the name of the owner and to his patronymic. When he found himself pressed for space he began to squeeze his words together, letters became thinner, some were missed out (or perhaps we should say ligatured), CNG for *cing*, 7N for *and in*. Can we argue then that the genitive endings were omitted towards the end of the inscription to save space? It was clear what was meant and so the grammatical indication was superfluous. This could be the explanation, but there is a slightly embarrassing feature: the text ends with a cross, and what is more, with a rather elaborate cross which occupies a good deal of room.[1] If the carver were really pressed for space, he could have omitted it and found room for at least one genitive ending. So the uninflected genitive may be a genuine local feature of either dialect, or date, or both. Such a genitive is well-known from the later Middle English period (Mustanoja 1960: 71), and this may be a very early example of it. In that case the Kirkdale examples should point to a date late in the Old English period at the earliest. However, Kirkdale may be a special case. Since this is an Anglo-Norse region, we may have here an early case of the decline of inflexional endings in a bilingual community.

We know nothing of the training of the carvers who produced the inscriptions of Anglo-Saxon England, how carefully they were taught and their epigraphical work supervised. Who wrote the text — the mason himself or his master, who handed to him writings written on, say, a wax tablet which the craftsman, rather slavishly, put on his object? Is there a single answer to this question, or does it have different answers for different circumstances? A runic graffito cut casually on a bit of bone could well be the composer's autograph, as that from Hamwih/Southampton (Page 1973: 170–1). A text incised in a sword-blade might be the work of a semi-literate smith, producing work to order, but perhaps not closely supervised, and that may explain some of the aberrations of the Thames (Battersea) scramasax (Wilson 1964: 144–6). The carver who cut the Crucifixion poem on the Ruthwell cross (Page 1973: 150–1) must have been literate, or following a carefully arranged plan of carving, for otherwise he would have had trouble accommodating his lengthy material. Some runic carvers were cognisant of non-runic as well as runic scripts. For instance, the craftsman who cut the carefully seriffed runes on a pair of tweezers found at Brandon (Suffolk) was presumably used to engraving Roman capitals, and it is not surprising that the excavators suggested that the site was ecclesiastical. The man who cut four runic words of Old English on a bone comb from Whitby could also manage a bit of simple Latin, so he was not entirely untrained in scholarly pursuits (Page 1966: 12).

From this survey I conclude that there was a good deal of literacy — or of careful copying of exemplars — among Anglo-Saxon carvers. Yet there also seems to be a high incidence of irregular, or slightly unusual spellings in the epigraphical texts. There is inorganic doubling of consonants and common doubling of vowels, as in 'a l m e ɨ t t i g', 'æ þ þ i l æ', 'g i s t o d d u n' and 'r i i c n æ' on the Ruthwell cross, 'g o o d', 'þ i i o s n e', 'c i i s m e e l' on the Mortain casket. There is an unusually large number of examples of the glide vowel between liquids and consonants: 'g e w a r a h t æ', Mortain, 'a l u w a l u d o', 'h e l i p æ', Whitby comb, 't o r o ɨ t r e d æ', Great Urswick stone, 'w o r o h t æ', Kirkheaton stone, as well as a number of cases of the element *-bereht* on name-stones and WYRICAN, BEROÞOR (2x) on the Brussels cross (Okasha 1971: 57). There are comparable examples to all of these in scribal texts, but what is striking in the inscriptions is the large proportion of cases, with the implication that the carvers are to some degree working in a different spelling tradition. As some have pointed out, producing an engraved text is a more laborious process than writing a manuscript, and this may influence spelling practice (D'Ardenne 1939: 151; Stanley 1987: 392—3). Further, as I suggested many years ago, it may be misleading to compare, in transliteration, different writing systems, runic and Roman (Page 1962).

The process of carving commits the writer more completely than that of writing on parchment. It is relatively easy to scratch out a writing error, as any reader of mediaeval manuscripts knows. Once a letter has been cut, either in relief or in intaglio, it is hard to get rid of; so errors may remain more extensively in engraved than in written texts. There are, of course, cases of epigraphical error corrected. The Ruthwell cross has examples. Its texts are long ones and laid out in a curious way, in short lines containing 2—4 letters. It is not easy to read this, but it obviously needed a good deal of planning in advance. It seems that the letters were cut in lightly at first, then checked and cut more deeply with a punch. Thus an error could be corrected in the second carving, provided there were space for it. In '[b] i s m æ r æ d u' the final letter was originally cut with two full verticals, and in 'l i m w œ r i g n æ' the rune 'œ' with two full cross-staves (as 'g'). Both errors were corrected in the second cutting. On the other hand, the form *bismæræcdu* may be an uncorrected error for *bismæradu*, though there is some dispute over the reading (Howlett 1974: 1—2).2

A related problem is that we have no idea how far the present state of an inscription represents what an Anglo-Saxon was supposed to see. The main shaft-stone of the Ruthwell cross has certainly been under cover for much of its long history, but we do not know whether it was sheltered from the first. There may have been colouring on the stone, outlining the cut letters, which would allow corrections to be incorporated at a late date. No colouring remains, I think, but that may be because it weathered away. There are certainly faint traces of paint on other Anglo-Saxon inscribed stones (and it is not uncommon on Scandinavian rune-stones too: Jansson 1962: 147—55) and in some cases suggestions of a skim of plaster on which the colour could be laid.

There are occasional inscriptions which reveal uncorrected errors that look too gross for correction. A clear example is the memorial stone from Overchurch (Cheshire). This has two lines of runes, partly defective, but those that remain are in general clear and deeply cut. The first line has the group 'f o l c æ a r æ r d o n', with a curious intrusive 'æ' which Dickins thought 'perhaps a blundered or damaged character abandoned by the carver' (Dickins 1932: 19). The second line has a form of the verb *(ge)biddan* with the sequence 'f o t e' following: there is no doubt that this is an error for the preposition *fore*. The cutting is so deep that it is unlikely that colouring could disguise it unless there was a thick covering of plaster.

The condition of many of our inscribed monuments makes any detailed examination of their language perilous. The Kirkdale inscription is well preserved because it is under cover and has probably been so for much of its life (though it is undoubtedly odd that a sundial should be inside a building).[3] Consequently, the only difficulty in reading it results from the fact that it has been painted over at some time or other, and it is not clear how much that can be read is in the painting rather than the engraving, while the position of the stone, above the doorway into the church nave, makes it difficult of access. The Brussels cross, a treasure kept in a treasury, is also in splendid condition. But these are exceptions. Thus the Bewcastle cross inscriptions, of vital importance as they are, are impossible to read in detail. The stone has been in the open for some 1300 years, suffering the attack of Cumbrian fell weather. When you see the main face from some distance, the first impression is that it is not so worn after all. Surely this time you will read it. But the nearer you get the less optimistic you are, and when you stand directly in front of the main inscribed face, you realise that, as usual, you are going to read only a few of the badly weathered runes.

Ruthwell, on the other hand, has been generally under shelter, and what remains of its main text is relatively easily read. But its shaft was much hacked about and battered in the storms of the Scottish Reformation, and bits of the edges (with some of the runes) are irretrievably lost. Even here, then, a good deal needs supplying, while occasional letter groups in incomplete sequences are ambiguous.

Clearly there is often difficulty in establishing a text. Even in unquestioned texts interpretation of the spelling may be a problem. For instance, the last line of the Thornhill II (W. Yorkshire) memorial stone is 'ea t e i n n e'. I take this to be the oblique personal name form *Eadþegne*, but why the doubled 'n'? This could be a case of the inorganic doubling of consonants that I discussed above as a possible indication of a divergent spelling tradition in inscriptions. But there is another explanation. The carver of this monument, fairly unusually for an Anglo-Saxon, set out his text carefully so as to avoid splitting words at line ends and to give each of the two personal names its own line. Thus 'ea t e i n n e' had to occupy a whole line and the cutter may have added a superfluous 'n' to spread it out more acceptably, as a sixteenth-century compositor would happily add an inorganic *-e* to a word to justify a line of type. If that is the case, the doubling of the consonant has no linguistic significance; only an artistic one.

A more complex pair of examples of the same sort of thing occurs on the Franks casket, which has two difficult forms, 'f i s c . f l o d u .' and 'g i u þ e a s u'. The first of these is particularly important since it has been taken as a significant form for dating the piece (Amos 1980: 23-24). In both texts involved there are problems of translation which I cannot go into here. The word *giuþeasu* has usually been interpreted as a nominative plural 'Jews', but then has a superfluous *-u*. *Flodu* may be either nominative or accusative, either singular or plural (I prefer accusative plural), but then also has an unnecessary *-u*, or very late retention of *-u* after a long stem syllable. Save on the cryptic side of the casket (which presents its own difficulties), the rune-master, in setting out his material, was scrupulous not to divide a word between two successive panels, except in the case of the long *fergenberig*, where he had no alternative. Can we explain these two superfluous *-u* endings as space fillers, put in because he had come to the end of a word without filling his panel, and did not want to begin another word which would have to be completed elsewhere? If we can take it thus, we should then note the occasional other runic case where *-u* is something of an embarrassment, as on the *skanomodu* solidus (if that is English: Page 1968: 21, but cf. Stewart 1978: 154).

It is the difficulty of establishing and assessing the linguistic significance of a text that provides the first obstacle to dating an inscription. A second is the amount of linguistic material an inscription is likely to contain, compared with even a short written text. One of our shortest Old English poems with significant dating features is Bede's Death Song, which consists of 25 words. Caedmon's Hymn has 42 words, the Leiden Riddle 88. Few inscriptions are as long. The Crucifixion poem of the Ruthwell cross, the longest of our runic inscriptions, has about 320 characters, some 72 words or fragments. The Kirkdale sundial has, in its three texts, a total of 49 words, the Brussels cross has 32 (+ 2 Latin), the Sutton, Isle of Ely, brooch 20. But these are long inscriptions. To take more common-sized ones: the Thornhill III memorial has 54 runes, 10 words; the Great Urswick cross 67 runes, 14 words, while several inscribed stones carry nothing but a single personal name. It is likely that in many cases there will be too few significant forms to give statistically valid results. Hence the tentative nature of much of our linguistic dating of monuments; as 'it can reasonably be claimed that the indications favour the seventh and eighth centuries, are not so favourable towards the ninth, and still less so towards the tenth' (Scott 1956: 205 on the Hartlepool name-stones).

To date an inscription we need control texts, datable written texts that can properly be compared with the epigraphical one. Of course, linguistic development varies according to local dialect. A sound change may take place earlier in one dialect than another, so that the control text must come from the same region as the inscription. This is a problem, for it may not be possible to find such a control. Up-to-date local distribution maps of the Anglo-Saxon inscriptions are not available, and of course some important examples are not provenanced in England at all — the Franks, Mortain and Brunswick caskets are cases in point. Moreover, in the case of portable objects the find-place is not necessarily the place of manufacture. Any distribution map must then be tentative: there are helpful preliminary ones in Okasha 1971: 140—1 and Page 1973: 26—7. These show intriguing patterns.

Taking the distribution of inscribed stones (and we regard this as more significant than that of the portable objects simply because they are in general less easily movable from the place they were made in), we can note clear concentrations in the North and North

Midlands. Elsewhere, taking the evidence of all the available maps, there is a general scatter of inscriptions over southern and eastern England, with gaps noticeable only in the central and West Midlands. Unfortunately, this distribution does not coincide with that known for the Old English written records. We know practically nothing of the Old English of East Anglia, so there is no control material for the inscriptions from Norfolk, Suffolk, Cambridgeshire or Essex. Though there are certainly Old English manuscripts from the North and North Midlands, they are limited in content and there is a limited range of provenances. For the middle and later period there are texts from Lindisfarne (Liber Vitae of Durham), Chester-le-Street (Lindisfarne Gospels gloss and Durham Ritual), as well as minor materials from Durham and elsewhere, together with the Rushworth$_2$ Gospels gloss from some place further to the south. For the earlier period we have a small number of lesser works, but none whose extant form can be localised precisely; though the early linguistic material from the *Historia Ecclesiastica* must derive ultimately from Monkwearmouth/Jarrow (Dahl 1938: 1—21 gives an account of these early Northumbrian texts). Thus there is nothing that we can certainly localise on the west coast of Northumbria; nothing therefore which is appropriate for comparison with the Ruthwell cross, the Great Urswick stone, the two rune-stones from Maughold, Isle of Man, and the Carlisle cross fragments.

To compare with the considerable numbers of inscriptions from the old West Riding of Yorkshire, there are no written texts closely localisable, except perhaps for Rushworth$_2$ in the tenth century. Whether that is a suitable control for the Thornhill and Dewsbury cross inscriptions, I do not know.

Yet there are more difficulties than I have outlined so far. For instance, I have assumed that the west coast inscriptions at Urswick and Ruthwell share the same local dialect; but the places are some 90 kilometres apart, separated by the fells of the Lake District and the waters of the Solway Firth. Campbell may describe Ruthwell as 'a spot in the heart of Northumbrian territory' (Campbell 1959: 4), but the heart is an organ notoriously off centre, and the main region for surviving written Northumbrian is likely to have been a good deal further east. I have asserted that the findspots of inscribed stones ought to be significant because stones are unlikely to be moved about much (which is true in general, if not in particular).[4] But though stones may be fixed, stone-carvers may travel, and it is possible, as Professor Cramp has suggested (Cramp 1965: 10-12), that the Ruthwell sculptors came from a distant part of Northumbria. What dialect they recorded on their cross can only be conjecture. There may, after all, have been a prestige sub-dialect within early Northumbrian which stone-carvers tended to use, whatever their own speech was. If so, we do not know about it.

So far I have assumed the integrity of an inscription: that its language does not intentionally deceive, but represents a genuine form of Old English roughly appropriate to the date the text was cut. However, some scholars have suggested that inscriptions are likely to be archaic in language. C.L. Wrenn argued this in the specific case of the Ruthwell cross (Wrenn 1943: 19–22). I do not believe his thesis myself (Page 1959a), but Professor Stanley has recently reinterpreted Wrenn's position in much modified and more acceptable form (Stanley 1987: 391–5). It is certainly evident that inscriptions containing fixed formulae, as *gibidæþ foræ* NN or NN *worohtæ*, may also contain fixed grammatical forms which remain unaffected by sound-changes in the current tongue. If an inscription contains such archaic — or even archaistic — spellings, it is liable to mislead the linguistic dater.

Finally, closely linked to linguistic but essentially distinct from it is palaeographical dating,

dating by reference to the forms of letters used. it is tempting to assume that letter forms found in inscriptions have their counterparts in manuscripts, and that it is feasible to date the one from the other. The occurrence of Gothic script on Victorian memorials should give us pause, for it is evident that display scripts may make use of archaic or unusual forms. Dr Okasha has presented a preliminary survey of the scripts of the non-runic monuments of Anglo-Saxon England (Okasha 1968), to which she has added, in a personal communication, the query 'whether it is legitimate to argue a direct dating link . . . from manuscripts to inscriptions'. Runic inscriptions give even less comfort, for inevitably there are few manuscript parallels and no adequate typology can be built up from the epigraphical material alone. There is the occasional clearly early form, as the variant *cen*—rune of the two Chessell Down inscriptions and the *skanomodu* solidus; while there is the occasional latish and local graph such as the *calc*—rune which seems restricted to the north-west and is not recorded before, say, 700. These distinctions are too blunt to base dating points on.

When a philologist suggests a date on linguistic grounds for an inscription, then, the non-philologist will do well to bear in mind the type of difficulty I have sketched in this paper, and be suitably cautious. Dating on the linguistic evidence alone will be barely even approximate. For dating an inscribed piece, it is important for the various experts, archaeologist, historian, technologist, palaeographer, philologist and art historian, each to reach an independent conclusion, and only thereafter to see if any harmony of opinion can be struck. Even if it can, it is unlikely that dating will be other than approximate until a lot more primary material comes to light.

APPENDIX

The following transcripts are not necessarily complete, and are given here only to clarify my argument. Other useful transcripts are in Okasha 1971 and Page 1973. Inscriptions in versions of the Roman alphabet are given in CAPITALS. Runic inscriptions are transliterated according to the system defined in Page 1984.

1. Auzon (Franks) casket, front:

'f i s c . f l o d u . || a h o f o n f e r g ||
  e n b e r i g ||
← w a r þ g a : s r i c g r o r n þ æ r h e o n
  g r e u t g i s w o m || → h r o n æ s b a n'

2. Auzon (Franks) casket, back:

'h e r f e g t a þ || t i t u s e n d g i u þ e a
s u' ||
HICFUGIANTHIERUSALIM || 'a f i t a t o r e s'

3. Caistor-by-Norwich astragalus:

r a ï h a n

4. Kirkdale sundial (I am uncertain of the punctuation in these transcripts):

left panel:

+ORM·GAMAL·
SVNA·BOHTE·SC̄S
GREGORIVS·MIN
STERÐONNEHI
T·WESÆL·TOBRO

right panel:

CAN·7TOFALAN·7Æ
HIT·LET·MACAN·NEWAN·FROM
GRVNDE·XPE:7SCSGREGORI
VS·IN·EADWARD·DAGVM·CN̄G
7N·TOSTI DAGVM·EORL+

dial panel:

+7HAWARÐ·MEWROHTE·7BRAND|PR̄S
+ÞISIS·DÆGES·SOLMERCA+||ÆTILCVMTIDE+

4. Mortain casket:

'+ g o o d h e l p e : æ a d a n
þ i i o s n e c i i s m e e l g e w a r
a h t æ'

5. Overchurch stone:

'f o l c {æ} a r æ r d o n b e [
] b i d d a þ f o <r> e æ þ e l m u n ['

6. Ruthwell cross:

parts of the east face:

'[+ . n d] g e r e | d æ | h i | n æ | ḡ o | d a |
l m | e ɨ | t t i | g'
'[.] | i c r | i i c n | æ k y | n i ŋ | c'

parts of west face:

'h w | e þ | r æ | þ e | r f | u s [æ] | f e a r |
r a n | k w [o] | m u [æ] | þ þ i l | æ t i l | a
n u | m'
'a l e | g d u | n h i æ | h i n æ | l i m w | œ r
i g | n æ g i | s t o | d d u | [n]'

7. Southampton/Hamwih bone:

'c a t æ'

8. Thames (Battersea) scramasax:

'f u þ o r c g w h n i j ɨ p x (s) t b e ŋ d l m
œ a æ y ea'
'b ea ḡ n o þ'

9. Thornhill II memorial stone:

'+ e a d r e d
* s e t e æ f t e
ea t e ɨ n n e'

10. Whitby comb:

'd͡[æ] u s m͡æ u s || g o d a l u w a l u || d͡o
hel i p æ c y || ['

NOTES

1. I suspect, however, that this cross was intended to act as a signe de renvoie, keying the main text to the maker formula on the dial, for the latter begins with a similar form of cross.

2. Dr Howlett suggests that in fact the error is not in the cross text, but in the work of scholars who have read 'b i s m æ r æ d u' here. He bases his argument on (1) the correct verbal form, (2) his own reading of 'a' rather than 'æ' for the seventh rune, (3) the, as he thinks it, consistent reporting of 'a' by early recorders of the inscription (Howlett 1974: 1–2). My own note-book shows that I read the rune as 'æ', but queried a possible alternative 'a'. In my dissertation I preferred 'æ' (Page 1959: 121), but when, a few years later, I came to write this entry up for the projected corpus of runic inscriptions, I changed my mind. I wrote the revised version some years before I saw Howlett's 1974 article, and it is worth repeating what I put then since in some degree it acts as independent confirmation of Howlett's position: 'This (i.e. the disputed rune) is faint but seems to be 'æ', presenting the reader with the embarrassing verbal form *bismærædu* which most editors emend to *bismæradu*. The difficulty is that the early drawings are unanimous in reading 'a' here: so, clearly, Gordon, Cardonnel and Ridell; Nicolson, though uncertain about the form, shows something a little nearer 'a' than 'æ', and Duncan too. Modern scholars commonly read 'æ' and what appears on the cross makes it tempting to do so. Viëtor implies that the rune may have been 'a' weathered to look like 'æ'. In view of the unanimity of early readings I prefer to put 'a' here, though I do it with some hesitation'. However, I suspect that neither Howlett nor I have given full consideration to all the early drawings of this passage —

there are several by Nicolson which do not always coincide —
so the matter remains in some doubt.

3. The sundial is set over the south door of the church, but
now protected by a porch. Whether the sundial is in situ or not
is a matter of uncertainty (Taylor 1965—78: 740). For what it
is worth, the earliest drawing of this dial that I know
describes it as 'over the South Door on the outside of
Kirkdale Church' (British Library MS, Stowe 1024 fo.199,
which, from its connection with John Anstis, must antedate
that of Brooke: Okasha 1971: 87).

4. It is something of a commonplace that stone monuments were
not transported over distances in the Anglo-Saxon period
despite the well-recorded case of the stone cross carried
from Lindisfarne by the community of St Cuthbert (Bailey
1980: 22—23). We tend to think of such monuments as huge and
heavy chunks of material, forgetting such tiny pieces as the
Hartlepool name-stones, which would fit easily into a brief
case.

BIBLIOGRAPHY

Amos, Ashley Crandell. 1980. *Linguistic Means of Determining the Dates of Old English Literary Texts.* (= *Medieval Academy Books*, 90.) Cambridge, Massachusetts: Medieval Academy of America.

Bailey, Richard N. 1980. *Viking Age Sculpture in Northern England*. London: Collins.

Bailey, Richard N. and Cramp, Rosemary. 1988. *The British Academy Corpus of Anglo-Saxon Stone Sculpture.* Vol. 2: *Cumberland, Westmorland and Lancashire North-of-the-Sands*. Oxford: British Academy.

Campbell, A. 1959. *Old English Grammar*. Oxford: Clarendon Press.

Collingwood, W.G. 1927. *Northumbrian Crosses of the Pre-Norman Age*. London: Faber and Gwyer.

Cramp, Rosemary. 1965. *Early Northumbrian Sculpture* (= *Jarrow Lecture* 1965.) Jarrow.

Cramp, Rosemary. 1984. *The British Academy Corpus of Anglo-Saxon Stone Sculpture.* Vol. 1: *County Durham and Northumberland*. Oxford: British Academy.

Dahl, Ivar. 1938. *Substantival Inflexion in Early Old English: Vocalic stems.* (=

Lund Studies in English, 7.) Lund: C.W.K. Gleerup.

D'Ardenne, S.T.R.O. 1939. "The Old English inscription on the Brussels cross". *ES* 21. 145–64, 271–2.

Dickins, Bruce. 1932. "A system of transliteration for Old English runic inscriptions". *LSE* 1. 15–19.

Dickins, Bruce. 1956. "The Inscriptions upon the Coffin". *The Relics of Saint Cuthbert* ed. by C.F. Battiscombe, 305–7. Durham: Dean and Chapter of Durham Cathedral.

Hawkes, Sonia Chadwick and Page, R.I. 1967. "Swords and runes in south-east England". *Antiquaries Journal* 47. 1–26.

Howlett, D.R. 1974. "Three forms in the Ruthwell text of The Dream of the Rood". *ES* 55. 1–5.

Jansson, Sven B.F. 1962. *The Runes of Sweden*. London: Phoenix House.

Moltke, Erik. 1985. *Runes and their Origin: Denmark and elsewhere*. Trans. by Peter G. Foote. Copenhagen: National Museum of Denmark.

Mustanoja, Tauno F. 1960. *A Middle English Syntax*. Vol. 1: *Parts of speech*. (= *Mémoires de la Société Néophilologique de Helsinki*, 23.) Helsinki.

Myres, J.N.L. and Green, Barbara. 1973. *The Anglo-Saxon Cemeteries of Caistor-by-Norwich and Markshall, Norfolk*. (= *Reports of the Research Committee of the Society of Antiquaries of London*, 30.) London.

Okasha, Elisabeth. 1968. "The non-runic scripts of Anglo-Saxon inscriptions". *Transactions of the Cambridge Bibliographical Society* 4. 321–38.

Okasha, Elisabeth. 1971. *Hand-list of Anglo-Saxon Non-runic Inscriptions*. Cambridge: Cambridge University Press.

Page, R.I. 1959. *The Inscriptions of the Anglo-Saxon Rune-stones*. Unpublished Ph.D. thesis, University of Nottingham.

Page, R.I. 1959a. "Language and dating in OE inscriptions". *Anglia* 77. 385–406.

Page, R.I. 1962. "A note on the transliteration of Old English runic inscriptions". *ES* 43. 1–6.

Page, R.I. 1966. "The Whitby runic comb". *Whitby Literary and Philosophical Society: Annual Report* 11–15.

Page, R.I. 1968. "The runic solidus of Schweindorf, Ostfriesland, and related runic solidi". *Medieval Archaeology* 12. 12—25.

Page, R.I. 1973. *An Introduction to English Runes*. London: Methuen.

Page, R.I. 1984. "On the transliteration of English runes". *Medieval Archaeology* 28. 22—45.

Scott, Forrest S. 1956. "The Hildithryth stone and the other Hartlepool name-stones". *Archaeologia Aeliana* 4. Series 34. 196—212.

Stanley, Eric Gerald. 1987. *A Collection of Papers with Emphasis on Old English Literature*. (= *Publications of the Dictionary of Old English*, 3.) Toronto: Pontifical Institute of Mediaeval Studies.

Stewart, I. 1978. "Anglo-Saxon Gold Coins". *Scripta Nummaria Romana: Essays presented to Humphrey Sutherland* ed. by R.A.G. Carson and Colin M. Kraay, 143—72. London: Spink and Son.

Taylor, H.M. and Taylor, Joan. 1965—78. *Anglo-Saxon Architecture*. Cambridge: Cambridge University Press.

Wilson, David M. 1964. *Anglo-Saxon Ornamental Metalwork 700—1100*. (= *Catalogue of Antiquities of the Later Saxon Period*, 1.) London: British Museum.

Wrenn, C.L. 1943. "The value of spelling as evidence". *TPhS* 14—39. (Repr. in *Word and Symbol: Studies in English language* by C.L. Wrenn, 129—49. London: Longmans, 1967.)

PARADIGM ARRANGEMENT AND INFLECTIONAL HOMONYMY: OLD ENGLISH CASE

FRANS PLANK
Universität Konstanz

Probably the single most important practical consideration behind the conventions of paradigm designers since the days of Panini and his ancient Indian colleagues is a formal one: the entries of an inflectional paradigm should be the closer to one another in arrangement the closer they are in form. Homonymous entries, representing the extreme of similarity, accordingly ought to be adjacent to one another. The basic purpose of paradigms in reference grammars is to provide information about the inflectional categories of inflecting words (such as Case), about the terms realising these categories (such as Nominative, Accusative, Dative), and about the exponents (affixes, segmental or suprasegmental modifications, root exchanges, zero) expressing these terms or, if exponents cumulatively express terms of more than one category, combinations of terms. Apart

from the possible drawbacks of formal similarities
between exponents of different terms or term
combinations (such as the confusion they might cause on
the part of the hearer), identical exponents tend to
have one advantage: they reduce the number of
grammatical forms that need to be memorised by the
speaker, and in particular the learner, of the
language.[1] The problem that remains, however, is to
know precisely which distinctions are neutralised[2] in
which paradigms. Unless there is some general strategy
of delimiting the range of possible victims of homonymy,
little is gained by formal parsimony as such; those who
are above all faced with this problem, language
learners, might just as well acquire distinct exponents.
It is here that the judicious arrangement of paradigms
proves pedagogically useful: the convention which places
next to each other those paradigm members which may be
expressed by the same exponents authorises an
appropriate generalisation. It rules out non-
neighbouring members as possible homonyms, unless they
are linked by members also sharing the same exponent.

Lists are one familiar method of presenting
paradigms; but they are not the only one. And obviously,
which and how many members of a paradigm may be
considered neighbours depends on the kinds of order we
are prepared to endorse.

If a paradigm is presented in the form of a list
all n elements of which are linearly ordered, there will
be $n-1$ pairs, $n-2$ triples (etc.) of neighbours, with two
elements, the first and the last on the list, having

only one neighbour, and *n-2* elements having two neighbours each, as is shown schematically in (1):

(1) *linear order*

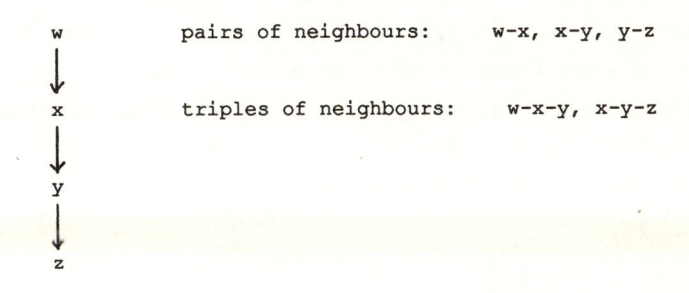

w
↓↑
x   pairs of neighbours: w-x, x-y, y-z
↓↑
y   triples of neighbours: w-x-y, x-y-z
↓↑
z

If the ordering is permitted not to be asymmetric, so that one element may precede as well as follow another, neighbourhood relations multiply. If the number of elements exceeds two, there are then at least as many pairs and (with more than three elements) triples of neighbours as there are elements directly linked to one another in a circle (all of which have two neighbours), and in the extreme case any element ends up a neighbour of any other, as shown in (2):[3]

(2) *circular order*

a. w←z   pairs of neighbours: w-x, x-y, y-z, z-w
    ↓ ↑
    x→y   triples of neighbours: w-x-y, x-y-z, y-z-w,
                                       z-w-x

b. w←z   pairs of neighbours: w-x, x-y, y-z, z-w, w-y
    ↓↘↑
    x→y   triples of neighbours: w-x-y, x-y-z, y-z-w,
                                       z-w-x

c. w←z   pairs of neighbours: w-x, x-y, y-z, z-w, w-y, z-w
    ↓⨯↑
    x→y   triples of neighbours: w-x-y, x-y-z, y-z-w, z-w-x

If the ordering is permitted not to be connex, so that
not all *n* elements are linearly ordered relative to all
others, there will be no more than *n*-1 pairs of
neighbours (as with linear and unlike circular orders),
but particular elements may have more than two
neighbours (as in circular but not in linear orders);
and as also shown in (3), there will also be more
triples (etc.) of neighbours than in a linear order.

(3)   *partial linear order*

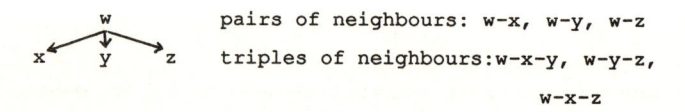

```
         w
         ↓
   x ← y → z      pairs of neighbours: w-x, w-y, w-z
                  triples of neighbours: w-x-y, w-y-z,
                                         w-x-z
```

Apart from being favoured by extraneous
considerations like that of saving space on a page, the
traditionally often preferred method of arranging
paradigms in the form of a list, with all entries
linearly ordered, is, thus, also the most restrictive
one as regards the connections between neighbours among
those entries.

Whichever order they opt for, paradigm designers
usually abide by a kind of meta-condition requesting
that the arrangement of terms be uniform throughout all
relevant paradigms or parts of them of the language
described. For example, one might well present the Case
terms of a language such as Sanskrit in different
orders, linear or non-linear, for the different
declensions of nouns, or for nouns and other Case-
inflecting parts of speech, or for the Singular, Dual,

and Plural parts of Case paradigms; but such variation would no doubt jar on the aesthetic sense of the reader of grammars. Of course, individual grammarians or schools may well disagree, with most inflectional categories, which is the most appropriate order of terms, invoking perhaps different kinds of criteria in justification of their decisions. What, nevertheless, unites them is that they subscribe to the uniformity principle that we have become so accustomed to as essential feature of a well-organised grammar.[4]

Now there is also a theoretical dimension, rarely recognised, to these practical and aesthetic matters. What is of some theoretical interest is to determine whether it will in fact always be possible for the ordinary working grammarian who wishes to oblige his readers to comply with our three requirements of good paradigm design, viz. that inflectional homonyms be adjacent, that terms be arranged linearly, and that term orders be uniform. If this *is* possible, it would imply that inflectional homonymy in the languages of the world is subject to quantitative constraints, because the well-meaning grammarian would be unable to succeed if a language confronted him with such a diverse pattern of homonymies that it cannot be defined in terms of neighbourhood in uniformly ordered lists. It is flective rather than agglutinative languages which are the best testing ground for these constraints. Here paradigms multiply, and they are rife with homonymies. If the terms of inflectional categories are expressed by alternative sets of exponents whose distribution needs to be stipulated lexically, we have to set up parallel paradigms for these categories; and in each of them all terms recur depending on the number of terms of the categories they are cumulated with. Term distinctions are susceptible to homonymy in all these separate paradigms and subparadigms, and the patterns of homonymies may, thus, differ arbitrarily. They could of course always be accounted for individually in accordance with the neighbourhood and linearity conditions by adopting different orders for different paradigms or subparadigms. This policy, however, would imply abandoning the uniformity condition. Our constraints on the permissible diversity of language particular patterns of homonymy, if valid, would forestall any such conflict. If such conflicts in fact do materialise, the most restrictive position one can take in these terms is proven untenable. However, instead of immediately conceding that inflectional homonymy is random, our representational framework provides sufficient flexibility to weaken our constraints gradually. A closer look at the Case system of Old English, more complex in relevant respects than those of many another flective-type language, is instructive here, for it will give us an idea of just how much ground it may be necessary to cede.

With five Cases[5], of which one, the Instrumental, is presumably best recognised only with adjectives and non-personal pronouns, the diversity of patterns of homonymy is potentially great. To be precise, the sum total of possible two-, three-, four-, and five-term homonymies is twenty-six:

(4)   1. Nom=Acc   11. Nom=Acc=Gen   21. Nom=Acc=Gen=Dat
       2. Nom=Gen   12. Nom=Acc=Dat   22. Nom=Acc=Gen=Ins
       3. Nom=Dat   13. Nom=Acc=Ins   23. Nom=Gen=Dat=Ins

PARADIGM ARRANGEMENT AND INFLECTIONAL HOMONYMY

4.	Nom=Ins	14.	Nom=Gen=Dat	24.	Nom=Acc=Dat=Ins
5.	Acc=Gen	15.	Nom=Gen=Ins	25.	Acc=Gen=Dat=Ins
6.	Acc=Dat	16.	Nom=Dat=Ins		
7.	Acc=Ins	17.	Acc=Gen=Dat		
8.	Gen=Dat	18.	Acc=Gen=Ins		
9.	Gen=Ins	19.	Acc=Dat=Ins		
10.	Dat=Ins	20.	Gen=Dat=Ins	26.	Nom=Acc=Gen=Dat=Ins

Any linear arrangement of five terms licenses no more than ten such patterns, as shown abstractly in (5).

(5) *list of terms: permitted neutralisations:*

```
a                      a=b, b=c, c=d, d=e;
b                      a=b=c, b=c=d, c=d=e;
c                      a=b=c=d, b=c=d=e;
d                      a=b=c=d=e.
e
```

With five terms, the alternative linear arrangements number no less than 120, which for our purposes may be reduced by half since neighbourhood relations are the same in corresponding inverted sequences. There are, thus, sixty different *sets* of homonymy patterns which could in principle be accommodated by choosing an appropriate linear term order. Since there are numerous classes of nominal, pronominal, and adjectival lexical items differing in the set of Case exponents they require, and also numerous subparadigms of Case, owing to the various categories Case is cumulated with in different classes of words (two- or three-term Number in nouns, adjectives, and pronouns; three-term Gender in adjectives and pronouns; two-term Definiteness in adjectives), the potential for a very diverse composite picture of Case homonymies is also enormous.

Here is a summary of the patterns of Case homonymies and their instances as actually attested in Old English, keyed to the enumeration in (4).

1. *Nom=Acc:* Singular of all masculine and neuter a/wa-nouns and phonologically identifiable subclasses of ja-nouns (suffix -∅), heavy-stem masculine and neuter i-nouns (-∅), feminine i-nouns (where Acc may also have distinct exponent -e), u-nouns (-u/-∅), neuter weak nouns (-e), athematic nouns (masc. -∅, fem. -u/-∅, plus appropriate root vowel), nouns in nd- (-∅), nouns in IE -es/-os (-∅), dental stems (with or without final -þ, suffix -∅), Indefinite ('strong') Neuter adjectives (-u/-∅), Indefinite Feminine adjectives with final -h such as hēah (hēa - hēa), Definite ('weak') Neuter adjectives (-e), Neuter 3rd Person personal pronoun (hit), Neuter demonstrative and interrogative pronouns (þæt, þis; hwæt); Plural of a/ja/wa-nouns (masc. -as, neut. -u/-∅), masculine and neuter i-nouns (-e/-as, -u/-∅), weak nouns (-an), athematic nouns (masc. -∅, fem. -e/-∅, plus appropriate root vowel), nouns of relationship (-as, -∅, -a/-u), nouns in -nd- (-∅/-e/-as), es/os-stems (-u), dental stems (-∅ and final -þ), Indefinite adjectives (Masc -e, Fem -e/-a, Neut. -∅/-u), Definite adjectives (-an), 3rd Person personal pronoun (hīe/hī/heo), demonstrative pronouns (bā, bās).

2. *Nom=Gen:* In the Plural, ō/jō/wō-nouns have normally -a in Nominative, Accusative, and Genitive in West-Saxon, but in early West-Saxon Accusative has occasionally -e, distinguishing this Case from Nominative and Genitive (late West-Saxon also has Gen - ena).

6. *Acc=Dat:* Singular, Dual, and Plural of 1st and 2nd Person personal pronouns (me, unc, ūs; þe, inc, ēow); outside West-Saxon, however, there tends to occur a distinctive Accusative (mec, unket, ūsic; þec, incit, ēowic), but these forms may later be generalised also to Dative function.

8. *Gen=Dat:* Singular of feminine i-nouns (-e, which may, however, also extend to Acc), u-nouns (-a), neuter weak nouns (-an), feminine athematic nouns (-e/-Ø, but there may be a difference in root vowels), dental stems (-Ø and final -þ), Definite Neuter adjectives (-an; Definite adjectives also lack a distinct Instrumental), Feminine 3rd Person personal pronoun (hire).

10. *Dat=Ins:* Plural of all adjectival and pronominal forms having a separate Instrumental in the Singular.

11. *Nom=Acc=Gen:* Plural of ō/jō/wō-nouns (-a. cf. No. 2 above), feminine i-nouns (-a, where Acc may alternatively be -e), u-nouns (-a), athematic feminine noun ēa (-Ø); Singular of the nouns of relationship brōþor, mōdor, and dohtor (-Ø).

12. *Nom=Acc=Dat:* Singular of masculine and neuter ja-nouns retaining the original stem formative (-i > -e) other than those with stem-final -r (i.e. the phonological subclass complementary to that in No. 1) (suffix -e), light-stem masculine and neuter i-nouns (-e), heavy-stem i-masculine sǣ (where sǣ-e -> sǣ DatSg),

heavy-stem feminine athematic nouns (-∅ and unumlauted root; but mutation is common, hence usually Dat≠Nom=Acc).

17. *Acc=Gen=Dat:* Singular of ō/jō/wō-nouns (-e), feminine i-nouns (-e; but Acc may have -∅, hence Acc≠Gen=Dat), masculine and feminine weak nouns (-an), Definite Masculine and Feminine adjectives (-an).

20. *Gen=Dat=Ins:* Singular of Indefinite Feminine adjectives (-re) and Feminine demonstratives (bǣre, bisse).

21. *Nom=Acc=Gen=Dat:* Singular of nouns of relationship fæder and sweostor (-∅), dental stems (-∅, and -b extended to Nom and Acc), feminine i-nouns sǣ (cf. No. 12 for its use as a masculine) and ǣ (-∅, because sǣ-e, ǣ-e -> sǣ, ǣ), feminine athematic noun ēa (-∅, but West-Saxon has frequently īe in GenSg and DatSg).

There are thus exactly ten homonymy patterns, which is the maximum number permitted by the neighbourhood condition if five terms are linearly ordered. This particular set, however, is not among those licensed by any of the sixty possible linear arrangements of our five Cases. The cause of the predicament is easily seen if only two linear alternatives are examined.[6]

(6) a. Nom   b. Nom
       Acc   Acc
       Gen   Dat
       Dat   Ins
       Ins   Gen

Seven of the ten homonymy patterns permitted by (6a) are
actually attested in Old English: Nos. 1 (Nom=Acc), 8
(Gen =Dat), 10 (Dat=Ins), 11 (Nom=Acc=Gen), 17 (Acc=Gen
=Dat), 20 (Gen=Dat=Ins), and 21 (Nom=Acc=Gen=Dat). In
fact, if Definite adjectives too are attributed an
Instrumental, on the analogy of Indefinites, one further
permissible pattern is exemplified by Masculine and
Feminine Definite adjectives in the Singular, which
conflate all Cases except the Nominative (No. 25).
(Extending the Instrumental to nouns and all pronouns as
well would shift our examples of pattern No. 21 to the
fully neutralising pattern No. 26, but would in addition
eliminate all instances of pattern Nos. 6, 8, 12, and
17, because the Instrumental here would have to be added
as a Case coinciding with the Dative.) Permitted by
(6a), but not attested are only three, or even two,
homonymy patterns: Nos. 5 (Acc=Gen), 26 (Nom=Acc=Gen
=Dat=Ins), and, provided Definite adjectives are refused
an Instrumental, 25 (Acc=Gen=Dat=Ins). Not permitted by
(6a), but attested are three further patterns: Nos. 2
(Nom=Gen), 6 (Acc=Dat), and 12 (Nom=Acc=Dat). Of these,
the first is somewhat dubious, homonymies of Nominative
and Genitive being highly uncharacteristic of $\bar{o}$/$j\bar{o}$/$w\bar{o}$-
nouns in later West-Saxon. On balance arrangement (6a)
fares better than (6b), and indeed all other
permutations. Permitted by (6b) and actually attested
are five homonymy patterns: Nos. 1 (Nom=Acc), 6
(Acc=Dat), 10 (Dat=Ins), 12 (Nom=Acc=Dat), 20
(Dat=Ins=Gen). Permitted but not attested are also five
patterns: Nos. 9 (Gen=Ins), 19 (Acc=Dat=Ins), 24
(Nom=Acc=Dat=Ins), 25 (Acc=Gen=Dat=Ins), and 26
(Nom=Acc=Gen=Dat=Ins). With the Instrumental also

extended to Definite adjectives, pattern No. 25 would strengthen the ranks of attestations. Not permitted by (6b), but attested are five patterns, one again being doubtful: Nos 2 (Nom=Gen, the uncertain one), 8 (Gen=Dat), 11 (Nom=Acc=Gen), 17 (Acc=Gen= Dat), and 21 (Nom=Acc=Gen=Dat).

The weaknesses of (6a) and (6b) are essentially complementary. What (6a) cannot cope with are homonymies involving Accusative and Dative, which are unproblematic for (6b), where these two terms are neighbours. (6b), on the other hand, is defeated by homonymies involving Accusative and Genitive, terms adjacent in (6a). An additional disadvantage of (6b) is that the Instrumental, a term not realised in all Case paradigms, intervenes between Dative and Genitive, two terms homonymous in three patterns. The regularity that Accusative does not coincide with Genitive unless Dative or Nominative or both share the same exponent as well, escapes (6a) completely, where Accusative and Genitive are adjacent, and is only partly captured by (6b), where Dative (and Instrumental) but not Nominative is intermediate between Accusative and Genitive.

Evidently, in no single linear arrangement is there a way out of the dilemma that both Dative and Genitive may separately coincide with Accusative, a Case most frequently neutralised with Nominative.[7] An invariant order where all Case terms anywhere involved in homonymies, and as few others as possible, are adjacent has got to be non-linear. To withdraw no further than to partial linear ordering, as illustrated in (3), unfortunately does not suffice: at least some terms must be allowed to form a circle. The partly circular arrangements in (7) are two candidates on which it seems difficult to improve.[8]

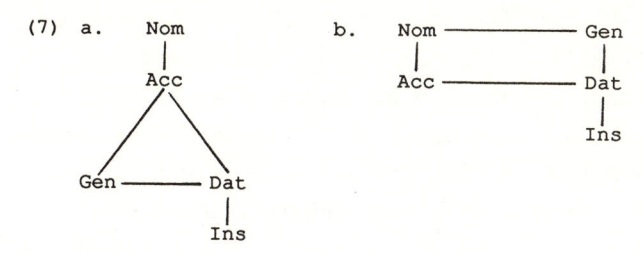

(7) a.
```
        Nom
         |
        Acc
        / \
       /   \
     Gen———Dat
           |
          Ins
```

b.
```
    Nom ——————— Gen
     |           |
    Acc ——————— Dat
                 |
                Ins
```

Unequal distances between neighbouring terms are intended to reflect unequal homonymy proclivities. Thus (7b) implies that vertical neighbours neutralise more commonly than horizontal ones, while according to (7a) both vertical and horizontal neighbours neutralise more commonly than diagonal ones.

To compute the scores of these less familiar arrangements, (7a) permits fourteen homonymy patterns, of which nine or ten are attested: Nos. 1 (Nom=Acc), 6 (Acc= Dat), 8 (Gen=Dat), 10 (Dat=Ins), 11 (Nom=Acc=Gen), 12 (Nom= Acc=Dat), 17 (Acc=Gen=Dat), 20 (Gen=Dat=Ins), 21 (Nom=Acc= Gen=Dat), and possibly, if an Instrumental is recognised with Definite adjectives, 25 (Acc=Gen=Dat=Ins). Permitted but unattested are five or four patterns: Nos. 5 (Acc=Gen), 19 (Acc=Dat=Ins), 24 (Nom=Acc=Dat=Ins), 26 (Nom=Acc=Gen =Dat=Ins), and possibly 25. Pattern No. 2 (Nom=Gen), which is only marginally attested in West-Saxon, if at all, is disallowed by (7a). The eleven further homonymy patterns which are logically possible but incompatible with (7a) do not occur. Of the sixteen homonymy patterns permitted

by (7b), ten or eleven are attested: Nos. 1 (Nom=Acc), 2
(Nom=Gen, at best marginal), 6 (Acc=Dat), 8 (Gen=Dat),
10 (Dat=Ins), 11 (Nom=Acc=Gen), 12 (Nom=Acc=Dat), 17
(Acc=Gen =Dat), 20 (Gen=Dat=Ins), 21 (Nom=Acc=Gen=Dat),
and possibly 25 (Acc=Gen=Dat=Ins). Permitted but
unattested are six or five patterns: Nos. 14
(Nom=Gen=Dat), 19 (Acc=Dat=Ins), 23 (Nom=Gen =Dat=Ins),
24 (Nom=Acc=Dat=Ins), 26 (Nom=Acc=Gen=Dat=Ins), and
possibly 25. None of the ten logically possible
patterns that are incompatible with (7b) are attested.
Although (7a) could seem slightly superior to (7b) on
the grounds of its greater restrictiveness (14 vs. 16
patterns permitted) and its higher ratio of actual to
permitted patterns (64.29% vs. 62.5%, or 71.43% vs.
68.75%), the only material difference in arrangement
rather tends to argue for (7b). In (7b) Genitive is
directly linked to Nominative rather than, as in (7a),
Accusative, which fits in well with two observations:
Gen=Nom is on record, if marginally, as one of the two-
term homonymies, while Gen=Acc is not; and the
Nominative, intermediate between Genitive and Accusative
only in (7b), is one of the Cases whose identity is a
prerequisite of the neutralisability of these two terms.
In favour of (7a), on the other hand, is one regularity:
Nominative and Dative do not coincide unless they also
coincide with the Accusative - and the only path from
Nominative to Dative is via the Accusative in (7a) but
not in (7b).[9]

Instead of sacrificing linearity, the diversity
of Case homomymies in Old English could also be
accounted for by weakening the neighbourhood condition.
With (6a) serving as the invariant linear order, what

would have to be admitted are homonymies across not more than one intervening term with a distinct exponent. The resultant possibilities are in fact not exhausted in Old English, where Accusative is homonymous with Dative across the Genitive (Nos. 6 and 12), Nominative at best marginally with Genitive across the Accusative (No. 2), but not Genitive with Instrumental across the Dative. If (6b) were selected as the linear invariant, allowances would have to be made for homonymies across two or even three intervening terms (and three, in a five-term sequence, indeed is the theoretical maximum), because Genitive can be homonymous with Dative across the Instrumental (Nos. 8, 17, 21), with Accusative across the Instrumental and Dative (No. 11), and marginally with Nominative across the Instrumental, Dative, and Accusative (No. 2).[10] The third way of coping with the complexities of Case homonymy is to back down from the invariance requirement. Between them, the two linear arrangements (6a) and (6b) would suffice to take care of virtually all attested patterns in terms of neighbourhood. Only the homonymy of Nominative and Genitive, of dubious standing in West-Saxon, would necessitate yet a third linear alternative. Needless to say, admitting three different linear orders in principle creates a vast potential of homonymy variability, much in excess of that actually observed in Old English. It is gratifying, therefore, that there is a better partner of (6a) than (6b):

(6) c. Gen
Nom
Acc
Dat
Ins

Order (6c), not without merits of its own despite its unorthodoxy, neatly complements (6a), licensing precisely those homonymies prohibited by (6a), viz. Acc=Dat and Nom=Gen, and very few extra patterns that are unattested (Acc=Dat=Ins, Nom=Acc=Dat=Ins).[11] (Independently, if chosen as the linear invariant, (6c) would have to put up with homonymies across one (Gen=Acc) or two (Gen=Dat) intervening terms.)

It is time to assess the damage caused by the facts of Old English to our set of constraints. In several respects, it is less severe than it could seem at first sight.

Case is realised by five terms in Old English, but it suffices to accommodate all homonymies if only three (7a) or four (7b) of them, rather than all five, are arranged in a circle, or alternatively if only one intervening term in a linear arrangement (viz. 6a), rather than the maximum of three, is allowed to be skipped, or if only two linear permutations (viz. 6a and 6c), rather than the maximum of sixty, are made use of in combination. If any of the five Case terms were directly linked to any other, fully exploiting the capacities of circular ordering, there would be no less than ten pairs, ten triples, five quadruples, and one quintuple of neighbours, which is far in excess of the five pairs, five triples, three (7a) or four (7b) quadruples, and one quintuple of neighbours definable in (7). The number especially of pairs and triples of neighbours in the partly circular arrangements in (7) is in fact closer to that obtained in linear orders of five terms.[12]

What this suggests is that deviations from the linear mode can be restrained in a principled manner. On the present evidence they need only be *minimal:* If terms need to be arranged circularly, they cannot form more than one circle (which rules out representations such as (2b/c)), and only three or at most four terms can be members of this circle, irrespective of how many terms a category happens to be realised by. In effect, categories with the lowest number of terms amenable to circular ordering, i.e. three, would thus set the limit also for categories of arbitrarily many terms with regard to the permissible diversity of homonymy patterns.[13] Violations of the neighbourhood condition are minimal, correspondingly, if only a single intervening term may be skipped by homonymies. And violations of the invariance requirement are minimal if recourse is had to no more than two linear orders in combination.

What should also be taken into consideration is the systemic relevance of the patterns of homonymy which caused these minimal relaxations of our constraints. Since (6a) has had the best marks of all linear permutations, it is the homonymies inconsistent with this arrangement whose status in the inflectional system of Old English deserves closer scrutiny – viz. those of Nominative and Genitive (No. 2), Accusative and Dative (No. 6), and Nominative, Accusative, and Dative (No. 12).

As was mentioned before, the Nom=Gen pattern is dubious and probably unattested in later West-Saxon.

The Acc=Dat pattern likewise is not met with in all regional and historical varieties of Old English. As to systemic relevance, homonymies of Nominative and Genitive across a distinct Accusative are completely *isolated* insofar as these two terms do not participate in any further, otherwise permissible patterns where more than two terms are homonymous. Unlike, for example, Nom=Acc, which recurs in three- and four-term homonymies (Nom=Acc=Gen and Nom=Acc=Gen=Dat), the Nom=Gen pattern is not accompanied by Nom=Gen=Dat and Nom=Gen=Dat=Ins. The Acc=Dat pattern is slightly less isolated, as there is one corresponding three-term pattern, Nom=Acc=Dat; unattested are, however, Acc=Dat=Ins and Nom=Acc=Dat=Ins, which would imply no additional infractions of the neighbourhood condition. Equally unattested is Nom=Acc=Dat=Ins, the only more extensive pattern to contain Nom=Acc=Dat(≠Gen).

The three offensive patterns, furthermore, are clearly surpassed by all inoffensive ones, except one or two, in the number of their instances throughout subparadigms. As Case is cumulated with two- or three-term Number (with all relevant words), two-term Definiteness (only adjectives), three-term Gender (adjectives, pronouns except 1st and 2nd Person personal ones),[14] and three-term Person (only personal pronouns), there is a wide variety of subparadigms across which homonymy patterns could be distributed. The Nom=Gen and the Nom=Acc=Dat patterns are in fact limited to a single Number subparadigm each: Nom=Gen to Plural and Nom=Acc=Dat to Singular. The Acc=Dat pattern is also limited to Number subparadigms, but is found in all three of them; its domain further includes 1st and 2nd

Person subparadigms. With the exception of pattern No. 21 and perhaps No. 11, all inoffensive ones are distributed more widely across subparadigms:

1. Nom=Acc: Singular, Plural; Indefinite, Definite; Neuter, Feminine; 3rd Person.
8. Gen=Dat: Singular; Definite; Neuter, Feminine; 3rd Person.
10. Dat=Ins: Plural; Indefinite; Masculine, Neuter, Feminine.
11. Nom=Acc=Gen: Singular, Plural.
17. Acc=Gen=Dat: Singular; Definite; Masculine, Feminine.
20. Gen=Dat=Ins: Singular; Indefinite; Feminine.
21. Nom=Acc=Gen=Dat: Singular.
25. Acc=Gen=Dat=Ins?: Singular; Definite; Masculine,

In this sense, offences against the neighbourhood condition can, thus, be characterised as *local*, inoffensive patterns being generally more pervasive.

Moreover, with one exception, all individual subparadigms of Case as well as their appropriate combinations are consistent with some linear ordering of Case terms. The homonymies in Indefinite (Nom=Acc, Dat=Ins, Gen=Dat= Ins), Definite (Nom=Acc, Gen=Dat, Acc=Gen=Dat, Acc=Gen=Dat=Ins?), Masculine (Nom=Acc, Acc=Gen=Dat, Acc=Gen=Dat=Ins?), Neuter (Nom=Acc, Gen=Dat), Feminine (Nom=Acc, Gen=Dat, Acc=Gen=Dat, Gen=Dat=Ins, Acc=Gen=Dat=Ins?), and 3rd Person (Nom=Acc, Gen=Dat) subparadigms can all be accounted for by (6a) alone. If 1st and 2nd Person subparadigms (Acc=Dat) are collated with that of 3rd Person, the ordering Nom-Acc-Dat-Gen (i.e.(6b), with Ins, not realised in Person paradigms, omitted) takes care of all homonymies. The Dual (Acc=Dat) and Plural (Nom=Acc, Nom=Gen, Acc=Dat, Dat=Ins, Nom=Acc=Gen) subparadigms square with (6c). Only the Singular subparadigm, richest in homonymy patterns (Nom=Acc, Acc=Dat, Gen=Dat, Nom=Acc=Gen, Nom=Acc=Dat, Acc=Gen=Dat, Gen=Dat=Ins, Nom=Acc=Gen=Dat, Acc=Gen= Dat=Ins?), does not admit of a uniform linear arrangement of the five Cases. The offence against linearity is, therefore, local as well.

Many attested homonymy patterns are found with different parts of speech inflecting for Case:

    1. Nom=Acc: nouns, adjectives, personal (3rd Person), demonstrative, interrogative pronouns;
    8. Gen=Dat: nouns, adjectives, personal pronouns (3rd Person);
  10. Dat=Ins: adjectives, demonstratives;
  17. Acc=Gen=Dat: nouns, adjectives;
  20. Gen=Dat=Ins: adjectives, demonstratives.

Five or six patterns, among which the three offensive ones, are restricted to single parts of speech: Nos. 2 (Nom=Gen), 11 (Nom=Acc=Gen), 12 (Nom=Acc=Dat), 21 (Nom=Acc=Gen=Dat) to nouns; No. 25 (Acc=Gen=Dat=Ins?) to adjectives; and No. 6 (Acc=Dat) to personal pronouns (1st and 2nd Person). This is another sense, then, in which some homonymy patterns can be said to be local.

Among nouns, the illicit homonymy of Accusative (plus Nominative) and Dative (No. 12) is indeed a peculiarity of phonologically identifiable groups of members of various inflection classes, viz. *ja*- and *i*- masculines and neuters and, less regularly, athematic feminines. Owing to their syllabic structure, the relevant nouns were able to avoid the loss, by regular phonological rule or analogy, of a final high vowel, and therefore retained final -*e* (< -*i*) as the exponent of Nominative and Accusative Singular, identical to the originally distinct exponent of Dative Singular; or, in one case, it was as a result of the phonological contraction of the Dative Singular exponent -e with the stem-final vowel (sǣ-e -> sǣ) that Dative happened to coincide with Accusative. This homonymy pattern is, therefore, an accident of Old English phonology rather than a deep-seated trait of the morphological system, hence deserves to be dismissed as *superficial*.

If this phonologically conditioned pattern and the Nom=Gen pattern, occasionally found with ō/jō/wō-nouns in early West-Saxon, are disregarded, *all* Old English words inflecting for Case except 1st and 2nd Person personal pronouns are in their Case homonymies consistent with the linear arrangement (6a). The cause of the insufficiency of linear ordering (or of the invariance or neighbourhood assumptions) can thus be localised very precisely: it is the homonymy behaviour of two items, the only ones which neither inflect for Gender nor have Case exponents sensitive to Gender, viz. the personal pronouns of 1st and 2nd Person. They alone require linear orders where Dative is adjacent to Accusative (as it is, for example, in (6b), (6c), or the circles of (7)), or permission to neutralise these two terms at a minimal distance, if their linear order as in (6a) is to be invariant. If Nom=Acc=Dat and Nom=Gen are not disregarded, the inflection classes where they are at home turn out to show only such further homonymy patterns as are consistent with linear Case orders. Nom=Acc=Dat is accompanied by Nom=Acc with the relevant ja-, i-, and athematic nouns, and with the latter also by Gen=Dat, which is compatible with (6b) if the Instrumental, not realised with nouns, is omitted. And

Nom=Gen is accompanied by Acc=Gen=Dat with $\bar{o}/j\bar{o}/w\bar{o}$-nouns, which squares for example with the arrangement Nom-Gen-Dat-Acc, the 'old' order of Cases once predominant in grammars of the Germanic languages.

We have seen that such *minimal* violations of the linearity, neighbourhood, or invariance conditions as are to be found in the Old English Case system are due to homonymy patterns which are *isolated, superficial,* and in various respects *local*.[15] If even homonymies of such marginal systemic relevance do not commit more than minor offences, there are grounds to suspect that the laws intended to control their behaviour are reasonably effective. In the case at hand, it should have become evident that homonymies, far from being randomly diverse, can be constrained in terms of the arrangement of paradigms almost as tightly as a grammarian could wish who wants to comply with three time-honoured conventions of good paradigm design. A preliminary survey of Case and further inflectional categories in other flective-type languages suggests that this conclusion in fact is of more general validity.[16]

What has been ignored here are motives for the arrangement of paradigms other than that exploiting homonymies. It is the heterogeneity of such possible semantic, syntagmatic, and formal motives which is commonly held responsible for disagreements about the single most natural order of particular paradigms, like those of Case. On the other hand, there has also been a belief, sometimes branded as wishful thinking, that different criteria ideally ought to harmonise, with formal similarities of paradigm entries iconically

reflecting semantic similarities, and with semantic
relatedness in particular being conducive to homonymy.
Old English Case tends to reassure this belief: the term
arrangements which best account for homonymies are, at
the same time, semantically not unnatural.

It is possible to recognise in the several linear
orders that were found expedient (6a/b/c) as well as in
both of the alternative partly circular orderings (7a/b)
a grouping of core syntactic clause-level Cases
(Nominative and Accusative), adverbial Cases (Dative,
Instrumental, and also Genitive),[17] and of a phrase-level
Case (Genitive). It is exclusively the Genitive whose
homonymy patterning militates against the completely
linear ordering of Old English Case terms, and the
variability of its ordering relative to the Nominative-
Accusative and the Dative- Instrumental group, manifest
from the ensemble of arrangements in (6) and (7), may be
taken to reflect the functional versatility of this Case
employed at phrase- as well as at clause-level. However
the Genitive links up with the two other groups, it
never intervenes between the members of either.
Syntactic operations likewise betray functional
affinities between Cases, and those in evidence in Old
English seem to fit in best with the partly circular
arrangement (7a). There is, for example, the subject-
centred diathesis of passive, which pairs Accusative
with Nominative, while object-centred alternations (as
in *se him fultum tiþaþ* 'who grant them (Dat) help (Acc)'
vs. *ne hine mon his bene typigean wolde* ('one did not
want to grant him (Acc) his request (Gen)') pair Dative
with Accusative and Accusative with Genitive.
Nominalisations pair Accusative as well as Nominative

with Genitive (*objectivus* and *subjectivus*, respectively), and it is only the first of these associations which is compatible with (7a), the second being more in line with (7b) or also (6c). Thus, in analogy to the picture potentially emerging from the patterning of inflectional homonymy, we must reckon with a network of functional-semantic affinities whose complexity transcends the representational power of uniform, linear arrangements.

This glance at Old English case ordering as inspired by semantic and functional motives was superficial, and also needs to be complemented by a cross-linguistic perspective. Its purpose merely was to act as an incentive to further effort in the search for form-meaning correspondence in the paradigmatic domain.

NOTES

1. This effect is more dramatic with cumulative than with separatist exponents, which accounts for the higher incidence of inflectional homonymy in flective-type as compared to agglutinative languages, as observed by early morphological typologists (cf. Plank 1989) and, more recently, by Skalicka (1979), Carstairs (1984), and Plank (1986).

2. I preferably use the term 'homonymy' to refer to the suspension of a paradigmatic distinction, but sometimes, if in need of a verb, I also employ 'to neutralise', well aware that 'homonymy' and 'neutralisation' are not synonymous for everybody.

3. Equivalent to the circular orders in (2a) and (2b) are these matrices with two columns and two rows of cells:

   a. | w | z |
      |---|---|
      | x | y |

   b. | w | z |
      |---|---|
      | x | y |

In this format, less convenient to model (2c), those cells are neighbours which share a boundary line. Such effectively circular arrangements are employed, for example, by Jakobson (1936) and Stewart (1975) for the Case paradigms of Russian and Old English.

4. The earliest known grammarians, those of ancient Babylon, were not very consistent on this count in their paradigms of Sumerian verbs and nouns; cf. Jacobsen (1974).

5. An endingless kind of Locative, as found in early Old English, is ignored here, as are early distinct Instrumental forms of nouns.

6. (6a) is the widely favoured 'new' order of Cases, followed also by Campbell (1959), the main source of the preceding account of homonymies. It never appealed to Rasmus Rask, though, perhaps the most persistent seeker of the true natural order of paradigms (cf. Allen & Brink 1980, esp. 77-83), who for Old English preferred Nom-Acc-Dat-Gen (1817) or, with the Instrumental distinguished from Dative, Nom-Acc-Ins-Dat-Gen (1830).

7. This difficulty was not appreciated by Rask, who in both the original Danish (1817) and the revised English (1830) versions of his Anglo-Saxon grammar has the Dative closer to Accusative than the Genitive. It is only in his grammar of Old Norse (1818) that he toys with the idea of reversing this order, but more on the analogy of Slavonic (where animate nouns may employ the Genitive in lieu of an Accusative) than on language-internal grounds.

8. Incidentally, both arrangements in (7) avoid a diachronic problem facing (6a): Nominative, Accusative, and Dative are later syncretised, while the Genitive, interrupting their sequence in (6a), continues to be distinguished.

9. A further alternative would be to switch Dative and Instrumental, and to put the latter in parentheses, thus indicating its limitation to particular inflection classes and maybe subparadigms:

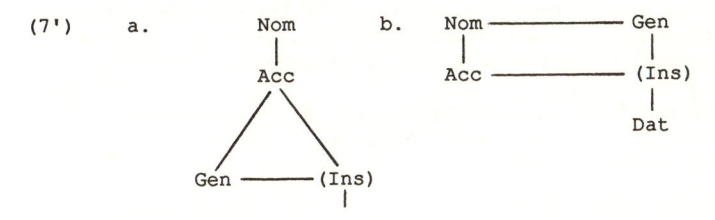

(7')   a.   Nom   b.   Nom ——————— Gen
                  | |
                 Acc   Acc ——————— (Ins)
                 / \ |
                /   \   Dat
              Gen ——— (Ins)
                      |

                              Dat

This would account for the regularity that Dative does not
coincide with Genitive or Accusative or both unless it also
coincides with Instrumental (cf. pattern No. 20) or unless
the relevant inflection   class lacks an Instrumental (cf.
instances of Nos. 6, 8, 12, 17, 21). On the other hand,
unlike (7), (7') misses the generalisation that Instrumental,
where realised, is not homonymous with Genitive without also
coinciding with Dative (cf. Nos. 10, 20). This also holds for
an analogous permutation of the linear arrangement (6a):

(6')   a.   Nom
                Acc
                Gen
                (Ins)
                Dat

10. The situation could be slightly improved by again putting the
    Instrumental in parentheses, in recognition of its limited
    occurrence.

11. This does not exhaust the range of possible complementary
    linear orders. A perfect partner of (6c), for example, would
    be the sequence Nom-Acc-Dat-Gen-Ins.

12. If translated into the Jakobsonian format, both (7a) and (7b)
    turn out to be more restrictive than the paradigm of Old
    English Cases as   arranged by Stewart (1975).

    (7) a. | Nom | b. | Nom | Gen | (Stewart)
             | Acc | | Acc | Dat | | Nom | Acc | Gen |
             | Gen | Dat | | Ins | | Ins | Dat |
             | | Ins|

    There are five shared boundary lines in (7a) (Nom/Acc,
    Acc/Gen, Acc/Dat, Gen/Dat, Dat/Ins) as well as in (7b)
    (Nom/Acc, Nom/Gen, Acc/Dat, Gen/Dat, Dat/Ins), whereas
    Stewart has seven (Nom/Acc, Nom/Ins, Acc/Gen, Acc/Ins,
    Acc/Dat, Gen/Dat, Ins/Dat).

13. Among the three-term categories of Old English, Gender and
    Mood indeed do require circular ordering if invariance and
    neighbourhood requirements are to be upheld.

14. With nouns, inflectional exponents are assumed to be
    sensitive to, but not really to express, Gender.

15. On the convention adopted in (7), it should, thus, be impossible for all terms to be equidistant in circular arrangements, if distance is used to depict systemic relevance. - In terms developed by Wurzel (1984), our isolated, superficial, and local patterns could be characterised as 'system-incongruous'. Wurzel (1984: ch. 3) in fact discusses the gamut of homonymy patterns of Old and Middle High German, but without recognising any principled constraints. For him it seems an arbitrary choice which and how many patterns particular languages decide on as constitutive of their inflectional systems. In the terminology of Carstairs (1987: ch. 4), our isolated, superficial, or local patterns would be 'accidental' rather than 'systematic' homonymies. Most of Carstairs's accidental homonymies are phonologically conditioned, but his main criterion of systematicity is recurrence in several word classes.

16. For Case, see Plank (1988).

17. The Genitive is not contiguous to the other two adverbial Cases in (6c). - For Old English, drawing a clear-cut boundary between syntactic-core (Acc) and adverbial (Dat, Ins, Gen) object Cases in fact is an oversimplification, as I have argued elsewhere (Plank 1982).

REFERENCES

Allen, W.S. & C.O. Brink. 1980. 'The Old Order and the New: A Case History.' *Lingua* 50.61-100.
Campbell, A. 1959. *Old English Grammar*. Oxford: Clarendon Press.
Carstairs, A. 1984. 'Outlines of a Constraint on Syncretism.' *Folia Linguistica* 18.73-85.
----. 1987. *Allomorphy in Inflexion*. London: Croom Helm.
Jacobsen, T. 1974. 'Very Ancient Linguistics: Babylonian Grammatical Texts.' In D. Hymes, ed. *Studies in the History of Linguistics. Traditions and Paradigms*, 41-62. Bloomington: Indiana University Press.
Jakobson, R. 1936. 'Beitrag zur allgemeinen Kasuslehre.' *Travaux du Cercle Linguistique de Prague* 6.240-288.
Plank, F. 1982. 'Coming into Being among the Anglo-Saxons.' *Folia Linguistica* 16.73-118.

----. 1986. 'Paradigm Size, Morphological Typology, and Universal Economy.' *Folia Linguistica* 20.29-48.
----. 1988. 'Rasmus Rask's Dilemma.' In F. Plank, ed. *Paradigms: The Economy of Inflection*. Berlin: Mouton de Gruyter (to appear).
----. 1989. 'Of the Wealth of Languages and the Division of Grammatical Labour.' In P. Jones & A. Skinner, eds. *Adam Smith*. Edinburgh: Edinburgh University Press (to appear).
Rask, R. 1817. *Angelsaksisk sproglære tilligemed en kort læsebog*. Stockholm: Wiborg.
----. 1818. *Undersøgelse om det gamle nordiske eller islandske sprogs oprindelse*. Kjøbenhavn: Gyldendal.
----. 1830. *A Grammar of the Anglo-Saxon Tongue, with a Praxis*. A new edition enlarged by the author. Translated from the Danish by B. Thorpe. Copenhagen: S.L. Møller.
Skalička, V. 1979. *Typologische Studien*. Braunschweig: Vieweg.
Stewart, A.H. 1975. 'A Note on Case Conflation in the Old English Nominal Declension.' *Papers in Linguistics* 8.165-176.
Wurzel, W.U. 1984. *Flexionsmorphologie und Natürlichkeit. Ein Beitrag zur morphologischen Theoriebildung*. Berlin: Akademie-Verlag.

A CONTACT-UNIVERSALS ORIGIN FOR PERIPHRASTIC *DO*, WITH SPECIAL CONSIDERATION OF OE-CELTIC CONTACT

PATRICIA POUSSA
University of Helsinki

1.0. *Introduction*. The aims of this paper are twofold. Firstly, I present a more general explanation of the origin of periphrastic DO[1] than development from causative DO by semantic bleaching, the explanation favoured by Ellegård (1953). My proposal is in essence a creolization-decreolization model. Secondly, I examine the applicability of this model to the development of western dialects of English in particular. I argue here, by a comparison of western dialectal forms with the forms of southern Hiberno-English, that, while the functional need for dummy auxiliaries will rise in any bilingual contact situation, the forms of the DO auxilliary recorded in modern western and south-western mainland dialects of English can best be explained specifically as the result of an early English-Celtic contact situation in Wessex. I conclude that the rise of periphrastic DO in the spoken language should be assigned to the OE period, though it apparently first enters the written mode in ME texts.

1.1. *Objections to Ellegard*. A basic objection to Ellegard's account is his tendency to reject speech-based explanations, dismissing the spoken dialect evidence referred to by Engblom (1938: 112), in favour of a purely literary account of the spread of periphrastic *do*. However, the developments in sociolinguistics over the last thirty-five years make a purely literary account of language change suspect. Recently studies of the grammaticalization of *do* in questions (Stein 1983, 1985) have shown without doubt that phonotactic considerations have been crucial in the later development of the peraphrasis. Other scholars (Tieken 1983, Kytö and Rissanen 1983) have shown that some correlation exists between textual styles (of speech-like vs. literary genres) and frequency of *do*-support in other sentence types at particular periods.

A more particular objection to Ellegård's bleached-causative model is that it fails to explain his own finding that the *do* periphrasis appears first (in the 13th century) in western texts, about one century before it appears in eastern texts. The problem here is that the causative use of *do* was not strong in western EME, because the ME reflexes of OE *lǣtan* and *macian* continued to be used with the infinitive to express causality in western texts, while causative *do* predominated in eastern texts. Kuhn has suggested that *macian* was borrowed into OE from Old Saxon first in Alfredian texts, and that it could have spread from Wessex in the OE period during the 10th and 11th centuries, when Wessex was politically and culturally dominant (1977, 1986). I infer from this that DO was not convenient for these purposes in the dialect of Wessex, perhaps because it had acquired another use, and that periphrastic DO and causative MAKE could have both spread from the west at the same time. I do not consider the absence of periphrastic *do* in OE texts is as significant as has been supposed.[2]

It appears, therefore, that the causative construction may be a red herring, and that, using the same data as Ellegård, we could argue that the disappearance of the causative *do*-construction could equally well be interpreted as the result of the emergence of periphrastic *do*, rather than its cause. This puts the onus on us to come up with a more powerful model which would account for both eastern and western data.

FIGURE 1.

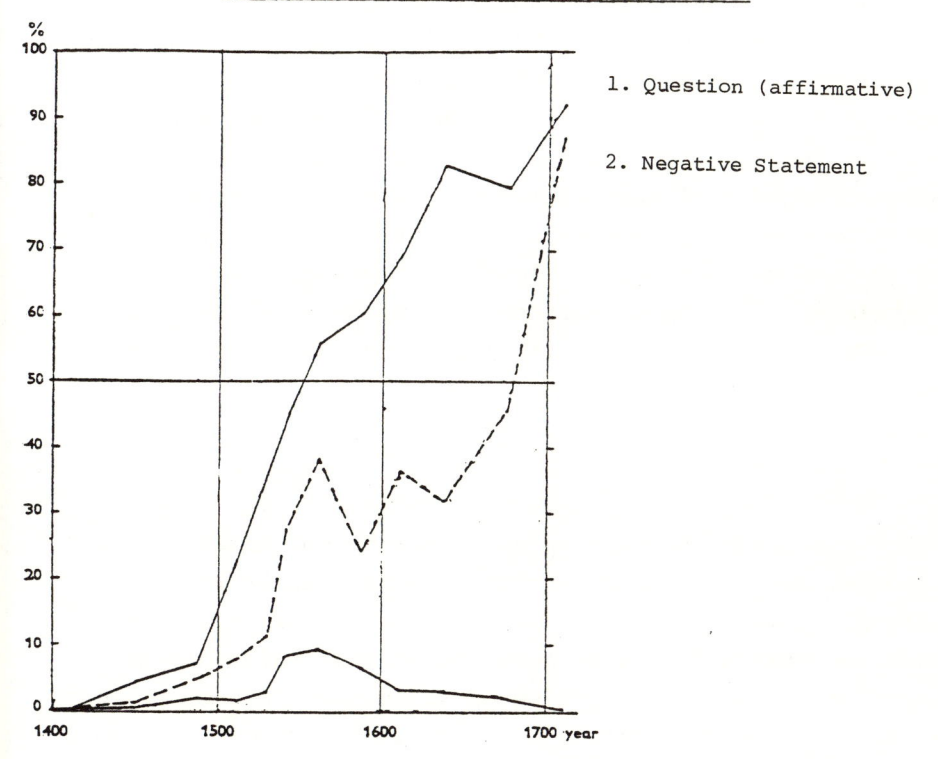

Percentage of do-forms in 3 sentence types

1. Question (affirmative)
2. Negative Statement

(Adapted from Ellegård 1953: 162)

The main outlines of the grammaticalization of *do* in (mostly standard) texts from 1400-1700 are shown in Figure 1. (somewhat simplified from Ellegård's by omission of the values for Neg Q and Neg Imp). For my purposes this is sufficient to illustrate that before 1400 the *do* seems to require a unified explanation. I agree with Ellegård on this. Afterwards the different sentence types undergo separate development, which leads to 100% *do* by PE in most cases. However, in the weak affirmative sentence type *do* support is gradually lost, apart from a rise in the graph in the mid 16th century, which marks the last period in which there is an undifferentiated rise in *do* across all sentence types in written standard English. Weak and strong affirmatives are conflated by Ellegård, as they cannot easily be separated in written texts. From the evidence of PE, however, we can say that *do* has been entirely lost in the weak affirmative in the written standard British English of the Lancaster Oslo/Bergen Corpus, but still appears to some extent in the spoken educated English of the London-Lund corpus (Nevalainen and Rissanen 1986). Therefore it is conceivable that we might still be able to glean something from the examination of variation in the use of DO-support in this sentence type in large spoken corpora in the future.

2.1. *A creolization-decreolization model.* However, there exist some present spoken varieties of English, e.g. pidgins, creoles, child language and L2 learner interlanguages, which show very much higher levels of DO-support than the standard, and it seems to me that reference to examples of the proliferation of DO in these non-mainstream varieties of English might be helpful. As several of these varieties involve bi- or multilingual contact, it is convenient to begin with the general phenomenon of the use of dummy verbs in the performance of bilingual speakers engaged in code-mixing or switching.

Following Di Sciullio et al (1986), it appears that a dummy auxiliary can enter a language as a performance feature in the speech of adult bilinguals who habitually mix and switch language codes. In mixing, foreign material can be incorporated into the stream of speech with no phonological adaptation (as visitors, not loans). As incorporating visiting verbs raises problems of how to attach native inflections, the strategy of using a native verb as head of the verbal complex, with the alien verb in either a nominal or infinitive form is utilized. Thus a single word in the foreign language may be incorporated easily in the stream of speech as two words: invariant stem + dummy inflection-carrier. Examples are given from several language pairs. The process would seem to be encouraged by the prior existence of such a dummy in one of the languages: thus in their Hindi-English bilingual sentence the use of the inflected verb *kar* 'do' as head of the English verb *prove* might be thought of as a borrowing from English. However, the writers note that both the Hindi structures with *karana* 'do' and *hona* 'be' are typically made up of a word of Persian or Arabic origin plus the dummy verb (Di Sciullio et al. 1986; 18). It is also possible that the strategy is the more favoured, the further the two languages differ in structure (according to Poplack, in discussion after a paper given in Helsinki, 1986). Further examples, with an application to ME, are given by Ihalainen (1982). Bilingual code-mixers may be highly fluent, as in some stable contact situtations, or non-fluent. The extreme case of the latter is met in a pre-pidgin situation. Bickerton

(1981;11) quotes the following example from the jargon phase of Hawaiian Pidgin, in which an elderly Japanese woman, asked if she spoke English, recollected:

> "No, *hapa-hapa* (Hawaiian 'half-half') *shite* (Japanese 'do') - i.e. 'I speak a mixture' - and added (in Japanese), "I never know whether I'm speaking one thing or the other".

The usefulness of an invariant verbal marker meaning 'do' is very clearly seen in its development in some pidgins and creoles, where morphology is reduced to the minimum. West African pidgins such as Cameroonian Pidgin English and the Caribbean creoles use preverbal markers derived from English DO and BE. The new forms function as tense/aspect markers. Not all English-based pidgins have selected DO and BE, however. (Mühlhäusler 1986: 186 gives parallel Tok Pisin forms.)

The Caribbean creoles use markers derived from English DO and BE (among others), and there would appear to be an underlying DO BE form in the early history of many of them. The different varieties have different verb paradigms. The following examples are from Le Page (1985: 89). (The *a* forms correspond to an earlier *da*, by an initial consonant deletion rule.)

	1. Jamaica	2. St Vincent
Unmarked for tense:		
habitual	ga	doz gu
Continuative or progressive aspect		
(I) am going	a gwoen	a gu
(she) was going	ena gou	ben gwoing
(where) were (they) going?	bena go, de go	bina gu
Past punctual		
he went	him gaa	i di bin, i bin
she went	him in/en go	i gu

As one of the known inputs to the Caribbean creoles is 17th century English dialects, particularly west-of-England dialects, these kind of forms may throw some light on the nature of the 17th vernacular English which became creolized. The early settlers in some islands, such as Barbados, a key early settlement, were overwhelmingly from the west of England (Rickford 1986: 252). The West African substratum influence is of course undeniable (Alleyne 1980), but the influence of the superstrate English dialects (including the possibility of influence from Hiberno-English) has been much discussed in the last decade, most recently in Harris (1985) and Rickford (1986), who gives a good overview. I will return to the western English and Hiberno-English dialects in the next section. Here it is sufficient to say that it appears that in the formation of the Caribbean creoles it is the earliest generations of migrants that have had the decisive influence in the formation of the new language varieties.

By common consent, creolization involves children, and simplification and analogical formations are typical of the developmental interlanguages of both child language acquirers and L2 learners. Analogical extension of DO to the weak affirmative construction can be observed the past tense formation rules of English monolingual children about the age of 3 years (Fletcher 1979: 272). I can attest the same for a Finnish English bilingual girl aged 2:10, in both past and present tense.

Naturalistic language acquisition is compared to creolization-decreolization (Schumann 1978, Andersen 1979, Rickford 1983), and it is to be expected that the monolingual child or L2 learner will abandon his or her early generalizations and will ultimately decreolize to the adult target model. However, in certain circumstances of language contact bilingual acquisition can lead to language deterioration, when the simplest rules and those common to both languages are learned first and generalized. The result can be accelerated language change, simplification, creolization, language convergence or language death, which may be rapid or take many generations.³

As naturalistic acquirers of DO seem to go through a similar developmental continuum with regard to the early generalization of DO, it seems that this is a natural weak spot in English, which each child finds independently at the same stage in its career as a English learner. Syntax is constructed anew by each learner. It is for this reason that I believe that the study of learner developmental continua is important to the study of historical syntax, especially in contact situations where societal restraints on the learner's linguistic behaviour are relaxed or removed, as in cases of language contact, especially where migration is involved. Such situations would be likely to lead to the proliferation of dummy verbs like DO, which would subsequently be available for new functions, whether grammatical, semantic, or stylistic.

In the case of English, such exceptional language contact situations have existed (a) in Celtic-Germanic contacts in the early OE period, (b) following the Scandinavian settlements, (c) possibly after the Norman conquest. I have argued earlier (Poussa 1982) that (c) is less likely than (b), but have not so far addressed alternative (a). The fact that nearly all surviving OE texts are in standardized LWS, and that standardization began even earlier, in the reign of Alfred, means that written OE effectively conceals variety of all kinds which must have existed in the spoken dialects, even in Wessex itself. Thus it is quite possible that periphrastic DO was well developed in spoken OE dialects, though not written, until it appears as a *fait accompli* in EME, by which time the status and use of written English had radically altered as a result of the Norman conquest.[4]

In favour of the universalist dummy aux innovation theory, we could point to the functions of the ME verbs *gar* (a northern form, from ON *gara*) and *gan*. When texts are translated into other dialects, both can be replaced by *do* or the simple past tense (Visser 1969: 1350), which argues that these verbs were dummies to ME speakers. The ON derivation of *gar* argues a bilingual and early origin. *Gar*, like *do* is involved in the causative/factitive construction, but *gan* has only an ingressive, never causative meaning (ibid: 1572).

If we go further back into the history of Germanic, we can find further suggestions that the DO verb has been used as an inflection carrier, e.g. in the Gothic weak verb past tense forms, which are, according to some Germanists, derived from a cliticized post-poned form of the IE auxiliary *$dh\bar{e}$-/$dh\bar{o}$- 'do'. It was argued by Franz Bopp (1816; 151-7) and later scholars that this explanation of the source of the /d/ element in the weak conjugation past tense marker holds for the whole of Germanic, though this is not universally accepted (Prokosch 1939: 194-9). At any rate, for our argument it is sufficient to note that the grammaticalization of a verb meaning 'do' as a tense marker is not an unlikely development in language history, and has possibly happened in the earliest written form of Germanic. We can say with certainty that the forms of the DO verb have been available for exploitation as a dummy aux from the very dawn of Germanic. (Though we do not need to enter the arena of whether Germanic should be regarded as creolized IE.)

The general advantages of this creolization-decreolization model are:

a) The crucial triggering changes in English are placed in a period marked by general language restructuring. Langenfelt (1933: 99) remarked that:

> "It stands to reason that the *do* auxiliary is a product of spoken language, most probably developing during a period of decaying grammar".

The LME period (when the causative sense of *do* was lost) is less suitable than EME, or OE, if we discount the written standard.

b) Decreolization would explain why DO was lost in the weak affirmative though not in the other sentence types. Ihalainen (1985: 65) observed that in dialect contact old forms first disappear from weak affirmatives. Question, negative and strong affirmative are conservative environments. He noted that the relative order of the sentence types was the same in as in Ellegård's data. This observation on mixed grammars is substantiated by Ihalainen (1986: 371-374) in Somerset and West Midland dialect forms, and he advances an explanation based on "prominence". Phonologically non-prominent forms allow weakening and contraction, and these forms tend to be deleted and replaced. So there is an implicational rule operating here very like that for copula deletion in North American Black English. If it is accepted that the relative frequency of *do*-support in ME texts found by Ellegård over these same sentence types can be explained in this way, then it follows that the written *do* must represent an old spoken form, and sufficient time must have elapsed for DO to have been dropped from the paradigm in the weak affirmative. Which leads us back to the proposition that the ME texts most probably record the results of processes which had taken place in the spoken language before the ME period.[5]

c) The same considerations would also explain the periphrastic use of the auxiliary *tun* in the modern German dialects. It seems to occur in question, negative and strong affirmative environments. The phenomenon is geographically widespread, and recorded from the 14th and 15th centuries (Erben 1969). The very existence of these similar German examples suggests that the DO periphrasis could have developed when the two branches were at a similar stage of development, though not necessarily before separation. As far as I know, the dialects of modern Dutch do not have periphrastic DO, though the causative construction with DO does occur, as Visser notes (1969: 1346), and he thinks it not impossible that the causative meaning existed in PrGmc (though he thinks the origin of the periphrasis lies in a factitive, not causative use (p. 1497, and Denison 1985)).

3.1. *The Celtic substratum.* To return to the specific problem of the first appearances of dummy DO in ME texts: because they appear in south-western texts a century before they are adopted in the east, it seems that we have to reconsider one of the explanations rejected by both Ellegård and Visser: the influence of the Celtic substratum in spoken dialects.

Since the appearance of Ellegård's work, the extent of the survival of Celtic-speaking communities in the OE period has been under reassessment. There has recently been much discussion of the possibility that the British population may have survived in much larger numbers than the traditional historical picture, based on Bede, allows. These suggestions have come from archeologists, e.g. Hope-Taylor in his discussion of Yeavering (1977), place-namists - a review is given by Gelling (1978: 87-88) and historians concerned with settlement studies, e.g. Jones (1978). Jackson (1953: 220) examined the evidence for the amount of Celtic-English bilingualism in the early English period by counting the survival of Celtic names for streams and rivers in modern English. On this basis, he divides the map of England and Wales into four linguistic areas. His conclusions are summarized in map form in Figure 2.

Jackson argues that the survival of topographical names, especially of features such as smaller waterways, gives a better picture of the survival of the Celtic languages than settlement names. Societal bilingualism seems clearly to have existed during the shift from a Celtic to a Germanic language, and most strongly in area III. Here some remarkable cases of remnants of Primitive Welsh counting systems, etc., are attested, even this century.

The boundary between area II and III corresponds roughly to the line of Anglo-Saxon conquest c550, and to the east-west division in modern regional dialects. It seems therefore that we have here the ingredients of a post-creole continuum in the OE dialects, with the

FIGURE 2

Celtic river and stream names

(Adapted from Jackson)

basilect, the most creolized, most Celtic influenced varieties, to the west. The most unexpected of these areas is the south-western one, for this fell within the boundaries of Wessex soon after the battle of Dyrham, 577 AD. It must be that an exceptionally large number of Britons remained in this Saxon-ruled area, and in fact the Laws of Ine confirm that Britons formed the lowest rank of society in Wessex. The confusions in the Chronicle

account of the conquest of western Wessex, combined with
some British-sounding names among the ruling dynasty
(Myres 1986: 146-48) and the scarcity of unambiguously
Germanic archeological finds suggests that the Germanic
settlers were comparatively thin on the ground in western
Wessex. These circumstances could have led in the OE
period to the development of contact varieties of Germanic
which favoured the use of dummy aux constructions,
especially in the modern counties of Devon, Somerset and
Dorset.

Some support for this view can be gathered from the
present dialects of the south west. In the historical
comments on the south-western dialects collected by
Wakelin (1986), it is remarkable that the dialect of
Somerset area in particular is singled out for its rude-
ness and barbarity, while Cornwall (Area IV in Jackson)
and western Devon have a dialect closer to the standard,
as a consequence of English having been originally learned
as a second language taught in schools. Cornwall has
therefore undergone a language shift in the modern period,
with comparatively little substratum influence. In my
interpretation, therefore, the most conservative rural
dialects of the Somerset area represent the lowest lects
in the remains of a post-creole continuum extending both
west and east, though the eastern dialect continuum is far
older. Like any creole continuum, it exists in the
geographical, social and temporal dimensions. As Bickerton
(1973, 1975) has demonstrated, the tendency is for speakers
to move up the continuum by a series of implicational
rules, so that in time the original basilect vanishes, and
then the next lowest lect, and so on - but the individual
speaker's basilectal floor is not impervious, so that a

mesolectal speaker can dip into a slightly lower lect in such situations as joke-telling, imitating older speakers, etc.

3.2. *Western and south-western DO forms*. The present western dialects of English are characterized by "redundant DO", and in the Somerset area a habitual use of DO is attested. A comparison with developments in present Hiberno-English dialects, discussed in Harris (1985), suggests the possibility that the south-western habitual DO has developed from earlier DO BE forms, which, in Hiberno-English at least, have been ascribed to the influence of the aspect categories of the Celtic verb. (I return to the evidence for this in the next section.)

In mainland English, we do not meet with DO BE forms in ME or ModE texts, but sporadic DO BE forms were encountered in materials collected in the 19th century for Oxfordshire, Dorset, Cornwall, Surrey and Sussex, according to the EDD. Some examples (discussed in Harris 1985: 90) are given below:

3. She do be so strict with us gals. (Oxfordshire) (Wright: EDD)

4. They do be getting all their bad ways again. (Sussex)

5. The childer do be laffen at me. (Cornwall)

6. Men and hosses don't be kept for nothing. (Surrey)

Peculiar habitual forms were found in Dorset:

7. The dog do jumpy (Dorset) (Barnes, 1886)

8. He do markety (Dorset (Elworthy, 1886: xlvi),

and many examples were found of the DO + verb habitual which is still in use in the south-west today:

9. I du zay zom prayers now and again. (Devon)
   (Elworthy: xx)

In addition to the above-mentioned counties, DO + verb is listed by the EDD for Cheshire, Wiltshire and West Hampshire. The natural inference is that all these forms were earlier more general in the spoken language. Though no DO BE forms seem to have been found in the mid 20th century, the DO + verb form was found used for reference to habitual action in Somerset by elderly speakers in the 1970s by Ihalainen (1976: 615, 1981, and forthcoming). It is also found in South Wales, and "the use of redundant DO" is reported in Herefordshire (Leeds, 1974). The present geographical distribution of habitual DO + verb is not yet clear, according to Trudgill, Edwards and Weltens (1983: 29). However the coincidence of the 19th and 20th-century finds of DO BE and habitual DO with Jackson's Area III and IV are suggestive, and support the substratumist view.

3.3. *Hiberno-English DO forms*. The classic case of Celtic-English contact is modern Hiberno-English. It has long been averred that the HE verb forms are due to the substratum influence of the Irish tense/aspect system. Bliss (1984: 143) states that "Southern Hiberno-English has precisely the same range of tenses as Irish has, but the forms are built up out of English material". Irish, like modern Welsh, is remarkable for having, both in the present and past tenses, three durative verbal forms, versus only one punctual (past-tense) form (Wagner 1959: 23, 64). The boundaries of southern and northern (Ulster Scots-influenced) dialects can only be drawn approximately (see map in Bliss: 117). DO BE and DO + verb forms (consuetudinal present) are in common use in southern HE, though "normally avoided by educated speakers" (Bliss 1984: 143-4). Some examples (from Harris 1984: 306):

10. They do be fighting among other. (Henry, 1957: 170)

11. Well, when you put them on to the barrow you do have them in heaps and then you do spread them and turn them over and all. (Derrygonnelly, Fermanagh)

In addition, HE has an extra tense/aspect form, Perfect I, termed the hot-news form by Harris, which has no equivalent in standard English.

12. A young man's only after getting shot out there. (Belfast)

(Like Irish, HE does not have a fully grammaticalized perfect form).

Harris differs from earlier writers in arguing that only the latter, PI, can be said to be directly calqued on Irish, and that the other forms quoted are possibly to be explained as results of decreolization of the most Irish basilect towards the English vernacular dialect of the superstrate. In southern Ireland this was originally a mixture of ME West of England dialects (Samuels: 108-9), with further immigrations of other dialect speakers in the 17th century, whereas in parts of Northern Ireland the decreolization is towards present Ulster Scots, which uses the habitual BE form, by deleting the "redundant DO". Harris (1984: 306-7) gives the following examples:

13. They be shooting and fishing out at the Forestry lakes. (Derrygonnelly)

14. Q: What kind of jobs do they be doing? (Tyrone)

A: Well, they be planting trees and they be digging drains and they be sowing manure. (Derrygonnelly)

3.4. *Inferences for the history of mainland English.* Though such DO BE habitual forms are not found in present mainland English dialects, DO + Verb habituals are attested in the south west (and both types in the Caribbean creoles). This leads us to ask: could both the southern HE types of DO BE and DO habituals have existed previously in early western English dialects on the mainland? After all, the tense/aspect system of modern Welsh makes exactly the same semantic distinctions as that of modern Irish. Cornish, which became extinct about 1800, apparently had two auxiliary verbs, *gil* and *bos*, corresponding in meaning to German *tun* and *sein*, and the excessive use of DO in the south west was ascribed to this Cornish substratum by Franz in *Shakespeare Grammatik*, sect. 597 (Wagner 1959: 94). As these branches of Celtic separated by the 6th century, they have presumably maintained their similar tense/aspect system in the spoken language all this time. Though Harris (1985: 93) regards the claim that a Celtic (Cornish) substratum influence on the habitual DO found in south-western dialects of English as virtually untestable, I think that a better case can be made than he allows.

I offer therefore the hypothesis that the Somerset habitual DO + verb forms may have arisen as the result of decreolization from DO BE, by copula deletion, rather than deletion of DO, which seems to be happening in northern HE, and has happened in some of the Caribbean creoles.[6] The next stage of decreolization towards the more easterly dialects would be to the loss of the habitual meaning of DO, which bleaching would then give us a dummy verb, redundant or periphrastic DO. The final stage would be to delete DO altogether in the weak affirmative, and this is apparently what is happening in younger West Somerset speakers now, according to Ihalainen (this conference). We thus have in PE a full geographical, social and (apparent time) temporal continuum extending from the basilect of oldest West Somerset rural speakers who have habitual DO but no periphrastic DO expressing completed action (Ihalainen 1976: 611), via lects with variable frequencies of "redundant DO" in the weak affirmative, with the LL spoken corpus and the LOB written corpus of British standard English as the acrolectal varieties. I fully agree with Harris that the testing of this model is problematic, but it seems to me to fit the known facts of DO periphrasis better than most earlier explanations given by philologists.

To return to ME: The very slow working through of this chain of restructurings in the western dialect continuum could have produced redundant DO's in the south west before and during the 13th century, and the time needed for the creolization-decreolization process would explain the time lag which caused Ellegård (1953: 119) and Visser (1969: 1496) to reject the Celtic influence origin theory advanced by Preusler (1938, 1939-40) for ME periphrastic DO. The very long time-span is not so very remarkable, however, when viewed in the light of the situation of the DO periphrasis in PE. Though in Ellegård's texts weak affirmative DO seems to have vanished c1700, yet we have noted the spoken examples in the LL corpus.

In this connection it is worth comparing the history of the rise of the progressive IS/WAS + ING verb form, which has also been ascribed to Celtic influence in the OE period (Braaten 1967: 174-5). He accounts for the late emergence of *-ing* participles in ME to the influence of the Norman conquest on the literary tradition:

> The fact that *-ing* participles occur with increasing frequency in the Middle English period may be accounted for by the circumstance that they had for a long time been felt to be strictly colloquial and inelegant, and that they now had a chance of being accepted. In any case, the originally colloquial *-ing* and the traditional, literary *-ind* are not infrequently found side by side" (Braaten 1977: 177).

The use of the progressive has continued to gain ground in writing since the 19th century.

4.1. *The London standard.* The reasons why periphrastic DO captured the standard in English while the comparable constructions with *tun* remained substandard and dialectal in German cannot be explained solely by the comparative strength of the Celtic substratum influence in England. Among the early factors influencing the outcome in England must be numbered subsequent invasions involving societal bilingualism (Scandinavian, Norman French), and dialect contact, particularly in London. The importance of London in the formation and dissemination through printed books of the early modern standard is obvious and indisputable. The stages of the formation of the spoken standard, and its relationship to the written standard are vaguer, through lack of evidence. However, dialect mixture because of in-migration from the countryside can be assumed from onomastic studies on the names of prominent citizens, which show increased immigration from the East Midlands and East Anglia in particular in the late ME period (Ekwall 1956).

The usefulness of the dummy aux strategy to fluent bilinguals is also likely to have been felt in situations of dialect clash between conflicting forms of the past tense. There is a great variety of conflicting (strong vs. weak) preterite forms in the dialects of PE (Trudgill, Edwards & Weltens 1983: 23). In the EModE period in London the mixing of southern with later east and central Midland dialect speakers must have given rise to a remarkable number of such clashes. Samuels (1972: 174) demonstrates how the instability of verb forms in the EModE period may have contributed to the rise of the DO periphrasis in texts of this period. As the present East Anglian dialects contain many non-standard preterite forms, the late ME immigrations to London from these areas are probably significant here.[7] In addition, as the EModE period was a period of high social mobility, hypercorrection would be a very likely factor in the language of social risers (Samuels p. 172-3).

Writing of course had its own needs, and it seems to me highly likely that the need for a compromise past tense form in writing was increased by the introduction of the printing press. This would be an additional motivation for the remarkable rise in all kinds of DO periphrasis in mid 16th century texts in linguistically highly aware writers such as Caxton, Ascham and Boorde, and which also affected the weak affirmative. Thus in the standardization period we probably have a conspiracy of pressures from above and below, both encouraging the DO-periphrasis. Though of course we cannot do Labovian urban sociolinguistics without live speakers, it seems a reasonable supposition that it was this kind of combination of factors in the spoken language of the London area that finally pushed the frequency of periphrastic DO over the hump, i.e. into the fast phase of Bailey's S-curve, after which the natural processes of the spoken language, such as the phonotactic factors analysed by Stein, took the change through to completion in standard English. Weak affirmative DO was presumably not frequent enough at this period to be caught in the general development. But how well the spoken and the written developments synchronized, it is impossible to say, even in this comparatively well-documented period.

I have argued throughout this paper for the possibility that some syntactic features of the Low spoken language, insulated by diglossia, have remained remarkably constant since ME, and that the conventions of the written language have obscured this, particularly in the older periods where we have no informal text-types available.

However, one small piece of evidence survives which suggests that some advanced speakers in the south east of England may already have had a near-PE system of DO-support even before 1400. It lies in a piece of literary child speech in Chaucer's *Monk's Tale*:

>"His yonge sone that three year was of age
>Unto him seyde, fader, why do ye wepe?
>Whan wol the gayler bringen our potage,
>Is there no morsel breed that ye do kepe? (441-444)

The last line contains one of the rare examples of weak affirmative periphrastic DO in Chaucer, and is taken by Ellegård (p. 22) as a metrical filler, rare for this poet. Langenfelt (1933: 111) regards it as "the prattle of children". As so often, I find myself on the side of Langenfelt. So far as I know, no commentator has remarked on the coincidence of the age Chaucer assigns to the child –

which is precisely the age at which 20th century English
children overgeneralize DO. I am thus inclined to trust
Chaucer's ear here, and conclude that children in the
south-east of England in the late 14th century could have
grammars rather like their modern counterparts in this
respect. If this is accepted, then it follows that DO-
support must have been quite common in the speech that the
adults in Chaucer's circle addressed to children, presumably in questions and negatives, where Chaucer does
occasionally use them in writing, more in prose than verse.
Now the speech of Chaucer's social circle - upper civil
servants attached to the court - must have been influential in the formation of the written and spoken standards,
though on the latter we have very little evidence.
Chaucer's child could be a key witness to the modernity of
the syntax of a very influential group of late ME London
speakers: the post-Chaucer generation.

NOTES

*   I wish to thank M. Briody for bibliographical advice on Celtic.
1. As the distinction between speech and writing is essential to the argument, I reserve *do* for the written form only, and use DO for the spoken form and in general.
2. Reports of work on the compilation of historical text corpora support this point. The compilers of the Helsinki Corpus of diachronic texts found no material to place under the prototype category "Private Letters" or "Drama" before late ME. The reasons are both accident of survival, and also no doubt the different role of writing in a more oral society with a pre-paper technology. This means that the OE corpus is unavoidably skewed, even though it represents the total of OE running text. The formal-ization achieved by Biber and Finegan (1986, and Biber 1986) only goes to show how deficient the total surviving OE corpus is in the most-speech like written genres. In terms of Biber's "dimensions", the OE corpus would seem to be weighted towards the linguistic forms characteristic of Informational vs. Involved Production, Explicit vs. Situation-Dependent Reference, and Abstract vs. Non-Abstract Information. Thus it is not surprising that some forms which were possibly typical of spoken OE should fail to appear in

the OE corpus, but begin to appear in written ME, because of the more genres represented, as well as the availability of regional dialect texts. (DO-support is a significant factor in Biber's analyses.)

3. On the role of children in creating simplified language varieties, see Trudgill (1978), Poussa (1985), Giacalone Ramat (1986: 318-19), on generational contact in language death, Dorian (1981) and Schmidt (1985), on language convergence, Gumperz & Wilson (1971). (The last is a study of accomplished convergence, and does not consider the possible role of children as agents.)

4. Hiltunen (1983: 92) remarks in a discussion of the apparently sudden loss of the OE verbal prefixes in ME:
   "Right from the first pages of *Ancr*, for instance, one cannot avoid the impression of the prefixes having been swept away almost overnight".
   As the decline of the prefixes and emergence of the phrasal verb is significantly linked with the changeover to SVO word order, this is a telling observation.

5. The process by which phonological weakening precedes deletion of the DO-marker was observed by Rickford (1986: 270-1) in younger speakers of Sea Island Gullah, who deleted the earlier habitual marker *does*, still in use by older speakers. The order was:
   does (be) > /z/ > 0
   Sea Islands Gullah is a very conservative variety, probably descended from Barbados English, which was very little creolized from the English 17th-century south-western settlers (Cassidy 1980, Rickford 1986: 252). The older speakers' DO BE forms may well be derived from those of 17th century western English dialects, and thus may demonstrate the rules underlying the present Somerset forms.
   The process of phonological wear of non-prominent pre-verbal markers can be seen widely in the Caribbean creoles, e.g. in the Jamaican forms shown as Example 1. In this paradigm the original initial consonant of the verbal marker has been deleted, except in the case of the question form, as in Somerset. A similar deletion of the past punctual marker /di/ is possibly going on in the St Vincent paradigm given earlier (Example 2).

6. The theory that the modern south-western dialects represent the remaining upper lects of an English-Celtic creole continuum that once stretched across western England has an interesting corollary: it may provide the source of the DO BE base forms in the Caribbean creoles, with no need to posit HE speakers where they cannot be found in the historical record. HE would be bound to resemble the lower lects of such a continuum. The same problem is raised in lexis by Holm (1981: 46-51): how can we tell the difference between what is genuinely regional and what was once common spoken material, but fallen out of use except in conservative peripheral dialects, such as HE or Scots?

7. Rissanen (1985) comments that in 17th century New England texts, texts classified as speech-based show a significantly higher count

of periphrastic DO when compared to formal written styles of the same provenance. This differential is not found in contemporary Old World texts, and vanishes in the New England texts after the first century of settlement. The initial circumstances of the migration caused many ordinary people to express themselves in writing who in normal settled circumstances would not have needed to. Hence the idiom of the spoken language is less heavily filtered than usual, and Rissanen argues (1985: 177) that the source of periphrastic *do* have a spoken, not a literary origin. It should be pointed out that the settlers in the Plymouth Plantation were not from the west of England, but from the east, the Lincolnshire-Cambridgeshire area in particular. Dialect mixture (social rather than areal in this case), resulting in the syntactic avoidance of conflicting preterites, could be a contributory factor in the rise of weak affirmative *do* in the 17th century New England texts.

REFERENCES

Alleyne, M.C. 1980. *Comparative Afro-American: An historical study of English-based Afro-American dialects of the New World*. (= *Linguistica Extranea* 11. Ann Arbor: Karoma.
Andersen, R. 1979. "Expanding Schumann's pidginization hypothesis". *Language Learning* 29. 105-119.
Barnes, W. 1886. *A glossary of the Dorset Dialect with a Grammar*. London: Trübner; Reprinted 1970, St Peter Port, Guernsey: Stevens-Cox.
Biber, D. 1986. "Spoken and written textual dimensions in English: resolving the contradictory findings". *Lg* 62. 384-414.
Biber, D. & E. Finegan. 1986. "An initial typology of text types". *Corpus Linguistics* 2. 19-45.
Bickerton, D. 1973. "The nature of a creole continuum". *Lg* 49:3. 640-669.
Bickerton, D. 1975. *Dynamics of a creole system*. Cambridge: University Press.
Bickerton, D. 1981. *The roots of language*. Ann Arbor: Karoma.
Bliss, A. 1984. "English in the south of Ireland". *Language in the British Isles*. ed. by Peter Trudgill. 135-51. Cambridge: University Press.
Bopp, F. 1816. *Das Konjugationssystem der Sanskritsprache*. Frankfurt am Main: Andreä.
Braaten, B. 1967. "Notes on continuous tenses in English". *Norsk Tidskrift fur Sprogvidenskap* 21. 167-80.
Cassidy, F.G. 1980. "The place of Gullah". *AM* 55. 3-16.
Denison, D. 1985. "The origins of periphrastic *Do*: Ellegard and Visser reconsidered". In Eaton et al. 45-60.
Di Sciullo, U., P. Muysken & R. Singh. 1986. "Government and code-mixing". *JL* 22. 1-24.

Dorian, N. 1981. *Language death: the life cycle of a Scottish Gaelic dialect.* Philadelphia: University of Pennsylvania Press.

Eaton, R. et al. eds. *Papers from the 4th International Conference on English Historical Linguistics. (Amsterdam studies in the theory and history of linguistic science.* Vol. 41.) Amsterdam/Philadelphia: John Benjamins.

Ekwall, E. 1956. *Studies on the population of medieval London.* Stockholm: Almqvist & Wiksell.

Ellegård, A. 1953. *The Auxiliary Do: The establishment and regulation of its use in English.* (= Gothenburg Studies in English 2.) Stockholm: Almqvist & Wiksell.

Elworthy, T. 1877. An outline of the grammar of the dialect of West Somerset. *TPhS* 1877-8-9. Part II. 143-257. Reprinted 1878. London: Trübner.

Engblom, V. 1938. *On the Origin and Early Development of the Auxiliary Do.* (= Lund Studies in English, 6) Lund: Gleerup.

Erben, J. 1969. "*Tun* als Hilfsverb im heutigen Deutsch". *Festschrift für Hugo Moser.* ed. by Engel, U., P. Grebe, H. Rupp. 46-52. Düsseldorf: Pädegogischer Verlag Schwann.

Fisiak, J. ed. 1984. *Historical syntax.* (= Trends in linguistics: Studies and monographs 23. Berlin/New York: Mouton.

Fletcher, P. 1979. "The development of the verb phrase". *Language Acquisition.* ed. by Paul Fletcher & Michael Garman, 261-84.

Gelling, M. 1978. *Signposts to the past. Place-names and the history of England.* London: Dent.

Giacalone Ramat, A. 1986. "On language contact and syntactic change". In Kastovsky & Szwedek. 317-328.

Gumperz, J. and R. Wilson. 1971. "Convergence and creolization: a case from the Indo-Aryan/Dravidian border". *Pidginization and Creolization of Languages.* ed. by Del Hymes, 151-67. Cambridge: University Press.

Harris, J. 1984. "Syntactic variation and dialect divergence". *JL* 20. 303-27.

Harris, J. 1985. "Expanding the superstrate: habitual aspect markers in Atlantic Englishes". *Sheffield Working Papers in Linguistics.* 72-97.

Henry, P.L. 1957. *An Anglo-Irish Dialect of North Roscommon.* Dublin: University Press.

Hiltunen, R. 1983. *The decline of the prefixes and the beginnings of the English phrasal verb.* (= Annales Universitatis Turkuensis Ser. B. Tom. 160.) Turku.

Holm, J. 1981. "Sociolinguistic history and the creolist". *Historicity and Variation in Creole Studies.* ed. by A. Highfield & A. Valdman. 40-51. Ann Arbor: Karoma.

Hope-Taylor, B. 1977. *Yeavering: an Anglo-British centre of early Northumbria.* London: HMSO.

Ihalainen, O. 1976. "Periphrastic DO in affirmative sentences in the dialect of East Somerset". *NphM* 77. 608-622.

Ihalainen, O. 1981. "A note on eliciting data in dialectology: the case of periphrastic *do*". *NphM* 82. 25-7.

Ihaiainen, O. 1982. "On the notion 'possible grammatical change': a look at a perfectly good change that did not quite make it". *SAP* 3-11.
Ihalainen, O. 1985. "Synchronic variation and linguistic change: evidence from British English Dialects". In Eaton et al. 61-72.
Ihalainen, O. 1986. "An inquiry into the nature of mixed grammars: two cases of grammatical variation in dialectal British English". In Kastovsky & Szwedek. 372-9.
Ihalainen, O. (1987, forthcoming). "Towards a grammar of the Somerset dialect: a case study of the language of JM". *NphM* 88. 71-86.
Jackson, K. 1953. *Language and History in Early Britain*. Edinburgh: University Press.
Jones, G. 1976. "Multiple estates and early settlement". In Sawyer, P. ed. *Medieval settlement: continuity and change*. Reprinted in Sawyer, P. ed. 1979. *English medieval settlement*. 9-34. London: Arnold.
Kastovsky, D. & A. Szwedek, eds. 1986. *Linguistics across Historical and Geographical Boundaries*. Vol. 1: *Linguistic Theory and Historical Linguistics*. Berlin, New York, Amsterdam: Mouton.
Kuhn, S.M. 1977. "Middle English *don* and *maken*: some observations on semantic patterns". *AS* 52. 5-18.
Kuhn, S.M. 1986. "Old English *macian*: its origin and dissemination". *JEL* 19. 49-93.
Kytö, M. and M. Rissanen. 1983. "The syntactic study of early American English". *NphM* 34. 470-90.
Langenfelt, G. 1933. *Select Studies in Colloquial English of the Late Middle Ages*. Lund: Gleerup.
Leeds, W. 1974. *Herefordshire Speech: The South-west Midland Dialect as Spoken in Herefordshire and its Environs*. Pound Cottage, Upton Crews, Ross-on-Wye: the author.
Le Page, R. and A. Tabouret-Keller. 1985. *Acts of Identity. Creole-based approaches to language and ethnicity*. Cambridge: University Press.
Myres, J.N.L. 1986. *The English Settlements*. Oxford: Clarendon Press.
Mühlhäusler, P. 1986. *Pidgin and Creole Linguistics*. Oxford: Basil Blackwell.
Nevalainen, T. & M. Rissanen. 1986. "Do you support the DO support? Emphatic and non-emphatic DO in affirmative statements in present-day spoken English". *Papers from the 3rd Scandinavian Symposium on Syntactic Variation*. ed. by Sven Jacobson, 35-50. (= *Stockholm Studies in English* 65). Stockholm: Almqvist & Wiksell International.
Poussa, P. 1982. "The evolution of early standard English: the creolization hypothesis". *SAP* 14. 70-85.
Poussa, P. 1985. "The development of the 3rd person singular pronoun system in the English of a bilingual Finnish-English child". *Scandinavian Working Papers in Bilingualism* 5. 1-39. Stockholm: University of Stockholm Institute of Linguistics.
Preusler, W. 1938, 1939-40. "Keltischer Einfluss im Englischen". *Indogermanische Forschungen* 56, 57.
Prokosch, E. 1939. *A comparative Germanic grammar*. Philadelphia: Yale University.

Rickford, J. 1983. "What happens in decreolization". *Pidginization and creolization as language acquisition.* ed. by R. Andersen, 298-319. Rowley, Mass: Newberry House.
Rickford, J. 1986. "Social contact and linguistic diffusion: Hiberno-English and New World Black English". *Lg* 62. 245-89.
Rissanen, M. 1985. "Periphrastic *do* in affirmative sentences in early American English", *JEL* 18. 163-183.
Samuels, M. 1972. *Linguistic evolution.* Cambridge: University Press.
Schmidt, A. 1985. *Young people's Dyirbal: an example of language death from Australia.* Cambridge: University Press.
Schumann, J. 1978. *The pidginization process.* Rowley, Mass: Newberry House.
Stein, D. 1983. "Stylistic aspects of syntactic change". *FoLH* 6. 153-178.
Stein, D. 1985. *Natürlicher syntaktischer Sprachwandel. Untersuchungen zur Entstehung der englischen 'Do'-Periphrase in Fragen.* (= Tuduv Studie: Reihe Sprach- und Literatur-wissenschaften, 19.) München: Tuduv-Verlagsgesellschaft.
Tieken, I. van Ostade. 1983. "*Do*-support in the writings of Lady Mary Wortley Montagu: a change in progress". *FoLH* 6. 127-151.
Trudgill, P. 1978. "Creolization in reverse". *TPhS* 1976-7. 32-50.
Trudgill, P., V.K. Edwards & B. Weltens. 1983. *Grammatical Characteristics of Non-Standard Dialects of English in the British Isles: A Survey of Research.* (Report to the Social Service Research Council.)
Visser, F. 1969. *An historical syntax of the English language.* Vol. III. Leiden: E.J. Brill.
Wagner, H. 1959. *Das Verbum in den Sprachen der Britischen Inseln.* (= *Buchreihe der Zeitschrift für Celtische Philologie* 1.) Tübingen: Max Niemeyer.
Wakelin, M. 1986. *The Southwest of England.* (= *Varieties of English Around the World: Text Series* 5.) Amsterdam & Philadelphia: John Benjamins.
Wright, J. 1905. *English dialect grammar.* Oxford: Clarendon Press.

A NEW KIND OF METRICAL EVIDENCE IN OLD ENGLISH POETRY

GEOFFREY RUSSOM
Brown University

It is now more than a decade since the appearance of Liberman and Prince (1977), which presented a theory of metrical phonology employing the concept of the metrical tree. The authors introduced the metrical tree with two familiar observations. They noted, first, that in phrases like black bird (any bird of that color), the last constituent is typically most prominent, whereas in lexical compounds like blackbird (Turdus merula), the first constituent predominates. The other familiar observation had to do with preservation of relative prominence under embedding. In a phrase like blackbird pie, the final constituent has the greatest prominence, as we would expect, and -bird remains subordinate to black-.

A tree diagram for blackbird pie appears below:

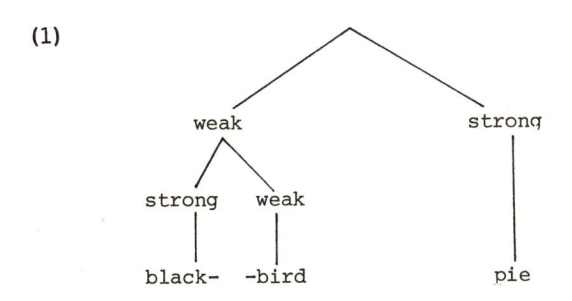

(1)

```
            weak              strong
           /    \               |
        strong  weak            |
          |      |              |
        black-  -bird          pie
```

Such a diagram differs signficantly from the type of representation employed in The Sound Pattern of English (Chomsky and Halle (1968)). In an SPE representation, each stressed syllable is labeled with a

number corresponding to its degree of prominence. No theoretical
limit is imposed on the number of such degrees. The metrical tree has
only two types of labels, strong and weak. Degrees of prominence are
represented not as features of segments but in terms of phonological
constituency. The first constituent in (1) at the level of the phrase
is blackbird, which is assigned to a weak node indicating its
subordination to the second constituent, pie. The relative prominence
of black- and -bird is indicated by their respective assignment
to strong and weak nodes embedded under the weak node that represents
blackbird. Possibilities of embedding are narrowly constrained by the
requirement of binary branching. At any given level of structure, the
only permissible branchings are strong-weak and weak-strong.

Stress trees pose two distinct but interrelated problems for the
theoretician. One is a problem familiar also in syntax: that of
determining how much hierarchical information in a tree is available
to rules of the grammar. Each node on the tree has a well-defined
relationship to every other node, but some of these relationships seem
to have no linguistic significance. Another problem has to do with
rhythmic disturbance of the expected relative prominence pattern for a
given constituent structure. The rising stress in compound adjectives
like good-looking, for instance, is not always preserved under
embedding. In the familiar example good-looking lifeguard, the
adjective has falling rather than rising stress.[1]

Phonetic contours of this type have been explained in terms of a
"rhythm rule" that modifies relative prominence relations among
stressed syllables to produce a more euphonic strong-weak alternation.
Liberman and Prince (1977: 316) illustrate the role of rhythm by means
of a relative prominence projection rule that eliminates phonetically
insignificant structure from trees to produce "grid patterns". The
grid patterns are then evaluated for euphony and modified when found
wanting. The obscuring effect of rhythm makes it difficult to justify
claims about the geometry of tree structures. Prince (1983) and
Selkirk (1984) have in fact suggested that an enriched theory of grids

might dispense with phonological trees altogether. However, Hayes (1984) has subsequently called attention to certain rules that seem to act on underlying tree structure, and which cannot be accommodated by the pure-grid theories.

A remarkable feature of the tree-versus-grid debate has been the systematic use of evidence from poetic meter, notably in the work of Hayes and Kiparsky.[2] Kiparsky (1977) showed that some metrical rules apply to underlying strong-weak patterns of phonological constituency rather than to patterns of relative phonetic prominence. Hayes (1983: 389-91) pointed out that such rules cannot be formulated within the pure-grid theories proposed since Kiparsky wrote. I would like to suggest that the constraints on alliteration in Old English poetry provide a new kind of evidence for a level of phonological structure best represented by trees. In fact, the placement of alliteration depends on features of arboreal geometry so subtle that they are generally dismissed as insignificant.

The methodology I sketch below will be somewhat different from that employed by Hayes and Kiparsky. These researchers deal with canonical poets of the modern English period, and they are primarily interested in the underlying structure of linguistic material to which the metrical rules apply. The metrical rules themselves have a mode of operation so uncomplicated that detailed inquiry into their nature seems unnecessary. The most important rule, for example, simply forbids placement of a strong syllable on a weak metrical position. There are many interesting problems with respect to what counts as a strong syllable in canonical English poetry, but the rest seems almost self-evident. My intention here, on the other hand, is to discuss a rule with a rather complex mode of operation, and I shall attempt to obtain linguistic evidence from the rule itself.

Kuryłowicz (1970: 16-20) suggested that the rule determining the placement of alliterating syllables in Beowulf could be regarded as a poeticized version of the Old English compound stress rule. Kuryłowicz made no attempt to state the alliteration rule in general terms. When properly formalized, however, his suggestion can be

supported with several types of evidence, as we shall see below. The
alliteration rule has special significance because it is not
restricted to the domain of Old English lexical compounds, which
rarely have more than two constituents, but creates patterns of
relative prominence that can involve four, five, or even six
constituents. In addition, it seems best, for reasons I have
discussed in detail elsewhere,[3] to assume that the rule does not apply
to the stressed syllables of actual phonetic material, rather to the
strong metrical positions occupied by those stressed syllables.
Consider for a moment how implausible it would be to claim that
alliteration actually changed the stress contour of an Old English
utterance. When we use alliteration today in a phrase like big, bad
wolf, the nuclear stress rule operates just as usual, assigning the
greatest prominence to non-alliterating wolf. Alliteration certainly
foregrounds the pairing of big and bad, but without any acoustic
distortion. If rules that create alliterative prominence do not apply
to phonetic material, of course, we would expect them to operate
without interference from the rhythmic factors that obscure underlying
phonological structure.

Several lines of inquiry suggest an intimate connection between
Old English stress and alliteration. We notice, first, a strong
tendency for alliterating syllables to occur in major category words
such as nouns and adjectives (see OEM, section 7.2). Root syllable in
these morphological types would be expected to bear strong stress.
Finite verbs have a significantly lower probability of alliteration.
It is generally assumed that these forms underwent subordination at
the level of the phrase like the finite verbs of modern German (cf.
Kiparsky (1966)). Proclitic function words such as prepositions and
conjunctions never alliterate, and pronouns alliterate only in a
handful of cases where they seem to have borne contrastive stress.

Old English lexical compounds behave very consistently with
regard to alliteration. Such compounds have primary stress on the
root syllable of the first constituent, and this is the syllable that

alliterates as well. In a compound like hand-ge-weorc "handiwork", for example, only the h- of hand- may alliterate; the -w- of the subordinated root -weorc may never do so. Alliteration does count as signficiant in the secondary constituent of a self-alliterating compound like brȳd-būr "bride-bower, women's dwelling-place". When a self-alliterating compound appears in poetry, its subordinated constituent must occupy a metrical position where alliteration is permitted. The relative prominence of constituents in Old English compounds seems to be unaffected by rhythmic factors, at least so far as alliteration is concerned. The secondary constituent never achieves sufficient prominence to take the alliteration away from the primary constituent.[4]

The domain of alliteration in Old English poetry is the line. Representative lines from Beowulf appear in (2) below,[5] with alliterating consonants indicated by capital letters:

(2) (a) [Wado] [Weallende],   [Wedera] [cealdost] 546
         water welling, of-weathers coldest
         "surging sea and very cold weather"

    (b) [Lēod] [scyldunga],   [Lange] [hwile] 2159
         prince of-the-Scyldings, for-a-long while
         "the prince of the Scyldings, for a long while"

Manuscript punctuation, which correlates with a prominent line-internal syntactic break, justifies a subdivision of the line into half-lines (cf. Klaeber (1950:c)). The half-lines displayed above are separated by extra spaces according to standard editorial practice. Like several other metrists, I also subdivide the half-line into two feet. The boundaries of the feet are indicated by brackets. In the present theoretical context I should point out that I use the term "foot" simply to indicate the smallest significant domain within the poetic line. I do not mean to evoke the technical sense of "foot" sometimes employed in phonology (e.g. in Hayes (1981)).

Although metrists are generally in agreement about the location of Old English line and half-line boundaries, there has been no consensus about the location of foot boundaries. The theories of Sievers (1885, 1893) and Pope (1942) divide the half-line differently in a number of cases. Deciding between these alternatives is difficult because there is a bewildering variety of foot patterns, and because neither theorist can derive the set of foot patterns from more general principles. I have been arguing for some time that when we adopt the definition of "word" required for Old English word-level phonology, the principles defining the set of Old English feet come clearly into view. As it turns out, there is a foot pattern for every word pattern of the language, and those patterns unattested as feet are not characteristic of native words.[6] In (3), I provide representative examples of Old English word patterns and a notation for the corresponding feet.[7] An upper-case S represents the <u>primary arsis</u>, a metrical position abstracted from a fully stressed syllable. A lower-case s represents the <u>secondary arsis</u>, a position abstracted from a syllable with secondary stress. Each lower-case x represents a weak position abstracted from a syllable with less than secondary stress:

(3) FOOT PATTERNS   CORRESPONDING WORDS[8]

x	ond ("and")
S	gōd ("good"), n.sg.fem.
xx	oþþe ("or")
Sx	dryhten ("lord")
Ss	brȳd-būr ("bride-bower")
Sxx	bealdode ("he encouraged")
Ssx	sǣ-mannes ("Sailor's"), g.sg.
Sxs	hand-ge-weorc ("handiwork")
Sxxs	sibbe-ge-driht ("band of kinsmen")

The definition of the foot proposed here makes it possible to
provide a simple definition of the half-line as a pair of easily
recoverable feet.⁹ As we shall see, this concept of the half-line has
significant implications for our understanding of alliteration and
stress. The hypothesis that feet derive from words is quite compatible
with Kuryłowicz's hypothesis that the alliteration rule derives from
the rule for compound stress. Since compound stress integrates
smaller words into larger words, a poeticized compound stress would
provide a natural device for integrating feet, the metrical analogues
of words, into the larger metrical constituents of half-line and line.
The rule governing foot patterns and the rule governing alliterative
patterns would be relatively easy to learn in conjunction, since they
would interact in accord with the native speaker's expectations.¹⁰

Permissible combinations of the feet listed in (3) yield a
considerable number of half-line types. I do not have space here to
develop the constraints on foot pairings or to discuss the
alliterative patterns attested in each type of half-line.
Fortunately, since we are interested in complex patterns of
subordination, we can confine our attention for the most part to the
so-called "heavy half-lines" with three stressed syllables. The rule
I propose for these heavy types will apply straightforwardly to the
other types as well (see OEM, chapters 7, 8).

Consider the following:

(4) (a)   [Flet] [innan-weard]   1976b
           floor   within

           "the floor inside the hall"
           [S] [Sxs]

     (b)   [Hond] [rond gefēng]   2609b
           hand   shield seized

           "the hand seized the shield"
           [S] [Sxs]

(c)   [Sweord] [[Swāte] [fāh]]   1286a
sword with-blood stained
"sword stained with blood"
[s] [[Sx] [s]]

(d)   [[Sunu] [dēoð]] [wrecan]   1278b
son's death to avenge
"to avenge the son's death"
[[S] [s]] [Sx]

The least complex sort of half-line with three stressed syllables is represented by (4a), which contains an underived word of major category accompanied by a compound. Such a word pair conforms in the most obvious way to the requirement that each half-line should be analyzable as a pair of wordlike feet. Half-lines like (4b) also appear in Old English poems. If feet correspond to words, such half-lines might seem to consist of three feet. When we divide the half-line at the major constituent break, however, we can see that its two natural subconstituents conform rather closely to available foot patterns. Since Hond is a single word, of course, there is no question about its ability to constitute a foot. In the more complex second foot, note that the line-final -fēng is the root syllable of a finite verb, which has relatively weak stress. The natural constituent rond gefēng therefore has a stress contour much like the contour of a lexical compound such as innanweard or handgeweorc. Word groups like rond gefēng behave exactly like compounds with respect to alliteration. Like handgeweorc, which alliterates only on h-, the word group rond gefēng alliterates only on r-, and may never alliterate on the -f- of the verbal root -fēng.

We are now ready to consider some ways in which alliteration mimics the integrating effect of the compound stress rule. Let us begin with a kind of metrical subordination not noticed by Kuryłowicz, which occurs at the level of the foot in certain half-lines with three strongly stressed words, as for example in (4c). Nothing in the history of the Germanic languages would lead us to expect subordination of stress on the adjective fāh, which seems unsuitable as a substitute for the secondary constituent of a compound. The relations of relative prominence that help the audience recover the underlying pattern of (4b) are absent here, and it is difficult at first to see how such a half-line could be analyzed into two feet. However, when we divide half-lines of this type at the major syntactic break, a striking generalization emerges. In every case, the first word of the heavy foot alliterates.[11] Alliteration on swāte in (4c) seems to act as a principle of cohesion, rendering what would otherwise constitute two feet equivalent to one.[12] I represent the integrity of the heavy foot in (4c) by means of an additional pair of brackets enclosing the bracketed words [swāte] and [fāh]. Not all half-lines with three strongly stressed syllables require a second alliteration. In (4d), for example, the major constituent break falls after the second word. Only the alliteration on sunu is required to make the heavy first foot cohesive.[13]

We can state the rule for alliteration below:

(5) When two metrical constituents appear within the same metrical domain, and each constituent contains a primary arsis, label the first constituent strong and the second constituent weak, and mark the leftmost primary arsis for alliteration.[14]

Rule (5) is essentially the Old English compound rule, but it is not confined to any morphological domain and it assigns alliteration to metrical positions rather than assigning prominence to phonological consitutents.

At the level of the foot, the metrical subordination applies to small foot pairs like those exemplified in (4c-d), marking the first arsis for alliteration. We rule out unacceptable heavy half-lines by requiring that the strongly stressed syllable of a noun or adjective must always occupy a primary arsis. The only feet that will accommodate two such syllables will now be those in which the first arsis is marked for alliteration by (5). A half-line like the hypothetical *[Sweord] [blōde] [fāh], which is identical to (4c) in syntax and meaning, will be interpreted as an unmetrical three-foot sequence [S] [Sx] [S]. Note that (5) will not apply within a foot that contains a primary arsis and a secondary arsis. The secondary arsis is defined in advance as weaker than the primary arsis, and need not undergo further subordination to make the foot cohesive.

Within the domains of half-line and line, rule (5) produces the patterns of relative metrical prominence discussed by Kuryłowicz. Refer once more to (2a-b). These exemplify the permissible alliterative patterns for lines consisting of four strongly stressed words. Each foot in (2a) and (2b) contains a single noun or adjective, with the main stress of the word obligatorily assigned to a primary arsis. The lines differ significantly in rhythm, but rule (5), which recognizes only the primary arsis and the domain boundary, will apply to both in the same way. So far as alliteration is concerned, we can treat such lines as if they had four feet of the form S, disregarding x positions. The resulting metrical tree structure is displayed below:

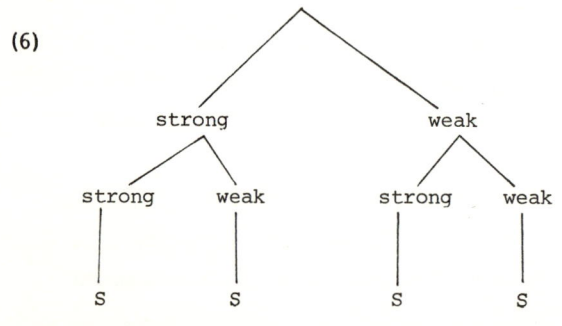

(6)
```
              /\
         strong     weak
          /\         /\
    strong weak  strong weak
      |     |      |     |
      S     S      S     S
```

Within each half-line, (5) has subordinated the second S position and assigned alliteration to the first. At the level of the line, (5) has subordinated the second half-line and assigned alliteration to the leftmost S of the first half-line, redundantly in this particular structure.[15]

Constraints on alliteration for the second half-line are not identical to those for the first. In the first half-line, a subordinated primary arsis need not contain an alliterating syllable, as example (2b) shows, but may optionally contain such a syllable, as in example (2a). The corresponding arsis of the second half-line never contains an alliterating syllable, however. What sort of rule would produce an asymmetry of this kind?

The rule we require can be expressed in tree-structural terms as a prohibition against alliterating syllables in a weak constituent of a weak constituent. Note that in (6) the path through the tree from the fourth S position to the unlabeled root node at the top passes through two weak nodes. No such position may contain an alliterating syllable.[16] The path from the second S position to the root node, on the other hand, passes through only one weak node. Alliteration is not ruled out for a position of this kind. The distinction between a weak constituent of a weak constituent and a weak constituent of a strong constituent is so subtle that it has never been exploited, to my knowledge, by phonological theory. The pervasive influence of rhythm always seems to disrupt the underlying prominence relations of such weak nonprimary stresses. It is only because metrical subordination operates on metrical positions rather than on phonetic material that the hierarchical structure of the tree becomes accessible to observation.

A closer look at details of alliteration again reveals evidence not noticed by Kuryłowicz that would tend to support his hypothesis. Consider first some half-line patterns in which the second foot is heavy:

(7) (a) [Lēof] [Lēod-cyning]   54a
          beloved nation-king
          "beloved high king"

     (b) [þrȳðlīc] [[þegna] [hēap]]   400a
          splendid thanes' troop
          "splendid troop of thanes"

Here as usual we divide the line at the major constituent break to define the foot domains. The corresponding tree structure is given below:

(8)

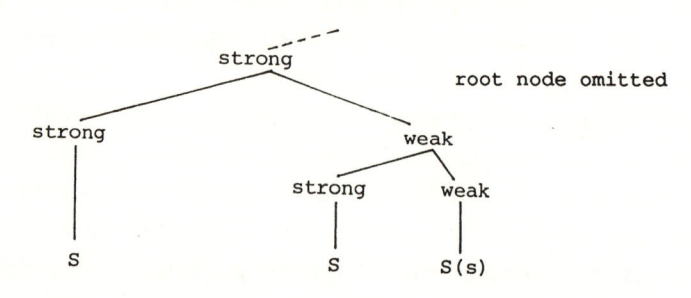

```
              strong
             /      \
         strong     weak          root node omitted
           |       /    \
           S   strong   weak
                 |        |
                 S      S(s)
```

Since (7a-b) appear in the first half of the line, the highest-level node in (0) will be marked strong. Note that -cyning of (7a) and heap of (7b) correspond to weak constituents of weak constituents, and should not be replaceable with alliterating words. In fact, this type of half-line never has two alliterating syllables in the heavy second foot.

Now consider the following, which also appear in the first half of the line:

(9) (a) Gūð- Gēata / lēod   1538a
         War- Geats' prince
         "Prince of the War- Geats"

    (b) Syn-Snǣdum / Swealh 743a
         in-great-gulps gobbled
         "gobbled in great gulps"

    (c) Swutol Sang / scopes 90a
         clear song of-the-poet
         "clear song of the poet"

    (d) Beorht Bēacen / godes 570a
         bright beacon of-God
         "bright beacon of God"

In these examples the major constituent break falls after the second stressed syllable, and the first foot is heavy. The corresponding tree diagram differs significantly from diagram (8):

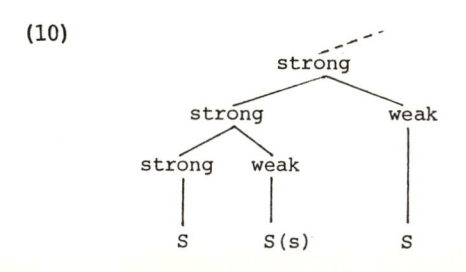

(10)

```
              strong
           /        \
       strong        weak
       /    \          |
   strong   weak       |
     |       |         |
     S      S(s)       S
```

The first arsis in (10) will be marked for obligatory alliteration when (5) applies at the level of the line. If an optional alliterating syllable appears, it usually occupies the last arsis, which is the weak constituent of a strong constituent (see (9b) for example). Note, however, that the more deeply embedded second arsis is also a weak constituent of a strong constituent. Half-lines like (9a-d) show that this arsis may contain an alliterating syllable, just as we would expect. The significance of such half-lines has gone almost entirely unnoticed, probably because there are only four of them in Beowulf (see OEM, p. 78). Yet all four yield perfectly good sense, and no editor, to my knowledge, has ever suggested that they should be emended. Moreover, it seems clear that alliterative patterns like those in (9) are uncommon because the linguistic preconditions for them are usually absent, and for no other reason. A foot with two alliterating syllables necessarily contains either a self-alliterating compound or a pair of stressed words; but self-alliterating compounds are of course quite difficult to obtain,[17] and the Beowulf poet has a marked tendency to place stressed word groups in the second foot rather than in the first foot (see OEM, section 2.5). Only eighteen compounds like Gūð-Gēata appear in Beowulf. The two half-lines like (9a-b) constitute a considerable percentage of this small total.[18] The two half-lines like (9c-d) are members of an even more select group of nine verses with a pair of stressed words in the first foot.[19] There is no evidence, then, for a rule forbidding double alliteration in the first foot. Unless we wish to propose twenty-seven new emendations, we must regard the alliterative patterns of (9a-d) as acceptable.

The importance of evidence from obscure corners of the poetic system has been emphasized in recent work on phonology. Kiparsky (1977: 201) reflects that "such minutiae are unlikely to have ever been the subject of much reflection by even the most technique conscious of poets". Accordingly, "any system that we discover in them is that much more sure to reflect not some self-imposed learned or artifical convention but the very nature of rhythm and language" (cf. Hayes (1983: 390)). It is worth noting, I think, that the metrical constraints of Old English verse evolved as part of a pre-literate, formulaic technique of composition (see Magoun (1953), Lord (1960)).[20] In a tradition of this kind, we would expect learning to take place almost entirely by intuition rather than by precept. The Yugoslavian bards described in Jakobson (1963), for example, knew immediately when a novice had violated a constraint on syllable count or placement of the caesura, but had no ability whatever to describe the violation. They could only object that the novice was "singing out of tune" (see Jakobson (1979: 195-6)). It is hard to imagine such bards learning constraints on poetic form that were both complex and purely artificial. To the extent that principles of poetic form derive from principles of linguistic form, on the other hand, the bard's task reduces to one of identifying metrical rules as analogues of rules known in advance. Ever since Sievers published his description of the meter in 1885, scholars have been attempting to explain Old English alliterative patterns in terms of a "simple" rule that would be suitable for explicit instruction. Several rules of this type have been proposed, but they all leave important facts unexplained, and none has achieved consensus.[21] The only simple rule that seems to work is the one proposed by Kuryłowicz, which equates alliteration with stress assignment in compounds; and this rule is only simple if we factor out of it what the learner already knew. The ability of Old English poets to acquire rule (5) testifies to the value of alliterative constraints as linguistic evidence.

Let us now apply some of the models proposed in generative phonology to the Old English poetic data. The best model will be the one that assigns the correct relative prominence to metrical positions in the same way that it assigns relative prominence to phonological constituents. We begin with an SPE-type compound rule, which will operate on bracketed segment strings. The elements of the poetic string will be strong metrical positions; in a corresponding large compound word, they would be stressed syllables. The bracketed string corresponding to (2a-b) and many similar lines can be represented as [[[S] [S]] [[S] [S]]]. Only strong metrical positions need to be included, since only they are affected by the subordination rule. The derivation proceeds as below (cf. SPE, 21, for the comparable procedures with linguistic material):

(11) [[[1] [1]] [[1] [1]]]   unsubordinated S's with 1-stress
     [[1   1] [1   1]]   bracket erasure
     [[1   2] [1   2]]   subordination within half-line
     [1   2   1   2   ]   bracket erasure
     [1   3   2   3   ]   subordination within line

In the first step of the derivation, each strong constituent has been assigned 1-stress, and no subordination has yet occurred (for typographical convenience, I simply replace the S's with the stress numerals rather than placing the stress numerals above the S's). Next the "Bracket Erasure Convention" removes the innermost brackets, which in this case are foot boundaries. The compound rule then applies within each half-line domain, assigning 1-stress to the first element. The "Stress Subordination Convention" reduces the prominence of the second element in each half-line by one degree. After erasure of the half-line boundaries, the compound rule applies a second time,

assigning 1-stress to the leftmost element of the line, and the Stress
Subordination Convention again lowers the prominence of all other
elements by one degree. The resulting pattern is 1323, yet what we
need to explain the alliterative patterns is 1324. This type of rule
also fails to capture the relative prominence distinctions represented
in tree structures (8) and (10). Alliterative patterns testify to a
contrast between 124 in (8) and 132 in (10), but the SPE rule gives us
123 and 132 instead:

(12) (a) [[S] [[S] [S]]]   bracketed string for (8)
         [[1] [[1] [1]]]   first assignment of 1-stress
         [[1] [1   1]]   bracket erasure
         [[1] [1   2]]   subordination within foot
         [1   1   2   ]   bracket erasure
         [1   2   3   ]   subordination within half-line

     (b) [[[S] [S]] [S]]   bracketed string for (10)
         [[[1] [1]] [1]]   first assignment of 1-stress
         [[1   1   ] [1]]   bracket erasure
         [[1   2   ] [1]]   subordination within foot
         [1   2   1]   bracket erasure
         [1   3   2]   subordination within half-line

The trees introduced by Liberman and Prince (1977) will of course
provide a way of capturing the necessary distinctions. It should be
noted, however, that such distinctions are filtered out by the
Relative Prominence Projection Rule (RPPR), quoted below from Liberman
and Prince (1977: 316):

(13) RPPR

In any constituent on which the strong-weak relation is defined,
the designated terminal element[22] of its strong subconstituent
is metrically stronger than the designated terminal element of
its weak subconstituent.

The RPPR captures only relations of relative prominence that involve strong constituents. When applied to the tree in (6), the RPPR will preserve the information that the leftmost S of the first half-line is stronger than the leftmost S of the second half-line, but it will not transmit any information about the relative strength of the other two S positions. In this model, there is no systematic attempt to deny the existence of underlying prominence distinctions such as those we have considered here.[23] Liberman and Prince simply leave open the question of how much tree structure is psychologically real. What the authors do suggest is that the subtler distinctions are lost in the course of a phonological derivation, and will never surface as distinctions of syllable stress. The poetic evidence suggests that this claim should be subjected to further inspection, but does not provide decisive evidence against it.

In the pure-grid theories, a stress-assignment rule will strengthen the first or last prominent constituent within a given domain (cf. Prince (1983: 19-20)). The Germanic compound rule formulated by Selkirk (1984: 50), strengthens the first stressed syllable relative to all other stressed syllables within the domain of the word. Applied to the structure [[[S][S]][[S][S]]], Selkirk's rule would produce something like the following derivation (with S's of the metrical pattern replaced by X's on the lowest level of the grid):

(14)
```
                          X
      X  X      ⟹         X  X    (within half-line)


                          X
      X  X      ⟹         X  X    (within line)
      X X X X             X X X X
```

In grid notation, relative prominence is proportional to the height of the column of X's. Strengthening is represented in (14) by adding X's above the leftmost element of a domain in such a way that its column becomes the highest. When one column becomes relatively higher, of

course, other columns become relatively lower. There is no need for a
distinct Stress Subordination Convention. Within the half-line,
Selkirk's rule strengthens the leftmost element. Within the line,
strengthening of the leftmost element yields a 1323 contour identical
to that produced by the SPE rule. The desired 1324 contour cannot be
derived by the pure-grid theories. What is special about pure-grid
rules is that they apply directly to syntactic surface structures.
Subtle features of relative prominence represented by metrical trees
will not be created at any level. This amounts to a claim that the
distinction between weak constituents of weak constituents and weak
constituents of strong constituents is never accessible to linguistic
intuition. I do not see how such a claim can be reconciled with the
poetic evidence.[24]

It is especially instructive to view our data within the
framework proposed by Hayes (1983, 1984). Although he advocates a
larger role for the grid than do Liberman and Prince (1977) or
Kiparsky (1977), Hayes concludes that trees are indispensible after
all. The two elements of the model are not redundant, but represent
separate theoretical components or modules, with trees being the
domain of relative prominence rules, while grids are the domain of
phonetically conditioned rhythmic rules. The rhythmic rules may not
even be linguistic rules, understood as competencies uniquely
associated with language use. According to Hayes (1984: 73), they
might instead reflect general principles of well-formed rhythmic
behaviour. If relative prominence assignment is independent of
euphony constraints in the way Hayes describes, we can begin to see
how a linguistic stress rule could become a rule of poetic
foregrounding. The process would appear to involve disconnecting the
phonetic "output device" and reconnecting the relative prominence
component to an output device that produces metrical patterns:
something like the "metrical pattern generator" of Kiparsky (1988:
190).

What I have tried to show is that a poetic text of interest to historical linguists can be made to yield a new kind of metrical evidence. Metrical constraints of the sort we have considered here allow the linguist to extract rules from phonological systems somewhat as the microbiologist extracts functioning subcomponents from the cellular structures that normally confine them. There is no reason to suppose that the Old English situation is unique. Research into other poetic traditions should allow us to extract a variety of linguistic rules for study in isolation. The extraction procedure is sure to involve doubt and difficulty, though perhaps less than that confronting a physicist interested in quarks. Rapid progress may require a kind of cooperation between theoreticians and philologists that many now find it difficult to imagine. Considering what we stand to gain, however, it seems worthwhile to proceed.

NOTES

1. Although this example is widely cited in American work on metrical phonology, it does not seem to work for some speakers. One of my readers claimed to get *good-looking* as SW in all positions..The WS value of my dialect is evident in the cliché question, "*What's cookin', good-lookin'*?" As traditionally uttered, this divides into two short "lines" with the same rhythm, and gives a normal English rhyme, not the sort of "Celtic" rhyme provided e.g. by *rain* and *freight-train*.
2. Metrical phonology and metrics have become so intertwined that technical terms in one field often bear a confusing resemblance to technical terms in the other. At this point, for example, I should probably make it clear that I use the phrases *metrical rule* and *metrical position* below in reference to poetic form.
3. The present argument is based in part on Russom (1987a), cited henceforth as OEM. The theory of Old English meter presented in that work cannot of course be defended in detail here; I can only attempt to demonstrate some implications of OEM for generative phonology.
4. Apparent exceptions to this rule in lines 445a and 1379a of *Beowulf* may be otherwise explained (see OEM, pp. 97, 122-3).
5. Citations from *Beowulf* are based on the edition of Klaeber (1950).
6. For detailed discussion of the relationship between word and foot in Old English, see OEM, chapter 1. Since the OEM theory derives "word feet" from morphological constituents, it may not be possible to reduce the "word foot" concept to the phonologist's concept of "foot" (cf. OEM, notes 5 and 6 to chapter 1, pp. 156-57). Any such reduction would have to accommodate the fundamental rule that Old English half-lines contain two feet (see OEM, pp. 2, 57, 145).
7. Readers may observe that large compound forms like g. sg. *handgeweorces* are missing from the list. These forms correspond to feet only in the so-called "hypermetrical patterns" (see OEM, chapter 6).
8. For detailed discussion of feet derived from unstressed words, see OEM, pp. 10-14. With regard to the analysis of verbs like *bealdode* as Sxx rather than Ssx, see OEM, pp. 13, 48-9.
9. The conditions under which a half-line may contain more than two stressed words will be specified below. On the use of extrametrical unstressed words, see OEM, chapter 3.
10. The theory of alliteration in Suzuki (1985) employs the concept of relative prominence proposed in Kuryłowicz (1970), but adds to it a poeticized version of the Universal Association Concention, which bars crossing of association lines in autosegmental representations. Since the theory proposed here requires only the concept of relative prominence, it is significantly simpler than Suzuki's. It should be noted, moreover, that Suzuki considers only half-lines of the most common type, without accounting for the alliterative peculiarities of heavy half-lines that concern us here.

11. For discussion of apparent exceptions in *Beowulf* 2714b, 2717b, see OEM, pp. 91-2, 124-5.
12. The sharp distinction between word groups like *swāte fāh* and word groups like *rond gefēng* would appear to rule out the hypothesis of Kaling (1971) that phrase-final nouns and adjectives underwent subordination in Old English. The concept of a heavy foot derived from smaller feet is required independently to explain hypermetrical patterns (see OEM, sections 8.7-8).
13. The word *sunu* is assigned to a single S position rather than to a trochaic foot because of a well-known rule of "resolution" that has no significant bearing on the present argument. For discussion of this rule see OEM, section 4.8.
14. Since the features of interest to us here occur only in heavy half-lines, we do not consider the case in which the first foot of the half-line is "light" (has the patter x of xx). A foot of this sort has no primary arsis, and (5) will not mark it for alliteration (see OEM, section 7.5.1).
15. A number of common half-line patterns which we need not consider here have only one primary arsis. Since (5) will not apply to these at the level of the half-line, the application of (5) to them at the level of the line will not be redundant (cf. note 12 above). For further discussion of "light" verses, see OEM, sections 7.5.1, 7.5.5. The concept of "subordination" introduced here has nothing to do with the traditional concept of the "head-stave" as a conspicuous feature of the alliterative line. The head-stave stands out because it is the only alliterating syllable in the line with an invariant position (the first S position of the second half-line). However, the placement of alliterating syllables in the first half-line, which I undertake to explain here, is no way dependent on the head-stave. The metrical subordination rule must explain *all* aspects of alliterative placement, including the fact that the head-stave has a fixed position (cf. OEM, pp. 72, 75).
16. I do not distinguish weak constituents immediately dominated by weak constituents from weak constituents dominated by strong constituents which are dominated in turn by weak constituents. Alliteration is blocked for all positions dominated by two weak nodes, no matter how those nodes are embedded.
17. Here I do not distinguish between "poetic compounds" like *Gūð-Gēata* and ordinary compounds like *mancynnes*. There are indications, however, that forms like *Gūð-Gēata* actually counted as two words, and would have occupied the complex foot pattern [[S][Sx]] rather than the pattern [Ssx]. For discussion see OEM, section 8.5.
18. The others are 178a, 187a, 324a, 707a, 792a, 840a, 851a, 885a, 921a, 1149a, 1704a, 2560a, 2652a, 2946a, 3150a. Double alliteration in the first foot is also possible, though not certain, in 1584a, 1809a, and 2603a.

19. The others are 147a, 517a, 545a, 1395a, 2313a, 2650b, 2987a.
20. I do not mean here to endorse all the claims about the composition of *Beowulf* put forward by Lord and Magoun. It seems clear, however, that the metrical *rules* employed by the *Beowulf* poet were inherited from preliterate times. A plausible theory of Old English meter would account for its preliterate transmission as well as for its employment in later works. For further discussion, see Russom (1987b).
21. A recent attempt to provide "simple" rules for various features of Old English verse, with detailed discussion of previous scholarship, can be found in Hoover (1985).
22. The *designated terminal element* is the strongest element in a subconstituent. In a maximally simple tree structure that branches only once, the designated terminal element will correspond to the only strong node. Iterative application of the RPPR identifies the stronger strong node at each level of embedding.
23. The assumption of the authors that every syllable is to be accounted for metrically (p. 294) implies intuitive access to the whole tree. The RPPR is put forward as an interesting hypothesis because it is the minimal theory of tree interpretation consistent with the concepts *strong* and *weak* (cf. Prince (1983: 24)).
24. I do not mean to claim, of course, that all features of tree structure have phonological significance. Regularities of alliteration provide no evidence for, say, a sixth degree of stress such as would be assigned by the SPE rule system (cf. Prince (1983: 22)).

REFERENCES

Chomsky, N., and M. Halle. 1968. *The Sound Pattern of Enlish*. New York: Harper and Row. (Cited as SPE.)

Hayes, B. 1981. *A Metrical Theory of Stress Rules*. Doctoral dissertation, MIT, Cambridge, MA. Distributed by the Indians University Linguistics Club, Bloomington.

─────── 1983. 'A Grid-based Theory of English Meter'. *LIn* 14.357-93.

─────── 1984. 'The Phonology of Rhythm in English'. *LIn* 15.33-74.

Hoover, D. 1985. *A New Theory of Old English Meter*. New York: Peter Lang.

Jakobson, R. 1963. 'On the So-Called Vowel Alliteration in Germanic Verse'. *ZPhon* 16.85-92. (Repr. in R. Jakobson (1979), *Selected Writings*, 5.189-97. The Hague: Mouton.)

Kiparsky, P. 1966. 'Über den deutschen Akzent'. *Untersuchungen über Akzent und Intonation im Deutschen* (= *Studia Grammatica*, 7) ed. by M. Bierwisch, 69-98. Berlin: Akademie-Verlag.

─────── 1977. 'The Rhythmic Structure of English Verse'. *LIn* 8.189-247.

Klaeber, Fr., ed. 1950. *Beowulf and the Fight at Finnsburg*. 3rd edition. Boston: Heath.

Kuryłowicz, J. 1970. *Die sprachlichen Grundlagen der altgermanischen Metrik*. (= *Innsbrucker Beiträge zur Sprachwissenschaft*, 1.) Innsbruck: Institut für vergleichende Sprachwissenschaft der Universität Innsbruck.

Liberman, M., and A. Prince. 1977. 'On Stress and Linguistic Rhythm'. *LIn* 8.249-336.

Lord, A.B. 1960. *The Singer of Tales*. Cambridge, MA: Harvard University Press.

Magoun, F.P., Jr. 1953. 'Oral-Formulaic Character of Anglo-Saxon Narrative Poetry'. *Speculum* 28.446-67.

Maling, J. 1971. 'Sentence Stress in Old English'. *LIn* 11.379-99.

OEM: see Russom (1987a).

Pope, J.C. 1942. *The Rhythm of Beowulf*. New Haven: Yale University Press.

Prince, A. 1983. 'Relating to the Grid'. *LIn* 14.19-100.

Russom, G. 1987a. *Old English Meter and Linguistic Theory*. Cambridge: Cambridge University Press. (Cited as OEM.)

_____ 1987b. 'Verse Translations and the Question of Literacy in *Beowulf*'. In J.M. Foley, ed. *Comparative Research on Oral Traditions: A Memorial for Milman Parry*. 567-80. Columbus, Ohio: Slavica.

Selkirk, E. 1984. *Phonology and Syntax: The relation between sound and structure*. Cambridge, MA: MIT Press.

Sievers, E. 1985. 'Zur Rhythmik des germanischen Alliterationsverses'. *PBB* 10.209-314, 451-545.

_____ 1893. *Altgermanische Metrik*. Halle: Niemeyer.

SPE: see Chomsky and Halle (1968).

Suzuki, S. 1985. 'The Role of Syllable Structure in Old English Poetry'. *Lingua* 67.97-119.

THE DEVELOPMENT OF ME ǭ FROM OPEN SYLLABLE LENGTHENING
IN THE WEST MIDLANDS

MAŁGORZATA TECŁAW
University of Gdańsk

1. *Introduction.* The present paper is an attempt to reconstruct the dialectal evolution of ME ǭ resulting from Open Syllable Lengthening (OSL) in the West Midlands (WM). The reconstruction is based exclusively on dialectal reflexes of ME ǭ < OSL attested in the WM area. The methodology follows Lass (1976, 1978) whereby mappings postulated for each of the dialects will constitute a basis for the uniform history of OSL of ME ŏ in the WM. In this paper I am trying not to neglect any phonetic detail attested in the data because sound changes are viewed here as 'changes from below', i.e. below the level of speaker's awareness. However, since the data provides us with certain phonetic properties which are insignificant for qualitative changes, I will ignore them in the proposed derivations. Moreover, only the evolutive type of change is of interest here, so consequently any non-evolutive data will not be discussed.

2. *Data Collection*. The data has been collected from the questionnaires for *SED* referring to the WM area. Of the lexical items with ME ǭ surveyed in ModE dialects of the WM, there are surprisingly few examples which could result from OSL of ME ŏ. It is worth mentioning here that I accept a modified version of the environment for OSL, i.e. V̆ -> V̄ / __ C^1_1 e ## as suggested by Minkova (1982)[1]. Her argument is that either the process was peripheral, since there are only 36 ModE disyllables which show lengthening (out of 225 disyllabic words in ModE), or the process operated in a more restricted environment, i.e. __ C^1_1 e#. Assuming that the latter was the case, I was able to find only 11 items in the appropriate environment, surveyed in *SED*, which could be eligible for ME OSL[2]. These are the following words:[3]

ModE	ME	OE	ModE	ME	OE
boot	bote	--	foal	fole	fola
coal	col	col	hole	hol	hol(a)
coat	cote	--	nose	nose	nosu
cote	cote, cot	cote	smoke	smoke	smoca
choke	cheoke	ceocian	sole	sole	sole
throat	throte	protu			

In spite of a very limited implementation of OSL, the change itself is assumed to have had serious effects on the ME vowel system, contributing to the rise of new vowel phonemes /ę̄ ǭ/ (besides the phonetically close counterparts ē̦, ō̦ already existing in the phonological system). Therefore, the pursuit of the dialectal evolution of ME ŏ in OS may throw some light on the phonological status of ME ǭ, at least in the WM.

The examples above were examined in all ModE dialects covering the WM area[4]. All the possible phonetic realisations of the root vowel are shown with the WM dialect map (see Appendix).

3.   *Methodology and application.* Within the vast amount of phonetic material there are pronunciations which are relevant for the reconstruction of stages in the evolution of ME ǭ < OSL and pronunciations which may vary from performance to performance. I have extracted the relevant nuclear types, each covering the area in the vowel space which additionally may be filled with slightly modified pronunciations of a given type[5]. Thus, the following nuclei emerge as significant:

[ɔː] including [ǫː , ɔː , ǫː]   [oː] including [oːᵊ, o.ə, oə, ǫː , ǫə]
[oω] including [oːᵂ, oːω, o.ω, oω:, ǫω] [ɔω] including [oːᵂ, oːφ, ǫ.ω, ǫω, ʔω]
[ωː] including [ωː, ωə, ᵊωə, φə]   [uː] including [uːᵊ, ʉː]
[ωu] including [ᵂuː, ᵂʉː, ωuː, ö̆u, wω] [üː] including [üə, ʉ̈ə, ᵊʉ̈ə]
[ɤː] including [ɤ.ə, ᶫɤə, ᶫɤ.ə, ᶫɤː]   [ʟu] including [ᶫuː]
     [ωü]   [ᵂüː]   [ɒω]   [ɒω]   [ɔ̈ω]   [əω]
     [εω]   [aω]   [ɑː]   [ɤʉ]   [yː]   [ɒɩ]

In order to reconstruct the evolution of ME o < OSL I adopt Lass's (1976, 1978) methodology and specifically, the following assumptions:

   (i) the synchronic evidence is a constraint on the reconstruction of both entities and events.

   (ii) The condition with regard to entities is: 'No segment is well formed if it does not appear in surface phonetic representations in the same etymological category that is being reconstructed in the same language in question' (1978:254).

(iii) A historical event is reconstructed by the technique of mapping which makes use of well-formed entities plus the principle of gradualness of sound changes.

(iv) A well-formed mapping is the one in which all the intermediate stages are attested to and form a graded continuum.

(v) Interdialectal borrowing will give a disjunctive picture, whereas internal evolutive change should give a graded continuum (cf. Lass, 1978).

The 'units' of change size (cf. assumptions iii-v) in the developments are determined by the primitive elements that come into play within the vowel space:

```
i ɪ        y ʏ        ʉ        ü   u
e                              o
  ɛ                  ə     ö   ɔ
       a                   ɑ   ɒ
```

Assumptions (i)-(v) allow us to organise the dialectal material and derive a tentative account of the processes operating in each of the dialects in question.

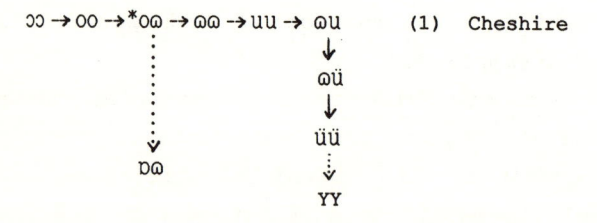

```
ɔː → oo → *oɷ → ɷɷ → uu → ɷu       (1)  Cheshire
 ⋮                         ↓
 ⋮                        ɷü
 ⋮                         ↓
 ⋮                        üü
 ↓                         ⋮
 ɒɷ                        ↓
                          ʏʏ
```

There are two problematic developments (suggested by the broken arrow in diagram (1)), i.e. [*oɷ] -> [ɒɷ] and [üü] -> [ʏʏ]. First, the [*oɷ] stage is hypothetical in this dialect but still a legitimate inference: this stage is attested in all other dialects of the WM. Second, in both cases the intermediate stages are lacking, which might suggest a non-evolutive change.

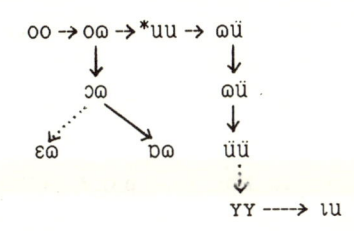

(2) Derbyshire

```
          oo → oω → *uu → ωü
             ↓            ↓
            ɔω           ωü
           ↙    ↘         ↓
         ɛω      ɒω       üü
                          ⋮
                          ↓
                         YY ----→ ɩu
```

This derivation supplies the missing intermediate stage in [Oω] -> [Dω]. Thus, in Derbyshire the [Oω] -> [ɔω] -> [Dω] string seems to be well-formed. The *[uu] stage must have been reached in this dialect, although it is not attested, since otherwise the subsequent gradual development would not have been evidenced. A new problem arises, however, with the evolution of [ɔω] -> [ɛω]. The same questionable development is attested in Staffordshire:

(3) Staffordshire

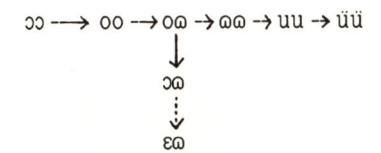

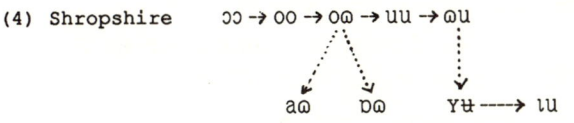

```
   ɔɔ ──→ oo ─→ oω → ωω → uu → üü
             ↓
            ɔω
             ⋮
             ↓
            ɛω
```

(4) Shropshire

```
   ɔɔ → oo → oω → uu → ωu
         ↙  ↘        ⋮
        aω   ɒω      ↓
                    Yʉ ----→ ɩu
```

In Shropshire, the occurrence of both [aω] and [Dω] cannot be ascribed to any evolutive process. There is nothing like [ɔω] stage, which exists in Derbyshire, to sanction the development of [Dω]. The existence of [aω] may be viewed as an evolutive substitute for [εω] in Staffordshire and Derbyshire. This will reduce the problem with [aω] to the possibility of the [ɔω] -> [εω] development.

The presence of [Yʉ] takes us back to the questionable development of [üü] --> [YY] in Cheshire and Derbyshire. On the one hand, this development may be considered a natural one if the following string is postulated: [üü] --> *[ʉʉ] --> [Yʉ] --> [YY]. In both Cheshire and Derbyshire as well as in neighbouring Staffordshire the pronunciation [üü] is the result of a natural process. On the other hand, in the case of Shropshire [Yʉ] must be treated as a borrowing since there are no reflexes furnishing intermediate stages from [ωU] to [Yʉ] there.

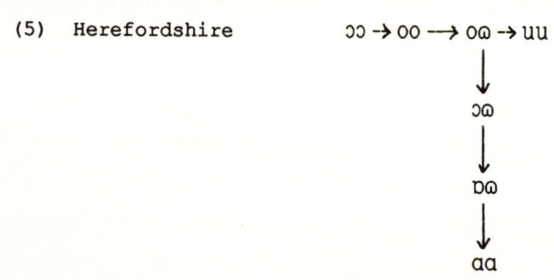

(5) Herefordshire   ɔɔ → oo → oω → uu
$$\downarrow$$
ɔω
$$\downarrow$$
Dω
$$\downarrow$$
ɑɑ

The derivations for Herefordshire and Worcestershire introduce a new step in the dialectal evolution of ME ō̧, i.e. [Dω] --> [ɑɑ]. My suggestion is that this monophthongisation must have gone through an intermediate stage [ɑω] which is attested in the dialectal evolution of ME o from other sources in the WM[6].

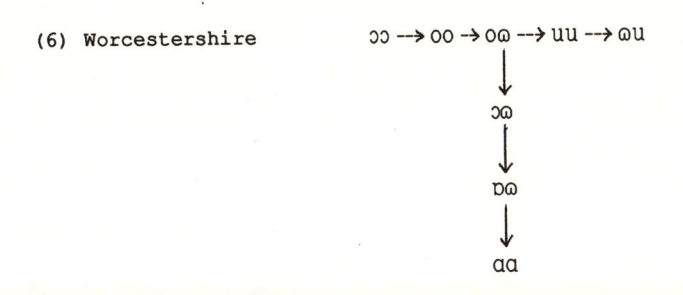

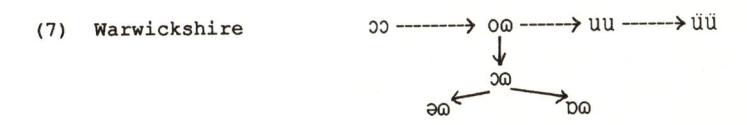

(6) Worcestershire   ɔɔ → oo → oω → uu → ωu
                              ↓
                              ɔω
                              ↓
                              ɒω
                              ↓
                              aɑ

(7) Warwickshire   ɔɔ --------→ oω -----→ uu ------→ üü
                                  ↓
                                  ɔω
                              ↙   ↘
                           əω   ɒω

What is interesting here is the [əω] quality. The change [ɔω] --> [əω] looks plausible and provides the missing link in [ɔω] --> [ɛω] (in 12St, 8Db). Now, if we add [öω] attested in Oxfordshire as well, the possible evolution of [ɔω] will appear thus: [ɔω] --> [öω] --> [əω] --> [ɛω] --> [aω]. This derivation does not suggest of course that [ɛω] is an evolutive result in Staffordshire and Derbyshire. In these dialects some earlier stage in the above derivation must have been transported and adopted as [ɛω]. The fact that the counties: Oxfordshire, Warwickshire, Staffordshire, Derbyshire form a contiguous area supports the plausibility of an evolutive process on the one hand,

and on the other, it points to Oxfordshire as the innovatory area in this kind of development.

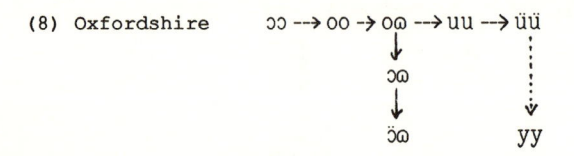

(8) Oxfordshire   ɔɔ --> oo --> oω --> uu --> üü
                       ↓   ⋮
                       ɔω   ⋮
                       ↓   ↓
                       ɔ̈ω   yy

As far as [yy] is concerned, the evolutive path is ruled out here, since none of the neighbouring dialects reveals a tendency towards fronting larger than the [üü] stage. Nevertheless, if we accept the gradualness of [üü] --> [YY] as suggested for Cheshire and Derbyshire, [yy] would naturally fit the hypothetical derivation:
[üü] --> *[ʉʉ] --> [Yʉ] --> [YY] --> [yy].

(9) Gloucestershire   ɔɔ --> oo --> oω --> uu --> ωu
                                ⋮   ⋮
                                ↓   ↓
                                ɑɑ   ɩu

In this dialect, both [ɑɑ] and [ɩu] are interdialectal borrowings; [ɑɑ] being borrowed from adjacent Herefordshire and Worcestershire.

4. *Conclusions*. The analysis of the possible processes operating in each of the dialects of the WM leads to a uniform history of ME $\bar{\varrho}$ < OSL which may be presented graphically. This mapping suggests that all the dialects follow the same route from [ɔɔ] to [uu] and that there are two stages at which the dialects could

```
ɔɔ ----> oo ---> oω --------> ωω --------> uu ---->ωu
              ↓                                      ↓
             ɔω                                     ωü
            ↙  ↘                                    ↓
           ɔ̈ω    ɒω                                 üü
           ↓     ↓                                   ↓
           əω    ɑɑ                                 *ʉʉ
           ↓                                         ↓
           εω                                       ʏʉ ----> ɯ
           ↓                                         ↓
           aω                                       ʏʏ
                                                     ↓
                                                    yy
```

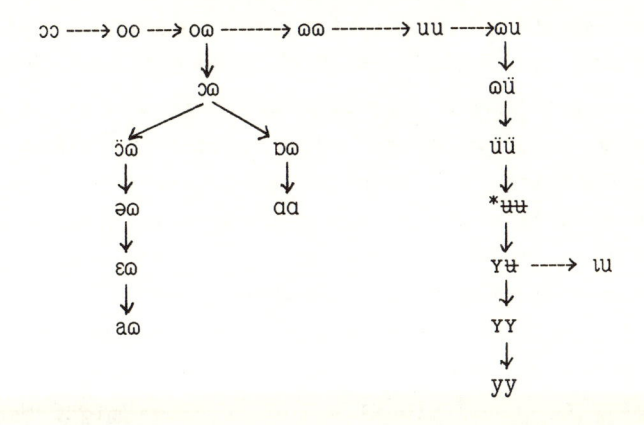

diversify: [Oω] and [UU]. In two of the dialects, Shropshire and Gloucestershire, nothing more than the evolution from [ɔɔ] to [UU] happened. Cheshire utilises the tendency towards [Uː]-fronting. In Derbyshire, both lines of development are attested, i.e. [Uː]-fronting and the evolution of [Oω]. In two dialects, Herefordshire and Worcestershire, the [Uː] stage is kept stable whereas [Oω] evolves into the stage of [ɑː]. In neighbouring Warwickshire as well as in Staffordshire and Oxfordshire (adjacent to Warwickshire), the evolution of [Oω] seems to prevail over the tendency to [Uː]-fronting. Thus it is only in Derbyshire that the two possible lines of evolution might be detected. In the remaining dialects some sort of choice has been made out of three options: '[Oω]-evolution', '[Uː]-fronting' or 'doing nothing'.

The last problem which should be addresses is the existence of [Dl] in Derbyshire and Shropshire. There is virtually no possibility of deriving [Dl] from any of the intermediate stages. The only one might be a dissimilation of [Dɵ] --> [Dl]. However, [Dɵ] is a natural development only in Derbyshire and it is a borrowing in Shropshire, which reduces the likelihood of such a solution. And even in Derbyshire there are no reflexes which could serve as intermediate stages. We cannot treat this change as a massive one either (for a detailed discussion see Lass 1978).

The present paper is a proposal for the history of ME ō̜ in the WM. For this account to be accepted, we obviously need additional evidence which might be provided by the analysis of localised ME texts. We can however, postulate the value [ǫ] as the result of OSL because of the uniformity of the development in the first stage in the whole of the WM area. The question whether it can be given a separate phonological status or not could be answered only after we have confronted our analysis with the development of related entities, i.e. ME ō̜ < OE ō, ME ō̜ < OSL of ME ŭ, and ME ǭ < OE ā. Theoretically, there should be a difference in the histories of ME ō̜ (of whatever origin) and ME ǭ (coming from either OE ā or OSL of ME ŏ), since the first one participated in the Great Vowel Shift of the fifteenth century, whereas ME ǭ was unaffected by this process.

NOTES

1. For a more detailed discussion and cross-references, see Minkova (1982).

2. In the list of items given by Minkova (1982) there are 26 items with ME ŏ in the appropriate environment. Apparently, not all

of them were included in the questionnaires for *SED*, besides, 3 of those 26 are marked as dialectal in OED.

3. Only 9 of my 11 items are included in the list by Minkova. The two which are not are *coat* and *boot*. I would consider them relevant because they were borrowed from AN with ŏ, and so the lengthening may have been a ME process (cf. Bliss 1952).

4. Professor Jacek Fisiak suggests that the dialect of Monmouthshire should be excluded because of probable Welsh influence.

5. This was suggested to me by Professor Roger Lass. First of all, too minute phonetic details will obscure the process involved. Since on the phonological level both diphthongs and long vowels are treated as sequences of VV, the reconstruction will reveal the relevant processes even though low-level phonetic distinctions have been ignored. Such details as interdiphthongal length or somewhat opener pronunciations of particular variants still fall within the same area in the vowel space. Needless to say, all the details can be put back, if needed.

6. Moreover, it seems very unlikely for the [D] quality to be lengthened and preserved as [DD]. Besides, in all the dialects I have examined, [D] is always a short vowel.

REFERENCES

Bliss, A.J. 1952-53. Vowel quantity in Middle English Borrowings from Anglo-Norman. In R. Lass (ed.) 164-207.
Fisiak, J. (ed.) 1978. *Recent Developments in Historical Phonology*. The Hague: Mouton.
Lass, R. (ed.) 1969. *Approaches to English Historical Linguistics*. New York: Holt, Rinehart & Winston.
_____. 1976. *English Phonology and Phonological Theory*. Cambridge: Cambridge University Press.
_____. 1978. Mapping constraints in phonological reconstruction: on climbing down trees without falling out of them. In Fisiak (ed.) 245-286.
_____. 1980. *On Explaining Language Change*. Cambridge: Cambridge University Press.
Minkova, D. 1982. The environment for Open Syllable Lengthening in Middle English. *Folia Linguistica Historica III*. 1. 29-59.
Orton, H. et. al. 1962-71. *Survey of English Dialects*. Leeds: Arnold.

APPENDIX: West Midlands Dialect Map:

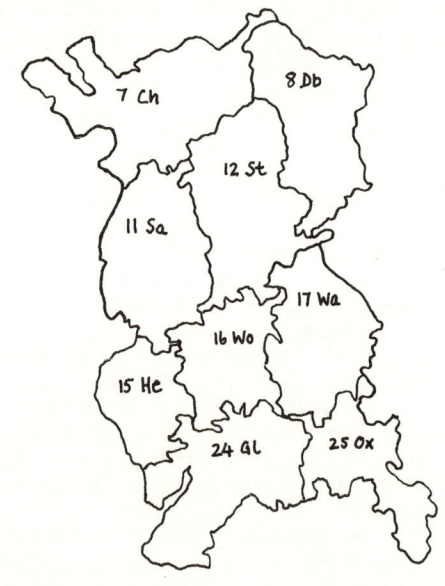

7 Ch (Cheshire) [ɔː oː ɒː oᵊː ɒ̈ː ɑː ɑʊ ᵊɑə ɥː ᵚɥː uː ᵚuː ᵚüː üː üə ᵊɥ̈ə
                   ʏː ˡʏə ˡʏ.ə ˡʏː ɒʊ ɒ ə]

8 Db (Derbyshire) [oː o.ə ɒː oːᵚ ɑ.ʊ ɛʊ ɒʊ oːʊ o.ʊ oʊ ʊə ɑ̈ə ᵚuː
                    ᵚüː ᵚü üː ˡuː ʏː ʏ.ə ɒʟ ə]

11 Sa (Shropshire) [ɔː oː oːᵊ oːᵚ uː ᵚuː ʏɤː ʟuː aʊ ɒʊ ɒʟ]

12 St (Staffordshire) [ɔː oː oʊ ɒʊ ɑː uː üː ɒʊ ɛʊ ɔʊ ʊ ɒ ə]

15 He (Hertfordshire) [ɔː oː oːᵊ oːᵚ oːʊ oʊ uː ɑʊ ɒʊ ɑː ɒ ə]

16 Wo (Worcestershire) [ɔː ɒː oː oːᵊ oə oʊ oʊː ɒʊ ʊə uː ŏu ᵚuː
                        ɑ̈u ɔʊ ɒʊ ɑː ᵂɒ ɒ ɒ. ʊ ə]

17 Wa (Warwickshire) [ɔː ɒə oʊ ɒʊ ɔʊ ɒʊ ɒʊ əʊ ʊə ɥː uː üː ʊ ʟ ɒ ə]

24 Gl (Gloucestershire) [ɔ̈ː ɒ̈ː ŏ̈ː ŏ̈ːᵚ ŏ̈ːᵂ oːɑ uː uːᵊ ᵚuː ɒʊː wʊ wə
                         ᵂə ˡuː ɑː ʊ ɒ̈ ə ɒ]

25 Ox (Oxfordshire) [ɔː ɒ̈ː ɒ̈ː oː oə ɒə oːᵚ oːʊ oʊ ʊə uː üː ü̈ː ʏː ɒʊ ɔʊ
                     öʊ ɔʊ ɛ ʊ ɒ ə]

SOME MODERN STANDARD ENGLISH FILTERS

JAMES P. THORNE
University of Edinburgh

The term 'filter' here is used to refer to constraints on the representations formed by deletion rules. More precisely, they are constraints on the structure of complements in these representations. Chomsky and Lasnik (1977) describe these as constraints on surface structures, but since deletion rules are rules which map from Surface Structure to Phonological Form it would seem to be the case that they are, in fact, constraints on phonological forms. Chomsky and Lasnik (1977: 436-7) make the point that the first step in the discussion of any such constraint is to determine whether "it is a true universal (that is, a principle of U[niversal] G[rammar]), or whether it is specific to the language which is under analysis". The filters I shall be discussing are not just language specific but dialect specific.

As an example of what I am calling a 'dialect specific' filter consider the constraints on the contents of the complements of restrictive relative clauses in Modern Standard English. An optimally simple phrase structure grammar of Modern Standard English would contain the following rules.[1]

(1) (i) $\bar{S}$ -->   COMP + S
     (ii)   S   -->   NP + INFL + VP
     (iii) COMP   -->   ± WH
     (iv)   + WH   -->   *whether*
     (v)   - WH   -->   *that*

It would, of course, also have to contain rules for expanding NP and
VP together with rules for generating S-daughters such as sentential
adverbs, all of which I have omitted because I am concerned here
almost exclusively with the structure of complements. I am, however,
assuming that lexical insertion rules can insert relative pronouns
into noun nodes and that such a rule must have operated in the case of
any well-formed restrictive relative clause, irrespective of whether
or not a relative pronoun occurs in its representation at Phonological
Form. The reason for this is that restrictive relative clauses must
contain a variable at Logical Form and that the trace left as a result
of the relative pronoun being moved into the complement at Surface
Structure is interpreted as a variable at Logical Form. I am also
assuming that although all the rules in (1) are optional there are
constraints which insure that rules (i), (ii) and (iii) apply in the
case of all well-formed sentences so that, in effect, it is only rules
(iv) and (v) that are optional. This means that the grammar will
assign the deep structure (2) to the restrictive relative clauses in
Sentences (3) and (4).

(2) [$_{NP}$ [$_{\bar{S}}$ [$_{comp}$ [$_{-WH}$]] [$_S$NP [$_{VP}$V [$_{NP}$who]]]]]

(3) Every girl who I liked left early.

(4) Every girl I liked left early.

And it will assign the deep structure (5) to Sentence (6).

(5) [$_{NP}$ [$_{\bar{S}}$ [[$_{-WH}$that]] [$_S$NP [$_{VP}$V [$_{NP}$who]]]]]
        comp

(6) Every girl that I liked left early.

Wh-movement will produce a surface structure from (2) in which the
structure of the complement is (7) and a surface structure from (5) in
which the structure of the complement is (8).

(7) [who   [   ]]
    COMP   -WH

(8) [who   [that]]
    COMP   -WH

The fact that the grammar assigns the same analyses to (3) and (4) but different analyses to (6) is in no way incompatible with the claim that in all three sentences the subordinate clauses are of the same kind - restrictive relative clauses. They are all clauses which have -WH complements and contain relative pronouns at Deep and Surface Structure, and hence variables in this position at Logical Form. Nor is it incompatible with the fact that Sentences (3), (4) and (6) are all synonymous. The only difference is that (6) contains the complementizer _that_ and (3) and (4) do not. But like all expressions introduced by syntactic rules rather than by lexical insertion rules the complementizer _that_ has no semantic content.

However, it still has to be explained how the surface structure (2) maps into the phonological forms of (3) and (4) and the surface structure (5) maps into the phonological form of (6). The simplest explanation is to postulate an optional rule that deletes the relative pronoun in the complement. When the rule does not operate on (7) the result is (3). When it does operate the result is (4). When it operates on (8) the result is (6). But when it does not operate on (7) (and notice the rule must be an optional rule or the grammar would not generate (3)) the result is the ungrammatical sentence (9).

(9) * The girl who that I liked left early.

Thus the cost (as it were) of adopting the simplest form of deletion rule is that the grammar generates a phonological form for restrictive relative clauses that is not well-formed. Still seeking the simplest account, sentences like (9) are marked as not well-formed by adding to the grammar the filter (10) - a statement that there is a constraint on the structure of the complement at Phonological Form preventing it from containing both a complementizer and a relative pronoun

(10) * [who   that]
         COMP

But this filter is specific to Modern Standard English, because although sentences with doubly filled complements are not well-formed

in Modern Standard English they are well-formed in, for example,
Middle English.

(11)   Euery wyght wheche þat to Rome went.
                    Chaucer *Troilus* II, 37.

(12)   What sholde I tellen ech proporcion
       Of thinges whiche that we werche upon
                    Chaucer *Chanouns Yemannes* I, 755-6.

(13)   þe woundes . . ./ w3uche þat weoren on honden and feet.
                    Cast. Love 1434.

This makes it clear that the concept of filters is essential to the understanding of one kind of language change. We can assume that with respect to restrictive relative clauses the grammar of Middle English and Modern Standard English are exactly the same, assigning identical representations at Deep Structure and Surface Structure, except that the grammar of Modern Standard English contains a filter ruling out the occurrence of both a complementizer and a relative pronoun in the complement at the level of Phonological Form. The result is that there was, as it were, one more pronunciation of restrictive relative clauses in Middle English.[2]

There is an additional constraint on the structure of the complement of restrictive relative classes in Modern Standard English. When the relative pronoun originates in subject position the complement cannot be empty.

(14)   The girl who liked me left early.

(15)   The girl that liked me left early.

(16)   *The girl liked me left early.

Chomsky and Lasnik's formulation of the filter that marks sentences like (16) as not well-formed is (17).

(17)   * [$_{NP}$ NP Tns VP]

This too is a dialect-specific filter. Sentences containing restrictive relative clauses with empty complements can be found in English up to about the middle of the Eighteenth Century.

(18) Lete fetche the best hors maye be found.
      Malory 137.

(19) My father had a daughter lou'd a man.
      Shakespeare *Twelfth Night* II iv 110.

(20) Or like the snow falls in the river . . .
      Burns *Tam O'Shanter* 281.

In the case of nonrestrictive relative clauses the grammar given in (1) will generate three phonological forms which are not well-formed in Modern Standard English.

(21) * Marietta, who that I liked, left early.
(22) * Marietta, that I liked, left early.
(23) * Marietta, I liked, left early.

The filter (10) will rule out (21) but since the constraint that demands that the complement contains a relative pronoun applies only to the complement of a nonrestrictive relative clause the filter that rules out (22) and (23) in Modern Standard English must refer to this fact. Unlike restrictive relative clauses, which are NP-daughters, nonrestrictive relative clauses are S-daughters. The filter required, therefore, is

(24) * $[_S \; [_{\bar{S}} \; [_{comp} \; \sigma \;] \;] \;]$ where $\sigma \neq$ wh-

But as the following examples show (24) is not part of the grammar of earlier forms of English

(25) 7 on þys ilcan ȝere forþferde Aethelred,
      was in Devon ealdorman.
      A.S. Chron. 901.

(26) Aleyn the clerk, that herd this melodye...
      Chaucer *Reeve's Tale* 248.

(27) Fleance his son, that keeps him company.
      Shakespeare *Macbeth* III.i.134.

Turning from −WH complements to +WH complements it will be seen that as well as subordinate clauses (indirect questions) with complements containing the complementizer whether the grammar in (1) would also generate main clauses (direct questions) with complements having this structure.

(28) * Whether she will come?

Since in Modern Standard English it is only direct questions without the complementizer whether that are well-formed it is necessary to include in the grammar the filter (29) which will mark sentences like (28) as ungrammatical.

(29) * $[_{\bar{S}_0} [_{comp} [_{+WH}$ whether]] S]

(adopting a convention whereby the highest S node in the tree is indexed $\bar{S}_0$ and all lower ones $\bar{S}_1$, $\bar{S}_2$ etc).

But direct questions with whether were permissible in Old, Middle and Early Modern English.

(30) Hwæðer æniʒ man him mete brohte?
                                    A.S. Gospel. John IV.33

(31) Hweþer she sholde be Quen and leuedi ouer me?
                                 Havelok 202.

(32) Whither wyl he alowe a subject to much?
                               Latimer, 1st Sermon before Edward VI.

This too, therefore, is a case where the development of Modern Standard English from earlier dialects can be explained in terms of the addition of a filter to the grammar reducing the number of phonological forms of certain kinds of structures.

But the grammar in (1) will not only 'overgenerate' main clauses with +WH complements with the complementizer whether. It will also overgenerate main clauses with −WH complements with the complementizer that. Sentences like

(33)   * That I like it.

A grammar of Modern Standard English must contain a filter (34) which will rule out sentences like (33).

(34)   * [$_S$ [$_{comp}$ [$_{-WH}$ that]] S]

But the fact that there are dialects which have main clauses with whether prompts the question whether there were also dialects which have main clauses with that. The following sentences, all taken from Mitchell (1985:23), suggest that Old English was such a dialect

(35)   Æfter þæm þe Romeburʒ ʒetimbred wæs IIII hunde wintra 7
       II, ðætte Cartina þære burʒe ærendracan comon to Rome.
                               King Alfred's Orosius 104.1

(36)   Ðæs ymb feower niht // þætte Martinus mære ʒeleorde.
                               Menologium 207.

(37)   . . .and no seoððan // þæt hie up þonan æfre moton.
                               Christ and Satan 632.

These are all clearly main clauses with a -WH complement and containing the complementizer that. In each case there is a prepositional or adverbial expression before the complementizer. This must mean that they cannot be in the clause itself but must be either in the complement or the topic. I assume the latter, that is, that the structure of these sentences is

(38)   [$_S$ [$_{Topic}$ Prepositional/Adverbial Phrase] [$_S$ [$_{comp}$ [that]] S]]

If this analysis is correct then as well as having prepositional and adverbial expressions in clause initial position Old English was able to have them in topic position in front of the complement, which in this case could contain the complementizer that.

Mitchell views these sentences quite differently, describing them as subordinate clauses. But it is difficult to see how a clause that is not in construction with a main clause can be a subordinate clause.

The mistake, I believe, arises from the assumption that a clause with a complement containing a complementizer cannot be a main clause because complementizers always have the function of marking a clause as subordinate. But it has already been shown that this is not necessarily the case with whether. Sentences like (35)-(37) show that it is not necessarily the case with that. One could perhaps go further. The fact that that does not always have the function of marking a clause as subordinate could, perhaps, be an indication that there was a time when it never had this function.

There is evidence to show that sentences like (39) where the presence of the complementizer marks the subordinate clause as subordinate are easier to process than sentences like (40) where it is absent.[3]

(39)   I said that she was crazy.
(40)   I said she was crazy.

One would, therefore, expect languages to have ways of marking subordinate clauses. If my conjecture is correct one would also expect there to be evidence that English had a means other than the that complementizer of marking clauses as subordinate, which grammatical changes rendered inoperative. At the beginning of the Old English period subordinate clauses have the verb in final position and main clauses have the verb in second position. By the end of the period subordinate clauses too have the verb in second position. Word order, therefore, no longer distinguished subordinate clauses from main clauses. The addition of (34) to the grammar would have provided another means of doing this.

The fact that we find Old English sentences like (35)-(37) is not inconsistent with this account. It is characteristic of filters that under certain circumstances they can be over-ridden. For example, (17) should (and for some speakers does) rule out sentences like (41).

(41)   There is a student wants to see you.

Yet for many speakers (41) is well-formed. Chomsky and Lasnik argue convincingly that the function of (17) is to enable us to make use of a simple heuristic in processing utterances - when a noun phrase comes in front of finite verb take it as the subject of that verb. But in the case of (41) by the time the listener hears the verb <u>wants</u> he has already made the noun phrase <u>a student</u> the subject of <u>is</u>, so the possibility of taking it as the subject of <u>wants</u> does not arise.[4] In the case of Sentences (35)-(37) there could be a connection between the over-riding of (34) and the fact that (at least in Modern English) clauses with preposed topic-NPs cannot be subordinate clauses.

(42)   Joe she approves of.

(43) * Matthew believes Joe she approves of.

I have left until the end a discussion of the most interesting of Mitchell's examples.

(44)   No þæt þin aldor æfre wolde
       ʒodes ʒoldfatu in ʒylp beran . . .
                          Daniel 753.

What makes (44) interesting is, of course, the fact that sentences like this occur in Modern Standard English

(45)   Not that your lord would ever wish vauntingly
       to bear away God's golden vessels.

Other examples are

(46)   Not that I cared.
(47)   Not that anybody paid the least attention
       to him.

The fact that <u>not</u> occurs before <u>that</u> together with the fact that clauses like (46) and (47) cannot be subordinate clauses indicate that the structure of these clauses is (38).

(48)   *I said that not that I cared.

The main point I have been making in this paper is that in the case of at least some Old English and Middle English sentences there are advantages to be gained from looking at them in the context of the grammar of Modern Standard English. An optimally simple grammar of Modern Standard English allows for the possibility of a dialect with sentences like (35)-(37). It also of course allows for the possibility of sentences like (45)-(47) within Modern Standard English. But it could equally well be argued that in the case of these sentences there are advantages to be gained from looking at them in the context of Old English. In Modern Standard English, sentences like (45)-47) appear not only exceptional but inexplicable. Why should (34) be over-ridden just in the case of clauses with a topicalized not? When the Old English evidence is taken into account sentences with this structure can be seen to be only survivors of a type which (because Old English allowed other types of expressions as well as not to occur in the topic) was at one time considerably more productive.

NOTES

1. For a full discussion of this grammar see Chomsky (1981).
2. For further discussion see Lightfoot (1979) 313 ff.
3. See Hawkes (1972).
4. It is probably for the same kind of reason that in the vast majority of the sentences recorded in Old, Middle and Early Modern English in which (17) is over-ridden the head noun phrase to which the restrictive relative clause is attached is the object either of a verb or a preposition.

REFERENCES

Chomsky, N. 1981. *Lectures on Government and Binding* Dordrecht: Foris Publications.

Chomsky, N. and Lasnik, H. 1977. "Filters and Control" <u>LI</u> 8, 425-505.

Hakes, D.T. 1972. "Effects of reducing complement constructions on sentence comprehension". *Journal of Verbal Learning and Verbal Behaviour*, 11, 278-86.

Lightfoot, D. 1979. *Principles of Diachronic Syntax*. Cambridge: Cambridge University Press.

Mitchell, B. 1985. *Old English Syntax*. Oxford: Clarendon Press.

EXEMPLIFICATION IN EIGHTEENTH-CENTURY ENGLISH GRAMMARS

INGRID TIEKEN-BOON VAN OSTADE

University of Leiden

1. Introduction

The function of examples in a grammar, according to Fenning in his *New Grammar of the English Language* (1771: v), is 'to impress the rules of Syntax the more deeply in the reader's memory'. He continues on the next page:

> In my quotations in general, I had an eye, not only to their being applicable to the rules they were intended to exemplify, but also to the elegance of style, and to the beauty of Sentiment they displayed, and to the purity of the moral they inculcated. They may, therefore, be considered not merely as illustrations of the Rules of grammar, but likewise as specimens of fine writing.

To this he adds:

> As to examples of *bad English*, I not only think that they make a very awkward appearance, but I am even of opinion, that they may have a very bad effect. They are more likely to perplex a young Scholar, and to confirm an old one in error, than to direct the judgment of the one, or correct the bad habit of the other. (Fenning 1771: vi-vii)

These quotations tell us a number of things. To begin with, Fenning makes use of examples as a teaching method, and his examples, or at least some of them, take the form of quotations that are at the same time 'specimens of fine writing'. Furthermore, there was apparently a controversy going on at the time as to the usefulness of examples of 'bad English'. And finally, the very fact that Fenning so elaborately discusses his use of examples in the preface to his grammar demonstrates his concern with the practicalities of the teaching of English grammar, and particularly with methods of exemplification. In being concerned with what might be the best methods of exemplification, he does not stand alone, though such a concern is by no means universal among eighteenth-century English grammarians and with one exception, i.e. Lane (1700: xviii), is found primarily in the second half of the century.

The aim of this paper is to describe the nature of the examples—and of exemplification in general—in a number of eighteenth-century grammars which I have analysed for this paper, the first published in 1700 and the last in 1798 (see appendix). In so doing I hope to shed some light on the methods used in studying, describing and teaching the English language in the eighteenth century. At the same time, my findings will serve to elucidate some of the normative grammarians' attitudes towards the language spoken and written in and before the eighteenth century. I have based myself to some extent on work I have done previously in the area of eighteenth-century grammar on the subject of double negation, shall/will and the auxiliary do (Tieken 1982, 1985 and 1987). For this paper, I have in particular studied the examples illustrating the rules for these three aspects of syntax, and in addition, in order to be able to analyse the authors' views on the matter of exemplification, the prefaces to the grammars analysed.

2. The nature of the examples.

All the grammars analysed contain examples in some form or other. A grammar without any illustrations to clarify its rules indeed seems inconceivable—after all, a grammar is a teaching instrument, and for a grammar to be successful in any way, that is, for a grammar to 'rather incite, than discourage the Curiosity of such who whould have a clear Notion of what they speak or write' (Greenwood 1711: A3), examples are indispensible. However, the nature of the examples found in the grammars is widely different, and the following four categories may be distinguished:

a. examples that have obviously been made up by the author, such as Kirkby's It was n't good for nothing (1746: 127) and Ann Fisher's (1750: 120) I cannot eat none. That these examples bear no relationship to actual usage may be illustrated from the fact that neither Austin (1984: 146) nor myself (Tieken 1982: 281-2) have come across any such instances of double negation in our respective analyses of eighteenth-century usage;

b. examples that have been translated from those traditionally found in Latin grammars, such as I shall love; I will love, provided by *The English Accidence* (1733: 49); cf. Lily's grammar (1549: Blll): Amabo 'I shall or wyll loue';[1]

c. examples that have been copied, or translated from grammars published previously, such as Greenwood (1711:128) whose use of the verb burn in I burn, I burned ... I do burn, I did burn, derives from Wallis (1653; 1765: 106) 'Uro, urebam, I burn, I burned... I do burn, I did burn',[2] and Kirkby (1746: 127), Ann Fisher (1750: 120) and Gough (1754: 114) who all give the example It was not good for nothing, and Ann Fisher (1750: 120), Buchanan (1762: 179) and Ussher (1785: 77) who all provide I cannot eat none;

d. examples that are quotations:
   1. literary: "Why do you look on us, and shake your head,
      And call us orphans, wretches, castaways"?
      (from Shakespeare; White 1761; 71)
   2. biblical: DO WE BEGIN again to command ourselves?
      (New Testament; Ward 1765: 449)
   3. sayings, maxims, proverbs: Virtue alone is happiness below (Ussher 1785: 93).

The purpose of the latter two subcategories of examples is

obvious: as Murray (1795: v) puts it, he 'has been studious ... not only to avoid all examples and illustrations which might have an improper effect on the minds of youth; but also to introduce, on many occasions, such as have a moral and religious tendency'. See also Fenning quoted above.

3. Literary quotations

The literary quotations represent by far the most interesting category from the point of view of the aim of this paper, and it is on these that I shall henceforth mainly concentrate. I have come across literary quotations in Bayly (1758), Fell (1784), Fenning (1771), Fogg (1792/6), Johnson (1755), Murray (1795), Webster (1784) and White (1761). Only one of these, White, was not designed as a teaching grammar. The work is a linguistic monograph dealing with the English verb, described by Alston as 'the first attempt at a systematic treatment of the English verb' (White 1761: Alston's introductory note). Johnson's grammar functions as a grammatical supplement that adds information to what is found in the dictionary entries. The other works are all teaching grammars. One might perhaps argue that literary quotations are somewhat out of place in a teaching grammar, but the fact that we do find them in the above-mentioned grammars, all of them produced in the second half of the eighteenth century, indicates that contrary to earlier practice, greater attention is paid to usage. As a result grammatical writing acquired the potential of improving in quality, in that actual usage might be described rather than a kind of idealised form of the language; however, this potential was not always realised.

Who do the grammarians quote from? Fogg merely observes that his examples 'have been generally extracted from approved authors' (1796: iii), and so does Webster (1784: 6). Some are silent on the subject altogether, while White (1761: xii) laments the fact that through lack

of time he has been unable to include examples 'from the works of
SWIFT, and some productions still more modern, which are of Classic
excellence'. In his admiration of Swift, White is supported by Lowth
(1762: ii), who claims that 'Swift ... is one of our most correct, and
perhaps our very best prose writer'. In Dr Johnson's view, Swift
would have been too modern a source to quote from. According to
Johnson, the best authors are those writing

> before the restoration, whose works I regard as the *wells of
> English undefiled*, as the pure sources of genuine diction ...
> I have fixed *Sidney's* work for the boundary, beyond which I
> make few excursions. (1755: Cl*)*

Johnson even specifies for which areas of usage certain authors are
most authoritative in his eyes:

> If the language of theology were extracted from *Hooker* and the
> translation of the Bible; the terms of natural knowledge from
> *Bacon*; the phrases of policy, war and navigation from *Raleigh*;
> the dialect of poetry and fiction from *Spenser* and *Sidney*; and
> the diction of common life from *Shakespeare*, few ideas would be
> lost to mankind, for want of *English* words, in which they might
> be expresses. (1755: Cl)

However, when it comes to the actual practice of exemplification
Johnson turns out to be not such a strict adherent to his own
principles: he does occasionally quote from contemporary sources, and
even admits to this himself in his preface (1755: B2ᵛ):

> nor have I departed from this resolution, but when some performance
> of uncommon excellence excited my veneration, when my memory
> supplied me, from late [i.e. recent] books with an example that was
> wanting, or when my heart, in the tenderness of friendship,
> solicited admission for a certain name.

It will be shown below that a certain amount of favouritism was not
uncommon among the eighteenth-century grammarians studied. Fell is
likewise highly specific as to the sources of his quotations. In the
'Advertisement' to his *Essay towards an English Grammar* (1784: xv) he
mentions 'the Holy Scriptures, Shakespeare, Milton [also praised by
Bayly (1772: xii)], Chillingworth, Algernon Sidney, Locke, Tillotson,
and Addison'. Dilworth (1751: ix) and Gough (1754: xvi) both mention
the authors of the *Spectator* (1711-12), the *Tatler* (1709-11) and the

Guardian (1713) as the best English writers. It is clear that the grammarians are on the whole not particularly interested in contemporary usage--strictly speaking, not even the language of the *Spectator*, the *Tatler* and the *Guardian* can be said to represent contemporary usage in the 1750s.[3] The admiration for the language of Swift, expressed by White and Lowth, seems exceptional in this respect.

As to the actual quotations found, a variety of authors is quoted from, mostly dating from the sixteenth and seventeenth centuries. Fogg is somewhat exceptional in that approximately half his quotations illustrating the use of do represent eighteenth-century usage, though most of his examples of the use of shall/will date from the seventeenth century. The most popular sources used by the grammarians are Shakespeare, the Bible and Pope, though by far the majority of the instances from Shakespeare (36 out of the 45 instances for do and 55 out of the 65 instances for shall / will) and from Pope are found in White's work, and those from the Bible in that of Fogg. The number of quotations provided by White is so large that he appears to have worked with a corpus; Baker (1770), who has not yet been referred to, and Fogg appear to have done so, too (see for the latter author Alston's introductory note to the facsimile reprint of the *Elementa Anglicana*). None of these three authors refer to their method of working with a corpus. It is apparently a new method at the time--at least among English grammarians--and it seems to have introduced by White whose corpus in the largest of all. Baker must have conceived of the method independently, for he claims in his preface:

> It will undoubtedly be thought strange, when I declare that I have never yet seen the folio Edition of *Mr. Johnson's* Dictionary: but knowing Nobody that has it, I have never been able to borrow it, and I have myself no Books; at least not many more that what a Church-going old Woman may by [sic] supposed to have of devotional Ones upon her mantle-piece. (1770: iv-v)

There is a somewhat incredulous note written opposite page 1 of the copy of the book which was reproduced by Alston, which reads:

> When this Book was published the Author was entirely ignorant
> that ever any man has published an English grammar either in
> our own language or any other. He had not heard of Lowth's,
> or Wallis's which was printed about a hundred years ago & is
> in Latin ... He had not seen Johnson's Dict. [t]ill he had
> written his Rem[arks].

It seems even more unlikely that Baker would have heard of White--the work was not very popular, and it was never reprinted (see Alston 1970).[4] In his Advertisement to Vol. II of the *Elementa Anglicana* Fogg refers to Lowth and Wallis only (1796: iv), and he may not have seen White either. Thus it appears that all three authors arrived at the method of basing grammatical description on a corpus of literary examples independently of each other.

From the actual quotations found, the conclusion drawn above that the grammarians analysed show no particular interest in contemporary eighteenth-century usage may be confirmed. Out of the 153 instances found, at least 128 date from before the eighteenth century. In his illustrations of the use of *do*, Fogg is apparently exceptional, but then he wrote towards the end of the eighteenth-century and to find fairly large numbers of eighteenth-century illustrations of the use of *do* in his work consequently need not surprise us; White once quotes from a contemporary source as well, the poet Grainger (1721?-1766; 1761: 72). Nevertheless, Fogg's quotations for *do* are the most recent of all grammars providing literary illustrations to their rules: I have found quotations from Moore, Goldsmith, Priestley, Blair, Wesley, Hume, Knox and Mason (1792: 154-5), all of whom were more or less his contemporaries.

4. Older Usage

The question presents itself whether the grammarians discussed so far, including those providing biblical illustrations such as Ward (1765) and others (subcategory d.2 distinguished above), were aware of the problem that by exemplifying with older quotations they might be describing archaic or obsolete patterns of usage. All three grammatical problems I have looked at, viz. double negation, <u>shall</u> / <u>will</u> and the auxiliary <u>do</u>, were undergoing change at the time: double negation was for the first time proscribed in the eighteenth century (Tieken 1982); usage of <u>shall</u> and <u>will</u> in the Authorized Version differed from that in the eighteenth century (Tieken 1985; see also Aijmer 1987), and there is considerable variation in the use of <u>do</u> in the eighteenth century (Tieken 1987). Some authors were clearly aware of the existence of older patterns of usage: when discussing double negation, Benjamin Martin, for instance, refers to usage of the construction in older stages of the language:

> We use but one negative, though the Saxons used two, as, Ne om ic na Crist, I am not the Christ. And hence Chaucer *I ne said none ill* (1748: 93)

And likewise Fogg on the subject of <u>shall</u> / <u>will</u> (1796: 128):

> The original sense of *shall* was duty, as
> The faithe I shalle to God.   *Chaucer.*

Others provide examples to demonstrate that usage has changed, such as Bayly (1758: 101-2):

> In the old *English* Writers *shall* is of general Use, and in all Cases of Certainty; but *will* only for mere Volition, somewhat differing from the modern Use and Sense.

After providing a quotation from Ascham, he adds, 'The same is observable throughout the BIBLE, in reading of which this old Use and Sense of the Future and not the modern should be attended to'. And Coote (1788: 101), quoted by Visser (1969: 1509), claims that 'the old English writers frequently used this verb [i.e. <u>do</u>] as an auxiliary in affirmative sentences, whether an emphasis was required or not'; the quotations he provides are from Henry VIII, Spenser and Shakespeare. He adds that 'at present, we do not use this auxiliary in mere affirmations, unless we wish to lay some stress on what we affirm'. A similar awareness of the changing language may be found in Priestley (1761: 22), Lowth (1762: 59) and Ward (1765: 198). Others may not have been aware of the extent to which usage in their time differed from that of earlier periods. This, as it happens, was especially a problem to those working with a corpus. Thus, White feels he has to make an exception in his discussion of do for do-less questions (i.e. questions in which nowadays a form of do would be required, such as Saw you her?). First he claims '... Do and Did are very frequently employ'd in putting a question'; but on the next page he adds: 'Yet the Signs Do and Did may often, on this occasion be well enough omitted' (1761: 71-2). However, from my own analysis of the use of do in the eighteenth century (Tieken 1987: 192) it appears that do-less questions are not nearly as frequent as White's remark would seem to suggest. The reverse may be found in his discussion of emphatic do: most of the illustrations he supplies are not emphatic, yet he describes them as though they were, because that was how do in affirmative sentences was generally used in his time, at least in the language of prose. Some examples are the following quotations:

"Brief as the lightning in the collied night,
"That in a spleen unfolds both heaven and earth;
"And, ere a man hath pow'r to say Behold,
"The Jaws of darkness *do* devour it up."   (from Shakespeare;
1761: 69)

"There spake my brother, there my father's grave
"*Did* utter forth a voice!"   (from Shakespeare; 1761: 70)

All this seems to originate from White's decision to work with a corpus consisting largely of older instances, and of his wish to accommodate each and every item in his corpus in his description of do. Fogg, too, through his inclusion of instances of shall/ will from the Bible in his corpus has to allow for a usage that differs from that generally current in his day: 'and in poetical or very solemn language, [shall] expresses that the thing will happen' (1792: 156). Johnson likewise notes that 'the difficulty [in explaining the use of shall / will] is increased by the poets who sometimes give to shall an emphatical sense of will (dictionary entry for shall); in prose texts of the time such a use of shall was no longer very common (see Hulbert 1947 and Taglicht 1970). Johnson's observation clearly derives from his practice, referred to above, of drawing largely on older patterns of usage.

It is clear, then, that the practice of illustrating with older
examples forces certain grammarians, as well as Johnson in his
Dictionary, to allow for usage that is no longer generally current in
their day; what is more, certain aspects of current usage are
occasionally even mistakenly illustrated with older examples that are
in effect illustrations of a different construction.

5. Examples of bad English.

The description of older uses of do induces Coote (1788: 101) to
criticise the poet Gray for an instance of incorrect usage of the
auxiliary do: ' "The moping owl does to the moon complain" - Here does
is superfluous, unless it be allowed that the repetition of the bird's
cries is better expressed by the auxiliary than without it'. To
censure contemporary writers is quite common practice in the
eighteenth century, for, says Lowth (1762: ix), 'our best Authors for
want of some rudiments of this kind have sometimes fallen into
mistakes, and been guilty of palpable errors in point of Grammar'. It
is felt that even 'the best authors' would benefit from studying a
grammar of their mother tongue, and that from citing their mistakes
the general public would benefit. Baker is especially straightforward
in this matter:

> ... I have paid no Regard to Authority. I have censured even
> our best Penmen, where they have departed from what I conceive
> to be the Idiom of the Tongue, or where I have thought they
> violate grammar without Necessity. To judge by the Rule of
> *Ipse Dixit* is the Way to perpetuate Error. [5] (1770: iv)

Some writers are strongly opposed to the idea that one might learn
from the errors of others. Fenning's opinion on the matter has
already been referred to at the beginning of this paper; Buchanan is
of the same opinion, and so is Priestley, the first 'for fear of
introducing Confusion, and distracting the Learner too much at his
first setting out' (1762: iii-iv) and the second, though 'they are
really useful; but that they make so uncouth an appearance in print'
(1761: xi). What these authors are referring to are very likely

exercises containing deliberately garbled sentences that were to be corrected by the pupil (see Fenning 1771: vii, as well as the exercises provided by Fisher 1750: 127-32), of which one might well doubt the pedagogical value. Even so, on the whole the practice of providing examples of 'bad English', first introduced by Ann Fisher (1750) after the example of Latin grammars (see Alston's introductory note to the facsimile reprint), seems to be much approved of. Murray sums up what may be the predominant attitude on the matter: 'a proper selection of faulty composition is more instructive to the young grammarian, than any rules and examples of propriety that can be given' (1795: iv).

As to the criticism of actual writers, it seems that there is no consensus as to whose English is worst. What is more, we find authors who are both praised and criticised, such as Blair (cited with approval by Fogg, and condemned by Webster 1789 as well as by Fogg), and Goldsmith (cited by Fogg as well as condemned by him) and Addison (condemned by Webster, but apparently praised by Dilworth and Gough; see above). Baker presents the most interesting case, because of his strong disapproval of some authors: Richardson he refers to as a 'bad Writer' (1770: 10), and of Lord Shaftesbury he says that he passes for a good one (1770: 13); his attitude towards others is, to say the least, biased--thus of Swift and Bolingbroke, both of whom he had criticised elsewhere (1770: 60, 56, 57), he says:

> Nay, if I mistake not, I have met with it [i.e. *demean* in the sense of 'debase' or 'lessen'] once or twice in *Swift;* and I think it likewise once occurs in my Lord *Bolingbroke's Oldcastle's Remarks upon English History*. If these two Writers have really employed the Word in that Sense, it must undoubtedly have been thro' Oversight. (1770: 10)

Obviously, these two writers do not bear comparison with Richardson. And on a 'mistake' he found in Pope's 'The King of Dikes, than whom no sluice of Mud/ With deeper Sable blots the silver Flood', he says 'But, as there is a Force in the Word Whom which there is not in Who, the using this last Word would have enfeebled the Sentence, and in a great Measure have spoil'd two of the most beautiful Lines in English Poetry' (1770: 47). The argument he provides here in favour of Pope's use of <u>whom</u> is irrational; obviously, again, good poetry bears no blemish.

From all this it is clear that anyone can come in for censure, and that it was generally felt to be profitable to show and discuss mistakes made, especially those by the 'approved authors'. What is interesting is that some authors, and especially Baker, can be particularly harsh in their criticism, and that it is mostly contemporary writing that comes in for criticism. It is striking that women writers are not criticised in the grammars--nor are they ever cited to illustrate <u>good</u> usage--even though their language, spoken as well as written, was often enough disapproved of at the time (see Tucker 1961: 96 and 1967: 78-80). This demonstrates that in the eighteenth century the language of men constituted the only norm by which good as well as bad usage was measured.

6. Conclusion.

In the above analysis I have argued that eighteenth-century grammarians were on the whole interested only in the written language produced by male authors in a not too distant past. This conclusion was drawn on the basis of my findings in a relatively small number of works as these were the only ones to include literary examples. Even so, this conclusion is of considerably wider validity for a number of reasons. To begin with, those grammarians who show any interest in usage, whether written or spoken, wrote in the second half of the eighteenth century. Before that time, grammarians tended to make up their own examples, or they derived much of their material from influential older grammarians. But even if these older grammarians based their descriptions on actual usage, they did not show a great interest in the spoken language, as may be concluded from the absence in the grammars of a description of certain constructions that are particularly characteristic of speech, such as tag questions (Tieken 1987: 221). Though the possibility should not be entirely discarded, it is not always the case that the examples deliberately made up to illustrate the rules reflect spoken usage. Of the examples of double negation provided by Ann Fisher and others no instances were found even in the most illiterate letters analysed by Austin (1984: 146). Even in the second half of the period spoken usage is only rarely taken into account. There are occasional exceptions, such as Baker when he discusses double negation:

> This is, as I have said, the correct Way of speaking. But we ought not to resolve never to deviate from it. In very animated Speeches, where a man were delivering himself with Vehemence and Heat, *neither* and *nor*, as having a more forcible Sound than *either* and *or* might perhaps be used not with an ill grace. (1770: 112)

Webster (1784) may likewise be referred to here (Leonard 1929: 189). But such exceptions are rare. One further illustration of the supreme importance of the written language in the eyes of the grammarians is the method of working with a corpus as a basis of grammatical description, a truly eighteenth-century innovation in the grammar writing of the time. The idea that doing so against the belief in the existence of a more perfect state of the English language in the past might have serious disadvantages, as has been demonstrated by the case of White and Fogg, had not presented itself yet.

NOTES

1. The use of examples such as these may often enough have been prompted by the author's thorough knowledge of his Latin grammar, acquired in his schoolboy days. A comparison between the 'Latin' examples and those in the Latin grammars published in England at the time, and in particular Lily's, may well produce interesting results.
2. Greenwood's indebtedness to Wallis is commonly known (Greenwood 1711: Alston's introductory note), and he even admits to it in his preface (1711: A4^r. Occasionally his rules are literal translations of Wallis's (see Tieken 1987: 212).
3. Dobson notes that it takes thirty to forty years, or even longer, for a new development in pronunciation as found in early modern English rhyme words to be taken notice of by the grammarians (1969: 431). This is exactly what seems to have happened here, too.
4. That White's study of the English verb did not go entirely unnoticed either may be illustrated from William Ward's reference to it (1765: xiii, see Tieken 1985: 141).
5. Baker's opinion as to what constitutes correct English is a highly idiosyncratic one. For one thing, he claims in his preface (Baker 1770: ii) to have received hardly any education -- he is 'ignorant of Greek and but indifferently skilled in the Latin ... (he) quitted the School at fifteen ... injudiciously instructed' -- and for another he was severely criticised for his pronouncements by the owner of the second edition of the *Reflections on the English language* (1779)- see Leonard (1929: 37).

REFERENCES

Alston, R.C. (ed.). 1965 and 1970. *A Bibliography of the English Language from the Invention of Printing to the Year 1800*. Vols I and III. Leeds: E.J. Arnold and Sons Limited, and The Scholar Press, Menston, respectively.

Alston, R.C. (ed.) 1974. *English Linguistics 1500-1800*. London: The Scolar Press.

Austin, Frances. 1984. "Double Negatives and the Eighteenth Century". *English Historical Linguistics: Studies in Development*. ed. by N.F. Blake and Charles Jones, 138-48. Sheffield: CECTAL.

Aijmer, K. 1987. "Principles of Semantic Change and Lexical Variation-- The Variation between *Shall* and *Will* in Early Modern English". Paper presented at the Fifth International Conference on English Historical Linguistics, Cambridge, April 1987.

Dobson, E.J. 1969. "Early Modern Standard English". *Approaches to English Historical Linguistics. An Anthology* ed. by Roger Lass, 419-39. New York: Holt, Rinehart and Winston Inc. (Repr. from *Transactions of the Philological Society* 1955, 25-54).
Hulbert, J.R. 1947. "On the Origin of the Grammarians' Rules for the Use of *Shall* and *Will*". *P.M.L.A.* 62. 1178-82.
Leonard, Sterling Andrus. 1929. *The Doctrine of Correctness in English Usage 1700-1800*. Madison: University of Wisconsin.
Taglicht, J. 1970. "The Genesis of the Conventional Rules for the use of *Shall* and *Will*". *English Studies* 51. 193-213.
Tieken-Boon van Ostade, Ingrid. 1982. "Double Negation and Eighteenth-century English Grammars". *Neophilologus* IX VI. 278-85.
Tieken-Boon van Ostade, Ingrid. 1985. "'I Will Be Drowned and No Man Shall Save Me': The Conventional Rules for *Shall* and *Will* in Eighteenth-century English Grammars". *English Studies* 66. 123-42.
Tieken-Boon van Ostade, Ingrid. 1987. *The Auxiliary Do in Eighteenth-century English: A Sociohistorical-linguistic Approach*. Geschiedenis van de Taalkunde 6. Dordrecht: Foris Publications.
Tucker, Susie I. 1961. *English Examined. Two Centuries of Comment on the Mother-tongue*. London: The Athlone Press.
Visser, F.Th. 1969. *An Historical Syntax of the English Language*. Part III, first half. Leiden: E.J. Brill.

APPENDIX

With the exception of those works indicated by an asterisk, all grammars and other works on the English language listed below are reprinted in facsimile by Alston 1974.

a. Eighteenth-century grammars and other works on the English language analysed:
anon., *The English Accidence*, London, 1733.
John Ash, *Grammatical Institutes*, 4th ed. (1st ed. 1760), London, 1763.
Robert Baker, *Reflections on the English Language*, London 1770.
Anselm Bayly, *An Introduction to Languages, Literary and Philosophical*, London, 1772.
John Brightland and Charles Gildon, *A Grammar of the English Tongue*, London 1711.
Richard Browne, *The English-School Reformed*, London, 1700.
James Buchanan, *The British Grammar*, London 1762.
John Collyer, *The General Principles of Grammar*, Nottingham, 1735.
*Charles Coote, *Elements of the Grammar of the English Language*, London, 1788 (as quoted by Visser 1969: 1509).
Thomas Dilworth, *A New Guide to the English Tongue*, 13th ed. (1st ed. 1740), London, 1751.
Daniel Duncan, *A New English Grammar*, London, 1731.

John Fell, *An Essay towards an English Grammar*, London, 1784.
Daniel Fenning, *A New Grammar of the English Language*, London, 1771.
Ann Fisher, *A New Grammar*, 2nd ed., Newcastle upon Tyne, 1750.
Peter Walkden Fogg, *Elementa Anglicana*, Stockport, 1792/6.
James Gough, *A Practical Grammar of the English Tongue*, Dublin, 1754.
James Greenwood, *An Essay towards a Practical English Grammar*, London, 1711.
Ralph Harrison, *Institutes of English Grammar*, Manchester, 1777.
*Samuel Johnson, *A Dictionary of the English Language*, London, 1755, repr. in facsimile Hildesheim, 1968.
Hugh Jones, *An Accidence to the English Tongue*, London, 1724.
John Kirkby, *A New English Grammar*, London, 1746.
A. Lane, *A Key to the Art of Letters*, London, 1700.
Solomon Lowe, *Four Tracts on Grammar*, 1723-38; 'English Grammar Reformed;', 1737.
Robert Lowth, *A Short Introduction to English Grammar*, London, 1762.
Duncan Mackintosh, *A Plain Rational Essay on English Grammar*, Boston, 1797.
Benjamin Martin, *Institutions of Language*, London, 1748.
Lindley Murray, *English Grammar*, York, 1795.
James Pickbourn, *A Dissertation of the English Verb*, London, 1789.
Joseph Priestley, *The Rudiments of English Grammar*, London, 1761.
Samuel Saxon, *The English Schollar's Assistant*, 2nd ed., Reading, 1737.
John Sedger, *The Structure of the English Language*, London, 1798.
George Neville Ussher, *The Elements of English Grammar*, Glocester (sic), 1785.
John Ward, *Four Essays upon the English Language*, London, 1758.
William Ward, *An Essay on Grammar*, London, 1765.
Noah Webster, *A Grammatical Institute of the English Language*, Part II, Hartford, 1784.
Noah Webster, *Dissertations on the English Language*, Boston, 1789.
James White, *The English Verb*, London, 1761.

b. Other works consulted:
William Lily and John Colet, *A Short Introduction of Grammar*, n.p., 1549
*John Wallis, *Grammatica Linguae Anglicanae*, Oxford, 1653; 6th ed. 1765; translated by J.A. Kemp. 1972. London: Longman.

FROM LESS TO MORE SITUATED IN LANGUAGE:
THE UNIDIRECTIONALITY OF SEMANTIC CHANGE

ELIZABETH CLOSS TRAUGOTT
Stanford University

1. *Introduction*. In Traugott (1982) I argued that semantic-pragmatic change in the early stages of grammaticalization was unidirectional:[1] meanings with largely propositional (ideational) content could gain textual (cohesion-making) and/or expressive (presuppositional, and other pragmatic) meanings, in short:

propositional ((> textual) > (expressive))

An example is the development of OE þa hwile þe 'at the time that' > ME *while (that)* 'during' > PDE *while* 'although'. 'At times' refers to a situation viewed as existing in the world. *While* in the sense of 'during' signals a cohesive time-relation between two clauses, and therefore has a primarily text-making function. And *while* in the sense of 'although' is primarily expressive of the speaker's attitude. The reverse change, from expressive > textual > propositional is highly unlikely in the history of any one grammatical marker.

Since writing that paper, I have extended my study of semantic change to lexical change (cf. Traugott, In Press a; Traugott and Dasher 1987). It turns out that the process of semantic change outlined for the semantics of grammaticalization belongs to a larger set of processes of semantic change that are in general quite regular.[2] Indeed, they are so regular that it is possible to develop predictive hypotheses. They are predictive in the sense that one can test them against historical data and show their correctness. Further, they are predictive in the sense that one can take synchronic polysemies from any period in any language and project change back into the past, in other words, one can do internal semantic-pragmatic reconstruction (Traugott 1986a). It is the purpose of this paper to show in some greater detail how this may be done.

2. *Some assumptions*. Before proceeding to discuss the paths of change and how they permit semantic internal reconstruction to be done, some assumptions need to be stated:

a) As is true of all linguistic change, the tendencies that I will outline are possible and not necessary (i.e. there was no necessity for *while* in the temporal sense to develop the concessive sense).

b) A form typically maintains its original meaning alongside its newer one, as in the case of *while*. Alternatively, only the newer meaning may survive, while the original meaning is expressed by another form. For example, OE *butan* could serve as a preposition introducing either an NP or, later, an S (in which case it was a subordinating conjunction); the former was replaced by 'except, unless' in all but a few contexts (such as the one just used), but was retained in the newer, connective sense and reanalized as a coordinate conjunction (cf. the paper by Nevalainen in this volume).

c) The semantic theory underlying an account of semantic change must allow for polysemy as well as homonymy, since widely-attested connections among meanings could not otherwise be shown. For example, if only homonymy were permitted in a semantic theory, then it would be impossible to show either synchronically or across time how the later meanings of <u>but</u> are related to and constrained by the earlier meanings, or how the attested meaning-changes share properties with similar changes in other semantic domains.

d) The semantic theory must also allow for invited inferences to become lexicalized (cf. Geis and Zwicky 1971).[3] For example, in *Since Phil left Bill has been despressed*, *since* has a temporal meaning but invites the inference of a causal relation. Invited inferences become lexicalized as part of the meaning of a form when what was formerly only an inference must be construed as the actual meaning of the form, as in *Since Phil is leaving, Bill is depressed*. (OE *siþþan* meant only 'after(ward)', but had a causal invited inference. This invited inference became lexicalized in ME, with the result that the form became polysemous; in one of its meanings it was temporal, and could have an invited inference of causality; in the other, it was causal.)

e) All languages as we know them have both semantic and pragmatic meanings. Both are equally present, although pragmatic meanings may be expressed in different ways at different times in different languages (e.g. by intonation, morphology, etc.). To say that textual or expressive (i.e. pragmatic) meanings are newer than propositional (i.e. semantic) ones does not mean that a language can at some stage have only semantic meanings, or only pragmatic ones. It means simply that, given a form X, the pragmatic meanings associated with it, if any, will be later than the semantic/propositional meanings associated with it, etc.

3. *Paths of semantic change*. I turn now to the paths of semantic change. I will argue that there are three closely-related tendencies, the first of which can feed the second and either of which can feed the third. The tendencies are characterized in terms loosely related to some current views of semantics that regard linguistic meanings not as independent entities but as relations between situations (or rather situation-types), and minds (cf. Barwise and Perry 1983). 'Described situations' are situations relevant to the truth or falsity of the utterance as interpreted. 'External' described situations are those events or states of affairs in the world about which we learn from being told about them, and sometimes through verification; 'internal' described situations are perceptions such as *hearing* and states of mind such as *knowing* which we learn about primarily by being told about them.

The first tendency can be stated as follows:

Tendency I.
Meanings based in the external described situation > meanings based in the internal (evaluative/ perceptual/cognitive) situation

This subsumes most of the familiar meaning changes known as pejoration and amelioration (e.g. *churl* 'man' > 'lowest rank of freeman (in the Anglo-Saxon laws)' >

'serf' > 'rude, ill-bred person'(cf. Dahlgren 1983), and a wide range of metaphorical extensions, most of them shifts from concrete to abstract (e.g. early OE *felan* meant only 'touch'; it did not acquire a perceptual sense until late OE). Tendency I also subsumes the tendency 'to use vocabulary from the external (sociophysical) domain in speaking of the internal (emotional and psychological) domain' (Sweetser 1984:56).

The second tendency is as follows:

Tendency II.
Meanings based in the described situation > meanings based in the metalinguistic situation.

It subsumes the shift from propositional to textual meanings illustrated by *þa hwile þe* in its shift from 'at the time that' > 'during' (for similar semantic developments in other connective domains, cf. Lord 1976, Traugott 1986b). It also includes shifts from mental to speech act verb meanings (e.g. *observe*, which had the mental verb meaning of 'perceive (that)' in the early 1500's and was used as a speech act verb in the sense 'state that' in the early 1600's (the mental verb meaning of *observe* was preceded by a more concrete meaning 'pay attention to rule'; in other words, it had already undergone Tendency I).

Finally, the third tendency can be stated as follows:

Tendency III.
Meanings tend to become increasingly based in the speaker's subjective belief state/attitude toward the situation.

This tendency subsumes the shift of temporal to concessive *while*, and a large number of other changes, such as the development of the action verb *go* into a marker of immediate, expected future. Of shifts such as the latter, Langacker has said:
> Whereas the basic meaning profiles *physical* motion by an *objectively*-construed mover (namely the *subject*, one (unprofiled) facet of the extended meaning is *abstract* motion by a *subjectively*-construed mover, specifically the *conceptualizer*. The pivotal factor in this type of semantic shift is therefore *subjectification*' (1986:467).

I will argue that this kind of subjectification is a major factor in semantic change.

All three tendencies share one property in common: the later meanings presuppose not only a world of objects and states of affairs, but of values and of linguistic relations that cannot exist without language; in other words, the later meanings are licensed by the function of language.

The hypothesis that the three tendencies correlate and that Tendency III is the dominant one, fed by Tendencies I and II, encourages us to look at synchronically-defined dictionary entries in a language for any period of that language with new eyes. In many (but certainly not all) cases, hypotheses about the order of development can readily be made, at least for the more general classes of meaning differences. Just as in the case of internal phonological reconstruction, loss or merger may obscure some actual paths of change. But the project can be remarkably successful nonetheless. I will devote the rest of this paper to illustrating some examples of backward-projecting hypotheses that can be made from the meanings of words in three semantic fields in English: 'presuppositional' terms like *very* (as in *the very answer I was looking for*), speech act verbs like *insist*, and modal expressions such as auxiliaries like *must* and modal adverbs like *apparently*.

4. *Presuppositional terms*. I will start with a brief study of presuppositional terms like *very*, *just*, *even*. I have discussed the development of *just* in detail elsewhere (Traugott, In Press b), and will therefore only summarize the main arguments here.

Any standard dictionary of contemporary English will include the following kinds of entries:

(1) Adj.: a) honorable, fair: *just ruler*; righteous, legitimate: *just cause*

b) properly due: *just deserts*; fitting: *a just touch of solemnity*

c) exact, precise: *a just measure*

These adjectival meanings all share the property of legitimacy, fairness, rightness, and being in harmony with some norm. In this they are supported by the meanings of words derived from *just*, such as *justice*, and *justify* (in the sense of both 'demonstrate the validity of' and 'space properly in printing'). The adverbial meanings may at first seem somewhat different:

(2) Adv.: a) precisely, exactly: *just enough good sense*; precisely at the moment: *it's just three* (scalar particle)

b) in immediate future or past: *she has just arrived; she's just arriving* (deictic temporal)

c) merely: *she's just a linguist*; barely: *you just missed the bull's eye* (downtoner)

However, the relation between doing something legitimately or fittingly and doing it exactly, precisely as it should be done are not really so far apart, especially when the adjectival usage in connection with weights and measures (1.c) is taken into account. Both the adjectival and the adverbial meanings bring into play various alternative values. Fairness and fittingness bring into play certain types of behavior, while excluding others that are valued less highly or considered excessive; preciseness, too, brings into play and excludes various alternatives that are neither too little nor too much (cf. König, In Press).

As a class, the adjectival meanings are based more in the external/described situation than the adverbial ones. Within the adverbial class, those meanings related to 'precisely' are based more in the described situation than the deictic temporals (*It's just three*, *She has just arrived*) and the scalar particles (*just a linguist*). Furthermore, although all the meanings are to some extent evaluative, those related to honesty and fairness are based in the social situation, those with precision in the perceptual realm, and those related to temporal deixis and especially scalarity are based almost entirely in the speaker's attitude.

Given these facts, the three tendencies outlined above, and the evidence that Tendency I can feed Tendency II, and that either can feed Tendency III, I hypothesized that the meanings came in as follows:

(3) ? > righteous/fitting/precise >⟨temporal / downtoner⟩

The question mark signals that since 'righteous/fitting/ precise' is in fact evaluative, there may have been an earlier, less evaluative meaning that no longer exists.

The historical evidence bears the hypothesis out well. Briefly, just ultimately derives from the Latin adjective iust- and the adverb iuste, which pertain to actions and decisions in accordance with ritual, law, and good reason. According to Benveniste, Lat. iustus 'just' is related to IE *yous 'state of regularity, of the normality required by the rules of ritual' (1973:391). He argues that in Latin the verb iurare, the past participle of which gave rise to the adjective, means to engage in 'the act of repeating a certain form of words' (ibid.:395), and the noun ius, which we usually translate as 'law', 'in general, is a *formula* and not an abstract concept' (ibid.:391). This suggests that the hypothesis is correct that *just* in the sense of 'righteous, legitimate', etc. originated in a more concrete, less evaluative, meaning.

By Classical Latin times, evaluative meanings associated with ceremonious and legal norms and with exactness had developed for the root *iust-*; the adverb had also developed a meaning associated with precise measure: 'to the extent described, fully' (cf. Oxford Latin Dictionary). These continued into Medieval French (MF), but were partially differentiated in morphology. An adjective *juste* was used in earlier Old French in connection with religious norms, i.e. in the sense 'righteous' (Wartburg 1950). From the twelfth century on there appear legal and normative meanings ('conforming to that which is legal, legitimate'), and from the end of the thirteenth century also the meaning 'precise, exact' in contexts involving measures and balances (cf. *juste mesure* 'just/exact measure'). In addition, there developed an adverb *justement*, which apparently was used only in the legal sense, and not in the sense 'precisely'. The latter sense did not develop until the sixteenth century (Wartburg 1950 and Larousse 1975).

We may ask how the meaning 'exact, precise' came into being. Righteousness and justness, whether established by religious canons or by law, bring into play alternatives on a scale; in this case the scale, by convention, is implicated to be behavioral--conforming to the regulation of law, religious doctrine, good manners, or other appropriate form. Extremes of behavior are normally not tolerated in these contexts. We may assume that in Classical Latin and Medieval French, as in PDE, to say that something is just or is justly done is to invite the inference that it is done in precisely the right way, with the appropriate balance. The shift from 'honorable, fair, legitimate' > 'precise' can best be understood as involving the lexicalization of this invited inference. It is hardly surprising that expansion of meaning occurred in the context of measures.

In sum, when *juste* was borrowed into English there was an MF adjective of this form and an adverb marked by *-ment* (as well at Latin forms; it is not clear, however, to what extent they influenced Middle English directly). The ME adjective appears in meanings essentially similar to those of MF *juste*: 'righteous, (legally) fair, exact':

(4) a) 1384 I cam not to clepe *iust* men but synful men to penaunce
'I came to call not righteous but sinful men to penance'

b) 1385 She...*juste* cause hadde hym to triste
'She...had reasonable cause to trust him'

c) 1380 Hir paleys...stant eke in so *juste* a place/That every soun mot to hyt pace
'Her (Fame's) palace...stood in so correct a place that every sound could reach it'

There was also an adverb *justli*. This might appear to be a form part borrowed, part calqued from *justement*. However, it meant not only 'righteously, fairly' as did MF *justement*, but also 'exactly' in contexts of measurement and fit:

(5) c.1391. Yif thou drawe a cross-lyne overthwart the compas *justly* over the lyne meridional, than hast thou est and west and south
'If you draw a line across the compass exactly over the meridian line, then you have E and W and S'

In other words, the English adverb *justli* had approximately the same meanings as the adjective. Within a couple of decades a new adverb *juste* appeared in the meaning 'exactly, precisely' of measurement and location. The deictic temporal meaning does not occur regularly until the seventeenth century, cf.

(6) a) 1697 pleasant Casia *just* renew'd in prime

    b) 1719 the captain replied, 'Tell his excellence I am *just* a coming'

Furthermore, the OED cites the earliest examples of the downtoner toward the end of the seventeenth century, and points out that they are often in the environment of *but* and *only*, e.g.

(7) 1693 Let Horace, who is the Second, and but *just* the Second, carry off the Quivers

It is possible that the downtoner derives metonymically from constructions with *but* (as in (7)), or *only*. However, in view of the fact that even from the beginning bare *just* also occurs in downtoning function, it is also possible that once more an invited inference has become lexicalized. As in the case of *merely* and *only*, *just* excludes 'more' in so far as it means 'precisely'. The negative downtoning meaning may well derive from social inferencing associated with such principles as 'the more the better', and conversely, 'if you can't get more, that's bad'.

    We see, then, that the semantic predictions made in (3) are in general correct. The earliest recorded meaning is relatively concrete. The meanings associated with righteousness, fittingness, and precision precede the temporal and downtoner meanings. Although the downtoner develops later than the temporal, there is no more evidence from the historical data than from the synchronic to assume that it derived out of the temporal rather than directly from the scalar particle.

    Just is, of course, only one of a whole class of so-called 'presuppositional' terms that presuppose, entail, or implicate relations to a scale. Other such terms include *mere*, *even*, *utter*, and *very*. All of them, at least in some of their meanings, express speaker attitudes. Given the process of subjectification, we can hypothesize that all these words once had meanings that referred primarily to external situations. As we will see, *mere* originally meant 'undiluted' (as of wine), *even* meant 'horizontal, equal', *utter* comes from 'outer' (later in the sense of 'outermost'), and *very* from 'true' (cf. the use of *truly* in *truly awful*; here the same semantic change is reoccurring in PDE).

Let us look a little more closely at *very*, for which Brugman (1984) has given a detailed synchronic analysis. She identifies two major classes of meanings. The first is those that involve the extreme end of a scale, as in:

(8) a) the very pinnacle of her career; the very back of the room; the very best croissants;

or the extreme end of an implicational scale, as in:

(9) b) the very thought of writing a dissertation puts me into a cold sweat (downtoner)

The second class means something like 'precise', 'identical', as in:

(9) the very person I have been waiting to see; Chomsky's very words.

Granted that all these meanings of adjectival *very* are discourse-based, can one hypothesize in what order they developed? What seems precise to the speaker may not always seem precise to the addressee; nevertheless, there are often external-means of verification: for example, interlocutors have external means of judging whether some string was or was not actually Chomsky's words. Therefore, *very* in its meaning 'precise' has some reference to the described situation. But verifying the very back of the room would be more difficult. Verification is barely the issue when we talk of *the very pinnacle* of someone's career and it is not an issue at all in the implicational use of *very* as in *the very thought of writing a dissertation*. Here the meaning is entirely speaker-based. In other words, the meanings typified by *Chomsky's very words*, *the very back of the room*, *the very thought* are on a scale of less to more indicative of speaker attitude. We may conjecture that the meanings developed in this order. The OED confirms that they did, although the gap in time between the first two is too small to provide strong evidence for the ordering between them:

(10) 1338 'precise' (cf. the *very* center; and uses in (9))

1386 'extreme' (cf. the *very* end; and uses in (8a))
1550 'implicational extreme' (cf. the *very* mountains; the *very* mention; and uses in (8b))

We have noted that both *just* and *very* have meanings related to 'precision' and 'truth' and that these preceded more 'up-toning' and 'down-toning' meanings. Up-toning meanings focus on the high end of a scale, down-toning meanings on the low end. *Very* is mostly an up-toner in the 'extreme' meanings, but serves as a down-toner in *the very (=mere) thought of writing a dissertation*, i.e. something as low on the probability scale as the thought of writing a dissertation. Since up-toning and down-toning meanings identify points at the extremes of a scale, they imply asymmetric relations (more, less, not equal). The shift from meanings referring to preciseness, sameness, parallelism, simultaneity, and so forth to asymmetric meanings is in fact quite frequent. We have seen this shift in the case of *just*. As I pointed out at the beginning, *while* meaning 'during', and therefore involving at least partial simultaneity of events, came to mean 'although' (or 'contrary to what might be expected', that is, non-parallelism with expectation). *Besides*, which used to mean 'at the sides of', i.e. symmetrically on both sides, came to mean *in addition*. We may, then, be fairly confident in hypothesizing that a word like *mere*, which is only a down-toner in contemporary English, may once have meant something like 'true' or 'precise'. Indeed, the Latin source *mer-* meant 'undiluted'; in French it was used as a legal term to mean 'true, absolute'. The first uses in English are in the Latin and French senses. The IE root *mer-* meant 'shine, flicker', and suggests that the Latin itself had undergone Tendency I, as would be predicted by the hypothesis outlined in this paper. An interesting example of *mere* in the sense 'true' from the mid-sixteenth century, which also includes *very* in the sense of 'precise' is:

(11) 1559-60 That your Majestie...is, and in *verie* deed, and of most *meere* right ought to be...our most rightful...soveraigne

From 'true' *mere* came to mean 'not more than specified':

(12) 1581 If I speeke rather lyke a *meere* Citizen, than a Philosopher

This brings us to *even*. The adjectival senses listed by the American Heritage Dictionary are:

(13) 'having a horizontal surface', 'parallel', 'regular', 'equal', 'having equal probability' (an *even* chance).

The adverbial ones are:

(14) 'to a higher extent' (*even* more), 'in spite of' (*even* with his head start).

We hardly need the extra entry 'arch. identical with: *It is I, even I*', to guess the relation between the adjective and the adverb, or to reconstruct the main outlines of the meaning change. For the adverb we find in OE the meanings 'regularly', 'in equal parts', 'exactly', 'precisely'. 'In spite of' is a late sixteenth century meaning, and 'even more' developed in the mid-eighteenth century.

5. *Speech act verbs*. So far I have focussed on 'presuppositional' words. They belong to a small lexical set which is rather special type, and might be considered inadequate evidence for the large-scale claim that it is possible to project semantic change backwards. I turn now to a brief summary of evidence from a rather different kind of lexical domain: that of speech act verbs.

Many speech act verbs, like *observe* discussed above, have several meanings. Thus *assume*, *commit*, and *insist* have the following polysemies (among others):

(15) a) *assume*: 'put on' (as of clothes), 'take for granted', 'claim', 'pretend that something is the case'

   b) *commit*: 'do' (*commit* a murder), 'place in trust', 'confine' (in prison), 'pledge oneself to do something'

Given the claim that Tendency I (meanings based in the external described situation shift to meanings based in the internal described situation) feeds Tendency II (meanings based in the described situation shift to meanings based in the metalinguistic situation), it follows that a reasonable hypothesis should be that where both non-speech act verb and speech act verb meanings coexist, the former precede the latter. This is because the speech act meaning is a metalinguistic one that at a minimum refers to the discourse situation as a described situation, and in some cases (those called performative uses) is actually constitutive of the discourse situation. Again, the hypothesis proves to be correct, cf. the following lexical entries (based on the OED and MED):

(16) a) *assume*: 1420 'arrogate to oneself' 'adopt' (cf. Lat. *ad-sumere* 'to take on'); 1450 'suppose' (in the sense of 'imagine'); 1714 'claim that something is the case'

   b) *commit*: borrowed into English in the 14th century meaning 'give in trust'; 15th century 'put' (in prison), 'do' (something bad, e.g. murder); 18th century 'pledge oneself to do X'.

Insist is particularly interesting because it involves two speech act meanings, one directive, the other assertive:

(17) *insist*: 'demand something', 'assert something vehemently' (cf. *I insist that he not smoke* vs. *I insist that he doesn't smoke*).

These and similar distinctions will be discussed further in the next section.

   6. *Weakly > strongly subjective epistemicity in modal auxiliaries and adverbs*. The last set of polysemies I will touch on involve weaker and stronger subjective epistemicity. Logicians and some semanticists (cf. Lyons 1982) have argued that both the deontic and the epistemic meanings are ambiguous between less and more subjective meanings. (Lyons refers to 'objective' epistemicity. However, it is not clear whether truly objective modality exists, especially in the epistemic domain, cf. Palmer (1986:16); hence the use here of 'weakly' and 'strongly subjective'.) For example, *He must be married* can be argued to be four ways ambiguous:

(18) a) He is required to marry (deontic, weakly subjective)

   b) I require him to marry (deontic, strongly subjective)

c) It is obvious from evidence that he is married (epistemic, weakly subjective)

d) I conclude that he is married (epistemic, strongly subjective)

Given the theory of semantic change I have outlined, we would expect not only that where non-epistemic (e.g. deontic) meanings coexist with epistemic ones, the former will be older than the latter, but also that the less subjective meanings will precede the more subjective ones. Interpretation of the data is particularly difficult in the domain of degrees of epistemicity, and significantly more work needs to be done before the results can be held to be conclusive. However, preliminary investigation of the prediction that weaker epistemicity precedes stronger epistemicity is encouraging.

As far as the modal auxiliaries in English are concerned, it is well known that all originated in main verbs, specifically verbs of mental ability (*cunnan*), physical ability (*magan*), permission (**motan*), owing (**sculan*), volition (*willan*), etc. In other words, they originated with meanings based in the described world. It is also well known that the deontic generally preceded the epistemic meanings (Shepherd 1982, Bybee and Pagliuca 1985).[4] Goossens (1982) has suggested that epistemicity was only beginning to be grammaticalized in OE. If this is the case, one would expect such epistemics as occur to be only weakly subjective.

In his paper arguing that 'there was already a distinctive grouping of modal properties in Old English, and possibly even a category auxiliary', Warner (this volume) shows that there are not only some deontic uses of the modal verbs, but also some possible epistemic uses of <u>magan</u>, *<u>sculan</u>, and <u>willan</u>. Furthermore, he suggests that some of the epistemic uses are relatively subjective (cf. his examples (4) and (5)). Two things are significant for the prediction being tested here. One is that deontic meanings already exist (and may indeed have subjective coloring, cf. Warner's examples in (3)), so we do not have an epistemic stage without a deontic one. In addition, the strength of the subjectivity of the epistemics can be interpreted as deriving largely from invited inference. This is because all Warner's examples include a context which forces a pragmatically subjective reading, but do not require that meaning to have been fully lexicalized. These contexts are: indirect quotation (associated in many languages of the world with evidentials) (Warner's (4)); concessive or conditional protases (Warner's (5a, 5b)); and the adverb *eaþe* 'easily, obviously' which may itself have an epistemic meaning (his (5c, 5d)). Fully lexicalized subjective *will* epistemics of the type *He will be here by now*, meaning 'I conclude that he is here by now', apparently do not occur until the ME period. Similarly, a weakly subjective (indeed relatively objective) epistemic meaning of *must* preceded the strongly subjective one; the latter apparently did not develop fully until ENE. The following lexicalized examples are cited in the OED (earlier examples are in the context of epistemic adverbs such as *needs* 'necessarily'):

(19) a) 1652 The continent [that which contains, ET] *must* be incorporeal, the contained corporeal (relatively objective; claimed to be based in the laws of rational thought and logic)

b) 1762 This *must* have been a sad shock to the poor disconsolate parent (strongly subjective; based in the speaker's assessment of the proposition)

A parallel can be drawn between deontic and epistemic *must* and speech act meanings such as *insist that you do* vs. *insist that something is the case* (cf. (17)). The directive meaning (*insist that someone do something*) is in a general sense oriented toward the hearer, that is, it has to do with setting up obligations for others and therefore is deontic. The assertive meaning (*insist that something is the case*) is speaker-oriented and has to do with the speaker's assessment of the truth of the proposition; in other words, it is epistemic. In Traugott (In Press a) and Traugott and Dasher (1987) it was hypothesized that the deontic meanings would precede the epistemic meanings on the grounds that this order of development is generally true of modal verbs in English. This is borne out by the data. Thus:

(20) *insist*: 1590s 'stand on, dwell at length on, persevere'; 1697 'demand that...' (deontic); 1768 'maintain that...' (epistemic).

Similarly, *postulate* occurs in the following senses:

(21) *postulate*: 1533 'ask an ecclesiatical authority to admit a nominee (or postulant)'; 1593 'demand' (deontic); 1646 'claim the existence of truth'; 1855 'claim that something is the case' in 1855 (epistemic).

It appears to me now that the deontic > epistemic change in the modals and the speech act verbs are both instances of Tendency III, in other words of the shift to meanings situated in the speaker's mental attitude toward the proposition.

Hanson (1987) has shown that similar kinds of changes are also attested in the history of modal adverbs like *possibly*, *probably*, *evidently*, *apparently*, *obviously*, etc. Exactly as would be expected, where manner and epistemic (sentential) adverb meanings coexist, the former is earlier than the latter, in other words, the meaning situated in the sociophysical world precedes that situated in the speaker's mental attitude. Indeed in many cases an adverb that now no longer has a non-epistemic meaning originally had one. For example, in the fifteenth century, *probably* meant 'in a way that approves itself to one's reason for acceptance or belief'. A particularly clear example comes from the early fifteen hundreds:

(22) a) 1535 You wrote so *probably* that it put me in feare of daungers to come

The epistemic meaning develops in the seventeenth century:

(23) b) 1647 A source, from whence those waters of bitterness...have...*probably* flowed

Some epistemic adverbs have developed strongly subjective meanings, and again the hypothesis that weaker epistemicity precedes stronger epistemicity seems to be borne out. An especially good example is provided by *evidently*. First a manner adverb, as in (24a), it became a weakly subjective epistemic as in (24b), and then a strongly subjective one as in (24c) (this usage appears to have been too recent or colloquial to have been recorded in the OED):

(24) a) 1584 We have here most manifestlie and *evidentlie* written the contrarie (non-epistemic, manner adv.)

b) 1690 No Idea, therefore, can be undinstinguishable from another...for from all other, it is *evidently* different (weak subjective epistemic)

c) 20th C? Sarah has *evidently* left (strong subjective epistemic; introduces implicature of some concession or uncertainty on the speaker's part)

7. *Conclusion*. In conclusion, I have shown that if meaning changes, it changes in the direction of becoming increasingly based in constructs that result from the fact that language exists and is used by speakers to evaluate, to refer to mental and perceptual states of affairs, to mark texts as coherent, to refer to linguistic events, and above all to express the speaker's subjective attitude to what is being said.

It has been my purpose in this paper to focus on the successes of predicting semantic change, especially in terms of predicting the order of change backward from synchronic polysemies. There are, of course, limitations, and not only limitations of the kind that are well known for internal phonological reconstruction.

Among the limitations particulaly relevant to the changes discussed above is the effect of borrowing. Borrowing can be expected to obscure natural changes. For example, *magnify* was borrowed into English from Latin as a speech act verb meaning 'praise', but was later restricted to its original more concrete meaning of 'enlarge' in the context of optics (Sylvia Adamson, personal communication), i.e. *magnify* is a counterexample in the history of English, the donor language but not in the history of Latin, the source language, to the tendencies outlined above. Also, if concrete meanings are borrowed, they may be very short-lived, as in the case of *insist*, whereas they are likely to be far longer-lived in the source language. However, it is remarkable that in most cases of speech act verbs and modal adverbs, the majority of which were borrowed, the tendencies are still borne out. Indeed, Nigel Vincent (personal communication), has pointed out that, in Italian, Latin *assumere* has the sense 'take on' (of staff, responsibilities, etc.). The mental sense of 'take for granted, suppose' is found only in scientific contexts and is an anglicism. It is significant to note, however, that even though the mental meaning is a borrowing, it follows the order of development predicted by the tendencies, so this particular limitation in Italian seems to be one on natural native development rather than on the sequence of semantic changes themselves.

Another apparent limitation is that semantic change very rarely applies to items of the same lexical field at the same time, and thus is rarely capturable in a rule. Thus while we know that words for smell are likely to become pejorative (as witness OE *stincan* 'smell' > *stink*, and *smell* itself), that spatial terms are likely to acquire temporal meanings, that words for 'precise' are likely to become up-toners and down-toners, and that mental verbs are likely to become speech act verbs, we cannot begin to predict either when that will occur, or which lexical item in a given field will change and which will not. Furthermore, the only rule of semantic change that is claimed to have gone to completion that I know of is Stern's much-cited rule (1968[1931]:189): 'rapidly' > 'immediately' before 1400, but not after. However, since this change is actually yet another example involving greater to less verifiability in the external world, and increasing subjectivity of evaluation, there is no principled reason why it should have come to completion, and may be new instances will occur.

A further problem is that, although we know that meanings will become increasingly based in the speaker's attitude, we do not know whether a specific word will become a down-toner (like *just*) or an up-toner (like *right* and, in many of its senses, *very*).

The limitations should not discourage us but rather prompt us to look for finer-grained regularities. What is important to recognize is that semantic change, an area of language often thought to be rather random, does in fact turn out to be subject to linguistic analysis, and to have predictive power.

Before I end, a word or two is in order about motivations for the regularities I have been discussing. My view is that the meaning changes are the result of language use in strategic interaction and goal-oriented activity. While I am not ruling out the role of perception, I see the changes as primarily showing evidence of speakers injecting themselves into the flow of speech, creating coherent discourses, and expressing attitudes toward people, hearers, propositions, and generally whatever is talked about. This is one of the reasons that the semantic changes illustrated here work equally well in the area of lexical change and in the early stages of grammaticalization, when new elements are being recruited to express grammatical relations. Of these early stages of grammaticalization Lehmann has said: 'Every speaker wants to give the fullest possible expression' to what he or she means (1985:315). In so far as this is true, I would add that the three tendencies identified at the beginning can give us some insight into the channelling of what Lehmann calls 'fullest expression'.

NOTES

1. This paper is an expanded and revised version of Traugott 1986a. Thanks are due to Sylvia Adamson, Charles Ferguson, Terry Moore, Robert Stockwell, Nigel Vincent, and Anthony Warner for their comments on the present paper, and to Judith Hochberg and Suzanne Kemmer who helped collect the data on which the generalizations are based. They are of course on no way responsible for any errors of fact or interpretation.

2. This is not to deny that there are irregularities. What is being denied is the claim that there are no or few regularities.

3. The important question of what constraints there are on invited inference must await further study.

A note is in order here on terminology. Geis and Zwicky (1971) use the word 'lexicalized' to characterize the fact that a meaning has become an inherent part of the word (either as a conventional implicature, or as a semantic 'feature' (in the loose sense of this term). The form *since* is actually a grammatical function word, and the process could in this case and in the case of particles such as *just* or auxiliaries such as *must* to be discussed below be termed 'grammaticalization', in the sense that a meaning has become part of the grammatical structure of the language. The term 'lexicalization' will be used here in keeping with general linguistic usage.

4. However, *can* and *may* acquired the permission use later than the possibility use. Bybee and Pagliuca (1985) argue that the deontic meaning arises independently of the epistemic, and that these modals do not provide a counterexample to the generalization that deontic precede epistemic modals.

REFERENCES

Barwise, J. and J. Perry. 1983. *Situations and Attitudes*. Cambridge, Mass.: The MIT Press.
Benveniste, E. 1973. *Indo-European Language and Society*, translated by Mary Elizabeth Meek. Coral Gables, Florida: University of Miami Press.
Brugman, C. 1984. 'The very Idea: a Case Study in Polysemy and Cross-lexical Generalization.' *CLS Papers from the Parasession on Lexical Semantics*, 21-38.
Bybee, J., and W. Pagliuca. 1985. 'Cross-linguistic Comparison and the Development of Grammatical Meaning.' In J. Fisiak, ed. *Historical Semantics and Historical Word Formation*, 60-83. Berlin: de Gruyter.
Dahlgren, K. 1983. 'Social Terms and Social Reality.' *Folia Linguistica Historica* 6.107-25.
Geis, M., and A. Zwicky. 1971. 'On Invited Inferences.' *LI* 2.561.66.
Goossens, L. 1982. 'On the Development of the Modals and of the Epistemic Function in English.' In A. Ahlqvist, ed. *Papers from the Fifth International Conference on Historical Linguistics*, 74-84. Amsterdam: Benjamins.
Hanson, K. 1987. 'On Subjectivity and the History of Epistemic Expressions in English'. *CLS* 23.132-47.
König, E. In Press. '"Just"': Polysemy or Vagueness.' Chapter of *The Meaning of Focus Particles: a Comparative Perspective*. London: Croom Helm.
Langacker, R.W. 1986. 'Abstract Motion.' *BLS* 12.455-71.
Larousse. 1975. *Grand Larousse de la langue francaise*. Paris: Librairie Larousse.
Lehmann, C. 1985. 'Grammaticalization: Synchronic Variation and Diachronic Change.' *Lingua e Stile* 20.303-18.

Lord, C. 1976. 'Evidence for Syntactic Reanalysis: from Verb to Complementizer in Kwa.' *CLS Papers from the Parasession on Diachronic Syntax,* 179-91.

Lyons, J. 1982. 'Deixis and Subjectivity. *Loquor ergo sum?*' In R.J. Jarvella and W. Klein, eds. *Speech, Place, and Action: Studies in Deixis and Related Topics,,* 101-24. New York: John Wiley and Sons, Ltd.

Palmer, F. R. 1986. *Mood and Modality.* Cambridge: Cambridge University Press.

Shepherd, S.C. 1982. 'From Deontic to Epistemic: an Analysis of Modals in the History of English, Creoles, and Language Acquisition.' In A. Ahlqvist, ed. *Papers from the Fifth International Conference on Historical Linguistics,* 316-23. Amsterdam: Benjamins.

Stern, G. 1968[1931]. *Meaning and Change of Meaning; with Special Reference to the English Language.* Bloomington: Indiana University Press.

Sweetser, E. E. 1984. *Semantic Structure and Semantic Change: a Cognitive Linguistic Study of Modality, Perception, Speech Acts, and Logical Relations.* Ph.D. dissertation, University of California, Berkeley.

Traugott, E. C. 1982. 'From Propositional to Textual and Expressive Meanings; some Semantic-pragmatic Aspects of Grammaticalization.' In W. P. Lehmann and Y. Malkiel, eds. *Perspectives on Historical Linguistics,* 245-71. Amsterdam: John Benjamins B.V.

---- 1986a. 'From Polysemy to Internal Reconstruction.' *BLS* 12.539-50.

---- 1986b. 'On the Origins of 'And' and 'But' Connectives in English.' *Studies in Language* 10.137-50.

---- In Press a. 'English Speech Act Verbs: a Historical Perspective.' Paper given at the First International Roman Jakobson Conference, New York, Oct. 1985. Forthcoming in L. R. Waugh, ed. *New Vistas in Grammmar.*

---- In Press b. 'Is Internal Semantic Reconstruction Possible?' In C. Brooke-Rose, J. Fisiak, and T. Vennemann, eds. *Rhetorica, Phonologica, Syntactica.*

Traugott, E. C., and R. Dasher. 1987. 'On the Historical Relation between Mental and Speech Act Verbs in English and Japanese.' In A. G. Ramat, O. Carruba, and G. Bernini, eds. *Papers from the Seventh International Conference on Historical Linguistics,* 561-73. Amsterdam: John Benjamins B.V.

Wartburg, W. von. 1950. *Franzözisches etymologisches Wörterbuch.* Basel:Helbing und Lichtenhahn.

THE EASY-TO-PLEASE CONSTRUCTION IN
OLD AND MIDDLE ENGLISH

WIM VAN DER WURFF
University of Amsterdam

1. *Introduction*.* The aim of this paper will be threefold. First of all, I will present the empirical facts of the 'easy-to-please' construction in Old English (OE) and Middle English (ME). There is of course an extensive literature dealing with 'easy-to-please' in modern English, but as yet hardly any attention has been paid to the history of the construction, even at the descriptive level. I will also propose a theoretical analysis of the historical data, within the government-binding framework of Chomsky (1981, 1982). Finally, I will try to relate the changes in the 'easy-to-please' construction, which are seen in the late ME data, to other changes taking place in English around the same time or a little earlier. I will show that the extension of surface patterns of 'easy-to-please' follows from independent changes affecting basic word order, preposition stranding, morphological Case-marking and the rule of verb-second. These various changes led to an abductive change in 'easy-to-please' and some further consequences for the encoding of passive in this construction.

2. *The OE data.* For what follows, I have drawn mainly on Callaway (1913), Van der Gaaf (1928) and Mitchell (1985) to identify the relevant adjectives, and on Healey & Venezky (1980) to locate all the instances featuring these adjectives followed by an inflected infinitive. There are only a handful of examples with the adjective followed by a plain infinitive, and I will leave these out of account here. With this in mind, let me give an overview of the occurring patterns. First of all, OE had the basic type:

(1) bere is swiðe earfoðe to gearcigenne (ÆCHom I,12 188,4)[1]
beer is very difficult to make

In this sort of sentence, the infinitive is always that of a transitive verb which normally assigns accusative Case to its direct object, and this object is lacking in the surface form. The surface matrix subject can always be interpreted as the missing direct object, and there are no reasons to assume anything other than nominative Case for it. There are no recorded examples in OE of sentences like 'he is difficult to talk to', with preposition stranding. Another pattern in OE was the one with introductory *hit*:

(2) hit bið swiðe unieðe ægðer to donne (PastC 355.2)
it is very difficult either to do

Such sentences are obviously different from (1) in the presence of *hit* and in the fuller nature of the complement clause: all sorts of verbs appear in it, and there is no gap in the complement structure of the infinitive. There are also many examples in which *hit* is absent:

(3) nis me earfoðe to geþolianne þeodnes willan (Guth A,B 1065)
not is for me difficult to endure the lord's will

Usually, in sentences like this, there is some adverb in initial position. Otherwise, the pattern is similar to the one seen in (2). Apart from these three simple types, the construction also occurs as part of a relative clause. The following two surface forms are found:

(4) manige oðre þe is lang to arimane (GDPref 4(C) 4.266.17)
    many others which is long to recount
(5) fela oðre tacna ... þe sind lange to reccenne
    many other signs .. which are long to tell
    (ÆCHom II,18 173.124)

Neither of these two types ever has *hit*. In (4) the verb *is* is singular, which is surprising in view of the regular observance of concord of number in OE relatives; for this see Mitchell (1985:§§ 2342ff). Sentences like (5), on the other hand, are unproblematic and can be subsumed under type (1).

These then are the surface forms of the construction in OE. Each of the examples given is meant to be representative, and for all the patterns there are many more instances in my collection. The group of adjectives concerned, based on the observable distributional facts, would comprise *earfoð(lic)*'difficult', *earmlic* 'miserable, *leoht* 'easy', *hefig(time)* 'difficult', *eaðe(lic)*'easy', *lang(sum)* 'long' and possibly some others. The adjectives are semantically similar, in that they describe the relative ease or difficulty associated with some intentional proposition.

3. *The ME data*. An exhaustive gathering of all the ME data would be a major undertaking beyond the scope of this paper. However, relying on Van der Gaaf (1928), Visser (1963-1973:§§ 940,1388), Koma (1981) and using Kurath & Kuhn (1952-   ) and various concordances, it is possible to come to a fairly complete outline of the 'easy-to-please' construction during this period. Just as in OE, the basic type of the construction is quite frequent in ME:

(6) þey..beþ esy to teche (a1398 TrevBarth 284 a/b)[2]
    they..are easy to teach

The infinitive is always that of a transitive verb, and there is a gap in direct object position. Unlike in OE, which only has verbs that can assign accusative Case, there is no restriction on the type of transitive verb that can appear in this pattern in ME. This of course fits in with the disappearance of such distinctions in ME in general. The second type, i.e. the one with introductory *it*, is also used throughout the period. An example is (7), while (8) shows the type of sentence lacking *it*:

(7) itt niss nohht lihht to betenn hefiȝ sinne (?c1200 *Orm* 4500)
    it is not light to mend heavy sin
(8) himm wass lihht to lokenn himm fra þeȝȝre laþe wiless
    for him was light to keep himself from their evil wiles
    (?c1200 *Orm* 10316)

In type (7) the complement clause can contain all sorts of verbs, and there is no gap in object position. Sentences like (8) are the same in this respect; however, they are not so frequent, and I have not found examples later than about 1400. Around this time i.e. the end of the 14th century, two new patterns begin to appear. They are illustrated in (9), which has the adjective followed by *to be* plus past participle, and (10), which has preposition stranding in the complement.

(9) þo matters schulen be .. eesi to be vndirstonde
    those matters should be .. easy to be understood
    (c1454 Pecock *Fol.* 15/7)
(10) the grete Roches, þat ben stronge and daungerouse
     the great rocks, that are strong and dangerous
     to passe by (?a1425(c1400) *Mandev.* 29/10)
     to pass by

In sentences like (10), the stranded preposition immediately follows the infinitive, but there are also examples in which elements intervene, as in (11):

(11) þe gospel ..is most esi to wynne heuene by
the gospel ..is most easy to reach heaven by
(c1430 (c1383) Wycl. *Leaven Pharisees* 2/22)

We can say that early ME kept the various types of the construction that were possible in OE. Around 1400, however, one of these types (i.e. the one lacking introductory *it*) disappears, and two new types are found: sentences with a passive infinitive, and sentences with preposition stranding. The group of relevant adjectives in ME contains *ethe* 'easy', *esi* 'easy', *hefig* 'hard', *arveth* 'difficult', *nedful* 'necessary', *dredful* 'terrible', *hard, difficult, light, possible, dangerous*, and probably some others. Adjectives meaning 'easy' and 'difficult' still form the core of the group, but some others have been added. However, they still form a semantically coherent group, in that each of them gives a particular comment on an intentional proposition as a whole.

4. *The analysis for OE*. Government-binding theory severely limits possible analyses for particular linguistic phenomena. This can be considered an important advantage for historical work, for reasons discussed in detail in Lightfoot (1979:14ff). Assuming, then, the theory outlined in Chomsky (1981, 1982), and also the small-clause analysis of Stowell (1981, 1983), let us look a little more closely at the basic OE type, with a gap in the complement clause:

(12) þes traht is langsum eow to gehyrenne (ÆCHom II,41 308.138)
this exposition is long for you to hear

To account for the gap, we must assume that either NP-movement or Wh-movement has applied. If it is NP-movement, as I suggest is the case, the infinitive must have passive character, hence the construction should have the properties associated with regular OE passives. Basically this means that the verb, if active, must be able to assign accusative Case, that there is a gap in direct object position (so there should not be any preposition stranding), and also that the landing site for the moved NP must not be θ-marked. Wh-movement, on the other hand, can also be from other than direct object object positions, it can result in preposition stranding, as in many þe-relatives, and there must be an available COMP landing site. For Wh-movement in OE involving the *to*-infinitive, see Van Kemenade (1987).

As pointed out in section 2, the first two passive properties are indeed found in all sentences of type (12). The third property, it should be realized, entails that the adjective must not θ-mark its subject. That it does not can be concluded from sentences like (3) or (13):

(13) us is lang þæt eall to gerecanne
for us is long that all to tell
(HomS 34(PetersonVercHom 19) 79)

As in modern Dutch, for which see Koster (1987), the absence of an overt subject in OE seems restricted to sentences in which the subject lacks a θ-role. Thus it is frequently found with impersonal verbs, for which see Fischer & van der Leek (1987), and with impersonal passives. Whatever explanation for this phenomenon is adopted, it suggests that *is lang* in (13) does not θ-mark the subject. Combining this with the theory of small clauses, we arrive at the result that *lang* in (13) does not θ-mark the external argument. This result can also be derived from a comparison of (12) with (2) or (14), where the subject is *hit*, which we may take to be coindexed with the infinitival complement.

(14) hit bið langsum to awritene þa wundra
it is long to write down the miracles
(ÆLS (Chrysanthus) 219)

If *langsum* did assign a θ-role to its subject *hit*, this role would also be associated with the coindexed infinitival clause. In (12), however, this same θ-role would be associated with the direct object position of the infinitival clause. This state of affairs seems unlikely. Rather, we assume that the subject position is not θ-marked. The adjective only θ-marks its complement, which at DS will be an NP or an infinitival clause. This makes the adjective similar to an ergative verb: it assigns a θ-role, but not Case, only to its complement. In a simple sentence like (15), the derivation would roughly be as in (16), assuming a verb-final VP and an adjectival small clause:

(15) nis nan ðing earfoðe (AECHom I,4 62.10)
    not is no thing difficult
(16) e [e earfoðe [nan ðing]] nis
        AP   NP

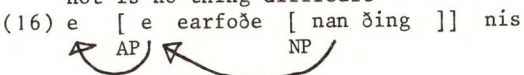

The NP, θ-marked complement of the adjective, is NP-moved twice, to end up in a Case-marked position. In (12) too, there has been NP-movement, and the *to*-infinitive is passive. Wh-movement is ruled out by the typically passive properties of the construction. For the derivation of (12) we may assume that the complement of the adjective is a verbal small clause, i.e. S, and that NP-movement applies three times, as follows (suppressing *eow*):

(17) e_3 [e_2 langsum [e_1 [[þes traht] to gehyrenne]]] is
            AP   S   VP NP

That the infinitive is passive here may be related to the presence of S rather than S'. S' would not be possible here, since e_1 would then not be governed, resulting in an ECP-violation. Now there is good evidence, discussed in Van Kemenade (1987) and references given there, that (18) is the correct structure for OE and other verb-second languages:

(18) [INFL [NP [NP V]]]
      S'   S   VP

This means that the *to*-infinitive in (17) is not governed by INFL, and I suggest that that is the reason why it is not active. If this is correct, we would expect that the OE *to*-infinitive should be passive in all cases involving a bare S, and active in all cases where we must postulate an S'. Both of these expectations are indeed fulfilled. Thus in (19), assuming the theory of small clauses, the infinitive should be passive, and in fact the construction satisfies the three conditions for passive discussed above; hence (20) would be the derivation:

(19) ðas ðing sint to donne (Lch II(2) 22.1.8)
     these things are to do
(20) e [e [[ðas ðing] to donne]] sint
       S   VP NP

On this construction, see Klöpzig (1922). An analysis of the modern Dutch counterpart is put forward in Hoekstra & Moortgat (1979). In the other uses of the OE *to*-infinitive, as far as I am aware, the projection must be S'. For example. in (21) it is used in a position where a tensed clause (so S') also occurs, as in (22):

(21) heo bið æfre geare men to acwellene (LS 29(Nicholas) 340)
     she is always ready men to kill
(22) ic eom gearo þæt ic gange (LS 1.1(AndrewBright) 306)
     I am ready that I go

The idea that in OE the *to*-infinitive is active only if governed by INFL thus gives the right result for (21) and also (17), the basic type of the construction in OE. Now turning to the other patterns, we can see that in (3) or (13) the DS complement to the adjective is not S, as in (17), but S'. Here no movement is necessary, because the *to*-infinitive will be active and Case-mark any object there may be. If any movement applies, it must be Wh-movement of such an object, and this is what seems to have happened in (4) or (23), for which the derivation would be (24):

(23) unþeawum þa þe nu longe to tellan is
vices which that now long to tell is
(ThCap 1 (Sauer) 32.361.8)

(24) unþeawum [þe [e [e longe[[PRO [þa to tellan]]]]is]]
     S'   S   AP   S' S   VP

Since the subject position of *is* is not involved, it will surface as a singular, just as in (3) or (13). For the remaining cases, like (2) and (14), we may assume an analysis similar to (16), with *hit* being NP-moved, and with a coindexed S' appearing in adjunct position. Thus, for (14) (disregarding possible movement of *þa wundra*) the derivation would be:

(25) e [e langsum [hit]] bið [PRO to awritene þa wundra]
       AP   NP$_i$ S'$_i$

Note that I take *hit* as an argument here, following ideas of Bennis & Wehrmann (1987) and references given there. This approach has the advantage that it can explain why there are no OE structures like 'miracles which it is hard to describe', a fact that was pointed out in section 2. In such sentences, there would have been Wh-movement from an adjunct S', and it is well-known that this is in general not possible. All relative structures that do occur are either like (23), which falls out quite naturally from the proposals I have put forward, or like (5), which would be derived in the manner of (17), with one application of Move Wh to be added at the end.

We may conclude that assuming 'ergative' status for the relevant adjectives has exactly the right results. The other properties of OE grammar hold as usual, and no extra mechanisms need be introduced.

5. *The analysis for ME*. In section 3, I showed that early ME had exactly the same types of 'easy-to-please' as OE. We may assume the same analysis for these data. In particular, the idea that the relevant adjectives do not θ-mark their subject still seems valid at this period. It is true that far-reaching changes were at this time taking place in the grammar of English, but it seems that most of these were only firmly established in the fourteenth century. Therefore it is not surprising that they had no direct effect on 'easy-to-please' until that time or a little later. For early ME, then, I would suggest analyses as in (16), (17), (25), possibly with a verb-initial rather than verb-final VP.

For the data of the 15th century, in which we find the use of passive morphology and the occurrence of preposition stranding, in addition to the two main patterns for OE, a different approach must be taken. If we start with sentences of type (11), here repeated as (26), we can easily see that assuming NP-movement would not be enough in such cases:

(26) þe gospel ..is most esi to wynne heuene by
     the gospel ..is most easy to reach heaven by

OE had no prepositional passive; it first starts occurring in early ME, and then (as now) the verb and the preposition must as a rule be adjacent. So passive sentences like (27) are grammatical, but not sentences like (28), where there is material intervening. However, if Wh-movement applies, material intervening between verb and preposition is allowed, so both (29) and (30) are grammatical:

(27) he was shot at
(28) *he was shot a bullet at
(29) who did he shoot at?
(30) who did he shoot a bullet at?

As a descriptive statement we may say that Move NP can only

strand a preposition if verb and preposition are adjacent
and reanalysable as a complex verb; for Wh-movement it is
enough that the preposition be inside the VP. See Chomsky
(1981:292ff) and work cited there for a number of theoretical proposals to account for this difference. Historically
speaking, there is good evidence that preposition stranding
by Wh-movement was possible already in OE, though with
heavy restrictions, and that stranding by NP-movement first
started in the course of the ME period, at the same time as
stranding by Wh-movement became more general; see Bennett
(1980), Koma (1981), Van Kemenade (1987)- but cf. Denison
(1985) for a note of caution concerning specific ME examples.

For (26) all this means that some form of Wh-movement
has applied. In present-day English, of course, there is
even more evidence for this, discussed in detail in
Chomsky (1977, 1981, 1982). A familiar problem for this
Wh-analysis is that it seems to imply a θ-marked subject
for the adjective. But these adjectives have throughout
their history also occurred in sentences introduced by *it*,
as in (31):

> (31) it is heuy to wrestil here sa lange
> it is heavy to wrestle here so long
> (a1500(c1340) Rolle *Psalter* (UC64)118.170)

As demonstrated in section 4, the co-occurrence of (31) and
(26) indicates that the adjective does not θ-mark its subject position. To overcome this problem my suggestion is
that (26) and similar sentences have undergone both Move NP
and Move Wh in their derivation. I would propose the following structure for (26):

> (32) e is [e esi [þe gospel]][COMP [PRO to wynne heuene by Wh]]
>   AP   NP   S'   S

The empty operator in the embedded S' is moved to COMP, and at SS will be coindexed with the matrix subject, which originates as complement to the adjective but is NP-moved twice to end up in a Case-marked position. In such a derivation, the adjective still has its 'ergative' θ-grid, so that sentences with passive morphology for the infinitive can be accounted for quite naturally. For (9) or (33), the analysis would be as in (34), which in the relevant respects is identical to the OE structure (17), except for the morphological expression of its passive character.

(33) þe blak of þe yge ..is ..hardest to be helid
the black of the eye ..is ..hardest to be healed
(a1398 *Trev Barth 42a/b)
(34) e is [e hardest [e [to be helid [þe blak]]]]
          AP   S   VP   NP

My analysis, then, reconciles the co-occurrence in the late ME data of clear signs of Wh-movement as well as NP-movement. Basically, the adjective will be involved in NP-movement as a direct consequence of its θ-marking properties and an adjunct S' can undergo internal Wh-movement. If the adjunct has no internal movement, a sentence like (31) would result, for which (35) could be the derivation, with *it* an argument as in the OE example (25). Note that, if *it* is not an argument here, we could adopt the familiar notion of *it* as a dummy element, and in that case the S' would be complement to the adjective. Structures like 'miracles which it is hard to decribe' should then be grammatical in late ME. In the absence of relevant data, this point is difficult to decide, so I will stick to the analysis of (35).

(35) e is [e heuy [it]][PRO to wrestil here sa lange]
        AP   NP   S'

Finally, we have to consider what would be the derivation for the basic type, as in (6) or (36), and also the type with verb and adjacent preposition, as in (10) or (37):

(36) a fool is eythe to bigyle (c1400 *Rom.Rose* 3955)
   a fool is easy to beguile
(37) an oute cry ..whiche were hevy to here off
   an outcry ..which were heavy to hear of
   (c1465 *Stonor Lett.* (Cam.) 74, 69)

Both of these sentences can be analyzed as containing a passive *to*-infinive, in (37) with an adjacent stranded preposition, which was allowed for passives at that time, as in (27). The use of the *to*-infinitive as a passive is also shown by the continued existence of sentences like (19), i.e. of the type 'these things are to do', in late ME and beyond; Visser (1963-1973:§1384) gives a lot of examples. This means that (36) and (37) can be analyzed along the lines of (34), with NP-movement. However, both sentences would also be generated automatically by the Wh-option of (32), as can easily be verified. We conclude, therefore, that the basic type of the construction in late ME had two possible derivations, resulting in identical strings (but not identical structures) at surface level. I should like to point out that these findings provide a principled explanation for a number of properties of 'easy-to-please' in present-day English discussed in Nanni (1980). In my ME material, however, relevant examples are lacking, and I intend to deal with the present-day data elsewhere.

6. *Causes of the changes*. A survey of the primary data in OE and ME makes clear that, after a long period of apparent stability, a number of changes took place towards the end of the 14th century. Most importantly, we find sentences with preposition stranding and sentences with passive morphology on the infinitive. In this section I want to suggest some specific language-internal reasons for these changes.

If we start with preposition stranding, especially those cases in which the verb is separated from the preposition,

we can say that at some time in the 14th century, people
started assigning a Wh-analysis to 'easy-to-please'. If we
adopt the ideas sketched in the previous section, the Wh-
analysis does not entail any special rules or mechanisms,
so we can also ask the question: why was this possibility
first utilized in the 14th century? The answer can be found
in a close consideration of the surface properties of 'easy-
to-please' in late ME as compared with OE. The language
learner would assign a particular analysis to the construction on the basis of these surface properties, given the in-
ternalized rules and principles of his grammar. Now we saw
that there were at least three good surface clues in OE to
an analysis involving Move NP rather than Move Wh for
'easy-to-please'. The first was the fact that only verbs
that can assign accusative Case appear in the complement of
the basic type, the second that this type always has a gap
in direct object position (and never preposition stranding),
and the third that the adjective need not have a subject.

In the course of the ME period, however, all three of
these properties were lost as a result of other, general
changes in the language. Thus, the possibility of having
empty subjects virtually disappeared, not only in this construction but also with other impersonal constructions; see
the references cited in section 3. Another specific clue to
NP-movement was lost through the reduction in the OE Case-
marking system. As dative and accusative became indistinguishable, passive was no longer restricted to a subset
of the transitive verbs. The third clue was lost when preposition stranding became widespread in both NP-movement
and Wh-movement constructions, a change which itself was
a consequence of the change from verb-final to verb-initial
VP; for details see Koma (1981) and Van Kemenade (1987).

Given the surface opacity of the construction, and the disappearance, due to several factors, of a number of properties obviously signalling NP-movement, it is not surprising that at some point an analysis involving Move Wh was assigned to the basic type of the construction, i.e. to sentences such as (36) or also (37). At first, therefore, the same output would be generated but a different derivation would be associated with it, at least as a possibility. We may hypothesize that this new derivation initially was not extended to generate new surface forms, which means that this change could have taken place somewhat earlier than 1400. In the course of time, however, a new output, characterized by a wider use of preposition stranding, would have resulted. The change can therefore be described as an abductive one. In over-all terms the change leads to an extension of possibilities rather than a substitution of possibilities, since, as I argued, for the basic type of the construction the OE/early ME analysis with NP-movement was not replaced but supplemented by the derivation involving Wh-movement. This idea has strong empirical support, since an extension of surface forms is exactly what we find in the late ME data. Only the subjectless type of 'easy-to-please' disappears, but under any interpretation this must be due to other factors, i.e. the decline of such empty subjects in general. The various other patterns continued into the early Modern English period and beyond.

To account for the occasional use of passive morphology in the construction after 1400, we may start out from the leading idea that passive, or Case-absorption, usually has some morphological expression. The question then is why OE and early ME should not have passive morphology in this construction or in sentences like 'these things are to do', and also why it appeared around 1400 rather than at some other time. We saw in section 4 that OE probably had an underlying structure as in (38):

(38) [INFL [NP [NP V]]]
      S'   S   VP

The main reason for assuming this particular position for INFL is the verb-second character of OE, as argued in Van Kemenade (1987); compare also modern Dutch, for which a similar analysis is proposed in Koopman (1984). We also established a regular correspondence, perhaps of a causal nature, between the presence or absence of INFL (i.e. the choice of S or S') and the voice of the *to*-infinitive. For a *to*-infinitive to be active, there must be an INFL governing it. If all this is correct, we can account for the simultaneity of the following three changes: (i) systematic verb-second disappears towards the end of the 14th century, see Van Kemenade (1987); (ii) sentences like 'these things are to be done' become frequent towards 1400, see Visser (1963-1973:§1384); (iii) 'the work is easy to be done' is first found around 1400. From the loss of verb-second we must conclude that around 1400 INFL no longer occurred in pre-S position; instead the structure would then be as in modern English:

(39) [[NP INFL [V NP]]]
     S' S   VP

This means that S would contain INFL, hence an active *to*-infinitive could appear in a small clause complement. In particular, the use of *to be* followed by a past participle would be possible, and this is exactly what constitutes the other two changes. According to this line of reasoning, the loss of verb-second and the concomitant change in the position of INFL was a necessary condition for the appearance of *to be* plus past participle in the 'easy-to-please' construction. However, there is no rule or principle forcing the use of this passive form in late ME. Thus, although intuitively this change is a particularly natural one considering our analysis for 'easy-to-please' in OE and early ME, it is very difficult to translate this intuition into a fully formalized statement. Nevertheless, the idea that Case-absorption is usually morphologically expressed, interacting with certain assumptions about INFL, does yield some quite precise predictions, which are borne out by the available data.

7. *Conclusion*. In this paper I have first presented the empirical data for 'easy-to-please' in OE and ME. Around 1400, an increase in the number of occurring patterns is found. Then I proposed an analysis for the construction in OE in terms of Move NP. For late ME I argued that an analysis involving both NP-movement and Wh-movement should be adopted. The evidence points to 'ergative' status for the adjective in both OE and ME, and there is no reason to postulate any change in the θ-marking properties of the adjective during these two periods. Finally I showed a connection between the surface changes in 'easy-to-please' around 1400 and changes affecting empty subjects, morphological Case-marking, preposition stranding (itself dependent on the change in basic word order) and the verb-second phenomenon.

NOTES

* I wish to thank David Denison for suggesting a number of improvements in an earlier draft of this paper.
1. I use the system of Healey & Venezky (1980) for identification of the OE examples.
2. I use the system of Kurath & Kuhn (1952-) for identification of the ME examples.

REFERENCES

Bennett, P.A. 1980. 'English Passives: A Study in Syntactic Change and Relational Grammar'. *Lingua* 51.101-114.
Bennis, H. & P. Wehrmann. 1987. 'Adverbial Arguments'. In F. Beukema & P. Coopmans, eds. *Linguistics in the Netherlands 1987*. 1-11. Dordrecht: Foris.
Callaway, M. 1913. *The Infinitive in Anglo-Saxon*. Washington: Carnegie Institution.
Chomsky, N. 1977. 'On Wh-movement'. In P. Culicover et al., eds. *Formal Syntax*. 71-132. New York: Academic Press.
Chomsky, N. 1981. *Lectures on Government and Binding*. Dordrecht: Foris.
Chomsky, N. 1982. *Some Concepts and Consequences of the Theory of Government and Binding*. Cambridge: MIT Press.
Denison, D. 1985. 'Why Old English had no Prepositional Passive'. *English Studies* 66.189-204.
Fischer, O. & F. van der Leek. 1987. 'A "Case" for the Old English Impersonal'. In W. Koopman et al., eds. *Explanation and Linguistic Change*. 79-120. Amsterdam: John Benjamins.
Gaaf, W. van der. 1928. 'The Post-adjectival Passive Infinitive'. *English Studies* 10.129-138.
Healey, A. & R. Venezky. 1980. *A Microfiche Concordance to Old English*. Dictionary of Old English Project, University of Toronto.
Hoekstra, T.A. & M. Moortgat. 1979. 'Passief en het lexicon'. *Forum der Letteren* 20.137-161.
Kemenade, A. van. 1987. *Syntactic Case and Morphological Case in the History of English*. Dissertation, University of Utrecht.
Klöpzig, W. 1922. 'Der Ursprung der *to be to* Konstruktion'. *Englische Studien* 56.378-389.
Koma, O. 1981. 'Word Order Change and Preposition Stranding in ME'. *Studies in English Linguistics* 9.132-144.
Koopman, H. 1984. *The syntax of verbs*. Dordrecht: Foris.
Koster, J. 1987. *Domains and Dynasties*. Dordrecht: Foris.
Kurath, H. & S.M. Kuhn. 1952- . *Middle English Dictionary*. Ann Arbor: University of Michigan Press.
Lightfoot, D. 1979. *Principles of diachronic syntax*. Cambridge: CUP.
Mitchell, B. 1985. *Old English Syntax*. Oxford: Clarendon Press.
Nanni, D. 1980. 'On the surface syntax of constructions with *easy*-type adjectives. *Language* 56.568-581.
Stowell, T.A. 1981. *Origins of Phrase Structure*. Dissertation, MIT.
Stowell, T.A. 1983. 'Subjects across categories'. *The Linguistic Review* 2.285-312.
Visser, F. 1963-1973. *An historical syntax of the English language*. Leiden: E.J. Brill.

REWORKING THE HISTORY OF ENGLISH AUXILIARIES

ANTHONY R. WARNER
University of York

I want to look at the history of English auxiliaries using a couple of ideas about categories taken from the work of Rosch and her associates (cf. Rosch 1977, 1978) to characterize the apparent shift that occurs at the beginning of Early Modern English.[1] I shall also suggest that Old English modals already formed a distinctive grouping, and that a further shift in the grammar of auxiliaries took place from about 1800. It seems reasonable to suggest that a general word-class account will contribute to any comprehensive history of these words, whatever else is also required, and my aim is partly to illuminate such an account.

I assume a surface syntax of little abstractness which introduces Present-day auxiliaries in such structures as (1), cf. in particular Gazdar, Pullum and Sag (1982), Warner (1985). I shall also assume that categories are defined in terms of opposing clusters of properties, and the familiar idea (found in Rosch) that certain groups of properties (hence perhaps certain members of a class) may be more central or 'prototypical', others less so.

(1)(a)

```
           S
          / \
        NP   VP
        |   /  \
        |  V[+AUX] VP
        |   |     / \
        |   |   V[+AUX] VP
        |   |    |      |
        |   |    |      V
        |   |    |      |
       Paul may have  come
```

(b)

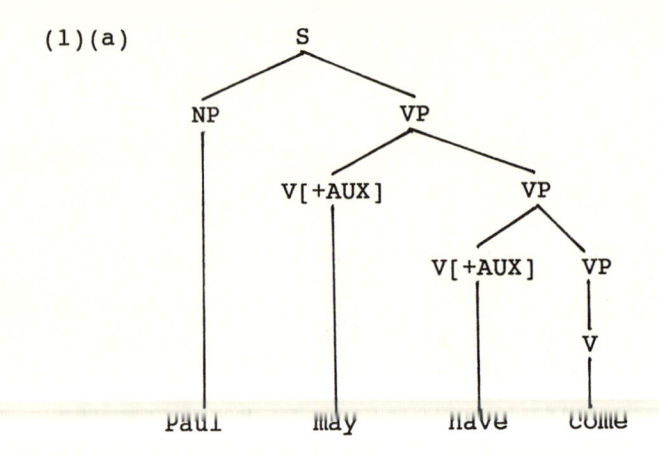

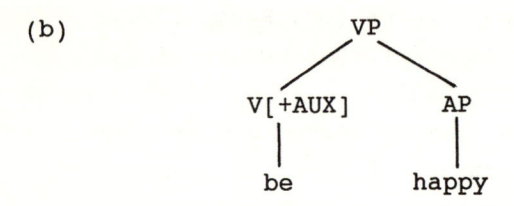

```
        VP
       /  \
   V[+AUX]  AP
     |      |
     be   happy
```

Today's auxiliaries, then, form a class rather clearly distinguished from nonauxiliary verbs by a series of characteristics, principally by their distinctive occurrence in inversion, with *not* and *-n't*, and before the site of ellipsis. Within that class occurs the group of modals, which I take to be prototypical auxiliaries. They show further properties distinguishing them from nonauxiliary verbs, of which I will be particularly interested in the following three. The first is the restriction of modals to finite categories. The second is that modals are typically 'sentence modifiers', modifying the clause they stand in as a whole without imposing selectional restrictions on their subject. This lack of selection is probably a major property of auxiliaries in general, holding also for periphrastic *do*, for *be*, and for 'perfect' *have*. It is, however, only a peripheral property of verbs. The third property is that modals are often subjective in that they encode aspects of a speaker's attitude to or evaluation of a proposition or event, as a matter of fact, or within a framework of authority, law or morality. Since these two semantic properties are so typical of auxiliaries and modals respectively, and so far from the actional transitive verbal prototype, it seems reasonable to suggest that they may themselves be prototypical properties for auxiliaries, and modals.

The modals' final loss of nonfinite categories and of nonmodal constructions and senses in Early Modern English seems to indicate a fundamental shift in their grammar. Both Lightfoot (1979) and his most detailed critic, Plank (1984), agree that there was a category change in modals at this period. But there were other developments too which (to someone with my word-class assumptions) imply that there was also a change in the status of a broader category auxiliary. The adoption of periphrastic *do* itself implies the existence of such a category by Early Modern English since it seems never to occur in construction with *be* or *have* in England in Middle English or in the developing Early Modern English standard. And there are several pieces of evidence which suggest a new importance for such a category in Early Modern English. It is then that a distinctive grouping of auxiliaries reduced by cliticization is first found: *we'll*, *thou'rt*, *thou'lt*, etc. (cf. the relevant OED entries). The contracted negative *-n't* also appears, round about 1600 in spoken English if we follow Jespersen (1909-49, part 5: 429), with such seventeenth century forms as *shan't* and *won't* implying that a distinct inflection or word form rather than a phonological process is already involved. There is also some indirect evidence. According to Visser (1963-73: section 1928) the passive participle *had* is 'anything but rare' in Middle English, though it is much restricted today. The decline seems to belong to Early Modern English. Concordances to Shakespeare and Blake, and to the verse of Ben Jonson, Milton and Pope show very few instances. This decline would make sense if 'possessive' *have* was an auxiliary and rejected the passive as a nonauxiliary construction. In favour of its being an auxiliary, note that it never occurs in the infinitive after periphrastic *do* at this period: in this respect it is like *be* but unlike all or virtually all 'full' verbs (Ellegård 1953: 199ff., 206f.). There is also the substitution of plural *are*, a form originally typical of the north, for earlier *ben*. I take this to be not a puzzling increase in the irregularity of *be*, but as motivated in part by the preterite-present correspondance *thou art - they are*, and hence as pointing to an increased correlation between preterite-present morphology and the category auxiliary at this period.[2]

So it makes sense to suggest that what develops in Early Modern English (or slightly before) isn't so much a class of modals as a wider class auxiliary, containing a group of modals. But this immediately sets someone with my impoverished assumptions about syntax the problem of accounting for the earlier grouping of relevant properties in verbs which generally also had 'main verb' properties. I will briefly defend the importance of this grouping by looking at modal characteristics of Old English *mæg*, *mot*, *sceal* and *wile*. My examples come from various sources, principally Visser (1963-73) and Venezky and Healey (1980).

The first and most important point is that these verbs may be 'sentence modifiers'. At least, this seems a reasonable interpretation of the fact that they may occur with impersonals, and in passives whose subject is not selected by the verb. I give some examples in (2). So in (2)(a) it is the infinitive *ofþyncan* which dictates the genitive *þæs* and the dative *þeodne*; and *mæg* has no nominative subject. Or in (2)(b) it seems unlikely in context to be a property of the apostolic word that it may be repeated: what is permitted is rather the repetition of the word. In my collection of impersonal examples, based largely on a search through Venezky and Healey (1980) under the infinitives of a range of impersonal verbs, such instances are plentiful with *sceal*, as also with *onginnan*, adequately attested with *mæg*, *wile* and also with *þearf*, and uncommon with *mot*. Similar examples may be found in Middle English. This is a rather distinctive property in Old English when 'subject raising' structures barely existed (Traugott 1972: 102). Note incidentally that the occurrence of *wile* in a construction type where it has no subject is convincing evidence that notions of volition and intention are absent, and that *wile* is capable of functioning as a marker of mere futurity already in Old English, as suggested by Visser (1963-73, section 1581, and cf. 1591) and more cautiously by Mitchell (1985, section 1023) on the basis of examples where *wile* has a grammatical subject but is best interpreted as semantically bleached.

(2) OE modals with impersonals and passives.

mæg

(a) Mæg þæs þonne ofþyncan ðeodne Heaðobeardna
"That may then [lit: may of-that then] displease (the) prince [dat] (of the) Heathobards ..."
Beowulf (ed. Dobbie) 2032.

(b) be þam mæg þæt apostolice word cweden beon, ...
"concerning whom may the apostolic word be repeated [lit: said be]".
de quibus apostolicum illum licet proferre sermonem
Bede (ed. Miller, EETS OS 95,96) 472.10

mot

(c) Me mæig ... gif hit mot gewiderian, mederan settan, ...
"One can ... if it may be-fair-weather, plant madder,..."
Law Ger 12

(d) manna gehwylc, ... mot he beon ærost ðinga gemynegad & gewisod þæt he cunne hu he of hæþendome mæge to cristendome ... cuman.
"each man [lit: of-men each] ... must (he) be above all things [lit: first of-things] warned and instructed so-that he should-know how he may come from heathendom to christendom [lit: from heathendom may to christendom come]."
Wulfstan Homilies (ed. Bethurum) 8c.8

sceal

(e) Ða cwæð ic: Hwy ne sceolde me swa þyncan?
"Then said I: Why should it not seem so to me [lit: not should to-me so seem]?"
Boethius (ed. Sedgefield) 38.119.9

(f) getacnod wæs, hwær gesette beon sceoldon þa lichaman
haligra fæmnena
"(it) was shown where the bodies of holy virgins should be
buried [lit: where buried be should, etc.]" Bede (ed.
Miller, EETS OS 95,96) 18.16.

wile

(g) ic wat, þæt hine wile tweogan, hwæðer heo him soð secge.
"I know, that he [lit: him (accusative)] will doubt,
whether she tells him the truth [lit: she him truth tell
(subjunctive)]".
Wulfstan Homilien (ed. Napier) 3.7
[BT and BTS give *tweogan* with experiencer subject, or
impersonal. With the impersonal an NP object of doubt is
in the genitive (though accusative plus clause may render
Latin accusative plus infinitive). So þæt is best taken
as the complementizer, and the clause as oblique rather
than subject in function.]

(h) Gif me seo godcunde geofu in dære stowe forgifen beon
wile, þæt ic lifgan mote be minum hondgewinne, ic dær
lustlice wunige.
"If the divine grace that I may live by the labour of my
hands will be vouchsafed to me in that place, I will live
there cheerfully. [lit: If to-me the divine grace in that
place vouchsafed be will, that I live may by my hand-work,
I there cheerfully will-live]".
Bede (ed. Miller, EETS OS 95,96) 366.5

Secondly, there are apparent cases of epistemic modality, and both epistemic and deontic modality may have a subjective element. In the subjective deontics an interlocutor is, at least in part, the source of authority. Their existence is well established for *sceal* (cf. OED Shall, 5, though 'Chiefly in Biblical language'). Instances also occur at least with *mot*, cf. (3) and note the imperative *hrepa* in (3)(a).

(3)(a) God ... him to cwæð, "Ealra þæra þinga þe on neorxna
    wange syndon þu most brucan ... buton anum treowe ... ne
    hrepa þu þæs treowes wæstm,..."
    "God ... (brought Adam into Paradise and) ... said unto
    him [lit: him to said], "(Of) all the things which are in
    Paradise [lit: in Paradise are] thou mayest eat, ... save
    one tree ... touch thou not the fruit of this tree [lit:
    not touch (imperative) thou that tree's fruit], ..."
    (Thorpe's translation.)
    ÆCHom I (ed. Thorpe) 12.34
    Cf. Ex omni ligno paradisi comede, de ligno autem
    scientiae boni et mali ne comedas,... Gen 2.16-17.

(b) Ða cwæð placidas, Drihten leof mot ic þis cyðan minum
    wife, and minum cildum, þæt hi gelyfan on þe? Ða cwæð
    drihten to him, far nu, and sege hiom þæt hi fulwiht
    onfon,...
    "Then said Placidas, "Dear Lord [lit: lord dear], may I
    make this known (to) my wife and (to) my children, that
    they may believe on Thee?" Then said the-Lord to him, "Go
    now and bid them receive baptism [lit: that they baptism
    should-receive],...". " Skeat's translation.
    Ælfric Lives of Saints ii (ed. Skeat, EETS OS 94,114)
    194.70

In referring to apparently epistemic uses with a subjective element, I follow Palmer (1979) in distinguishing the epistemic modality of propositions from the dynamic modality of events. I take it that the use of *sceolde* as in (4) 'in the oblique report of another's statement in order to imply that the speaker does not commit himself to the truth of the alleged fact' (OED Shall, 15) is both epistemic and subjective.[3] Standop (1957) and Goossens (1982) noted a few epistemic or near epistemic instances for *mæg* and *wile*, and I give further relevant examples in (5). The examples of (5)(a) and (b) occur in contexts where Ælfric excuses himself from developing a topic of discussion on the ground that it would be inappropriate for his audience. His use of *wile* here is OED Will, $v.^1$ 15. 'As auxiliary of future expressing a contingent event'. The corresponding modern category is epistemic prediction to most recent analysts, though not all (cf. Palmer 1979). The examples of (5)(c) and (d) also correspond to modern epistemics (cf. the oddity of *It can easily be* ... in these). It is, however, notable that these do not correspond to central or prototypical epistemics. The type of (5)(a) and (b) is closely related to (even a subcategory of) the future, that of (5)(c) and (d) is related to the dynamic (which is presumably its historical antecedent) in that a verb of being or becoming mediates between the modal and the proposition centrally concerned. Consider now the possibility of an element of subjectivity in these examples. This is extremely difficult to assess. But a comparison of 5(a) and (b) (with *wene we*), and the circumstances of (c), make it seem reasonably likely that these examples contain an element of subjective assessment, and (d) is compatible with such a possibility. I leave open the question of how such epistemic instances should be treated in an account of Old English (see Traugott's paper in-this volume for a view on the extent to which subjectivity was lexicalized here). For my purposes it is enough that the presence of uses with these elements gives further support to the notion that modals already formed a distinct grouping within the class of verbs.

(4) Eustatius hæfde gecydd þam cynge þet hit sceolde beon mare gylt þære burhwaru þonne his. ac hit næs na swa.
"Eustace had informed the king that it was [lit: should be] more the fault [lit: greater fault] of the townsfolk than his. But it was not so at all."
ChronE (ed. Plummer) 1048.38

(5)(a) Wucan & monðas sind mannum cuðe æfter heora andgite,
& ðeah ðe we hi æfter boclicum andgite awriton, hit
wile ðincan ungelæredum mannum to deoplic &
ungewunelic;...
(After naming and glossing the seven hours of the night)
"Weeks and months are clear to men [lit: to-men clear]
from their (native) understanding, and even if we (do)
describe them according to scholarly understanding [lit:
we them after scholarly understanding describe (= present
subjunctive)], it will seem to unlearned men too profound
and unwonted."
Ælfric De Temporibus Anni (ed. Henel EETS OS 213) 3.26

(b) Gif we deoplicor ymbe þis sprecað, þonne wene we þæt hit
wile ðincan ðam ungelæredum to manigfeald;...
"If we speak more deeply about this [lit: more-deeply
about this speak], then we think that it will seem too
complex to the unlearned [lit: (to) the unlearned too
complex]".
ÆCHom II (ed. Thorpe) 582.25.

(c) Eaðe mæg gewurðan þæt þu wite þæt ic nat, ðu þe þar
andweard wære.
(the king gives Apollonius a letter to read in the hope
that he will be able to explain what it means, and says:)
"(It) easily may be that you know what I do-not-know, you
who were present there [lit: there present were]."
Potest enim fieri ut quod ego minus novi, tu intelligas
qui praesens affuisti.
Apollonius of Tyre (ed. P. Goolden 1958) 21.10
[Although he characterizes the text as a "faithful
translation", the editor notes "the independent character
of the Old English style" in which "Latin constructions
are carefully avoided" (xxiii-xxv)].

(d) Swa hit eaþe beon mæg þæt se halga heahengel of heofenum
cumen wære, & wære gemyndig manna tyddernesse, þæt he hine
geeaðmedde þæt he hie mid his sylfes handum gesette &
geworhte,...
"So it easily may be that the holy archangel came from
heaven [lit: from heavens come was (subjunctive)], and was
mindful (of) men's infirmity, so-that he deigned [lit:
himself humbled] that he established and made it (= the
cave which forms St Michael's church) with his own hands
[lit: he it with his own hands established and made]".
Blickling Homilies (ed. Morris, EETS 58, 63, 73) 197.10.

A third modern property to be found in earlier English is the restriction to finite forms. This holds for both *mot* and *sceal* throughout both Old and Middle English. No nonfinite forms of either verb are given in the major standard sources. The Middle English Dictionary specifically states that no infinitives or participles of *mot* have been found. And Professor Lewis, its Editor-in-Chief, kindly informs me that no nonfinite forms of *shal* appear in the dictionary's material for any sense or construction. These absences seem unlikely to be merely accidental. Nonfinites are found elsewhere in Germanic, and Ælfric interestingly seems to avoid the infinitive of *mot* just when he has need of it in (6) to render the paradigm of Latin *licere* in his *Grammar*.

(6)   *licet mihi bibere* mot ic drincan, *mihi licuit* ic moste,
         tibi licet, nobis licet, si nobis liceret gyf we moston;
         INFINITIVVM *licere* beon alyfed
         ÆGram (ed. Zupitza) 207.1.

Clearly, then, even Old English had a grouping of 'less verbal' verbs or uses of verbs with some of the properties characteristic of today's modals, and it was a grouping whose historical development shows that it must have been real to speakers. It may even be necessary to recognize a category auxiliary with some strictly syntactic properties, though this is to some extent a theory-particular matter. The best evidence for it is the occurrence of a group of verbs (most importantly the modals discussed above and 'be') in two types of construction: firstly in impersonal constructions, such as those in (2) with modals; secondly in elliptical constructions like those found today with auxiliaries.

The fact that Old English 'be' is a member of this group, being found with ellipsis of its complement and in a parallel type of impersonal construction (most obviously in the impersonal passive), shows that the relevant category is wider than the semantic group of modals. This 'transparency' of modals and 'be' to the case-assigning properties of the verb form which follows them, and the coincidence of this property with that of occurrence in elliptical constructions, constitutes potentially important evidence for the grammatical status of a class of auxiliaries in Old English.[4]

But if the category was in some sense already there in Old English, how can we interpret the apparent evidence for category change found in Early Modern English? What kind of difference is involved here? I suggest we should borrow from Rosch (and other taxonomists) the idea that there are not only different levels of categorization, but, crucially, that they have different properties. There is a central level which Rosch calls 'basic'. At this level categories are at once most internally coherent within themselves and most sharply distinguished from one another. I cite one of Rosch's examples in (7). Here the subordinate-level terms *kitchen chair* and *living-room chair* share many properties in common, and are harder to distinguish from one another than the category *chair* is from other basic-level categories such as *table*. The superordinate-level term *furniture* on the other hand is less internally coherent.

(7) Example of Taxonomy used in basic object research, Rosch (1978: 32).

Superordinate	Basic Level	Subordinate
Furniture	Chair	Kitchen chair
		Living-room chair
	Table	Kitchen table
		Dining-room table
	Lamp	Floor lamp
		Desk lamp

Now it is clear that we could describe what happens in the sixteenth century or shortly before as the development of a basic-level category auxiliary, as the properties of modals and auxiliaries become more coherent and more sharply distinguished from those of nonauxiliary verbs. Earlier, 'modal' and 'auxiliary' were subordinate-level categories, relatively poorly distinguished from other verbs. Rosch does not tell us what such categories ought to look like, since her essential concern is with the basic level. But we might find a parallel in Old and Middle English impersonals. Verbs which appear in impersonal constructions without a nominative subject share most of their properties with other verbs, and in no few cases this includes the property of possible occurrence with a nominative cause or experiencer subject in other constructions. Thus the impersonal group, though distinctive in particular respects, is not sharply set off from other verbs, and could only form a subordinate-level category in Rosch's sense (cf. the discussion of the group's fuzzy boundaries in Denison's paper in this volume). To return to modals, they behave as we would expect of a less distinctive grouping, in that they not only develop peculiarities in

earlier English: they also undergo some general verbal
developments. There are some new nonfinites (notably past
participles of *may* and *will*); some develop impersonal
constructions (*mot* and *þarf*); and in some Southern
dialects preterite-presents adopt the regular verbal
plural, giving *conneþ*, *shulleþ*, and even *moweþ* (see OED,
MED).

    This way of looking at mediaeval English and the
Early Modern developments has important implications,
which give us a view of these changes entirely different
from that developed in Lightfoot (1979).[5] In the first
place, we can give some account of the developing
coherency of the group of modals (and of auxiliaries) in
mediaeval English. These developments are not the chance
piling up of irregularities, as in Lightfoot's view, but
throughout constitute a subordinate regularity.

    Secondly, the major changes evidenced in Early
Modern English can be interpreted as successive
implementations of a basic-level distinction. Rosch
characterizes her basic level as being the way it is as
the result of pressure for cognitive efficiency. Given
that related considerations hold for linguistic
categories, then once an opposition becomes basic its
internal coherency and external distinctiveness should
tend to increase, if opportunity offers. Thus we should
expect a succession of changes, rather than the set of
ideally instantaneous changes which corresponds to
Lightfoot's cataclysmic reanalysis. So this type of
account provides directly for the more typically gradual
development of auxiliary characteristics in both mediaeval

and Modern English, while admitting that there was a fundamental word-class change in (or shortly before) the sixteenth century, cf. Plank (1984). Thirdly, it predicts a wider group of changes than Lightfoot's account. Lightfoot focusses on the loss of properties shared between modal and verb, such as the modals' loss of nonfinite categories. But within a Rosch-style framework we should expect not only such losses, but also changes which widen the gap between auxiliary and 'full' verb by adding distinguishing properties to one category but not the other, such as the development of negative or clitic forms for auxiliaries only. These points of interpretation seem entirely appropriate for Early Modern English developments in auxiliaries, and they offer a closer modelling of events than Lightfoot's account. And I will suggest in a moment that the gap continues to widen in the later period, as we might expect.

Finally, we can interpret the developing coherency of the class as itself an agent of change, as we should surely wish to. This is especially clear if we consider the loss of *wite* 'know', the last preterite-present to lack modal senses and constructions. Its decline seems to be rapid and to belong mainly to the fifteenth century. It sharply increases the internal coherency and external distinctiveness of auxiliaries, since it removes the major exception to the statement 'a preterite-present is an auxiliary'. Without getting involved in the interesting question of the extent to which it fell out of the language or was pushed, it is clear that the increasing coherency of the class may itself have been a factor promoting change. Similar comments may hold also for

periphrastic *do* which is adopted into the English of the
London area from the second half of the fifteenth century
according to Ellegård (1953). Since for Rosch frequency
increases salience, this may have increased the importance
of auxiliary properties.

This way of describing the facts seems quite
appealing. It enables us to keep both properties and
categories in view, to interpret the development of
auxiliaries as gradual, yet involving a fundamental change
occurring at a specific period, and to make sense of a
situation where major semantic and constructional
properties of a basic category are around some centuries
earlier. It is also a framework within which reference
can straightforwardly be made to function and frequency.
Although Rosch's most relevant work involves the
categorization of concrete objects it seems reasonable to
import these ideas essentially for the reason offered by
Lakoff (1982) in discussing prototypes: that it would be
surprising if language did not use general principles of
human categorization.

The gap between auxiliary and 'full' verb continues
to widen with the generalization of periphastic *do*, with
the loss of directional phrases after modals and their
continuing erosion of tense distinctions, and with the
final loss of agreement categories in modals after the
loss of *thou* in colloquial Standard English, which I place
in the second half of the eighteenth century (see Warner
(1986) for a brief account of the evidence). I suggest
that these changes led to a further shift in the
characterization of auxiliaries. Its consequences are to

be found mainly within the verb *be*, which develops some idiosyncratic restrictions from the turn of the eighteenth century.

One group of developments restricts the complements which may follow individual members of the paradigm of *be*, as when an *ing*-form may not follow *being*. I take this to be a fully grammaticized restriction today, unlike the more stylistic restriction with other verbs which is frequently violated, cf. the attested (8). Instances of *being* with an *ing*-form complement as in (9) are found throughout Early Modern English, though they are never common, last appearing in straightforward examples, as far as I know, in Jane Austen, cf. Visser (1963-73: section 1834), Phillipps (1970), Denison (1985).

(8) You see what I mean about him never stopping talking!

(9) And exclaimed quite as much as was necessary (or being acting a part, perhaps rather more).
Jane Austen, Emma. 1816. ed. by R.W. Chapman, Oxford: OUP 1923: 145, cited from Phillipps (1970: 115).

Secondly, a directional *to*-phrase or infinitive of purpose is found today only after *been*, as in (10), not after other members of the paradigm. But finites at least were also found until the second half of the eighteenth century according to the OED (Be, *v.* 6). Thirdly, in the late 19th and early 20th century, English generally adopts the restriction that only finites may precede the infinitive in the *is to* construction. The copula appears to have no separate semantics here, since the exclamatory (11) gets by without it, so we need not recognise a special 'modal' *be*, any more than a special 'progressive' or 'passive' *be*, cf. Warner (1985). Rather, finite *be* is followed by wider range of VP-complements than nonfinite *be* is, just as *been* and *being* also have distinct complements. The development of these idiosyncracies suggests that from the beginning of the 19th century the morphosyntactic categories of *be* became less tightly interrelated than those of nonauxiliary verbs, and this in turn suggests that the gap between auxiliary and nonauxiliary verbs was widening.

(10) I have never been to Helsinki, and I look forward to going there.

(11) What, Paul to cook dinner! I don't believe it!

There is a similar implication in the loss of the ellipsis possibility represented by (12), where a *be*-phrase is retrieved from a finite *am*-phrase. This is quite impossible today but is found throughout Middle and Early Modern English. Jane Austen, linguistically conservative as ever, is the last to use this construction as far as I know. But with other verbs such retrieval in ellipsis is in general readily permitted. Thus the relationship between finite and nonfinite forms of *be* changes in the early 19th century, ceasing to be the same as that for other verbs. Here then is another case where the paradigm of *be* is fragmenting, and interrelationships normal for verbs do not obtain. I have given a particular account of this in Warner (1986) and here I just want to note that these developments are consistent with an increased gap between auxiliary and nonauxiliary verb, and that this increase is in line with the general development we might expect of a 'basic-level' distinction.

(12)(a) I think, added he, all the Charges attending it, and
the Trouble you had, were defray'd by my Attorney: I
order'd that they should [sc. be defrayed - ARW]. They
were, Sir, said he; and Ten Thousand Thanks to you for
this Goodness,...   Samuel Richardson, 1740-1.
Pamela, London: third edition 1741, vol 2 p129.

(b) I wish our opinions were the same. But in time they will
[sc. be the same - ARW].   Jane Austen, Emma. 1816. ed.
by R.W. Chapman, Oxford: OUP 1923: 471 (cited from
Phillipps 1970: 142).

A further development is also consistent with an increasing tendency for auxiliaries to lack verbal interrelationships. It is the sudden flowering of *to* before ellipsis sites in the mid 19th century noted by Visser (1963-73: section 1000) and OED (To, *prep.*, *conj.*, *adv.* B 21). If *to* is an auxiliary today, as Pullum (1984) has claimed, this is presumably when it became one. The development would have been natural enough if by that time the existence of a infinitival auxiliary no longer carried implications for the existence of other morphosyntactic categories of that word.

In conclusion: Rosch's distinction between basic-level categories which are maximally coherent and distinct and subordinate categories which are less well distinguished, along with the dynamic implications of this distinction, is important for the interpretation of the history of English auxiliaries. Some general account along the lines sketched above will surely be required even if we also need an account in terms of more particular grammatical parameters. And I am led to three points of interpretation. (1) that there was already a distinctive grouping of modal properties in Old English, and possibly even a category auxiliary; (2) that the Early Modern English changes essentially result from the development of a basic-level category auxiliary, which leads to a succession of changes that widen the gap between verb and auxiliary; and (3), that there is a tendency in the last couple of centuries for members of the paradigm of *be* to acquire distinct properties, which may also be interpreted as a consequence of a widening gap between the copula and nonauxiliary verbs.

NOTES

1. I am grateful to Jacek Fisiak and Richard Hogg for information relevant to particular points made in this paper, and to Elizabeth Closs Traugott for comments and especially for helpful discussion of the OE examples. But they may not agree with what I say, and should not be blamed for my mistakes. Where convenient, short references to OE texts have been taken from Venezky and Healey (1980), but I have also used transparent short titles.

2. Is it also the case that the modern tag-question construction as in the example below is (relatively) new in the sixteenth century, when it is found not just with modals but with *do*, *be* and *have*? This would jibe well with a change in the status of auxiliaries at this period.
    Slender I must wait on myself, must I? You have not the book of
    riddles about you, have you? Shakes. Wiv. 1.01.201
In favour of this possibility note that when Visser (1963-73) discusses this construction (though only with *do*, *be* and *will*), he gives no examples before 1550. And ME concordances have not led me to examples. But this needs more work, and I would be very grateful to hear from readers who know of ME examples of this construction, or who feel confident of its absence from some corpus.

3. Such uses are not restricted to clauses of indirect statement, cf. the apparently subjective epistemic instance at Peterborough Chronicle (ed. Clark 1970) anno 1100.5.

4. Although the central members of the group show both properties, the properties may not always cooccur. Thus OE *onginnan* is found with impersonals, but I do not yet know convincing evidence for an elliptical as distinct from an intransitive use. Note also that "transparency" with impersonals is an obvious candidate for semantic motivation. The question of the coherency and further membership of this group, involving the status of *habban*, *uton*, *cunnan*, *onginnan*, etc. will be taken up in Warner, forthcoming. The importance of the occurrence of OE modals with impersonals has also been noted independently by David Denison in unpublished work.

5. Different too, in related ways, from Roberts' (1985) reworking of Lightfoot (1979). It is also clear that some of the claims I make in this paper provide difficulties for Roberts' account.

REFERENCES

BT = *An Anglo-Saxon Dictionary based on the manuscript collections of the late Joseph Bosworth*, ed. and enlarged by T. Northcote Toller. London: Oxford University Press. 1898.
BTS = *An Anglo-Saxon Dictionary based on the manuscript collections of the late Joseph Bosworth. Supplement*, ed. by T. Northcote Toller. London: Oxford University Press. 1921, and *Enlarged Addenda and Corrigenda to the Supplement*, ed. by A. Campbell, Oxford: Clarendon Press. 1972.
Coates, Jennifer. 1983. *The Semantics of the Modal Auxiliaries*. London: Croom Helm.
Denison, David. 1985. "Some Observations on *Being Teaching*. *Studia Neophilologica* 57.157-159.
Ellegård, A. 1953. *The Auxiliary "Do": The establishment and regulation of its use in English*. (=Gothenburg Studies in English, 2.) Stockholm: Almqvist & Wiksell.
Gazdar, Gerald; Geoffrey K. Pullum; and Ivan A. Sag. 1982. "Auxiliaries and Related Phenomena in a Restrictive Theory of Grammar". *Language* 58.591-638.
Goossens, Louis. 1982. "On the Development of the Modals and of the Epistemic Function in English". *Papers from the 5th International Conference on Historical Linguistics*, ed. by Anders Ahlqvist, 74-84. (=Current Issues in Linguistic Theory, 21.) Amsterdam and Philadelphia: John Benjamins.
Jespersen, Otto. 1909-49. *A Modern English Grammar on Historical Principles*. 7 parts. Published and reprinted in London: George Allen and Unwin.
Lakoff, George. 1982. *Categories and Cognitive Models*. Berkeley Cognitive Science Report no. 2.

Lightfoot, David W. 1979. *Principles of Diachronic Syntax*. Cambridge: Cambridge University Press.
MED = *Middle English Dictionary*, ed. by Hans Kurath, Sherman M. Kuhn, Robert E. Lewis and John Reidy. Ann Arbor: University of Michigan Press (1954-).
Mitchell, Bruce. 1985. *Old English syntax*. 2 vols. Oxford: Clarendon Press.
OED = *The Oxford English Dictionary*, ed. by J.A.H. Murray, H. Bradley, W.A. Craigie, and C.T. Onions. Oxford: Clarendon Press. 1933.
Palmer, F.R. 1979. *Modality and the English Modals*. London: Longman.
Phillipps, K.C. 1970. *Jane Austen's English*. London: Andre Deutsch.
Plank, Frans. 1984. "The Modals Story Retold". *Studies in Language* 8.305-364.
Pullum, Geoffrey K. 1982. "Syncategorematicity and English Infinitival *To*". *Glossa* 16.181-215.
Roberts, Ian G. 1985. "Agreement Parameters and the Development of English Modal Auxiliaries". *Natural Language and Linguistic Theory* 3.21-58.
Rosch, Eleanor. 1977. "Human Categorization". *Studies in Cross-cultural Psychology*, vol 1, ed. by Neil Warren. 1-49. London: Academic Press.
——, 1978. "Principles of Categorization". *Cognition and Categorization* ed. by Eleanor Rosch and Barbara B. Lloyd, 27-48. Hillsdale NJ: Erlbaum.
Standop, Ewald. 1957. *Syntax und Semantik der Modalen Hilfsverben im Altenglischen: Magan, motan, sculan, willan.* (=*Beiträge zur Englischen Philologie*, 38.) Bochum-Langendreer: Pöppinghaus.
Traugott, Elizabeth Closs. 1972. *A History of English Syntax: A transformational approach to the history of English sentence structure.* New York: Holt, Rinehart and Winston.
Venezky, Richard L. and Antonette diPaolo Healey. 1980. *A Microfiche Concordance to Old English*. Newark, Del. and Toronto: Pontifical Institute of Mediaeval Studies.
Visser, F.Th. 1963-73. *An Historical Syntax of the English Language*. 3 parts. Leiden: E.J. Brill.
Warner, Anthony R. 1985. *The Structuring of English Auxiliaries: A phrase structure grammar*. Bloomington: IULC.
——, 1986. "Ellipsis Conditions and the Status of the English Copula". *York Papers in Linguistics* 12.153-172.
——, forthcoming. *English Auxiliaries: Structure and history.* Cambridge: Cambridge University Press.

ON GROUNDING IN ENGLISH NARRATIVES:
A DIACHRONIC PERSPECTIVE

Brita Wårvik
Åbo Akademi

1. One of the questions that has intrigued students of discourse in the last decade or so is the marking of grounding distinctions.[1] The term grounding refers to the distinction between the most essential, main line, or foregrounded material, and the supportive, secondary, or backgrounded material.[2] Linguists have found that such a distinction is potentially universal in that it is made in a great number of unrelated languages. What is even more interesting is that this distinction is frequently signalled by morphosyntactic markers. Such foreground markers or background markers vary greatly in form and explicitness from one language to another. They may also change from one stage of a language to another.[3]

Many, if not most, of the elements of a clause play a role in giving the clause a grounding value. Thus, in addition to the potential explicit grounding markers, the foregroundedness of a clause can be defined by the types of participants (referentiality, definiteness, agentivity, humanness, affectedness of the object, etc.) and the types of verb or predicate (tense, aspect, mood, affirmation,

Aktionsart, etc.), as well as by the syntactic status of the clause (i.e., whether it is a main clause, a subclause or some other dependent construction). According to such criteria we can define a prototypical, maximally foregrounded clause in a narrative text as follows. In such a clause the participants are individuated or identified human or humanlike beings. The clause typically depicts a unique, dynamic and punctual action performed by the human subject purposefully and entirely, so that it affects the human object to as high a degree as possible. Moreover, these clauses are main clauses, usually those forming the temporally sequential story-line.

This simplified definition, though usable, needs certain additional specifications. First, as implied in the definition above, the distinction between foreground and background is not a dichotomy, but forms a scale along which clauses can be placed according to their degrees of foregroundedness or backgroundedness. Hence, the foregroundedness of a clause depends on several criteria, each of which affects its grounding value, but none of which is alone decisive (cf. the Transitivity Scale by Hopper & Thompson (1980) and the Saliency Hierarchy by Chvany (1985, 1986)). Secondly, the real grounding value of a clause is, of course, dependent on the context. In other words, the degrees of foregroundedness or backgroundedness of individual clauses must be compared to each other before we can know what is foregrounded and what backgrounded, and in relation to what, in the text.

Thirdly, in contrast to some early work on the subject (e.g. the narrative analysis of Labov & Waletzky (1967)), it has become evident that narrative foreground is not the same as the sequential story-line, which is defined as the events and actions following each other in chronological order, even though temporal sequentiality and foregrounding often merge. Instead, temporal sequentiality is one of the component criteria of foregrounding in narrative texts, functioning together with or against the other grounding criteria (cf. Chvany 1985, 1986; Kalmár 1982). Other such content criteria cover a number of features which could be collectively labelled as Salience, with a term borrowed from Osgood (1980). In the framework of grounding, Salience arises out of (1) the vividness of the event or action depicted in the clause, (2) its human importance as defined by speaker-motivation (cf. the Me-first principle of Cooper & Ross (1975)), and (3) the topicality of the action or event, which is related to the unity of hero in the sequence of foregrounded clauses, and thus to the nearness or familiarity of the participants in the context. (For more detailed discussions of grounding criteria see Chvany 1985, Hopper & Thompson 1980, Reinhart 1984, Wårvik 1987).

In the fourth place, the linguistic distinction between foreground and background can be seen as a parallel to the perceptual distinction between figure and ground (cf. Reinhart 1984; Talmy 1978; Wallace 1982). This parallelism is obvious when we compare the features which allow us to recognize figures and foreground as distinct from grounds and background. In a similar way, we can draw a parallel between grounding and Salience, as defined by Osgood (1980). When grounding is thus seen as an exponent of more general perceptual phenomena, the pervasiveness of grounding distinctions in language after language becomes less surprising.

Finally, the numerous interdependent and sometimes contradictory grounding criteria should be organized into some sort of hierarchy, so that they could be efficiently used in the analysis of more elaborate texts than the ones dealt with here. Such hierarchies are likely to vary according to the functions or aims of the discourse, and they are probably to some extent culture specific.

2. The distinctions between foregrounded and backgrounded elements in a text are better illustrated by texts than by definitions. Text 1 is an extract from *The Old English Orosius*, dating from around the year 900, and Text 2 is from Ælfric's Catholic Homilies, from around 1000.

(1) On þæm dagum on Tracia þæm londe wæron twegen cyningas ymb þæt rice winnende, þa wæron gebroþor. þa sendan hie to Philippuse 7 bædon þæt he hie ymb þæt rice gesemde 7 on þære gewitnesse wære þæt hit emne gedæled wære. He þa Philippus to heora gemote com mid micelre firde 7 þa cyningas begen ofslog 7 ealle þa witan, 5
7 feng him to þæm ricum bæm. Æfter þæm Atheniense bædan Philippus þæt he heora ladteow wære wið Focenses þæm folce, þeh hie ær hiera clusan him ongean beluce, 7 þæt he oðer ðara dyde, oþþe hie gesemde, oþþe him gefultumade þæt hi hie oferwinnan mehten. He him þa gehet þæt he him gefultuman wolde þæt hie hie ofer- 10
wunnen. Eac æt þæm ilcan cirre bædan Focense his fultumes wið Athene. He him þa gehet þæt he hie geseman wolde. Siþþan he buta þa clusan on his gewealde hæfde, þa dyde he him eac þa ricu to gewealdon, 7 his here geond þa byrig todælde 7 him bebead þæt hie ðæt lond hergiende wæron oþ hie hit awesten, þæt þæm folce 15
wæs ægþres waa, ge þæt hie þæt mæste yfel forberan sceoldon, ge eac þæt hie his sciran ne dorstan. Ac he ealle þa ricestan forslean het 7 þa oðre sume on wræcsið forsende, sume on oðra mearca gesette. Swa he Philippus þa miclan ricu geniþerade, þeh þe ær anra gehwelc wende þæt hit ofer monig oþru anwald habban 20
mehte, þæt hie þa æt nihstan hie selfe to nohte bemætan.

(2) On sumere tide com micel hungor on ðam lande. and gehwær þæt landfolc micclum geangsumode; þa getimode swa micel hafenleast on benedictes mynstre. þæt ða gebroðra næfdon buton fif hlafas to heora ealra gereorde; Se halga wer ða benedictus mid geswæsum wordum his gebroðra unrotnysse gefrefrode. and cwæð; Nu todæg 5
we habbað hwonlice behlaf. ac tomerigen we sceolon habban genihtsumlice; Hwæt ða þæs on merigen wurdon gemette ætforan heora gedyrum twa hund mittan meluwes on fætelsum. ða se ælmihtiga god his ðeowum asende. ac swa ðeah næs nanum men cuð hu hi ðider comon; 10

Sum eawfæst ðegen bæd ðone halgan wer þæt he mid his munecum
on his lande him munuclif aræran sceolde. and he lustbære ðæs
getiðode. and cwæð to ðam gebroðrum þæt he wolde sylf on ðam dæge
ðe he gecwæð ðær gecuman. and þæs mynstres getimbrunge gedihtan;
Ða munecas ða ferdon be his hæse and bletsunge to ðæs ðegenes 15
lande. and georne ðæs andagan cepton; þa æteowode se halga wer
benedictus on swefne hine sylfne ðam munece þe he to ealdre geset
hæfde. ofer ðam mynstre. and his profoste samod. and hi gewissode
swiðe smeaðancellice ymbe ðæs mynstres gebytlungum. on þære nihte
þe se andaga on merigen wæs; þa ða hi awocon se ealdor and his 20
profost. ða rehte heora ægðer oðrum hwæt hi on swefene gesawon.
and þæs micclum wundrodon; Eft siððan þa se andaga agan wæs. and
se halga wer ne com swa swa he gecweden hæfde. ða comon hi eft wið
his. ðus cwedende; We andbidodon ðin halga fæder þæt ðu us þæs
mynstres gebytlu dihtan sceoldest. and þu ne come swa swa ðu us 25
behete; Ða andwyrde se halga. and cwæð; Mine gebroðra. hwi secge
ge þæt ic ne come? Hwæt la. ne æteowode ic inc bam slapendum.
and ealle ða gebytlunge gewisslice tæhte? Farað nu. and aræræð
þæt mynster swa swa ic eow on swefne gedihte; Hi ða mid micelre
wundrunge to ðam lande gewendon. and swa ða gebytlunge gefade- 30
don swa swa him on swefene æteowod wæs;

Old English provides us with an example of an explicit grounding marker: in Old English narrative texts the adverbial *þa* functions as a foreground marker (Enkvist 1972, 1986). In Texts 1 and 2 the clauses marked by *þa* depict actions and events that constitute the main points in the stories. Though these clauses do not always satisfy all the criteria for foregrounding, they are characterized by several of them. For instance, the subjects in *þa* -clauses are human beings, which are well identified and individuated in the text: they are the heroes of the story, such as Philippus in 1 and Benedict and his brethren in 2. The same applies to some of the objects, for example the two kings and the peoples in 1. More characteristically, the objects are often highly affected, such as the two kings, who are killed. The events are also typical of foreground: they are all unique, neither repeated nor habitual; they are usually dynamic in being actions; they are punctual, such as *sendan, biddan, cuman,* and *ofslean* , though duratives, such as *bemetan* and *wundrian* are also found.

The actions are purposeful, not accidental, and further, they are completed.

Moreover, these narratives are typical of Old English story-telling in being simple stories whose events are depicted in the same order as they are supposed to have happened in the real world: the presentation of the events follows what has been called the Naturalness principle (Osgood 1980) or Experiential iconicity (Enkvist 1981). In such narratives the temporally sequential story-line tends to appear as foreground. Story-line sequentiality can be signalled by various means, such as adverbials of temporal succession like *aefter þaem*, *siþþan-* and *þa þa*-clauses, and uses of tenses and aspects. Even without such explicit signals, we can infer sequentiality on the basis of the content criteria as well as of the context, for instance when we have a sequence of clauses coordinated with *and*. As temporal sequentiality is the basic, 'natural' or 'iconic' ordering principle in narratives, we take conformity to it for granted, unless another order is indicated.

þa is, of course, also a time adverbial, and as such it is linked with the other expressions of temporal relations in the narrative. It cooperates with them in indicating the structure of the text. In addition to signalling story-line sequentiality, time adverbials also have another text-structuring function in narratives, which is the marking of textual units at different levels (on the text-structuring functions of adverbials see Enkvist 1987, Grimes 1975, Longacre 1979, Thompson & Longacre 1985, Virtanen 1987). In the example texts the beginnings of each of the four substories give the settings for the following episodes[4]. In 1 we are first given the temporal setting *on þaem dagum* and the local setting *on Tracia þaem londe*, and the second substory about Philippus and the two peoples starts with a temporal setting: *aefter þaem* (1:6). In 2 the first substory begins with a new temporal setting for the 'hunger'-episode, *on sumere tide*. Within the substories the time adverbials other than *þa* are used for indicating divisions into minor episodes, as in 1:11 *aet þaem ilcan cirre* and in 1:12 the *siþþan*-clause.

Finally, we can consider some of the ways of indicating background. We can think of backgrounded elements as textually subordinate, and, as an iconic parallel to this, syntactic subordination is one of the signals of backgrounding. Relative clauses, for instance, may function as identifications, which are part of the background of a narrative, as in 2:17 *þe he to ealdre geset haefde*. Temporal subordinate clauses, such as the *þa þa*-clause in 2:20, can well be part of the sequential story-line, but they are nevertheless backgrounded, giving settings for the following foregrounded clauses and thus introducing new episodes (cf. Thompson 1987). This illustrates why temporal sequentiality never alone implies foregrounding, and why, consequently, the two concepts have to be kept separate in spite of the mergings.

Another type of material which is typically backgrounded in simple stories consists of elements off the story-line, which can be 'flashforwards', simultaneous events, or 'flashbacks'. Flashforwards or not-yet-realized events are, like all irreal events, off the story-line and can be used as explanations for and comments on the foregrounded elements. Simultaneous events may be marked by, for instance, the progressive form, as in 1:1-2. They are presented as backgrounded to a more punctual and thus more foregrounded event, such as here, the sending after Philippus. 'Flashbacks' are expressed in these texts by subordinate clauses, where they are also otherwise marked as off-story-line elements, for instance in 1:7, where the adverbial *aer* signals previousness, and in 2:17, where the tense is pluperfect.

To sum up. The system of indicating grounding distinctions in Old English narratives consists of the foreground marker *þa* functioning in an interplay with content criteria, such as temporal sequentiality, and with certain linguistic criteria, such as clause status and the tense-aspect system.

3. A description of a past synchronic state will further increase in interest, if that state differs from another state in the past or in the present. In fact, the narrative grounding signals in Old English are different from those in Modern English narratives. Some characteristics of narratives can of course be found in both, in particular content criteria, such as the unity of hero and temporal sequentiality, which can be violated but not ignored. It is rather in the linguistic criteria, and especially in the use made of the grounding signals, that differences can be found. The forms as such have correspondences in all stages of English; for instance, the Old English foreground marker *þa* can be related to *then* in Modern English, and, similarly, the Modern English background-marking progressive form and pluperfect find their correlates in the Old English periphrastic forms *bēon/wesan* + -*ende* and *habban* + past participle. But the status of these forms in the system of signals of grounding distinctions is not the same in Old English as in Modern English.

As has been pointed out by Nickel (1966) and Mitchell

(1985:681ff.) among many others, the Old English progressive forms and pluperfects are fairly often found in contexts similar to those where they are found in Modern English, which, from the perspective of grounding, can be called narrative background, as we saw in 1 and 2. But the uses made of these forms in Old English coincide only partially with those in Modern English, even so partially that some linguists have denied any overlap of functions (cf. Aristar & Dry 1982). For instance, the 'pluperfect'-meaning, indicating events preceding those on the story-line, can be expressed by the *habban* + past participle periphrasis corresponding to the Modern English form, as in 2:17 and 2:23, but it can also be expressed by the simple past tense + the adverbial *aer*, as in 1:7, or the simple past alone, as in 2:21.

Whatever the expressions used, the sequential story-line and grounding distinctions in the narrative text presumably had to be comprehensible to the receivers. Thus, there has to be an explanation why this kind of off-story-line, backgrounded material in Old English could be given without explicit background markers distinguishing it from story-line foregrounded material. One reason is the existence of a foreground marker. In Old English, the foregrounding particle *þa* was used to make grounding distinctions more explicit in narratives. Therefore the tense-aspect system did not have to carry the burden of expressing all the distinctions between different types of material and their degrees of foregroundedness vs. back-groundedness, as in Modern English for instance. It is less economical to mark both ends of the grounding scale, if marking one end is enough.

4. Text 3 exemplifies an intermediary stage between

the system of narrative grounding signals of Old English and that of Modern English. This text is an extract from *Barlam and Iosaphat*, dating from the mid-15th century.

(3) Than afterwarde he toke one of þe pryncis þat he loued wel, þat was an holy man and good, whos name was Barachias, whych was with him aʒens þe philosophers whan Nachor made hym Barlam, as it is seide before. And Iosaphat praide hym meekly and goodly to take þe kyngdom vpon hym for to gouerne þe peple of God in drede,   5
þat he myʒt go and performe his promys þat he had made to God. Barachias refused it, and seide:'Treuly, Syr, þy dome is fulunrichtful, and dost noþynge after þe comaundement of God. For if þou loue þy neghbore as þyself, why wylt þou put such a charge to me, þat þou wylt nat take þyself? For if it be good to be a   10
kynge, kepe þat is goode and holde it faste. And if it be nat profitable to þy soule, why wylt þou put it vpon me?' And whan he had seide þes wordis, þe kynge wolde no more speke as at þat tyme. Than at nyʒt he made a lettre, and þerin he wrote how þe peple sholde gouerne hem, and how þey sholde truste to God, and 15
what lyf þey sholde lyue, and what praiers þei sholde make to God, and bade hem þat þei sholde make non oþer kynge but Barachias. And whan þis lettre was wryten he lefte it in his chamber vpon his bedde, and wente preuely out of his palice. But he myʒt nat ascape so awey, for erly on þe morowe þe peple myste hym,   20
and þan þei were wonder sory, and faste þey wente aboute to seke hym. They souʒt hym aboute valeies and mounteynes, and at laste þey fonde hym in a valei holdynge vp his hondis to heuene, and seide þe .vj. houre. And whan þey sawe hym þei wepte for ioye, and asked hym why he wente so fro hem, and preide hym to come   25
aʒen and be here kynge. He seide aʒen vnto hem:'Treuly, ʒe laboure al in vayne, for ʒe shul haue me no more to be ʒoure kynge, and þerfor Y pray ʒou desyre it nat.' And ʒit by þe gret instance of the peple, and by here praier, he turned aʒen with hem to his palice. And whan al men were gadered togydre he declared open-   30
ly, and tolde hem his counseile, and þan he swore his oth þat he wolde nat one day abyde with hem longer:...

Here *than* does not function as a foreground marker. It is far less frequent in the foregrounded clauses than was Old English *þa* in 1 and 2. What *than* is doing in this text could rather be defined as 'marking episodic shifts or turning-points': the first two instances of *than* occur together with a time adverbial at the beginnings of minor episodes, in 3:1 and 3:14, and the two others come near the beginnings of episodes, which are also introduced by time adverbials, in 3:21 and 3:31. As to signals of backgrounding in 3, we find the pluperfect used in the same way as in the Old English texts. It occurs in subordinate clauses which contain the flashback-type of background, for instance in 3:6 *þat he had made to God* and 3:12 *whan he had seide þes wordis*, but it is not used every time Modern English would prefer a pluperfect, as in 3:2 *whych was with hym*, which would rather be rendered by 'who had been with him' and in 3:18 *whan þis lettre was wryten*, which would be 'when this letter had been written'.

5. To compare these texts with a simple narrative in Modern English we can look at the signals of grounding distinctions in Text 4. This text comes from a simplified version of a detective story, which is typically an event-centred type of narrative.

(<u>4</u>) I could not sleep that night. I felt that something was wrong. It was a wild night. The wind was blowing outside, and the rain was beating on the windows. Suddenly I heard a woman screaming in terror. It was my sister's voice. I sprang from my bed, and ran into the corridor. When I opened my door I seemed to hear a   5
low whistle and then the sound of a piece of heavy metal falling. As I ran down the corridor, my sister's door opened, and I saw her coming out with her face white with terror and her hands held out, moving from one side to the other as if she was drunk. I ran to her and threw my arms around her, but she fell   10
to the ground. And she cried in a voice which I shall never forget. "O, my God, Helen! It was the band. The speckled band." There was something else she wanted to say but was not able to; she only pointed her finger at the doctor's door. I ran away, calling for my stepfather, and met him coming out of his room.   15
When we came to my sister's side, she was dead.

Here the first clauses, until *suddenly*, present the setting for the incident: in them we find a negation, durative verbs, and progressive forms, which are typically associated with backgrounded contexts in narrative texts.

The progressive form as well as the present participle are used, in addition to indicating the setting, for simultaneous events as calling and coming in 4:14-15, and for descriptions of what the main character hears or sees, as in 4:3 and 4:8ff. Certain elements are also signalled as backgrounded by subordination. For instance in 4:7ff, running is presented as backgrounded to the opening of the door and to seeing the sister come out, and, in the last sentence, their coming to the sister's side, depicted in the subordinate clause, is less foregrounded than the fact that she is dead, presented in the main clause. Subordinate clauses also present comments on the events, which are part of the background in a narrative, as in 4:9 *as if she was drunk* and 4:11 *which I shall I never forget*. *Then*, which is the probable heir of the grounding functions of *þa* , does not behave like a foreground marker in this narrative text: it occurs only once, in 4:6, indicating the sequentiality as opposed to simultaneity of the sounds heard by the main character.

6. It may be significant that Text 4 is a sample of written narrative. When we listen to impromptu storytelling in Modern English, we may find that *then* is frequent in story-line clauses, which are often foregrounded. Such a strategy can also be found in written stories, but there it is typically used to reproduce or give an impression of reproducing a spoken original. However, this organization with *then* is far from the only alternative available in Modern English spoken narratives (cf. e.g. the use of *then* in the stories cited in Chafe (ed.) 1980 and Labov & Waletzky 1967). The strategy of marking story-line with *then* would thus qualify as a stylistic option in Modern English narrative.

In Old English, on the contrary, the narrators had perforce to rely on the foreground marker *þa*. As the existence of styles always, by definition, presupposes choice (Enkvist 1964, 1973), the use of *þa* Old English narratives cannot be a feature of style.

There is one common denominator in Old English narratives and today's spoken stories which is not shared by Modern English written narratives, namely an influence of orality. Though the Old English stories that we know have all been written down, they can be presumed to mirror oral traditions. This can be seen, for instance, in the addresses to the hearer instead of reader, and in certain structural features, such as parataxis rather than hypotaxis, which characterize oral discourse (Ong 1982; Rynell 1952). It must be noted, however, that orality in Old and Middle English is no longer the primary orality of languages untouched by writing, but rather the residue of an oral culture still strong in the unstable period of change from orality to a literacy-dominated culture.[5]

We should in fact make a distinction between two parameters: orality/literacy and speech/writing, the former referring to cultures, the latter to modes of presentation. In these terms, we can characterize the Old and Middle English narratives discussed here as written texts produced in an oral culture. The Modern English narratives with high frequencies of *then* would thus be classified as spoken discourse in a literate culture.

In this light, it can be hypothesized that the Old English foreground-marking type of narration arose out of the oral story-telling tradition, which was still dominant at that time. As our modern literate standards of story-telling gradually started to dominate over the traditional oral standards, this old type of narrating lost its status as 'worthy of writing', but survived as a stylistic alternative in the spoken mode. Thus stylistic variation enters into the development of grounding signals through the changes in story-telling traditions. We may assume that the increasingly literate culture gave rise to a larger repertoire of styles, which were needed for the new, literate models of story-telling.

7. To conclude, the changes in the uses and functions of the adverbial *þa*, later *then*, the progressive form, and the pluperfect in the written narrative suggest a development from a dominantly foreground-marking system of grounding distinctions in Old English narrative to the Modern English system where background marking is preferred. When we look for signals of grounding distinctions in Modern English narratives, what we find are special forms indicating certain types of backgrounded material, whereas it is more difficult to point at an explicit foreground marker. However, Modern English could perhaps best be classified as a fuzzy-grounding language, that is, a language where grounding judgements are based on the number of grounding criteria satisfied by the textual element rather than the presence or absence of specific, discrete grounding markers (cf. Hopper & Thompson 1980). If languages can be grouped according to their means of signalling grounding distinctions into foreground-marking, background-marking, fuzzy-grounding, and other types of languages, it is tempting to classify the change undergone by English narrative as a typological shift from a predominantly foreground-marking type to a fuzzy-grounding type which favours background-marking.

NOTES

1. I wish to thank the following persons for their valuable comments on earlier versions of this paper: Nils Erik Enkvist, Aleksander Szwedek, Jan-Ola Östman, and the members of the Research Group Style and Text at Åbo Akademi, Finland.
2. Accounts of previous research on related topics can be found in Chvany 1985, 1986, Pollack 1976, Reinhart 1984, and Weber 1982.
3. For studies on grounding markers in various languages see e.g. Grimes (ed.) 1978, Hopper 1979, Hopper & Thompson 1980, Hopper & Thompson (eds.) 1982, Longacre 1981. Earlier stages of individual languages have been investigated by Enkvist 1986, Enkvist & Wårvik 1987, Fleischman 1985, and Wårvik 1987 among others.
4. On the terminology of story grammars see e.g. de Beaugrande 1982.
5. On the relationship between orality and literacy in the Middle Ages see e.g. Bäuml 1984, Maas 1985, and Ong 1984.

SOURCES

Aelfric's Catholic Homilies. Second Series. Ed. Malcolm Godden. (= EETS S.S. 5). London, etc.: Oxford University Press. 1979. (2).
Barlam and Iosaphat. Ed. John C. Hirsh. (= EETS 290). London, etc: Oxford University Press. 1986. (3).
Doyle, Sir Arthur Conan. 1977. *The Speckled Band* . (Easy Readers A). Copenhagen: Grafisk Forlag A/S. (4).
The Old English Orosius. Ed. Janet Bately. (= EETS S.S. 6. London, etc: Oxford University Press. 1980. (1).

REFERENCES

Aristar, Anthony & Helen Dry. 1982. "The Origins of Backgrounding Tenses in English". *PCLS* 18.1-13.
Bäuml, Franz H. 1984. "Medieval Texts and the Two Theories of Oral-Formulaic Composition: A proposal for a third theory". *New Literary History* 16.31-49.
Beaugrande, Robert de. 1982. "The Story of Grammars and the Grammar of Stories". *JPrag* 6.383-422.
Chafe, Wallace L. (ed.). 1980. *The Pear Stories* . (= Advances in Discourse Processes, 3). Norwood, NJ: Ablex.
Chvany, Catherine V. 1985. "Foregrounding, 'Transitivity', Saliency (in sequential and non-sequential prose)". *Essays in Poetics* 10.2.1-27.

_____ 1986. "Backgrounded Perfectives and Plot-line Imperfectives: Toward a theory of grounding in text". *The Scope of the Slavic Aspect* (= UCLA Slavic Studies), ed. by Michael S.Flier & Alan M. Timberlake, 247-73. Columbus: Slavica.

Cooper, William E. & John R.Ross. 1975. "World Order". *Papers from the Parasession on Functionalism*, ed. by Robin E.Grossman, L.James San, & Timothy J.Vance, 63-111. Chicago: Chicago Linguistic Society.

Enkvist, Nils Erik. 1964. "On Defining Style: An essay in applied linguistics". *Linguistics and Style*, ed. by John Spencer, 1-56. London, etc: Oxford University Press.

_____ 1972. "Old English þa - An action marker?". *NphM* 73.90-96.

_____ 1973. *Linguistic Stylistics* (= Janua Linguarum. Series Critica, 5). The Hague & Paris: Mouton.

_____ 1981. "Experiential Iconicism in Text Strategy". *Text* 1.77-111.

_____ 1986. "More about the Textual Functions of Old English Adverbial þa". *Linguistics across Historical and Geographical Boundaries : in honour of Jacek Fisiak on the occasion of his fiftieth birthday* (= Trends in Linguistics: Studies and Monographs, 32), ed. by Dieter Kastovsky & Aleksander Szwedek. Vol. 1: *Linguistic theory and historical Linguistics*, 301-09. Berlin etc.: Mouton de Gruyter.

_____ 1987. "A Note towards the Definition of Text Strategy". *ZPhon* 40.1.19-27.

_____ & Brita Wårvik. 1987. "Old English þa, Temporal Chains, and Narrative Structure". *Papers from the 7th International Conference on Historical Linguistics*, ed. by Anna G. Ramat, Onofrio Carruba, & Giuliano Bernini, 221-37. Amsterdam & Philadelphia: John Benjamins.

Fleischman, Suzanne. 1985. "Discourse Functions of Tense-aspect Oppositions in Narrative: Toward a theory of grounding". *Linguistics* 23.851-82.

Givon, Talmy (ed.). 1979. *Discourse and Syntax* (= Syntax and Semantics, 12). New York, etc: Academic Press.

Grimes, Joseph E. 1975. *The Thread of Discourse* (= Janua Linguarum. Series Minor, 207). The Hague & Paris: Mouton.

_____ (ed.). 1978. *Papers on Discourse*. Arlington, Texas: Summer Institute of Linguistics.

Hopper, Paul J. 1979. "Aspect and Foregrounding in Discourse". In Givon (ed.) 1979, 213-44.

_____ & Sandra A.Thompson. 1980. "Transitivity in Grammar and Discourse". *Lg* 56.251-99.

_____ & _____ (eds.). 1982. *Studies in Transitivity* (= Syntax and Semantics, 15). New York, etc: Academic Press.

Kalmár, Ivan. 1982. "Transitivity in a Czech Folk Tale". In Hopper & Thompson (eds.) 1982, 241-59.

Labov, William & Joshua Waletzky. 1967. "Narrative Analysis: Oral versions of personal experiences". *Essays on Verbal and Visual Arts: Proceedings of the 1966 Annual Spring Meeting of the American Ethnological Society*, ed. by June Helm, 12-44. Seattle: University of Washington Press.

Lindblad, Ishrat & Magnus Ljung (eds.).1987. *Proceedings from the Third Nordic Conference on English Studies*, Vol.1 (= Stockholm Studies in

English, 73). Stockholm: Almqvist & Wiksell.
Longacre, Robert E. 1979. "The Paragraph as a Grammatical Unit". In Givon (ed.) 1979, 115-34.
───── 1981. "A Spectrum and Profile Approach to Discourse Analysis". *Text* 1.337-59.
Maas, Utz. 1985. "Lesen - Schreiben - Schrift. Die Demotisierung eines professionellen Arkanums im Spätmittelalter und in die fruhen Neuzeit". *Zeitschrift für Literaturwissenschaft und Linguistik* 59.55-81.
Mitchell, Bruce. 1985. *Old English Syntax*. Oxford: Clarendon Press.
Nickel, Gerhard. 1966. *Die Expanded Form im Altenglischen*. Neumunster: Karl Wachholtz Verlag.
Ong, Walter J. 1982. *Orality and Literacy : The technologizing of the word* (New Accents). London & New York: Methuen.
───── 1984. "Orality, Literacy, and Medieval Textualization". *New Literary History* 16.1-12.
Osgood, Charles E. 1980. *Lectures on Language Performance* (= Springer Series in Language and Communication, 7). New York, etc.: Springer-Verlag.
Pollack, Wolfgang. 1976. "Un modele explicatif de l'opposition aspectuelle: le schema d'incidence". *FM* 44.289-311.
Reinhart, Tanya. 1984. "Principles of Gestalt Perception in the Temporal Organization of Narrative Texts". *Linguistics* 22.779-809.
Rynell, Alarik. 1952. "Parataxis and Hypotaxis as a Criterion of Syntax and Style". *Lunds Universitets Årsskrift* . N. F. Avd.1. Bd.48:3. Lund: C.W.K.Gleerup.
Talmy, Leonard. 1978. "Figure and Ground in Complex Sentences". *Universals of Human Language* , ed. by Joseph Greenberg, Vol. 4, 625-49. Stanford: Stanford University Press.
Thompson, Sandra A. 1987. ""Subordination" and Narrative Event Structure". *Coherence in Grounding and Discourse* (TSL, 11) ed. by Russell Tomlin, 435-54. Amsterdam & Philadelphia: John Benjamins.
───── & Robert E.Longacre. 1985. "Adverbial Clauses". *Language Typology and Syntactic Description* . Vol. 2: *Complex Constructions* , ed. by Timothy Shopen, 171-234. Cambridge etc.: Cambridge University Press.
Wårvik, Brita. 1987. "On Grounding in Narratives". In Lindblad & Ljung (eds.) 1987, 379-93.
Wallace, Stephen. 1982. "Figure and Ground: The interrelationships of linguistic categories". *Tense-Aspect : Between Semantics and Pragmatics* (= TSL, 1), ed. by Paul J.Hopper, 201-23. Amsterdam & Philadelphia: John Benjamins.
Weber, Jean Jacques. 1983. "The Foreground-Background Distinction: A survey of its definitions and applications". *Linguistics in Literature* 8.1-15.
Virtanen, Tuija. 1987. "On the Textual Functions of Adverbial Placement". In Lindblad & Ljung (eds.) 1987, 347-61.

AUTHOR INDEX

Aarsleff, H., 170-1, 172
Abercrombie, D., 3
Adams, M., 285
Adamson, S., 276, 513, 515
Addison, J., 485, 491
Aelfric, 112, 139, 544, 547, 562
Agutter, A., 1, 5
Aijmer, K., 488
Aitken, A. J., 9, 250, 270, 274
Alexander, H., 26
Alfred, 477
Algeo, J., 13, 29
Allen, H.B., 272
Allen, C. L., 90, 116, 131, 134, 135, 139, 230, 289
Allen, W. S., 403
Alleyne, M. C., 413
Alston, R. C., 484, 486, 487, 491
Altenberg, B., 340
Amos, A. C., 161, 163, 367
Andersen, R., 413
Anderson, J., 112, 119, 120, 122, 141-2, 147-55, 158-9, 161, 162-3, 215-6, 219, 289
Anstis, J., 375
Aristar, A., 567
Arndt, W. W., 85
Arnold, M., 176
Aronoff, M., 221
Ascham, R., 427, 488
Ashby, W. J., 343
Atwood, E. B., 26
Austen, Jane, 553, 554
Austin, F., 483, 493
Avery, E., 22,
Ayres, H.M., 25
Babbitt, G., 22
Bacon, Sir Francis, 485

Bailey, C-J. N., 276, 277, 338, 345, 349, 352, 428
Bailey, R. N., 359, 375
Bailey, R. W., 29
Baker, R., 486, 487, 490, 491, 492, 493, 494
Bald, M., 4
Ball, C. J. E., 161
Barber, C.,3
Barfield, O., 24
Barker, H.F., 23, 24, 25
Barlow, J., 16, 23
Barnes, W., 421
Barnes, W., 189-203
Barrett, C.R., 228
Barwise, C., 499
Bastiaensens, A., 96, 98
Batchelor, T., 256
Batteaux, C., 171, 180, 184
Bauml, F. H., 573
Bayly, A., 484, 485, 488
Beale, J., 251
Beattie, J., 166, 182
Beaugrande, R. de, 573
Beauzee, N., 171, 172, 178, 179, 180, 184-5
Bede, 115, 120, 367, 418
Behaghel, O., 94
Bennett, P. A., 529
Bennis, H., 527
Benveniste, E., 503
Berendsen, E., 228, 233
Bergsland, Ќ., 70, 84
Beschorner, F., 41, 46, 47-8
Bever, T., 100
Biber, D., 429-30
Bickerton, D., 411-2, 420
Bihl, J., 331-2
Birss, J. W., 24
Bishop, T. A. M., 360
Blair, H., 165-87
Blake, W., 540

Blandford, F., 23
Bliss, A., 293, 295, 296, 298, 302, 304, 423, 469
Bloomfield, L., 177, 184
Bolingbroke, L., 491
Bolinger, D.L., 32, 327, 329, 334
Bonaparte, L. -L., 189
Bopp, F., 415
Bossuyit, A., 343
Bosworth, J., 71
Bourcier, G., 96, 314
Braaten, B., 426
Bresnan, J., 87
Bridges, R., 24
Brink, C. O., 403
Brinton, D.G., 40
Briody, M., 429
Brown, C., 349
Brown, G., 39, 40
Brown, W.H., 228
Brugman, C., 506
Bryce, J., 182
Buchanan, J., 483, 490
Buck, C. D., 71, 72
Buckhurst, H., 22,
Burnley, D., 315-6, 317, 327, 330, 331
Burns, R., 475
Butters, R. R., 29
Buxbaum, K., 24
Bybee, J., 510, 516
Byington, S., 23, 25
Caedmon, 367
Callaway, M., 520
Cameron, A., 141, 155-7, 161, 163
Campbell, A., 142, 144, 155, 161, 370, 403
Campbell, G., 180, 182
Canale, W., 225
Canfield, D. L., 25
Carstairs, A., 402, 405
Cassidy, F.G., 28, 273, 430
Caxton, W., 427
Chafe, W., 39, 570
Chaucer, G., 10, 33, 36, 41-3, 47, 48, 92, 93, 100, 135, 315, 316, 318, 326, 340, 428-9, 474, 475, 488
Chevillet, F., 97, 99, 100, 101
Chomsky, N., 284, 287, 291, 435, 471, 479, 480, 506, 519, 523, 529
Chvany, C.V., 560, 561, 573
Cicero, 351

Clark, C., 314
Claudius, R.H., 22, 23
Coates, J., 139
Collingwood, W. G., 359
Collins, R., 349
Colman, F., 141-2, 147-55, 158-9, 161, 162 -3
Condillac, E.B. de, 171, 184
Cooper, C., 258, 262
Cooper, W. E., 561
Coote, C., 488, 490
Cowen, J.M., 331
Craigie, T., 181
Cramp, R., 359, 370
Curme, G. O., 23, 95, 96, 97
d'Ardenne, S. R. T. O., 161, 361
Dahl, I., 369
Dahl, O., 342
Dahlgren, K., 500
Dal, I., 94, 96, 97, 98, 104
Dasher, R., 497, 511
Davis, J.,15, 24
de Brosses, C., 171, 172, 174, 183, 184
Dekeyser, X., 97, 98, 100, 101, 102, 104, 139
den Besten, H., 226, 241
Denison, D., 32, 47, 93, 138, 241, 417, 529, 535, 549, 553, 557
Devitt, A., 1, 4
Di Sciullio, U. P., 411
Dickens, C., 19, 23, 26
Dickins, B., 357, 365
Dillard, J.L., 246-7, 268, 274
Dilworth, T., 485, 491
Dobson, E.J., 494
Donaldson, E. T., 315, 340
Downing, B.T., 106
Dresher, B.E., 141, 144, 152, 153, 154, 159, 161, 162
Dry, H., 567
Du Marsais, C.C., 171, 179
Dunbar, J., 182
Dunbar, W., 10, 11
Duncan-Rose, C., 35, 40, 44, 46, 47
Eagleson, R. D., 277
Edward VI, 476
Edward VIII, 25
Edwards, V. K., 422, 427
Ekwall, E. 25, 426
Elizabeth I, 8
Ellegård, A., 32, 35, 407-10, 416-8, 425, 428, 540, 552

AUTHOR INDEX

Ellis, A. J., 251, 254, 255, 256, 257, 264, 277
Elmer, W., 116, 119, 120, 122, 125, 126, 139, 289
Elworthy, T., 189-203, 421, 422
Engblom, V., 408
Enkvist, N.E., 563, 564, 571, 573
Erben, J., 417
Feather, W., 22, 23, 26
Fell, J., 484, 485
Fenning, D., 481-2, 484, 490, 491
Ferguson, C., 515
Finegan, E., 429
Firth, J. R., 25
Fischer, O., 111-40, 225, 241, 289, 524
Fisher, A., 483, 491, 493
Fisiak, J., 314, 469, 556
Fleischman, S., 573
Fletcher, P., 413
Flint, M., 258
Fogg, P.W., 484, 486, 487, 488, 489, 491, 493
Franz, W., 424
Friedrich, P., 47
Fudge, E.C., 266, 267
Funke, O., 32-5, 36, 40, 43, 44, 45, 46, 47
Gachelin, J-M., 202
Galsworthy, J., 18, 25
Gardner, F.F., 228
Gazdar, G., 537
Geis, M., 498, 515
Gelling, M., 418
Geoghegan, S.G., 89
Giacalone Ramat, A., 430
Giegerich, H., 333
Girard, G., 171, 179
Godden, M., 139
Goldsmith, W., 487, 491
Goossens, L., 544
Gordon, T., 182
Görlach, M., 29, 276
Gossens, L., 510
Gough, J., 483, 485, 491
Gower, J., 316, 318, 323, 324, 326
Grainger, J., 487
Gray, T., 490
Green, B., 359
Greenberg, J., 205
Greenwood, J., 482, 483, 494
Grimes, J.E., 564, 573

Grimshaw, J.B., 87, 89, 92, 93, 105
Grommersch, C., 97
Gumperz, J., 430
Hackett, J., 17-8
Haider, H., 239, 240
Halle, M., 435
Halliday, M.A.K., 294, 295, 337, 338, 340
Hannula, J. ,352
Hanson, K., 512
Harris, J.M., 270, 276, 277, 413, 421, 423, 424, 425
Harris, J., 167, 169, 171, 177, 182, 183
Hasan, R., 340
Haugen, E., 94, 103
Hausermann, H., 34
Hawkes, D.T., 480
Hawkes, S.C., 359
Hayes, B., 322-3, 333, 334, 437, 439, 448, 452
Healy, A. DiPaolo, 114, 139, 241, 520, 535, 541, 556
Helgander, J., 95, 96
Hench, A.L., 24
Henry, P.L., 423
Henry VIII, 488
Herder, J.G., 170
Herslund, M., 94, 105
Hewett, M., 189, 191
Hibbitt, G.W., 27
Higden, R., 277
Hills, C., 359
Hiltunen, R., 430
Hochberg, J., 515
Hockett, C.F., 154
Hoekstra, T.A., 526
Hogg, R.M., 144, 161, 162, 163, 556
Holm, J., 430
Holmberg, B., 258
Homann, E.R., 33, 46, 48
Hooker, R., 485
Hoover, D., 456
Hope-Taylor, B., 418
Hopper, P.J., 32, 37-8, 47, 353, 560, 561, 572, 573
Hornstein, N., 285
Horvath, B., 276
Howlett, D.R., 364, 374
Hulbert, J.R., 489
Hume, D., 172, 487
Hume, A. 3
Humphries, W.R., 182
Ihalainen, O., 190, 202, 276, 411, 416, 422, 425

AUTHOR INDEX

Ingels, M., 92, 102
Jack, G.B., 343
Jack, R.D. S., 8
Jackson, K., 418-9, 420, 422
Jacobson, R., 403, 404, 448
James IV, 10
James VI and I, 2, 8
Jansson, S.B.F., 365
Jefferson, J.A., 331
Jefferson, T., 15
Jennings, J., 189, 194, 197
Jespersen, O., 103, 113, 256, 262, 342, 540
Johnson, Dr. S., 16, 484, 485, 486, 487, 489, 490
Joly, A., 352, 353
Jones, D., 265
Jones, G., 418
Jones, W.M., 201
Jonson, B., 540
Kalmar, I., 561
Kames, Lord, 182
Karttunen, F., 276, 352
Kastovsky, D., 205, 206, 221, 22
Keating, P., 161
Kemble, F., 19,
Kemmer, S., 515
Kendall, C.B., 304
Kennedy, A.G., 22, 23, 24, 25
Kerkhof, J., 34, 36, 46
Kerstens, J., 227-8, 233
Keyser, S.J., 221
Kinsley, J., 11
Kiparsky, P., 437, 438, 448, 452
Kirkby, J., 483
Kivimaa, K., 91
Klaeber, F., 439, 454
Klopzig, W., 526
Knox, John 8, 11, 487
Kohonen, V., 228
Koma, O., 521, 529, 532
Konig, E., 342, 352, 502
Koopman, H., 534
Koopman, W., 232, 240
Koskinen, L., 352
Koster, J., 524
Koziol, H., 34, 35, 36, 46
Krapp, G.P., 24, 25
Kruisinga, E., 189
Kuhn, H., 293-312
Kuhn, S. M., 146, 152, 153, 408, 521, 535
Kurath, H., 27, 268, 276, 521, 535

Kurylowicz, J., 437, 441, 442, 445, 449, 454
Kurzova, H., 97, 106
Kytö, M., 352, 408
Labov, W., 42, 277, 427, 560, 570
Lahiri, A., 161
Lakoff, G., 552
Lane, A., 482
Langacker, R.W., 500
Langendoen, D.T., 100
Langenfelt, G., 416, 428
Lasnik, H., 471, 479
Lass, R., 215-6, 219, 221, 245, 250, 251, 252, 253, 258, 260, 266, 269, 272, 276, 276, 277, 278, 459, 461, 462, 468, 469
Latimer, H., 476
Layamon, 92
Le Page, R., 412
Leechman, W., 167, 183
Leeds, W., 422
Lees, R.B., 85
Lehmann, C., 515
Lehnert, M., 332, 333
Lenerz, J., 104
Leonard, S.A., 493, 494
Liberman, M., 435, 436, 450-1, 452
Lightfoot, D.W., 113, 283, 285, 286, 291, 480, 523, 539, 550-1, 557
Lily, J., 483, 494
Locke, J., 485
Longacre, R.E., 32, 37, 38, 39, 564, 573
Lord, A.B., 295, 448, 456
Lord, C., 500
Lowth, R., 485, 486, 487, 488, 490
Lucas, P.J., 294, 296, 303
Luick, K., 277
Lutz, A., 221, 22
Lydgate, J., 10
Lyons, J., 206, 509
Maas, U., 573
Macaulay, G.C., 316-7, 324, 325-6
Macpherson, J., 175
Magoun, F.P., 448, 456
Maling, J.M., 94, 455
Malone, K., 22, 24
Malory, T., 135, 475
Mandeville, J., 317
Marchand, H., 207
Marckwardt, A.H., 314, 333

Maroldt, K., 276
Martens, L., 97, 100
Martin, B., 488
Mason, W., 487
Matthews, P.H., 206
McDavid, R.I., 27, 28, 268
Meier, A.J., 221
Mencken, H., 17, 22, 24, 25, 26
Meritt, H.D., 75, 83, 95
Millar, J., 166
Milton, J., 485, 540
Minkova, D., 221, 313, 332, 334, 460, 468, 469
Mitchell, B., 88, 90, 91, 96, 117, 129, 131, 132, 139, 227, 228, 232, 297, 303, 304, 339, 352, 471, 479, 520, 521, 542, 566
Moltke, E., 361
Monboddo, Lord (James Burnett), 171, 172, 178, 183
Moore, S., 314, 333
Moore, Terry, 515
Moore, Thomas, 487
Moortgat, M., 526
Morsbach, L., 314
Mossé, F., 277, 314, 323
Mülhäusler, P., 412
Murray, L., 484, 491
Mustanoja, T.F., 33, 34, 36, 43, 44, 46, 47, 88, 93, 101, 362
Myres, J.N.L., 359, 420
Nanni, D., 531
Nares, R., 262, 277
Ness, L., 35, 40, 44, 46, 47
Nevalainen, T., 345, 349, 352, 353, 410, 498
Nevanlinna, S., 352
Nickel, G., 566
Nisbet, M., 8
O'Neil, W., 221
Ogura, M., 117, 120, 121, 122, 132, 139
Okasha, E., 358, 361, 363, 368, 371, 372, 375
Omont, H., 156
Ong, W.J., 571, 573
Osgood, C.E., 561, 564
Ossian, 175
Ostmann, J-O., 573
Otfrid, 96
Outakoski, T., 352
Page, R.I., 359, 363, 364, 367, 368, 370, 372, 374

Pagliuca, W. 510, 516
Palmer, F.R., 139, 509, 544, 545
Partridge, A.C., 350
Paul, H., 94, 97
Peck, R., 325, 326
Peitsara, K., 352
Penzl, H., 26, 27
Perry, J., 499
Peters, S., 352
Phillipps, K.C., 97, 553
Plank, F., 135, 184, 402, 405, 539, 551
Plummer, C., 88, 90, 96
Polanyi, L., 38, 39
Pollack, W., 573
Pope, A., 486, 491-2, 540
Pope, J.C., 440
Poplack, S., 411
Porset, C., 172, 179
Poussa, P., 276, 414, 430
Preusler, W., 425
Priestley, J., 169
Priestley, Joseph, 487, 488, 490
Prince, A., 435, 436, 450-1, 452, 456
Prokosch, E., 415
Ptolemy, 57
Pullum, G.K., 537, 555
Quintillian, 176
Quirk, R., 27, 92, 99, 112, 127-8, 130, 132, 136, 214, 334, 350, 352
Raleigh, Sir Walter, 485
Rask, R., 403
Rastorguyeva, T.A., 314
Reid, T., 172
Reinhart, T., 561, 573
Richardson, S., 491
Rickford, J., 413, 430
Rissanen, M., 276, 349, 352, 408, 410, 430-1
Rizzi, L., 284
Roberts, I.G., 557
Robinson, F.N., 48
Rolle, R., 135
Romaine, S., 100, 102
Rosch, E., 537, 548-52, 555
Ross, J.R., 561
Rousseau, J-J., 171, 173
Russom, G., 454, 456
Rynell, A., 44, 571
Sag, I.A., 537
Saito, T., 102
Samuels, M.L., 313, 315, 319, 326, 331, 350, 423, 427

Scha, R.J.H., 38, 39
Schauman, B., 141, 155-6
Schiffrin, D., 340
Schlauch, M., 314
Schmidt, A., 430
Schumann, J., 413
Scott, F.S., 368
Selkirk, E., 320, 322, 333, 436, 451-2
Seymour, M.C., 317, 331, 334
Shaftesbury, Lord, 491
Shakespeare, W., 475, 483, 485, 486, 488, 489, 540
Shannon, A., 228
Shepherd, S.C., 510
Shores, D.L., 228
Sidney, A., 485
Sidney, Sir Philip, 485
Sievers, E., 440, 448
Silverstein, T., 349
Skalicka, V., 402
Skeat, W.W., 71
Skene, G., 182
Slay, D., 296, 298
Smith, A., 165-7, 169, 171, 177, 181-2, 183-4
Smithers, G.V., 324, 332
Smyser, H.M., 34, 35, 36, 41, 46, 47
Sorensen, K., 350
Spenser, E., 485, 488
Standop, E., 544
Stanley, E.G., 364, 370
Stein, D., 40, 43, 46, 47, 408, 428
Stern, G., 514
Stewart, A.H., 403, 404
Stewart, D., 166, 169-70
Stewart, I., 367
Stockwell, R., 276, 515
Stoett, F.A., 104
Stowell, T.A., 523
Stubbs, M., 32, 40
Stiles, P., 162
Suzuki, S., 454
Swadesh, M., 76, 85
Sweet, B., 264
Sweet, H., 333
Sweetser, E.E., 500
Swift, J., 485, 486, 491
Szwedek, A., 573
Taavtsainen, I., 352
Taglicht, J., 342, 352, 489
Tajima, M., 36, 46
Talmy, L., 561
Taylor, H.M., 375
Taylor, R., 37, 46

Tempeton, J., 9
Thiersch, C., 230
Thompson, S.A., 353, 560, 561, 564, 565, 572, 573
Tieken-Boon, I. van Ostade, 408, 482, 483, 488, 489, 493, 494
Tillotson, J., 485
Toller, T.N., 71
Toon, T.E., 153, 158
Topliff, D., 314-5, 316, 317, 319, 325, 330
Trail, J., 182-3
Traugott, E.C., 31, 32, 39-40, 46, 47, 89, 139, 337, 338, 343, 351, 497-8, 500, 501, 511, 515, 541, 545, 556
Trevisa, J., 97, 277
Trnka, B., 44, 46
Trudgill, P., 29, 196, 422, 427, 430
Tucker, S.I., 492
Tudor, M., 10
Tyndale, W., 344
Ussher, G.N., 483
Van den Eynden, N.N., 97, 100
van der Gaaf, W., 113, 520, 521
van der Leek, F., 111-40, 225, 241, 289, 524
van der Wurff, W., 241
van Dijk, T.A., 38-9, 40
van Draat, P.F., 329, 334
van Kemenade, A., 225, 228, 233, 235, 237, 241, 524, 525, 529, 532, 534
Varnhagen, H., 352
Venezky, R.L., 114, 139, 241, 520, 535, 541, 556
Viereck, W., 29, 245
Vincent, N.B., 284, 513, 515
Virtanen, T., 564
Visser, F.Th., 31, 32, 34, 35, 44-5, 46, 48, 91, 92, 93, 98, 99, 100, 135, 139, 241, 415, 417, 425, 488, 521, 531, 534, 540, 541, 542, 553, 555, 556
Vogt, H., 70, 84
Wagner, H., 422, 424
Wakelin, M., 196, 251, 254, 277, 420
Waletzky, J., 560, 570
Walker, W., 347, 350
Wallace, S., 561
Wallis, J., 483, 487, 494
Walshe, M.O., 103

Ward, I.C., 24, 264
Ward, J., 487, 488
Ward, W., 494
Wardale, E.E., 314
Warner, A.R., 129, 138, 139,
    286, 289, 510-1, 515, 537,
    552, 554, 557
Wartburg, W. von, 503
Wårvik, B., 561, 573
Watson, R., 166, 167, 182-3
Weber, J.J., 573
Webster, N., 14-5, 16, 22, 23,
    484, 491, 493
Wehrmann, P., 527
Weinberg, A., 291
Weinreich, U., 269
Wells, J.C., 253, 272, 277
Weltens, B., 422, 427
Wesley, J., 487
Wessen, E., 98, 103
White, J., 483, 484, 486, 487,
    489, 493, 494
Wilkins, J., 176-7
Wilson, D.M., 360, 363
Wilson, R., 430
Wolfson, N., 44, 48
Wrenn, C.L., 214, 334, 370
Wright, J., 255, 259, 262,
    264, 421
Wright, S., 245, 258, 269,
    276, 278
Wright, T., 317
Wurzel, W.U., 221, 405
Wuth, A., 34, 46
Wycliffe, J., 93, 129, 344
Yule, G., 39, 40
Zandvoort, R.W., 25
Zviadadze, G., 28
Zwicky, A., 498, 515

In the CURRENT ISSUES IN LINGUISTIC THEORY (CILT) series (Series Editor: E.F. Konrad Koerner) the following volumes have been published thus far, and will be published during 1990:

1. KOERNER, E.F. Konrad (ed.): *The Transformational-Generative Paradigm and Modern Linguistic Theory*. Amsterdam, 1975.
2. WEIDERT, Alfons: *Componential Analysis of Lushai Phonology*. Amsterdam, 1975.
3. MAHER, J. Peter: *Papers on Language Theory and History I: Creation and Tradition in Language*. Foreword by Raimo Anttila. Amsterdam, 1977.
4. HOPPER, Paul J. (ed.): *Studies in Descriptive and Historical Linguistics: Festschrift for Winfred P. Lehmann*. Amsterdam, 1977. Out of print.
5. ITKONEN, Esa: *Grammatical Theory and Metascience: A critical investigation into the methodological and philosophical foundations of 'autonomous' linguistics*. Amsterdam, 1978.
6. ANTTILA, Raimo: *Historical and Comparative Linguistics*. Amsterdam/Philadelphia, 1989.
7. MEISEL, Jürgen M. & Martin D. PAM (eds): *Linear Order and Generative Theory*. Amsterdam, 1979.
8. WILBUR, Terence H.: *Prolegomena to a Grammar of Basque*. Amsterdam, 1979.
9. HOLLIEN, Harry & Patricia (eds): *Current Issues in the Phonetic Sciences, Proceedings of the IPS-77 Congress, Miami Beach, Fla., 17-19 December 1977*. Amsterdam, 1979. 2 vols.
10. PRIDEAUX, Gary (ed.): *Perspectives in Experimental Linguistics. Papers from the University of Alberta Conference on Experimental Linguistics, Edmonton, 13-14 Oct. 1978*. Amsterdam, 1979.
11. BROGYANYI, Bela (ed.): *Studies in Diachronic, Synchronic, and Typological Linguistics: Festschrift for Oswald Szemerényi on the Occasion of his 65th Birthday*. Amsterdam, 1980.
12. FISIAK, Jacek (ed.): *Theoretical Issues in Contrastive Linguistics*. Amsterdam, 1980.
13. MAHER, J. Peter with coll. of Allan R. Bomhard & E.F. Konrad Koerner (ed.): *Papers from the Third International Conference on Historical Linguistics, Hamburg, August 22-26, 1977*. Amsterdam, 1982.
14. TRAUGOTT, Elizabeth C., Rebecca LaBRUM, Susan SHEPHERD (eds): *Papers from the Fourth International Conference on Historical Linguistics, Stanford, March 26-30, 1980*. Amsterdam, 1980.
15. ANDERSON, John (ed.): *Language Form and Linguistic Variation. Papers dedicated to Angus McIntosh*. Amsterdam, 1982.
16. ARBEITMAN, Yoël & Allan R. BOMHARD (eds): *Bono Homini Donum: Essays in Historical Linguistics, in Memory of J. Alexander Kerns*. Amsterdam, 1981.
17. LIEB, Hans-Heinrich: *Integrational Linguistics*. 6 volumes. Amsterdam, 1984-1986. Vol. I available; Vol. 2-6 n.y.p.
18. IZZO, Herbert J. (ed.): *Italic and Romance. Linguistic Studies in Honor of Ernst Pulgram*. Amsterdam, 1980.
19. RAMAT, Paolo et al. (eds): *Linguistic Reconstruction and Indo-European Syntax. Proceedings of the Coll. of the 'Indogermanische Gesellschaft' Univ. of Pavia, 6-7 Sept. 1979*. Amsterdam, 1980.
20. NORRICK, Neal R.: *Semiotic Principles in Semantic Theory*. Amsterdam, 1981.
21. AHLQVIST, Anders (ed.): *Papers from the Fifth International Conference on Historical Linguistics, Galway, April 6-10, 1981*. Amsterdam, 1982.

22. UNTERMANN, Jürgen & Bela BROGYANYI (eds): *Das Germanische und die Rekonstruktion der Indogermanische Grundsprache*. Akten, Proceedings from the Colloquium of the Indogermanische Gesellschaft, Freiburg, 26-27 February 1981. Amsterdam, 1984.
23. DANIELSEN, Niels: *Papers in Theoretical Linguistics*. Amsterdam, n.y.p.
24. LEHMANN, Winfred P. & Yakov MALKIEL (eds): *Perspectives on Historical Linguistics*. Papers from a conference held at the meeting of the Language Theory Division, Modern Language Ass., San Francisco, 27-30 December 1979. Amsterdam, 1982.
25. ANDERSEN, Paul Kent: *Word Order Typology and Comparative Constructions*. Amsterdam, 1983.
26. BALDI, Philip (ed.) *Papers from the XIIth Linguistic Symposium on Romance Languages, University Park, April 1-3, 1982*. Amsterdam, 1984.
27. BOMHARD, Alan: *Toward Proto-Nostratic*. Amsterdam, 1984.
28. BYNON, James: *Current Progress in Afroasiatic Linguistics: Papers of the Third International Hamito-Semitic Congress, London, 1978*. Amsterdam, 1984.
29. PAPROTTÉ, Wolf & Rene DIRVEN (eds): *The Ubiquity of Metaphor: Metaphor in Language and Thought*. Amsterdam, 1985.
30. HALL, Robert A., Jr.: *Proto-Romance Morphology*. Amsterdam, 1984.
31. GUILLAUME, Gustave: *Foundations for a Science of Language*. Translated and with an introd. by Walter Hirtle and John Hewson. Amsterdam, 1984.
32. COPELAND, James E. (ed.): *New Directions in Linguistics and Semiotics*. Houston/Amsterdam, 1984. No rights for US/Can. *Customers from USA and Canada: please order from Rice University*.
33. VERSTEEGH, Kees: *Pidginization and Creolization: The Case of Arabic*. Amsterdam, 1984.
34. FISIAK, Jacek (ed.): *Papers from the VIth International Conference on Historical Linguistics, Poznan, 22-26 August 1983*. Amsterdam, 1985.
35. COLLINGE, N.E.: *The Laws of Indo-European*. Amsterdam, 1985.
36. KING, Larry D. & Catherine A. MALEY (eds): *Selected Papers from the XIIIth Linguistics Symposium on Romance Languages*. Amsterdam, 1985.
37. GRIFFEN, T.D.: *Aspects of Dynamic Phonology*. Amsterdam, 1985.
38. BROGYANYI, Bela & Thomas KRÖMMELBEIN (eds): *Germanic Dialects: Linguistic and Philological Investigations*. Amsterdam, 1986.
39. BENSON, James D., Michael J. CUMMINGS & William S. GREAVES (eds): *Linguistics in a Systemic Perspective*. Amsterdam, 1988.
40. FRIES, Peter Howard and Nancy (eds): *Toward an Understanding of Language: Charles C. Fries in Perspective*. Amsterdam, 1985.
41. EATON, Roger, et al. (eds): *Papers from the 4th International Conference on English Historical Linguistics*. Amsterdam, 1985.
42. MAKKAI, Adam & Alan K. MELBY (eds): *Linguistics and Philosophy. Essays in honor of Rulon S. Wells*. Amsterdam, 1985.
43. AKAMATSU, Tsutomu: *The Theory of Neutralization and the Archiphoneme in Functional Phonology*. Amsterdam, 1988.
44. JUNGRAITHMAYR, Herrmann & Walter W. MUELLER (eds): *Proceedings of the 4th International Hamito-Semitic Congress*. Amsterdam, 1987.
45. KOOPMAN, W.F., F.C. VAN DER LEEK, O. FISCHER & R. EATON (eds): *Explanation and Linguistic Change*. Amsterdam, 1987.
46. PRIDEAUX, Gary D., and William J. BAKER: *Strategies and Structures: The Processing of Relative Clauses*. Amsterdam, 1986.

47. LEHMANN, Winfred P.: *Language Typology 1985. Papers from the Linguistic Typology Symposium, Moscow, 9-13 Dec. 1985.* Amsterdam, 1986.
48. RAMAT, Anna Giacalone (ed.): *Proceedings of the VII International Conference on Historical Linguistics, Pavia 9-13 September 1985.* Amsterdam, 1987.
49. WAUGH, Linda R. & Stephen RUDY (eds): *New Vistas in Grammar: Invariance and Variation.* Amsterdam/Philadelphia, 1990. n.y.p.
50. RUDZKA-OSTYN, Brygida (ed.): *Topics in Cognitive Linguistics.* Amsterdam/Philadelphia, 1988.
51. CHATTERJEE, Ranjit: *Aspect and Meaning in Slavic and Indic.* Amsterdam/Philadelphia, 1988.
52. FASOLD, Ralph & Deborah SCHIFFRIN (eds): *Language Change and Variation.* Amsterdam/Philadelphia, 1989.
53. SANKOFF, David (ed.): *Diversity and Diachrony.* Amsterdam, 1986.
54. WEIDERT, Alfons: *Tibeto-Burman Tonology. A Comparative Analysis.* Amsterdam, 1987.
55. HALL, Robert A. Jr.: *Linguistics and Pseudo-Linguistics.* Amsterdam, 1987.
56. HOCKETT, Charles F.: *Refurbishing our Foundations. Elementary Linguistics from an Advanced Point of View.* Amsterdam, 1987.
57. BUBENIK, Vít: *Hellenistic and Roman Greece as a Sociolinguistic Area.* Amsterdam/Philadelphia, 1989.
58. ARBEITMAN, Yoël L.: *FUCUS. A Semitic/Afrasian Gathering in Remembrance of Albert Ehrman.* Amsterdam/Philadelphia, 1988.
59. VOORST, Jan van: *Event Structure.* Amsterdam/Philadelphia, 1988.
60. KIRSCHNER, Carl and Janet DECESARIS (eds): *Studies in Romance Linguistics.* Amsterdam/Philadelphia, 1989.
61. CORRIGAN, Roberta, Fred ECKMAN and Michael NOONAN (eds): *Linguistic Categorization.* Amsterdam/Philadelphia, 1989.
62. FRAJZYNGIER, Zygmunt (ed.): *Current Progress in Chadic Linguistics.* Amsterdam/Philadelphia, 1989.
63. EID, Mushira (ed.): *New Perspectives on Arabic Linguistics.* Amsterdam/Philadelphia, 1990. n.y.p.
64. BROGYANYI, Bela and Reiner LIPP (eds): *Essays in Linguistics. Offered in honor of Oswald Szemerényi on the occasion of his 75th birthday.* Amsterdam/Philadelphia, n.y.p. 1990.
65. ADAMSON, Sylvia, Vivien A. LAW, Nigel VINCENT and Susan WRIGHT (eds): *Papers from the 5th International Conference of English Historical Linguistics.* Amsterdam/Philadelphia, 1990.
66. ANDERSEN, Henning and Konrad KOERNER (eds): *Historical Linguistics 1987. Papers from the 8th International Conference on Historical Linguistics, Lille, August 30-September 4, 1987.* Amsterdam/Philadelphia, 1990.
67. LEHMANN, Winfred (ed.): *Language Typology 1987. Systematic Balance in Language. Papers from the Linguistic Typology Symposium, Berkeley, 1-3 December 1987.* Amsterdam/Philadelphia, 1990.
68. BALL, Martin, James FIFE, Erich POPPE and Jenny ROWLAND (eds): *Celtic Linguistics / Ieithyddiaeth Geltaidd. Readings in the Brythonic Languages. Festschrift for T. Arwyn Watkins.* Amsterdam/Philadelphia, n.y.p.
69. WANNER, Dieter and Douglas A. KIBBEE (eds): *New Analyses in Romance Linguistics. Papers from the XVIII Linguistic Symposium on Romance Languages, Urbana-Champaign, April 7-9, 1988.* Amsterdam/Philadelphia, n.y.p.
70. JENSEN, John T.: *Morphology. Word Structure in Generative Grammar.* Amsterdam/Philadelphia, 1990.